THE CAXTONS:

A FAMILY PICTURE

"Now beat me, do beat me"

Page 14.

THE CAXTONS

A FAMILY PICTURE

BY

LORD LYTTON

WITH SIXTEEN ILLUSTRATIONS BY
CHRIS. HAMMOND

NEW YORK: G. P. PUTNAM'S SONS
LONDON: SERVICE & PATON
1898

Republished 1971
Scholarly Press, Inc., 22929 Industrial Drive East
St. Clair Shores, Michigan 48080

Library of Congress Catalog Card Number: 75-145149
ISBN 0-403-00763-1

PREFACE

IF it be the good fortune of this work to possess any interest for the Novel reader, that interest, perhaps, will be but little derived from the customary elements of fiction. The plot is extremely slight; the incidents are few, and with the exception of those which involve the fate of VIVIAN, such as may be found in the records of ordinary life.

Regarded as a Novel, this attempt is an experiment somewhat apart from the previous works of the author; it is the first of his writings in which Humour has been employed less for the purpose of satire than in illustration of amiable characters;—it is the first, too, in which man has been viewed less in his active relations with the world, than in his repose at his own hearth:—in a word, the greater part of the canvas has been devoted to the completion of a simple FAMILY PICTURE. And thus, in any appeal to the sympathies of the human heart, the common household affections occupy the place of those livelier or larger passions which usually (and not unjustly) arrogate the foreground in Romantic composition.

In the Hero whose autobiography connects the different characters and events of the work, it has been the Author's intention to imply the influences of Home upon the conduct and career of youth; and in the ambition which estranges PISISTRATUS for the time from the sedentary occupations in which the man of civilised life must usually serve his apprenticeship to Fortune or to Fame, it is not designed to describe the fever of Genius conscious of superior powers and aspiring to high destinies, but the natural tendencies of a fresh and buoyant mind, rather vigorous than contemplative, and in which the desire of action is but the symptom of health.

Pisistratus, in this respect (as he himself feels and implies), becomes the specimen or type of a class the numbers of which are daily increasing in the inevitable progress of modern civilisation. He is one too many in the midst of the crowd: he is the representative of the exuberant energies of youth, turning, as with the instinct of nature for space and development, from the Old World to the New. That which may be called the interior meaning of the whole is sought to be completed by the inference that, whatever our wanderings, our happiness will always be found within a narrow compass, and amidst the objects more immediately within our reach; but that we are seldom sensible of this truth (hackneyed though it be in the Schools of all Philosophies) till our researches have spread over a wider area. To ensure the blessing of repose, we require a brisker excitement than a few turns up and down our room. Content is like that humour in the crystal, on which Claudian has lavished the wonder of a child and the fancies of a Poet—

"Vivis gemma tumescit aquis."

E. B. L.

October 1849.

LIST OF ILLUSTRATIONS

By CHRIS. HAMMOND

THE CAXTONS:

A FAMILY PICTURE

PART I

CHAPTER I

"SIR—sir, it is a boy!"

"A boy," said my father, looking up from his book, and evidently much puzzled; "what is a boy?"

Now my father did not mean by that interrogatory to challenge philosophical inquiry, nor to demand of the honest but unenlightened woman who had just rushed into his study, a solution of that mystery, physiological and psychological, which has puzzled so many curious sages, and lies still involved in the question, "What is man?" For, as we need not look further than Dr. Johnson's Dictionary to know that a boy is "a male child"— *i.e.*, the male young of man; so he who would go to the depth of things, and know scientifically what is a boy, must be able to ascertain "what is a man." But, for aught I know, my father may have been satisfied with Buffon on that score, or he may have sided with Monboddo. He may have agreed with Bishop Berkeley—he may have contented himself with Professor Combe—he may have regarded the genus spiritually, like Zeno, or materially, like Epicurus. Grant that boy is the male young of man, and he would have had plenty of definitions to choose from. He might have said, "Man is a stomach—*ergo*, boy a male young stomach. Man is a brain—boy a male young brain. Man is a bundle of habits—boy a male young bundle of habits. Man is a machine—boy a male young machine. Man is a tailless monkey—boy a male young tailless monkey. Man is a combination of gases—boy a male young combination of gases. Man is an appearance—boy a male young appearance,"

A

&c., &c., and et cetera, *ad infinitum!* And if none of these definitions had entirely satisfied my father, I am perfectly persuaded that he would never have come to Mrs. Primmins for a new one.

But it so happened that my father was at that moment engaged in the important consideration whether the Iliad was written by one Homer—or was rather a collection of sundry ballads, done into Greek by divers hands, and finally selected, compiled, and reduced into a whole by a Committee of Taste, under that elegant old tyrant Pisistratus; and the sudden affirmation, "It is a boy," did not seem to him pertinent to the thread of the discussion. Therefore he asked, " What is a boy ? " vaguely, and, as it were, taken by surprise.

" Lord, sir ! " said Mrs. Primmins, " what is a boy ? Why, the baby ! "

" The baby ? " repeated my father, rising. " What, you don't mean to say that Mrs. Caxton is—eh ? "

" Yes, I do," said Mrs. Primmins, dropping a curtsey; " and as fine a little rogue as ever I set eyes upon."

" Poor dear woman," said my father with great compassion. " So soon, too—so rapidly ; " he resumed in a tone of musing surprise. " Why, it is but the other day we were married ! "

" Bless my heart, sir," said Mrs. Primmins, much scandalised, " it is ten months and more."

" Ten months ! " said my father with a sigh. " Ten months ! and I have not finished fifty pages of my refutation of Wolfe's monstrous theory ! In ten months a child ! and I'll be bound complete—hands, feet, eyes, ears, and nose !—and not like this poor Infant of Mind (and my father pathetically placed his hand on the treatise) of which nothing is formed and shaped—not even the first joint of the little finger ! Why, my wife is a precious woman ! Well, keep her quiet. Heaven preserve her, and send me strength—to support this blessing ! "

" But your honour will look at the baby ?—come, sir ! " and Mrs. Primmins laid hold of my father's sleeve coaxingly.

" Look at it—to be sure," said my father kindly ; " look at it, certainly ; it is but fair to poor Mrs. Caxton ; after taking so much trouble, dear soul ! "

Therewith my father, drawing his dressing-robe round him in more stately folds, followed Mrs. Primmins upstairs into a room very carefully darkened.

" How are you, my dear ? " said my father with compassionate tenderness, as he groped his way to the bed.

A faint voice muttered, " Better now, and so happy !" And, at the same moment, Mrs. Primmins pulled my father away, lifted a coverlid from a small cradle, and, holding a candle within an inch of an undeveloped nose, cried emphatically, " There—bless it !"

" Of course, ma'am, I bless it," said my father rather peevishly. " It is my duty to bless it—Bless it ! And this, then, is the way we come into the world !—red, very red,—blushing for all the follies we are destined to commit."

My father sat down on the nurse's chair, the women grouped round him. He continued to gaze on the contents of the cradle, and at length said musingly, " And Homer was once like this !"

At this moment—and no wonder, considering the propinquity of the candle to his visual organs—Homer's infant likeness commenced the first untutored melodies of nature.

" Homer improved greatly in singing as he grew older," observed Mr. Squills, the accoucheur, who was engaged in some mysteries in a corner of the room.

My father stopped his ears. " Little things can make a great noise," said he philosophically ; " and the smaller the thing the greater noise it can make."

So saying, he crept on tiptoe to the bed, and clasping the pale hand held out to him, whispered some words that no doubt charmed and soothed the ear that heard them, for that pale hand was tenderly drawn from his own, and thrown tenderly round his neck. The sound of a gentle kiss was heard through the stillness.

" Mr. Caxton, sir," cried Mr. Squills in rebuke, " you agitate my patient—you must retire."

My father raised his mild face, looked round apologetically, brushed his eyes with the back of his hand, stole to the door, and vanished.

" I think," said a kind gossip seated at the other side of my mother's bed, " I think, my dear, that Mr. Caxton might have shown more joy,—more natural feeling, I may say,—at the sight of the baby : and such a baby ! But all men are just the same, my dear—brutes—all brutes, depend upon it."

" Poor Austin !" sighed my mother feebly ; " how little you understand him !"

" And now I shall clear the room," said Mr. Squills. " Go to sleep, Mrs. Caxton."

" Mr. Squills," exclaimed my mother, and the bed-curtains trembled, " pray see that Mr. Caxton does not set himself on

fire ;—and, Mr. Squills, tell him not to be vexed and miss me,—
I shall be down very soon—shan't I ? "

"If you keep yourself easy, you will, ma'am."

"Pray, say so ;—and Primmins——"

"Yes, ma'am."

"Every one, I fear, is neglecting your master. Be sure,—
(and my mother's lips approached close to Mrs. Primmins' ear,)
—be sure that you—air his nightcap yourself."

"Tender creatures those women," soliloquised Mr. Squills,
as after clearing the room of all present, save Mrs. Primmins and
the nurse, he took his way towards my father's study. Encountering the footman in the passage,—"John," said he, "take
supper into your master's room, and make us some punch, will
you—stiffish ? "

CHAPTER II

MR. CAXTON, how on earth did you ever come to marry ? "
asked Mr. Squills abruptly, with his feet on the hob, while
stirring up his punch.

That was a home question which many men might reasonably
resent ; but my father scarcely knew what resentment was.

"Squills," said he, turning round from his books, and laying
one finger on the surgeon's arm confidentially,—"Squills," said
he, "I myself should be glad to know how I came to be
married."

Mr. Squills was a jovial, good-hearted man—stout, fat, and
with fine teeth, that made his laugh pleasant to look at as well
as to hear. Mr. Squills, moreover, was a bit of a philosopher in
his way ;—studied human nature in curing its diseases ;—and
was accustomed to say, that Mr. Caxton was a better book in
himself than all he had in his library. Mr. Squills laughed and
rubbed his hands.

My father resumed thoughtfully, and in the tone of one who
moralises—

"There are three great events in life, sir—birth, marriage,
and death. None know how they are born, few know how they
die. But I suspect that many can account for the intermediate
phenomenon—I cannot."

"It was not for money,—it must have been for love," observed
Mr. Squills ; "and your young wife is as pretty as she is good."

"Ha !" said my father, "I remember."

"Do you, sir!" exclaimed Squills, highly amused. "How was it?"

My father, as was often the case with him, protracted his reply, and then seemed rather to commune with himself than to answer Mr. Squills.

"The kindest, the best of men," he murmured—"*Abyssus Eruditionis:* and to think that he bestowed on me the only fortune he had to leave, instead of to his own flesh and blood, Jack and Kitty. All at least that I could grasp *deficiente manu,* of his Latin, his Greek, his Orientals. What do I not owe to him?"

"To whom?" asked Squills. "Good Lord, what's the man talking about?"

"Yes, sir," said my father, rousing himself, "such was Giles Tibbets, M.A., *Sol Scientiarum,* tutor to the humble scholar you address, and father to poor Kitty. He left me his Elzevirs; he left me also his orphan daughter."

"Oh! as a wife——"

"No, as a ward. So she came to live in my house. I am sure there was no harm in it. But my neighbours said there was, and the widow Weltraum told me the girl's character would suffer. What could I do?—Oh yes, I recollect all now! I married her, that my old friend's child might have a roof to her head, and come to no harm. You see I was forced to do her that injury; for, after all, poor young creature, it was a sad lot for her. A dull book-worm like me—*cochleæ vitam agens,* Mr. Squills—leading the life of a snail. But my shell was all I could offer to my poor friend's orphan."

"Mr. Caxton, I honour you," said Squills emphatically, jumping up, and spilling half a tumblerful of scalding punch over my father's legs. "You have a heart, sir; and I understand why your wife loves you. You seem a cold man; but you have tears in your eyes at this moment."

"I dare say I have," said my father, rubbing his shins; "it was boiling!"

"And your son will be a comfort to you both," said Mr. Squills, reseating himself, and, in his friendly emotion, wholly abstracted from all consciousness of the suffering he had inflicted. "He will be a dove of peace to your ark."

"I don't doubt it," said my father ruefully; "only those doves, when they are small, are a very noisy sort of birds—*non talium avium cantus somnum reducent.* However, it might have been worse. Leda had twins."

"So had Mrs. Barnabas last week," rejoined the accoucheur.

"Who knows what may be in store for you yet? Here's a health to Master Caxton, and lots of brothers and sisters to him."

"Brothers and sisters! I am sure Mrs. Caxton will never think of such a thing, sir," said my father, almost indignantly. "She's much too good a wife to behave so. Once, in a way, it is all very well; but twice—and as it is, not a paper in its place, nor a pen mended the last three days: I, too, who can only write ' *cuspide duriusculâ* '—and the baker coming twice to me for his bill too! The Ilithyiæ are troublesome deities, Mr. Squills."

"Who are the Ilithyiæ?" asked the accoucheur.

"You ought to know," answered my father, smiling. "The female dæmons who presided over the Neogilos or New-born. They take the name from Juno. See Homer, Book XI. By-the-bye, will my Neogilos be brought up like Hector or Astyanax—*videlicet*, nourished by its mother or by a nurse?"

"Which do you prefer, Mr. Caxton?" asked Mr. Squills, breaking the sugar in his tumbler. "In this I always deem it my duty to consult the wishes of the gentleman."

"A nurse by all means, then," said my father. "And let her carry him *upo kolpo*, next to her bosom. I know all that has been said about mothers nursing their own infants, Mr. Squills; but poor Kitty is so sensitive, that I think a stout healthy peasant woman will be the best for the boy's future nerves, and his mother's nerves, present and future, too. Heigh-ho! I shall miss the dear woman very much; when will she be up, Mr. Squills?"

"Oh, in less than a fortnight!"

"And then the Neogilos shall go to school! *upo kolpo*—the nurse with him, and all will be right again," said my father, with a look of sly mysterious humour, which was peculiar to him.

"School! when he's just born?"

"Can't begin too soon," said my father positively; "that's Helvetius' opinion, and it is mine too!"

CHAPTER III

THAT I was a very wonderful child I take for granted; but, nevertheless, it was not of my own knowledge that I came into possession of the circumstances set down in my former chapters. But my father's conduct on the occasion of my birth made a notable impression upon all who witnessed it;

and Mr. Squills and Mrs. Primmins have related the facts to me sufficiently often to make me as well acquainted with them as those worthy witnesses themselves. I fancy I see my father before me, in his dark-grey dressing-gown, and with his odd, half-sly, half-innocent twitch of the mouth, and peculiar puzzling look, from two quiet, abstracted, indolently handsome eyes, at the moment he agreed with Helvetius on the propriety of sending me to school as soon as I was born. Nobody knew exactly what to make of my father—his wife excepted. The people of Abdera sent for Hippocrates to cure the supposed insanity of Democritus, "who at that time," saith Hippocrates dryly, " was seriously engaged in philosophy." That same people of Abdera would certainly have found very alarming symptoms of madness in my poor father; for, like Democritus, " he esteemed as nothing the things, great or small, in which the rest of the world were employed." Accordingly, some set him down as a sage, some as a fool. The neighbouring clergy respected him as a scholar, " breathing libraries " ; the ladies despised him as an absent pedant, who had no more gallantry than a stock or stone. The poor loved him for his charities, but laughed at him as a weak sort of man, easily taken in. Yet the squires and farmers found that, in their own matters of rural business, he had always a fund of curious information to impart ; and whoever, young or old, gentle or simple, learned or ignorant, asked his advice, it was given with not more humility than wisdom. In the common affairs of life, he seemed incapable of acting for himself; he left all to my mother; or, if taken unawares, was pretty sure to be the dupe. But in those very affairs—if *another* consulted him—his eye brightened, his brow cleared, the desire of serving made him a new being : cautious, profound, practical. Too lazy or too languid where only his own interests were at stake—touch his benevolence, and all the wheels of the clockwork felt the impetus of the master-spring. No wonder that, to others, the nut of such a character was hard to crack ! But, in the eyes of my poor mother, Augustine (familiarly Austin) Caxton was the best and the greatest of human beings ; and she ought to have known him well, for she studied him with her whole heart, knew every trick of his face, and, nine times out of ten, divined what he was going to say before he opened his lips. Yet certainly there were deeps in his nature which the plummet of her tender woman's wit had never sounded ; and, certainly it sometimes happened that, even in his most domestic colloquialisms, my mother was in doubt whether he was the simple straightforward person he was mostly taken for. There was, indeed, a kind of suppressed, subtle irony about him, too unsubstantial to be popularly called humour, but dimly implying some sort of jest, which he kept all to himself; and this was only noticeable when he said something that sounded very grave, or appeared to the grave very silly and irrational.

That I did not go to school—at least to what Mr. Squills understood by the word school—quite so soon as intended, I need scarcely observe. In fact, my mother managed so well—my nursery, by means of double doors, was so placed out of hearing—that my father, for the most part, was privileged, if he pleased, to forget my existence. He was once vaguely recalled to it on the occasion of my christening. Now, my father was a shy man, and he particularly hated all ceremonies and public spectacles. He became uneasily aware that a great ceremony, in which he might be called upon to play a prominent part, was at hand. Abstracted as he was, and conveniently deaf at times, he had heard such significant whispers about "taking advantage of the bishop's being in the neighbourhood," and "twelve new jelly-glasses being absolutely wanted," as to assure him that some deadly festivity was in the wind. And when the question of godmother and godfather was fairly put to him, coupled with the remark that this was a fine opportunity to return the civilities of the neighbourhood, he felt that a strong effort at escape was the only thing left. Accordingly, having, seemingly without listening, heard the day fixed, and seen, as they thought, without observing, the chintz chairs in the best drawing-room uncovered (my dear mother was the tidiest woman in the world), my father suddenly discovered that there was to be a great book-sale, twenty miles off, which would last four days, and attend it he must. My mother sighed; but she never contradicted my father, even when he was wrong, as he certainly was in this case. She only dropped a timid intimation that she feared "it would look odd, and the world might misconstrue my father's absence—had not she better put off the christening?"

"My dear," answered my father, "it will be *my* duty, by-and-by, to christen the boy—a duty not done in a day. At present, I have no doubt that the bishop will do very well without me. Let the day stand, or, if you put it off, upon my word and honour I believe that the wicked auctioneer will put off the book-sale also. Of one thing I am quite sure, that the sale and the christening will take place at the same time."

There was no getting over this; but I am certain my dear mother had much less heart than before in uncovering the chintz chairs in the best drawing-room. Five years later this would not have happened. My mother would have kissed my father, and said " Stay," and he would have stayed. But she was then very young and timid ; and he, wild man, not of the woods, but the cloisters, not yet civilised into the tractabilities of home. In short, the post-chaise was ordered and the carpet-bag packed.

" My love," said my mother, the night before this Hegira, looking up from her work—" my love, there is one thing you have quite forgot to settle—I beg pardon for disturbing you, but it is important !—baby's name ; shan't we call him Augustine ? "

" Augustine," said my father dreamily ; " why, that name's mine."

" And you would like your boy's to be the same ? "

" No," said my father, rousing himself. " Nobody would know which was which. I should catch myself learning the Latin accidence or playing at marbles. I should never know my own identity, and Mrs. Primmins would be giving me pap."

My mother smiled ; and putting her hand, which was a very pretty one, on my father's shoulder, and looking at him tenderly, she said, " There's no fear of mistaking you for any other, even your son, dearest. Still, if you prefer another name, what shall it be ? "

" Samuel," said my father. " Dr. Parr's name is Samuel."

" La, my love ! Samuel is the ugliest name——"

My father did not hear the exclamation, he was again deep in his books ; presently he started up—" Barnes says Homer is Solomon. Read Omeros backwards, in the Hebrew manner——"

" Yes, my love," interrupted my mother. " But baby's Christian name ? "

" Omeros—Soremo—Solemo—Solomo ! "

" Solomo ! shocking ! " said my mother.

"Shocking, indeed," echoed my father : "an outrage to common sense." Then, after glancing again over his books, he broke out musingly—" But, after all, it is nonsense to suppose that Homer was not settled till *his* time."

" Whose ? " asked my mother mechanically.

My father lifted up his finger.

My mother continued, after a short pause, " Arthur is a pretty name. Then there's William—Henry—Charles—Robert. What shall it be, love?"

"Pisistratus!" said my father (who had hung fire till then), in a tone of contempt—"Pisistratus, indeed!"

"Pisistratus! a very fine name," said my mother joyfully—"Pisistratus Caxton. Thank you, my love: Pisistratus it shall be."

"Do you contradict me? Do you side with Wolfe and Heyne, and that pragmatical fellow, Vico? Do you mean to say that the Rhapsodists——"

"No, indeed," interrupted my mother. "My dear, you frighten me."

My father sighed and threw himself back in his chair. My mother took courage and resumed.

"Pisistratus is a long name too! Still, one could call him Sisty."

"Sisty, Viator," muttered my father; "that's trite!"

"No, Sisty by itself—short. Thank you, my dear."

Four days afterwards, on his return from the book-sale, to my father's inexpressible bewilderment, he was informed that "Pisistratus was growing the very image of him."

When at length the good man was made thoroughly aware of the fact, that his son and heir boasted a name so memorable in history as that borne by the enslaver of Athens, and the disputed arranger of Homer—and it was asserted to be a name that he himself had suggested—he was as angry as so mild a man could be. "But it is infamous!" he exclaimed. "Pisistratus christened! Pisistratus! who lived six hundred years before Christ was born. Good Heavens, madam! you have made me the father of an Anachronism."

My mother burst into tears. But the evil was irremediable. An anachronism I was, and an anachronism I must continue to the end of the chapter.

CHAPTER IV

"OF course, sir, you will begin soon to educate your son yourself?" said Mr. Squills.

"Of course, sir," said my father, "you have read Martinus Scriblerus?"

"I don't understand you, Mr. Caxton."

"Then you have *not* read Martinus Scriblerus, Mr. Squills!"

"Consider that I have read it, and what then?"

"Why then, Squills," said my father familiarly, "you would know, that though a scholar is often a fool, he is never a fool so supreme, so superlative, as when he is defacing the first unsullied page of the human history, by entering into it the commonplaces of his own pedantry. A scholar, sir—at least one like me—is of all persons the most unfit to teach young children. A mother, sir—a simple, natural, loving mother—is the infant's true guide to knowledge."

"Egad, Mr. Caxton, in spite of Helvetius, whom you quoted the night the boy was born—egad, I believe you are right."

"I am sure of it," said my father; "at least as sure as a poor mortal can be of anything. I agree with Helvetius, the child should be educated from its birth; but how?—there is the rub: send him to school forthwith! Certainly, he is at school already with the two great teachers, Nature and Love. Observe, that childhood and genius have the same master-organ in common—inquisitiveness. Let childhood have its way, and as it began where genius begins, it may find what genius finds. A certain Greek writer tells us of some man, who, in order to save his bees a troublesome flight to Hymettus, cut their wings, and placed before them the finest flowers he could select. The poor bees made no honey. Now, sir, if I were to teach my boy, I should be cutting his wings, and giving him the flowers he should find himself. Let us leave Nature alone for the present, and Nature's loving proxy, the watchful mother."

Therewith my father pointed to his heir sprawling on the grass, and plucking daisies on the lawn; while the young mother's voice rose merrily, laughing at the child's glee.

"I shall make but a poor bill out of your nursery, I see," said Mr. Squills.

Agreeably to these doctrines, strange in so learned a father, I thrived and flourished, and learned to spell, and make pot-hooks, under the joint care of my mother and Dame Primmins. This last was one of an old race fast dying away—the race of old faithful servants—the race of old tale-telling nurses. She had reared my mother before me; but her affection put out new flowers for the new generation. She was a Devonshire woman —and Devonshire women, especially those who have passed their youth near the sea-coast, are generally superstitious. She had a wonderful budget of fables. Before I was six years old, I was erudite in that primitive literature, in which the legends of all nations are traced to a common fountain—*Puss in Boots, Tom Thumb, Fortunio, Fortunatus, Jack the Giant Killer,*—tales

like proverbs, equally familiar, under different versions, to the
infant worshippers of Budh and the hardier children of Thor.
I may say, without vanity, that in an examination in those venerable classics, I could have taken honours!

My dear mother had some little misgivings as to the solid
benefit to be derived from such fantastic erudition, and timidly
consulted my father thereon.

" My love," answered my father, in that tone of voice which
always puzzled even my mother, to be sure whether he was in
jest or earnest—"in all these fables, certain philosophers could
easily discover symbolic significations of the highest morality.
I have myself written a treatise to prove that *Puss in Boots* is an
allegory upon the progress of the human understanding, having
its origin in the mystical schools of the Egyptian priests, and
evidently an illustration of the worship rendered at Thebes and
Memphis to those feline quadrupeds, of which they make both
religious symbols and elaborate mummies."

" My dear Austin," said my mother, opening her blue eyes,
"you don't think that Sisty would discover all those fine things
in *Puss in Boots!*"

" My dear Kitty," answered my father, "you don't think,
when you were good enough to take up with me, that you
found in me all the fine things I have learned from books. You
knew me only as a harmless creature, who was happy enough to
please your fancy. By-and-by you discovered that I was no
worse for all the quartos that have transmigrated into ideas
within me—ideas that are mysteries even to myself. If Sisty,
as you call the child (plague on that unlucky anachronism!
which you do well to abbreviate into a dissyllable),—if Sisty
can't discover all the wisdom of Egypt in *Puss in Boots*, what
then? *Puss in Boots* is harmless, and it pleases his fancy. All
that wakes curiosity is wisdom, if innocent—all that pleases the
fancy now, turns hereafter to love or to knowledge. And so,
my dear, go back to the nursery."

But I should wrong thee, oh best of fathers! if I suffered the
reader to suppose, that because thou didst seem so indifferent
to my birth, and so careless as to my early teaching, therefore
thou wert, at heart, indifferent to thy troublesome Neogilos.
As I grew older, I became more sensibly aware that a father's
eye was upon me. I distinctly remember one incident, that
seems to me, in looking back, a crisis in my infant life, as
the first tangible link between my own heart and that calm
great soul.

My father was seated on the lawn before the house, his straw hat over his eyes (it was summer), and his book on his lap. Suddenly a beautiful delf blue-and-white flower-pot, which had been set on the window-sill of an upper storey, fell to the ground with a crash, and the fragments spluttered up round my father's legs. Sublime in his studies as Archimedes in the siege, he continued to read; *Impavidum ferient ruinæ!*

"Dear, dear!" cried my mother, who was at work in the porch, "my poor flower-pot that I prized so much! Who could have done this? Primmins, Primmins!"

Mrs. Primmins popped her head out of the fatal window, nodded to the summons, and came down in a trice, pale and breathless.

"Oh," said my mother mournfully, "I would rather have lost all the plants in the greenhouse in the great blight last May,— I would rather the best tea-set were broken! The poor geranium I reared myself, and the dear, dear flower-pot which Mr. Caxton bought for me my last birthday! That naughty child must have done this!"

Mrs. Primmins was dreadfully afraid of my father—why, I know not, except that very talkative social persons are usually afraid of very silent shy ones. She cast a hasty glance at her master, who was beginning to evince signs of attention, and cried promptly, "No, ma'am, it was not the dear boy, bless his flesh, it was I!"

"You? how could you be so careless? and you knew how I prized them both. O Primmins!"

Primmins began to sob.

"Don't tell fibs, nursey," said a small shrill voice; and Master Sisty (coming out of the house as bold as brass) continued rapidly—"Don't scold Primmins, mamma; it was I who pushed out the flower-pot."

"Hush!" said nurse, more frightened than ever, and looking aghast towards my father, who had very deliberately taken off his hat, and was regarding the scene with serious eyes wide awake.

"Hush! And if he did break it, ma'am, it was quite an accident; he was standing so, and he never meant it. Did you, Master Sisty? Speak! (this in a whisper) or Pa will be so angry."

"Well," said my mother, "I suppose it was an accident; take care in future, my child. You are sorry, I see, to have grieved me. There's a kiss; don't fret."

"No, mamma, you must not kiss me ; I don't deserve it. I pushed out the flower-pot on purpose."

"Ha ! and why ? " said my father, walking up.

Mrs. Primmins trembled like a leaf.

"For fun !" said I, hanging my head—"just to see how you'd look, papa; and that's the truth of it. Now beat me, do beat me ! "

My father threw his book fifty yards off, stooped down, and caught me to his breast. "Boy," he said, "you have done wrong : you shall repair it by remembering all your life that your father blessed God for giving him a son who spoke truth in spite of fear ! O Mrs. Primmins, the next fable of this kind you try to teach him, and we part for ever ! "

From that time I first date the hour when I felt that I loved my father, and knew that he loved me ; and from that time, too, he began to *converse* with me. He would no longer, if he met me in the garden, pass by with a smile and nod ; he would stop, put his book in his pocket, and though his talk was often above my comprehension, still somehow I felt happier and better, and less of an infant, when I thought over it, and tried to puzzle out the meaning ; for he had a way of suggesting, not teaching—putting things into my head, and then leaving them to work out their own problems. I remember a special instance with respect to that same flower-pot and geranium. Mr. Squills, who was a bachelor, and well-to-do in the world, often made me little presents. Not long after the event I have narrated, he gave me one far exceeding in value those usually bestowed on children,—it was a beautiful large domino-box in cut ivory, painted and gilt. This domino-box was my delight. I was never weary of playing at dominoes with Mrs. Primmins, and I slept with the box under my pillow.

"Ah !" said my father one day, when he found me ranging the ivory parallelograms in the parlour, "ah ! you like that better than all your playthings, eh ? "

"Oh yes, papa."

"You would be very sorry if your mamma were to throw that box out of the window, and break it for fun." I looked beseechingly at my father, and made no answer.

"But perhaps you would be very glad," he resumed, "if suddenly one of those good fairies you read of could change the domino-box into a beautiful geranium in a beautiful blue-and-white flower-pot, and you could have the pleasure of putting it on your mamma's window-sill."

"Indeed I would ! " said I, half-crying.

"My dear boy, I believe you; but good wishes don't mend bad actions—good actions mend bad actions."

So saying, he shut the door and went out. I cannot tell you how puzzled I was to make out what my father meant by his aphorism. But I know that I played at dominoes no more that day. The next morning my father found me seated by myself under a tree in the garden; he paused and looked at me with his grave bright eyes very steadily.

"My boy," said he, "I am going to walk to —— (a town about two miles off), will you come? and, by-the-bye, fetch your domino-box: I should like to show it to a person there." I ran in for the box, and, not a little proud of walking with my father upon the high-road, we set out.

"Papa," said I by the way, "there are no fairies now."

"What then, my child?"

"Why—how then can my domino-box be changed into a geranium and a blue-and-white flower-pot?"

"My dear," said my father, leaning his hand on my shoulder, "everybody who is in earnest to be good, carries two fairies about with him—one here," and he touched my heart; "and one here," and he touched my forehead.

"I don't understand, papa."

"I can wait till you do, Pisistratus! What a name!"

My father stopped at a nursery gardener's, and, after looking over the flowers, paused before a large double geranium. "Ah, this is finer than that which your mamma was so fond of. What is the cost, sir?"

"Only 7s. 6d.," said the gardener.

My father buttoned up his pocket. "I can't afford it to-day," said he gently, and we walked out.

On entering the town, we stopped again at a china-warehouse.

"Have you a flower-pot like that I bought some months ago? Ah, here is one, marked 3s. 6d. Yes, that is the price. Well, when your mamma's birthday comes again, we must buy her another. That is some months to wait. And we can wait, Master Sisty. For truth, that blooms all the year round, is better than a poor geranium; and a word that is never broken is better than a piece of delf."

My head, which had drooped before, rose again; but the rush of joy at my heart almost stifled me.

"I have called to pay your little bill," said my father, entering the shop of one of those fancy stationers, common in country towns, and who sell all kinds of pretty toys and nick-nacks.

"And by the way," he added, as the smiling shopman looked over his books for the entry, "I think my little boy here can show you a much handsomer specimen of French workmanship than that work-box which you enticed Mrs. Caxton into raffling for, last winter. Show your domino-box, my dear."

I produced my treasure, and the shopman was liberal in his commendations. "It is always well, my boy, to know what a thing is worth, in case one wishes to part with it. If my young gentleman gets tired of his plaything, what will you give him for it?"

"Why, sir," said the shopman, "I fear we could not afford to give more than eighteen shillings for it, unless the young gentleman took some of these pretty things in exchange!"

"Eighteen shillings!" said my father; "you would give *that* sum. Well, my boy, whenever you do grow tired of your box, you have my leave to sell it."

My father paid his bill and went out. I lingered behind a few moments, and joined him at the end of the street.

"Papa, papa!" I cried, clapping my hands, "we can buy the geranium—we can buy the flower-pot." And I pulled a handful of silver from my pockets.

"Did I not say right?" said my father, passing his hand-kerchief over his eyes—"You have found the two fairies!"

Oh! how proud, how overjoyed I was, when, after placing vase and flower on the window-sill, I plucked my mother by the gown, and made her follow me to the spot.

"It is his doing and his money!" said my father; "good actions have mended the bad."

"What!" cried my mother, when she had learned all; "and your poor domino-box that you were so fond of! We will go back to-morrow, and buy it back, if it costs us double."

"Shall we buy it back, Pisistratus?" asked my father.

"Oh no—no—no! It would spoil all," I cried, burying my face on my father's breast.

"My wife," said my father solemnly, "this is my first lesson to our child—the sanctity and the happiness of self-sacrifice—undo not what it should teach to his dying day."

CHAPTER V

WHEN I was between my seventh and my eighth year, a change came over me, which may perhaps be familiar to the notice of those parents who boast the anxious blessing of an only child. The ordinary vivacity of childhood forsook me; I became quiet, sedate, and thoughtful. The absence of playfellows of my own age, the companionship of mature minds, alternated only by complete solitude, gave something precocious, whether to my imagination or my reason. The wild fables muttered to me by the old nurse in the summer twilight, or over the winter's hearth—the effort made by my struggling intellect to comprehend the grave, sweet wisdom of my father's suggested lessons—tended to feed a passion for reverie, in which all my faculties strained and struggled, as in the dreams that come when sleep is nearest waking. I had learned to read with ease, and to write with some fluency, and I already began to imitate, to reproduce. Strange tales, akin to those I had gleaned from fairy-land—rude songs, modelled from such verse-books as fell into my hands, began to mar the contents of marble-covered pages, designed for the less ambitious purposes of round text and multiplication. My mind was yet more disturbed by the intensity of my home affections. My love for both my parents had in it something morbid and painful. I often wept to think how little I could do for those I loved so well. My fondest fancies built up imaginary difficulties for them, which my arm was to smooth. These feelings, thus cherished, made my nerves over-susceptible and acute. Nature began to affect me powerfully ; and from that affection rose a restless curiosity to analyse the charms that so mysteriously moved me to joy or awe, to smiles or tears. I got my father to explain to me the elements of astronomy; I extracted from Squills, who was an ardent botanist, some of the mysteries in the life of flowers. But music became my darling passion. My mother (though the daughter of a great scholar—a scholar at whose name my father raised his hat if it happened to be on his head) possessed, I must own it fairly, less book-learning than many an humble tradesman's daughter can boast in this more enlightened generation ; but she had some natural gifts which had ripened, Heaven knows how ! into womanly accomplishments. She drew with some elegance, and painted flowers to exquisite perfection. She

B

played on more than one instrument with more than boarding-school skill; and though she sang in no language but her own, few could hear her sweet voice without being deeply touched. Her music, her songs, had a wondrous effect on me. Thus, altogether, a kind of dreamy yet delightful melancholy seized upon my whole being; and this was the more remarkable, because contrary to my early temperament, which was bold, active, and hilarious. The change in my character began to act upon my form. From a robust and vigorous infant, I grew into a pale and slender boy. I began to ail and mope. Mr. Squills was called in.

"Tonics!" said Mr. Squills; "and don't let him sit over his book. Send him out in the air—make him play. Come here, my boy—these organs are growing too large;" and Mr. Squills, who was a phrenologist, placed his hand on my forehead. "Gad, sir, here's an ideality for you; and, bless my soul, what a constructiveness!"

My father pushed aside his papers, and walked to and fro the room with his hands behind him; but he did not say a word till Mr. Squills was gone.

"My dear," then said he to my mother, on whose breast I was leaning my aching ideality—"my dear, Pisistratus must go to school in good earnest."

"Bless me, Austin!—at his age?"

"He is nearly eight years old."

"But he is so forward."

"It is for that reason he must go to school."

"I don't quite understand you, my love. I know he is getting past me; but you who are so clever——"

My father took my mother's hand—"We can teach him nothing now, Kitty. We send him to school to be taught——"

"By some schoolmaster who knows much less than you do——"

"By little schoolboys, who will make him a boy again," said my father, almost sadly. "My dear, you remember that, when our Kentish gardener planted those filbert trees, and when they were in their third year, and you began to calculate on what they would bring in, you went out one morning, and found he had cut them down to the ground. You were vexed, and asked why. What did the gardener say? 'To prevent their bearing too soon.' There is no want of fruitfulness here—put back the hour of produce, that the plant may last."

"Let me go to school," said I, lifting my languid head, and smiling on my father. I understood him at once, and it was as if the voice of my life itself answered him.

CHAPTER VI

A YEAR after the resolution thus come to, I was at home for the holidays.

"I hope," said my mother, "that they are doing Sisty justice. I do think he is not nearly so quick a child as he was before he went to school. I wish you would examine him, Austin."

"I have examined him, my dear. It is just as I expected; and I am quite satisfied."

"What! you really think he has come on?" said my mother joyfully.

"He does not care a button for botany now," said Mr. Squills.

"And he used to be so fond of music, dear boy!" observed my mother, with a sigh. "Good gracious, what noise is that?"

"Your son's pop-gun against the window," said my father. "It is lucky it is only the window; it would have made a less deafening noise, though, if it had been Mr. Squill's head, as it was yesterday morning."

"The left ear," observed Squills; "and a very sharp blow it was, too. Yet you are satisfied, Mr. Caxton?"

"Yes; I think the boy is now as great a blockhead as most boys of his age are," observed my father with great complacency.

"Dear me, Austin—a great blockhead?"

"What else did he go to school for?" asked my father. And observing a certain dismay in the face of his female audience, and a certain surprise in that of his male, he rose and stood on the hearth, with one hand in his waistcoat, as was his wont when about to philosophise in more detail than was usual to him.

"Mr. Squills," said he, "you have had great experience in families."

"As good a practice as any in the county," said Mr. Squills proudly; "more than I can manage. I shall advertise for a partner."

"And," resumed my father, "you must have observed almost invariably that, in every family, there is what father, mother, uncle, and aunt pronounce to be one wonderful child."

"One at least," said Mr. Squills, smiling.

"It is easy," continued my father, "to say this is parental partiality,—but it is not so. Examine that child as a stranger, and it will startle yourself. You stand amazed at its eager curiosity—its quick comprehension—its ready wit—its delicate perception. Often, too, you will find some faculty strikingly developed; the child will have a turn for mechanics, perhaps, and make you a model of a steam-boat—or it will have an ear tuned to verse, and will write you a poem like that it has got by heart from 'The Speaker'—or it will take to botany (like Pisistratus), with the old maid its aunt—or it will play a march on its sister's pianoforte. In short, even you, Squills, will declare that it is really a wonderful child."

"Upon my word," said Mr. Squills thoughtfully, "there's a great deal of truth in what you say. Little Tom Dobbs *is* a wonderful child—so is Frank Stepington—and as for Johnny Styles, I must bring him here for you to hear him prattle on Natural History, and see how well he handles his pretty little microscope."

"Heaven forbid!" said my father. "And now let me proceed. These *thaumata*, or wonders, last till when, Mr. Squills? —last till the boy goes to school, and then, somehow or other, the *thaumata* vanish into thin air, like ghosts at the cockcrow. A year after the prodigy has been at the academy, father and mother, uncle and aunt, plague you no more with his doings and sayings; the extraordinary infant has become a very ordinary little boy. Is it not so, Mr. Squills?"

"Indeed you are right, sir. How did you come to be so observant? you never seem to——"

"Hush!" interrupted my father; and then, looking fondly at my mother's anxious face, he said soothingly,—"Be comforted: this is wisely ordained—and it is for the best."

"It must be the fault of the school," said my mother, shaking her head.

"It is the necessity of the school, and its virtue, my Kate. Let any one of these wonderful children—wonderful as you thought Sisty himself—stay at home, and you will see its head grow bigger and bigger, and its body thinner and thinner—eh, Mr. Squills?—till the mind take all nourishment from the frame, and the frame, in turn, stint or make sickly the mind. You see that noble oak from the window. If the Chinese had brought it up, it would have been a tree in miniature at five years old, and at a hundred, you would have set it in a flower-pot on your table, no bigger than it was at five—a curiosity for its maturity at one age—a show for its diminutiveness at the other. No! the ordeal for talent is school; restore the stunted mannikin to the growing child, and then let the child, if it can, healthily, hardily, naturally, work its slow way up into greatness. If

greatness be denied it, it will at least be a man, and that is
better than to be a little Johnny Styles all its life—an oak in a
pill-box."

At that moment I rushed into the room, glowing and panting
health on my cheek—vigour in my limbs—all childhood at my
heart. "Oh, mamma, I have got up the kite—so high! come
and see. Do come, papa."

"Certainly," said my father; "only don't cry so loud—kites
make no noise in rising; yet, you see how they soar above the
world. Come, Kate. Where is my hat? Ah—thank you, my
boy."

"Kitty," said my father, looking at the kite, which, attached
by its string to the peg I had stuck into the ground, rested calm
in the sky, "never fear but what our kite shall fly as high; only,
the human soul has stronger instincts to mount upward than a
few sheets of paper on a framework of lath. But observe, that
to prevent its being lost in the freedom of space, we must attach
it lightly to earth; and observe again, my dear, that the higher
it soars, the more string we must give it."

PART II

CHAPTER I

WHEN I had reached the age of twelve, I had got to the head of the preparatory school to which I had been sent. And having thus exhausted all the oxygen of learning in that little receiver, my parents looked out for a wider range for my inspirations. During the last two years in which I had been at school, my love for study had returned; but it was a vigorous, wakeful, undreamy love, stimulated by competition, and animated by the practical desire to excel.

My father no longer sought to curb my intellectual aspirings. He had too great a reverence for scholarship not to wish me to become a scholar if possible; though he more than once said to me somewhat sadly, " Master books, but do not let them master you. Read to live, not live to read. One slave of the lamp is enough for a household; my servitude must not be a hereditary bondage."

My father looked round for a suitable academy; and the fame of Dr. Herman's " Philhellenic Institute" came to his ears.

Now, this Dr. Herman was the son of a German music-master, who had settled in England. He had completed his own education at the University of Bonn; but finding learning too common a drug in that market to bring the high price at which he valued his own, and having some theories as to political freedom which attached him to England, he resolved upon setting up a school, which he designed as an "Era in the History of the Human Mind." Dr. Herman was one of the earliest of those new-fashioned authorities in education, who have, more lately, spread pretty numerously amongst us, and would have given, perhaps, a dangerous shake to the foundations of our great classical seminaries, if those last had not very wisely, though very cautiously, borrowed some of the more sensible principles which lay mixed and adulterated amongst the crotchets and chimeras of their innovating rivals and assailants.

22

Dr. Herman had written a great many learned works against every pre-existing method of instruction : that which had made the greatest noise was upon the infamous fiction of Spelling Books : " A more lying, roundabout, puzzle-headed delusion than that by which we confuse the clear instincts of truth in our accursed system of spelling, was never concocted by the father of falsehood." Such was the exordium of this famous treatise. " For instance, take the monosyllable Cat. What a brazen forehead you must have, when you say to an infant, c, a, t,—spell Cat : that is, three sounds forming a totally opposite compound—opposite in every detail, opposite in the whole—compose a poor little monosyllable, which, if you would but say the simple truth, the child will learn to spell merely by looking at it ! How can three sounds, which run thus to the ear *see—eh—tee,* compose the sound *cat ?* Don't they rather compose the sound *see-eh-té,* or *ceaty ?* How can a system of education flourish that begins by so monstrous a falsehood, which the sense of hearing suffices to contradict ? No wonder that the hornbook is the despair of mothers ! " From this instance, the reader will perceive that Dr. Herman, in his theory of education, began at the beginning !—he took the bull fairly by the horns. As for the rest, upon a broad principle of eclecticism, he had combined together every new patent invention for youthful idea-shooting. He had taken his trigger from Hofwyl ; he had bought his wadding from Hamilton ; he had got his copper-caps from Bell and Lancaster. The youthful idea ! he had rammed it tight !—he had rammed it loose !—he had rammed it with pictorial illustrations !—he had rammed it with the monitorial system !—he had rammed it in every conceivable way, and with every imaginable ramrod ; but I have mournful doubts whether he shot the youthful idea an inch farther than it did under the old mechanism of flint and steel ! Nevertheless, as Dr. Herman really did teach a great many things too much neglected at schools ; as, besides Latin and Greek, he taught a vast variety in that vague infinite nowadays called " useful knowledge ; " as he engaged lecturers on chemistry, engineering, and natural history ; as arithmetic and the elements of physical science were enforced with zeal and care ; as all sorts of gymnastics were intermingled with the sports of the playground ; —so the youthful idea, if it did not go farther, spread its shots in a wider direction ; and a boy could not stay there five years without learning *something,* which is more than can be said of all schools ! He learned at least to use his eyes, and his ears, and his limbs; order, cleanliness, exercise, grew into habits; and the school pleased the ladies and satisfied the gentlemen; in a word, it thrived: and Dr. Herman, at the time I speak of, numbered more than one hundred pupils. Now, when the worthy man first commenced the task of tuition, he had proclaimed the humanest abhorrence to the barbarous system of corporal punishment. But, alas! as his school increased in numbers, he had proportionately recanted these honourable and anti-birchen ideas. He had, reluctantly, perhaps,—honestly, no doubt, but with full determination—come to the conclusion that there are secret springs which can only be detected by the twigs of the divining rod; and having discovered with what comparative ease the whole mechanism of his little government could be carried on by the admission of the birch regulator, so, as he grew richer, and lazier, and fatter, the Philhellenic Institute spun along as glibly as a top kept in vivacious movement by the perpetual application of the lash.

I believe that the school did not suffer in reputation from this sad apostasy on the part of the head-master; on the contrary, it seemed more natural and English—less outlandish and heretical. And it was at the zenith of its renown, when, one bright morning, with all my clothes nicely mended, and a large plum-cake in my box, I was deposited at its hospitable gates.

Amongst Dr. Herman's various whimsicalities, there was one to which he had adhered with more fidelity than to the anti-corporal punishment articles of his creed; and, in fact, it was upon this that he had caused those imposing words, "Philhellenic Institute," to blaze in gilt capitals in front of his academy. He belonged to that illustrious class of scholars who are now waging war on our popular mythologies, and upsetting all the associations which the Etonians and Harrovians connect with the household names of ancient history. In a word, he sought to restore to scholastic purity the mutilated orthography of Greek appellatives. He was extremely indignant that little boys should be brought up to confound Zeus with Jupiter, Ares with Mars, Artemis with Diana—the Greek deities with the Roman; and so rigidly did he inculcate the doctrine that these two sets of personages were to be kept constantly contradistinguished from each other, that his cross-examinations kept us in eternal confusion.

" Vat," he would exclaim, to some new boy fresh from some grammar-school on the Etonian system—" Vat do you mean by dranslating _Zeus_ Jupiter? Is dat amatory, irascible, cloud-com-

pelling god of Olympus, vid his eagle and his ægis, in the
smallest degree resembling de grave, formal, moral Jupiter
Optimus Maximus of the Roman capitol?—a god, Master
Simpkins, who would have been perfectly shocked at the idea
of running after innocent Fräulein dressed up as a swan or a
bull! I put dat question to you vonce for all, Master Simpkins."
Master Simpkins took care to agree with the Doctor. "And
how could you," resumed Dr. Herman majestically, turning to
some other criminal alumnus—"how could you presume to
dranslate de *Ares* of Homer, sir, by the audacious vulgarism
Mars? *Ares*, Master Jones, who roared as loud as ten thousand
men when he was hurt; or as you vill roar if I catch you calling
him Mars again! *Ares*, who covered seven plectra of ground;
confound *Ares*, the manslayer, with the Mars or Mavors whom
de Romans stole from de Sabines! Mars, de solemn and calm
protector of Rome! Master Jones, Master Jones, you ought to
be ashamed of yourself!" And then waxing enthusiastic, and
warming more and more into German gutturals and pronuncia-
tion, the good Doctor would lift up his hands, with two great
rings on his thumbs, and exclaim—"Und Du! and dou, *Aphro-
ditè;* dou, whose bert de seasons velcomed! dou, who didst put
Atonis into a coffer, and den tid durn him into an anemone;
dou to be called *Venus* by dat snivel-nosed little Master Budderfield! Venus, who presided over Baumgartens and funerals, and
nasty tinking sewers! Venus Cloacina—O mein Gott! Come
here, Master Budderfield; I must flog you for dat; I must indeed,
liddle boy!" As our Philhellenic preceptor carried his archæo-
logical purism into all Greek proper names, it was not likely
that my unhappy baptismal would escape. The first time I
signed my exercise I wrote "Pisistratus Caxton" in my best
round-hand. "And dey call your baba a scholar!" said the
doctor contemptuously. "Your name, sir, is Greek; and, as
Greek, you vill be dood enough to write it, vith vat you call an
e and an *o*—P, E, I, S, I, S, T, R, A, T, O, S. Vat can you expect for
to come to, Master Caxton, if you don't pay de care dat is proper
to your own dood name—de *e*, and de *o?* Ach! let me see no
more of your vile corruptions! Mein Gott! Pi! ven de name
is Pei!"

The next time I wrote home to my father, modestly implying
that I was short of cash, that a trap-bat would be acceptable,
and that the favourite goddess amongst the boys (whether
Greek or Roman was very immaterial) was *Diva Moneta*, I
felt a glow of classical pride in signing myself "your affec-

tionate Peisistratos." The next post brought a sad damper to my scholastic exultation. The letter ran thus :—

"My dear Son,—I prefer my old acquaintances Thucydides and Pisistratus to Thoukudides and Peisistratos. Horace is familiar to me, but Horatius is only known to me as Cocles. Pisistratus can play at trap-ball; but I find no authority in pure Greek to allow me to suppose that that game was known to Peisistratos. I should be too happy to send you a drachma or so, but I have no coins in my possession current at Athens at the time when Pisistratus was spelt Peisistratos.—Your affectionate father,   A. Caxton."

Verily, here indeed was the first practical embarrassment produced by that melancholy anachronism which my father had so prophetically deplored. However, nothing like experience to prove the value of compromise in this world! Peisistratos continued to write exercises, and a second letter from Pisistratus was followed by the trap-bat.

CHAPTER II

I WAS somewhere about sixteen when, on going home for the holidays, I found my mother's brother settled among the household *Lares*. Uncle Jack, as he was familiarly called, was a light-hearted, plausible, enthusiastic, talkative fellow, who had spent three small fortunes in trying to make a large one.

Uncle Jack was a great speculator; but in all his speculations he never affected to think of himself,—it was always the good of his fellow-creatures that he had at heart, and in this ungrateful world fellow-creatures are not to be relied upon! On coming of age, he inherited £6000 from his maternal grandfather. It seemed to him then that his fellow-creatures were sadly imposed upon by their tailors. Those ninth parts of humanity notoriously eked out their fractional existence by asking nine times too much for the clothing which civilisation, and perhaps a change of climate, render more necessary to us than to our predecessors, the Picts. Out of pure philanthropy, Uncle Jack started a "Grand National Benevolent Clothing Company," which undertook to supply the public with inexpressibles of the best Saxon cloth at 7s. 6d. a pair; coats, superfine, £1 18s. ! and waistcoats at so much per dozen—they were all to be worked off by steam. Thus the rascally tailors were to be put down, humanity clad, and the philanthropists rewarded (but that was a secondary consideration) with a clear return of 30 per cent. In spite of the evident charitableness of this Christian design, and the irrefragable calculations upon which it was based, this company died a victim to the ignorance and unthankfulness of our fellow-creatures. And all that remained of Jack's £6000 was a fifty-fourth share in a small steam-engine, a large assortment of ready-made pantaloons, and the liabilities of the directors.

Uncle Jack disappeared, and went on his travels. The same spirit of philanthropy which characterised the speculations of his purse attended the risks of his person. Uncle Jack had a natural leaning towards all distressed communities : if any tribe, race, or nation was down in the world, Uncle Jack threw himself plump into the scale to redress the balance. Poles, Greeks (the last were then fighting the Turks), Mexicans, Spaniards—Uncle Jack thrust his nose into all their squabbles !—Heaven forbid I should mock thee, poor Uncle Jack ! for those generous predilections towards the unfortunate ; only, whenever a nation is in a misfortune, there is always a job going on ! The Polish cause, the Greek cause, the Mexican cause, and the Spanish cause, are necessarily mixed up with loans and subscriptions. These Continental patriots, when they take up the sword with one hand, generally contrive to thrust the other hand deep into their neighbour's breeches-pockets ! Uncle Jack went to Greece, thence he went to Spain, thence to Mexico. No doubt he was of great service to those afflicted populations, for he came back with unanswerable proof of their gratitude, in the shape of £3000. Shortly after this appeared a prospectus of the " New, Grand, National, Benevolent Insurance Company, for the Industrious Classes." This invaluable document, after setting forth the immense benefits to society arising from habits of providence, and the introduction of insurance companies—proving the infamous rate of premiums exacted by the existent offices, and their inapplicability to the wants of the honest artisan, and declaring that nothing but the purest intentions of benefiting their fellow-creatures, and raising the moral tone of society, had led the directors to institute a new society, founded on the noblest principles and the most moderate calculations—proceeded to demonstrate that twenty-four and a half per cent. was the smallest possible return the shareholders could anticipate. The company began under the fairest auspices : an archbishop was caught as president, on the condition always that he should give nothing but his name to the society. Uncle Jack—more euphoniously designated as "the celebrated philanthropist, John Jones Tibbets, Esquire"—was honorary secretary, and the capital stated at two millions. But such was the obtuseness of the industrious classes, so little did they perceive the benefits of subscribing one-and-ninepence a week from the age of twenty-one to fifty, in order to secure at the latter age the annuity of £18, that the company dissolved into thin air, and with it dissolved Uncle Jack's £3000. Nothing more was then seen or heard of him for three years. So obscure was his existence, that on the death of an aunt who left him a small farm in Cornwall, it was necessary to advertise that "If John Jones Tibbets, Esq., would apply to Messrs. Blunt & Tin, Lothbury, between the hours of ten and four, he would hear of something to his advantage." But, even as a conjuror declares that he will call the ace of spades, and the ace of spades, that you thought you had safely under your foot, turns up on the table—so with this advertisement suddenly turned up Uncle Jack. With inconceivable satisfaction did the new landowner settle himself in his comfortable homestead. The farm, which was about two hundred acres, was in the best possible condition, and saving one or two chemical preparations, which cost Uncle Jack, upon the most scientific principles, thirty acres of buckwheat, the ears of which came up, poor things, all spotted and speckled, as if they had been inoculated with the small-pox, Uncle Jack for the first two years was a thriving man. Unluckily, however, one day Uncle Jack discovered a coal-mine in a beautiful field of Swedish turnips; in another week the house was full of engineers and naturalists, and in another month appeared, in my uncle's best style, much improved by practice, a prospectus of the "Grand National Anti-Monopoly Coal Company, instituted on behalf of the poor householders of London, and against the Monster Monopoly of the London Coal Wharfs.

"A vein of the finest coal has been discovered on the estate of the celebrated philanthropist, John Jones Tibbets, Esq. This new mine, the Molly Wheel, having been satisfactorily tested by that eminent engineer, Giles Compass, Esq., promises an inexhaustible field to the energies of the benevolent and the wealth of the capitalist. It is calculated that the best coals may be delivered, screened, at the mouth of the Thames, for 18s. per load, yielding a profit of not less than forty-eight per cent. to the shareholders. Shares, £50, to be paid in five instalments. Capital to be subscribed, one million. For shares, early application must be made to Messrs. Blunt & Tin, solicitors, Lothbury."

Here, then, was something tangible for fellow-creatures to go on—there was land, there was a mine, there was coal, and there actually came shareholders and capital. Uncle Jack was so persuaded that his fortune was now to be made, and had, moreover, so great a desire to share the glory of ruining the monster monopoly of the London wharfs, that he refused a very large offer to dispose of the property altogether, remained chief shareholder, and removed to London, where he set up his carriage, and gave dinners to his fellow-directors. For no less than three years did this company flourish, having submitted the entire direction and working of the mines to that eminent engineer, Giles Compass—twenty per cent. was paid regularly by that gentleman to the shareholders, and the shares were at more than cent. per cent., when one bright morning Giles Compass, Esq., unexpectedly removed himself to that wider field for genius like his, the United States ; and it was discovered that the mine had for more than a year run itself into a great pit of water, and that Mr. Compass had been paying the shareholders out of their own capital. My uncle had the satisfaction this time of being ruined in very good company ; three doctors of divinity, two county members, a Scotch lord, and an East India director, were all in the same boat—that boat which went down with the coal-mine into the great water-pit !

It was just after this event that Uncle Jack, sanguine and light-hearted as ever, suddenly recollected his sister, Mrs. Caxton, and not knowing where else to dine, thought he would repose his limbs under my father's *trabes citrea*, which the ingenious W. S. Landor opines should be translated " mahogany." You never saw a more charming man than Uncle Jack. All plump people are more popular than thin people. There is something jovial and pleasant in the sight of a round face ! What conspiracy could succeed when its head was a lean and hungry-looking fellow, like Cassius ? If the Roman patriots had had Uncle Jack amongst them, perhaps they would never have furnished a tragedy to Shakspeare. Uncle Jack was as plump as a partridge—not unwieldy, not corpulent, not obese, not " *vastus*," which Cicero objects to in an orator—but every crevice comfortably filled up. Like the ocean, " time wrote no wrinkles on his glassy (or brassy) brow." His natural lines were all upward curves, his smile most ingratiating, his eye so frank, even his trick of rubbing his clean, well-fed, English-looking hands, had something about it coaxing and *débonnaire*, something that actually decoyed you into trusting your money into hands so prepossessing. Indeed, to him might be fully applied the expression —" Sedem animæ in extremis digitis habet ;" " He had his soul's seat in his finger-ends." The critics observe that few men have ever united in equal perfection the imaginative with the scientific faculties. " Happy he," exclaims Schiller, " who combines the enthusiast's warmth with the worldly man's light"—light and warmth, Uncle Jack had them both. He was a perfect symphony of bewitching enthusiasm and convincing calculation. Dicæopolis in the *Acharnenses*, in presenting a gentleman called Nicharchus to the audience, observes—" He is small, I confess, but there is nothing lost in him; all is knave that is not fool." Parodying the equivocal compliment, I may say that though Uncle Jack was no giant, there was nothing lost in him. Whatever was not philanthropy was arithmetic, and whatever was not arithmetic was philanthropy. He would have been equally dear to Howard and to Cocker. Uncle Jack was comely, too—clearskinned and florid, had a little mouth, with good teeth, wore no whiskers, shaved his beard as close as if it were one of his grand national companies; his hair, once somewhat sandy, was now rather greyish, which increased the respectability of his appearance; and he wore it flat at the sides and raised in a peak at the top; his organs of constructiveness and ideality were pronounced by Mr. Squills to be prodigious, and those freely developed bumps gave great breadth to his forehead. Well-shaped, too, was Uncle Jack, about five feet eight, the proper height for an active man of business. He wore a black coat; but to make the nap look the fresher, he had given it the relief of gilt buttons, on which were wrought a small crown and anchor; at a distance this button looked like the king's button, and gave him the air of one who has a place about Court. He always wore a white neckcloth without starch, a frill, and a diamond pin, which last furnished him with observations upon certain mines of Mexico, which he had a great, but hitherto unsatisfied, desire of seeing worked by a grand National United Britons Company. His waistcoat of a morning was pale buff—of an evening, embroidered velvet; wherewith were connected sundry schemes of an "association for the improvement of native manufactures." His trousers, matutinally, were of the colour vulgarly called "blotting-paper"; and he never wore boots, which, he said, unfitted a man for exercise, but short drab gaiters and square-toed shoes. His watch-chain was garnished with a vast number of seals : each seal, indeed, represented the device of some defunct company, and they might be said to resemble the scalps of the slain, worn by the aboriginal Iroquois—concerning whom, indeed, he had once entertained philanthropic designs, compounded of conversion to Christianity on the principles of the English Episcopal Church, and of an advantageous exchange of beaver-skins for Bibles, brandy, and gunpowder.

That Uncle Jack should win my heart was no wonder; my mother's he had always won from her earliest recollection of his having persuaded her to let her great doll (a present from her godmother) be put up to a raffle for the benefit of the chimney-sweepers. "So like him—so good!" she would often say pensively ; "they paid sixpence apiece for the raffle—twenty tickets, and the doll cost £2. Nobody was taken in, and the doll, poor thing (it had such blue eyes !), went for a quarter of its value. But Jack said nobody could guess what good the ten shillings did to the chimney-sweepers." Naturally enough, I say, my mother liked Uncle Jack ; but my father liked him quite as well, and that was a strong proof of my uncle's powers of captivation. However, it is noticeable that when some retired scholar is once interested in an active man of the world, he is more inclined to admire him than others are. Sympathy with such a companion gratifies at once his curiosity and his indolence ; he can travel with him, scheme with him, fight with him, go with him through all the adventures of which his own books speak so eloquently, and all the time never stir from his easy-chair. My father said "that it was like listening to Ulysses to hear Uncle Jack !" Uncle Jack, too, had been in Greece and Asia Minor, gone over the site of the siege of Troy, ate figs at Marathon, shot hares in the Peloponnesus, and drank three pints of brown stout at the top of the Great Pyramid.

Therefore, Uncle Jack was like a book of reference to my father. Verily at times he looked on him *as* a book, and took him down after dinner as he would a volume of Dodwell or Pausanias. In fact, I believe that scholars who never move from their cells are not the less an eminently curious, bustling, active race, rightly understood. Even as old Burton saith of himself—"Though I live a collegiate student, and lead a monastic life, sequestered from those tumults and troubles of the world, I hear and see what is done abroad, how others run, ride, turmoil, and macerate themselves in town and country;" which citation sufficeth to show that scholars are naturally the most active men of the

world, only that while their heads plot with Augustus, fight with
Julius, sail with Columbus, and change the face of the globe with
Alexander, Attila, or Mahomet, there is a certain mysterious
attraction, which our improved knowledge of mesmerism will
doubtless soon explain to the satisfaction of science, between
that extremer and antipodal part of the human frame, called in
the vulgate "the seat of honour," and the stuffed leather of an
armed chair.   Learning somehow or other sinks down to that
part into which it was first driven, and produces therein a
leaden heaviness and weight, which counteract those lively
emotions of the brain, that might otherwise render students
too mercurial and agile for the safety of established order.   I
leave this conjecture to the consideration of experimentalists
in the physics.

I was still more delighted than my father with Uncle Jack.
He was full of amusing tricks, could conjure wonderfully,
make a bunch of keys dance a hornpipe, and if ever you gave
him half-a-crown, he was sure to turn it into a halfpenny.
He was only unsuccessful in turning my halfpennies into half-
crowns.

We took long walks together, and in the midst of his most
diverting conversation my uncle was always an observer.   He
would stop to examine the nature of the soil, fill my pockets
(not his own) with great lumps of clay, stones, and rubbish, to
analyse when he got home, by the help of some chemical apparatus he had borrowed from Mr. Squills.   He would stand
an hour at a cottage door, admiring the little girls who were
straw-platting, and then walk into the nearest farm-houses, to
suggest the feasibility of "a national straw-plat association."
All this fertility of intellect was, alas! wasted in that *ingrata
terra* into which Uncle Jack had fallen.   No squire could be
persuaded into the belief that his mother-stone was pregnant
with minerals; no farmer talked into weaving straw-plat into a
proprietary association.   So, even as an ogre, having devastated
the surrounding country, begins to cast a hungry eye on his
own little ones, Uncle Jack's mouth, long defrauded of juicier
and more legitimate morsels, began to water for a bite of my
innocent father.

CHAPTER III

A T this time **we** were living in what may be called a very respectable style for people who made no pretence to ostentation. On the skirts of a large village stood a square red brick house, about the date of Queen Anne. Upon the top of the house was a balustrade; why, Heaven knows—for nobody, except our great tom-cat Ralph, ever walked upon the leads—but so it was, and so it often is in houses from the time of Elizabeth, yea, even to that of Victoria. This balustrade was divided by low piers, on each of which was placed a round ball. The centre of the house was distinguishable by an architrave, in the shape of a triangle, under which was a niche, probably meant for a figure, but the figure was not forthcoming. Below this was the window (encased with carved pilasters) of my dear mother's little sitting-room; and lower still, raised on a flight of six steps, was a very handsome-looking door, with a projecting porch. All the windows, with smallish panes and largish frames, were relieved with stone copings;—so that the house had an air of solidity, and well-to-do-ness about it—nothing tricky on the one hand, nothing decayed on the other. The house stood a little back from the garden gates, which were large, and set between two piers surmounted with vases. Many might object, that in wet weather you had to walk some way to your carriage; but we obviated that objection by not keeping a carriage. To the right of the house the enclosure contained a little lawn, a laurel hermitage, a square pond, a modest green-house, and half-a-dozen plots of mignonette, heliotrope, roses, pinks, sweet-william, &c. To the left spread the kitchen-garden, lying screened by espaliers yielding the finest apples in the neighbourhood, and divided by three winding gravel walks, of which the extremest was backed by a wall, whereon, as it lay full south, peaches, pears, and nectarines sunned themselves early into well-remembered flavour. This walk was appropriated to my father. Book in hand, he would, on fine days, pace to and fro, often stopping, dear man, to jot down a pencil-note, gesticulate, or soliloquise. And there, when not in his study, my mother would be sure to find him. In these deambulations, as he called them, he had generally a companion so extraordinary, that I expect to be met with a hillalu of incredulous contempt when I specify it. Nevertheless I vow and protest

c

that it is strictly true, and no invention of an exaggerating romancer. It happened one day that my mother had coaxed Mr. Caxton to walk with her to market. By the way they passed a sward of green, on which sundry little boys were engaged upon the lapidation of a lame duck. It seemed that the duck was to have been taken to market, when it was discovered not only to be lame, but dyspeptic; perhaps some weed had disagreed with its ganglionic apparatus, poor thing. However that be, the goodwife had declared that the duck was good for nothing; and upon the petition of her children, it had been consigned to them for a little innocent amusement, and to keep them out of harm's way. My mother declared that she never before saw her lord and master roused to such animation. He dispersed the urchins, released the duck, carried it home, kept it in a basket by the fire, fed it and physicked it till it recovered; and then it was consigned to the square pond. But lo! the duck knew its benefactor; and whenever my father appeared outside his door, it would catch sight of him, flap from the pond, gain the lawn, and hobble after him (for it never quite recovered the use of its left leg), till it reached the walk by the peaches; and there sometimes it would sit, gravely watching its master's deambulations; sometimes stroll by his side, and, at all events, never leave him till, at his return home, he fed it with his own hands; and, quacking her peaceful adieus, the nymph then retired to her natural element.

With the exception of my mother's favourite morning-room, the principal sitting-rooms—that is, the study, the dining-room, and what was emphatically called "the best drawing-room," which was only occupied on great occasions—looked south. Tall beeches, firs, poplars, and a few oaks backed the house, and indeed surrounded it on all sides but the south; so that it was well sheltered from the winter cold and the summer heat. Our principal domestic, in dignity and station, was Mrs. Primmins, who was waiting gentlewoman, housekeeper, and tyrannical dictatrix of the whole establishment. Two other maids, a gardener, and a footman, composed the rest of the serving household. Save a few pasture-fields, which he let, my father was not troubled with land. His income was derived from the interest of about £15,000, partly in the Three per Cents., partly on mortgage; and what with my mother and Mrs. Primmins, this income always yielded enough to satisfy my father's single hobby for books, pay for my education, and entertain our neighbours, rarely, indeed, at dinner, but very often at tea. My

dear mother boasted that our society was very select. It consisted chiefly of the clergyman and his family, two old maids
who gave themselves great airs, a gentleman who had been in
the East India service, and who lived in a large white house at
the top of the hill ; some half-a-dozen squires and their wives
and children; Mr. Squills, still a bachelor : and once a year
cards were exchanged—and dinners too—with certain aristocrats
who inspired my mother with a great deal of unnecessary awe ;
since she declared they were the most good-natured, easy people
in the world, and always stuck their cards in the most conspicuous part of the looking-glass frame over the chimney-piece
of the best drawing-room. Thus you perceive that our natural
position was one highly creditable to us, proving the soundness
of our finances and the gentility of our pedigree—of which last
more hereafter. At present I content myself with saying on
that head, that even the proudest of the neighbouring squirearchs
always spoke of us as a very ancient family. But all my father
ever said, to evince pride of ancestry, was in honour of William
Caxton, citizen and printer in the reign of Edward IV.—" Clarum
et venerabile nomen ! " an ancestor a man of letters might be
justly vain of.

"Heus," said my father, stopping short, and lifting his eyes
from the Colloquies of Erasmus, " salve multum, jucundissime."

Uncle Jack was not much of a scholar, but he knew enough
of Latin to answer, " Salve tantundem, mi frater."

My father smiled approvingly. " I see you comprehend true
urbanity, or politeness, as we phrase it. There is an elegance in
addressing the husband of your sister as brother. Erasmus com-
mends it in his opening chapter, under the head of ' Salutandi
formulæ.' And, indeed," added my father thoughtfully, " there
is no great difference between politeness and affection. My
author here observes that it is polite to express salutation in
certain minor distresses of nature. One should salute a gentleman in yawning, salute him in hiccuping, salute him in sneezing,
salute him in coughing ; and that evidently because of your
interest in his health ; for he may dislocate his jaw in yawning, and the hiccup is often a symptom of grave disorder, and
sneezing is perilous to the small blood-vessels of the head, and
coughing is either a tracheal, bronchial, pulmonary, or ganglionic
affection."

"Very true. The Turks always salute in sneezing, and they
are a remarkably polite people," said Uncle Jack. " But, my
dear brother, I was just looking with admiration at these apple-

trees of yours.   I never saw finer.   I am a great judge of
apples.   I find, in talking with my sister, that you make very
little profit by them.   That's a pity.   One might establish a
cider orchard in this county.   You can take your own fields in
hand ; you can hire more, so as to make the whole, say a
hundred acres.   You can plant a very extensive apple-orchard
on a grand scale.   I have just run through the calculations ;
they are quite startling.   Take 40 trees per acre—that's the
proper average—at 1s. 6d. per tree ; 4000 trees for 100 acres,
£300 ; labour of digging, trenching, say £10 an acre—total for
100 acres, £1000.   Pave the bottoms of the holes to prevent
the tap-root striking down into the bad soil—oh, I am very
close and careful, you see, in all minutiæ ! always was—pave
'em with rubbish and stones, 6d. a hole ; that for 4000 trees
the 100 acres is £100.   Add the rent of the land at 30s. an
acre, £150.   And how stands the total ?"   Here Uncle Jack
proceeded rapidly ticking off the items with his fingers :—

" Trees	.	.	.	.	.	£ 300
Labour	.	.	.	.	.	1000
Paving holes	.	.	.	.	100
Rent	.	.	.	.	.	150
		Total	.	.	£1550

That's your expense.   Mark.—Now to the profit.   Orchards in
Kent realise £100 an acre, some even £150 ; but let's be
moderate, say only £50 an acre, and your gross profit per year,
from a capital of £1550, will be £5000,—£5000 a year.   Think
of that, brother Caxton.   Deduct 10 per cent., or £500 a year,
for gardeners' wages, manure, &c., and the net product is £4500.
Your fortune's made, man—it is made—I wish you joy !"   And
Uncle Jack rubbed his hands.

"Bless me, father," said eagerly the young Pisistratus, who
had swallowed with ravished ears every syllable and figure of
this inviting calculation, "why, we should be as rich as Squire
Rollick ; and then, you know, sir, you could keep a pack of
fox-hounds."

"And buy a large library," added Uncle Jack, with more
subtle knowledge of human nature as to its appropriate temptations.   "There's my friend the archbishop's collection to be
sold."

Slowly recovering his breath, my father gently turned his
eyes from one to the other ; and then, laying his left hand on

my head, while with the right he held up Erasmus rebukingly to Uncle Jack, said—

"See how easily you can sow covetousness and avidity in the youthful mind. Ah, brother!"

"You are too severe, sir. See how the dear boy hangs his head! Fie!—natural enthusiasm of his years—'gay hope my fancy fed,' as the poet says. Why, for that fine boy's sake, you ought not to lose so certain an occasion of wealth, I may say, untold. For, observe, you will form a nursery of crabs; each year you go on grafting and enlarging your plantation, renting, nay, why not buying, more land? Gad, sir! in twenty years you might cover half the country; but say you stop short at 2000 acres, why, the net profit is £90,000 a year. A duke's income—a duke's—and going a-begging, as I may say."

"But stop," said I modestly; "the trees don't grow in a year. I know when our last apple-tree was planted—it is five years ago—it was then three years old, and it only bore one half-bushel last autumn."

"What an intelligent lad it is!—Good head there. Oh, he'll do credit to his great fortune, brother," said Uncle Jack approvingly. "True, my boy. But in the meanwhile we could fill the ground, as they do in Kent, with gooseberries and currants, or onions and cabbages. Nevertheless, considering we are not great capitalists, I am afraid we must give up a share of our profits to diminish our outlay. So hark-ye, Pisistratus—(look at him, brother—simple as he stands there, I think he is born with a silver spoon in his mouth)—hark-ye, now to the mysteries of speculation. Your father shall quietly buy the land, and then, presto! we will issue a prospectus, and start a company. Associations can wait five years for a return. Every year, meanwhile, increases the value of the shares. Your father takes, we say, fifty shares at £50 each, paying only an instalment of £2 a share. He sells 35 shares at cent. per cent. He keeps the remaining 15, and his fortune's made all the same; only it is not quite so large as if he had kept the whole concern in his own hands. What say you now, brother Caxton? '*Visne edere pomum?*' as we used to say at school."

"I don't want a shilling more than I have got," said my father resolutely. "My wife would not love me better; my food would not nourish me more; my boy would not, in all probability, be half so hardy, or a tenth part so industrious; and——"

"But," interrupted Uncle Jack, pertinaciously, and reserving his grand argument for the last, "the good you would confer on the community—the progress given to the natural productions of your country, the wholesome beverage of cider, brought within cheap reach of the labouring classes. If it was only for your sake, should I have urged this question? should I now? is it in my character? But for the sake of the public! mankind! of our fellow-creatures! Why, sir, England could not get on if gentlemen like you had not a little philanthropy and speculation."

"Papæ!" exclaimed my father, "to think that England can't get on without turning Austin Caxton into an apple-merchant! My dear Jack, listen. You remind me of a colloquy in this book; wait a bit—here it is—*Pamphagus and Cocles.*—Cocles recognises his friend, who had been absent for many years, by his eminent and remarkable nose.—Pamphagus says, rather irritably, that he is not ashamed of his nose. 'Ashamed of it! no, indeed,' says Cocles: 'I never saw a nose that could be put to so many uses!' 'Ha,' says Pamphagus (whose curiosity is aroused), 'uses! what uses?' Whereon (*lepidissime frater!*) Cocles, with eloquence as rapid as yours, runs on with a countless list of the uses to which so vast a development of the organ can be applied. 'If the cellar was deep, it could sniff up the wine like an elephant's trunk,—if the bellows were missing, it could blow the fire,—if the lamp was too glaring, it could suffice for a shade,—it would serve as a speaking-trumpet to a herald, —it could sound a signal of battle in the field,—it would do for a wedge in wood-cutting—a spade for digging—a scythe for mowing—an anchor in sailing;' till Pamphagus cries out, 'Lucky dog that I am! and I never knew before what a useful piece of furniture I carried about with me.'" My father paused and strove to whistle, but that effort of harmony failed him—and he added, smiling, "So much for my apple-trees, brother John. Leave them to their natural destination of filling tarts and dumplings."

Uncle Jack looked a little discomposed for a moment; but he then laughed with his usual heartiness, and saw that he had not yet got to my father's blind side. I confess that my revered parent rose in my estimation after that conference; and I began to see that a man may not be quite without common sense, though he is a scholar. Indeed, whether it was that Uncle Jack's visit acted as a gentle stimulant to his relaxed faculties, or that I, now grown older and wiser, began to see his character more clearly, I date from those summer holidays the commencement of that familiar and endearing intimacy which ever after existed between my father and myself. Often I deserted the more extensive rambles of Uncle Jack, or the greater allurements of a cricket-match in the village, or a day's fishing in Squire Rollick's preserves, for a quiet stroll with my father by the old peach wall;—sometimes silent, indeed, and already musing over the future, while he was busy with the past, but amply rewarded when, suspending his lecture, he would pour forth hoards of varied learning, rendered amusing by his quaint comments, and that Socratic satire which only fell short of wit because it never passed into malice. At some moments, indeed, the vein ran into eloquence; and with some fine heroic sentiment in his old books, his stooping form rose erect, his eye flashed; and you saw that he had not been originally formed and wholly meant for the obscure seclusion in which his harmless days now wore contentedly away.

CHAPTER IV

EGAD, sir, the country is going to the dogs! Our sentiments are not represented in Parliament or out of it. The *County Mercury* has ratted, and be hanged to it! and now we have not one newspaper in the whole shire to express the sentiments of the respectable part of the community!"

This speech was made on the occasion of one of the rare dinners given by Mr. and Mrs. Caxton to the grandees of the neighbourhood, and uttered by no less a person than Squire Rollick, of Rollick Hall, chairman of the quarter-sessions.

I confess that I (for I was permitted on that first occasion not only to dine with the guests, but to outstay the ladies, in virtue of my growing years, and my promise to abstain from the decanters)—I confess, I say, that I, poor innocent, was puzzled to conjecture what sudden interest in the county newspaper could cause Uncle Jack to prick up his ears like a war-horse at the sound of the drum, and rush so incontinently across the interval between Squire Rollick and himself. But the mind of that deep and truly knowing man was not to be plumbed by a chit of my age. You could not fish for the shy salmon in that pool with a crooked pin and a bobbin, as you would for minnows; or, to indulge in a more worthy illustration, you could not say

of him, as St. Gregory saith of the streams of Jordan, " A lamb
could wade easily through that ford."

" Not a county newspaper to advocate the rights of——"
here my uncle stopped, as if at a loss, and whispered, in my
ear, " What are his politics ? "   " Don't know," answered I.
Uncle Jack intuitively took down from his memory the phrase
most readily at hand, and added with a nasal intonation, " the
rights of our distressed fellow-creatures ! "

My father scratched his eyebrow with his forefinger, as he
was apt to do when doubtful ; the rest of the company—a silent
set—looked up.

" Fellow-creatures !" said Mr. Rollick—" fellow-fiddlesticks !"

Uncle Jack was clearly in the wrong box.   He drew out
of it cautiously—" I mean," said he, " our *respectable* fellow-
creatures ; " and then suddenly it occurred to him that a
County Mercury would naturally represent the agricultural
interest, and that if Mr. Rollick said that the " *County Mercury*
ought to be hanged," he was one of those politicians who had
already begun to call the agricultural interest " a Vampire."
Flushed with that fancied discovery, Uncle Jack rushed on,
intending to bear along with the stream, thus fortunately
directing all the " rubbish " [1] subsequently shot into Covent
Garden and Hall of Commerce.

" Yes, respectable fellow-creatures, men of capital and enterprise !   For what are these country squires compared to our
wealthy merchants ?   What is this agricultural interest that
professes to be the prop of the land ? "

" Professes ! " cried Squire Rollick —" it *is* the prop of the
land ; and as for those manufacturing fellows who have bought
up the *Mercury*——"

" Bought up the *Mercury*, have they, the villains ? " cried
Uncle Jack, interrupting the Squire, and now bursting into full
scent—" Depend upon it, sir, it is a part of a diabolical system
of buying up, which must be exposed manfully.—Yes, as I was
saying, what is that agricultural interest which they desire to
ruin ? which they declare to be so bloated—which they call a
' vampire !' they the true blood-suckers, the venomous millocrats !
Fellow-creatures, sir !   I may well call distressed fellow-creatures
the members of that much-suffering class of which you yourself
are an ornament.   What can be more deserving of our best

---

[1] " We talked sad rubbish when we first began," says Mr. Cobden in
one of his speeches.

efforts for relief, than a country gentleman like yourself, we'll say—of a nominal £5000 a year—compelled to keep up an establishment, pay for his fox-hounds, support the whole population by contributions to the poor-rates, support the whole Church by tithes; all justice, jails, and prosecutions by the county rates — all thoroughfares by the highway rates — ground down by mortgages, Jews, or jointures; having to provide for younger children; enormous expenses for cutting his woods, manuring his model farm, and fattening huge oxen till every pound of flesh costs him five pounds sterling in oil-cake; and then the lawsuits necessary to protect his rights; plundered on all hands by poachers, sheep-stealers, dog-stealers, churchwardens, overseers, gardeners, gamekeepers, and that necessary rascal, his steward. If ever there was a distressed fellow-creature in the world, it is a country gentleman with a great estate."

My father evidently thought this an exquisite piece of banter, for by the corner of his mouth I saw that he chuckled inly.

Squire Rollick, who had interrupted the speech by sundry approving exclamations, particularly at the mention of poor-rates, tithes, county-rates, mortgages, and poachers, here pushed the bottle to Uncle Jack, and said civilly—"There's a great deal of truth in what you say, Mr. Tibbets. The agricultural interest is going to ruin; and when it does, I would not give *that* for Old England!" and Mr. Rollick snapped his finger and thumb. "But what is to be done—done for the country? There's the rub."

"I was just coming to that," quoth Uncle Jack. "You say that you have not a county paper that upholds your cause, and denounces your enemies."

"Not since the Whigs bought the ——shire *Mercury.*"

"Why, good heavens! Mr. Rollick, how can you suppose that you will have justice done you, if at this time of day you neglect the press? The press, sir—there it is—air we breathe! What you want is a great national—no, not a national—A PROVINCIAL proprietary weekly journal, supported liberally and steadily by that mighty party whose very existence is at stake. Without such a paper, you are gone, you are dead, extinct, defunct, buried alive; *with* such a paper, well conducted, well edited by a man of the world, of education, of practical experience in agriculture and human nature, mines, corn, manure, insurances, acts of Parliament, cattle-shows, the state of parties, and the best interests of society—with such a man and such a paper, you will carry all before you. But it must be done by subscription, by

association, by co-operation, by a Grand Provincial Benevolent
Agricultural Anti-Innovating Society."

"Egad, sir, you are right!" said Mr. Rollick, slapping his
thigh; "and I'll ride over to our Lord-Lieutenant to-morrow.
His eldest son ought to carry the county."

"And he will, if you encourage the press and set up a journal,"
said Uncle Jack, rubbing his hands, and then gently stretching
them out, and drawing them gradually together, as if he were
already enclosing in that airy circle the unsuspecting guineas of
the unborn association.

All happiness dwells more in the hope than the possession;
and at that moment, I dare be sworn that Uncle Jack felt a
livelier rapture, *circum præcordia*, warming his entrails, and dif-
fusing throughout his whole frame of five feet eight the prophetic glow of the Magna Diva Moneta, than if he had enjoyed
for ten years the actual possession of King Crœsus's privy purse.

"I thought Uncle Jack was not a Tory," said I to my father
the next day.

My father, who cared nothing for politics, opened his eyes.

"Are you a Tory or Whig, papa?"

"Um," said my father—"there's a great deal to be said on
both sides of the question. You see, my boy, that Mrs. Primmins
has a great many moulds for our butter-pats; sometimes they
come up with a crown on them, sometimes with the more
popular impress of a cow. It is all very well for those who dish
up the butter to print it according to their taste, or in proof of
their abilities; it is enough for us to butter our bread, say
grace, and pay for the dairy. Do you understand?"

"Not a bit, sir."

"Your namesake Pisistratus was wiser than you, then," said
my father. "And now let us feed the duck. Where's your
uncle?"

"He has borrowed Mr. Squills' mare, sir, and gone with Squire
Rollick to the great lord they were talking of."

"Oho!" said my father, "brother Jack is going to print his
butter!"

And indeed Uncle Jack played his cards so well on this occasion, and set before the Lord-Lieutenant, with whom he had a
personal interview, so fine a prospectus, and so nice a calculation,
that before my holidays were over, he was installed in a very
handsome office in the county town, with private apartments
over it, and a salary of £500 a year—for advocating the cause
of his distressed fellow-creatures, including noblemen, squires,

Egad, Sir, you're right!

yeomanry, farmers, and all yearly subscribers in the NEW PRO-
PRIETARY AGRICULTURAL ANTI-INNOVATING —— SHIRE WEEKLY
GAZETTE. At the head of his newspaper Uncle Jack caused to
be engraved a crown supported by a flail and a crook, with the
motto, " Pro rege et grege : "—And that was the way in which
Uncle Jack printed his pats of butter.

CHAPTER V

I SEEMED to myself to have made a leap in life when I returned to school. I no longer felt as a boy. Uncle Jack, out
of his own purse, had presented me with my first pair of Wellington boots ; my mother had been coaxed into allowing me a
small tail to jackets hitherto tailless ; my collars, which had been
wont, spaniel-like, to flap and fall about my neck, now, terrier-
wise, stood erect and rampant, encompassed with a circumvalla-
tion of whalebone, buckram, and black silk. I was, in truth,
nearly seventeen, and I gave myself the airs of a man. Now, be
it observed, that that crisis in adolescent existence wherein we
first pass from Master Sisty into Mr. Pisistratus, or Pisistratus
Caxton, Esq.—wherein we arrogate, and with tactic concession
from our elders, the long-envied title of " young man "—always
seems a sudden and imprompt upshooting and elevation. We
do not mark the gradual preparations thereto ; we remember
only one distinct period in which all the signs and symptoms
burst and effloresced together ; Wellington boots, coat tail, cravat,
down on the upper lip, thoughts on razors, reveries on young
ladies, and a new kind of sense of poetry.

I began now to read steadily, to understand what I did read,
and to cast some anxious looks towards the future, with vague
notions that I had a place to win in the world, and that nothing
is to be won without perseverance and labour ; and so I went
on till I was seventeen, and at the head of the school, when
I received the two letters I subjoin.

1.—FROM AUGUSTINE CAXTON, ESQ.

" MY DEAR SON,—I have informed Dr. Herman that you will
not return to him after the approaching holidays. You are
old enough now to look forward to the embraces of our beloved
Alma Mater, and I think studious enough to hope for the

honours she bestows on her worthier sons. You are already entered at Trinity,—and in fancy I see my youth return to me in your image. I see you wandering where the Cam steals its way through those noble gardens; and, confusing you with myself, I recall the old dreams that haunted me when the chiming bells swung over the placid waters. 'Verum secretumque *Mouseion*, quam multa dictatis, quam multa invenitis!' There at that illustrious college, unless the race has indeed degenerated, you will measure yourself with young giants. You will see those who, in the Law, the Church, the State, or the still cloisters of Learning, are destined to become the eminent leaders of your age. To rank amongst them you are not forbidden to aspire; he who in youth 'can scorn delight, and love laborious days,' should pitch high his ambition.

"Your Uncle Jack says he has done wonders with his newspaper,—though Mr. Rollick grumbles, and declares that it is full of theories, and that it puzzles the farmers. Uncle Jack, in reply, contends that he creates an audience, not addresses one,—and sighs that his genius is thrown away in a provincial town. In fact, he really is a very clever man, and might do much in London, I dare say. He often comes over to dine and sleep, returning the next morning. His energy is wonderful—and contagious. Can you imagine that he has actually stirred up the flame of my vanity, by constantly poking at the bars? Metaphor apart—I find myself collecting all my notes and commonplaces, and wondering to see how easily they fall into method, and take shape in chapters and books. I cannot help smiling when I add, that I fancy I am going to become an author; and smiling more when I think that your Uncle Jack should have provoked me into so egregious an ambition. However, I have read some passages of my book to your mother, and she says, 'It is vastly fine,' which is encouraging. Your mother has great good sense, though I don't mean to say that she has much learning,—which is a wonder, considering that Pic de la Mirandola was nothing to her father. Yet he died, dear great man, and never printed a line,—while I—positively I blush to think of my temerity!

"Adieu, my son; make the best of the time that remains with you at the Philhellenic. A full mind is the true Pantheism, *plena Jovis:* It is only in some corner of the brain which we leave empty that Vice can obtain a lodging. When she knocks at your door, my son, be able to say, 'No room for your ladyship—pass on.' Your affectionate father,   A. CAXTON."

2.—From Mrs. Caxton.

"My dearest Sisty,—You are coming home!—My heart is so full of that thought that it seems to me as if I could not write anything else. Dear child, you are coming home, as you have done with school, you have done with strangers,—you are our own, all our own son again! You are mine again, as you were in the cradle, the nursery, and the garden, Sisty, when we used to throw daisies at each other! You will laugh at me so, when I tell you, that as soon as I heard you were coming home for good, I crept away from the room, and went to my drawer where I keep, you know, all my treasures. There was your little cap that I worked myself, and your poor little nankeen jacket that you were so proud to throw off—oh! and many other relics of you when you were little Sisty, and I was not the cold, formal 'Mother' you call me now, but 'dear Mamma.' I kissed them, Sisty, and said, 'my little child is coming back to me again!' So foolish was I, I forgot all the long years that have passed, and fancied I could carry you again in my arms, and that I should again coax you to say 'God bless papa.' Well, well! I write now between laughing and crying. You cannot be what you were, but you are still my own dear son—your father's son—dearer to me than all the world—except that father.

"I am so glad, too, that you will come so soon: come while your father is really warm with his book, and while you can encourage and keep him to it. For why should he not be great and famous? Why should not all admire him as we do? You know how proud of him I always was; but I do so long to let the world know *why* I was so proud. And yet, after all, it is not only because he is so wise and learned,—but because he is so good, and has such a large noble heart. But the heart must appear in the book too, as well as the learning. For though it is full of things I don't understand—every now and then there *is* something I do understand—that seems as if that heart spoke out to all the world.

"Your uncle has undertaken to get it published; and your father is going up to town with him about it, as soon as the first volume is finished.

"All are quite well except poor Mrs. Jones, who has the ague very bad indeed; Primmins has made her wear a charm for it, and Mrs. Jones actually declares she is already much better. One can't deny that there may be a great deal in such things, though it seems quite against the reason. Indeed your father says, 'Why not? A charm must be accompanied by a strong wish on the part of the charmer that it may succeed,—and what is magnetism but a wish?' I don't quite comprehend this; but, like all your father says, it has more than meets the eye, I am quite sure.

"Only three weeks to the holidays, and then no more school, Sisty—no more school! I shall have your room all done freshly, and made so pretty; they are coming about it to-morrow.

"The duck is quite well, and I really don't think it is quite as lame as it was.

"God bless you, dear, dear child. Your affectionate happy mother, K. C."

The interval between these letters and the morning on which I was to return home seemed to me like one of those long, restless, yet half-dreamy days which in some infant malady I had passed in a sick-bed. I went through my task-work mechanically, composed a Greek ode in farewell to the Philhellenic, which Dr. Herman pronounced a *chef-d'œuvre*, and my father, to whom I sent it in triumph, returned a letter of false English with it, that parodied all my Hellenic barbarisms by imitating them in my mother tongue. However, I swallowed the leek, and consoled myself with the pleasing recollection that, after spending six years in learning to write bad Greek, I should never have any further occasion to avail myself of so precious an accomplishment.

And so came the last day. Then alone, and in a kind of delighted melancholy, I revisited each of the old haunts. The robber's cave we had dug one winter, and maintained, six of us, against all the police of the little kingdom. The place near the pales where I had fought my first battle. The old beech stump on which I sate to read letters from home! With my knife, rich in six blades (besides a corkscrew, a pen-picker, and a button-hook), I carved my name in large capitals over my desk. Then night came, and the bell rang, and we went to our rooms. And I opened the window and looked out. I saw all the stars, and wondered which was mine—which should light to fame and fortune the manhood about to commence. Hope and Ambition were high within me;—and yet, behind them, stood Melancholy. Ah! who amongst you, readers, can now summon back all those thoughts, sweet and sad—all that untold, half-conscious regret for the past—all those vague longings for the future, which made a poet of the dullest on the last night before leaving boyhood and school for ever.

PART III

CHAPTER I

IT was a beautiful summer afternoon when the coach set me
down at my father's gate. Mrs. Primmins herself ran out to
welcome me; and I had scarcely escaped from the warm clasp
of her friendly hand, before I was in the arms of my mother.

As soon as that tenderest of parents was convinced that I was
not famished, seeing that I had dined two hours ago at Dr.
Herman's, she led me gently across the garden towards the
arbour. "You will find your father so cheerful," said she, wiping
away a tear. "His brother is with him."

I stopped. *His* brother! Will the reader believe it?—I had
never heard that he had a brother, so little were family affairs
ever discussed in my hearing.

"*His* brother!" said I. "Have I then an Uncle Caxton as
well as an Uncle Jack?"

"Yes, my love," said my mother. And then she added,
"Your father and he were not such good friends as they ought
to have been, and the Captain has been abroad. However,
thank Heaven! they are now quite reconciled."

We had time for no more—we were in the arbour. There, a
table was spread with wine and fruit—the gentlemen were at
their dessert; and those gentlemen were my father, Uncle Jack,
Mr. Squills, and—tall, lean, buttoned-to-the-chin — an erect,
martial, majestic, and imposing personage, who seemed worthy
of a place in my great ancestor's "Boke of Chivalrie."

All rose as I entered; but my poor father, who was always
slow in his movements, had the last of me. Uncle Jack had
left the very powerful impression of his great seal-ring on my
fingers; Mr. Squills had patted me on the shoulder, and pronounced me "wonderfully grown"; my new-found relative had
with great dignity said, "Nephew, your hand, sir—I am Captain
de Caxton;" and even the tame duck had taken her beak from
her wing, and rubbed it gently between my legs, which was her

usual mode of salutation, before my father placed his pale hand
on my forehead, and, looking at me for a moment with unutterable sweetness, said, "More and more like your mother—God
bless you!"

A chair had been kept vacant for me between my father and
his brother. I sat down in haste, and with a tingling colour on
my cheeks and a rising at my throat, so much had the unusual
kindness of my father's greeting affected me; and then there
came over me a sense of my new position. I was no longer a
schoolboy at home for his brief holiday: I had returned to the
shelter of the roof-tree to become myself one of its supports.
I was at last a man, privileged to aid or solace those dear ones
who had ministered, as yet without return, to me. That is a
very strange crisis in our life when we come home *"for good."*
Home seems a different thing: before, one has been but a
sort of guest after all, only welcomed and indulged, and little
festivities held in honour of the released and happy child. But
to come home *for good*—to have done with school and boyhood
—is to be a guest, a child no more. It is to share the everyday
life of cares and duties—it is to enter into the *confidences* of home.
Is it not so? I could have buried my face in my hands, and wept!

My father, with all his abstraction and all his simplicity, had
a knack now and then of penetrating at once to the heart. I
verily believe he read all that was passing in mine as easily as if
it had been Greek. He stole his arm gently round my waist
and whispered, "Hush!" Then lifting his voice, he cried
aloud, "Brother Roland, you must not let Jack have the best of
the argument."

"Brother Austin," replied the Captain, very formally, "Mr.
Jack, if I may take the liberty so to call him."

"You may indeed," cried Uncle Jack.

"Sir," said the Captain, bowing, "it is a familiarity that does
me honour. I was about to say that Mr. Jack has retired from
the field."

"Far from it," said Squills, dropping an effervescing powder
into a chemical mixture which he had been preparing with great
attention, composed of sherry and lemon-juice—"far from it,
Mr. Tibbets—whose organ of combativeness is finely developed,
by-the-bye—was saying——"

"That it is a rank sin and shame in the nineteenth century," quoth Uncle Jack, "that a man like my friend Captain
Caxton——"

"*De* Caxton, sir—Mr. Jack."

"De Caxton—of the highest military talents, of the most illustrious descent—a hero sprung from heroes—should have served so many years, and with such distinction, in his Majesty's service, and should now be only a captain on half-pay. This, I say, comes of the infamous system of purchase, which sets up the highest honours for sale as they did in the Roman empire——"

My father pricked up his ears; but Uncle Jack pushed on before my father could get ready the forces of his meditated interruption.

"A system which a little effort, a little union, can so easily terminate. Yes, sir,"—and Uncle Jack thumped the table, and two cherries bobbed up and smote Captain de Caxton on the nose—"yes, sir, I will undertake to say that I could put the army upon a very different footing. If the poorer and more meritorious gentlemen, like Captain de Caxton, would, as I was just observing, but unite in a grand anti-aristocratic association, each paying a small sum quarterly, we could realise a capital sufficient to out-purchase all these undeserving individuals, and every man of merit should have his fair chance of promotion."

"Egad, sir," said Squills, "there is something grand in that —eh, Captain?"

"No, sir," replied the Captain, quite seriously; "there is in monarchies but one fountain of honour. It would be an interference with a soldier's first duty—his respect for his sovereign."

"On the contrary," said Mr. Squills, "it would still be to the sovereigns that one would owe the promotion."

"Honour," pursued the Captain, colouring up, and unheeding this witty interruption, "is the reward of a soldier. What do I care that a young jackanapes buys his colonelcy over my head? Sir, he does not buy from me my wounds and my services. Sir, he does not buy from me the medal I won at Waterloo. He is a rich man, and I am a poor man; he is called—colonel, because he paid money for the *name*. That pleases him; well and good. It would not please me: I had rather remain a captain, and feel my dignity, not in my title, but in the services by which it has been won. A beggarly, rascally association of stockbrokers, for aught I know, buy *me* a company! I don't want to be uncivil, or I would say damn 'em—Mr.—sir— Jack!"

A sort of thrill ran through the Captain's audience—even Uncle Jack seemed touched, for he stared very hard at the grim veteran, and said nothing. The pause was awkward—Mr. Squills

D

broke it. "I should like," quoth he, "to see your Waterloo medal—you have it not about you?"

"Mr. Squills," answered the Captain, "it lies next to my heart while I live. It shall be buried in my coffin, and I shall rise with it, at the word of command, on the day of the Grand Review!" So saying, the Captain leisurely unbuttoned his coat, and, detaching from a piece of striped ribbon as ugly a specimen of the art of the silversmith (begging its pardon) as ever rewarded merit at the expense of taste, placed the medal on the table.

The medal passed round, without a word, from hand to hand.

"It is strange," at last said my father, "how such trifles can be made of such value—how in one age a man sells his life for what in the next age he would not give a button! A Greek esteemed beyond price a few leaves of olive twisted into a circular shape, and set upon his head—a very ridiculous head-gear we should now call it. An American Indian prefers a decoration of human scalps, which, I apprehend, we should all agree (save and except Mr. Squills, who is accustomed to such things) to be a very disgusting addition to one's personal attractions; and my brother values this piece of silver, which may be worth about five shillings, more than Jack does a gold mine, or I do the library of the London Museum. A time will come when people will think that as idle a decoration as leaves and scalps."

"Brother," said the Captain, "there is nothing strange in the matter. It is as plain as a pike-staff to a man who understands the principles of honour."

"Possibly," said my father mildly. "I should like to hear what you have to say upon honour. I am sure it would very much edify us all."

CHAPTER II

MY UNCLE ROLAND'S DISCOURSE UPON HONOUR

GENTLEMEN," began the Captain, at the distinct appeal thus made to him—"Gentlemen, God made the earth, but man made the garden. God made man, but man re-creates himself."

"True, by knowledge," said my father.

"By industry," said Uncle Jack.

"By the physical conditions of his body," said Mr. Squills. "He could not have made himself other than he was at first in the woods and wilds if he had fins like a fish, or could only chatter gibberish like a monkey. Hands and a tongue, sir; these are the instruments of progress."

"Mr. Squills," said my father, nodding, "Anaxagoras said very much the same thing before you, touching the hands."

"I can't help that," answered Mr. Squills; "one could not open one's lips, if one were bound to say what nobody else had said. But, after all, our superiority is less in our *hands* than the greatness of our *thumbs*."

"Albinus, *de Sceleto,* and our own learned William Lawrence, have made a similar remark," again put in my father.

"Hang it, sir!" exclaimed Squills, "what business have you to know everything?"

"Everything! No; but thumbs furnish subjects of investigation to the simplest understanding," said my father modestly.

"Gentlemen," recommenced my Uncle Roland, "thumbs and hands are given to an Esquimaux, as well as to scholars and surgeons—and what the deuce are they the wiser for them? Sirs, you cannot reduce us thus into mechanism. Look within. Man, I say, re-creates himself. How? BY THE PRINCIPLE OF HONOUR. His first desire is to excel some one else—his first impulse is distinction above his fellows. Heaven places in his soul, as if it were a compass, a needle that always points to one end,—viz., to honour in that which those around him consider honourable. Therefore, as man at first is exposed to all dangers from wild beasts, and from men as savage as himself, COURAGE becomes the first quality mankind must honour: therefore the savage is courageous; therefore he covets the praise for courage; therefore he decorates himself with the skins of the beasts he has subdued, or the scalps of the foes he has slain. Sirs, don't tell me that the skins and the scalps are only hide and leather; they are trophies of honour. Don't tell me that they are ridiculous and disgusting; they become glorious as proofs that the savage has emerged out of the first brute-like egotism, and attached price to the praise which men never give except for works that secure or advance their welfare. By-and-by, sirs, our savages discover that they cannot live in safety amongst themselves, unless they agree to speak the truth to each other: therefore TRUTH becomes valued, and grows into a principle of honour; so, brother Austin will tell us that in the primitive times, truth was always the attribute of a hero."

"Right," said my father; "Homer emphatically assigns it to Achilles."

"Out of truth comes the necessity for some kind of rude justice and law. Therefore men, after courage in the warrior, and truth in all, begin to attach honour to the elder, whom they entrust with preserving justice amongst them. So, sirs, LAW is born——"

"But the first lawgivers were priests," quoth my father.

"Sirs, I am coming to that. Whence arises the desire of honour, but from man's necessity of excelling—in other words, of improving his faculties for the *benefit* of others,—though, unconscious of that consequence, man only strives for their *praise?* But that desire for honour is unextinguishable, and man is naturally anxious to carry its rewards beyond the grave. Therefore, he who has slain most lions or enemies is naturally prone to believe that he shall have the best hunting fields in the country beyond, and take the best place at the banquet. Nature, in all its operations, impresses man with the idea of an invisible Power; and the principle of honour—that is, the desire of praise and reward—makes him anxious for the approval which that Power can bestow. Thence comes the first rude idea of RELIGION; and in the death-hymn at the stake, the savage chants songs prophetic of the distinctions he is about to receive. Society goes on; hamlets are built; property is established. He who has more than another has more power than another. Power is honoured. Man covets the honour attached to the power which is attached to possession. Thus the soil is cultivated; thus the rafts are constructed; thus tribe trades with tribe; thus COMMERCE is founded, and CIVILISATION commenced. Sirs, all that seems least connected with honour, as we approach the vulgar days of the present, has its origin in honour, and is but an abuse of its principles. If men nowadays are hucksters and traders—if even military honours are purchased, and a rogue buys his way to a peerage—still all arise from the desire for honour, which society, as it grows old, gives to the outward signs of titles and gold, instead of, as once, to its inward essentials,—courage, truth, justice, enterprise. Therefore, I say, sirs, that honour is the foundation of all improvement in mankind."

"You have argued like a schoolman, brother," said Mr. Caxton admiringly; "but still, as to this round piece of silver—don't we go back to the most barbarous ages in estimating so highly such things as have no real value in themselves—as could not give us one opportunity for instructing our minds?"

"Could not pay for a pair of boots," added Uncle Jack.

"Or," said Mr. Squills, "save you one twinge of the cursed rheumatism you have got for life from that night's bivouac in the Portuguese marshes—to say nothing of the bullet in your cranium, and that cork-leg, which must much diminish the salutary effects of your constitutional walk."

"Gentlemen," resumed the Captain, nothing abashed, "in going back to those barbarous ages, I go back to the true principles of honour. It is precisely because this round piece of silver has no value in the market that it is priceless, for thus it is only a proof of desert. Where would be the sense of service in this medal, if it could buy back my leg, or if I could bargain it away for forty thousand a year? No, sirs, its value is this—that when I wear it on my breast, men shall say, 'that formal old fellow is not so useless as he seems. He was one of those who saved England and freed Europe.' And even when I conceal it here" (and, devoutly kissing the medal, Uncle Roland restored it to its ribbon and its resting-place), "and no eye sees it, its value is yet greater in the thought that my country has not degraded the old and true principles of honour, by paying the soldier who fought for her in the same coin as that in which you, Mr. Jack, sir, pay your bootmaker's bill. No, no, gentlemen. As courage was the first virtue that honour called forth—the first virtue from which all safety and civilisation proceed, so we do right to keep that one virtue at least clear and unsullied from all the money-making, mercenary, pay-me-in-cash abominations which are the vices, not the virtues, of the civilisation it has produced."

My Uncle Roland here came to a full stop; and, filling his glass, rose and said solemnly—"A last bumper, gentlemen,—'To the dead who died for England!'"

CHAPTER III

INDEED, my dear, you must take it. You certainly *have* caught cold: you sneezed three times together."

"Yes, ma'am, because I would take a pinch of Uncle Roland's snuff, just to say that I *had* taken a pinch out of his box—the honour of the thing—you know."

"Ah, my dear! what was that very clever remark you made at the same time, which so pleased your father—something about Jews and the college?"

" Jews and—oh! '*pulverem Olympicum collegisse juvat*,' my dear
mother—which means that it is a pleasure to take a pinch out
of a brave man's snuff-box. I say, mother, put down the posset.
Yes, I'll take it; I will, indeed. Now, then, sit here—that's
right—and tell me all you know about this famous old Captain.
Imprimis, he is older than my father."

" To be sure!" exclaimed my mother indignantly; " he looks
twenty years older; but there is only five years' real difference.
Your father must always look young."

"And why does Uncle Roland put that absurd French *de* before
his name—and why were my father and he not good friends—and
is he married—and has he any children?"

Scene of this conference—my own little room, new papered
on purpose for my return *for good*—trellis-work paper, flowers
and birds—all so fresh, and so new, and so clean, and so gay—
with my books ranged in neat shelves, and a writing-table by
the window; and, without the window, shines the still summer
moon. The window is a little open—you scent the flowers and
the new-mown hay. Past eleven; and the boy and his dear
mother are all alone.

" My dear, my dear! you ask so many questions at once."

" Don't answer them, then. Begin at the beginning, as Nurse
Primmins does with her fairy tales, ' Once on a time.' "

" Once on a time, then," said my mother—kissing me between
the eyes—" once on a time, my love, there was a certain clergyman in Cumberland, who had two sons; he had but a small
living, and the boys were to make their own way in the world.
But close to the parsonage, on the brow of a hill, rose an old
ruin, with one tower left, and this, with half the country round
it, had once belonged to the clergyman's family; but all had
been sold—all gone piece by piece, you see, my dear, except
the presentation to the living (what they call the advowson was
sold too), which had been secured to the last of the family. The
elder of these sons was your Uncle Roland—the younger was
your father. Now I believe the first quarrel arose from the
absurdest thing possible, as your father says; but Roland was
exceedingly touchy on all things connected with his ancestors.
He was always poring over the old pedigree, or wandering
amongst the ruins, or reading books of knight-errantry. Well,
where this pedigree began I know not, but it seems that King
Henry II. gave some lands in Cumberland to one Sir Adam de
Caxton; and from that time, you see, the pedigree went regularly
from father to son till Henry V.; then, apparently from the dis-

orders produced, as your father says, by the Wars of the Roses, there was a sad blank left—only one or two names, without dates or marriages, till the time of Henry VII., except that in the reign of Edward IV. there was one insertion of a William Caxton (named in a deed). Now in the village church there was a beautiful brass monument to one Sir William de Caxton, who had been killed at the battle of Bosworth, fighting for that wicked King Richard III. And about the same time there lived, as you know, the great printer, William Caxton. Well, your father, happening to be in town on a visit to his aunt, took great trouble in hunting up all the old papers he could find at the Heralds' College; and sure enough he was overjoyed to satisfy himself that he was descended, not from that poor Sir William, who had been killed in so bad a cause, but from the great printer, who was from a younger branch of the same family, and to whose descendants the estate came in the reign of Henry VIII. It was upon this that your Uncle Roland quarrelled with him; and, indeed, I tremble to think that they may touch on that matter again."

"Then, my dear mother, I must say my uncle was wrong there, so far as common sense is concerned; but still, somehow or other, I can understand it. Surely, this was not the only cause of estrangement?"

My mother looked down, and moved one hand gently over the other, which was her way when embarrassed. "What was it, my own mother?" said I coaxingly.

"I believe—that is, I—I think that they were both attached to the same young lady."

"How! you don't mean to say that my father was ever in love with any one but you?"

"Yes, Sisty—yes, and deeply! and," added my mother, after a slight pause, and with a very low sigh, "he never was in love with me; and what is more, he had the frankness to tell me so!"

"And yet you——"

"Married him—yes!" said my mother, raising the softest and purest eyes that ever a lover could have wished to read his fate in—"Yes, for the old love was hopeless. I knew that I could make him happy. I knew that he would love me at last, and he does so! My son, your father loves me!"

As she spoke, there came a blush as innocent as virgin ever knew, to my mother's smooth cheek; and she looked so fair, so good, and still so young, all the while, that you would have said that either Dusius, the Teuton fiend, or Nock, the Scandinavian sea-imp, from whom the learned assure us we derive our modern Daimones, "The Deuce," and Old Nick, had indeed possessed my father, if he had not learned to love such a creature.

I pressed her hand to my lips, but my heart was too full to speak for a moment or so; and then I partially changed the subject.

"Well, and this rivalry estranged them more? And who was the lady?"

"Your father never told me, and I never asked," said my mother simply. "But she was very different from me, I know. Very accomplished, very beautiful, very high-born."

"For all that, my father was a lucky man to escape her. Pass on. What did the Captain do?"

"Why, about that time your grandfather died, and shortly after an aunt, on the mother's side, who was rich and saving, died, and unexpectedly left them each sixteen thousand pounds. Your uncle, with his share, bought back, at an enormous price, the old castle and some land round it, which they say does not bring him in three hundred a year. With the little that remained he purchased a commission in the army; and the brothers met no more till last week, when Roland suddenly arrived."

"He did not marry this accomplished young lady?"

"No! but he married another, and is a widower."

"Why, he was as inconstant as my father; and I am sure without so good an excuse. How was that?"

"I don't know. He says nothing about it."

"Has he any children?"

"Two, a son—by-the-bye, you must never speak about *him*. Your uncle briefly said, when I asked him what was his family, 'A girl, ma'am. I had a son, but——'

"'He is dead,' cried your father in his kind pitying voice.

"'Dead to me, brother—and you will never mention his name!' You should have seen how stern your uncle looked. I was terrified."

"But the girl—why did not he bring her here?"

"She is still in France, but he talks of going over for her; and we have half promised to visit them both in Cumberland. But bless me! is that twelve? and the posset quite cold!"

"One word more, dearest mother—one word. My father's book—is he still going on with it?"

"Oh yes, indeed!" cried my mother, clasping her hands; "and he must read it to you, as he does to me—*you* will understand it so well. I have always been so anxious that the world

should know him, and be proud of him as we are, so—so anxious !
—for, perhaps, Sisty, if he had married that great lady, he would
have roused himself, been more ambitious—and I could only
make him happy, I could not make him great !"

"So he has listened to you at last ?"

"To me !" said my mother, shaking her head and smiling
gently : "No, rather to your Uncle Jack, who, I am happy to
say, has at length got a proper hold over him."

"A proper hold, my dear mother ! Pray beware of Uncle
Jack, or we shall all be swept into a coal-mine, or explode with
a grand national company for making gunpowder out of tea
leaves !"

"Wicked child !" said my mother, laughing ; and then, as she
took up her candle and lingered a moment while I wound my
watch, she said musingly,—"Yet Jack is very, very clever,—and
if for your sake we *could* make a fortune, Sisty !"

"You frighten me out of my wits, mother ! You are not in
earnest ?"

"And if *my* brother could be the means of raising *him* in the
world——"

"Your brother would be enough to sink all the ships in the
Channel, ma'am," said I quite irreverently. I was shocked before
the words were well out of my mouth ; and throwing my arms
round my mother's neck, I kissed away the pain I had inflicted.

When I was left alone, and in my own little crib, in which my
slumber had ever been so soft and easy,—I might as well have
been lying upon cut straw. I tossed to and fro—I could not sleep.
I rose, threw on my dressing-gown, lighted my candle, and sat
down by the table near the window. First I thought of the
unfinished outline of my father's youth, so suddenly sketched
before me. I filled up the missing colours, and fancied the
picture explained all that had often perplexed my conjectures.
I comprehended, I suppose by some secret sympathy in my own
nature (for experience in mankind could have taught me little
enough), how an ardent, serious, inquiring mind—struggling
into passion under the load of knowledge, had, with that stimulus
sadly and abruptly withdrawn, sunk into the quiet of passive,
aimless study. I comprehended how, in the indolence of a happy
but unimpassioned marriage, with a companion so gentle, so provident and watchful, yet so little formed to rouse, and task
and fire an intellect naturally calm and meditative,—years upon
years had crept away in the learned idleness of a solitary scholar.
I comprehended, too, how gradually and slowly, as my father

entered that stage of middle life, when all men are most prone
to ambition—the long-silenced whispers were heard again ; and
the mind, at last escaping from the listless weight which a
baffled and disappointed heart had laid upon it, saw once more,
fair as in youth, the only true mistress of Genius—Fame.

Oh ! how I sympathised, too, in my mother's gentle triumph.
Looking over the past, I could see, year after year, how she had
stolen more and more into my father's heart of hearts—how
what had been kindness had grown into love,—how custom and
habit, and the countless links in the sweet charities of home,
had supplied that sympathy with the genial man which had
been missed at first by the lonely scholar.

Next I thought of the grey, eagle-eyed old soldier, with his
ruined tower and barren acres,—and saw before me his proud,
prejudiced, chivalrous boyhood, gliding through the ruins or
poring over the mouldy pedigree. And this son, so disowned,—
for what dark offence ?—an awe crept over me. And this girl
—his ewe-lamb—his all—was she fair ? had she blue eyes like
my mother, or a high Roman nose and beetle brows like
Captain Roland ? I mused, and mused, and mused—and the
candle went out—and the moonlight grew broader and stiller ;
till at last I was sailing in a balloon with Uncle Jack, and
had just tumbled into the Red Sea—when the well-known
voice of Nurse Primmins restored me to life with a "God
bless my heart ! the boy has not been in bed all this 'varsal
night !"

CHAPTER IV

AS soon as I was dressed I hastened downstairs, for I longed
to revisit my old haunts—the little plot of garden I had
sown with anemones and cresses ; the walk by the peach wall ;
the pond wherein I had angled for roach and perch.

Entering the hall, I discovered my Uncle Roland in a great
state of embarrassment. The maid-servant was scrubbing the
stones at the hall-door ; she was naturally plump,—and it is
astonishing how much more plump a female becomes when
she is on all-fours !—the maid-servant, then, was scrubbing the
stones, her face turned from the Captain ; and the Captain,
evidently meditating a sortie, stood ruefully gazing at the
obstacle before him and hemming aloud. Alas, the maid-

servant was deaf! I stopped, curious to see how Uncle Roland would extricate himself from the dilemma.

Finding that his hems were in vain, my uncle made himself as small as he could, and glided close to the left of the wall : at that instant the maid turned abruptly round towards the right, and completely obstructed, by this manœuvre, the slight crevice through which hope had dawned on her captive. My uncle stood stock-still,—and, to say the truth, he could not have stirred an inch without coming into personal contact with the rounded charms which blockaded his movements. My uncle took off his hat and scratched his forehead in great perplexity. Presently, by a slight turn of the flanks, the opposing party, while leaving him an opportunity of return, entirely precluded all chance of egress in that quarter. My uncle retreated in haste, and now presented himself to the right wing of the enemy. He had scarcely done so when, without looking behind her, the blockading party shoved aside the pail that crippled the range of her operations, and so placed it that it formed a formidable barricade, which my uncle's cork leg had no chance of surmounting. Therewith Captain Roland lifted his eyes appealingly to heaven, and I heard him distinctly ejaculate—

" Would to heaven she were a creature in breeches ! "

But happily at this moment the maid-servant turned her head sharply round, and, seeing the Captain, rose in an instant, moved away the pail, and dropped a frightened curtsey.

My Uncle Roland touched his hat, " I beg you a thousand pardons, my good girl," said he ; and, with a half bow, he slid into the open air.

" You have a soldier's politeness, uncle," said I, tucking my arm into Captain Roland's.

" Tush, my boy," said he, smiling seriously, and colouring up to the temples ; " tush, say a gentleman's ! To us, sir, every woman is a lady, in right of her sex."

Now, I had often occasion later to recall that aphorism of my uncle's ; and it served to explain to me how a man, so prejudiced on the score of family pride, never seemed to consider it an offence in my father to have married a woman whose pedigree was as brief as my dear mother's. Had she been a Montmorenci, my uncle could not have been more respectful and gallant than he was to that meek descendant of the Tibbetses. He held, indeed, which I never knew any other man, vain of family, approve or support, — a doctrine deduced from the

following syllogisms: 1st, that birth was not valuable in itself, but as a transmission of certain qualities which descent
from a race of warriors should perpetuate, viz., truth, courage,
honour; 2ndly, That, whereas from the woman's side we derive
our more intellectual faculties, from the man's we derive our
moral; a clever and witty man generally has a clever and witty
mother; a brave and honourable man, a brave and honourable
father.   Therefore, all the qualities which attention to race
should perpetuate, are the manly qualities traceable only from
the *father's* side.   Again, he held that while the aristocracy
have higher and more chivalrous notions, the people generally
have shrewder and livelier ideas.   Therefore, to prevent gentlemen from degenerating into complete dunderheads, an admixture with the people, provided always it was on the female side,
was not only excusable, but expedient; and, finally, my uncle
held, that, whereas a man is a rude, coarse, sensual animal, and
requires all manner of associations to dignify and refine him,
women are so naturally susceptible of everything beautiful in
sentiment and generous in purpose, that she who is a true
woman is a fit peer for a king.   Odd and preposterous notions,
no doubt, and capable of much controversy, so far as the doctrine
of race (if that be any way tenable) is concerned; but then the
plain fact is, that my Uncle Roland was as eccentric and con-
tradictory a gentleman—as—as—why, as you and I are, if we
once venture to think for ourselves.

"Well, sir, and what profession are you meant for?" asked
my uncle—"not the army, I fear?"

"I have never thought of the subject, uncle."

"Thank Heaven," said Captain Roland, "we have never yet
had a lawyer in the family! nor a stockbroker, nor a tradesman
—ahem!"

I saw that my great ancestor the printer suddenly rose up in
that hem.

"Why, uncle, there are honourable men in all callings."

"Certainly, sir.   But in all callings honour is not the first
principle of action."

"But it may be, sir, if a man of honour pursue it!   There are
some soldiers who have been great rascals!"

My uncle looked posed, and his black brows met thoughtfully.

"You are right, boy, I dare say," he answered somewhat
mildly.   "But do you think that it ought to give me as much
pleasure to look on my old ruined tower, if I knew it had been
bought by some herring-dealer, like the first ancestor of the

Poles, as I do now, when I know it was given to a knight and gentleman (who traced his descent from an Anglo-Dane in the time of King Alfred), for services done in Aquitaine and Gascony, by Henry the Plantagenet? And do you mean to tell me that I should have been the same man if I had not from a boy associated that old tower with all ideas of what its owners were, and should be, as knights and gentlemen? Sir, you would have made a different being of me, if at the head of my pedigree you had clapped a herring-dealer ; though, I dare say, the herring-dealer might have been as good a man as ever the Anglo-Dane was ! God rest him ! ''

"And for the same reason, I suppose, sir, that you think my father never would have been quite the same being he is, if he had not made that notable discovery touching our descent from the great William Caxton, the printer."

My uncle bounded as if he had been shot ; bounded so incautiously, considering the materials of which one leg was composed, that he would have fallen into a strawberry-bed if I had not caught him by the arm.

"Why, you—you—you young jackanapes," cried the Captain, shaking me off as soon as he had regained his equilibrium. "You do not mean to inherit that infamous crotchet my brother has got into his head? You do not mean to exchange Sir William de Caxton, who fought and fell at Bosworth, for the mechanic, who sold black-letter pamphlets in the Sanctuary at Westminster ? "

"That depends on the evidence, uncle ! "

"No, sir, like all noble truths, it depends upon *faith*. Men, nowadays," continued my uncle, with a look of ineffable disgust, "actually require that truths should be proved."

"It is a sad conceit on their part, no doubt, my dear uncle. But till a truth is proved, how can we know that it is a truth ? "

I thought that in that very sagacious question I had effectually caught my uncle. Not I. He slipped through it like an eel.

"Sir," said he, "whatever, in Truth, makes a man's heart warmer, and his soul purer, is a belief, not a knowledge. Proof, sir, is a handcuff—belief is a wing ! Want proof as to an ancestor in the reign of King Richard ! Sir, you cannot even prove to the satisfaction of a logician that you are the son of your own father. Sir, a religious man does not want to reason about his religion—religion is not mathematics. Religion is to be felt, not proved. There are a great many things in the religion of a good man which are not in the catechism. Proof ! "

continued my uncle, growing violent—"Proof, sir, is a low, vulgar, levelling, rascally Jacobin—Belief is a loyal, generous, chivalrous gentleman! No, no—prove what you please, you shall never rob me of one belief that has made me——"

"The finest-hearted creature that ever talked nonsense," said my father, who came up, like Horace's deity, at the right moment. "What is it you must believe in, brother, no matter what the proof against you?"

My uncle was silent, and with great energy dug the point of his cane into the gravel.

"He will not believe in our great ancestor the printer," said I maliciously.

My father's calm brow was overcast in a moment.

"Brother," said the Captain loftily, "you have a right to your own ideas, but you should take care how they contaminate your child."

"Contaminate!" said my father; and for the first time I saw an angry sparkle flash from his eyes, but he checked himself on the instant: "change the word, my dear brother."

"No, sir, I will not change it! To belie the records of the family!"

"Records! A brass plate in a village church against all the books of the College of Arms!"

"To renounce your ancestor, a knight, who died in the field!"

"For the worst cause that man ever fought for!"

"On behalf of his king!"

"Who had murdered his nephews!"

"A knight! with our crest on his helmet."

"And no brains underneath it, or he would never have had them knocked out for so bloody a villain!"

"A rascally, drudging, money-making printer!"

"The wise and glorious introducer of the art that has enlightened a world. Prefer for an ancestor, to one whom scholar and sage never name but in homage, a worthless, obscure, jolter-headed booby in mail, whose only record to men is a brass plate in a church in a village!"

My uncle turned round perfectly livid. "Enough, sir! enough! I am insulted sufficiently. I ought to have expected it. I wish you and your son a very good day."

My father stood aghast. The Captain was hobbling off to the iron gate; in another moment he would have been out of our precincts. I ran up and hung upon him. "Uncle, it is all my fault. Between you and me, I am quite of your side; pray forgive us both. What could I have been thinking of, to vex you so? And my father, whom your visit has made so happy!"

My uncle paused, feeling for the latch of the gate. My father had now come up, and caught his hand. "What are all the printers that ever lived, and all the books they ever printed, to one wrong to thy fine heart, brother Roland? Shame on me! A bookman's weak point, you know! It is very true—I should never have taught the boy one thing to give you pain, brother Roland;—though I don't remember," continued my father, with a perplexed look, "that I ever did teach it him either! Pisistratus, as you value my blessing, respect as your ancestor Sir William de Caxton, the hero of Bosworth. Come, come, brother!"

"I am an old fool," said Uncle Roland, "whichever way we look at it. Ah, you young dog! you are laughing at us both!"

"I have ordered breakfast on the lawn," said my mother, coming out from the porch, with her cheerful smile on her lips; "and I think the devil will be done to your liking to-day, brother Roland."

"We have had enough of the devil already, my love," said my father, wiping his forehead.

So, while the birds sang overhead, or hopped familiarly across the sward for the crumbs thrown forth to them, while the sun was still cool in the east, and the leaves yet rustled with the sweet air of morning, we all sat down to our table, with hearts as reconciled to each other, and as peaceably disposed to thank God for the fair world around us, as if the river had never run red through the field of Bosworth, and the excellent Mr. Caxton had never set all mankind by the ears with an irritating invention, a thousand times more provocative of our combative tendencies than the blast of the trumpet and the gleam of the banner!

CHAPTER V

BROTHER," said Mr. Caxton, "I will walk with you to the Roman encampment."

The Captain felt that this proposal was meant as the greatest peace-offering my father could think of; for, 1st, it was a very long walk, and my father detested long walks; 2ndly, it was the sacrifice of a whole day's labour at the Great Work. And yet, with that quick sensibility which only the generous possess, Uncle Roland accepted at once the proposal. If he had not done so, my father would have had a heavier heart for a month to come. And how could the Great Work have got on while the author was every now and then disturbed by a twinge of remorse?

Half-an-hour after breakfast, the brothers set off arm-in-arm; and I followed, a little apart, admiring how sturdily the old soldier got over the ground, in spite of the cork leg. It was pleasant enough to listen to their conversation, and notice the contrasts between these two eccentric stamps from Dame Nature's ever-variable mould,—Nature who casts nothing in stereotype, for I do believe that not even two fleas can be found identically the same.

My father was not a quick or minute observer of rural beauties. He had so little of the organ of locality, that I suspect he could have lost his way in his own garden. But the Captain was exquisitely alive to external impressions—not a feature in the landscape escaped him. At every fantastic gnarled pollard he halted to gaze; his eye followed the lark soaring up from his feet; when a fresher air came from the hill-top, his nostrils dilated, as if voluptuously to inhale its delight. My father, with all his learning, and though his study had been in the stores of all language, was very rarely eloquent. The Captain had a glow and a passion in his words which, what with his deep, tremulous voice and animated gestures, gave something poetic to half of what he uttered. In every sentence of Roland's, in every tone of his voice, and every play of his face, there was some outbreak of pride; but, unless you sat him on his hobby of that great ancestor the printer, my father had not as much pride as a homœopathist could have put into a globule. He was not proud even of not being proud. Chafe all his feathers, and still you could rouse but a dove. My father was slow and mild, my uncle quick and fiery,; my father reasoned, my uncle imagined; my father was very seldom wrong, my uncle never quite in the right; but, as my father once said of him, " Roland beats about the bush till he sends out the very bird that we went to search for. He is never in the wrong without suggesting to us what is the right." All in my uncle was stern, rough, and angular; all in my father was sweet, polished, and rounded into a natural grace. My uncle's character cast out a multiplicity of shadows, like a Gothic pile in a northern sky. My father stood serene in the light, like a Greek temple at mid-day in a southern clime. Their persons corresponded with their natures. My uncle's high aquiline features, bronzed hue, rapid fire of eye, and upper lip that always quivered, were a notable contrast to my father's delicate profile, quiet, abstracted gaze, and the steady sweetness that rested on his musing smile. Roland's forehead was singularly high, and rose to a peak in the summit where phrenologists place the organ of veneration, but it was narrow and deeply furrowed. Augustine's might be as high, but then soft, silky hair waved carelessly over it—concealing its height, but not its vast breadth—on which not a wrinkle was visible. And yet, withal, there was a great family likeness between the two brothers. When some softer sentiment subdued him, Roland caught the very look of Augustine; when some high emotion animated my father, you might have taken him for Roland. I have often thought since, in the greater experience of mankind which life has afforded me, that if, in early years, their destinies had been exchanged—if Roland had taken to literature, and my father had been forced into action—that each would have had greater worldly success. For Roland's passion and energy would have given immediate and forcible effect to study; he might have been a historian or a poet. It is not study alone that produces a writer; it is *intensity*. In the mind, as in yonder chimney, to make the fire burn hot and quick, you must narrow the draught. Whereas, had my father been forced into the practical world, his calm depth of comprehension, his clearness of reason, his general accuracy in such notions as he once entertained and pondered over, joined to a temper that crosses and losses could never ruffle, and utter freedom from vanity and self-love, from prejudice and passion, might have made him a very wise and enlightened counsellor in the great affairs of life—a lawyer, a diplomatist, a statesman, for what I know, even a great general—if his tender humanity had not stood in the way of his military mathematics.

But, as it was—with his slow pulse never stimulated by action, and too little stirred by even scholarly ambition—my father's mind went on widening and widening, till the circle was lost in the great ocean of contemplation; and Roland's passionate energy, fretted into fever by every let and hindrance, in the struggle with his kind—and narrowed more and more as it was curbed within the channels of active discipline and duty—missed its due career altogether; and what might have been the poet, contracted into the humourist.

Yet, who that had ever known ye, could have wished you other than ye were—ye guileless, affectionate, honest, simple creatures? simple both, in spite of all the learning of the one, all the prejudices, whims, irritabilities, and crotchets of the other? There you are, seated on the height of the old Roman camp, with a volume of the Stratagems of Polyœnus (or is it Frontinus?) open on my father's lap; the sheep grazing in the furrows of the circumvallations; the curious steer gazing at you where it halts in the space whence the Roman cohorts glittered forth. And your boy-biographer standing behind you with folded arms; and—as the scholar read or the soldier pointed his cane to each fancied post in the war—filling up the pastoral landscape with the eagles of Agricola and the scythed cars of Boadicea!

CHAPTER VI

IT is never the same two hours together in this country," said my Uncle Roland, as, after dinner, or rather after dessert, we joined my mother in the drawing-room.

Indeed, a cold drizzling rain had come on within the last two hours; and, though it was July, it was as chilly as if it had been October. My mother whispered to me, and I went out; in ten minutes more, the logs (for we live in a wood country) blazed merrily in the grate. Why could not my mother have rung the bell, and ordered the servant to light a fire? My dear reader, Captain Roland was poor, and he made a capital virtue of economy!

The two brothers drew their chairs near to the hearth, my father at the left, my uncle at the right; and I and my mother sat down to "Fox and geese."

Coffee came in—one cup for the Captain, for the rest of the party avoided that exciting beverage. And on that cup was a picture of—His Grace the Duke of Wellington!

During our visit to the Roman camp, my mother had borrowed Mr. Squills' chaise, and driven over to our market-town, for the express purpose of greeting the Captain's eyes with the face of his old chief.

My uncle changed colour, rose, lifted my mother's hand to his lips, and sat himself down again in silence.

"I have heard," said the Captain after a pause, "that the Marquis of Hastings, who is every inch a soldier and a gentleman—and that is saying not a little, for he measures seventy-five

" *When she was warming my bed* "

inches from the crown to the sole—when he received Louis XVIII. (then an exile) at Donnington, fitted up his apartments exactly like those his Majesty had occupied at the Tuileries. It was a kingly attention (my Lord Hastings, you know, is sprung from the Plantagenets), a kingly attention to a king. It cost some money and made some noise. A woman can show the same royal delicacy of heart in this bit of porcelain, and so quietly, that we men all think it a matter of course, brother Austin."

"You are such a worshipper of women, Roland, that it is melancholy to see you single. You must marry again !"

My uncle first smiled, then frowned, and lastly sighed somewhat heavily.

"Your time will pass slowly in your old tower, poor brother," continued my father, "with only your little girl for a companion."

"And the past !" said my uncle ; "the past, that mighty world——"

"Do you still read your old books of chivalry, Froissart and the Chronicles, Palmerin of England, and Amadis of Gaul ?"

"Why," said my uncle, reddening, "I have tried to improve myself with studies a little more substantial. And " (he added with a sly smile) "there will be your great book for many a long winter to come."

"Um !" said my father bashfully.

"Do you know," quoth my uncle, "that Dame Primmins is a very intelligent woman ; full of fancy, and a capital story-teller ?"

"Is not she, uncle ?" cried I, leaving my fox in the corner. "Oh, if you could hear her tell the tale of King Arthur and the Enchanted Lake, or the Grim White Woman !"

"I have already heard her tell both," said my uncle.

"The deuce you have, brother ! My dear, we must look to this. These captains are dangerous gentlemen in an orderly household. Pray, where could you have had the opportunity of such private communications with Mrs. Primmins ?"

"Once," said my uncle readily, "when I went into her room, while she mended my stock ; and once "—he stopped short, and looked down.

"Once when ?—out with it."

"When she was warming my bed," said my uncle, in a half-whisper.

"Dear !" said my mother innocently, "that's how the sheets

came by that bad hole in the middle. I thought it was the warming-pan."

" I am quite shocked ! " faltered my uncle.

" You well may be," said my father. " A woman who has been heretofore above all suspicion ! But come," he said, seeing that my uncle looked sad, and was no doubt casting up the probable price of twice six yards of Holland—" but come, you were always a famous rhapsodist or tale-teller yourself. Come, Roland, let us have some story of your own ; something which your experience has left strong in your impressions."

" Let us first have the candles," said my mother.

The candles were brought, the curtains let down—we all drew our chairs to the hearth. But, in the interval, my uncle had sunk into a gloomy reverie ; and when we called upon him to begin, he seemed to shake off with effort some recollections of pain.

" You ask me," he said, " to tell you some tale which my own experience has left deeply marked in my impressions—I will tell you one apart from my own life, but which has often haunted me. It is sad and strange, ma'am."

" Ma'am, *brother ?* " said my mother reproachfully, letting her small hand drop upon that which, large and sunburnt, the Captain waved towards her as he spoke.

" Austin, you have married an angel ! " said my uncle ; and he was, I believe, the only brother-in-law who ever made so hazardous an assertion.

CHAPTER VII

MY UNCLE ROLAND'S TALE

IT was in Spain, no matter where or how, that it was my fortune to take prisoner a French officer of the same rank that I then held—a lieutenant ; and there was so much similarity in our sentiments, that we became intimate friends—the most intimate friend I ever had, sister, out of this dear circle. He was a rough soldier, whom the world had not well treated ; but he never railed at the world, and maintained that he had had his deserts. Honour was his idol, and the sense of honour paid him for the loss of all else.

" We were both at that time volunteers in a foreign service— in that worst of service, civil war,—he on one side, I on the other,—both, perhaps, disappointed in the cause we had severally espoused. There was something similar, too, in our domestic relationships. He had a son—a boy—who was all in life to him, next to his country and his duty. I, too, had then such a son, though of fewer years." (The Captain paused an instant; we exchanged glances, and a stifling sensation of pain and suspense was felt by all his listeners.) "We were accustomed, brother, to talk of these children—to picture their future, to compare our hopes and dreams. We hoped and dreamed alike. A short time sufficed to establish this confidence. My prisoner was sent to headquarters, and soon afterwards exchanged.

"We met no more till last year. Being then at Paris, I inquired for my old friend, and learned that he was living at R——, a few miles from the capital. I went to visit him. I found his house empty and deserted. That very day he had been led to prison, charged with a terrible crime. I saw him in that prison, and from his own lips learned his story. His son had been brought up, as he fondly believed, in the habits and principles of honourable men; and, having finished his education, came to reside with him at R——. The young man was accustomed to go frequently to Paris. A young Frenchman loves pleasure, sister; and pleasure is found at Paris. The father thought it natural, and stripped his age of some comforts to supply luxuries for the son's youth.

"Shortly after the young man's arrival, my friend perceived that he was robbed. Moneys kept in his bureau were abstracted he knew not how, nor could guess by whom. It must be done in the night. He concealed himself, and watched. He saw a stealthy figure glide in, he saw a false key applied to the lock—he started forward, seized the felon, and recognised his son. What should the father have done? I do not ask *you*, sister! I ask these men, son and father, I ask you."

"Expelled him the house," cried I.

"Done his duty, and reformed the unhappy wretch," said my father. "*Nemo repentè turpissimus semper fuit*—No man is wholly bad all at once."

"The father did as you would have advised, brother. He kept the youth; he remonstrated with him; he did more—he gave him the key of the bureau. 'Take what I have to give,' said he: 'I would rather be a beggar than know my son a thief.'"

"Right; and the youth repented, and became a good man?" exclaimed my father.

Captain Roland shook his head. "The youth promised

amendment, and seemed penitent. He spoke of the temptations of Paris, the gaming-table, and what not. He gave up his
daily visits to the capital. He seemed to apply to study.
Shortly after this, the neighbourhood was alarmed by reports of
night robberies on the road. Men, masked and armed, plundered
travellers, and even broke into houses.

"The police were on the alert. One night an old brother
officer knocked at my friend's door. It was late : the veteran
(he was a cripple, by the way, like myself—strange coincidence !)
was in bed. He came down in haste, when his servant woke
and told him that his old friend, wounded and bleeding, sought
an asylum under his roof. The wound, however, was slight.
The guest had been attacked and robbed on the road. The
next morning the proper authority of the town was sent for.
The plundered man described his loss—some *billets* of five
hundred francs in a pocket-book, on which was embroidered his
name and coronet (he was a vicomte). The guest stayed to
dinner. Late in the forenoon, the son looked in. The guest
started to see him : my friend noticed his paleness. Shortly
after, on pretence of faintness, the guest retired to his room,
and sent for his host. ' My friend,' said he, ' can you do me a
favour ?—go to the magistrate and recall the evidence I have
given.'

" ' Impossible,' said the host. ' What crotchet is this ? '

" The guest shuddered. ' *Peste !* ' said he, ' I do not wish in
my old age to be hard on others. Who knows how the robber
may have been tempted, and who knows what relations he may
have—honest men, whom his crime would degrade for ever !
Good heavens ! if detected, it is the galleys, the galleys ! '

" ' And what then ?—the robber knew what he braved.'

" ' But did his father know it ? ' cried the guest.

" A light broke upon my unhappy comrade in arms : he
caught his friend by the hand—' You turned pale at my son's
sight—where did you ever see him before ? Speak ! '

" ' Last night on the road to Paris. The mask slipped aside.
Call back my evidence ! '

" ' You are mistaken,' said my friend calmly. ' I saw my son
in his bed, and blessed him, before I went to my own.'

" ' I will believe you,' said the guest; ' and never shall my
hasty suspicion pass my lips—but call back the evidence.'

" The guest returned to Paris before dusk. The father conversed with his son on the subject of his studies ; he followed
him to his room, waited till he was in bed, and was then about

to retire, when the youth said, ' Father, you have forgotten your blessing.'

" The father went back, laid his hand on the boy's head and prayed. He was credulous—fathers are so ! He was persuaded that his friend had been deceived. He retired to rest, and fell asleep. He woke suddenly in the middle of the night, and felt (I here quote his words)—' I felt,' said he, ' as if a voice had awakened me—a voice that said " Rise and search." I rose at once, struck a light, and went to my son's room. The door was locked. I knocked once, twice, thrice,—no answer. I dared not call aloud, lest I should rouse the servants. I went down the stairs—I opened the back-door—I passed to the stables. My own horse was there, *not* my son's. My horse neighed ; it was old, like myself—my old charger at Mount St. Jean. I stole back, I crept into the shadow of the wall by my son's door, and extinguished my light. I felt as if I were a thief myself.' "

" Brother," interrupted my mother under her breath, " speak in your own words, not in this wretched father's. I know not why, but it would shock me less."

The Captain nodded.

" Before daybreak my friend heard the back-door open gently ; a foot ascended the stair—a key grated in the door of the room close at hand—the father glided through the dark into that chamber behind his unseen son.

" He heard the clink of the tinder-box ; a light was struck ; it spread over the room, but he had time to place himself behind the window-curtain which was close at hand. The figure before him stood a moment or so motionless, and seemed to listen, for it turned to the right, to the left, its visage covered with the black hideous mask which is worn in carnivals. Slowly the mask was removed ; could that be his son's face ? the son of a brave man ?—it was pale and ghastly with scoundrel fears ; the base drops stood on the brow ; the eye was haggard and bloodshot. He looked as a coward looks when death stands before him.

" The youth walked, or rather skulked, to the secretaire, unlocked it, opened a secret drawer ; placed within it the contents of his pockets and his frightful mask : the father approached softly, looked over his shoulder, and saw in the drawer the pocket-book embroidered with his friend's name. Meanwhile, the son took out his pistols, uncocked them cautiously, and was about also to secrete them, when his father arrested his arm. ' Robber, the use of these is yet to come ! '

"The son's knees knocked together, an exclamation for mercy burst from his lips; but when, recovering the mere shock of his dastard nerves, he perceived it was not the gripe of some hireling of the law, but a father's hand that had clutched his arm, the vile audacity which knows fear only from a bodily cause, none from the awe of shame, returned to him.

"'Tush, sir,' he said, 'waste not time in reproaches, for, I fear, the *gens-d'armes* are on my track. It is well that you are here; you can swear that I have spent the night at home. Unhand me, old man—I have these witnesses still to secrete,' and he pointed to the garments wet and bedabbled with the mud of the roads. He had scarcely spoken when the walls shook; there was the heavy clatter of hoofs on the ringing pavement without.

"'They come!' cried the son. 'Off, dotard! save your son from the galleys.'

"'The galleys, the galleys!' said the father, staggering back; 'it is true'—he said—'the galleys.'

"There was a loud knocking at the gate. The *gens-d'armes* surrounded the house. 'Open in the name of the law.' No answer came, no door was opened. Some of the *gens-d'armes* rode to the rear of the house, in which was placed the stable-yard. From the window of the son's room the father saw the sudden blaze of torches, the shadowy forms of the men-hunters. He heard the clatter of arms as they swung themselves from their horses. He heard a voice cry, 'Yes, this is the robber's grey horse—see, it still reeks with sweat!' And behind and in front, at either door, again came the knocking, and again the shout, 'Open in the name of the law.'

"Then lights began to gleam from the casements of the neighbouring houses; then the space filled rapidly with curious wonderers startled from their sleep; the world was astir, and the crowd came round to know what crime or what shame had entered the old soldier's home.

"Suddenly, within, there was heard the report of a firearm; and a minute or so afterwards the front door was opened, and the soldier appeared.

"'Enter,' he said to the *gens-d'armes*: 'what would you?'

"'We seek a robber who is within your walls.'

"'I know it; mount and find him: I will lead the way.'

"He ascended the stairs; he threw open his son's room; the officers of justice poured in, and on the floor lay the robber's corpse.

"They looked at each other in amazement. 'Take what is left you,' said the father. 'Take the dead man rescued from the galleys; take the living man on whose hands rests the dead man's blood!'

"I was present at my friend's trial. The facts had become known beforehand. He stood there with his grey hair, and his mutilated limbs, and the deep scar on his visage, and the cross of the Legion of Honour on his breast; and when he had told his tale, he ended with these words—'I have saved the son whom I reared for France from a doom that would have spared the life to brand it with disgrace. Is this a crime? I give you my life in exchange for my son's disgrace. Does my country need a victim? I have lived for my country's glory, and I can die contented to satisfy its laws; sure that, if you blame me, you will not despise; sure that the hands that give me to the headsman will scatter flowers over my grave. Thus I confess all. I, a soldier, look round amongst a nation of soldiers; and in the name of the star which glitters on my breast, I dare the Fathers of France to condemn me!'

"They acquitted the soldier—at least they gave a verdict answering to what in our courts is called 'justifiable homicide.' A shout rose in the court which no ceremonial voice could still; the crowd would have borne him in triumph to his house, but his look repelled such vanities. To his house he returned indeed, and the day afterwards they found him dead, beside the cradle in which his first prayer had been breathed over his sinless child. Now, father and son, I ask you, do you condemn that man?"

CHAPTER VIII

MY father took three strides up and down the room, and then, halting on his hearth, and facing his brother, he thus spoke —"I condemn his deed, Roland! At best he was but a haughty egotist. I understand why Brutus should slay his sons. By that sacrifice he saved his country! What did this poor dupe of an exaggeration save?—nothing but his own name. He could not lift the crime from his son's soul, nor the dishonour from his son's memory. He could but gratify his own vain pride; and, insensibly to himself, his act was whispered to him by the fiend that ever whispers to the heart of man, 'Dread men's opinions more than God's law!' Oh, my dear brother, what minds like yours should guard against the most is not the meanness of evil—it is the evil that takes false nobility, by garbing itself in the royal magnificence of good." My uncle walked to the window, opened it, looked out a moment, as if to draw in fresh air, closed it gently, and came back again to his seat; but during the short time the window had been left open, a moth flew in.

"Tales like these," renewed my father pityingly—"whether told by some great tragedian, or in thy simple style, my brother, —tales like these have their uses: they penetrate the heart to make it wiser; but all wisdom is meek, my Roland. They invite us to put the question to ourselves that thou hast asked —'Can we condemn this man?' and reason answers, as I have answered—'We pity the man, we condemn the deed.' We—— take care, my love! that moth will be in the candle. We—— *whish!—whish!*"—and my father stopped to drive away the moth. My uncle turned, and taking his handkerchief from the lower part of his face, of which he had wished to conceal the workings, he flapped away the moth from the flame. My mother moved the candles from the moth. I tried to catch the moth in my father's straw-hat. The deuce was in the moth! it baffled us all, now circling against the ceiling, now sweeping down at the fatal lights. As if by a simultaneous impulse, my father approached one candle, my uncle approached the other; and just as the moth was wheeling round and round, irresolute which to choose for its funeral pyre, both candles were put out. The fire had burned down low in the grate, and in the sudden dimness my father's soft sweet voice came forth, as if from an invisible being: "We leave ourselves in the dark to save a moth from the flame, brother! shall we do less for our fellow-men? Extinguish, oh! humanely extinguish the light of our reason, when the darkness more favours our mercy." Before the lights were relit my uncle had left the room. His brother followed him; my mother and I drew near to each other and talked in whispers.

PART IV

CHAPTER I

I WAS always an early riser. Happy the man who is! Every morning, day comes to him with a virgin's love, full of bloom, and purity, and freshness. The youth of Nature is contagious, like the gladness of a happy child. I doubt if any man can be called "old" so long as he is an early riser, and an early *walker*. And oh, Youth!—take my word of it—youth in dressing-gown and slippers, dawdling over breakfast at noon, is a very decrepit ghastly image of that youth which sees the sun blush over the mountains, and the dews sparkle upon blossoming hedgerows.

Passing by my father's study, I was surprised to see the windows unclosed—surprised more, on looking in, to see him bending over his books—for I had never before known him study till after the morning meal. Students are not usually early risers, for students, alas! whatever their age, are rarely young. Yes; the Great Book must be getting on in serious earnest. It was no longer dalliance with learning : this was work.

I passed through the gates into the road. A few of the cottages were giving signs of returning life ; but it was not yet the hour for labour, and no "Good morning, sir," greeted me on the road. Suddenly, at a turn, which an overhanging beech-tree had before concealed, I came full upon my Uncle Roland.

"What! you, sir? So early? Hark, the clock is striking five!"

"Not later! I have walked well for a lame man. It must be more than four miles to —— and back."

"You have been to —— : not on business? No soul would be up."

"Yes, at inns there is always some one up. Ostlers never sleep! I have been to order my humble chaise and pair. I leave you to-day, nephew."

"Ah, uncle, we have offended you. It was my folly, that cursed print——"

"Pooh!" said my uncle quickly. "Offended me, boy! I defy you!" and he pressed my hand roughly.

"Yet this sudden determination! It was but yesterday, at the Roman camp, that you planned an excursion with my father to C—— Castle."

"Never depend upon a whimsical man. I must be in London to-night."

"And return to-morrow?"

"I know not when," said my uncle gloomily; and he was silent for some moments. At length, leaning less lightly on my arm, he continued—"Young man, you have pleased me. I love that open, saucy brow of yours, on which Nature has written 'Trust me.' I love those clear eyes, that look one manfully in the face. I must know more of you—much of you. You must come and see me some day or other in your ancestor's ruined keep."

"Come! that I will. And you shall show me the old tower——"

"And the traces of the outworks!" cried my uncle, flourishing his stick.

"And the pedigree——"

"Ay, and your great-great-grandfather's armour, which he wore at Marston Moor——"

"Yes, and the brass plate in the church, uncle."

"The deuce is in the boy! Come here, come here; I've three minds to break your head, sir!"

"It is a pity somebody had not broken the rascally printer's, before he had the impudence to disgrace us by having a family, uncle."

Captain Roland tried hard to frown, but he could not. "Pshaw!" said he, stopping, and taking snuff. "The world of the dead is wide; why should the ghosts jostle us?"

"We can never escape the ghosts, uncle. They haunt us always. We cannot think or act, but the soul of some man, who has lived before, points the way. The dead never die, especially since——"

"Since what, boy?—you speak well."

"Since our great ancestor introduced printing," said I majestically.

My uncle whistled "*Malbrouk s'en va-t-en guerre.*"

I had not the heart to plague him further.

"Peace!" said I, creeping cautiously within the circle of the stick.

"No! I forewarn you——"

"Peace! and describe to me my little cousin, your pretty daughter—for pretty I am sure she is."

"Peace," said my uncle, smiling. "But you must come and judge for yourself."

CHAPTER II

UNCLE ROLAND was gone. Before he went he was closeted for an hour with my father, who then accompanied him to the gate; and we all crowded round him as he stepped into his chaise. When the Captain was gone, I tried to sound my father as to the cause of so sudden a departure. But my father was impenetrable in all that related to his brother's secrets. Whether or not the Captain had ever confided to him the cause of his displeasure with his son—a mystery which much haunted me—my father was mute on that score, both to my mother and myself. For two or three days, however, Mr. Caxton was evidently unsettled. He did not even take to his Great Work, but walked much alone, or accompanied only by the duck, and without even a book in his hand. But by degrees the scholarly habits returned to him; my mother mended his pens, and the work went on.

For my part, left much to myself, especially in the mornings, I began to muse restlessly over the future. Ungrateful that I was, the happiness of home ceased to content me. I heard afar the roar of the great world, and roved impatient by the shore.

At length, one evening, my father, with some modest hums and ha's, and an unaffected blush on his fair forehead, gratified a prayer frequently urged on him, and read me some portions of the Great Work. I cannot express the feelings this lecture created—they were something akin to awe. For the design of this book was so immense—and towards its execution a learning so vast and various had administered—that it seemed to me as if a spirit had opened to me a new world, which had always been before my feet, but which my own human blindness had hitherto concealed from me. The unspeakable patience with which all these materials had been collected, year after year —the ease with which now, by the calm power of genius, they seemed of themselves to fall into harmony and system—the unconscious humility with which the scholar exposed the stores of a laborious life ;—all combined to rebuke my own restlessness and ambition, while they filled me with a pride in my father, which saved my wounded egotism from a pang.   Here, indeed, was one of those books which embrace an existence ; like the Dictionary of Bayle, or the History of Gibbon, or the *Fasti Hellenici* of Clinton, it was a book to which thousands of books had contributed, only to make the originality of the single mind more bold and clear.   Into the furnace all vessels of gold, of all ages, had been cast ; but from the mould came the new coin, with its single stamp.   And, happily, the subject of the work did not forbid to the writer the indulgence of his naïve, peculiar irony of humour—so quiet, yet so profound.   My father's book was the " History of Human Error."   It was, therefore, the moral history of mankind, told with truth and earnestness, yet with an arch, unmalignant smile.   Sometimes, indeed, the smile drew tears.   But in all true humour lies its germ, pathos.   Oh ! by the goddess Moria or Folly, but he was at home in his theme !   He viewed man first in the savage state, preferring in this the positive accounts of voyagers and travellers to the vague myths of antiquity, and the dreams of speculators on our pristine state.   From Australia and Abyssinia he drew pictures of mortality unadorned, as lively as if he had lived amongst Bushmen and savages all his life.   Then he crossed over the Atlantic, and brought before you the American Indian, with his noble nature, struggling into the dawn of civilisation, when friend Penn cheated him out of his birthright, and the Anglo-Saxon drove him back into darkness.   He showed both analogy and contrast between this specimen of our kind, and others equally apart from the extremes of the savage state and the cultured.   The Arab in his tent, the Teuton in his forests, the Greenlander in his boat, the Fin in his reindeer car.   Up sprang the rude gods of the north, and the resuscitated Druidism, passing from its earliest templeless belief into the later corruptions of crommell and idol.   Up sprang, by their side, the Saturn of the Phœnicians, the mystic Budh of India, the elementary deities of the Pelasgian, the Naith and Serapis of Egypt, the Ormuzd of Persia, the Bel of Babylon, the winged genii of the graceful Etruria.   How nature and life shaped the religion ; how the religion shaped the manners ; how, and by what influences, some tribes were formed for progress ; how others were destined to remain stationary, or be swallowed up in war and slavery by their brethren, was told with a precision clear and strong as the voice of Fate. Not only an antiquarian and philologist, but an anatomist and philosopher—my father brought to bear on all these grave points the various speculations involved in the distinction of races. He showed how race in perfection is produced, up to a certain point, by admixture; how all mixed races have been the most intelligent—how, in proportion as local circumstance and religious faith permitted the early fusion of different tribes, races improved and quickened into the refinements of civilisation. He tracked the progress and dispersion of the Hellenes, from their mythical cradle in Thessaly; and showed how those who settled near the sea-shores, and were compelled into commerce and intercourse with strangers, gave to Greece her marvellous accomplishments in arts and letters— the flowers of the ancient world. How others, like the Spartans, dwelling evermore in a camp, on guard against their neighbours, and rigidly preserving their Dorian purity of extraction, contributed neither artists, nor poets, nor philosophers to the golden treasure-house of mind. He took the old race of the Celts, Cimry, or Cimmerians. He compared the Celt who, as in Wales, the Scotch Highlands, in Bretagne, and in uncomprehended Ireland, retains his old characteristics and purity of breed, with the Celt, whose blood, mixed by a thousand channels, dictates from Paris the manners and revolutions of the world. He compared the Norman, in his ancient Scandinavian home, with that wonder of intelligence and chivalry into which he grew, fused imperceptibly with the Frank, the Goth, and the Anglo-Saxon. He compared the Saxon, stationary in the land of Horsa, with the colonist and civiliser of the globe, as he becomes, when he knows not through what channels—French, Flemish, Danish, Welsh, Scotch, and Irish— he draws his sanguine blood. And out from all these speculations, to which I do such hurried and scanty justice, he drew the blessed truth, that carries hope to the land of the Caffre, the hut of the Bushman—that there is nothing in the flattened skull and the ebon aspect that rejects God's law—improvement; that by the same principle which raises the dog, the lowest of the animals in its savage state, to the highest after man—viz., admixture of race—you can elevate into nations of majesty and power the outcasts of humanity, now your compassion or your scorn. But when my father got into the marrow of his theme — when, quitting these preliminary discussions, he fell pounce amongst the would-be wisdom of the wise : when he dealt with civilisation itself, its schools, and porticoes, and academies; when he bared the absurdities couched beneath the colleges of the Egyptians, and the Symposia of the Greeks; when he showed that, even in their own favourite pursuit of metaphysics, the Greeks were children; and in their own more practical region of politics, the Romans were visionaries and bunglers;—when, following the stream of error through the Middle Ages, he quoted the puerilities of Agrippa, the crudities of Cardan, and passed, with his calm smile, into the *salons* of the chattering wits of Paris in the eighteenth century, oh! then his irony was that of Lucian, sweetened by the gentle spirit of Erasmus. For not even here was my father's satire of the cheerless and Mephistophelian school. From this record of error he drew forth the grand eras of truth. He showed how earnest men never think in vain, though their thoughts may be errors. He proved how, in vast cycles, age after age, the human mind marches on—like the ocean, receding here, but there advancing: how from the speculations of the Greeks sprang all true philosophy; how from the institutions of the Roman rose all durable systems of government; how from the robust follies of the north came the glory of chivalry, and the modern delicacies of honour, and the sweet, harmonising influences of woman. He tracked the ancestry of our Sidneys and Bayards from the Hengists, Generics, and Attilas. Full of all curious and quaint anecdote—of original illustration—of those niceties of learning which spring from a taste cultivated to the last exquisite polish —the book amused, and allured, and charmed; and erudition lost its pedantry now in the simplicity of Montaigne, now in the penetration of La Bruyère. He lived in each time of which he wrote, and the time lived again in him. Ah! what a writer of romances he would have been, if—if what? If he had had as sad an experience of men's passions, as he had the happy intuition into their humours. But he who would see the mirror of the shore, must look where it is cast on the river, not the ocean. The narrow stream reflects the gnarled tree, and the pausing herd, and the village spire, and the romance of the landscape; but the sea reflects only the vast outline of the headland, and the lights of the eternal heaven.

CHAPTER III

"IT is Lombard Street to a China orange," quoth Uncle Jack.

"Are the odds in favour of fame against failure so great? You do not speak, I fear, from experience, brother Jack," answered my father, as he stooped down to tickle the duck under the left ear.

"But Jack Tibbets is not Augustine Caxton. Jack Tibbets is not a scholar, a genius, a wond——"

"Stop!" cried my father.

"After all," said Mr. Squills, "though I am no flatterer, Mr. Tibbets is not so far out. That part of your book which compares the crania or skulls of the different races is superb. Lawrence or Dr. Prichard could not have done the thing more neatly. Such a book must not be lost to the world; and I agree with Mr. Tibbets that you should publish as soon as possible."

"It is one thing to write and another to publish," said my father irresolutely. "When one considers all the great men who have published; when one thinks one is going to intrude one's self audaciously into the company of Aristotle and Bacon, of Locke, of Herder—of all the grave philosophers who bend over Nature with brows weighty with thought—one may well pause, and——"

"Pooh!" interrupted Uncle Jack; "science is not a club, it is an ocean; it is open to the cockboat as the frigate. One man carries across it a freightage of ingots, another may fish there for herrings. Who can exhaust the sea? who say to intellect, 'The deeps of philosophy are preoccupied'?"

"Admirable!" cried Squills.

"So it is really your advice, my friends," said my father, who seemed struck by Uncle Jack's eloquent illustrations, "that I should desert my household gods, remove to London, since my own library ceases to supply my wants; take lodgings near the British Museum, and finish off one volume, at least, incontinently."

"It is a duty you owe to your country," said Uncle Jack solemnly.

"And to yourself," urged Squills. "One must attend to the natural evacuations of the brain. Ah! you may smile, sir; but I have observed that if a man has much in his head, he must

F

give it vent or it oppresses him; the whole system goes wrong. From being abstracted, he grows stupefied. The weight of the pressure affects the nerves. I would not even guarantee you from a stroke of paralysis."

"O Austin!" cried my mother tenderly, and throwing her arms round my father's neck.

"Come, sir, you are conquered," said I.

"And what is to become of you, Sisty!" asked my father. "Do you go with us, and unsettle your mind for the university?"

"My uncle has invited me to his castle; and in the meanwhile I will stay here, fag hard, and take care of the duck."

"All alone?" said my mother.

"No. All alone! Why, Uncle Jack will come here as often as ever, I hope."

Uncle Jack shook his head.

"No, my boy—I must go to town with your father. You don't understand these things. I shall see the booksellers for him. I know how these gentlemen are to be dealt with. I shall prepare the literary circles for the appearance of the book. In short, it is a sacrifice of interest, I know. My Journal will suffer. But friendship and my country's good before all things."

"Dear Jack!" said my mother affectionately.

"I cannot suffer it," cried my father. "You are making a good income. You are doing well where you are; and as to seeing the booksellers—why, when the work is ready, you can come to town for a week, and settle that affair."

"Poor dear Austin," said Uncle Jack, with an air of superiority and compassion. "A week! sir, the advent of a book that is to succeed requires the preparation of months. Pshaw! I am no genius, but I am a practical man. I know what's what. Leave me alone."

But my father continued obstinate, and Uncle Jack at last ceased to urge the matter. The journey to fame and London was now settled; but my father would not hear of my staying behind.

No; Pisistratus must needs go also to town and see the world; the duck would take care of itself.

CHAPTER IV

WE had taken the precaution to send, the day before, to secure our due complement of places—four in all (including one for Mrs. Primmins)—in, or upon, the fast family coach called the Sun, which had lately been set up for the special convenience of the neighbourhood.

This luminary, rising in a town about seven miles distant from us, described at first a very erratic orbit amidst the contiguous villages, before it finally struck into the high-road of enlightenment, and thence performed its journey, in the full eyes of man, at the majestic pace of six miles and a half an hour. My father with his pockets full of books, and a quarto of "Gebelin on the Primitive World," for light reading under his arm ; my mother with a little basket, containing sandwiches, and biscuits of her own baking; Mrs. Primmins, with a new umbrella purchased for the occasion, and a bird-cage containing a canary, endeared to her not more by song than age, and a severe pip through which she had successfully nursed it—and I myself, waited at the gates to welcome the celestial visitor. The gardener, with a wheelbarrow full of boxes and portmanteaus, stood a little in the van ; and the footman, who was to follow when lodgings had been found, had gone to a rising eminence to watch the dawning of the expected Sun, and apprise us of its approach by the concerted signal of a handkerchief fixed to a stick.

The quaint old house looked at us mournfully from all its deserted windows. The litter before its threshold and in its open hall; wisps of straw or hay that had been used for packing; baskets and boxes that had been examined and rejected ; others, corded and piled, reserved to follow with the footman—and the two heated and hurried serving-women left behind standing half-way between house and garden-gate whispering to each other, and looking as if they had not slept for weeks—gave to a scene, usually so trim and orderly, an aspect of pathetic abandonment and desolation. The Genius of the place seemed to reproach us. I felt the omens were against us, and turned my earnest gaze from the haunts behind with a sigh, as the coach now drew up with all its grandeur. An important personage, who, despite the heat of the day, was enveloped in a vast superfluity of belcher, in the midst of which galloped a gilt fox, and who rejoiced in the name of "guard," descended to inform us politely that only three places, two inside and one out, were at our disposal, the rest having been pre-engaged a fortnight before our orders were received.

Now, as I knew that Mrs. Primmins was indispensable to the comforts of my honoured parents (the more so, as she had once lived in London, and knew all its ways), I suggested that she should take the outside seat, and that I should perform the journey on foot—a primitive mode of transport, which has its charms to a young man with stout limbs and gay spirits. The guard's outstretched arm left my mother little time to oppose this proposition, to which my father assented with a silent squeeze of the hand. And, having promised to join them at a family hotel near the Strand, to which Mr. Squills had recommended them as peculiarly genteel and quiet, and waved my last farewell to my poor mother, who continued to stretch her meek face out of the window till the coach was whirled off in a cloud like one of the Homeric heroes, I turned within, to put up a few necessary articles in a small knapsack, which I remembered to have seen in the lumber-room, and which had appertained to my maternal grandfather; and with that on my shoulder, and a strong staff in my hand, I set off towards the great city at as brisk a pace as if I were only bound to the next village. Accordingly, about noon I was both tired and hungry; and seeing by the wayside one of those pretty inns yet peculiar to England, but which, thanks to the railways, will soon be amongst the things before the Flood, I sat down at a table under some clipped limes, unbuckled my knapsack, and ordered my simple fare with the dignity of one who, for the first time in his life, bespeaks his own dinner, and pays for it out of his own pocket.

While engaged on a rasher of bacon and a tankard of what the landlord called "No mistake," two pedestrians, passing the same road which I had traversed, paused, cast a simultaneous look at my occupation, and induced no doubt by its allurements, seated themselves under the same lime-trees, though at the farther end of the table. I surveyed the new-comers with the curiosity natural to my years.

The elder of the two might have attained the age of thirty, though sundry deep lines, and hues formerly florid and now faded, speaking of fatigue, care, or dissipation, might have made him look somewhat older than he was. There was nothing very prepossessing in his appearance. He was dressed with a pretension ill suited to the costume appropriate to a foot-traveller. His

coat was pinched and padded; two enormous pins, connected
by a chain, decorated a very stiff stock of blue satin, dotted
with yellow stars; his hands were cased in very dingy gloves,
which had once been straw-coloured, and the said hands played
with a whalebone cane surmounted by a formidable knob, which
gave it the appearance of a "life-preserver." As he took off a
white napless hat, which he wiped with great care and affection
with the sleeve of his right arm, a profusion of stiff curls instantly betrayed the art of man. Like my landlord's ale, in
that wig there was "no mistake:" it was brought (after the
fashion of the wigs we see in the popular effigies of George IV.
in his youth) low over his forehead and was raised at the top.
The wig had been oiled, and the oil had imbibed no small
quantity of dust; oil and dust had alike left their impression
on the forehead and cheeks of the wig's proprietor. For the rest
the expression of his face was somewhat impudent and reckless,
but not without a certain drollery in the corners of his eyes.

The younger man was apparently about my own age, a year
or two older, perhaps—judging rather from his set and sinewy
frame than his boyish countenance. And this last, boyish as it
was, could not fail to command the attention even of the most
careless observer. It had not only the darkness, but the character
of the gipsy face, with large brilliant eyes, raven hair, long and
wavy, but not curling; the features were aquiline, but delicate,
and when he spoke he showed teeth dazzling as pearls. It was
impossible not to admire the singular beauty of the countenance;
and yet, it had that expression, at once stealthy and fierce, which
war with society has stamped upon the lineaments of the race of
which it reminded me. But, withal, there was somewhat of the
air of a gentleman in this young wayfarer. His dress consisted
of a black velveteen shooting-jacket, or rather short frock, with
a broad leathern strap at the waist, loose white trousers, and a
foraging cap, which he threw carelessly on the table as he wiped
his brow. Turning round impatiently, and with some haughtiness, from his companion, he surveyed me with a quick, observant
flash of his piercing eyes, and then stretched himself at length on
the bench, and appeared either to doze or muse, till, in obedience
to his companion's orders, the board was spread with all the cold
meats the larder could supply.

"Beef!" said his companion, screwing a pinchbeck glass into
his right eye. "Beef;—mottled, cowey—humph! Lamb;—
oldish—rawish—muttony—humph! Pie;—stalish. Veal?—no,
pork. Ah! what will you have?"

"Help yourself," replied the young man peevishly, as he sat up, looked disdainfully at the viands, and, after a long pause, tasted first one, and then the other, with many shrugs of the shoulders and muttered exclamations of discontent. Suddenly he looked up, and called for brandy; and, to my surprise, and I fear admiration, he drank nearly half a tumblerful of that poison undiluted, with a composure that spoke of habitual use.

"Wrong!" said his companion, drawing the bottle to himself, and mixing the alcohol in careful proportions with water. "Wrong! coats of stomach soon wear out with that kind of clothes-brush. Better stick to the 'yeasty foam,' as sweet Will says. That young gentleman sets you a good example," and therewith the speaker nodded at me familiarly. Inexperienced as I was, I surmised at once that it was his intention to make acquaintance with the neighbour thus saluted. I was not deceived. "Anything to tempt *vou*, sir?" asked this social personage after a short pause, and describing a semicircle with the point of his knife.

"I thank you, sir, but I have dined."

"What then? 'Break out into a second course of mischief,' as the swan recommends—swan of Avon, sir! No? 'Well, then, I charge you with this sup of sack.' Are you going far, if I may take the liberty to ask?"

"To London."

"Oh!" said the traveller—while his young companion lifted his eyes; and I was again struck with their remarkable penetration and brilliancy.

"London is the best place in the world for a lad of spirit. See life there; 'glass of fashion and mould of form.' Fond of the play, sir?"

"I never saw one."

"Possible!" cried the gentleman, dropping the handle of his knife, and bringing up the point horizontally: "then, young man," he added solemnly, "you have—but I won't say what you have to see. I won't say—no, not if you could cover this table with golden guineas, and exclaim with the generous ardour so engaging in youth, 'Mr. Peacock, these are yours if you will only say what I have to see!'"

I laughed outright—may I be forgiven for the boast, but I had the reputation at school of a pleasant laugh. The young man's face grew dark at the sound: he pushed back his plate and sighed.

"Why," continued his friend, "my companion here, who, I

suppose, is about your own age, he could tell you what a play is —he could tell you what life is. He has viewed the manners of the town : ' perused the traders,' as the swan poetically remarks. Have you not, my lad, eh ? "

Thus directly appealed to, the boy looked up with a smile of scorn on his lips—

" Yes, I know what life is, and I say that life, like poverty, has strange bed-fellows. Ask me what life is now, and I say a melodrama ; ask me what it is twenty years hence, and I shall say——"

" A farce ? " put in his comrade.

" No, a tragedy—or comedy as Molière wrote it."

" And how is that ? " I asked, interested and somewhat surprised at the tone of my contemporary.

" Where the play ends in the triumph of the wittiest rogue. My friend here has no chance ! "

" ' Praise from Sir Hubert Stanley,' hem—yes, Hal Peacock may be witty, but he is no rogue."

" That was not exactly my meaning," said the boy dryly.

" ' A fico for your meaning,' as the swan says.—Hallo, you, sir ! Bully Host, clear the table,—fresh tumblers—hot water— sugar—lemon,—and——the bottle's out ! Smoke, sir ? " and Mr. Peacock offered me a cigar.

Upon my refusal, he carefully twirled round a very uninviting specimen of some fabulous havannah—moistened it all over, as a boa-constrictor may do the ox he prepares for deglutition ; bit off one end, and lighting the other from a little machine for that purpose which he drew from his pocket, he was soon absorbed in a vigorous effort (which the damp inherent in the weed long resisted) to poison the surrounding atmosphere. Therewith the young gentleman, either from emulation or in self-defence, extracted from his own pouch a cigar-case of notable elegance,—being of velvet, embroidered apparently by some fair hand, for " From Juliet " was very legibly worked thereon— selected a cigar of better appearance than that in favour with his comrade, and seemed quite as familiar with the tobacco as he had been with the brandy.

" Fast, sir—fast lad that," quoth Mr. Peacock, in the short gasps which his resolute struggle with his uninviting victim alone permitted—" nothing but (puff, puff) your true (suck, suck) syl—syl—sylva—does for him. Out, by the Lord ! ' the jaws of darkness have devoured it up ;'" and again Mr. Peacock applied to his phosphoric machine. This time patience and perseverance succeeded, and the heart of the cigar responded by a dull red spark (leaving the sides wholly untouched) to the indefatigable ardour of its wooer.

This feat accomplished, Mr. Peacock exclaimed triumphantly, " And now, what say you, my lads, to a game at cards?—three of us—whist and a dummy—nothing better—eh?" As he spoke he produced from his coat pocket a red silk handkerchief, a bunch of keys, a nightcap, a tooth-brush, a piece of shaving-soap, four lumps of sugar, the remains of a bun, a razor, and a pack of cards. Selecting the last, and returning its motley accompaniments to the abyss whence they had emerged, he turned up, with a jerk of his thumb and finger, the knave of clubs, and placing it on the top of the rest, slapped the cards emphatically on the table.

" You are very good, but I don't know whist," said I.

" Not know whist—not been to a .play—not smoke! Then pray tell me, young man," said he majestically, and with a frown, "what on earth you *do* know!"

Much consternated by this direct appeal, and greatly ashamed of my ignorance of the cardinal points of erudition in Mr. Peacock's estimation, I hung my head and looked down.

"That is right," renewed Mr. Peacock more benignly; "you have the ingenuous shame of youth. It is promising, sir —'lowliness is young ambition's ladder,' as the swan says. Mount the first step, and learn whist—sixpenny points to begin with."

Notwithstanding any newness in actual life, I had had the good fortune to learn a little of the way before me, by those much-slandered guides called novels—works which are often to the inner world what maps are to the outer; and sundry recollections of " Gil Blas " and the " Vicar of Wakefield " came athwart me. I had no wish to emulate the worthy Moses, and felt that I might not have even the shagreen spectacles to boast of in my negotiations with this new Mr. Jenkinson. Accordingly, shaking my head, I called for my bill. As I took out my purse—knit by my mother—with one gold piece in one corner, and sundry silver ones in the other, I saw that the eyes of Mr. Peacock twinkled.

" Poor spirit, sir! poor spirit, young man! "This avarice sticks deep,' as the swan beautifully observes. ' Nothing venture, nothing have.' "

"Nothing have, nothing venture," I returned, plucking up spirit.

"Nothing have!—Young sir, do you doubt my solidity—my capital—my 'golden joys'?"

"Sir, I spoke of myself. I am not rich enough to gamble."

"Gamble!" exclaimed Mr. Peacock, in virtuous indignation—"Gamble! what do you mean, sir? You insult me!" and he rose threateningly, and clapped his white hat on his wig.

"Pshaw! let him alone, Hal," said the boy contemptuously. "Sir, if he is impertinent, thrash him." (This was to me.)

"Impertinent!—thrash!" exclaimed Mr. Peacock, waxing very red; but catching the sneer on his companion's lip, he sat down, and subsided into sullen silence.

Meanwhile I paid my bill. This duty, rarely a cheerful one, performed, I looked round for my knapsack, and perceived that it was in the boy's hands. He was very coolly reading the address which, in case of accidents, I prudently placed on it—"Pisistratus Caxton, Esq., —— Hotel, —— Street, Strand."

I took my knapsack from him, more surprised at such a breach of good manners in a young gentleman who knew life so well, than I should have been at a similar error on the part of Mr. Peacock. He made no apology, but nodded farewell, and stretched himself at full length on the bench. Mr. Peacock, now absorbed in a game of patience, vouchsafed no return to my parting salutation, and in another moment I was alone on the high-road. My thoughts turned long upon the young man I had left; mixed with a sort of instinctive compassionate foreboding of an ill future for one with such habits, and in such companionship, I felt an involuntary admiration, less even for his good looks than his ease, audacity, and the careless superiority he assumed over a comrade so much older than himself.

The day was far gone when I saw the spires of a town at which I intended to rest for the night. The horn of a coach behind made me turn my head, and, as the vehicle passed me, I saw on the outside Mr. Peacock, still struggling with a cigar—it could scarcely be the same—and his young friend stretched on the roof amongst the luggage, leaning his handsome head on his hand, and apparently unobservant both of me and every one else.

CHAPTER V

I AM apt—judging egotistically, perhaps, from my own experience—to measure a young man's chance of what is termed
practical success in life, by what may seem at first two very
vulgar qualities; viz., his inquisitiveness and his animal vivacity.
A curiosity which springs forward to examine everything new
to his information—a nervous activity, approaching to restlessness, which rarely allows bodily fatigue to interfere with some
object in view—constitute, in my mind, very profitable stock-in-
hand to begin the world with.

Tired as I was, after I had performed my ablutions, and
refreshed myself in the little coffee-room of the inn at which I
put up, with the pedestrian's best beverage, familiar and oft-
calumniated tea, I could not resist the temptation of the broad,
bustling street, which, lighted with gas, shone on me through
the dim windows of the coffee-room. I had never before seen
a large town, and the contrast of lamp-lit, busy night in the
streets, with sober, deserted night in the lanes and fields, struck
me forcibly.

I sauntered out, therefore, jostling and jostled, now gazing at
the windows, now hurried along the tide of life, till I found myself before a cook-shop, round which clustered a small knot of
housewives, citizens, and hungry-looking children. While con-
templating this group, and marvelling how it comes to pass that
the staple business of earth's majority is how, when, and where
to eat, my ear was struck with " ' In Troy there lies the scene,'
as the illustrious Will remarks."

Looking round, I perceived Mr. Peacock pointing his stick
towards an open doorway next to the cook-shop, the hall beyond
which was lighted with gas, while, painted in black letters on a
pane of glass over the door, was the word " Billiards."

Suiting the action to the word, the speaker plunged at once
into the aperture, and vanished. The boy-companion was following more slowly when his eye caught mine. A slight blush came
over his dark cheek; he stopped, and leaning against the door-
jambs, gazed on me hard and long before he said—" Well met
again, sir ! You find it hard to amuse yourself in this dull place;
the nights are long out of London."

" Oh," said I ingenuously, " everything here amuses me; the
lights, the shops, the crowd; but, then, to me everything is new."

The youth came from his lounging-place and moved on, as if inviting me to walk; while he answered, rather with bitter sullenness, than the melancholy his words expressed—

"One thing, at least, cannot be new to you ; it is an old truth with us before we leave the nursery—' Whatever is worth having must be bought; *ergo*, he who cannot buy, has nothing worth having.'"

"I don't think," said I wisely, "that the things best worth having can be bought at all. You see that poor dropsical jeweller standing before his shop-door : his shop is the finest in the street, —and I dare say he would be very glad to give it to you or me in return for our good health and strong legs. Oh no! I think with my father—' All that are worth having are given to all ; '— that is, nature and labour."

"Your father says that; and you go by what your father says ! Of course, all fathers have preached that, and many other good doctrines, since Adam preached to Cain ; but I don't see that the fathers have found their sons very credulous listeners."

"So much the worse for the sons," said I bluntly.

"Nature," continued my new acquaintance, without attending to my ejaculation—"nature indeed does give us much, and nature also orders each of us how to use her gifts. If nature give you the propensity to drudge, you will drudge ; if she give me the ambition to rise, and the contempt for work, I may rise—but I certainly shall not work."

"Oh," said I, "you agree with Squills, I suppose, and fancy we are all guided by the bumps on our foreheads ?"

"And the blood in our veins, and our mothers' milk. We inherit other things besides gout and consumption. So you always do as your father tells you ! Good boy !"

I was piqued. Why we should be ashamed of being taunted for goodness, I never could understand ; but certainly I felt humbled. However, I answered sturdily—" If you had as good a father as I have, you would not think it so very extraordinary to do as he tells you."

"Ah ! so he is a very good father, is he ! He must have a great trust in your sobriety and steadiness to let you wander about the world as he does."

"I am going to join him in London."

"In London ! Oh, does he live there ?"

"He is going to live there for some time."

"Then, perhaps, we may meet. I, too, am going to town."

"Oh, we shall be sure to meet there !" said I, with frank

gladness; for my interest in the young man was not diminished by his conversation, however much I disliked the sentiments it expressed.

The lad laughed—and his laugh was peculiar: it was low, musical, but hollow and artificial.

"Sure to meet! London is a large place: where shall you be found?"

I gave him, without scruple, the address of the hotel at which I expected to find my father; although his deliberate inspection of my knapsack must already have apprised him of that address. He listened attentively, and repeated it twice over, as if to impress it on his memory; and we both walked on in silence, till, turning up a small passage, we suddenly found ourselves in a large churchyard,—a flagged path stretched diagonally across it towards the market-place, on which it bordered. In this churchyard, upon a gravestone, sat a young Savoyard; his hurdy-gurdy, or whatever else his instrument might be called, was on his lap; and he was gnawing his crust, and feeding some poor little white mice (standing on their hind-legs on the hurdy-gurdy) as merrily as if he had chosen the gayest resting-place in the world.

We both stopped. The Savoyard, seeing us, put his arch head on one side, showed all his white teeth in that happy smile so peculiar to his race, and in which poverty seems to beg so blithely, and gave the handle of his instrument a turn.

"Poor child!" said I.

"Aha, you pity him! but why? According to your rule, Mr. Caxton, he is not so much to be pitied; the dropsical jeweller would give him as much for his limbs and health as for ours! How is it—answer me, son of so wise a father—that no one pities the dropsical jeweller, and all pity the healthy Savoyard? Is it, sir, because there is a stern truth which is stronger than all Spartan lessons — Poverty *is* the master-ill of the world. Look round. Does poverty leave its signs over the graves? Look at that large tomb fenced round ; read that long inscription :—'Virtue' — 'best of husbands'—'affectionate father'— —'inconsolable grief'—'sleeps in the joyful hope,' &c., &c. Do you suppose these stoneless mounds hide no dust of what were men just as good? But no epitaph tells their virtues, bespeaks their wives' grief, or promises joyful hope to them!"

"Does it matter? Does God care for the epitaph and tomb-stone?"

"*Datemi qualche cosa!*" said the Savoyard, in his touching

patois, still smiling, and holding out his little hand; therein I dropped a small coin. The boy evinced his gratitude by a new turn of the hurdy-gurdy.

"That is not labour," said my companion; "and had you found him at work, you had given him nothing. I, too, have my instrument to play upon, and my mice to see after. Adieu!"

He waved his hand, and strode irreverently over the graves back in the direction we had come.

I stood before the fine tomb with its fine epitaph: the Savoyard looked at me wistfully.

CHAPTER VI

THE Savoyard looked at me wistfully. I wished to enter into conversation with him. That was not easy. However, I began:—

PISISTRATUS.—"You must be often hungry enough, my poor boy. Do the mice feed you?"

SAVOYARD puts his head on one side, shakes it and strokes his mice.

PISISTRATUS.—"You are very fond of the mice; they are your only friends, I fear."

SAVOYARD, evidently understanding Pisistratus, rubs his face gently against the mice, then puts them softly down on a grave, and gives a turn to the hurdy-gurdy. The mice play unconcernedly over the grave.

PISISTRATUS, pointing first to the beasts, then to the instrument. —"Which do you like best, the mice or the hurdy-gurdy?"

SAVOYARD shows his teeth—considers—stretches himself on the grass—plays with the mice—and answers volubly.

PISISTRATUS, by the help of Latin, comprehending that the Savoyard says that the mice are alive, and the hurdy-gurdy is not—"Yes, a live friend is better than a dead one. Mortua est hurda-gurda!"

SAVOYARD shakes his head vehemently.—"Nô—nô! Eccellenza, non è morta!" and strikes up a lively air on the slandered instrument. The Savoyard's face brightens—he looks happy: the mice run from the grave into his bosom.

PISISTRATUS, affected, and putting the question in Latin.— "Have you a father?"

SAVOYARD, with his face overcast.—"Nô—Eccellenza!" then

pausing a little, he says briskly, "Si si !" and plays a solemn air on the hurdy-gurdy—stops—rests one hand on the instrument, and raises the other to heaven.

Pisistratus understands : the father is like the hurdy-gurdy, at once dead and living. The mere form is a dead thing, but the music lives. Pisistratus drops another small piece of silver on the ground, and turns away.

God help and God bless thee, Savoyard. Thou hast done Pisistratus all the good in the world. Thou hast corrected the hard wisdom of the young gentleman in the velveteen jacket; Pisistratus is a better lad for having stopped to listen to thee.

I regained the entrance to the churchyard—I looked back: there sat the Savoyard, still amidst men's graves, but under God's sky. He was still looking at me wistfully ; and when he caught my eye, he pressed his hand to his heart, and smiled. God help and God bless thee, young Savoyard.

PART V

CHAPTER I

IN setting off the next morning, the Boots, whose heart I had won by an extra sixpence for calling me betimes, good-naturedly informed me that I might save a mile of the journey, and have a very pleasant walk into the bargain, if I took the footpath through a gentleman's park, the lodge of which I should see about seven miles from the town.

"And the grounds are showed too," said the Boots, "if so be you has a mind to stay and see 'em. But don't you go to the gardener, he'll want half-a-crown; there's an old 'oman at the lodge, who will show you all that's worth seeing—the walks and the big cascade—for a tizzy. You may make use of my name," he added proudly—"Bob, boots at the Lion. She be a *h*aunt o' mine, and she minds them that come from me pertiklerly."

Not doubting that the purest philanthropy actuated these counsels, I thanked my shock-headed friend, and asked carelessly to whom the park belonged.

"To Muster Trevanion, the great Parliament man," answered the Boots. "You has heard o' him, I guess, sir?"

I shook my head, surprised every hour more and more to find how very little there was in it.

"They takes in the *Moderate Man's Journal* at the Lamb; and they say in the tap there that he's one of the cleverest chaps in the House o' Commons," continued the Boots in a confidential whisper. "But we takes in the *People's Thunderbolt* at the Lion, and we knows better this Muster Trevanion: he is but a trimmer—milk and water, no *h*orator,—not the right sort,—you understand?"

Perfectly satisfied that I understood nothing about it, I smiled, and said, "Oh yes;" and slipping on my knapsack, commenced my adventures; the Boots bawling after me, "Mind, sir, you tells *h*aunt I sent you!"

The town was only languidly putting forth symptoms of re-

turning life as I strode through the streets; a pale sickly un-
wholesome look on the face of the slothful Phœbus had succeeded
the feverish hectic of the past night: the artisans whom I met
glided by me haggard and dejected; a few early shops were
alone open; one or two drunken men, emerging from the lanes,
sallied homeward with broken pipes in their mouths; bills, with
large capitals, calling attention to "Best family teas at 4s. a
pound;" "the arrival of Mr. Sloman's caravan of wild beasts;"
and Dr. Do'em's "Paracelsian Pills of Immortality," stared out
dull and uncheering from the walls of tenantless dilapidated
houses, in that chill sunrise which favours no illusion.   I was
glad when I had left the town behind me, and saw the reapers
in the corn-fields, and heard the chirp of the birds.   I arrived
at the lodge of which the Boots had spoken: a pretty rustic
building half-concealed by a belt of plantations, with two large
iron gates for the owner's friends, and a small turn-stile for the
public, who, by some strange neglect on his part, or sad want
of interest with the neighbouring magistrates, had still preserved
a right to cross the rich man's domains, and look on his grandeur,
limited to compliance with a reasonable request mildly stated
on the notice-board, "to keep to the paths."   As it was not yet
eight o'clock, I had plenty of time before me to see the grounds,
and profiting by the economical hint of the Boots, I entered the
lodge, and inquired for the old lady who was *haunt* to Mr. Bob.
A young woman, who was busied in preparing breakfast, nodded
with great civility to this request, and, hastening to a bundle of
clothes which I then perceived in the corner, she cried, "Grand-
mother, here's a gentleman to see the cascade."

The bundle of clothes then turned round, and exhibited a
human countenance, which lighted up with great intelligence
as the grand-daughter, turning to me, said with simplicity—
"She's old, honest cretur, but she still likes to earn a sixpence,
sir;" and taking a crutch-staff in her hand while her grand-
daughter put a neat bonnet on her head, this industrious gentlewoman sallied out at a pace which surprised me.

I attempted to enter into conversation with my guide; but
she did not seem much inclined to be sociable, and the beauty
of the glades and groves which now spread before my eyes reconciled me to silence.

I have seen many fine places since then, but I do not remember to have seen a landscape more beautiful in its peculiar
English character than that which I now gazed on.   It had
none of the feudal characteristics of ancient parks, with giant

oaks, fantastic pollards, glens covered with fern, and deer grouped upon the slopes; on the contrary, in spite of some fine trees, chiefly beech, the impression conveyed was, that it was a new place—a made place. You might see ridges on the lawns which showed where hedges had been removed; the pastures were parcelled out in divisions by new wire-fences; young plantations, planned with exquisite taste, but without the venerable formality of avenues and quincunxes, by which you know the parks that date from Elizabeth and James, diversified the rich extent of verdure; instead of deer, were short-horned cattle of the finest breed—sheep that would have won the prize at an agricultural show. Everywhere there was the evidence of improvement—energy—capital; but capital clearly not employed for the mere purpose of return. The ornamental was too conspicuously predominant amidst the lucrative, not to say eloquently—"The owner is willing to make the most of his land, but not the most of his money."

But the old woman's eagerness to earn sixpence had impressed me unfavourably as to the character of the master. "Here," thought I, "are all the signs of riches; and yet this poor old woman, living on the very threshold of opulence, is in want of a sixpence."

These surmises, in the indulgence of which I piqued myself on my penetration, were strengthened into conviction by the few sentences which I succeeded at last in eliciting from the old woman.

"Mr. Trevanion must be a rich man?" said I.

"O ay, rich eno'!" grumbled my guide.

"And," said I, surveying the extent of shrubbery or dressed ground through which our way wound, now emerging into lawns and glades, now belted by rare garden-trees, now (as every inequality of the ground was turned to advantage in the landscape) sinking into the dell, now climbing up the slopes, and now confining the view to some object of graceful art or enchanting nature—"And," said I, "he must employ many hands here—plenty of work, eh?"

"Ay, ay—I don't say that he don't find work for those who want it. But it ain't the same place it wor in my day."

"You remember it in other hands, then?"

"Ay, ay! When the Hogtons had it, honest folk! My good man was the gardener--none of those set-up fine gentlemen who can't put hand to a spade."

Poor faithful old woman!

G

I began to hate the unknown proprietor. Here clearly was
some mushroom usurper who had bought out the old simple
hospitable family, neglected its ancient servants, left them to
earn tizzies by showing waterfalls, and insulted their eyes by his
selfish wealth.

"There's the water all spil't—it warn't so in my day," said
the guide.

A rivulet, whose murmur I had long heard, now stole suddenly
into view, and gave to the scene the crowning charm.   As, re-
lapsing into silence, we tracked its sylvan course, under dipping
chestnuts and shady limes, the house itself emerged on the
opposite side—a modern building of white stone, with the
noblest Corinthian portico I ever saw in this country.

"A fine house, indeed," said I.   "Is Mr. Trevanion here
much?"

"Ay, ay—I don't mean to say that he goes away altogether,
but it ain't as it wor in my day, when the Hogtons lived here
all the year round in their warm house,—not that one."

Good old woman, and these poor banished Hogtons! thought
I; hateful parvenu! I was pleased when a curve in the
shrubberies shut out the house from view, though in reality
bringing us nearer to it.   And the boasted cascade, whose roar
I had heard for some moments, came in sight.

Amidst the Alps, such a waterfall would have been insignificant, but contrasting ground highly dressed, with no other bold
features, its effect was striking, and even grand.   The banks
were here narrowed and compressed; rocks, partly natural,
partly no doubt artificial, gave a rough aspect to the margin;
and the cascade fell from a considerable height into rapid
waters, which my guide mumbled out were "mortal deep."

"There wor a madman leapt over where you be standing,"
said the old woman, "two years ago last June."

"A madman! why," said I, observing, with an eye practised
in the gymnasium of the Hellenic Institute, the narrow space of
the banks over the gulf—"why, my good lady, it need not be a
madman to perform that leap."

And so saying, with one of those sudden impulses which it
would be wrong to ascribe to the noble quality of courage, I
drew back a few steps, and cleared the abyss.   But when from
the other side I looked back at what I had done, and saw that
failure had been death, a sickness came over me, and I felt as
if I would not have releapt the gulf to become lord of the
domain.

"And how am I to get back?" said I in a forlorn voice to the old woman, who stood staring at me on the other side—"Ah! I see there is a bridge below."

"But you can't go over the bridge; there's a gate on it; master keeps the key himself. You are in the private grounds now. Dear—dear! the squire would be so angry if he knew. You must go back; and they'll see you from the house! Dear me! dear—dear! What shall I do? Can't you leap back again?"

Moved by these piteous exclamations, and not wishing to subject the poor old lady to the wrath of a master evidently an unfeeling tyrant, I resolved to pluck up courage and releap the dangerous abyss.

"Oh yes—never fear," said I, therefore. "What's been done once ought to be done twice, if needful. Just get out of my way, will you?"

And I receded several paces over a ground much too rough to favour my run for a spring. But my heart knocked against my ribs. I felt that impulse can do wonders where preparation fails.

"You had best be quick, then," said the old woman.

Horrid old woman! I began to esteem her less. I set my teeth, and was about to rush on, when a voice close beside me said—

"Stay, young man; I will let you through the gate."

I turned round sharply, and saw close by my side, in great wonder that I had not seen him before, a man, whose homely (but not working) dress seemed to intimate his station as that of the head-gardener, of whom my guide had spoken. He was seated on a stone under a chestnut tree, with an ugly cur at his feet, who snarled at me as I turned.

"Thank you, my man," said I joyfully. "I confess frankly that I was very much afraid of that leap."

"Ho! Yet you said, what can be done once can be done twice."

"I did not say it *could* be done, but *ought* to be done."

"Humph! That's better put."

Here the man rose; the dog came and smelt my legs, and then, as if satisfied with my respectability, wagged the stump of his tail.

I looked across the waterfall for the old woman, and to my surprise saw her hobbling back as fast as she could.

"Ah!" said I, laughing, "the poor old thing is afraid you'll tell her master—for you're the head-gardener, I suppose? But I am the only person to blame. Pray say that, if you mention the circumstance at all!" and I drew out half-a-crown, which I proffered to my new conductor.

He put back the money with a low, "Humph—not amiss." Then, in a louder voice, "No occasion to bribe me, young man; I saw it all."

"I fear your master is rather hard to the poor Hogtons' old servants."

"Is he? Oh! humph! my master. Mr. Trevanion you mean?"

"Yes."

"Well, I dare say people say so. This is the way." And he led me down a little glen away from the fall.

Everybody must have observed, that after he has incurred or escaped a great danger, his spirits rise wonderfully—he is in a state of pleasing excitement. So it was with me. I talked to the gardener *à cœur ouvert*, as the French say: and I did not observe that his short monosyllables in rejoinder all served to draw out my little history—my journey, its destination; my schooling under Dr. Herman, and my father's Great Book. I was only made somewhat suddenly aware of the familiarity that had sprung up between us, when, just as, having performed a circuitous meander, we regained the stream and stood before an iron gate, set in an arch of rockwork, my companion said simply—"And your name, young gentleman? What's your name?"

I hesitated a moment; but having heard that such communications were usually made by the visitors of show places, I answered—"Oh! a very venerable one, if your master is what they call a bibliomaniac—Caxton."

"Caxton!" cried the gardener, with some vivacity: "there is a Cumberland family of that name——"

"That's mine; and my Uncle Roland is the head of that family."

"And you are the son of Augustine Caxton?"

"I am. You have heard of my dear father, then?"

"We will not pass by the gate now. Follow me—this way;" and my guide, turning abruptly round, strode up a narrow path, and the house stood a hundred yards before me ere I recovered my surprise.

"Pardon me," said I, "but where are we going, my good friend?"

Chris Hammond
oct '97

"My name is Trevanion"

"Good friend—good friend! Well said, sir. You are going amongst good friends. I was at college with your father. I loved him well. I knew a little of your uncle too. My name is Trevanion."

Blind young fool that I was! The moment my guide told his name, I was struck with amazement at my unaccountable mistake. The small insignificant figure took instant dignity; the homely dress, of rough dark broadcloth, was the natural and becoming dishabille of a country gentleman in his own demesnes. Even the ugly cur became a Scotch terrier of the rarest breed.

My guide smiled good-naturedly at my stupor; and patting me on the shoulder, said—

"It is the gardener you must apologise to, not me. *He* is a very handsome fellow, six feet high."

I had not found my tongue before we had ascended a broad flight of stairs under the portico; passed a spacious hall, adorned with statues and fragrant with large orange-trees; and, entering a small room, hung with pictures, in which were arranged all the appliances for breakfast, my companion said to a lady, who rose from behind the tea-urn, "My dear Ellinor, I introduce to you the son of our old friend Augustine Caxton. Make him stay with us as long as he can. Young gentleman, in Lady Ellinor Trevanion think that you see one whom you ought to know well—family friendships should descend."

My host said these last words in an imposing tone, and then pounced on a letter-bag on the table, drew forth an immense heap of letters and newspapers, threw himself into an arm-chair, and seemed perfectly forgetful of my existence.

The lady stood a moment in mute surprise, and I saw that she changed colour from pale to red, and red to pale, before she come forward with the enchanting grace of unaffected kindness, took me by the hand, drew me to a seat next to her own, and asked so cordially after my father, my uncle, my whole family, that in five minutes I felt myself at home. Lady Ellinor listened with a smile (though with moistened eyes, which she wiped every now and then) to my artless details. At length she said—

"Have you never heard your father speak of me—I mean of us—of the Trevanions?"

"Never," said I bluntly; "and that would puzzle me, only my dear father, you know, is not a great talker."

"Indeed! he was very animated when I knew him," said Lady Ellinor; and she turned her head and sighed.

At this moment there entered a young lady, so fresh, so blooming, so lovely, that every other thought vanished out of my head at once. She came in singing, as gay as a bird, and seeming to my adoring sight quite as native to the skies.

"Fanny," said Lady Ellinor, "shake hands with Mr. Caxton, the son of one whom I have not seen since I was little older than you, but whom I remember as if it were but yesterday."

Miss Fanny blushed and smiled, and held out her hand with an easy frankness which I in vain endeavoured to imitate. During breakfast, Mr. Trevanion continued to read his letters and glance over the papers, with an occasional ejaculation of "Pish!"—"Stuff!"—between the interval in which he mechanically swallowed his tea, or some small morsels of dry toast. Then rising with a suddenness which characterised his movements, he stood on his hearth for a few moments buried in thought; and now that a large-brimmed hat was removed from his brow, and the abruptness of his first movement, with the sedateness of his after pause, arrested my curious attention, I was more than ever ashamed of my mistake. It was a careworn, eager, and yet musing countenance, hollow-eyed, and with deep lines; but it was one of those faces which take dignity and refinement from that mental cultivation which distinguishes the true aristocrat, viz., the highly educated, acutely intelligent man. Very handsome might that face have been in youth, for the features, though small, were exquisitely defined; the brow, partially bald, was noble and massive, and there was almost feminine delicacy in the curve of the lip. The whole expression of the face was commanding, but sad. Often, as my experience of life increased, have I thought to trace upon that expressive visage the history of energetic ambition curbed by a fastidious philosophy and a scrupulous conscience; but then all that I could see was a vague, dissatisfied melancholy, which dejected me I knew not why.

Presently Trevanion returned to the table, collected his letters, moved slowly towards the door, and vanished.

His wife's eyes followed him tenderly. Those eyes reminded me of my mother's, as I verily believe did all eyes that expressed affection. I crept nearer to her, and longed to press the white hand that lay so listless before me.

"Will you walk out with us?" said Miss Trevanion, turning to me. I bowed, and in a few minutes I found myself alone. While the ladies left me, for their shawls and bonnets, I took

up the newspapers which Mr. Trevanion had thrown on the
table, by way of something to do.   My eye was caught by his
own name ; it occurred often, and in all the papers.   There was
contemptuous abuse in one, high eulogy in another ; but one
passage in a journal that seemed to aim at impartiality, struck
me so much as to remain in my memory ; and I am sure that I
can still quote the sense, though not the exact words.   The
paragraph ran somewhat thus :—

"In the present state of parties, our contemporaries have,
not unnaturally, devoted much space to the claims or demerits
of Mr. Trevanion.   It is a name that stands unquestionably
high in the House of Commons ; but, as unquestionably, it
commands little sympathy in the country.   Mr. Trevanion is
essentially and emphatically *a member of Parliament.*   He is a
close and ready debater ; and is an admirable chairman in
committees.   Though never in office, his long experience of
public life, his gratuitous attention to public business, have
ranked him high among those practical politicians from whom
ministers are selected.   A man of spotless character and excellent intentions, no doubt, he must be considered ; and in him
any cabinet would gain an honest and a useful member.   There
ends all we can say in his praise.   As a speaker, he wants the
fire and enthusiasm which engage the popular sympathies.   He
has the ear of the House, not the heart of the country.   An
oracle on subjects of mere business, in the great questions of
policy he is comparatively a failure.   He never embraces any
party heartily ; he never espouses any question as if wholly in
earnest.   The moderation on which he is said to pique himself,
often exhibits itself in fastidious crotchets, and an attempt at
philosophical originality of candour which has long obtained
him, with his enemies, the reputation of a trimmer.   Such a
man circumstances may throw into temporary power ; but can
he command lasting influence ?   No : let Mr. Trevanion remain
in what nature and position assign as his proper post—that of
an upright, independent, able member of Parliament ; conciliat-
ing sensible men on both sides, when party runs into extremes.
He is undone as a cabinet minister.   His scruples would break
up any government ; and his want of decision—when, as in all
human affairs, some errors must be conceded to obtain a great
good—would shipwreck his own fame."

I had just got to the end of this paragraph, when the ladies
returned.

My hostess observed the newspaper in my hand, and said,

with a constrained smile, "Some attack on Mr. Trevanion, I suppose?"

"No," said I awkwardly; for, perhaps, the paragraph that appeared to me so impartial, was the most galling attack of all—"No, not exactly."

"I never read the papers now—at least what are called the leading articles—it is too painful: and once they gave me so much pleasure—that was when the career began, and before the fame was made."

Here Lady Ellinor opened the window which admitted on the lawn, and in a few moments we were in that part of the pleasure-grounds which the family reserved from the public curiosity. We passed by rare shrubs and strange flowers, long ranges of conservatories, in which bloomed and lived all the marvellous vegetation of Africa and the Indies.

"Mr. Trevanion is fond of flowers?" said I.

The fair Fanny laughed. "I don't think he knows one from another."

"Nor I either," said I; "that is, when I fairly lose sight of a rose or a hollyhock."

"The farm will interest you more," said Lady Ellinor.

We came to farm buildings recently erected, and no doubt on the most improved principle. Lady Ellinor pointed out to me machines and contrivances of the newest fashion, for abridging labour, and perfecting the mechanical operations of agriculture.

"Ah, then, Mr. Trevanion is fond of farming?"

The pretty Fanny laughed again.

"My father is one of the great oracles in agriculture, one of the great patrons of all its improvements; but, as for being fond of farming, I doubt if he knows his own fields when he rides through them."

We returned to the house; and Miss Trevanion, whose frank kindness had already made too deep an impression upon the youthful heart of Pisistratus the Second, offered to show me the picture-gallery. The collection was confined to the works of English artists; and Miss Trevanion pointed out to me the main attractions of the gallery.

"Well, at least Mr. Trevanion is fond of pictures?"

"Wrong again," said Fanny, shaking her arched head. "My father is said to be an admirable judge; but he only buys pictures from a sense of duty—to encourage our own painters. A picture once bought, I am not sure that he ever looks at it again."

"What does he then——" I stopped short, for I felt my meditated question was ill-bred.

"What does he like then? you were about to say. Why, I have known him, of course, since I could know anything; but I have never yet discovered what my father does like. No, not even politics, though he lives for politics alone. You look puzzled; you will know him better some day, I hope; but you will never solve the mystery—what Mr. Trevanion likes."

"You are wrong," said Lady Ellinor, who had followed us into the room, unheard by us. "I can tell you what your father does more than like—what he loves and serves every hour of his noble life—justice, beneficence, honour, and his country. A man who loves these may be excused for indifference to the last geranium, or the newest plough, or even (though that offends you more, Fanny) the freshest masterpiece by Landseer, or the latest fashion honoured by Miss Trevanion."

"Mamma!" said Fanny, and the tears sprang to her eyes.

But Lady Ellinor looked to me sublime as she spoke, her eyes kindled, her breast heaved. The wife taking the husband's part against the child, and comprehending so well what the child felt not, despite its experience of every day, and what the world would never know, despite all the vigilance of its praise and its blame, was a picture, to my taste, finer than any in the collection.

Her face softened as she saw the tears in Fanny's bright hazel eyes; she held out her hand, which her child kissed tenderly; and whispering, "'Tis not the giddy word you must go by, mamma, or there will be something to forgive every minute," Miss Trevanion glided from the room.

"Have you a sister?" asked Lady Ellinor.

"No."

"And Trevanion has no son," she said mournfully. The blood rushed to my cheeks. Oh, young fool, again! We were both silent, when the door was opened, and Mr. Trevanion entered.

"Humph!" said he, smiling as he saw me—and his smile was charming though rare. "Humph, young sir, I came to seek for you—I have been rude, I fear: pardon it—that thought has only just occurred to me, so I left my Blue Books, and my amanuensis hard at work on them, to ask you to come out for half-an-hour,—just half-an-hour, it is all I can give you—a deputation at one! You dine and sleep here, of course?"

"Ah, sir, my mother will be so uneasy if I am not in town to-night."

"Pooh!" said the member, "I'll send an express."

"Oh, no indeed; thank you."

"Why not?"

I hesitated. "You see, sir, that my father and mother are both new to London; and though I am new too, yet they may want me—I may be of use." Lady Ellinor put her hand on my head, and sleeked down my hair as I spoke.

"Right, young man, right; you will do in the world, wrong as that is. I don't mean that you'll *succeed* as the rogues say—that's another question; but, if you don't rise, you'll not fall. Now, put on your hat and come with me; we'll walk to the lodge—you will be in time for a coach."

I took my leave of Lady Ellinor, and longed to say something about "compliments to Miss Fanny"; but the words stuck in my throat, and my host seemed impatient.

"We must see you soon again," said Lady Ellinor kindly, as she followed us to the door.

Mr. Trevanion walked on briskly and in silence—one hand in his bosom, the other swinging carelessly a thick walking-stick.

"But I must go round by the bridge," said I, "for I forgot my knapsack. I threw it off when I made my leap, and the old lady certainly never took charge of it."

"Come, then, this way. How old are you?"

"Seventeen and a half."

"You know Latin and Greek as they know them at schools, I suppose?"

"I think I know them pretty well, sir."

"Does your father say so?"

"Why, my father is fastidious; however, he owns that he is satisfied on the whole."

"So am I, then. Mathematics?"

"A little."

"Good."

Here the conversation dropped for some time I had found and restrapped the knapsack, and we were near the lodge, when Mr. Trevanion said abruptly, "Talk, my young friend, talk: I like to hear you talk—it refreshes me. Nobody has talked naturally to me these last ten years."

The request was a complete damper to my ingenuous eloquence: I could not have talked naturally now for the life of me.

"I made a mistake, I see," said my companion good-humouredly, noticing my embarrassment. "Here we are at the lodge. The coach will be by in five minutes: you can spend that time in hearing the old woman praise the Hogtons and abuse me. And hark you, sir, never care three straws for praise or blame—leather and prunella! praise and blame are *here!*" and he struck his hand upon his breast with almost passionate emphasis. "Take a specimen. These Hogtons were the bane of the place, uneducated and miserly; their land a wilderness, their village a pig-sty. I come, with capital and intelligence; I redeem the soil, I banish pauperism, I civilise all around me; no merit in me—I am but a type of capital guided by education—a machine. And yet the old woman is not the only one who will hint to you that the Hogtons were angels, and myself the usual antithesis to angels. And, what is more, sir, because that old woman, who has ten shillings a week from me, sets her heart upon earning her sixpences—and I give her that privileged luxury—every visitor she talks to goes away with the idea that I, the rich Mr. Trevanion, let her starve on what she can pick up from the sight-seers. Now, does that signify a jot? Good-bye. Tell your father his old friend must see him; profit by his calm wisdom; his old friend is a fool sometimes, and sad at heart. When you are settled, send me a line to St. James's Square, to say where you are. Humph! that's enough."

Mr. Trevanion wrung my hand, and strode off.

I did not wait for the coach, but proceeded towards the turn-stile, where the old woman (who had either seen, or scented from a distance, that tizzy of which I was the impersonation)—

"Hushed in grim repose, did wait her morning prey."

My opinions as to her sufferings, and the virtues of the departed Hogtons, somewhat modified, I contented myself with dropping into her open palm the exact sum virtually agreed on. But that palm still remained open, and the fingers of the other clawed hold of me as I stood, impounded in the curve of the turnstile, like a cork in a patent corkscrew.

"And threepence for Nephy Bob," said the old lady.

"Threepence for nephew Bob, and why?"

"'Tis his parquisites when he recommends a gentleman. You would not have me pay out of my own earnings; for he *will* have it, or he'll ruin my bizziness. Poor folk must be paid for their trouble."

Obdurate to this appeal, and mentally consigning Bob to a master whose feet would be all the handsomer for boots, I threaded the stile and escaped.

Towards evening I reached London. Who ever saw London for the first time and was not disappointed? Those long suburbs melting indefinably away into the capital, forbid all surprise. The gradual is a great disenchanter. I thought it prudent to take a hackney-coach, and so jolted my way to the —— Hotel, the door of which was in a small street out of the Strand, though the greater part of the building faced that noisy thoroughfare. I found my father in a state of great discomfort in a little room, which he paced up and down like a lion new caught in his cage. My poor mother was full of complaints— for the first time in her life, I found her indisputably crossish. It was an ill time to relate my adventures. I had enough to do to listen. They had all day been hunting for lodgings in vain. My father's pocket had been picked of a new India handker-chief. Primmins, who ought to know London so well, knew nothing about it, and declared it was turned topsy-turvy, and all the streets had changed names. The new silk umbrella, left for five minutes unguarded in the hall, had been exchanged for an old gingham with three holes in it.

It was not till my mother remembered that if she did not see herself that my bed was well aired I should certainly lose the use of my limbs, and therefore disappeared with Primmins and a pert chambermaid, who seemed to think we gave more trouble than we were worth, that I told my father of my new acquaintance with Mr. Trevanion.

He did not seem to listen to me till I got to the name *Trevanion*. He then became very pale, and sat down quietly. "Go on," said he, observing I stopped to look at him.

When I had told all, and given him the kind messages with which I had been charged by husband and wife, he smiled faintly; and then, shading his face with his hand, he seemed to muse, not cheerfully, perhaps, for I heard him sigh once or twice.

"And Ellinor," said he at last, without looking up —"Lady Ellinor, I mean; she is very—very——"

"Very what, sir?"

"Very handsome still?"

"Handsome! Yes, handsome, certainly; but I thought more of her manner than her face. And then Fanny, Miss Fanny, is so young!"

"Ah!" said my father, murmuring in Greek the celebrated lines of which Pope's translation is familiar to all:

"'Like leaves on trees, the race of man is found,
Now green in youth, now withering on the ground.'

"Well, so they wish to see me. Did Ellinor, Lady Ellinor, say that, or her—her husband?"

"Her husband, certainly—Lady Ellinor rather implied than said it."

"We shall see," said my father. "Open the window, this room is stifling."

I opened the window, which looked on the Strand. The noise, the voices, the trampling feet, the rolling wheels, became loudly audible. My father leant out for some moments, and I stood by his side. He turned to me with a serene face. "Every ant on the hill," said he, "carries its load, and its home is but made by the burden that it bears. How happy am I!—how I should bless God! How light my burden! how secure my home!"

My mother came in as he ceased. He went up to her, put his arm round her waist and kissed her. Such caresses with him had not lost their tender charm by custom: my mother's brow, before somewhat ruffled, grew smooth on the instant. Yet she lifted her eyes to his in soft surprise.

"I was but thinking," said my father apologetically, "how much I owed you, and how much I love you!"

CHAPTER II

AND now behold us, three days after my arrival, settled in all the state and grandeur of our own house in Russell Street, Bloomsbury: the library of the Museum close at hand. My father spends his mornings in those *lata silentia*, as Virgil calls the world beyond the grave. And a world beyond the grave we may well call that land of the ghosts, a book collection.

"Pisistratus," said my father, one evening as he arranged his notes before him, and rubbed his spectacles. "Pisistratus, a great library is an *awful* place! There, are interred all the remains of men since the Flood."

"It is a burial-place!" quoth my Uncle Roland, who had that day found us out.

"It is an Heraclea!" said my father.

"Please, not such hard words," said the Captain, shaking his head.

"Heraclea was the city of necromancers, in which they raised the dead. Do I want to speak to Cicero?—I invoke him. Do I want to chat in the Athenian market-place, and hear news two thousand years old?—I write down my charm on a slip of paper, and a grave magician calls me up Aristophanes. And we owe all this to our ancest——"

"Brother!"

"Ancestors, who wrote books—thank you."

Here Roland offered his snuff-box to my father, who, abhorring snuff, benignly imbibed a pinch, and sneezed five times in consequence; an excuse for Uncle Roland to say, which he did five times, with great unction, "God bless you, brother Austin!"

As soon as my father had recovered himself, he proceeded, with tears in his eyes, but calm as before the interruption—for he was of the philosophy of the Stoics:—

"But it is not *that* which is awful. It is the presuming to vie with these 'spirits elect': to say to them, 'Make way—I too claim place with the chosen. I too would confer with the living, centuries after the death that consumes my dust. I too'—Ah, Pisistratus! I wish Uncle Jack had been at Jericho before he had brought me up to London, and placed me in the midst of those rulers of the world!"

I was busy, while my father spoke, in making some pendent shelves for these "spirits elect": for my mother, always provident where my father's comforts were concerned, had foreseen the necessity of some such accommodation in a hired lodging-house, and had not only carefully brought up to town my little box of tools, but gone out herself that morning to buy the raw materials. Checking the plane in its progress over the smooth deal, "My dear father," said I, "if at the Philhellenic Institute I had looked with as much awe as you do on the big fellows that had gone before me, I should have stayed, to all eternity, the lag of the Infant Division."

"Pisistratus, you are as great an agitator as your namesake," cried my father, smiling. "And so, a fig for the big fellows!"

And now my mother entered in her pretty evening cap, all smiles and good humour, having just arranged a room for Uncle Roland, concluded advantageous negotiations with the laundress, held high council with Mrs. Primmins on the best mode of defeating the extortions of London tradesmen; and, pleased with herself and all the world, she kissed my father's forehead as it bent over his notes, and came to the tea-table, which only waited its presiding deity. My Uncle Roland, with his usual gallantry, started up, kettle in hand (our own urn—for we had one—not being yet unpacked), and having performed with soldier-like method the chivalrous office thus volunteered, he joined me at my employment, and said—

"There is a better steel for the hands of a well-born lad than a carpenter's plane."

"Aha! uncle—that depends——"

"Depends!—What on?"

"On the use one makes of it. Peter the Great was better employed in making ships than Charles XII. in cutting throats."

"Poor Charles XII.!" said my uncle, sighing pathetically— "a very brave fellow!"

"Pity he did not like the ladies a little better!"

"No man is perfect!" said my uncle sententiously. "But, seriously, you are *now* the male hope of the family—you are now——" My uncle stopped, and his face darkened. I saw that he thought of his son—that mysterious son! And, looking at him tenderly, I observed that his deep lines had grown deeper, his iron-grey hair more grey. There was the trace of recent suffering on his face; and though he had not spoken to us a word of the business on which he had left us, it required no penetration to perceive that it had come to no successful issue.

My uncle resumed—"Time out of mind, every generation of our house has given one soldier to his country. I look round now: only one branch is budding yet on the old tree; and——"

"Ah! uncle. But what would *they* say? Do you think I should not like to be a soldier? Don't tempt me!"

My uncle had recourse to his snuff-box: and at that moment —unfortunately, perhaps, for the laurels that might otherwise have wreathed the brows of Pisistratus of England,—private conversation was stopped by the sudden and noisy entrance of Uncle Jack. No apparition could have been more unexpected.

"Here I am, my dear friends. How d'ye do—how are you all? Captain de Caxton, yours heartily. Yes, I am released, thank Heaven! I have given up the drudgery of that pitiful provincial paper. I was not made for it. An ocean in a tea-cup! I was indeed! Little, sordid, narrow interests—and I, whose heart embraces all humanity. You might as well turn a circle into an isolated triangle."

"Isosceles!" said my father, sighing as he pushed aside his notes, and very slowly becoming aware of the eloquence that destroyed all chance of further progress that night in the Great Book. "Isosceles triangle, Jack Tibbets—not isolated."

"Isosceles or isolated, it is all one," said Uncle Jack, as he rapidly performed three evolutions, by no means consistent with his favourite theory of "the greatest happiness of the greatest number";—first, he emptied into the cup which he took from my mother's hands half the thrifty contents of a London cream-jug; secondly, he reduced the circle of a muffin, by the abstraction of three triangles, to as nearly an isosceles as possible; and thirdly, striding towards the fire, lighted in consideration of Captain de Caxton, and hooking his coat-tails under his arms, while he sipped his tea, he permitted another circle peculiar to humanity wholly to eclipse the luminary it approached.

"Isolated or isosceles, it is all the same thing. Man is made for his fellow-creatures. I had long been disgusted with the interference of those selfish Squirearchs. Your departure decided me. I have concluded negotiations with a London firm of spirit and capital, and extended views of philanthropy. On Saturday last I retired from the service of the oligarchy. I am now in my true capacity of protector of the million. My prospectus is printed—here it is in my pocket.—Another cup of tea, sister; a little more cream, and another muffin. Shall I ring?" Having disembarrassed himself of his cup and saucer, Uncle Jack then drew forth from his pocket a damp sheet of printed paper. In large capitals stood out "The ANTI-MONOPOLY GAZETTE, or POPULAR CHAMPION." He waved it triumphantly before my father's eyes.

"Pisistratus," said my father, "look here. This is the way your Uncle Jack now prints his pats of butter: a cap of liberty growing out of an open book! Good, Jack! good! good!"

"It is Jacobinical!" exclaimed the Captain.

"Very likely," said my father; "but knowledge and freedom are the best devices in the world to print upon pats of butter intended for the market."

"Pats of butter! I don't understand," said Uncle Jack.

"The less you understand, the better will the butter sell, Jack," said my father, settling back to his notes.

CHAPTER III

UNCLE JACK had made up his mind to lodge with us, and my mother found some difficulty in inducing him to comprehend that there was no bed to spare.

"That's unlucky," said he. "I had no sooner arrived in town than I was pestered with invitations; but I refused them all, and kept myself for you."

"So kind in you! so like you!" said my mother; "but you see——"

"Well, then, I must be off and find a room. Don't fret; you know I can breakfast and dine with you all the same; that is, when my other friends will let me. I shall be dreadfully persecuted." So saying, Uncle Jack re-pocketed his prospectus, and wished us good-night.

The clock had struck eleven; my mother had retired; when my father looked up from his books, and returned his spectacles to their case. I had finished my work, and was seated over the fire, thinking now of Fanny Trevanion's hazel eyes—now, with a heart that beat as high at the thought of campaigns, battle-fields, laurels, and glory; while, with his arms folded on his breast and his head drooping, Uncle Roland gazed into the low clear embers. My father cast his eyes round the room, and after surveying his brother for some moments, he said, almost in a whisper—

"My son has seen the Trevanions. They remember us, Roland."

The Captain sprang to his feet, and began whistling—a habit with him when he was much disturbed.

"And Trevanion wishes to see us. Pisistratus promised to give him our address; shall he do so, Roland?"

"If you like it," answered the Captain, in a military attitude, and drawing himself up till he looked seven feet high.

"I *should* like it," said my father mildly. "Twenty years since we met."

"More than twenty," said my uncle, with a stern smile; "and the season was—the fall of the leaf!"

"Man renews the fibre and material of his body every seven years," said my father; "in three times seven years he has time to renew the inner man. Can two passengers in yonder street be more unlike each other than the soul is to the soul after

H

an interval of twenty years? Brother, the plough does not pass over the soil in vain, nor care over the human heart. New crops change the character of the land; and the plough must go deep indeed before it stirs up the mother stone."

"Let us see Trevanion," cried my uncle; then, turning to me, he said abruptly, "What family has he?"

"One daughter."

"No son?"

"No."

"That must vex the poor foolish ambitious man. Oho! you admire this Mr. Trevanion much, eh? Yes, that fire of manner, his fine words, and bold thoughts were made to dazzle youth."

"Fine words, my dear uncle!—fire! I should have said, in hearing Mr. Trevanion, that his style of conversation was so homely, you would wonder how he could have won such fame as a public speaker."

"Indeed!"

"The plough has passed there," said my father.

"But not the plough of care: rich, famous, Ellinor his wife, and no son!"

"It is because his heart is sometimes sad that he would see us."

Roland stared first at my father, next at me. "Then," quoth my uncle heartily, "in God's name, let him come. I can shake him by the hand, as I would a brother soldier. Poor Trevanion! Write to him at once, Sisty."

I sat down and obeyed. When I had sealed my letter I looked up, and saw that Roland was lighting his bed-candle at my father's table; and my father, taking his hand, said something to him in a low voice. I guessed it related to his son, for he shook his head, and answered in a stern, hollow voice, "Renew grief if you please—not shame. On that subject—silence!"

CHAPTER IV

LEFT to myself in the earlier part of the day, I wandered, wistful and lonely, through the vast wilderness of London. By degrees I familiarised myself with that populous solitude—I ceased to pine for the green fields. That active energy all around, at first saddening, became soon exhilarating, and at last contagious. To an industrious mind nothing is so catching as industry. I began to grow weary of my golden holiday of unlaborious childhood, to sigh for toil, to look around me for a career. The University, which I had before anticipated with pleasure, seemed now to fade into a dull monastic prospect; after having trod the streets of London, to wander through cloisters was to go back in life. Day by day, my mind grew sensibly within me; it came out from the rosy twilight of boyhood—it felt the doom of Cain, under the broad sun of man.

Uncle Jack soon became absorbed in his new speculation for the good of the human race, and, except at meals (whereat, to do him justice, he was punctual enough, though he did not keep us in ignorance of the sacrifices he made, and the invitations he refused, for our sake), we seldom saw him. The Captain, too, generally vanished after breakfast, seldom dined with us, and it was often late before he returned. He had the latch-key of the house, and let himself in when he pleased. Sometimes (for his chamber was next to mine) his step on the stairs awoke me; and sometimes I heard him pace his room with perturbed strides, or fancied that I caught a low groan. He became every day more careworn in appearance, and every day the hair seemed more grey. Yet he talked to us all easily and cheerfully; and I thought that I was the only one in the house who perceived the gnawing pangs over which the stout old Spartan drew the decorous cloak.

Pity, blended with admiration, made me curious to learn how these absent days, that brought night so disturbed, were consumed. I felt that, if I could master the Captain's secret, I might win the right both to comfort and to aid.

I resolved at length, after many conscientious scruples, to endeavour to satisfy a curiosity excused by its motives.

Accordingly, one morning, after watching him from the house, I stole in his track, and followed him at a distance.

And this was the outline of his day: he set off at first with a firm stride, despite his lameness—his gaunt figure erect, the soldierly chest well thrown out from the threadbare but speckless coat. First he took his way towards the purlieus of Leicester Square; several times, to and fro, did he pace the isthmus that leads from Piccadilly into that reservoir of foreigners, and the lanes and courts that start thence towards St. Martin's. After an hour or two so passed, the step became more slow; and often the sleek, napless hat was lifted up, and the brow wiped. At length he bent his way towards the two great theatres, paused before the play-bills, as if deliberating seriously on the chances of entertainment they severally proffered, wandered slowly through the small streets that surround those temples of the Muse, and finally emerged into the Strand. There he rested himself for an hour, at a small cookshop; and as I passed the window and glanced within, I could see him seated before the simple dinner, which he scarcely touched, and poring over the advertisement columns of the *Times*. The *Times* finished, and a few morsels distastefully swallowed, the Captain put down his shilling in silence, receiving his pence in exchange, and I had just time to slip aside as he reappeared at the threshold. He looked round as he lingered, but I took care he should not detect me; and then struck off towards the more fashionable quarters of the town. It was now the afternoon, and, though not yet the season, the streets swarmed with life. As he came into Waterloo Place, a slight but muscular figure buttoned up across the breast like his own, cantered by on a handsome bay horse; every eye was on that figure. Uncle Roland stopped short, and lifted his hand to his hat; the rider touched his own with his forefinger, and cantered on—Uncle Roland turned round and gazed.

"Who," I asked of a shop-boy just before me, also staring with all his eyes—"who is that gentleman on horseback?"

"Why, the Duke to be sure," said the boy contemptuously.

"The Duke?"

"Wellington—stu-pid!"

"Thank you," said I meekly. Uncle Roland had moved on into Regent Street, but with a brisker step: the sight of the old chief had done the old soldier good. Here again he paced to and fro; till I, watching him from the other side of the way, was ready to drop with fatigue, stout walker though I was. But the Captain's day was not half done. He took out his watch, put it to his ear, and then, replacing it, passed into Bond Street, and thence into Hyde Park. There, evidently wearied out, he leant against the rails, near the bronze statue, in an attitude that spoke despondency. I seated myself on the grass near the statue, and gazed at him: the park was empty compared with the streets, but still there were some equestrian idlers, and many foot-loungers. My uncle's eye turned wistfully on each: once or twice some gentlemen of a military aspect (which I had already learned to detect) stopped, looked at him, approached, and spoke; but the Captain seemed as if ashamed of such greetings. He answered shortly, and turned again.

The day waned—evening came on: the Captain again looked

at his watch, shook his head, and made his way to a bench,
where he sat perfectly motionless—his hat over his brows, his
arms folded; till up rose the moon.   I had tasted nothing since
breakfast—I was famished ; but I still kept my post like an old
Roman sentinel.

At length the Captain rose, and re-entered Piccadilly ; but
how different his mien and bearing ! languid, stooping ; his
chest sunk, his head inclined ; his limbs dragging one after the
other ; his lameness painfully perceptible.   What a contrast in
the broken invalid at night from the stalwart veteran of the
morning !

How I longed to spring forward to offer my arm ! but I did
not dare.

The Captain stopped near a cab-stand.   He put his hand in
his pocket—he drew out his purse—he passed his fingers over
the net-work ; the purse slipped again into the pocket, and, as
if with a heroic effort, my uncle drew up his head, and walked
on sturdily.

"Where   next?"   thought I.   "Surely home !   No, he is
pitiless ! "

The Captain stopped not till he arrived at one of the small
theatres in the Strand ; then he read the bill, and asked if half
price was begun.   "Just begun," was the answer, and the Captain entered.   I also took a ticket and followed.   Passing by
the open doors of a refreshment-room, I fortified myself with
some biscuits and soda-water ; and in another minute, for the
first time in my life, I beheld a play.   But the play did not
fascinate me.   It was the middle of some jocular afterpiece ;
roars of laughter resounded round me.   I could detect nothing
to laugh at, and sending my keen eyes into every corner, I
perceived at last, in the uppermost tier, one face as saturnine
as my own.   *Eureka !*   It was the Captain's !   "Why should he
go to a play if he enjoys it so little ! " thought I ; "better have
spent a shilling on a cab, poor old fellow ! "

But soon came smart-looking men, and still smarter-looking
ladies, around the solitary corner of the poor Captain.   He grew
fidgety—he rose—he vanished.   I left my place, and stood without the box to watch for him.   Downstairs he stumped—I recoiled into the shade ; and after standing a moment or two, as
in doubt, he entered boldly the refreshment-room or saloon.

Now, since I had left that saloon, it had become crowded, and
I slipped in unobserved.   Strange was it, grotesque yet pathetic,
to mark the old soldier in the midst of that gay swarm.   He

towered above all like a Homeric hero, a head taller than the tallest; and his appearance was so remarkable, that it invited the instant attention of the fair. I, in my simplicity, thought it was the natural tenderness of that amiable and penetrating sex, ever quick to detect trouble and anxious to relieve it, which induced three ladies, in silk attire—one having a hat and plume, the other two with a profusion of ringlets—to leave a little knot of gentlemen with whom they were conversing, and to plant themselves before my uncle. I advanced through the press to hear what passed.

"You are looking for some one, I'm sure," quoth one familiarly, tapping his arm with her fan.

The Captain started. "Ma'am, you are not wrong," said he.

"Can I do as well?" said one of those compassionate angels with heavenly sweetness.

"You are very kind, I thank you; no, no, ma'am," said the Captain with his best bow.

"Do take a glass of negus," said another, as her friend gave way to her. "You seem tired, and so am I. Here, this way;" and she took hold of his arm to lead him to the table. The Captain shook his head mournfully; and then, as if suddenly aware of the nature of the attentions so lavished on him, he looked down upon these fair Armidas with a look of such mild reproach, such sweet compassion—not shaking off the hand, in his chivalrous devotion to the sex, which extended even to all its outcasts—that each bold eye fell abashed. The hand was timidly and involuntarily withdrawn from the arm, and my uncle passed his way.

He threaded the crowd, passed out at the further door, and I, guessing his intention, was in waiting for his steps in the street.

"Now home at last, thank Heaven!" thought I. Mistaken still! My uncle went first towards that popular haunt which I have since discovered is called "the Shades"; but he soon re-emerged, and finally he knocked at the door of a private house in one of the streets out of St. James's. It was opened jealously, and closed as he entered, leaving me without. What could this house be! As I stood and watched, some other men approached, —again the low single knock, again the jealous opening, and the stealthy entrance.

A policeman passed and repassed me. "Don't be tempted, young man," said he, looking hard at me; "take my advice, and go home."

"What is that house, then?" said I, with a sort of shudder at this ominous warning.

"Oh, you know."

"Not I. I am new to London."

"It is a hell," said the policeman, satisfied, by my frank manner, that I spoke the truth.

"God bless me—a what! I could not have heard you rightly?"

"A hell; a gambling-house!"

"Oh!" and I moved on. Could Captain Roland, the rigid, the thrifty, the penurious, be a gambler? The light broke on me at once: the unhappy father sought his son! I leant against the post, and tried hard not to sob.

By-and-by I heard the door open: the Captain came out and took the way homeward. I ran on before, and got in first, to the inexpressible relief both of father and mother, who had not seen me since breakfast, and who were in equal consternation at my absence. I submitted to be scolded with a good grace. "I had been sight-seeing, and lost my way;" begged for some supper, and slunk to bed; and five minutes afterwards the Captain's jaded step came wearily up the stairs.

PART VI

CHAPTER I

"I DON'T know that," said my father.

What is it my father does not know? My father does not know that "happiness is our being's end and aim."

And pertinent to what does my father reply, by words so sceptical, to an assertion so seldom disputed?

Reader, Mr. Trevanion has been half-an-hour seated in our little drawing-room. He has received two cups of tea from my mother's fair hand; he has made himself at home. With Mr. Trevanion has come another old friend of my father's, whom he has not seen since he left college—Sir Sedley Beaudesert.

Now, you must understand that it is a warm night, a little after nine o'clock — a night between departing summer and approaching autumn. The windows are open — we have a balcony, which my mother has taken care to fill with flowers —the air, though we are in London, is sweet and fresh— the street quiet, except that an occasional carriage or hackney cabriolet rolls rapidly by—a few stealthy passengers pass to and fro noiselessly on their way homeward. We are on classic ground—near that old and venerable Museum, the dark monastic pile which the taste of the age had spared then—and the quiet of the temple seems to hallow the precincts. Captain Roland is seated by the fireplace, and, though there is no fire, he is shading his face with a hand-screen; my father and Mr. Trevanion have drawn their chairs close to each other in the middle of the room; Sir Sedley Beaudesert leans against the wall near the window, and behind my mother, who looks prettier and more pleased than usual, since her Austin has his old friends about him; and I, leaning my elbow on the table, and my chin upon my hand, am gazing with great admiration on Sir Sedley Beaudesert.

O rare specimen of a race fast decaying!—specimen of the true fine gentleman, ere the word dandy was known, and before exquisite became a noun substantive—let me here pause to describe thee! Sir Sedley Beaudesert was the contemporary of Trevanion and my father; but, without affecting to be young, he still seemed so. Dress, tone, look, manner—all were young —yet all had a certain dignity which does not belong to youth. At the age of five-and-twenty he had won what would have been fame to a French marquis of the old *régime*, viz., the reputation of being "the most charming man of his day"—the most popular of our sex—the most favoured, my dear lady-reader, by yours. It is a mistake, I believe, to suppose that it does not require talent to become the fashion; at all events, Sir Sedley was the fashion, and he had talent. He had travelled much, he had read much—especially in memoirs, history, and belles-lettres, —he made verses with grace and a certain originality of easy wit and courtly sentiment—he conversed delightfully, he was polished and urbane in manner—he was brave and honourable in conduct; in words he could flatter—in deeds he was sincere.

Sir Sedley Beaudesert had never married. Whatever his years, he was still young enough in looks to be married for love. He was high-born, he was rich; he was, as I have said, popular; yet on his fair features there was an expression of melancholy; and on that forehead—pure from the lines of ambition, and free from the weight of study—there was the shadow of unmistakable regret.

"I don't know that," said my father; "I have never yet found in life one man who made happiness his end and aim. One wants to gain a fortune, another to spend it—one to get a place, another to build a name; but they all know very well that it is not happiness they search for. No Utilitarian was ever actuated by self-interest, poor man, when he sat down to scribble his unpopular crotchets to prove self-interest universal. And as to that notable distinction—between self-interest vulgar and self-interest enlightened—the more the self-interest is enlightened, the less we are influenced by it. If you tell the young man who has just written a fine book or made a fine speech, that he will not be any happier if he attain to the fame of Milton or the power of Pitt, and that, for the sake of his own happiness, he had much better cultivate a farm, live in the country, and postpone to the last the days of dyspepsia and gout, he will answer you fairly—'I am quite as sensible of that as you are. But I am not thinking whether or not I shall be happy. I have made up my mind to be, if I can, a great author or a prime minister.' So it is with all the active sons of the

world. To push on is the law of nature. And you can no more
say to men and to nations than to children, 'Sit still, and don't
wear out your shoes!'"

"Then," said Trevanion, "if I tell you I am not happy, your
only answer is, that I obey an inevitable law."

"No! I don't say that it is an inevitable law that man should
not be happy; but it is an inevitable law that a man, in spite
of himself, should live for something higher than his own happiness. He cannot live in himself or for himself, however egotistical he may try to be. Every desire he has links him with
others. Man is not a machine—he is a part of one."

"True, brother, he is a soldier, not an army," said Captain
Roland.

"Life is a drama, not a monologue," pursued my father.
"Drama is derived from a Greek verb, signifying *to do*. Every
actor in the drama has something to do, which helps on the
progress of the whole: that is the object for which the author
created him. Do your part, and let the Great Play get on."

"Ah!" said Trevanion briskly, "but to do the part is the
difficulty! Every actor helps to the catastrophe, and yet must
do his part without knowing how all is to end. Shall he help
the curtain to fall on a tragedy or a comedy? Come, I will tell
you the one secret of my public life—that which explains all
its failure (for, in spite of my position, I have failed), and its
regrets—I *want conviction!*"

"Exactly," said my father; "because to every question there
are two sides, and you look at them both."

"You have said it," answered Trevanion, smiling also. "For
public life a man should be one-sided; he must act with a
party; and a party insists that the shield is silver when, if it
will take the trouble to turn the corner, it will see that the
reverse of the shield is gold. Woe to the man who makes that
discovery alone, while his party are still swearing the shield is
silver, and that not once in his life, but every night!"

"You have said quite enough to convince me that you ought
not to belong to a party, but not enough to convince me why
you should not be happy," said my father.

"Do you remember," said Sir Sedley Beaudesert, "an anecdote
of the first Duke of Portland? He had a gallery in the great
stable of his villa in Holland, where a concert was given once a
week, to *cheer and amuse* his horses! I have no doubt the horses
thrived all the better for it. What Trevanion wants is a concert
once a week. With him it is always saddle and spur. Yet,

after all, who would not envy him ? If life be a drama, his name stands high in the play-bill, and is printed in capitals on the walls."

"Envy me!" cried Trevanion—"ME!—no, you are the enviable man—you who have only one grief in the world, and that so absurd a one, that I will make you blush by disclosing it. Hear, O sage Austin!—O sturdy Roland!—Olivares was haunted by a spectre, and Sedley Beaudesert by the dread of old age!"

"Well," said my mother seriously, "I do think it requires a great sense of religion, or, at all events, children of one's own, in whom one is young again, to reconcile oneself to becoming old."

"My dear ma'am," said Sir Sedley, who had slightly coloured at Trevanion's charge, but had now recovered his easy self-possession, "you have spoken so admirably that you give me courage to confess my weakness. I do dread to be old. All the joys of my life have been the joys of youth. I have had so exquisite a pleasure in the mere sense of living, that old age, as it comes near, terrifies me by its dull eyes and grey hairs. I have lived the life of a butterfly. Summer is over, and I see my flowers withering; and my wings are chilled by the first airs of winter. Yes, I envy Trevanion; for, in public life, no man is ever young; and while he can work, he is never old."

"My dear Beaudesert," said my father, "when St. Amable, patron saint of Riom, in Auvergne, went to Rome, the sun waited upon him as a servant, carried his cloak and gloves for him in the heat, and kept off the rain, if the weather changed, like an umbrella. You want to put the sun to the same use: you are quite right; but then, you see, you must first be a saint before you can be sure of the sun as a servant."

Sir Sedley smiled charmingly; but the smile changed to a sigh as he added, "I don't think I should much mind being a saint, if the sun would be my sentinel instead of my courier. I want nothing of him but to stand still. You see he moved even for St. Amable. My dear madam, you and I understand each other; and it is a very hard thing to grow old, do what one will to keep young."

"What say you, Roland, of these two malcontents?" asked my father. The Captain turned uneasily in his chair, for the rheumatism was gnawing his shoulder, and sharp pains were shooting through his mutilated limb.

"I say," answered Roland, "that these men are wearied with

marching from Brentford to Windsor—that they have never known the bivouac and the battle."

Both the grumblers turned their eyes to the veteran: the eyes rested first on the furrowed, careworn lines in his eagle face—then they fell on the stiff outstretched cork limb—and then they turned away.

Meanwhile my mother had softly risen, and under pretence of looking for her work on the table near him, bent over the old soldier and pressed his hand.

"Gentlemen," said my father, "I don't think my brother ever heard of Nichocorus, the Greek comic writer; yet he has illustrated him very ably. Saith Nichocorus, 'the best cure for drunkenness is a sudden calamity.' For chronic drunkenness, a continued course of real misfortune must be very salutary!"

No answer came from the two complainants; and my father took up a great book.

CHAPTER II

MY friends," said my father, looking up from his book and addressing himself to his two visitors, "I know of one thing, milder than calamity, that would do you both a great deal of good."

"What is that?" asked Sir Sedley.

"A saffron bag, worn at the pit of the stomach!"

"Austin, my dear," said my mother reprovingly.

My father did not heed the interruption, but continued gravely—"Nothing is better for the spirits! Roland is in no want of saffron, because he is a warrior; and the desire of fighting, and the hope of victory, infuse such a heat into the spirits as is profitable for long life, and keeps up the system."

"Tut!" said Trevanion.

"But gentlemen in your predicament must have recourse to artificial means. Nitre in broth, for instance—about three grains to ten—(cattle fed upon nitre grow fat); or earthy odours—such as exist in cucumbers and cabbage. A certain great lord had a clod of fresh earth, laid in a napkin, put under his nose every morning after sleep. Light anointing of the head with oil, mixed with roses and salt, is not bad; but, upon the whole, I prescribe the saffron bag at the——"

"Sisty, my dear, will you look for my scissors?" said my mother.

"What nonsense are you talking! Question! question!" cried Mr. Trevanion.

"Nonsense!" exclaimed my father, opening his eyes. "I am giving you the advice of Lord Bacon. You want conviction—conviction comes from passion—passion from the spirits—spirits from a saffron bag. You, Beaudesert, on the other hand, want to keep youth. He keeps youth longest who lives longest. Nothing more conduces to longevity than a saffron bag, provided always it is worn at the——"

"Sisty, my thimble!" said my mother.

"You laugh at us justly," said Beaudesert, smiling; "and the same remedy, I dare say, would cure us both."

"Yes," said my father, "there is no doubt of that. In the pit of the stomach is that great central web of nerves called the ganglions; thence they affect the head and the heart. Mr. Squills proved that to us, Sisty."

"Yes," said I; "but I never heard Mr. Squills talk of a saffron bag."

"Oh, foolish boy! it is not the saffron bag—it is the belief in the saffron bag. Apply BELIEF to the centre of the nerves, and all will go well," said my father.

CHAPTER III

BUT it is a devil of a thing to have too nice a conscience!" quoth the member of Parliament.

"And it is not an angel of a thing to lose one's front teeth!" sighed the fine gentleman.

Therewith my father rose, and putting his hand into his waistcoat, *more suo*, delivered his famous

SERMON UPON THE CONNECTION BETWEEN FAITH AND PURPOSE.

Famous it was in our domestic circle. But, as yet, it has not gone beyond. And since the reader, I am sure, does not turn to the Caxton Memoirs with the expectation of finding sermons, so to that circle let its fame be circumscribed. All I shall say about it is, that it was a very fine sermon, and that it proved indisputably, to me at least, the salubrious effects of a saffron bag applied to the great centre of the nervous system. But the wise Ali saith, that " a fool doth not know what maketh him look little, neither will he hearken to him that adviseth him." I cannot assert that my father's friends were fools, but they certainly came under this definition of Folly.

CHAPTER IV

FOR therewith arose, not conviction, but discussion ; Trevanion was logical, Beaudesert sentimental. My father held firm to the saffron bag. When James the First dedicated to the Duke of Buckingham his meditation on the Lord's Prayer, he gave a very sensible reason for selecting his Grace for that honour ; " For," saith the king, " it is made upon a very short and plain prayer, and, therefore, the fitter for a courtier, for courtiers are for the most part thought neither to have lust nor leisure to say long prayers ; liking best *courte messe et long disner*." I suppose it was for a similar reason that my father persisted in dedicating to the member of Parliament and the fine gentleman this " short and plaine " morality of his—to wit, the saffron bag. He was evidently persuaded, if he could once get them to apply that, it was all that was needful ; that they had neither lust nor leisure for longer instructions. And this saffron bag,— it came down with such a whack, at every round in the argument ! You would have thought my father one of the old plebeian combatants in the popular ordeal, who, forbidden to use sword and lance, fought with a sand-bag tied to a flail : a very stunning weapon it was when filled only with sand ; but a bag filled with saffron,—it was irresistible ! Though my father had two to one against him, they could not stand such a deuce of a weapon. And after tuts and pishes innumerable from Mr. Trevanion, and sundry bland grimaces from Sir Sedley Beaudesert, they fairly gave in, though they would not own they were beaten.

" Enough," said the member, " I see that you don't comprehend me ; I must continue to move by my own impulse."

My father's pet book was the Colloquies of Erasmus ; he was wont to say that those Colloquies furnished life with illustrations in every page. Out of the Colloquies of Erasmus he now answered the member—

" Rabirius, wanting his servant Syrus to get up," quoth my

father, "cried out to him to move. 'I do move,' said Syrus. 'I see you move,' replied Rabirius, 'but you *move nothing*.' To return to the saffron bag——"

"Confound the saffron bag!" cried Trevanion in a rage; and then softening his look as he drew on his gloves, he turned to my mother, and said, with more politeness than was natural to, or at least customary with him—

"By the way, my dear Mrs. Caxton, I should tell you that Lady Ellinor comes to town to-morrow, on purpose to call on you. We shall be here some little time, Austin; and though London is so empty, there are still some persons of note to whom I should like to introduce you and yours——"

"Nay," said my father; "your world and my world are not the same. Books for me, and men for you. Neither Kitty nor I can change our habits, even for friendship; she has a great piece of work to finish, and so have I. Mountains cannot stir, especially when in labour; but Mahomet can come to the mountain as often as he likes."

Mr. Trevanion insisted, and Sir Sedley Beaudesert mildly put in his own claims; both boasted acquaintance with literary men, whom my father would, at all events, be pleased to meet. My father doubted whether he could meet any literary men more eloquent than Cicero, or more amusing than Aristophanes; and observed, that if such did exist, he would rather meet them in their books than in a drawing-room. In fine, he was immovable; and so also, with less argument, was Captain Roland.

Then Mr. Trevanion turned to me.

"Your son, at all events, should see something of the world."

My mother's soft eye sparkled.

"My dear friend, I thank you," said my father, touched; "and Pisistratus and I will talk it over."

Our guests had departed. All four of us gathered to the open window, and enjoyed in silence the cool air and the moonlight.

"Austin," said my mother at last, "I fear it is for my sake that you refuse going amongst your old friends: you knew I should be frightened by such fine people, and——"

"And we have been happy for more than eighteen years without them, Kitty! My poor friends are not happy, and we are. To leave well alone is a golden rule worth all in Pythagoras. The ladies of Bubastis, my dear, a place in Egypt where the cat was worshipped, always kept rigidly aloof from the gentlemen in Athribis, who adored the shrew-mice. Cats are domestic animals,—your shrew-mice are sad gadabouts: you can't find a better model, my Kitty, than the ladies of Bubastis!"

"How Trevanion is altered!" said Roland musingly—"he who was so lively and ardent!"

"He ran too fast uphill at first, and has been out of breath ever since," said my father.

"And Lady Ellinor," said Roland hesitatingly, "shall you see her to-morrow?"

"Yes!" said my father calmly.

As Captain Roland spoke, something in the tone of his question seemed to flash a conviction on my mother's heart,—the woman there was quick: she drew back, turning pale, even in the moonlight, and fixed her eyes on my father, while I felt her hand which had clasped mine tremble convulsively.

I understood her. Yes, this Lady Ellinor was the early rival whose name till then she had not known. She fixed her eyes on my father, and at his tranquil tone and quiet look she breathed more freely, and, sliding her hand from mine, rested it fondly on his shoulder. A few moments afterwards, I and Captain Roland found ourselves standing alone by the window.

"You are young, nephew," said the Captain; "and you have the name of a fallen family to raise. Your father does well not to reject for you that opening into the great world which Trevanion offers. As for me, my business in London seems over: I cannot find what I came to seek. I have sent for my daughter; when she arrives I shall return to my old tower; and the man and the ruin will crumble away together."

"Tush, uncle! I must work hard and get money; and then we will repair the old tower, and buy back the old estate. My father shall sell the red brick house; we will fit him up a library in the keep; and we will all live united, in peace, and in state, as grand as our ancestors before us."

While I thus spoke my uncle's eyes were fixed upon a corner of the street, where a figure, half in shade, half in moonlight, stood motionless. "Ah!" said I, following his eye, "I have observed that man, two or three times, pass up and down the street on the other side of the way, and turn his head towards our window. Our guests were with us then, and my father in full discourse, or I should have——"

Before I could finish the sentence, my uncle, stifling an exclamation, broke away, hurried out of the room, stumped down the stairs, and was in the street, while I was yet rooted to the spot with surprise. I remained at the window, and my eye rested on the figure. I saw the Captain, with his bare head and his grey hair, cross the street; the figure started, turned the corner, and fled.

Then I followed my uncle, and arrived in time to save him from falling: he leant his head on my breast, and I heard him murmur,—"It is he—it is he! He has watched us!—he repents!"

CHAPTER V

THE next day Lady Ellinor called; but, to my great disappointment, without Fanny.

Whether or not some joy at the incident of the previous night had served to rejuvenate my uncle, I know not, but he looked to me ten years younger when Lady Ellinor entered. How carefully the buttoned-up coat was brushed! how new and glossy was the black stock! The poor Captain was restored to his pride, and mighty proud he looked! With a glow on his cheek, and a fire in his eye; his head thrown back, and his whole air composed, severe, Mavortian, and majestic, as if awaiting the charge of the French cuirassiers at the head of his detachment.

My father, on the contrary, was as usual (till dinner, when he always dressed punctiliously, out of respect to his Kitty) in his easy morning gown and slippers; and nothing but a certain compression in his lips, which had lasted all the morning, evinced his anticipation of the visit, or the emotion it caused him.

Lady Ellinor behaved beautifully. She could not conceal a certain nervous trepidation, when she first took the hand my father extended; and, in touching rebuke of the Captain's stately bow, she held out to him the hand left disengaged, with a look which brought Roland at once to her side. It was a desertion of his colours to which nothing, short of Ney's shameful conduct at Napoleon's return from Elba, affords a parallel in history. Then, without waiting for introduction, and before a word indeed was said, Lady Ellinor came to my mother so cordially, so caressingly—she threw into her smile, voice, manner, such winning sweetness, that I, intimately learned in my poor mother's simple loving heart, wondered how she re-

I

frained from throwing her arms round Lady Ellinor's neck and kissing her outright. It must have been a great conquest over herself not to do it! My turn came next; and talking to me, and about me, soon set all parties at their ease—at least apparently.

What was said I cannot remember; I do not think one of us could. But an hour slipped away, and there was no gap in the conversation.

With curious interest, and a survey I strove to make impartial, I compared Lady Ellinor with my mother. And I comprehended the fascination which the high-born lady must, in their earlier youth, have exercised over both brothers, so dissimilar to each other. For *charm* was the characteristic of Lady Ellinor—a charm indefinable. It was not the mere grace of refined breeding, though that went a great way: it was a charm that seemed to spring from natural sympathy. Whomsoever she addressed, that person appeared for the moment to engage all her attention, to interest her whole mind. She had a gift of conversation very peculiar. She made what she said like a continuation of what was said to her. She seemed as if she had entered into your thoughts, and talked them aloud. Her mind was evidently cultivated with great care, but she was perfectly void of pedantry. A hint, an allusion, sufficed to show how much she knew, to one well instructed, without mortifying or perplexing the ignorant. Yes, there probably was the only woman my father had ever met who could be the companion to his mind, walk through the garden of knowledge by his side, and trim the flowers while he cleared the vistas. On the other hand, there was an inborn nobility in Lady Ellinor's sentiments that must have struck the most susceptible chord in Roland's nature, and the sentiments took eloquence from the look, the mien, the sweet dignity of the very turn of the head. Yes, she must have been a fitting Oriana to a young Amadis. It was not hard to see that Lady Ellinor was ambitious—that she had a love of fame, for fame itself—that she was proud—that she set value (and that morbidly) on the world's opinion. This was perceptible when she spoke of her husband, even of her daughter. It seemed to me as if she valued the intellect of the one, the beauty of the other, by the gauge of the social distinction it conferred. She took measure of the gift, as I was taught at Dr. Herman's to take measure of the height of a tower—by the length of the shadow it cast upon the ground.

My dear father! with such a wife you would never have lived eighteen years, shivering on the edge of a Great Book.

My dear uncle, with such a wife you would never have been contented with a cork leg and a Waterloo medal! And I understand why Mr. Trevanion, "eager and ardent" as ye say he was in youth, with a heart bent on the practical success of life, won the hand of the heiress. Well, you see Mr. Trevanion has contrived not to be happy! By the side of my listening, admiring mother, with her blue eyes moist, and her coral lips apart, Lady Ellinor looks faded. Was she ever as pretty as my mother is now? Never. But she was much handsomer. What delicacy in the outline, and yet how decided in spite of the delicacy! The eyebrow so defined—the profile slightly aquiline, so clearly cut—with the curved nostril, which, if physiognomists are right, shows sensibility so keen; and the classic lip, that, but for the neighbouring dimple, would be so haughty. But wear and tear are in that face. The nervous excitable temper has helped the fret and cark of ambitious life. My dear uncle, I know not yet your private life. But as for my father, I am sure that, though he might have done more on earth, he would have been less fit for heaven if he had married Lady Ellinor.

At last this visit—dreaded, I am sure, by three of the party, was over, but not before I had promised to dine at the Trevanions' that day.

When we were again alone, my father threw off a long breath, and, looking round him cheerfully, said, " Since Pisistratus deserts us, let us console ourselves for his absence—send for brother Jack, and all four go down to Richmond to drink tea."

"Thank you, Austin," said Roland; "but I don't want it, I assure you!"

"Upon your honour?" said my father in a half-whisper.

"Upon my honour."

"Nor I either. So, my dear Kitty, Roland and I will take a walk, and be back in time to see if that young Anachronism looks as handsome as his new London-made clothes will allow him. Properly speaking, he ought to go with an apple in his hand, and a dove in his bosom. But now I think of it, that was luckily not the fashion with the Athenians till the time of Alcibiades!"

CHAPTER VI

YOU may judge of the effect that my dinner at Mr. Trevanion's, with a long conversation after it with Lady Ellinor, made upon my mind, when, on my return home, after having satisfied all questions of parental curiosity, I said nervously, and looking down,—" My dear father,—I should like very much, if you have no objection—to—to——"

" What, my dear ?" asked my father kindly.

" Accept an offer Lady Ellinor has made me, on the part of Mr. Trevanion. He wants a secretary. He is kind enough to excuse my inexperience, and declares I shall do very well, and can soon get into his ways. Lady Ellinor says (I continued with dignity) that it will be a great opening in public life for me ; and at all events, my dear father, I shall see much of the world, and learn what I really think will be more useful to me than anything they will teach me at college."

My mother look anxiously at my father. " It will indeed be a great thing for Sisty," said she timidly ; and then, taking courage, she added—"and that is just the sort of life he is formed for."

" Hem !" said my uncle.

My father rubbed his spectacles thoughtfully, and replied, after a long pause—

" You may be right, Kitty : I don't think Pisistratus is meant for study ; action will suit him better. But what does this office lead to ?"

" Public employment, sir," said I boldly ; " the service of my country."

" If that be the case," quoth Roland, " I have not a word to say. But I should have thought that for a lad of spirit, a descendant of the old De Caxtons, the army would have——"

" The army !" exclaimed my mother, clasping her hands, and looking involuntarily at my uncle's cork leg.

" The army !" repeated my father peevishly. " Bless my soul, Roland, you seem to think man is made for nothing else but to be shot at ! You would not like the army, Pisistratus ?"

" Why, sir, not if it pained you and my dear mother ; otherwise, indeed——"

" Papæ !" said my father, interrupting me. " This all comes of your giving the boy that ambitious, uncomfortable name,

Mrs. Caxton; what could a Pisistratus be but the plague of one's life? That idea of serving his country is Pisistratus ipsissimus all over. If ever I have another son (*Dii meliora!*) he has only got to be called Eratostratus, and then he will be burning down St. Paul's; which I believe was, by the way, first made out of the stones of a temple to Diana! Of the two, certainly, you had better serve your country with a goose-quill than by poking a bayonet into the ribs of some unfortunate Indian; I don't think there are any other people whom the service of one's country makes it necessary to kill just at present,—eh, Roland?"

"It is a very fine field, India," said my uncle sententiously; "it is the nursery of captains."

"Is it? Those plants take up a great deal of ground, then, that might be more profitably cultivated. And, indeed, considering that the tallest captains in the world will be ultimately set into a box not above seven feet at the longest, it is astonishing what a quantity of room that species of *arbor mortis* takes in the growing! However, Pisistratus, to return to your request, I will think it over, and talk to Trevanion."

"Or rather Lady Ellinor," said I imprudently; my mother slightly shivered, and took her hand from mine. I felt cut to the heart by the slip of my own tongue.

"That, I think, your mother could do best," said my father dryly, "if she wants to be quite convinced that somebody will see that your shirts are aired. For I suppose they mean you to lodge at Trevanion's."

"Oh, no!" cried my mother; "he might as well go to college then. I thought he was to stay with us; only go in the morning, but, of course, sleep here."

"If I know anything of Trevanion," said my father, "his secretary will be expected to do without sleep. Poor boy! you don't know what it is you desire. And yet, at your age, I"— my father stopped short. "No!" he renewed abruptly after a long silence, and as if soliloquising—"No: man is never wrong while he lives for others. The philosopher who contemplates from the rock is a less noble image than the sailor who struggles with the storm. Why should there be two of us? And *could* he be an *alter ego*, even if I wished it? Impossible!" My father turned on his chair, and laying the left leg on the right knee, said smilingly, as he bent down to look me full in the face—"But, Pisistratus, will you promise me always to wear the saffron bag?"

CHAPTER VII

I NOW make a long stride in my narrative. I am domesticated with the Trevanions. A very short conversation with the statesman sufficed to decide my father; and the pith of it lay in this single sentence uttered by Trevanion—"I promise you one thing—he shall never be idle!"

Looking back, I am convinced that my father was right, and that he understood my character, and the temptations to which I was most prone, when he consented to let me resign college and enter thus prematurely on the world of men. I was naturally so joyous, that I should have made college life a holiday, and then, in repentance, worked myself into a phthisis.

And my father, too, was right, that, though I could study, I was not meant for a student.

After all, the thing was an experiment. I had time to spare: if the experiment failed, a year's delay would not necessarily be a year's loss.

I am ensconced, then, at Mr. Trevanion's. I have been there some months—it is late in the winter; Parliament and the season have commenced. I work hard—Heaven knows, harder than I should have worked at college. Take a day for sample.

Trevanion gets up at eight o'clock, and in all weathers rides an hour before breakfast; at nine he takes that meal in his wife's dressing-room; at half-past nine he comes into his study. By that time he expects to find done by his secretary the work I am about to describe.

On coming home, or rather before going to bed, which is usually after three o'clock, it is Mr. Trevanion's habit to leave on the table of the said study a list of directions for the secretary. The following, which I take at random from many I have preserved, may show their multifarious nature :—

1. Look out in the Reports (Committee House of Lords) for the last seven years—all that is said about the growth of flax—mark the passages for me.

2. Do. do.—"Irish Emigration."

3. Hunt out second volume of Kames's History of Man, passage containing "Reid's Logic"—don't know where the book is!

4. How does the line beginning "Lumina conjurent, inter" something, end? Is it in Grey? See.

5. Fracastorius writes—"Quantum hoc *infecit* vitium, quot adiverit

*'At four, Fanny puts her head into
the room,—and I lose mine'*

urbes." Query, ought it not, in strict grammar, to be—*infecerit* instead of *infecit?*—if you don't know, write to father.

6. Write the four letters in full from the notes I leave, *i.e.*, about the Ecclesiastical Courts.

7. Look out Population Returns—strike average of last five years (between mortality and births) in Devonshire and Lancashire.

8. Answer these six begging letters, "No"—civilly.

9. The other six, to constituents—"that I have no interest with Government."

10. See, if you have time, whether any of the new books on the round table are not trash.

11. I want to know ALL about Indian corn.

12. Longinus says something, somewhere, in regret for uncongenial pursuits (public life, I suppose)—what is it? N.B. Longinus is not in my London catalogue, but is here, I know—I think in a box in the lumber-room.

13. Set right the calculation I leave on the poor-rates. I have made a blunder somewhere. &c. &c.

Certainly my father knew Mr. Trevanion; he never expected a secretary to sleep! To get through the work required of me by half-past nine, I get up by candle-light. At half-past nine I am still hunting for Longinus, when Mr. Trevanion comes in with a bundle of letters.

Answers to half the said letters fall to my share. Directions verbal—in a species of short-hand talk. While I write, Mr. Trevanion reads the newspapers—examines what I have done—makes notes therefrom, some for Parliament, some for conversation, some for correspondence—skims over the Parliamentary papers of the morning—and jots down directions for extracting, abridging, and comparing them with others, perhaps twenty years old. At eleven he walks down to a Committee of the House of Commons—leaving me plenty to do—till half-past three, when he returns. At four, Fanny puts her head into the room—and I lose mine. Four days in the week Mr. Trevanion then disappears for the rest of the day—dines at Bellamy's or a club—expects me at the House at eight o'clock, in case he thinks of something, wants a fact or a quotation. He then releases me—generally with a fresh list of instructions. But I have my holidays, nevertheless. On Wednesdays and Saturdays Mr. Trevanion gives dinners, and I meet the most eminent men of the day—on both sides. For Trevanion is on both sides himself—or no side at all, which comes to the same thing. On Tuesdays, Lady Ellinor gives me a ticket for the Opera, and I get there at least in time for the ballet. I have already invitations enough to balls and soirées, for I am regarded as an only son of great expectations. I am treated as becomes a Caxton who has the right, if he pleases, to put a De before his name. I have grown very smart. I have taken a passion for dress— natural to eighteen. I like everything I do, and every one about me. I am over head and ears in love with Fanny Trevanion—who breaks my heart, nevertheless; for she flirts with two peers, a life-guardsman, three old members of Parliament, Sir Sedley Beaudesert, one ambassador, and all his attachés, and, positively (the audacious minx!) with a bishop, in full wig and apron, who, people say, means to marry again.

Pisistratus has lost colour and flesh. His mother says he is very much improved,—*that* he takes to be the natural effect produced by Stultz and Hoby. Uncle Jack says he is "fined down."

His father looks at him and writes to Trevanion—

"Dear T.—I refused a salary for my son. Give him a horse, and two hours a day to ride it. Yours, A. C."

The next day I am master of a pretty bay mare, and riding by the side of Fanny Trevanion. Alas! alas!

CHAPTER VIII

I HAVE not mentioned my Uncle Roland. He is gone— abroad—to fetch his daughter. He has stayed longer than was expected. Does he seek his son still—there as here? My father has finished the first portion of his work, in two great volumes. Uncle Jack, who for some time has been looking melancholy, and who now seldom stirs out, except on Sundays (on which days we all meet at my father's and dine together)— Uncle Jack, I say, has undertaken to sell it.

"Don't be over sanguine," says Uncle Jack, as he locks up the MS. in two red boxes with a slit in the lids, which belonged to one of the defunct companies. "Don't be over sanguine as to the price. These publishers never venture much on a first experiment. They must be talked even into looking at the book."

"Oh!" said my father, "if they will publish it at all, and at their own risk, I should not stand out for any other terms. 'Nothing great,' said Dryden, 'ever came from a venal pen!'"

"An uncommonly foolish observation of Dryden's," returned Uncle Jack; "he ought to have known better."

"So he did," said I, "for he used his pen to fill his pockets—poor man!"

"But the pen was not venal, master Anachronism," said my father. "A baker is not to be called venal if he sells his loaves—he is venal if he sells himself: Dryden only sold his loaves."

"And we must sell yours," said Uncle Jack emphatically. "A thousand pounds a volume will be about the mark, eh?"

"A thousand pounds a volume!" cried my father. "Gibbon, I fancy, did not receive more."

"Very likely; Gibbon had not an Uncle Jack to look after his interests," said Mr. Tibbets, laughing and rubbing those smooth hands of his. "No! two thousand pounds the two volumes! a sacrifice, but still I recommend moderation."

"I should be happy, indeed, if the book brought in anything," said my father, evidently fascinated; "for that young gentleman is rather expensive; and you, my dear Jack;—perhaps half the sum may be of use to you!"

"To me! my dear brother," cried Uncle Jack—"to me! why, when my new speculation has succeeded, I shall be a millionaire!"

"Have you a new speculation, uncle?" said I anxiously. "What is it?"

"Mum!" said my uncle, putting his finger to his lip, and looking all round the room—"Mum!! Mum!!"

PISISTRATUS.—"A Grand National Company for blowing up both Houses of Parliament!"

MR. CAXTON.—"Upon my life, I hope something newer than that; for they, to judge by the newspapers, don't want Brother Jack's assistance to blow up each other!"

UNCLE JACK (mysteriously).—"Newspapers! you don't often read a newspaper, Austin Caxton?"

MR. CAXTON.—"Granted, John Tibbets!"

UNCLE JACK.—"But if my speculation make you read a newspaper every day?"

MR. CAXTON (astounded).—"Make me read a newspaper every day!"

UNCLE JACK (warming, and expanding his hands to the fire).—"As big as the *Times!*"

MR. CAXTON (uneasily).—"Jack, you alarm me!"

UNCLE JACK.—"And make you write in it too—a leader!"

MR. CAXTON, pushing back his chair, seizes the only weapon at

his command, and hurls at Uncle Jack a great sentence of Greek
"Τους μεν γαρ ειναι χαλεπους, όσε και ανθρωποφγειν!" *

UNCLE JACK (nothing daunted).—Ay, and put as much Greek
as you like into it!"

MR. CAXTON (relieved and softening).—"My dear Jack, you
are a great man—let us hear you!"

Then Uncle Jack began.   Now, perhaps my readers may have
remarked that this illustrious speculator was really fortunate in
his ideas.   His speculations in themselves always had something
sound in the kernel, considering how barren they were in the
fruit; and this it was that made him so dangerous.   The idea
Uncle Jack had now got hold of will, I am convinced, make a
man's fortune one of these days; and I relate it with a sigh,
in thinking how much has gone out of the family.   Know, then,
it was nothing less than setting up a daily paper on the plan
of the *Times*, but devoted entirely to Art, Literature, and
Science—*Mental* Progress, in short; I say on the plan of the
Times, for it was to imitate the mighty machinery of that
diurnal illuminator.   It was to be the Literary Salmoneus of
the Political Jupiter, and rattle its thunder over the bridge of
knowledge.   It was to have correspondents in all parts of the
globe; everything that related to the chronicle of the mind,
from the labour of the missionary in the South Sea Islands, or
the research of a traveller in pursuit of that mirage called
Timbuctoo, to the last new novel at Paris, or the last great
emendation of a Greek particle at a German university, was to
find a place in this focus of light.   It was to amuse, to instruct,
to interest—there was nothing it was not to do.   Not a man in
the whole reading public, not only of the three kingdoms, not
only of the British empire, but under the cope of heaven, that
it was not to touch somewhere, in head, in heart, or in pocket.
The most crotchety member of the intellectual community might
find his own hobby in those stables.

"Think," cried Uncle Jack,—"think of the march of mind—
think of the passion for cheap knowledge—think how little
quarterly, monthly, weekly journals can keep pace with the main
wants of the age.   As well have a weekly journal on politics, as
a weekly journal on all the matters still more interesting than
politics to the mass of the public.   My Literary Times once

* "Some were so barbarous as to eat their own species."   The sentence
refers to the Scythians, and is in Strabo.   I mention the authority, for
Strabo is not an author that any man engaged on a less work than the
History of Human Error is expected to have by heart.

started, people will wonder how they had ever lived without it! Sir, they have not lived without it—they have vegetated—they have lived in holes and caves, like the Troggledikes."

"Troglodytes," said my father mildly—"from *trogle*, a cave—and *dumi*, to go under. They lived in Ethiopia, and had their wives in common."

"As to the last point, I don't say that the public, poor creatures, are as bad as that," said Uncle Jack candidly; "but no simile holds good in all its points. And the public are no less Troggledummies, or whatever you call them, compared with what they will be when living under the full light of my Literary Times. Sir, it will be a revolution in the world. It will bring literature out of the clouds into the parlour, the cottage, the kitchen. The idlest dandy, the finest fine lady, will find something to her taste; the busiest man of the mart and counter will find some acquisition to his practical knowledge. The practical man will see the progress of divinity, medicine, nay, even law. Sir, the Indian will read me under the banyan; I shall be in the seraglios of the East; and over my sheets the American Indian will smoke the calumet of peace. We shall reduce politics to its proper level in the affairs of life—raise literature to its due place in the thoughts and business of men. It is a grand thought; and my heart swells with pride while I contemplate it!"

"My dear Jack," said my father seriously, and rising with emotion, "it *is* a grand thought, and I honour you for it. You are quite right—it would be a revolution! It would educate mankind insensibly. Upon my life, I should be proud to write a leader, or a paragraph. Jack, you will immortalise yourself!"

"I believe I shall," said Uncle Jack modestly; "but I have not said a word yet on the greatest attraction of all."

"Ah! and that?"

"THE ADVERTISEMENTS!" cried my uncle, spreading his hands with all the fingers at angles, like the threads of a spider's web. "The advertisements — oh, think of them!— a perfect *El Dorado*. The advertisements, sir, on the most moderate calculation, will bring us in £50,000 a year. My dear Pisistratus, I shall never marry; you are my heir. Embrace me!"

So saying, my Uncle Jack threw himself upon me, and squeezed out of breath the prudential demur that was rising to my lips.

My poor mother, between laughing and sobbing, faltered out —"And it is *my* brother who will pay back to *his* son all—all he gave up for me!" While my father walked to and fro the

room, more excited than ever I saw him before, muttering,
" A sad useless dog I have been hitherto! I should like to serve
the world! I should indeed!"

Uncle Jack had fairly done it this time. He had found out
the only bait in the world to catch so shy a carp as my father—
" *hæret lethalis arundo.*" I saw that the deadly hook was within
an inch of my father's nose, and that he was gazing at it with a
fixed determination to swallow.

But if it amused my father? Boy that I was, I saw no
further. I must own I myself was dazzled, and, perhaps with
childlike malice, delighted at the perturbation of my betters.
The young carp was pleased to see the waters so playfully in
movement, when the old carp waved his tail, and swayed himself on his fins.

"Mum!" said Uncle Jack, releasing me; "not a word to
Mr. Trevanion, to any one."

" But why?"

" Why? God bless my soul. Why? If my scheme gets
wind, do you suppose some one will not clap on sail to be before
me? You frighten me out of my senses. Promise me faith-
fully to be silent as the grave."

" I should like to hear Trevanion's opinion too."

" As well hear the town-crier! Sir, I have trusted to your
honour. Sir, at the domestic hearth all secrets are sacred.
Sir, I——"

" My dear Uncle Jack, you have said quite enough. Not a
word will I breathe!"

" I'm sure you may trust him, Jack," said my mother.

" And I do trust him—with wealth untold," replied my
uncle. " May I ask you for a little water—with a trifle of
brandy in it—and a biscuit, or indeed a sandwich. This talking
makes me quite hungry."

My eye fell upon Uncle Jack as he spoke. Poor Uncle Jack,
he had grown thin!

PART VII

CHAPTER I

SAITH Dr. Luther, "When I saw Dr. Gode begin to tell his puddings hanging in the chimney, I told him he would not live long!"

I wish I had copied that passage from "The Table Talk" in large round hand, and set it before my father at breakfast, the morn preceding that fatal eve in which Uncle Jack persuaded him to tell his puddings.

Yet, now I think of it, Uncle Jack hung the puddings in the chimney,—but he did not persuade my father to tell them.

Beyond a vague surmise that half the suspended "tomacula" would furnish a breakfast to Uncle Jack, and that the youthful appetite of Pisistratus would despatch the rest, my father did not give a thought to the nutritious properties of the puddings, —in other words, to the two thousand pounds which, thanks to Mr. Tibbets, dangled down the chimney. So far as the Great Work was concerned, my father only cared for its publication, not its profits. I will not say that he might not hunger for praise, but I am quite sure that he did not care a button for pudding. Nevertheless, it was an infaust and sinister augury for Austin Caxton, the very appearance, the very suspension and danglement of any puddings whatsoever, right over his ingle-nook, when those puddings were made by the sleek hands of Uncle Jack! None of the puddings which he, poor man, had all his life been stringing, whether from his own chimneys, or the chimneys of other people, had turned out to be real puddings,—they had always been the *eidola*, the *erscheinungen*, the phantoms and semblances of puddings. I question if Uncle Jack knew much about Democritus of Abdera. But he was certainly tainted with the philosophy of that fanciful sage. He peopled the air with images of colossal stature which impressed all his dreams and divinations, and from whose influences came his very sensations and thoughts. His whole being, asleep or waking, was thus but the reflection of great phantom puddings!

As soon as Mr. Tibbets had possessed himself of the two volumes of the " History of Human Error," he had necessarily established that hold upon my father which hitherto those lubricate hands of his had failed to effect. He had found what he had so long sighed for in vain, his *point d'appui*, wherein to fix the Archimedean screw. He fixed it tight in the " History of Human Error," and moved the Caxtonian world.

A day or two after the conversation recorded in my last chapter, I saw Uncle Jack coming out of the mahogany doors of my father's banker; and, from that time, there seemed no reason why Mr. Tibbets should not visit his relations on week-days as well as Sundays. Not a day, indeed, passed but what he held long conversations with my father. He had much to report of his interviews with the publishers. In these conversations he naturally recurred to that grand idea of the Literary Times, which had so dazzled my poor father's imagination; and, having heated the iron, Uncle Jack was too knowing a man not to strike while it was hot.

When I think of the simplicity my wise father exhibited in this crisis of his life, I must own that I am less moved by pity than admiration for that poor great-hearted student. We have seen that out of the learned indolence of twenty years, the ambition which is the instinct of a man of genius had emerged; the serious preparation of the Great Book for the perusal of the world, had insensibly restored the claims of that noisy world on the silent individual. And therewith came a noble remorse that he had hitherto done so little for his species. Was it enough to write quartos upon the past history of Human Error? was it not his duty, when the occasion was fairly presented, to enter upon that present, daily, hourly war with Error—which is the sworn chivalry of Knowledge? St. George did not dissect dead dragons, he fought the live one. And London, with that magnetic atmosphere which in great capitals fills the breath of life with stimulating particles, had its share in quickening the slow pulse of the student. In the country, he read but his old authors, and lived with them through the gone ages. In the city, my father, during the intervals of repose from the Great Book, and still more now that the Great Book had come to a pause,—inspected the literature of his own time. It had a prodigious effect upon him. He was unlike the ordinary run of scholars, and, indeed, of readers for that matter—who, in their superstitious homage to the dead, are always willing enough to sacrifice the living. He did justice to the marvellous fertility of intellect which characterises the authorship of the present age. By the present age, I do not only mean the present day, I commence with the century. "What," said my father one day in dispute with Trevanion—"what characterises the literature of our time is—its *human interest.* It is true that we do not see scholars addressing scholars, but men addressing men,—not that scholars are fewer, but that the reading public is more large. Authors in all ages address themselves to what interests their readers; the same things do not interest a vast community which interested half a score of monks or bookworms. The literary *polis* was once an oligarchy, it is now a republic. It is the general brilliancy of the atmosphere which prevents your noticing the size of any particular star. Do you not see that with the cultivation of the masses has awakened the Literature of the affections? Every sentiment finds an expositor, every feeling an oracle. Like Epimenides, I have been sleeping in a cave; and, waking, I see those whom I left children are bearded men; and towns have sprung up in the landscapes which I left as solitary wastes."

Thence the reader may perceive the causes of the change which had come over my father. As Robert Hall says, I think of Dr. Kippis, "he had laid so many books at the top of his head, that the brains could not move." But the electricity had now penetrated the heart, and the quickened vigour of that noble organ enabled the brain to stir. Meanwhile, I leave my father to these influences, and to the continuous conversations of Uncle Jack, and proceed with the thread of my own egotism.

Thanks to Mr. Trevanion, my habits were not those which favour friendships with the idle, but I formed some acquaintances amongst young men a few years older than myself, who held subordinate situations in the public offices, or were keeping their terms for the bar. There was no want of ability amongst these gentlemen; but they had not yet settled into the stern prose of life. Their busy hours only made them more disposed to enjoy the hours of relaxation. And when we got together, a very gay, light-hearted set we were! We had neither money enough to be very extravagant, nor leisure enough to be very dissipated; but we amused ourselves notwithstanding. My new friends were wonderfully erudite in all matters connected with the theatres. From an opera to a ballet, from Hamlet to the last farce from the French, they had the literature of the stage at the finger-ends of their straw-coloured gloves. They had a pretty large acquaintance with actors and actresses, and were perfect *Walpoluli* in the minor scandals of the day. To do them justice, however, they were not indifferent to the more masculine knowledge necessary in "this wrong world." They talked as familiarly of the real actors of life as of the sham ones. They could adjust to a hair the rival pretensions of contending statesmen. They did not profess to be deep in the mysteries of foreign cabinets (with the exception of one young gentleman connected with the Foreign Office, who prided himself on knowing exactly what the Russians meant to do with India— when they got it); but, to make amends, the majority of them had penetrated the closest secrets of our own. It is true that, according to a proper subdivision of labour, each took some particular member of the government for his special observation; just as the most skilful surgeons, however profoundly versed in the general structure of our frame, rest their anatomical fame on the light they throw on particular parts of it,—one man taking the brain, another the duodenum, a third the spinal cord, while a fourth, perhaps, is a master of all the symptoms indicated by a pensile finger. Accordingly, one of my friends appropriated to himself the Home Department; another the Colonies; and a third, whom we all regarded as a future Talleyrand (or a De Retz at least), had devoted himself to the special study of Sir Robert Peel, and knew, by the way in which that profound and inscrutable statesman threw open his coat, every thought that was passing in his breast! Whether lawyers or officials, they all had a great idea of themselves—high notions of what they were to *be*, rather than what they were to *do*, some day. As the king of modern fine gentlemen said of himself, in paraphrase of Voltaire, "they had letters in their pockets addressed to Posterity,—which the chances were, however, that they might forget to deliver." Somewhat "priggish" most of them might be; but, on the whole, they were far more interesting than mere idle men of pleasure. There was about them, as features of a general family likeness, a redundant activity of life—a gay exuberance of ambition—a light-hearted earnestness when at work—a schoolboy's enjoyment of the hours of play.

A great contrast to these young men was Sir Sedley Beaudesert, who was pointedly kind to me, and whose bachelor's house was always open to me after noon: Sir Sedley was visible to no one but his valet, before that hour. A perfect bachelor's house it was, too—with its windows opening on the Park, and sofas niched into the windows, on which you might loll at your ease, like the philosopher in Lucretius,—

> "Despicere unde queas alios, passimque videre,
>   Errare,"—

and see the gay crowds ride to and fro Rotten Row—without the fatigue of joining them, especially if the wind was in the east.

There was no affectation of costliness about the rooms, but a wonderful accumulation of comfort. Every patent chair that proffered a variety in the art of lounging found its place there ; and near every chair a little table, on which you might deposit your book or your coffee-cup, without the trouble of moving more than your hand. In winter, nothing warmer than the quilted curtains and Axminster carpets can be conceived. In summer, nothing airier and cooler than the muslin draperies and the Indian mattings. And I defy a man to know to what perfection dinner may be brought, unless he had dined with Sir Sedley Beaudesert. Certainly, if that distinguished personage had but been an egotist, he had been the happiest of men. But, unfortunately for him, he was singularly amiable and kind-hearted. He had the *bonne digestion*, but not the other requisite for worldly felicity—the *mauvais cœur*. He felt a sincere pity for every one else who lived in rooms without patent chairs and little coffee-tables—whose windows did not look on the Park, with sofas niched into their recesses. As Henry IV. wished every man to have his *pot au feu*, so Sir Sedley Beaudesert, if he could have had his way, would have every man served with an early cucumber for his fish, and a caraffe of iced water by the side of his bread and cheese. He thus evinced on politics a naïve simplicity, which delightfully contrasted his acuteness on matters of taste. I remember his saying, in a discussion on the Beer Bill, "The poor ought not to be allowed to drink beer, it is so particularly rheumatic ! The best drink in hard work is dry champagne—(not *mousseux*)—I found that out when I used to shoot on the moors."

Indolent as Sir Sedley was, he had contrived to open an extraordinary number of drains on his wealth.

First, as a landed proprietor, there was no end to applications from distressed farmers, aged poor, benefit societies, and poachers he had thrown out of employment by giving up his preserves to please his tenants.

Next, as a man of pleasure, the whole race of womankind had

K

legitimate demands on him.   From a distressed duchess, whose
picture lay *perdu* under a secret spring of his snuff-box, to a
decayed laundress, to whom he might have paid a compliment
on the perfect involutions of a frill, it was quite sufficient to be
a daughter of Eve to establish a just claim on Sir Sedley's
inheritance from Adam.

Again, as an amateur of art, and a respectful servant of every
muse, all whom the public had failed to patronise—painter,
actor, poet, musician—turned, like dying sunflowers to the sun,
towards the pitying smile of Sir Sedley Beaudesert.   Add to
these the general miscellaneous multitude who "had heard of
Sir Sedley's high character for benevolence," and one may well
suppose what a very costly reputation he had set up.   In fact,
though Sir Sedley could not spend on what might fairly be
called "himself," a fifth part of his very handsome income, I
have no doubt that he found it difficult to make both ends meet
at the close of the year.   That he did so, he owed perhaps
to two rules which his philosophy had peremptorily adopted.
He never made debts, and he never gambled.   For both
these admirable aberrations from the ordinary routine of fine
gentlemen, I believe he was indebted to the softness of his
disposition.   He had a great compassion for a wretch who was
dunned.   "Poor fellow!" he would say, "it must be so painful
to him to pass his life in saying No."   So little did he know
about that class of promisers,—as if a man dunned ever said No.
As Beau Brummell, when asked if he was fond of vegetables,
owned that he had once eat a pea, so Sir Sedley Beaudesert
owned that he had once played high at piquet.   "I was so unlucky as to win," said he, referring to that indiscretion, "and
I shall never forget the anguish on the face of the man who
paid me.   Unless I could always lose, it would be a perfect
purgatory to play."

Now nothing could be more different in their kinds of benevolence than Sir Sedley and Mr. Trevanion.   Mr. Trevanion
had a great contempt for individual charity.   He rarely put his
hand into his purse—he drew a great cheque on his bankers.
Was a congregation without a church, or a village without a
school, or a river without a bridge, Mr. Trevanion set to work
on calculations, found out the exact sum required by an algebraic
$x-y$, and paid it as he would have paid his butcher.   It must
be owned that the distress of a man, whom he allowed to be
deserving, did not appeal to him in vain.   But it is astonishing
how little he spent in that way; for it was hard, indeed, to

convince Mr. Trevanion that a deserving man ever was in such distress as to want charity.

That Trevanion, nevertheless, did infinitely more real good than Sir Sedley, I believe; but he did it as a mental operation —by no means as an impulse from the heart. I am sorry to say that the main difference was this,—distress always seemed to accumulate round Sir Sedley, and vanish from the presence of Trevanion. Where the last came, with his busy, active, searching mind, energy woke, improvement sprang up. Where the first came, with his warm kind heart, a kind of torpor spread under its rays ; people lay down and basked in the liberal sunshine. Nature in one broke forth like a brisk sturdy winter, in the other like a lazy Italian summer. Winter is an excellent invigorator, no doubt, but we all love summer better.

Now, it is a proof how lovable Sir Sedley was, that I loved him, and yet was jealous of him. Of all the satellites round my fair Cynthia, Fanny Trevanion, I dreaded most this amiable luminary. It was in vain for me to say with the insolence of youth that Sir Sedley Beaudesert was of the same age as Fanny's father;—to see them together, he might have passed for Trevanion's son. No one amongst the younger generation was half so handsome as Sedley Beaudesert. He might be eclipsed at first sight by the showy effect of more redundant locks and more brilliant bloom ; but he had but to speak, to smile, in order to throw a whole cohort of dandies into the shade. It was the expression of his countenance that was so bewitching ; there was something so kindly in its easy candour, its benign good-nature. And he understood women so well! He flattered their foibles so insensibly ; he commanded their affection with so gracious a dignity. Above all, what with his accomplishments, his peculiar reputation, his long celibacy, and the soft melancholy of his sentiments, he always contrived to *interest* them. There was not a charming woman by whom this charming man did not seem just on the point of being caught ! It was like the sight of a splendid trout in a transparent stream, sailing pensively to and fro your fly, in a will-and-a-won't sort of way. Such a trout ! it would be a thousand pities to leave him, when evidently so well disposed ! That trout, fair maid or gentle widow, would have kept you whipping the stream and dragging the fly from morning to dewy eve. Certainly I don't wish worse to my bitterest foe of five-and-twenty than such a rival as Sedley Beaudesert at seven-and-forty.

Fanny, indeed, perplexed me horribly. Sometimes I fancied

she liked me; but the fancy scarce thrilled me with delight,
before it vanished in the frost of a careless look, or the cold
beam of a sarcastic laugh.   Spoiled darling of the world as she
was, she seemed so innocent in her exuberant happiness, that
one forgot all her faults in that atmosphere of joy which she
diffused around her.   And, despite her pretty insolence, she
had so kind a woman's heart below the surface!   When she
once saw that she had pained you, she was so soft, so winning,
so humble, till she had healed the wound.   But *then*, if she saw
she had pleased you too much, the little witch was never easy
till she had plagued you again.   As heiress to so rich a father,
or rather perhaps mother (for the fortune came from Lady
Ellinor), she was naturally surrounded with admirers not wholly
disinterested.   She did right to plague *them*—but ME!   Poor
boy that I was, why should I seem more disinterested than
others! how should she perceive all that lay hid in my young
deep heart?   Was I not in all worldly pretensions the least
worthy of her admirers, and might I not seem, therefore, the
most mercenary?   I who never thought of her fortune, or if
that thought did come across me, it was to make me start and
turn pale!   And then it vanished at her first glance, as a ghost
from the dawn.   How hard it is to convince youth, that sees all
the world of the future before it, and covers that future with
golden palaces, of the inequalities of life!   In my fantastic and
sublime romance, I looked out into that Great Beyond, saw
myself orator, statesman, minister, ambassador—Heaven knows
what—laying laurels, which I mistook for rent-rolls, at Fanny's
feet.

Whatever Fanny might have discovered as to the state of my
heart, it seemed an abyss not worth prying into by either
Trevanion or Lady Ellinor.   The first, indeed, as may be supposed, was too busy to think of such trifles.   And Lady Ellinor
treated me as a mere boy—almost like a boy of her own, she
was so kind to me.   But she did not notice much the things
that lay immediately around her.   In brilliant conversation with
poets, wits, and statesmen—in sympathy with the toils of her
husband—or proud schemes for his aggrandisement, Lady Ellinor
lived a life of excitement.   Those large eager shining eyes of
hers, bright with some feverish discontent, looked far abroad as
if for new worlds to conquer—the world at her feet escaped
from her vision.   She loved her daughter, she was proud of her,
trusted in her with a superb repose—she did not watch over her.
Lady Ellinor stood alone on a mountain, and amidst a cloud.

CHAPTER II

ONE day the Trevanions had all gone into the country on a visit to a retired minister distantly related to Lady Ellinor, and who was one of the few persons Trevanion himself condescended to consult. I had almost a holiday. I went to call on Sir Sedley Beaudesert.—I had always longed to sound him on one subject, and had never dared. This time I resolved to pluck up courage.

"Ah, my young friend!" said he, rising from the contemplation of a villainous picture by a young artist, which he had just benevolently purchased, "I was thinking of you this morning.— Wait a moment, Sumners (this to the valet). Be so good as to take this picture, let it be packed up and go down into the country. It is a sort of picture," he added, turning to me, "that requires a large house. I have an old gallery with little casements that let in no light. It is astonishing how convenient I have found it!" As soon as the picture was gone, Sir Sedley drew a long breath, as if relieved; and resumed more gaily—

"Yes, I was thinking of you : and if you will forgive any interference in your affairs—from your father's old friend—I should be greatly honoured by your permission to ask Trevanion what he supposes is to be the ultimate benefit of the horrible labours he inflicts upon you."

"But, my dear Sir Sedley, I like the labours; I am perfectly contented."

"Not to remain always secretary to one who, if there were no business to be done among men, would set about teaching the ants to build hills upon better architectural principles! My dear sir, Trevanion is an awful man, a stupendous man—one *catches fatigue* if one is in the same room with him three minutes! At your age, an age that ought to be so happy," continued Sir Sedley, with a compassion perfectly angelic, "it is sad to see so little enjoyment!"

"But, Sir Sedley, I assure you that you are mistaken. I thoroughly enjoy myself; and have I not heard even you confess that one may be idle and not happy?"

"I did not confess that till I was on the wrong side of forty!" said Sir Sedley, with a slight shade on his brow.

"Nobody would ever think you were on the wrong side of

forty!" said I with artful flattery, winding into my subject.
"Miss Trevanion for instance?"

I paused. Sir Sedley looked hard at me, from his bright dark-
blue eyes. "Well, Miss Trevanion for instance?"

"Miss Trevanion, who has all the best-looking fellows in
London round her, evidently prefers you to any of them."

I said this with a great gulp. I was obstinately bent on
plumbing the depth of my own fears.

Sir Sedley rose; he laid his hand kindly on mine, and said,
"Do not let Fanny Trevanion torment you even more than her
father does!"

"I don't understand you, Sir Sedley!"

"But if I understand you, that is more to the purpose. A girl
like Miss Trevanion is cruel till she discovers she has a heart.
It is not safe to risk one's own with any woman till she has
ceased to be a coquette. My dear young friend, if you took
life less in earnest, I should spare you the pain of these hints.
Some men sow flowers, some plant trees—you are planting a
tree under which you will soon find that no flower will grow.
Well and good, if the tree could last to bear fruit and give
shade; but beware lest you have to tear it up one day or other;
for then—what then? why, you will find your whole life plucked
away with its roots!"

Sir Sedley said these last words with so serious an emphasis,
that I was startled from the confusion I had felt at the former
part of his address. He paused long, tapped his snuff-box,
inhaled a pinch slowly, and continued, with his more accustomed
sprightliness—

"Go as much as you can into the world—again I say 'enjoy
yourself.' And again I ask, what is all this labour to do for you?
On some men, far less eminent than Trevanion, it would impose
a duty to aid you in a practical career, to secure you a public
employment—not so on him. He would not mortgage an inch
of his independence by asking a favour from a minister. He so
thinks occupation the delight of life, that he occupies you out of
pure affection. He does not trouble his head about your future.
He supposes your father will provide for *that*, and does not consider that meanwhile your work leads to nothing! Think over
all this. I have now bored you enough."

I was bewildered—I was dumb: these practical men of the
world, how they take us by surprise! Here had I come to
sound Sir Sedley, and here was I plumbed, gauged, measured,
turned inside out, without having got an inch beyond the

surface of that smiling, *débonnaire*, unruffled ease. Yet with his invariable delicacy, in spite of all this horrible frankness, Sir Sedley had not said a word to wound what he might think the more sensitive part of my *amour propre*—not a word as to the inadequacy of my pretensions to think seriously of Fanny Trevanion. Had we been the Celadon and Chloë of a country village, he could not have regarded us as more equal, so far as the world went. And for the rest, he rather insinuated that poor Fanny, the great heiress, was not worthy of me, than that I was not worthy of Fanny.

I felt that there was no wisdom in stammering and blushing out denials and equivocations; so I stretched my hand to Sir Sedley, took up my hat,—and went. Instinctively I bent my way to my father's house. I had not been there for many days. Not only had I had a great deal to do in the way of business, but I am ashamed to say that pleasure itself had so entangled my leisure hours, and Miss Trevanion especially so absorbed them, that, without even uneasy foreboding, I had left my father fluttering his wings more feebly and feebly in the web of Uncle Jack. When I arrived in Russell Street, I found the fly and the spider cheek by jowl together. Uncle Jack sprang up at my entrance, and cried, " Congratulate your father. Congratulate *him !*—no; congratulate the world ! "

" What, uncle," said I, with a dismal effort at sympathising liveliness, " is the Literary Times launched at last ? "

" Oh, that is all settled—settled long since. Here's a specimen of the type we have chosen for the leaders." And Uncle Jack, whose pocket was never without a wet sheet of some kind or other, drew forth a steaming papyral monster, which in point of size was to the political *Times* as a mammoth may be to an elephant. " That is all settled. We are only preparing our contributors, and shall put out our programme next week or the week after. No, Pisistratus, I mean the Great Work."

" My dear father, I am so glad. What! it is really sold, then ? "

" Hum ! " said my father.

" Sold ! " burst forth Uncle Jack. " Sold—no, sir, we would not sell it ! No : if all the booksellers fell down on their knees to us, as they will some day, that book should not be sold ! Sir, that book is a revolution—it is an era—it is the emancipator of genius from mercenary thraldom ;—THAT BOOK ! "

I looked inquiringly from uncle to father, and mentally retracted my congratulations. Then Mr. Caxton, slightly blushing, and shyly rubbing his spectacles, said, "You see, Pisistratus, that though poor Jack has devoted uncommon pains to induce the publishers to recognise the merit he has discovered in the 'History of Human Error,' he has failed to do so."

"Not a bit of it; they all acknowledge its miraculous learning —its——"

"Very true; but they don't think it will sell, and therefore most selfishly refuse to buy it.   One bookseller, indeed, offered to treat for it if I would leave out all about the Hottentots and Caffres, the Greek philosophers and Egyptian priests, and confining myself solely to polite society, entitle the work 'Anecdotes of the Courts of Europe, ancient and modern.'"

"The wretch!" groaned Uncle Jack.

"Another thought it might be cut up into little essays, leaving out the quotations, entitled 'Men and Manners.'   A third was kind enough to observe, that though this particular work was quite unsaleable, yet, as I appeared to have some historical information, he should be happy to undertake an historical romance from 'my graphic pen '—that was the phrase, was it not, Jack ?"

Jack was too full to speak.

—"Provided I would introduce a proper love-plot, and make it into three volumes post octavo, twenty-three lines in a page, neither more nor less.   One honest fellow at last was found, who seemed to me a very respectable and indeed enterprising person.   And after going through a list of calculations, which showed that no possible profit could arise, he generously offered to give me half of those no-profits, provided I would guarantee half the very visible expenses.   I was just meditating the prudence of accepting this proposal, when your uncle was seized with a sublime idea, which has whisked up my book in a whirlwind of expectation."

"And that idea?" said I despondingly.

"That idea," quoth Uncle Jack, recovering himself, "is simply and shortly this.   From time immemorial, authors have been the prey of the publishers.   Sir, authors have lived in garrets, nay, have been choked in the street by an unexpected crumb of bread, like the man who wrote the play, poor fellow!"

"Otway," said my father.   "The story is not true—no matter."

"Milton, sir, as everybody knows, sold 'Paradise Lost' for ten pounds—ten pounds, sir!   In short, instances of a like nature are too numerous to quote. But the booksellers, sir—they are leviathans—they roll in seas of gold. They subsist upon authors as vampires upon little children. But at last endurance has reached its limit—the fiat has gone forth—the tocsin of liberty has resounded—authors have burst their fetters. And we have just inaugurated the institution of 'THE GRAND ANTI-PUBLISHER CONFEDERATE AUTHORS' SOCIETY,' by which, Pisistratus — by which, mark you, every author is to be his own publisher; that is, every author who joins the Society. No more submission of immortal works to mercenary calculators, to sordid tastes—no more hard bargains and broken hearts!—no more crumbs of bread choking great tragic poets in the streets — no more Paradises Lost sold at £10 apiece! The author brings his book to a select committee appointed for the purpose; men of delicacy, education, and refinement—authors themselves; they read it, the Society publish; and after a modest deduction, which goes toward the funds of the Society, the treasurer hands over the profits to the author."

"So that in fact, uncle, every author who can't find a publisher anywhere else, will of course come to the Society. The fraternity will be numerous."

"It will indeed."

"And the speculation—ruinous."

"Ruinous, why?"

"Because in all mercantile negotiations, it is ruinous to invest capital in supplies which fail of demand. You undertake to publish books that booksellers will not publish—why? because booksellers can't sell them. It is just probable that you'll not sell them any better than the booksellers. Ergo, the more your business, the larger your deficit; and the more numerous your society, the more disastrous your condition. Q.E.D."

"Pooh! The select committee will decide what books are to be published."

"Then, where the deuce is the advantage to the authors? I would as lief submit my work to a publisher as I would to a select committee of authors. At all events, the publisher is not my rival; and I suspect he is the best judge, after all, of a book—as an accoucheur ought to be of a baby."

"Upon my word, nephew, you pay a bad compliment to your father's Great Work, which the booksellers will have nothing to do with."

That was artfully said, and I was posed: when Mr. Caxton observed, with an apologetic smile—

"The fact is, my dear Pisistratus, that I want my book published without diminishing the little fortune I keep for you some day. Uncle Jack starts a society so to publish it.—Health and long life to Uncle Jack's society. One can't look a gift horse in the mouth."

Here my mother entered, rosy from a shopping expedition with Mrs. Primmins ; and in her joy at hearing that I could stay dinner, all else was forgotten. By a wonder, which I did not regret, Uncle Jack really was engaged to dine out. He had other irons in the fire besides the Literary Times and the Confederate Authors' Society : he was deep in a scheme for making house-tops of felt (which, under other hands, has, I believe, since succeeded); and he had found a rich man (I suppose a hatter) who seemed well inclined to the project, and had actually asked him to dine and expound his views.

CHAPTER III

HERE we three are seated round the open window—after dinner—familiar as in the old happy time—and my mother is talking low, that she may not disturb my father, who seems in thought.——

Cr-cr-crrr-cr-cr !   I feel it — I have it. — Where !   What ! Where !   Knock it down—brush it off !   For Heaven's sake, see to it !—Crrrr—crrrrr—there—here—in my hair—in my sleeve—in my ear.—Cr-cr.

I say solemnly—and on 'the word of a Christian, that, as I sat down to begin this chapter, being somewhat in a brown study, the pen insensibly slipt from my hand, and leaning back in my chair, I fell to gazing into the fire. It is the end of June, and a remarkably cold evening—even for that time of year. And while I was so gazing I felt something crawling just by the nape of the neck, ma'am. Instinctively and mechanically, and still musing, I put my hand there, and drew forth—What ? That *what* it is which perplexes me. It was a thing—a dark thing—a much bigger thing than I had expected. And the sight took me so by surprise, that I gave my hand a violent shake, and the thing went—where I know not. The what and the where are the knotty points in the whole question ! No sooner had it gone, than I was seized with repentance not to have examined it more closely—not to have ascertained what the creature was. It might have been an earwig—a very large motherly earwig—an earwig far gone in that way in which earwigs wish to be who love their lords. I have a profound horror of earwigs—I firmly believe that they do get into the ear. That is a subject on which it is useless to argue with me upon philosophical grounds. I have a vivid recollection of a story told me by Mrs. Primmins—How a lady for many years suffered under the most excruciating headaches; how, as the tombstones say, " physicians were in vain ; " how she died ; and how her head was opened, and how such a nest of earwigs— ma'am—such a nest !—Earwigs are the prolifickest things, and so fond of their offspring ! They sit on their eggs like hens— and the young, as soon as they are born, creep under them for protection—quite touchingly ! Imagine such an establishment domesticated at one's tympanum !

But the creature was certainly larger than an earwig. It might have been one of that genus in the family of *Forficulidæ*, called *Labidoura*—monsters whose antennæ have thirty joints ! There is a species of this creature in England, but to the great grief of naturalists, and to the great honour of Providence, very rarely found, infinitely larger than the common earwig, or *Forficulida auriculana*. Could it have been an early hornet ? It had certainly a black head, and great feelers. I have a greater horror of hornets, if possible, than I have of earwigs. Two hornets will kill a man, and three a carriage-horse sixteen hands high. However, the creature was gone.—Yes, but where ? Where had I so rashly thrown it ? It might have got into a fold of my dressing-gown or into my slippers—or, in short, any- where, in the various recesses for earwigs and hornets which a gentleman's habiliments afford. I satisfy myself at last, as far as I can, seeing that I am not alone in the room—that it is not upon me. I look upon the carpet—the rug—the chair—under the fender. It is *non inventus*. I barbarously hope it is frizzling behind that great black coal in the grate. I pluck up courage —I prudently remove to the other end of the room. I take up my pen—I begin my chapter—very nicely, too, I think upon the whole. I am just getting into my subject, when—cr-cr-cr- cr-cr—crawl—crawl—crawl—creep—creep—creep. Exactly, my dear ma'am, in the same place it was before ! Oh, by the Powers ! I forgot all my scientific regrets at not having scrutinised its genus before, whether *Forficulida* or *Labidoura*. I made a desperate lunge with both hands—something between thrust and cut, ma'am. The beast is gone. Yes, but again where? I say that that *where* is a very horrible question. Having come twice, in spite of all my precautions—and exactly on the same spot, too—it shows a confirmed disposition to habituate itself to its quarters—to effect a parochial settlement upon me; there is something awful and preternatural in it. I assure you that there is not a part of me that has not gone cr-cr-cr!—that has not crept—crawled and forficulated ever since; and I put it to you what sort of a chapter I can make after such a——My good little girl, will you just take the candle, and look carefully under the table?—that's a dear! Yes, my love, very black indeed, with two horns, and inclined to be corpulent. Gentlemen and ladies who have cultivated an acquaintance with the Phœnician language, are aware that Belzebub, examined etymologically and entomologically, is nothing more nor less than Baalzebub—"the Jupiter-fly"—an emblem of the Destroying Attribute, which attribute, indeed, is found in all the insect tribes more or less. Wherefore, as Mr. Payne Knight, in his "Inquiry into Symbolical Languages," hath observed, the Egyptian priests shaved their whole bodies, even to their eyebrows, lest unaware they should harbour any of the minor Zebubs of the great Baal. If I were the least bit more persuaded that that black cr-cr were about me still, and that the sacrifice of my eyebrows would deprive him of shelter, by the souls of the Ptolemies! I would,—and I will too. Ring the bell, my little dear! John, my—my cigar-box! There is not a cr in the world that can abide the fumes of the Havannah! Pshaw! sir, I am not the only man who lets his first thoughts upon cold steel end, like this chapter, in—Pff—pff—pff!

CHAPTER IV

EVERYTHING in this world is of use, even a black thing crawling over the nape of one's neck! Grim unknown! I shall make of thee—a simile.

I think, ma'am, you will allow that if an incident such as I have described had befallen yourself, and you had a proper and ladylike horror of earwigs (however motherly and fond of their offspring), and also of early hornets,—and indeed of all unknown things of the insect tribe with black heads and two great horns, or feelers, or forceps, just by your ear—I think, ma'am, you will allow that you would find it difficult to settle back to your former placidity of mood and innocent stitch-work. You would feel a something that grated on your nerves—and cr'd-cr'd "all over you like," as the children say. And the worst is, that you would be ashamed to say it. You would feel obliged to look pleased and join in the conversation, and not fidget too much, nor always be shaking your flounces, and looking into a dark corner of your apron. Thus it is with many other things in life besides black insects. One has a secret care—an abstraction—a something between the memory and the feeling, of a dark crawling cr, which one has never dared to analyse. So I sat by my mother, trying to smile and talk as in the old time,—but longing to move about and look around, and escape to my own solitude, and take the clothes off my mind, and see what it was that had so troubled and terrified me —for trouble and terror were upon me. And my mother, who was always (Heaven bless her!) inquisitive enough in all that concerned her darling Anachronism, was especially inquisitive that evening. She made me say where I had been, and what I had done, and how I had spent my time,—and Fanny Trevanion (whom she had seen, by the way, three or four times, and whom she thought the prettiest person in the world)—oh, she must know exactly what I thought of Fanny Trevanion!

And all this while my father seemed in thought; and so, with my arm over my mother's chair, and my hand in hers, I answered my mother's questions—sometimes by a stammer, sometimes by a violent effort at volubility; when at some interrogatory that went tingling right to my heart I turned uneasily, and there were my father's eyes fixed on mine—fixed as they had been—when, and none knew why, I pined and languished, and my father said "he must go to school." Fixed, with quiet watchful tenderness. Ah no!—his thoughts had not been on the Great Work—he had been deep in the pages of that less worthy one for which he had yet more an author's paternal care. I met those eyes, and yearned to throw myself on his heart—and tell him all. Tell him what? Ma'am, I no more knew what to tell him, than I know what that black thing was which has so worried me all this blessed evening!

"Pisistratus," said my father softly, "I fear you have forgotten the saffron bag."

"No, indeed, sir," said I, smiling.

"He," resumed my father,—"he who wears the saffron bag has more cheerful, settled spirits than you seem to have, my poor boy."

"My dear Austin, his spirits are very good, I think," said my mother anxiously.

My father shook his head—then he took two or three turns about the room.

"Shall I ring for candles, sir? It is getting dark, you will wish to read?"

"No, Pisistratus, it is you who shall read; and this hour of twilight best suits the book I am about to open to you."

So saying, he drew a chair between me and my mother, and seated himself gravely, looking down a long time in silence—then turning his eyes to each of us alternately.

"My dear wife," said he at length, almost solemnly, "I am going to speak of myself as I was before I knew you."

Even in the twilight I saw that my mother's countenance changed.

"You have respected my secrets, Katherine, tenderly—honestly. Now the time is come when I can tell them to you and to our son."

CHAPTER V

MY FATHER'S FIRST LOVE

I LOST my mother early; my father (a good man, but who was so indolent that he rarely stirred from his chair, and who often passed whole days without speaking, like an Indian dervish) left Roland and myself to educate ourselves much according to our own taste. Roland shot, and hunted, and fished,—read all the poetry and books of chivalry to be found in my father's collection, which was rich in such matters, and made a great many copies of the old pedigree;—the only thing in which my father ever evinced much vital interest. Early in life I conceived a passion for graver studies, and by good luck I found a tutor in Mr. Tibbets, who, but for his modesty, Kitty, would have rivalled Porson. He was a second Budæus for industry, and by the way, he said exactly the same thing that Budæus did, viz., 'that the only lost day in his life was that in which he was married; for on that day he had only had six hours for reading!' Under such a master I could not fail to be a scholar. I came from the university with such distinction as led me to look sanguinely on my career in the world.

"I returned to my father's quiet rectory to pause and consider what path I should take to fame. The rectory was just at the foot of the hill, on the brow of which were the ruins of the castle Roland has since purchased. And though I did not feel for the ruins the same romantic veneration as my dear brother (for my day-dreams were more coloured by classic than feudal recollections), I yet loved to climb the hill, book in hand, and built my castles in the air amidst the wrecks of that which time had shattered on the earth.

"One day, entering the old weed-grown court, I saw a lady seated on my favourite spot, sketching the ruins. The lady was young—more beautiful than any woman I had yet seen, at least to my eyes. In a word, I was fascinated, and as the trite phrase goes, 'spell-bound.' I seated myself at a little distance, and contemplated her without desiring to speak. By-and-by, from another part of the ruins, which were then uninhabited, came a tall, imposing, elderly gentleman, with a benignant aspect; and a little dog. The dog ran up to me barking. This drew the attention of both lady and gentleman to me. The gentleman approached, called off the dog, and apologised with much politeness. Surveying me somewhat curiously, he then began to ask questions about the old place and the family it had belonged to, with the name and antecedents of which he was well acquainted. By degrees it came out that I was the descendant of that family, and the younger son of the humble rector who was now its representative. The gentleman then introduced himself to me as the Earl of Rainsforth, the principal proprietor in the neighbourhood, but who had so rarely visited the county during my childhood and earlier youth that I had never before seen him. His only son, however, a young man of great promise, had been at the same college with me in my first year at the university. The young lord was a reading man and a scholar; and we had become slightly acquainted when he left for his travels.

"Now, on hearing my name, Lord Rainsforth took my hand cordially, and, leading me to his daughter, said, 'Think, Ellinor, how fortunate !—this is the Mr. Caxton whom your brother so often spoke of.'

"In short, my dear Pisistratus, the ice was broken, the acquaintance made, and Lord Rainsforth, saying he was come to atone for his long absence from the county, and to reside at Compton the greater part of the year, pressed me to visit him. I did so. Lord Rainsforth's liking to me increased; I went there often."

My father paused, and seeing my mother had fixed her eyes
upon him with a sort of mournful earnestness, and had pressed
her hands very tightly together, he bent down and kissed her
forehead.

"There is no cause, my child!" said he.   It was the only
time I ever heard him address my mother so parentally.   But
then I never heard him before so grave and solemn—not a
quotation, too—it was incredible ; it was not my father speaking,
it was another man.   "Yes, I went there often.   Lord Rainsforth was a remarkable person.   Shyness, that was wholly
without pride (which is rare), and a love for quiet literary pursuits,
had prevented his taking that personal part in public life for
which he was richly qualified ; but his reputation for sense and
honour, and his personal popularity, had given him no inconsiderable influence even, I believe, in the formation of cabinets,
and he had once been prevailed upon to fill a high diplomatic
situation abroad, in which I have no doubt that he was as
miserable as a good man can be under any infliction.   He was
now pleased to retire from the world, and look at it through the
loopholes of retreat.   Lord Rainsforth had a great respect for
talent, and a warm interest in such of the young as seemed to
him to possess it.   By talent, indeed, his family had risen, and
were strikingly characterised.   His ancestor, the first peer,
had been a distinguished lawyer; his father had been celebrated for scientific attainments; his children, Ellinor and Lord
Pendarvis, were highly accomplished.   Thus the family identified
themselves with the aristocracy of intellect, and seemed unconscious of their claims of the lower aristocracy of rank.   You
must bear this in mind throughout my story.

"Lady Ellinor shared her father's tastes and habits of thought
—(she was not then an heiress).   Lord Rainsforth talked to me
of my career.   It was a time when the French Revolution had
made statesmen look round with some anxiety to strengthen
the existing order of things, by alliance with all in the rising
generation who evinced such ability as might influence their
contemporaries.

"University distinction is, or was formerly, among the popular
passports to public life.   By degrees, Lord Rainsforth liked
me so well as to suggest to me a seat in the House of Commons.
A member of Parliament might rise to anything, and Lord
Rainsforth had sufficient influence to effect my return.   Dazzling
prospect this to a young scholar fresh from Thucydides, and
with Demosthenes fresh at his tongue's end.   My dear boy, I

was not then, you see, quite what I am now; in a word, I loved Ellinor Compton, and therefore I was ambitious. You know how ambitious she is still. But I could not mould my ambition to hers. I could not contemplate entering the senate of my country as a dependant on a party or a patron—as a man who must make his fortune there—as a man who, in every vote, must consider how much nearer he advanced himself to emolument. I was not even certain that Lord Rainsforth's views on politics were the same as mine would be. How could the politics of an experienced man of the world be those of an ardent young student? But had they been identical, I felt that I could not so creep into equality with a patron's daughter. No! I was ready to abandon my own more scholastic predilections—to strain every energy at the bar—to carve or force my own way to fortune—and if I arrived at independence, then—what then? why, the right to speak of love, and aim at power. This was not the view of Ellinor Compton. The law seemed to her a tedious, needless drudgery: there was nothing in it to captivate her imagination. She listened to me with that charm which she yet retains, and by which she seems to identify herself with those who speak to her. She would turn to me with a pleading look when her father dilated on the brilliant prospects of a parliamentary success; for he (not having gained it, yet having lived with those who had) overvalued it, and seemed ever to wish to enjoy it through some other. But when I, in turn, spoke of independence, of the bar, Ellinor's face grew overcast. The world—the world was with her, and the ambition of the world, which is always for power or effect! A part of the house lay exposed to the east wind. 'Plant half-way down the hill,' said I one day. 'Plant!' cried Lady Ellinor—'it will be twenty years before the trees grow up. No, my dear father, build a wall, and cover it with creepers!' That was an illustration of her whole character. She could not wait till trees had time to grow; a dead wall would be so much more quickly thrown up, and parasite creepers would give it a prettier effect. Nevertheless, she was a grand and noble creature. And I—in love! Not so discouraged as you may suppose; for Lord Rainsforth often hinted encouragement, which even I could scarcely misconstrue. Not caring for rank, and not wishing for fortune beyond competence for his daughter, he saw in me all he required—a gentleman of ancient birth, and one in whom his own active mind could prosecute that kind of mental ambition which overflowed in him, and yet had never had its vent. And

L

Ellinor !—Heaven forbid I should say she loved me,—but something made me think she could do so. Under these notions, suppressing all my hopes, I made a bold effort to master the influences round me, and to adopt that career I thought worthiest of us all. I went to London to read for the bar."

"The bar ! is it possible !" cried I. My father smiled sadly.

"Everything seemed possible to me then. I read some months. I began to see my way even in that short time ; began to comprehend what would be the difficulties before me, and to feel there was that within me which could master them. I took a holiday and returned to Cumberland. I found Roland there on my return. Always of a roving, adventurous temper, though he had not then entered the army, he had, for more than two years, been wandering over Great Britain and Ireland on foot. It was a young knight-errant whom I embraced, and who overwhelmed me with reproaches that I should be reading for the law. There had never been a lawyer in the family ! It was about that time, I think, that I petrified him with the discovery of the printer ! I knew not exactly wherefore, whether from jealousy, fear, foreboding—but it certainly *was* a pain that seized me—when I learned from Roland that he had become intimate at Compton Hall. Roland and Lord Rainsforth had met at the house of a neighbouring gentleman, and Lord Rainsforth had welcomed his acquaintance, at first, perhaps, for my sake, afterwards for his own.

"I could not for the life of me," continued my father, "ask Roland if he admired Ellinor; but when I found that he did not put that question to me, I trembled !

"We went to Compton together, speaking little by the way. We stayed there some days."

My father here thrust his hand into his waistcoat—all men have their little ways, which denote much ; and when my father thrust his hand into his waistcoat, it was always a sign of some mental effort—he was going to prove, or to argue, to moralise, or to preach. Therefore, though I was listening before with all my ears, I believe I had, speaking magnetically and mesmerically, an extra pair of ears, a new sense supplied to me, when my father put his hand into his waistcoat.

CHAPTER VI

WHEREIN MY FATHER CONTINUES HIS STORY

THERE is not a mystical creation, type, symbol, or poetical invention for meanings abstruse, recondite, and incomprehensible, which is not represented by the female gender," said my father, having his hand quite buried in his waistcoat. "For instance, the Sphinx and Isis, whose veil no man had ever lifted, were both ladies, Kitty! And so was Persephone, who must be always either in heaven or hell—and Hecate, who was one thing by night and another by day. The Sibyls were females; and so were the Gorgons, the Harpies, the Furies, the Fates, and the Teutonic Valkyrs, Nornies, and Hela herself: in short, all representations of ideas, obscure, inscrutable, and portentous, are nouns feminine."

Heaven bless my father! Augustine Caxton was himself again! I began to fear that the story had slipped away from him, lost in that labyrinth of learning. But, luckily, as he paused for breath, his look fell on those limpid blue eyes of my mother's and that honest open brow of hers, which had certainly nothing in common with Sphinxes, Fates, Furies, or Valkyrs; and, whether his heart smote him, or his reason made him own that he had fallen into a very disingenuous and unsound train of assertion, I know not, but his front relaxed, and with a smile he resumed—"Ellinor was the last person in the world to deceive any one willingly. Did she deceive me and Roland, that we both, though not conceited men, fancied that, if we had dared to speak openly of love, we had not so dared in vain? or do you think, Kitty, that a woman really can love (not much perhaps, but somewhat) two or three, or half-a-dozen at a time?"

"Impossible!" cried my mother. "And as for this Lady Ellinor, I am shocked at her—I don't know what to call it!"

"Nor I either, my dear," said my father, slowly taking his hand from his waistcoat, as if the effort were too much for him, and the problem were insoluble. "But this, begging your pardon, I do think, that before a young woman does really, truly, and cordially centre her affections on one object, she suffers fancy, imagination, the desire of power, curiosity, or Heaven knows what, to simulate even to her own mind, pale reflections of the luminary not yet risen—parhelia that precede the sun. Don't judge of Roland as you see him now, Pisistratus —grim, and grey, and formal; imagine a nature soaring high amongst daring thoughts, or exuberant with the nameless poetry of youthful life—with a frame matchless for bounding elasticity—an eye bright with haughty fire—a heart from which noble sentiments sprang like sparks from an anvil. Lady Ellinor had an ardent, inquisitive imagination. This bold, fiery nature must have moved her interest. On the other hand, she had an instructed, full, and eager mind. Am I vain if I say, now after the lapse of so many years, that in my mind her intellect felt companionship? When a woman loves, and marries, and settles, why then she becomes—a one whole, a completed being. But a girl like Ellinor has in her many women. Various herself, all varieties please her. I do believe that, if either of us had spoken the word boldly, Lady Ellinor would have shrunk back to her own heart—examined it, tasked it, and given a frank and generous answer. And he who had spoken first might have had the better chance not to receive a 'No.' But neither of us spoke. And perhaps she was rather curious to know if she had made an impression, than anxious to create it. It was not that she willingly deceived us, but her whole atmosphere was de- lusion. Mists come before the sunrise. However this be, Roland and I were not long in detecting each other. And hence arose, first coldness, then jealousy, then quarrel."

"Oh, my father, your love must have been indeed powerful, to have made a breach between the hearts of two such brothers!"

"Yes," said my father, "it was amidst the old ruins of the castle, there, where I had first seen Ellinor—that, winding my arm round Roland's neck, as I found him seated amongst the weeds and stones, his face buried in his hands—it was there that I said—'Brother, we both love this woman! My nature is the calmer of the two, I shall feel the loss less. Brother, shake hands, and God speed you, for I go!'"

"Austin!" murmured my mother, sinking her head on my father's breast.

"And therewith we quarrelled. For it was Roland who insisted, while the tears rolled down his eyes, and he stamped his foot on the ground, that he was the intruder, the interloper— that he had no hope—that he had been a fool and a madman— and that it was for him to go! Now, while we were disputing, and words began to run high, my father's old servant entered the desolate place, with a note from Lady Ellinor to me, asking for the loan of some book I had praised. Roland saw the hand-writing, and while I turned the note over and over irresolutely, before I broke the seal, he vanished.

"He did not return to my father's house. We did not know what had become of him. But I, thinking over that impulsive volcanic nature, took quick alarm. And I went in search of him; came on his track at last; and after many days, found him in a miserable cottage amongst the most dreary of the dreary wastes which form so large a part of Cumberland. He was so altered I scarcely knew him. To be brief, we came at last to a compromise. We would go back to Compton. This suspense was intolerable. One of us at least should take courage and learn his fate. But who should speak first? We drew lots, and the lot fell on me.

"And now that I was really to pass the Rubicon, now that I was to impart that secret hope which had animated me so long —been to me a new life—what were my sensations? My dear boy, depend on it that that age is the happiest, when such feelings as I felt then can agitate us no more : they are mistakes in the serene order of that majestic life which heaven meant for thoughtful man. Our souls should be as stars on earth, not as meteors and tortured comets. What could I offer to Ellinor— to her father? What but a future of patient labour? And in either answer, what alternative of misery !—my own existence shattered, or Roland's noble heart !

"Well, we went to Compton. In our former visits we had been almost the only guests. Lord Rainsforth did not much affect the intercourse of country squires, less educated then than now ; and in excuse for Ellinor and for us, we were almost the only men of our own age she had seen in that large dull house. But now the London season had broken up, the house was filled ; there was no longer that familiar and constant approach to the mistress of the Hall, which had made us like one family. Great ladies, fine people were round her ; a look, a smile, a passing word were as much as I had a right to expect. And the talk, too, how different ! Before, I could speak on books,— I was at home there ! Roland could pour forth his dreams, his chivalrous love for the past, his bold defiance of the unknown future. And Ellinor, cultivated and fanciful, could sympathise with both. And her father, scholar and gentleman, could sympathise too. But now——"

CHAPTER VII

WHEREIN MY FATHER BRINGS OUT HIS DENOUEMENT

IT is no use in the world," said my father, "to know all the languages expounded in grammars and splintered up into lexicons, if we don't learn the language of the world. It is a talk apart, Kitty," cried my father, warming up. "It is an ANAGLYPH—a spoken anaglyph, my dear! If all the hieroglyphs of the Egyptians had been A B C to you, still if you did not know the anaglyph, you would know nothing of the true mysteries of the priests.[1]

"Neither Roland nor I knew one symbol letter of the ana-glyph. Talk, talk—talk on persons we never heard of, things we never cared for. All *we* thought of importance, puerile or pedantic trifles—all we thought so trite and childish, the grand momentous business of life! If you found a little schoolboy, on his half-holiday, fishing for minnows with a crooked pin, and you began to tell him of all the wonders of the deep, the laws of the tides, and the antediluvian relics of iguanodon and ichthyosaurus—nay, if you spoke but of pearl-fisheries and coral-banks, or water-kelpies and naiads, would not the little boy cry out peevishly, 'Don't tease me with all that nonsense! let me fish in peace for my minnows.' I think the little boy is right after his own way—it was to fish for minnows that he came out, poor child, not to hear about iguanodons and water-kelpies!

"So the company fished for minnows, and not a word could we say about our pearl-fisheries and coral-banks! And as for fishing for minnows ourselves, my dear boy, we should have been less bewildered if you had asked us to fish for a mermaid! Do you see, now, one reason why I have let you go thus early into the world? Well, but amongst these minnow-fishers there was one who fished with an air that made the minnows look larger than salmons.

"Trevanion had been at Cambridge with me. We were even intimate. He was a young man like myself, with his way to make in the world. Poor as I—of a family upon a par with mine—old enough, but decayed. There was, however, this

---

[1] The anaglyph was peculiar to the Egyptian priests—the hieroglyph generally known to the well-educated.

difference between us : he had connections in the great world—
I had none. Like me, his chief pecuniary resource was a college
fellowship. Now, Trevanion had established a high reputation
at the University; but less as a scholar, though a pretty fair
one, than as a man to rise in life. Every faculty he had was an
energy. He aimed at everything—lost some things—gained
others. He was a great speaker in a debating society, a
member of some politico-economical club. He was an eternal
talker — brilliant, various, paradoxical, florid — different from
what he is now. For, dreading fancy, his career since has been
one effort to curb it. But all his mind attached itself to something that we Englishmen call solid : it was a large mind—not,
my dear Kitty, like a fine whale sailing through knowledge
from the pleasure of sailing—but like a polypus, that puts forth
all its feelers for the purpose of catching hold of something.
Trevanion had gone at once to London from the University :
his reputation and his talk dazzled his connections, not unjustly.
They made an effort—they got him into Parliament: he had
spoken, he had succeeded. He came to Compton in the flush of
his virgin fame. I cannot convey to you who know him now—
with his careworn face, and abrupt dry manner,—reduced by perpetual gladiatorship to the skin and bone of his former self—
what that man was when he first stepped into the arena of life.

"You see, my listeners, that you have to recollect that we
middle-aged folks were young then; that is to say, we were
as different from what we are now, as the green bough of
summer is from the dry wood, out of which we make a ship
or a gate-post. Neither man nor wood comes to the uses of
life till the green leaves are stripped and the sap gone. And
then the uses of life transform us into strange things with
other names : the tree is a tree no more—it is a gate or a
ship ; the youth is a youth no more, but a one-legged soldier ;
a hollow-eyed statesman ; a scholar spectacled and slippered !
When Micyllus "—(here the hand slides into the waistcoat
again !) — "when Micyllus," said my father, "asked the cock
that had once been Pythagoras,[1] if the affair of Troy was really
as Homer told it, the cock replied scornfully, 'How could
Homer know anything about it ?—at that time he was a camel
in Bactria.' Pisistratus, according to the doctrine of Metem-
psychosis, you might have been a Bactrian camel, when that
which to my life was the siege of Troy saw Roland and
Trevanion before the walls.

[1] Lucian, "The Dream of Micyllus."

"Handsome you can see that Trevanion has been; but the beauty of his countenance then was in its perpetual play, its intellectual eagerness; and his conversation was so discursive, so various, so animated, and above all, so full of the things of the day! If he had been a priest of Serapis for fifty years, he could not have known the anaglyph better. Therefore he filled up every crevice and pore of that hollow society with his broken, inquisitive, petulant light. Therefore he was admired, talked of, listened to; and everybody said, 'Trevanion is a rising man.'

"Yet I did not do him then the justice I have done since; for we students and abstract thinkers are apt too much, in our first youth, to look to the *depth* of a man's mind or knowledge, and not enough to the *surface* it may cover. There may be more water in a flowing stream, only four feet deep, and certainly more force and more health, than in a sullen pool thirty yards to the bottom. I did not do Trevanion justice. I did not see how naturally he realised Lady Ellinor's ideal. I have said that she was like many.women in one. Trevanion was a thousand men in one. He had learning to please her mind, eloquence to dazzle her fancy, beauty to please her eye, reputation precisely of the kind to allure her vanity, honour and conscientious purpose to satisfy her judgment; and, above all, he was ambitious; ambitious, not as I—not as Roland was, but ambitious as Ellinor was; ambitious, not to realise some grand ideal in the silent heart, but to grasp the practical positive substances that lay without.

"Ellinor was a child of the great world, and so was he.

"I saw not all this, nor did Roland; and Trevanion seemed to pay no particular court to Ellinor.

"But the time approached when I ought to speak. The house began to thin. Lord Rainsforth had leisure to resume his easy conferences with me; and one day, walking in his garden, he gave me the opportunity; for I need not say, Pisistratus," said my father, looking at me earnestly, "that before any man of honour, if of inferior worldly pretensions, will open his heart seriously to the daughter, it is his duty to speak first to the parent, whose confidence has imposed that trust." I bowed my head, and coloured.

"I know not how it was," continued my father, "but Lord Rainsforth turned the conversation on Ellinor. After speaking of his expectations in his son, who was returning home, he said, 'But he will of course enter public life—will, I trust, soon marry, have a separate establishment, and I shall see but little of him. My Ellinor!—I cannot bear the thought of parting wholly with her. And that, to say the selfish truth, is one reason why I have never wished her to marry a rich man, and so leave me for ever. I could hope that she will give herself to one who may be contented to reside at least great part of the year with me, who may bless me with another son, not steal from me a daughter. I do not mean that he should waste his life in the country; his occupations would probably lead him to London. I care not where my *house* is—all I want is to keep my *home*. You know' (he added, with a smile that I thought meaning), 'how often I have implied to you that I have no vulgar ambition for Ellinor. Her portion must be very small, for my estate is strictly entailed, and I have lived too much up to my income all my life to hope to save much now. But her tastes do not require expense; and while I live, at least, there need be no change. She can only prefer a man whose talents, congenial to hers, will win their own career, and ere I die that career may be made.' Lord Rainsforth paused; and then—how, in what words I know not—but out all burst!—my long-suppressed, timid, anxious, doubtful, fearful love. The strange energy it had given to a nature till then so retiring and calm! My recent devotion to the law—my confidence that, with such a prize, I could succeed—it was but a transfer of labour from one study to another. Labour could conquer all things, and custom sweeten them in the conquest. The bar was a less brilliant career than the senate; but the first aim of the poor man should be independence. In short, Pisistratus, wretched egotist that I was, I forgot Roland in that moment; and I spoke as one who felt his life was in his words.

"Lord Rainsforth looked at me, when I had done, with a countenance full of affection, but it was not cheerful.

"'My dear Caxton,' said he tremulously, 'I own that I once wished this—wished it from the hour I knew you; but why did you so long—I never suspected that—nor, I am sure, did Ellinor.' He stopped short, and added quickly—'However, go and speak, as you have spoken to me, to Ellinor. Go, it may not yet be too late. And yet—but go.'

"Too late!—what meant those words? Lord Rainsforth had turned hastily down another walk, and left me alone, to ponder over an answer which concealed a riddle. Slowly I took my way towards the house, and sought Lady Ellinor. half hoping, half dreading to find her alone. There was a little room com-

municating with a conservatory, where she usually sat in the
morning. Thither I took my course.

"That room—I see it still!—the walls covered with pictures
from her own hand; many were sketches of the haunts we had
visited together—the simple ornaments, womanly but not
effeminate—the very books on the table, that had been made
familiar by dear associations. Yes; there the *Tasso* in which we
had read together the episode of *Clorinda*—there the *Æschylus*
in which I translated to her the *Prometheus.* Pedantries these
might seem to some; pedantries, perhaps, they were; but they
were proofs of that congeniality which had knit the man of
books to the daughter of the world. That room, it was the
home of my heart.

"Such, in my vanity of spirit, methought would be the air
round a home to come. I looked about me, troubled and confused, and, halting timidly, I saw Ellinor before me, leaning her
face on her hand, her cheek more flushed than usual, and tears
in her eyes. I approached in silence, and as I drew my chair
to the table, my eye fell on a glove on the floor. It was a
man's glove. Do you know," said my father, "that once, when
I was very young, I saw a Dutch picture called The Glove, and
the subject was of murder? There was a weed-grown marshy
pool, a desolate dismal landscape, that of itself inspired thoughts
of ill deeds and terror. And two men, as if walking by chance,
came to this pool; the finger of one pointed to a blood-
stained glove, and the eyes of both were fixed on each other,
as if there were no need of words. The glove told its tale!
The picture had long haunted me in my boyhood, but it never
gave me so uneasy and fearful a feeling as did that real glove
upon the floor. Why? My dear Pisistratus, the theory of forebodings involves one of those questions on which we may ask
'why' for ever. More chilled than I had been in speaking to
her father, I took heart at last, and spoke to Ellinor."

My father stopped short, the moon had risen, and was shining
full into the room and on his face. And by that light the face
was changed; young emotions had brought back youth—my
father looked a young man. But what pain was there! If
the memory alone could raise what, after all, was but the ghost
of suffering, what had been its living reality? Involuntarily
I seized his hand; my father pressed it convulsively, and said
with a deep breath—"It was too late; Trevanion was Lady
Ellinor's accepted, plighted, happy lover. My dear Katherine,
I do not envy him now; look up, sweet wife, look up!"

"It was a man's glove"

CHAPTER VIII

ELLINOR (let me do her justice) was shocked at my silent emotion. No human lip could utter more tender sympathy, more noble self-reproach ; but that was no balm to my wound. So I left the house ; so I never returned to the law ; so all impetus, all motive for exertion, seemed taken from my being ; so I went back into books. And so, a moping, despondent, worthless mourner might I have been to the end of my days, but that Heaven, in its mercy, sent thy mother, Pisistratus, across my path ; and day and night I bless God and her ; for I have been, and am—oh, indeed, I am, a happy man ! "

My mother threw herself on my father's breast, sobbing violently, and then turned from the room without a word ; my father's eye, swimming in tears, followed her ; and then, after pacing the room for some moments in silence, he came up to me, and leaning his arm on my shoulder, whispered, " Can you guess why I have now told you all this, my son ? "

" Yes, partly ; thank you, father," I faltered, and sat down, for I felt faint.

" Some sons," said my father, seating himself beside me, " would find in their father's follies and errors an excuse for their own ; not so will you, Pisistratus."

" I see no folly, no error, sir ; only nature and sorrow."

" Pause ere you thus think," said my father. " Great was the folly and great the error, of indulging imagination that had no basis—of linking the whole usefulness of my life to the will of a human creature like myself. Heaven did not design the passion of love to be this tyrant ; nor is it so with the mass and multitude of human life. We dreamers, solitary students like me, or half-poets like poor Roland, make our own disease. How many years, even after I had regained serenity, as your mother gave me a home long not appreciated, have I wasted ! The mainstring of my existence was snapped—I took no note of time. And therefore now, you see, late in life, Nemesis wakes. I look back with regret at powers neglected, opportunities gone. Galvanically I brace up energies half palsied by disuse ; and you see me, rather than rest quiet and good for nothing, talked into what, I dare say, are sad follies, by an Uncle Jack ! And now I behold Ellinor again ; and I say in wonder—' All this—all this—

all this agony, all this torpor, for that haggard face, that worldly spirit!' So is it ever in life: mortal things fade; immortal things spring more freshly with every step to the tomb.

"Ah!" continued my father, with a sigh, "it would not have been so, if at your age I had found out the secret of the saffron bag!"

CHAPTER IX

AND Roland, sir," said I—"how did he take it?"

"With all the indignation of a proud unreasonable man. More indignant, poor fellow, for me than himself. And so did he wound and gall me by what he saïd of Ellinor, and so did he rage against me because I would not share his rage, that again we quarrelled. We parted, and did not meet for many years. We came into sudden possession of our little fortunes. His he devoted (as you may know) to the purchase of the old ruins, and the commission in the army, which had always been his dream—and so went his way, wrathful. My share gave me an excuse for indolence—it satisfied all my wants; and when my old tutor died, and his young child became my ward, and, somehow or other, from my ward my wife, it allowed me to resign my fellowship, and live amongst my books—still as a book myself. One comfort, somewhat before my marriage, I had conceived; and that, too, Roland has since said was comfort to him. Ellinor became an heiress. Her poor brother died; and all of the estate that did not pass in the male line devolved on her. That fortune made a gulf between us almost as wide as her marriage. For Ellinor, poor and portionless, in spite of her rank, I could have worked, striven, slaved; but Ellinor RICH! it would have crushed me. This was a comfort. But still, still the past—that perpetual aching sense of something that had seemed the essential of life withdrawn from life, evermore, evermore! What was left was not sorrow,—it was a void. Had I lived more with men, and less with dreams and books, I should have made my nature large enough to bear the loss of a single passion. But in solitude we shrink up. No plant so much as man needs the sun and the air. I comprehend now why most of our best and wisest men have lived in capitals; and therefore again I say, that one scholar in a family is enough. Confiding in your sound heart and strong honour, I turn you thus betimes on the world. Have I done wrong? Prove that

I have not, my child. Do you know what a very good man has said ? Listen, and follow my precept, not example.

"'The state of the world is such, and so much depends on action, that everything seems to say aloud to every man, Do something—do it—do it!'"[1]

I was profoundly touched, and I rose refreshed and hopeful, when suddenly the door opened, and who or what in the world should come in; but certainly he, she, it, or they, shall not come into this chapter ! On that point I am resolved. No, my dear young lady, I am extremely flattered ;—I feel for your curiosity; but really not a peep—not one ! And yet—well then, if you will have it, and look so coaxingly—who or what, I say, should come in abrupt, unexpected—taking away one's breath, not giving one time to say, "By your leave, or with your leave," but making one's mouth stand open with surprise, and one's eyes fix in a big round stupid stare, but—

THE END OF THE CHAPTER.

[1] "Remains of the Rev. Richard Cecil," p. 349.

PART VIII

CHAPTER I

THERE entered, in the front drawing-room of my father's house in Russell Street—an Elf!!! clad in white,—small, delicate, with curls of jet over her shoulders;—with eyes so large and so lustrous that they shone through the room, as no eyes merely human could possibly shine. The Elf approached, and stood facing us. The sight was so unexpected, and the apparition so strange, that we remained for some moments in startled silence. At length my father, as the bolder and wiser man of the two, and the more fitted to deal with the eerie things of another world, had the audacity to step close up to the little creature, and bending down to examine its face, said, "What do you want, my pretty child?"

Pretty child! was it only a pretty child after all? Alas, it would be well if all we mistake for fairies at the first glance could resolve themselves only into pretty children!

"Come," answered the child with a foreign accent, and taking my father by the lappet of his coat, "come, poor papa is so ill! I am frightened! come—and save him."

"Certainly," exclaimed my father quickly; "where's my hat, Sisty? Certainly, my child, we will go and save papa."

"But who is papa?" asked Pisistratus—a question that would never have occurred to my father. He never asked who or what the sick papas of poor children were, when the children pulled him by the lappet of his coat—"Who is papa?"

The child looked hard at me, and the big tears rolled from those large luminous eyes, but quite silently. At this moment a full-grown figure filled up the threshold, and emerging from the shadow, presented to us the aspect of a stout, well-favoured young woman. She dropped a curtsey, and then said, mincingly—

"Oh, miss, you ought to have waited for me, and not alarmed the gentlefolks by running upstairs in that way. If you please, sir, I was settling with the cabman, and he was so imperent : them low fellows always are, when they have only us poor women to deal with, sir—and——"

" But what is the matter ? " cried I, for my father had taken the child in his arms, soothingly, and she was now weeping on his breast.

" Why, you see, sir (another curtsey), the gent only arrived last night at our hotel, sir,—the Lamb, close by Lunnun Bridge —and he was taken ill—and he's not quite in his right mind like :—so we sent for the doctor, and the doctor looked at the brass plate on the gent's carpet-bag, sir,—and he then looked into the *Court Guide,* and he said, ' There is a Mr. Caxton in Great Russell Street,—is he any relation ? ' and this young lady said, ' That's my papa's brother, and we were going there.' And so, sir, as the Boots was out, I got into a cab, and miss would come with me, and——"

" Roland—Roland ill ! Quick—quick, quick ! " cried my father, and, with the child still in his arms, he ran down the stairs. I followed with his hat, which of course he had forgotten. A cab, by good luck, was passing our very door ; but the chambermaid would not let us enter it till she had satisfied herself that it was not the same she had dismissed. This preliminary investigation completed, we entered, and drove to the Lamb.

The chambermaid, who sate opposite, passed the time in ineffectual overtures to relieve my father of the little girl, who still clung nestling to his breast,—in a long epic, much broken into episodes, of the causes which had led to her dismissal of the late cabman, who, to swell his fare, had thought proper to take a " circumbendibus ! "—and with occasional tugs at her cap, and smoothings down of her gown, and apologies for being such a figure, especially when her eyes rested on my satin cravat, or drooped on my shining boots.

Arrived at the Lamb, the chambermaid, with a conscious dignity, led us up a large staircase, which seemed interminable. As she mounted the region above the third storey, she paused to take breath, and inform us, apologetically, that the house was full, but that, if the " gent " stayed over Friday, he would be moved into No. 54, " with a look-out and a chimbly." My little cousin now slipped from my father's arms, and, running up the stairs, beckoned to us to follow. We did so, and were led to a door, at which the child stopped and listened ; then, taking off her shoes, she stole in on tiptoe. We entered after her.

By the light of a single candle we saw my poor uncle's face; it was flushed with fever, and the eyes had that bright, vacant stare which it is so terrible to meet. Less terrible is it to find the body wasted, the features sharp with the great life-struggle, than to look on the face from which the mind is gone,—the eyes in which there is no recognition. Such a sight is a startling shock to that unconscious habitual materialism with which we are apt familiarly to regard those we love: for, in thus missing the mind, the heart, the affection that sprang to ours, we are suddenly made aware that it was the something *within* the form, and not the form itself, that was so dear to us. The form itself is still, perhaps, little altered; but that lip which smiles no welcome, that eye which wanders over us as strangers, that ear which distinguishes no more our voices,—the *friend* we sought is not there! Even our own love is chilled back—grows a kind of vague superstitious terror. Yes, it was not the matter, still present to us, which had conciliated all those subtle nameless sentiments which are classed and fused in the word "*affection*,"—it was the airy, intangible, electric *something*,—the absence of which now appals us.

I stood speechless—my father crept on, and took the hand that returned no pressure—the child only did not seem to share our emotions, but, clambering on the bed, laid her cheek on the breast, and was still.

"Pisistratus," whispered my father, at last, and I stole near, hushing my breath,—"Pisistratus, if your mother were here!"

I nodded: the same thought had struck us both. His deep wisdom, my active youth, both felt their nothingness then and there. In the sick chamber, both turned helplessly to miss the *woman*.

So I stole out, descended the stairs, and stood in the open air in a sort of stunned amaze. Then the tramp of feet, and the roll of wheels, and the great London roar, revived me. That contagion of practical life which lulls the heart and stimulates the brain,—what an intellectual mystery there is in its common atmosphere! In another moment I had singled out, like an inspiration, from a long file of those ministrants of our Trivia, the cab of the lightest shape and with the strongest horse, and was on my way, not to my mother's but to Dr. M—— H——, Manchester Square, whom I knew as the medical adviser to the Trevanions. Fortunately, that kind and able physician was at home, and he promised to be with the sufferer before I myself could join him. I then drove to Russell Street, and broke to my mother, as cautiously as I could, the intelligence with which I was charged.

When we arrived at the Lamb, we found the doctor already writing his prescription and injunctions: the activity of the treatment announced the danger. I flew for the surgeon who had been before called in. Happy those who are strange to that indescribable silent bustle which the sick-room at times presents—that conflict which seems almost hand to hand between life and death—when all the poor, unresisting, unconscious frame is given up to the war against its terrible enemy; the dark blood flowing—flowing; the hand on the pulse, the hushed suspense, every look on the physician's bended brow; then the sinaplasms to the feet, and the ice to the head; and now and then, through the lull of the low whispers, the incoherent voice of the sufferer—babbling, perhaps, of green fields and fairyland, while your hearts are breaking! Then, at length, the sleep—in that sleep, perhaps, the crisis—the breathless watch, the slow waking, the first *sane* words—the old smile again, only fainter—your gushing tears, your low "Thank God! thank God!"

Picture all this; it is past: Roland has spoken—his sense has returned—my mother is leaning over him—his child's small hands are clasped round his neck—the surgeon, who has been there six hours, has taken up his hat, and smiles gaily as he nods farewell—and my father is leaning against the wall, his face covered with his hands.

CHAPTER II

ALL this had been so sudden that, to use the trite phrase—for no other is so expressive—it was like a dream. I felt an absolute, an imperious want of solitude, of the open air. The swell of gratitude almost stifled me—the room did not seem large enough for my big heart. In early youth, if we find it difficult to control our feelings, so we find it difficult to vent them in the presence of others. On the spring side of twenty, if anything affects us, we rush to lock ourselves up in our room, or get away into the streets or fields; in our earlier years we are still the savages of Nature, and we do as the poor brute does,—the wounded stag leaves the herd, and if there is any-thing on a dog's faithful heart, he slinks away into a corner.

M

Accordingly, I stole out of the hotel, and wandered through the streets, which were quite deserted. It was about the first hour of dawn, the most comfortless hour there is, especially in London! But I only felt freshness in the raw air, and soothing in the desolate stillness. The love my uncle inspired was very remarkable in its nature: it was not like that quiet affection with which those advanced in life must usually content themselves, but connected with the more vivid interest that youth awakens. There was in him still so much of vivacity and fire, in his errors and crotchets so much of the self-delusion of youth, that one could scarce fancy him other than young. Those Quixotic exaggerated notions of honour, that romance of sentiment, which no hardship, care, grief, disappointment, could wear away (singular in a period when, at two-and-twenty, young men declare themselves *blasés!*) seemed to leave him all the charm of boyhood. A season in London had made me more a man of the world, older in heart than he was. Then, the sorrow that gnawed him with such silent sternness. No, Captain Roland was one of those men who seize hold of your thoughts, who mix themselves up with your lives. The idea that Roland should die—die with the load at his heart unlightened, was one that seemed to take a spring out of the wheels of nature, an object out of the aims of life—of my life at least. For I had made it one of the ends of my existence to bring back the son to the father, and restore the smile that must have been gay once, to the downward curve of that iron lip. But Roland was now out of danger,—and yet, like one who has escaped shipwreck, I trembled to look back on the danger past; the voice of the devouring deep still boomed in my ears. While rapt in my reveries, I stopped mechanically to hear a clock strike—four; and, looking round, I perceived that I had wandered from the heart of the City, and was in one of the streets that lead out of the Strand. Immediately before me, on the doorsteps of a large shop whose closed shutters wore as obstinate a stillness as if they had guarded the secrets of seventeen centuries in a street in Pompeii,—reclined a form fast asleep; the arm propped on the hard stone supporting the head, and the limbs uneasily strewn over the stairs. The dress of the slumberer was travel-stained, tattered, yet with the remains of a certain pretence: an air of faded, shabby, penniless gentility made poverty more painful, because it seemed to indicate unfitness to grapple with it. The face of this person was hollow and pale, but its expression, even in sleep, was fierce and hard. I drew near and nearer; I recognised the countenance, the regular features, the raven hair, even a peculiar gracefulness of posture: the young man whom I had met at the inn by the wayside, and who had left me alone with the Savoyard and his mice in the churchyard, was before me. I remained behind the shadow of one of the columns of the porch, leaning against the area rails, and irresolute whether or not so slight an acquaintance justified me in waking the sleeper, when a policeman, suddenly emerging from an angle in the street, terminated my deliberations with the decision of his practical profession; for he laid hold of the young man's arm and shook it roughly,—"You must not lie here; get up and go home!" The sleeper woke with a quick start, rubbed his eyes, looked round, and fixed them upon the policeman so haughtily, that that discriminating functionary probably thought that it was not from sheer necessity that so improper a couch had been selected, and with an air of greater respect he said, "You have been drinking, young man,—can you find your way home?"

"Yes," said the youth, resettling himself, "you see I have found it!"

"By the Lord Harry!" muttered the policeman, "if he ben't going to sleep again! Come, come, walk on, or I must walk you off."

My old acquaintance turned round. "Policeman," said he, with a strange sort of smile, "what do you think this lodging is worth?—I don't say for the night, for you see that is over, but for the next two hours? The lodging is primitive, but it suits me; I should think a shilling would be a fair price for it—eh?"

"You love your joke, sir," said the policeman, with a brow much relaxed, and opening his hand mechanically.

"Say a shilling, then—it is a bargain! I hire it of you upon credit. Good night, and call me at six o'clock."

With that the young man settled himself so resolutely, and the policeman's face exhibited such bewilderment, that I burst out laughing, and came from my hiding-place.

The policeman looked at me. "Do you know this—this——"

"This gentleman?" said I gravely. "Yes, you may leave him to me;" and I slipped the price of the lodging into the policeman's hand. He looked at the shilling—he looked at me —he looked up the street and down the street—shook his head, and walked off. I then approached the youth, touched him, and said—"Can you remember me, sir; and what have you done with Mr. Peacock?"

STRANGER (after a pause).—"I remember you; your name is Caxton."

PISISTRATUS.—"And yours?"

STRANGER.—"Poor devil, if you ask my pockets—pockets, which are the symbols of man; Dare-devil, if you ask my heart. (Surveying me from head to foot)—The world seems to have smiled on you, Mr. Caxton! Are you not ashamed to speak to a wretch lying on the stones?—but, to be sure, no one sees you."

PISISTRATUS (sententiously).—"Had I lived in the last century, I might have found Samuel Johnson lying on the stones."

STRANGER (rising).—"You have spoilt my sleep; you had a right, since you paid for the lodging. Let me walk with you a few paces; you need not fear—I do not pick pockets—yet!"

PISISTRATUS.—"You say the world has smiled on me; I fear it has frowned on you. I don't say 'courage,' for you seem to have enough of that; but I say '*patience,*' which is the rarer quality of the two."

STRANGER.—"Hem!" (again looking at me keenly) "Why is it that you stop to speak to me—one of whom you know nothing, or worse than nothing?"

PISISTRATUS.—"Because I have often thought of you; because you interest me; because—pardon me—I would help you if I can—that is, if you want help."

STRANGER.—"Want! I am one want! I want sleep—I want food:—I want the patience you recommend—patience to starve and rot. I have travelled from Paris to Boulogne on foot, with twelve sous in my pocket. Out of those twelve sous in my pocket I saved four; with the four I went to a billiard-room at Boulogne; I won just enough to pay my passage and buy three rolls. You see I only require capital in order to make a fortune. If with four sous I can win ten francs in a night, what could I win with a capital of four sovereigns, and in the course of a year?—that is an application of the Rule of Three which my head aches too much to calculate just at present. Well, those three rolls have lasted me three days; the last crumb went for supper last night. Therefore, take care how you offer me money (for that is what men mean by help). You see I have no option but to take it. But I warn you, don't expect gratitude!—I have none in me!"

PISISTRATUS.—"You are not so bad as you paint yourself. I would do something more for you if I can, than lend you the little I have to offer. Will you be frank with me?"

STRANGER. — "That depends — I have been frank enough hitherto, I think."

PISISTRATUS.—"True; so I proceed without scruple. Don't tell me your name or your condition, if you object to such confidence; but tell me if you have relations to whom you can apply? You shake your head: well, then, are you willing to work for yourself? or is it only at the billiard-table (pardon me) that you can try to make four sous produce ten francs?"

STRANGER (musing). — "I understand you. I have never worked yet—I abhor work. But I have no objection to try if it is in me."

PISISTRATUS.—"It is in you: a man who can walk from Paris to Boulogne with twelve sous in his pocket, and save four for a purpose—who can stake those four on the cool confidence in his own skill, even at billiards—who can subsist for three days on three rolls—and who, on the fourth day, can wake from the stones of a capital with an eye and a spirit as proud as yours, has in him all the requisites to subdue fortune."

STRANGER.—"Do you work?—you?"

PISISTRATUS.—"Yes—and hard."

STRANGER.—"I am ready to work, then."

PISISTRATUS.—"Good. Now, what can you do?"

STRANGER (with his odd smile).—"Many things useful. I can split a bullet on a penknife; I know the secret tierce of Coulon, the fencing-master; I can speak two languages (besides English) like a native, even to their slang; I know every game in the cards; I can act comedy, tragedy, farce; I can drink down Bacchus himself; I can make any woman I please in love with me—that is, any woman good-for-nothing. Can I earn a handsome livelihood out of all this—wear kid gloves and set up a cabriolet? You see my wishes are modest!"

PISISTRATUS.—"You speak two languages, you say, like a native—French, I suppose, is one of them?"

STRANGER.—"Yes."

PISISTRATUS.—"Will you teach it?"

STRANGER (haughtily).—"No. *Je suis gentilhomme,* which means more or less than a gentleman. *Gentilhomme* means well born, because free born—teachers are slaves!"

PISISTRATUS (unconsciously imitating Mr. Trevanion).—"Stuff!"

STRANGER (looks angry, and then laughs).—"Very true: stilts don't suit shoes like these! But I cannot teach; Heaven help those *I* should teach!—anything else?"

PISISTRATUS.—"Anything else!—you leave me a wide margin.

You know French thoroughly—to write as well as speak?—that is much. Give me some address where I can find you—or will you call on me?"

STRANGER.—"No! Any evening at dusk I will meet you. I have no address to give; and I cannot show these rags at another man's door."

PISISTRATUS.—"At nine in the evening, then, and here in the Strand, on Thursday next. I may then have found something that will suit you. Meanwhile——" (slides his purse into the Stranger's hand. N.B.—Purse not very full).

Stranger, with the air of one conferring a favour, pockets the purse; and there is something so striking in the very absence of all emotion at so accidental a rescue from starvation, that Pisistratus exclaims—

"I don't know why I should have taken this fancy to you, Mr. Daredevil, if that be the name that pleases you best. The wood you are made of seems cross-grained, and full of knots; and yet, 'in the hands of a skilful carver, I think it would be worth much."

STRANGER (startled).—"Do you? do you? None, I believe, ever thought that before. But the same wood, I suppose, that makes the gibbet, could make the mast of a man-of-war. I tell you, however, why you have taken this fancy to me—the strong sympathise with the strong. You, too, could subdue fortune!"

PISISTRATUS.—"Stop; if so—if there is congeniality between us, then liking should be reciprocal. Come, say that; for half my chance of helping you is in my power to touch your heart."

STRANGER (evidently softened).—"If I were as great a rogue as I ought to be, my answer would be easy enough. As it is, I delay it. Adieu.—On Thursday."

Stranger vanishes in the labyrinth of alleys round Leicester Square.

CHAPTER III

ON my return to the Lamb, I found that my uncle was in a soft sleep; and after a morning visit from the surgeon, and his assurance that the fever was fast subsiding, and all cause for alarm was gone, I thought it necessary to go back to Trevanion's house, and explain the reason for my night's absence. But the family had not returned from the country. Trevanion himself came up for a few hours in the afternoon, and seemed to feel much for my poor uncle's illness. Though, as usual, very busy, he accompanied me to the Lamb, to see my father, and cheer him up. Roland still continued to mend, as the surgeon phrased it; and as we went back to St. James's Square, Trevanion had the consideration to release me from my oar in his galley for the next few days. My mind, relieved from my anxiety for Roland, now turned to my new friend. It had not been without an object that I had questioned the young man as to his knowledge of French. Trevanion had a large correspondence in foreign countries which was carried on in that language, and here I could be but of little help to him. He himself, though he spoke and wrote French with fluency and grammatical correctness, wanted that intimate knowledge of the most delicate and diplomatic of all languages to satisfy his classical purism. For Trevanion was a terrible *word-weigher*. His taste was the plague of my life and his own. His prepared speeches (or rather perorations) were the most finished pieces of cold diction that could be conceived under the marble portico of the Stoics,—so filed and turned, trimmed and tamed, that they never admitted a sentence that could warm the heart, or one that could offend the ear. He had so great a horror of a vulgarism that, like Canning, he would have made a periphrasis of a couple of lines, to avoid using the word "cat." It was only in extempore speaking that a ray of his real genius could indiscreetly betray itself. One may judge what labour such a super-refinement of taste would inflict upon a man writing in a language not his own to some distinguished statesman, or some literary institution,—knowing that language just well enough to recognise all the native elegances he failed to attain. Trevanion, at that very moment, was employed upon a statistical document intended as a communication to a Society at Copenhagen, of which he was an honorary member. It had been for three weeks the torment of the whole house, especially of poor Fanny (whose French was the best at our joint disposal). But Trevanion had found her phraseology too mincing, too effeminate, too much that of the *boudoir*. Here, then, was an opportunity to introduce my new friend, and test the capacities that I fancied he possessed. I therefore, though with some hesitation, led the subject to " Remarks on the Mineral Treasures of Great Britain and Ireland " (such was the title of the work intended to enlighten the *savans* of Denmark); and, by certain ingenious circumlocutions, known to all able applicants, I introduced my acquaintance with a young gentleman who possessed the most familiar and intimate knowledge of French, and who might be of use in revising the manuscript.   I knew enough of Trevanion to feel that I could not reveal the circumstances under which I had formed that acquaintance, for he was much too practical a man not to have been frightened out of his wits at the idea of submitting so classical a performance to so disreputable a scape-grace.   As it was, however, Trevanion, whose mind at that moment was full of a thousand other things, caught at my suggestion, with very little cross-questioning on the subject, and before he left London, consigned the manuscript to my charge.

"My friend is poor," said I timidly.

"Oh! as to that," cried Trevanion hastily, "if it be a matter of charity, I put my purse in your hands; but don't put my manuscript in his! If it be a matter of business, it is another affair; and I must judge of his work before I can say how much it is worth—perhaps nothing!"

So ungracious was this excellent man in his very virtues!

"Nay," said I, "it is a matter of business, and so we will consider it."

"In that case," said Trevanion, concluding the matter, and buttoning his pockets, "if I dislike his work, *nothing;* if I like it, twenty guineas.   Where are the evening papers?" and in another moment the member of Parliament had forgotten the statist, and was pishing and tutting over the *Globe* or the *Sun.*

On Thursday, my uncle was well enough to be moved into our house; and on the same evening, I went forth to keep my appointment with the stranger.   The clock struck nine as we met.   The palm of punctuality might be divided between us. He had profited by the interval, since our last meeting, to re-pair the more obvious deficiencies of his wardrobe; and though there was something still wild, dissolute, outlandish, about his whole appearance, yet in the elastic energy of his step, and the resolute assurance of his bearing, there was that which Nature gives to her own aristocracy,—for, as far as my observation goes, what has been called the "grand air" (and which is wholly distinct from the polish of manner or the urbane grace of high breeding) is always accompanied, and perhaps produced, by two qualities—courage, and the desire of command.   It is more common to a half-savage nature than to one wholly civilised. The Arab has it, so has the American Indian; and I suspect that it was more frequent among the knights and barons of the

Middle Ages than it is among the polished gentlemen of the modern drawing-room.

We shook hands, and walked on a few moments in silence; at length thus commenced the Stranger—

"You have found it more difficult, I fear, than you imagined, to make the empty sack stand upright. Considering that at least one-third of those born to work cannot find it, why should I?"

PISISTRATUS.—"I am hard-hearted enough to believe that work never fails to those who seek it in good earnest. It was said of some man, famous for keeping his word, that 'if he had promised you an acorn, and all the oaks in England failed to produce one, he would have sent to Norway for an acorn.' If I wanted work, and there was none to be had in the Old World, I would find my way to the New. But to the point: I *have* found something for you, which I do not think your taste will oppose, and which may open to you the means of an honourable independence. But I cannot well explain it in the streets; where shall we go?"

STRANGER (after some hesitation).—"I have a lodging near here, which I need not blush to take you to—I mean, that it is not among rogues and castaways."

PISISTRATUS (much pleased, and taking the Stranger's arm).— "Come, then."

Pisistratus and the Stranger pass over Waterloo Bridge, and pause before a small house of respectable appearance. Stranger admits them both with a latch-key—leads the way to the third storey—strikes a light, and does the honours to a small chamber, clean and orderly. Pisistratus explains the task to be done, and opens the manuscript. The Stranger draws his chair deliberately towards the light, and runs his eye rapidly over the pages. Pisistratus trembles to see him pause before a long array of figures and calculations. Certainly it does not look inviting; but, pshaw! it is scarcely a part of the task which limits itself to the mere correction of words.

STRANGER (briefly).—"There must be a mistake here—stay!— I see——" (He turns back a few pages, and corrects with rapid precision an error in a somewhat complicated and abstruse calculation.)

PISISTRATUS (surprised).—"You seem a notable arithmetician."

STRANGER.—"Did I not tell you that I was skilful in all games of mingled skill and chance? It requires an arithmetical head for that: a first-rate card-player is a financier spoilt. I am certain that you never could find a man fortunate on the turf, or at the gaming-table, who had not an excellent head for figures. Well, this French is good enough apparently; there are but a few idioms, here and there, that, strictly speaking, are more English than French. But the whole is a work scarce worth paying for!"

PISISTRATUS.—" The work of the head fetches a price not proportioned to the quantity, but the quality. When shall I call for this?"

STRANGER.—" To-morrow." (And he puts the manuscript away in a drawer.)

We then conversed on various matters for nearly an hour; and my impression of this young man's natural ability was confirmed and heightened. But it was an ability as wrong and perverse in its directions or instincts as a French novelist's. He seemed to have, to a high degree, the harder portion of the reasoning faculty, but to be almost wholly without that arch beautifier of character, that sweet purifier of mere intellect—*the imagination*. For, though we are too much taught to be on our guard against imagination, I hold it, with Captain Roland, to be the divinest kind of reason we possess, and the one that leads us the least astray. In youth, indeed, it occasions errors, but they are not of a sordid or debasing nature. Newton says that one final effect of the comets is to recruit the seas and the planets by a condensation of the vapours and exhalations therein; and so even the erratic flashes of an imagination really healthful and vigorous deepen our knowledge and brighten our lights; they recruit our seas and our stars. Of such flashes my new friend was as innocent as the sternest matter-of-fact person could desire. Fancies he had in profusion, and very bad ones: but of imagination not a *scintilla!* His mind was one of those which live in a prison of logic, and cannot, or will not, see beyond the bars: such a nature is at once positive and sceptical. This boy had thought proper to decide at once on the numberless complexities of the social world from his own harsh experience. With him the whole system was a war and a cheat. If the universe were entirely composed of knaves, he would be sure to have made his way. Now this bias of mind, alike shrewd and unamiable, might be safe enough if accompanied by a lethargic temper; but it threatened to become terrible and dangerous in one who, in default of imagination, possessed abundance of passion: and this was the case with the young outcast. Passion, in him, comprehended many of the worst emotions which militate against human happiness. You could not contradict him, but you raised quick choler; you could not speak of wealth, but the cheek paled with gnawing envy. The astonishing natural advantages of this poor boy—his beauty, his readiness, the daring spirit that breathed around him like a fiery atmosphere—had raised his constitutional self-confidence into an arrogance that turned his very claims to admiration into prejudices against him. Irascible, envious, arrogant—bad enough, but not the worst, for these salient angles were all varnished over with a cold repellent cynicism—his passions vented themselves in sneers. There seemed in him no moral susceptibility; and, what was more remarkable in a proud nature, little or nothing of the true point of honour. He had, to a morbid excess, that desire to rise, which is vulgarly called ambition, but no apparent wish for fame, or esteem, or the love of his species; only the hard wish to succeed, not shine, not serve,—succeed that he might have the right to despise a world which galled his self-conceit, and enjoy the pleasures which the redundant nervous life in him seemed to crave. Such were the more patent attributes of a character that, ominous as it was, yet interested me, and yet appeared to me to be redeemable,—nay, to have in it the rude elements of a certain greatness. Ought we not to make something great out of a youth under twenty, who has, in the highest degree, quickness to conceive and courage to execute? On the other hand, all faculties that can make greatness, contain those that can attain goodness. In the savage Scandinavian, or the ruthless Frank, lay the germs of a Sidney or a Bayard. What would the best of us be, if he were suddenly placed at war with the whole world? And this fierce spirit *was* at war with the whole world—a war self-sought, perhaps, but it was war not the less. You must surround the savage with peace, if you want the virtues of peace.

I cannot say that it was in a single interview and conference that I came to these convictions; but I am rather summing up the impressions which I received as I saw more of this person, whose destiny I presumed to take under my charge.

In going away, I said, " But, at all events, you have a name in your lodgings; whom am I to ask for when I call to-morrow?"

" Oh, you may know my name now," said he, smiling; " it is Vivian—Francis Vivian."

CHAPTER IV

I REMEMBER one morning, when a boy, loitering by an old
wall, to watch the operations of a garden spider, whose web
seemed to be in great request. When I first stopped, she was
engaged very quietly with a fly of the domestic species, whom
she managed with ease and dignity. But just when she was
most interested in that absorbing employment, came a couple
of May-flies, and then a gnat, and then a blue-bottle,—all at
different angles of the web. Never was a poor spider so distracted by her good fortune ! She evidently did not know
which godsend to take first. The aboriginal victim being released, she slid half-way towards the May-flies ; then one of her
eight eyes caught sight of the blue-bottle ! and she shot off in
that direction :—when the hum of the gnat again diverted her ;
and in the middle of this perplexity, pounce came a young
wasp in a violent passion ! Then the spider evidently lost her
presence of mind ; she became clean demented : and after
standing, stupid and stock-still, in the middle of her meshes,
for a minute or two, she ran off to her hole as fast as she could
run, and left her guests to shift for themselves. I confess that
I am somewhat in the dilemma of the attractive and amiable
insect I have just described. I got on well enough while I had
only my domestic fly to see after. But now that there is something fluttering at every end of my net (and especially since
the advent of that passionate young wasp, who is fuming and
buzzing in the nearest corner !) I am fairly at a loss which I
should first grapple with—and alas ! unlike the spider, I have
no hole where I can hide myself, and let the web do the
weaver's work. But I will imitate the spider as far as I can ;
and while the rest hum and struggle away their impatient,
unnoticed hour, I will retreat into the inner labyrinth of my
own life.

The illness of my uncle, and my renewed acquaintance with
Vivian, had naturally sufficed to draw my thoughts from the
rash and unpropitious love I had conceived for Fanny Trevanion.
During the absence of the family from London (and they stayed
some time longer than had been expected), I had leisure, however, to recall my father's touching history, and the moral it
had so obviously preached to me ; and I formed so many good
resolutions, that it was with an untrembling hand that I welcomed

Miss Trevanion at last to London, and with a firm heart that I avoided, as much as possible, the fatal charm of her society. The slow convalescence of my uncle gave me a just excuse to discontinue our rides. What time Trevanion spared me, it was natural that I should spend with my family. I went to no balls nor parties. I even absented myself from Trevanion's periodical dinners. Miss Trevanion at first rallied me on my seclusion, with her usual lively malice. But I continued worthily to complete my martyrdom. I took care that no reproachful look at the gaiety that wrung my soul should betray my secret. Then Fanny seemed either hurt or disdainful, and avoided altogether entering her father's study; all at once, she changed her tactics and was seized with a strange desire for knowledge, which brought her into the room to look for a book, or ask a question, ten times a day. I was proof to all. But, to speak truth, I was profoundly wretched. Looking back now, I am dismayed at the remembrance of my own sufferings: my health became seriously affected; I dreaded alike the trial of the day and the anguish of the night. My only distractions were in my visits to Vivian, and my escape to the dear circle of home. And that home was my safeguard and preservative in that crisis of my life; its atmosphere of unpretending honour and serene virtue strengthened all my resolutions; it braced me for my struggles against the strongest passion which youth admits, and counteracted the evil vapours of that air in which Vivian's envenomed spirit breathed and moved. Without the influence of such a home, if I had succeeded in the conduct that probity enjoined towards those in whose house I was a trusted guest, I do not think I could have resisted the contagion of that malign and morbid bitterness against fate and the world, which love, thwarted by fortune, is too inclined of itself to conceive, and in the expression of which Vivian was not without the eloquence that belongs to earnestness, whether in truth or falsehood. But, somehow or other, I never left the little room that contained the grand suffering in the face of the veteran soldier, whose lip, often quivering with anguish, was never heard to murmur; and the tranquil wisdom which had succeeded my father's early trials (trials like my own), and the loving smile on my mother's tender face, and the innocent childhood of Blanche (by which name the Elf had familiarised herself to us), whom I already loved as a sister,—without feeling that those four walls contained enough to sweeten the world, had it been filled to its capacious brim with gall and hyssop.

Trevanion had been more than satisfied with Vivian's performance—he had been struck with it.   For though the corrections
in the mere phraseology had been very limited, they went beyond
verbal amendments—they suggested such words as improved
the thoughts; and, besides that notable correction of an arithmetical error, which Trevanion's mind was formed to over-
appreciate, one or two brief annotations on the margin were
boldly hazarded, prompting some stronger link in a chain of
reasoning, or indicating the necessity for some further evidence
in the assertion of a statement.   And all this from the mere
natural and naked logic of an acute mind, unaided by the
smallest knowledge of the subject treated of!   Trevanion threw
quite enough work into Vivian's hands, and at a remuneration
sufficiently liberal to realise my promise of an independence.
And more than once he asked me to introduce to him my
friend.   But this I continued to elude—Heaven knows, not
from jealousy, but simply because I feared that Vivian's manner
and way of talk would singularly displease one who detested
presumption, and understood no eccentricities but his own.

Still, Vivian, whose industry was of a strong wing, but only
for short flights, had not enough to employ more than a few
hours of his day, and I dreaded lest he should, from very
idleness, fall back into old habits, and re-seek old friendships.
His cynical candour allowed that both were sufficiently disreputable to justify grave apprehensions of such a result; accordingly, I contrived to find leisure in my evenings to lessen
his *ennui*, by accompanying him in rambles through the gaslit
streets, or occasionally, for an hour or so, to one of the theatres.

Vivian's first care, on finding himself rich enough, had been
bestowed on his person; and those two faculties of observation
and imitation which minds so ready always eminently possess,
had enabled him to achieve that graceful neatness of costume
peculiar to the English gentleman.   For the first few days of
his metamorphosis, traces indeed of a constitutional love of show,
or vulgar companionship, were noticeable; but one by one
they disappeared.   First went a gaudy neckcloth, with collars
turned down; then a pair of spurs vanished; and lastly, a
diabolical instrument that he called a cane—but which, by
means of a running bullet, could serve as a bludgeon at one end
and concealed a dagger in the other—subsided into the ordinary
walking-stick adapted to our peaceable metropolis.   A similar
change, though in a less degree, gradually took place in his
manner and his conversation.   He grew less abrupt in the one,

and more calm, perhaps more cheerful, in the other. It was
evident that he was not insensible to the elevated pleasure of
providing for himself by praiseworthy exertion—of feeling for
the first time that his intellect was of use to him *creditably*. A
new world, though still dim—seen through mist and fog—began
to dawn upon him.

Such is the vanity of us poor mortals, that my interest in
Vivian was probably increased, and my aversion to much in him
materially softened, by observing that I gained a sort of ascendency over his savage nature. When we had first met by the
roadside, and afterwards conversed in the churchyard, the
ascendency was certainly not on my side. But I now came
from a larger sphere of society than that in which he had yet
moved. I had seen and listened to the first men in England.
What had then dazzled me only, now moved my pity. On the
other hand, his active mind could not but observe the change
in me; and, whether from envy or a better feeling, he was
willing to learn from me how to eclipse me, and resume his
earlier superiority—not to be superior chafed him. Thus he
listened to me with docility when I pointed out the books
which connected themselves with the various subjects inci-
dental to the miscellaneous matters on which he was employed.
Though he had less of the literary turn of mind than any one
equally clever I had ever met, and had read little, considering
the quantity of thought he had acquired, and the show he
made of the few works with which he had voluntarily made
himself familiar, he yet resolutely sate himself down to study;
and though it was clearly against the grain, I augured the more
favourably from tokens of a determination to do what was at
the present irksome for a purpose in the future. Yet, whether
I should have approved the purpose had I thoroughly understood it is another question! There were abysses both in his
past life and in his character, which I could not penetrate.
There was in him both a reckless frankness and a vigilant
reserve: his frankness was apparent in his talk on all matters
immediately before us; in the utter absence of all effort to
make himself seem better than he was. His reserve was
equally shown in the ingenious evasion of every species of
confidence that could admit me into such secrets of his life as
he chose to conceal: where he had been born, reared, and
educated; how he came to be thrown on his own resources;
how he had contrived, how he had subsisted, were all matters
on which he had seemed to take an oath to Harpocrates, the

god of silence. And yet he was full of anecdotes of what he had seen, of strange companions whom he never named, but with whom he had been thrown. And, to do him justice, I remarked that, though his precocious experience seemed to have been gathered from the holes and corners, the sewers and drains of life, and though he seemed wholly without dislike to dishonesty, and to regard virtue or vice with as serene an indifference as some grand poet who views them both merely as ministrants to his art, yet he never betrayed any positive breach of honesty in himself. He could laugh over the story of some ingenious fraud that he had witnessed, and seemed insensible to its turpitude; but he spoke of it in the tone of an approving witness, not of an actual accomplice. As we grew more intimate, he felt gradually, however, that *pudor*, or instinctive shame, which the contact with minds habituated to the distinctions between wrong and right unconsciously produces, and such stories ceased. He never but once mentioned his family, and that was in the following odd and abrupt manner:

"Ah!" cried he one day, stopping suddenly before a printshop, "how that reminds me of my dear, dear mother!"

"Which?" said I eagerly, puzzled between an engraving of Raffaelle's "Madonna," and another of "The Brigand's Wife."

Vivian did not satisfy my curiosity, but drew me on in spite of my reluctance.

"You loved your mother, then?" said I, after a pause.

"Yes, as a whelp may a tigress."

"That's a strange comparison."

"Or a bull-dog may the prize-fighter, his master! Do you like that better?"

"Not much; is it a comparison your mother would like?"

"Like?—she is dead!" said he, rather falteringly.

I pressed his arm closer to mine.

"I understand you," said he, with his cynic repellent smile. "But you do wrong to feel for my loss. I feel for it; but no one who cares for me should sympathise with my grief."

"Why?"

"Because my mother was not what the world would call a good woman. I did not love her the less for that. And now let us change the subject."

"Nay; since you have said so much, Vivian, let me coax you to say on. Is not your father living?"

"Is not the Monument standing?"

"I suppose so; what of that?"

"Why, it matters very little to either of us; and my question answers yours."

I could not get on after this, and I never did get on a step farther. I must own that if Vivian did not impart his confidence liberally, neither did he seek confidence inquisitively from me. He listened with interest if I spoke of Trevanion (for I told him frankly of my connection with that personage, though you may be sure that I said nothing of Fanny), and of the brilliant world that my residence with one so distinguished opened to me. But if ever, in the fulness of my heart, I began to speak of my parents, of my home, he evinced either so impertinent an *ennui*, or assumed so chilling a sneer, that I usually hurried away from him, as well as the subject, in indignant disgust. Once especially, when I asked him to let me introduce him to my father—a point on which I was really anxious, for I thought it impossible but that the devil within him would be softened by that contact—he said, with his low, scornful laugh—

"My dear Caxton, when I was a child, I was so bored with 'Telemachus,' that, in order to endure it, I turned it into travesty."

"Well?"

"Are you not afraid that the same wicked disposition might make a caricature of your Ulysses?"

I did not see Mr. Vivian for three days after that speech; and I should not have seen him then, only we met, by accident, under the Colonnade of the Opera House. Vivian was leaning against one of the columns, and watching the long procession which swept to the only temple in vogue that Art has retained in the English Babel. Coaches and chariots, blazoned with arms and coronets—cabriolets (the brougham had not then replaced them) of sober hue, but exquisite appointment, with gigantic horses and pigmy "tigers," dashed on, and rolled off before him. Fair women and gay dresses, stars and ribbons—the rank and the beauty of the patrician world—passed him by. And I could not resist the compassion with which this lonely, friendless, eager, discontented spirit inspired me—gazing on that gorgeous existence in which it fancied itself formed to shine, with the ardour of desire and the despair of exclusion. By one glimpse of that dark countenance, I read what was passing within the yet darker heart. The emotion might not be amiable, nor the thoughts wise, yet, were they unnatural? I had experienced

N

something of them—not at the sight of gay-dressed people, of wealth and idleness, pleasure and fashion; but when, at the doors of Parliament, men who have won noble names, and whose word had weight on the destinies of glorious England, brushed heedlessly by to their grand arena; or when, amidst the holiday crowd of ignoble pomp, I had heard the murmur of fame buzz and gather round some lordly labourer in art or letters: that contrast between glory so near, and yet so far, and one's own obscurity, of course I had felt it—who has not? Alas! many a youth not fated to be a Themistocles, will yet feel that the trophies of a Miltiades will not suffer him to sleep! So I went up to Vivian and laid my hand on his shoulder.

"Ah!" said he, more gently than usual, "I am glad to see you, and to apologise—I offended you the other day. But you would not get very gracious answers from souls in purgatory if you talked to them of the happiness of heaven. Never speak to me about homes and fathers! Enough! I see you forgive me. Why are you not going to the opera? *You* can?"

"And you too, if you so please. A ticket is shamefully dear, to be sure; still, if you are fond of music, it is a luxury you can afford."

"Oh, you flatter me if you fancy the prudence of saving withholds me! I did go the other night, but I shall not go again. Music!—when you go to the opera, is it for the music?"

"Only partially, I own: the lights, the scene, the pageant, attract me quite as much. But I do not think the opera a very profitable pleasure for either of us. For rich, idle people, I dare say, it may be as innocent an amusement as any other, but I find it a sad enervator."

"And I just the reverse—a horrible stimulant! Caxton, do you know that, ungracious as it will sound to you, I am growing impatient of this 'honourable independence!' What does it lead to?—board, clothes, and lodging,—can it ever bring me anything more?"

"At first, Vivian, you limited your aspirations to kid gloves and a cabriolet: it has brought the kid gloves already; by-and-by it will bring the cabriolet!"

"Our wishes grow by what they feed on. You live in the great world—you can have excitement if you please it—I want excitement, I want the world, I want room for my mind, man! Do you understand me?"

"Perfectly—and sympathise with you, my poor Vivian; but it will all come. Patience, as I preached to you while dawn rose so comfortless over the streets of London. You are not losing time; fill your mind; read, study, fit yourself for ambition. Why wish to fly till you have got your wings? Live in books now: after all, they are splendid palaces, and open to us all, rich and poor."

"Books, books!—ah! you are the son of a bookman. It is not by books that men get on in the world, and enjoy life in the meanwhile."

"I don't know that; but, my good fellow, you want to do both—get on in the world as fast as labour can, and enjoy life as pleasantly as indolence may. You want to live like the butterfly, and yet have all the honey of the bee; and, what is the very deuce of the whole, even as the butterfly, you ask every flower to grow up in a moment; and, as a bee, the whole hive must be stored in a quarter of an hour! Patience, patience, patience."

Vivian sighed a fierce sigh. "I suppose," said he, after an unquiet pause, "that the vagrant and the outlaw are strong in me, for I long to run back to my old existence, which was all action, and therefore allowed no thought."

While he thus said, we had wandered round the Colonnade, and were in that narrow passage in which is situated the more private entrance to the opera; close by the doors of that entrance, two or three young men were lounging. As Vivian ceased, the voice of one of these loungers came laughingly to our ears.

"Oh!" it said, apparently in answer to some question, "I have a much quicker way to fortune than that: I mean to marry an heiress!"

Vivian started, and looked at the speaker. He was a very good-looking fellow. Vivian continued to look at him, and deliberately, from head to foot; he then turned away with a satisfied and thoughtful smile.

"Certainly," said I gravely (construing the smile), "you are right there; you are even better-looking than that heiress-hunter!"

Vivian coloured; but before he could answer, one of the loungers, as the group recovered from the gay laugh which their companion's easy coxcombry had excited, said—

"Then, by the way, if you want an heiress, here comes one of the greatest in England; but instead of being a younger son, with three good lives between you and an Irish peerage, one ought to be an earl at least to aspire to Fanny Trevanion!"

The name thrilled through me—I felt myself tremble; and, looking up, I saw Lady Ellinor and Miss Trevanion, as they hurried from their carriage towards the entrance of the opera. They both recognised me—and Fanny cried—

"You here! How fortunate! You must see us into the box, even if you run away the moment after."

"But I am not dressed for the opera," said I, embarrassed.

"And why not?" asked Miss Trevanion; then, dropping her voice, she added, "Why do you desert us so wilfully?"—and, leaning her hand on my arm, I was drawn irresistibly into the lobby. The young loungers at the door made way for us, and eyed me, no doubt, with envy.

"Nay!" said I, affecting to laugh, as I saw Miss Trevanion waited for my reply. "You forget how little time I have for such amusements now—and my uncle——"

"Oh, but mamma and I have been to see your uncle to-day, and he is nearly well—is he not, mamma? I cannot tell you how I like and admire him. He is just what I fancy a Douglas of the old day. But mamma is impatient. Well, you must dine with us to-morrow—promise!—not *adieu* but *au revoir*," and Fanny glided to her mother's arm. Lady Ellinor, always kind and courteous to me, had good-naturedly lingered till this dialogue, or rather monologue, was over.

On returning to the passage, I found Vivian walking to and fro; he had lighted his cigar, and was smoking energetically.

"So this great heiress," said he, smiling, "who, as far as I could see—under her hood—seems no less fair than rich, is the daughter, I presume, of the Mr. Trevanion whose effusions you so kindly submit to me. He is very rich, then! You never said so, yet I ought to have known it: but you see I know nothing of your *beau monde*—not even that Miss Trevanion is one of the greatest heiresses in England."

"Yes, Mr. Trevanion is rich," said I, repressing a sigh,— "very rich."

"And you are his secretary! My dear friend, you may well offer me patience, for a large stock of yours will, I hope, be superfluous to you."

"I don't understand you."

"Yet you heard that young gentleman, as well as myself: and you are in the same house as the heiress."

"Vivian!"

"Well, what have I said so monstrous?"

"Pooh! since you refer to that young gentleman, you heard,

too, what his companion told him,—'one ought to be an earl, at least, to aspire to Fanny Trevanion!'"

"Tut! as well say that one ought to be a millionaire to aspire to a million!—yet I believe those who make millions generally begin with pence."

"That belief should be a comfort and encouragement to you, Vivian. And now, good night,—I have much to do."

"Good night, then," said Vivian, and we parted.

I made my way to Mr. Trevanion's house, and to the study. There was a formidable arrear of business waiting for me, and I sat down to it at first resolutely; but by degrees I found my thoughts wandering from the eternal blue-books, and the pen slipped from my hand, in the midst of an extract from a Report on Sierra Leone. My pulse beat loud and quick; I was in that state of nervous fever which only emotion can occasion. The sweet voice of Fanny rang in my ears; her eyes, as I had last met them, unusually gentle—almost beseeching—gazed upon me wherever I turned: and then, as in mockery, I heard again those words,—"One ought to be an earl, at least, to aspire to" —Oh! did I aspire? Was I vain fool so frantic?—household traitor so consummate? No, no! Then what did I under the same roof?—why stay to imbibe this sweet poison, that was corroding the very springs of my life? At that self-question, which, had I been but a year or two older, I should have asked long before, a mortal terror seized me; the blood rushed from my heart, and left me cold—icy cold. To leave the house— leave Fanny!—never again to see those eyes—never to hear that voice! better die of the sweet poison than of the desolate exile! I rose—I opened the windows—I walked to and fro the room; I could decide nothing—think of nothing; all my mind was in an uproar. With a violent effort at self-mastery, I approached the table again. I resolved to force myself to my task, if it were only to re-collect my faculties, and enable them to bear my own torture. I turned over the books impatiently, when, lo! buried amongst them, what met my eye?—archly, yet reproachfully—the face of Fanny herself! Her miniature was there. It had been, I knew, taken a few days before by a young artist whom Trevanion patronised. I suppose he had carried it into his study to examine it and so left it there care-lessly. The painter had seized her peculiar expression, her ineffable smile—so charming, so malicious; even her favourite posture—the small head turned over the rounded Hebe-like shoulder—the eye glancing up from under the hair. I know not what change in my madness came over me; but I sank on my knees, and, kissing the miniature again and again, burst into tears. Such tears! I did not hear the door open—I did not see the shadow steal over the floor; a light hand rested on my shoulder, trembling as it rested—I started. Fanny herself was bending over me!

"What is the matter?" she asked tenderly. "What has happened?—your uncle—your family—all well? Why are you weeping?"

I could not answer; but I kept my hands clasped over the miniature, that she might not see what they contained.

"Will you not answer? Am I not your friend?—almost your sister? Come, shall I call mamma?"

"Yes—yes; go—go."

"No, I will not go yet. What have you there?—what are you hiding?"

And innocently, and sister-like, those hands took mine; and so—and so—the picture became visible! There was a dead silence. I looked up through my tears. Fanny had recoiled some steps, and her cheek was very flushed, her eyes downcast. I felt as if I had committed a crime—as if dishonour clung to me; and yet I repressed—yes, thank Heaven! I repressed the cry that swelled from my heart, and rushed to my lips—"Pity me, for I love you!" I repressed it, and only a groan escaped me—the wail of my lost happiness! Then, rising, I laid the miniature on the table, and said, in a voice, that I believe was firm—

"Miss Trevanion, you *have* been as kind as a sister to me, and therefore I was bidding a brother's farewell to your likeness; it *is* so like you—this!"

"Farewell!" echoed Fanny, still not looking up.

"Farewell—*sister!* There, I have boldly said the word; for —for"—I hurried to the door, and, there turning, added, with what I meant to be a smile—"for they say at home that I—I am not well; too much for me this; you know, mothers will be foolish; and—and—I am to speak to your father to-morrow: and —good night—God bless you, Miss Trevanion!"

*Fanny herself was bending
over me!*

PART IX

CHAPTER I

AND my father pushed aside his books.

O young reader, whoever thou art,—or reader, at least, who hast been young,—canst thou not remember some time when, with thy wild troubles and sorrows as yet borne in secret, thou hast come back from that hard, stern world which opens on thee when thou puttest thy foot out of the threshold of home—come back to the four quiet walls, wherein thine elders sit in peace—and seen, with a sort of sad amaze, how calm and undisturbed all is there? That generation which has gone before thee in the path of the passions—the generation of thy parents (not so many years, perchance, remote from thine own)—how immovably far off, in its still repose, it seems from thy turbulent youth! It has in it a stillness as of a classic age, antique as the statues of the Greeks. That tranquil monotony of routine into which those lives that preceded thee have merged—the occupations that they have found sufficing for their happiness, by the fireside—in the arm-chair and corner appropriated to each—how strangely they contrast thine own feverish excitement! And they make room for thee, and bid thee welcome, and then resettle to their hushed pursuits, as if nothing had happened! Nothing had happened! while in thy heart, perhaps, the whole world seems to have shot from its axis, all the elements to be at war! And you sit down, crushed by that quiet happiness which you can share no more, and smile mechanically and look into the fire ; and, ten to one, you say nothing till the time comes for bed, and you take up your candle, and creep miserably to your lonely room.

Now, if in a stage-coach in the depth of winter, when three passengers are warm and snug, a fourth, all besnowed and frozen, descends from the outside and takes place amongst them, straightway all the three passengers shift their places, uneasily pull up their cloak collars, re-arrange their "com-

forters," feel indignantly a sensible loss of caloric—the intruder
has at least made a sensation.   But if you had all the snows
of the Grampians in your heart, you might enter unnoticed ;
take care not to tread on the toes of your opposite neighbour,
and not a soul is disturbed, not a "comforter" stirs an inch!
I had not slept a wink, I had not even laid down all that night
—the night in which I had said farewell to Fanny Trevanion—
and the next morning, when the sun rose, I wandered out—
where I know not: I have a dim recollection of long, grey,
solitary streets—of the river that seemed flowing in dull, sullen
silence, away, far away, into some invisible eternity—trees and
turf, and the gay voices of children.   I must have gone from
one end of the great Babel to the other: but my memory only
became clear and distinct when I knocked, somewhere before
noon, at the door of my father's house, and, passing heavily
up the stairs, came into the drawing-room, which was the
rendezvous of the little family; for, since we had been in
London, my father had ceased to have his study apart, and
contented himself with what he called "a corner"—a corner
wide enough to contain two tables and a dumb waiter, with
chairs *à discrétion* all littered with books.   On the opposite
side of this capacious corner sat my uncle, now nearly con-
valescent, and he was jotting down, in his stiff, military hand,
certain figures in a little red account book — for you know
already that my Uncle Roland was, in his expenses, the most
methodical of men.

My father's face was more benign than usual, for before him
lay a proof—the first proof of his first work—his one work—
the Great Book !   Yes ! it had positively found a press.   And
the first proof of your first work—ask any author what *that* is !
My mother was out, with the faithful Mrs. Primmins, shopping
or marketing, no doubt; so, while the brothers were thus
engaged, it was natural that my entrance should not make as
much noise as if it had been a bomb, or a singer, or a clap of
thunder, or the last "great novel of the season," or anything
else that made a noise in those days.   For what makes a noise
now ?   Now, when the most astonishing thing of all is our easy
familiarity with things astounding—when we say, listlessly,
"Another revolution at Paris," or, "By-the-bye, there is the
deuce to do at Vienna !"—when De Joinville is catching fish
in the ponds at Claremont, and you hardly turn back to look
at Metternich on the pier at Brighton !

My uncle nodded and growled indistinctly ; my father—

" Put aside his books ; you have told us that already."

Sir, you are very much mistaken ; it was not then that he put aside his books, for he was not then engaged in them— he was reading his proof. And he smiled, and pointed to it (the proof I mean) pathetically, and with a kind of humour, as much as to say—"What can you expect, Pisistratus ?—my new baby in short clothes—or long primer, which is all the same thing !"

I took a chair between the two, and looked first at one, then at the other—Heaven forgive me !—I felt a rebellious, ungrate- ful spite against both. The bitterness of my soul must have been deep indeed, to have overflowed in that direction, but it did. The grief of youth is an abominable egotist, and that is the truth. I got up from the chair, and walked towards the window ; it was open, and outside the window was Mrs. Primmins' canary, in its cage. London air had agreed with it, and it was singing lustily. Now, when the canary saw me standing opposite to its cage, and regarding it seriously, and I have no doubt, with a very sombre aspect, the creature stopped short, and hung its head on one side, looking at me obliquely and suspiciously. Finding that I did it no harm, it began to hazard a few broken notes, timidly and interrogatively, as it were, pausing between each ; and at length, as I made no reply, it evidently thought it had solved the doubt, and ascer- tained that I was more to be pitied than feared—for it stole gradually into so soft and silvery a strain that, I verily believe, it did it on purpose to comfort me !—me, its old friend, whom it had unjustly suspected. Never did any music touch me so home as did that long, plaintive cadence. And when the bird ceased, it perched itself close to the bars of the cage, and looked at me steadily with its bright intelligent eyes. I felt mine water, and I turned back and stood in the centre of the room, irresolute what to do, where to go. My father had done with the proof, and was deep in his folios. Roland had clasped his red account-book, restored it to his pocket, wiped his pen carefully, and now watched me from under his great beetle- brows. Suddenly he rose, and stamping on the hearth with his cork-leg, exclaimed, " Look up from those cursed books, brother Austin ! What is there in your son's face ? Construe *that*, if you can ! "

CHAPTER II

AND my father pushed aside his books, and rose hastily. He took off his spectacles, and rubbed them mechanically, but he said nothing, and my uncle, staring at him for a moment, in surprise at his silence, burst out—

"Oh! I see; he has been getting into some scrape, and you are angry. Fie! young blood will have its way, Austin, it will. I don't blame that—it is only when—come here, Sisty. Zounds! man, come here."

My father gently brushed off the Captain's hand, and advancing towards me, opened his arms. The next moment I was sobbing on his breast.

"But what is the matter?" cried Captain Roland—"will no-body say what is the matter? Money, I suppose—money, you confounded extravagant young dog. Luckily you have got an uncle who has more than he knows what to do with. How much? Fifty?—a hundred?—two hundred? How can I write the cheque, if you'll not speak."

"Hush, brother! it is no money you can give that will set this right. My poor boy! Have I guessed truly? Did I guess truly? the other evening, when——"

"Yes, sir, yes! I have been so wretched. But I am better now—I can tell you all."

My uncle moved slowly towards the door; his fine sense of delicacy made him think that even he was out of place in the confidence between son and father.

"No, uncle," I said, holding out my hand to him, "stay; you too can advise me—strengthen me. I have kept my honour yet—help me to keep it still."

At the sound of the word honour, Captain Roland stood mute, and raised his head quickly.

So I told all—incoherently enough at first, but clearly and manfully as I went on. Now I know that it is not the custom of lovers to confide in fathers and uncles. Judging by those mirrors of life, plays and novels, they choose better; valets and chambermaids, and friends whom they have picked up in the street, as I had picked up poor Francis Vivian—to these they make clean breasts of their troubles. But fathers and uncles—to them they are close, impregnable, "buttoned to the chin." The Caxtons were an eccentric family, and never did anything like other people. When I had ended, I lifted up my eyes, and said pleadingly, " Now tell me, is there no hope—none ? "

" Why should there be none ? " cried Captain Roland hastily —" The De Caxtons are as good a family as the Trevanions ; and as for yourself, all I will say is, that the young lady might choose worse for her own happiness."

I wrung my uncle's hand, and turned to my father in anxious fear, for I knew that, in spite of his secluded habits, few men ever formed a sounder judgment on worldly matters, when he was fairly drawn to look at them. A thing wonderful is that plain wisdom which scholars and poets often have for others, though they rarely deign to use it for themselves. And how on earth do they get at it ? I looked at my father, and the vague hope Roland had excited fell as I looked.

" Brother," said he slowly, and shaking his head, " the world, which gives codes and laws to those who live in it, does not care much for a pedigree, unless it goes with a title-deed to estates."

" Trevanion was not richer than Pisistratus when he married Lady Ellinor," said my uncle.

" True ; but Lady Ellinor was not then an heiress ; and her father viewed these matters as no other peer in England per- haps would. As for Trevanion himself, I dare say he has no prejudices about station, but he is strong in common sense. He values himself on being a practical man. It would be folly to talk to him of love, and the affections of youth. He would see in the son of Austin Caxton, living on the interest of some fifteen or sixteen thousand pounds, such a match for his daughter as no prudent man in his position could approve. And as for Lady Ellinor——"

" She owes us much, Austin ! " exclaimed Roland, his face darkening.

" Lady Ellinor is now what, if we had known her better, she promised always to be—the ambitious, brilliant, scheming woman of the world. Is it not so,—Pisistratus ? "

I said nothing—I felt too much.

" And does the girl like you ?—but I think it is clear she does ! " exclaimed Roland. " Fate, fate ; it has been a fatal family to us ! Zounds ! Austin, it was your fault. Why did you let him go there ? "

" My son is now a man—at least in heart, if not in years— can man be shut from danger and trial ? They found me in the old parsonage, brother ! " said my father mildly.

My uncle walked, or rather stumped, three times up and down the room; and he then stopped short, folded his arms, and came to a decision—

"If the girl likes you, your duty is doubly clear—you can't take advantage of it. You have done right to leave the house, for the temptation might be too strong."

"But what excuse shall I make to Mr. Trevanion?" said I feebly—"what story can I invent? So careless as he is while he trusts, so penetrating if he once suspects, he will see through all my subterfuges, and—and——"

"It is as plain as a pikestaff," said my uncle abruptly—"and there need be no subterfuge in the matter. 'I must leave you, Mr. Trevanion.' 'Why?' says he. 'Don't ask me.' He insists. 'Well then, sir, if you must know, I love your daughter. I have nothing, she is a great heiress. You will not approve of that love, and therefore I leave you!' That is the course that becomes an English gentleman. Eh, Austin?"

"You are never wrong when your instincts speak, Roland," said my father. "Can you say this, Pisistratus, or shall I say it for you?"

"Let him say it himself," said Roland; "and let him judge himself of the answer. He is young, he is clever, he may make a figure in the world. Trevanion *may* answer, 'Win the lady after you have won the laurel, like the knights of old.' At all events you will hear the worst."

"I will go," said I firmly; and I took my hat and left the room. As I was passing the landing-place, a light step stole down the upper flight of stairs, and a little hand seized my own. I turned quickly, and met the full, dark, seriously sweet eyes of my cousin Blanche.

"Don't go away yet, Sisty," said she coaxingly. "I have been waiting for you, for I heard your voice, and did not like to come in and disturb you."

"And why did you wait for me, my little Blanche?"

"Why! only to see you. But your eyes are red. O cousin!"—and before I was aware of her childish impulse, she had sprung to my neck and kissed me. Now Blanche was not like most children, and was very sparing of her caresses. So it was out of the deeps of a kind heart that that kiss came. I returned it without a word; and putting her down gently, descended the stairs, and was in the streets. But I had not got far before I heard my father's voice; and he came up, and hooking his arm into mine, said, "Are there not two of us that

suffer ?—let us be together !" I pressed his arm, and we walked
on in silence. But when we were near Trevanion's house, I
said hesitatingly, "Would it not be better, sir, that I went in
alone ? If there is to be an explanation between Mr. Trevanion
and myself, would it not seem as if your presence implied either
a request to him that would lower us both, or a doubt of me
that——"

"You will go in alone, of course : I will wait for you——"

"Not in the streets—oh, no ! father," cried I, touched inexpressibly. For all this was so unlike my father's habits, that I
felt remorse to have so communicated my young griefs to the
calm dignity of his serene life.

"My son, you do not know how I love you. I have only
known it myself lately. Look you, I am living in you, now, my
first-born ; not in my other son—the Great Book : I must have
my way. Go in ; that is the door, is it not ? "

I pressed my father's hand, and I felt then, that while that
hand could reply to mine, even the loss of Fanny Trevanion
could not leave the world a blank. How much we have before
us in life, while we retain our parents ! How much to strive
and to hope for ! what a motive in the conquest of our sorrow—
that they may not sorrow with us !

CHAPTER III

I ENTERED Trevanion's study. It was an hour in which he
was rarely at home, but I had not thought of that ; and I
saw without surprise that, contrary to his custom, he was in
his arm-chair, reading one of his favourite classic authors,
instead of being in some committee-room of the House of
Commons.

"A pretty fellow you are," said he, looking up, " to leave me
all the morning, without rhyme or reason ! And my committee
is postponed—chairman ill ; people who get ill should not go
into the House of Commons. So here I am looking into
Propertius : Parr is right; not so elegant a writer as Tibullus.
But what the deuce are you about ?—why don't you sit down ?
Humph ! you look grave—you have something to say,—say it ! "

And, putting down Propertius, the acute, sharp face of
Trevanion instantly became earnest and attentive.

"My dear Mr. Trevanion," said I, with as much steadiness as

I could assume, "you have been most kind to me; and out of my own family there is no man I love and respect more."

TREVANION.—"Humph! What's all this? (In an undertone) —Am I going to be taken in?"

PISISTRATUS.—"Do not think me ungrateful, then, when I say I come to resign my office—to leave the house where I have been so happy."

TREVANION.—"Leave the house! Pooh! I have overtasked you. I will be more merciful in future. You must forgive a political economist; it is the fault of my sect to look upon men as machines."

PISISTRATUS (smiling faintly).—"No, indeed; that is not it! I have nothing to complain of; nothing I could wish altered—could I stay."

TREVANION (examining me thoughtfully).—"And does your father approve of your leaving me thus?"

PISISTRATUS.—"Yes—fully."

TREVANION (musing a moment).—"I see, he would send you to the University, make you a book-worm like himself: pooh! that will not do—you will never become wholly a man of books —it is not in you. Young man, though I may seem careless, I read characters, when I please it, pretty quickly. You do wrong to leave me; you are made for the great world—I can open to you a high career. I wish to do so! Lady Ellinor wishes it— nay, insists on it—for your father's sake as well as yours. I never ask a favour from ministers, and I never will. But (here Trevanion rose suddenly, and, with an erect mien and a quick gesture of his arm, he added)—but a minister can dispose as he pleases of his patronage. Look you, it is a secret yet, and I trust to your honour. But, before the year is out, I must be in the cabinet. Stay with me, I guarantee your fortunes— three months ago I would not have said that. By-and-by I will open Parliament for you—you are not of age yet—work till then. And now sit down and write my letters—a sad arrear!"

"My dear, dear Mr. Trevanion!" said I, so affected that I could scarcely speak, and seizing his hand, which I pressed between both mine—"I dare not thank you—I cannot! But you don't know my heart—It is not ambition. No! if I could but stay here on the same terms for ever—*here*"—looking ruefully on that spot where Fanny had stood the night before. "But it is impossible!—If you knew all, you would be the first to bid me go!"

"You are in debt," said the man of the world coldly. "Bad, very bad—still——"

"No, sir; no! worse."

"Hardly possible to be worse, young man—hardly! But, just as you will; you leave me, and will not say why. Good-bye. Why do you linger? Shake hands, and go!"

"I cannot leave you thus: I—I—sir, the truth shall out. I am rash and mad enough not to see Miss Trevanion without forgetting that I am poor, and——"

"Ha!" interrupted Trevanion softly, and growing pale, "this is a misfortune, indeed! And I, who talked of reading characters! Truly, truly, we would-be practical men are fools—fools! And you have made love to my daughter!"

"Sir? Mr. Trevanion!—no—never, never so base! In your house, trusted by you,—how could you think it? I dared, it may be, to love—at all events, to feel that I could not be insensible to a temptation too strong for me. But to say it to your heiress—to ask love in return—I would as soon have broken open your desk! Frankly I tell you my folly: it is a folly, not a disgrace."

Trevanion came up to me abruptly, as I leant against the bookcase, and, grasping my hand with a cordial kindness, said, "Pardon me! You have behaved as your father's son should— I envy him such a son! Now, listen to me—I cannot give you my daughter——"

"Believe me, sir, I never——"

"Tut, listen! I cannot give you my daughter. I say nothing of inequality—all gentlemen are equal; and if not, any impertinent affectation of superiority, in such a case, would come ill from one who owes his own fortune to his wife! But, as it is, I have a stake in the world, won not by fortune only, but the labour of a life, the suppression of half my nature—the drudging, squaring, taming down all that made the glory and joy of my youth—to be that hard matter-of-fact thing which the English world expect in a *statesman!* This station has gradually opened into its natural result—power! I tell you I shall soon have high office in the administration: I hope to render great services to England—for we English politicians, whatever the mob and the press say of us, are not selfish place-hunters. I refused office, as high as I look for now, ten years ago. We believe in our opinions, and we hail the power that may carry them into effect. In this cabinet I shall have enemies. Oh, don't think we leave jealousy behind us, at the doors of Downing Street!

I shall be one of a minority. I know well what must happen : like all men in power, I must strengthen myself by other heads and hands than my own. My daughter shall bring to me the alliance of that house in England which is most necessary to me. My life falls to the ground, like a child's pyramid of cards, if I waste—I do not say on you, but on men of ten times your fortune (whatever that be), the means of strength which are at my disposal in the hand of Fanny Trevanion. To this end I have looked; but to this end her mother has schemed—for these household matters are within a man's hopes, but belong to a woman's policy. So much for us. But to you, my dear, and frank, and high-souled young friend—to you, if I were not Fanny's father—if I were your nearest relation, and Fanny could be had for the asking, with all her princely dowry (for it is princely),—to you I should say, fly from a load upon the heart, on the genius, the energy, the pride, and the spirit, which not one man in ten thousand can bear; fly from the curse of owing everything to a wife !—it is a reversal of all natural position, it is a blow to all the manhood within us. You know not what it is ; I do ! My wife's fortune came not till after marriage—so far, so well ; it saved my reputation from the charge of fortune-hunting. But, I tell you fairly, that if it never came at all, I should be a prouder, and a greater, and a happier man than I have ever been, or ever can be, with all its advantages ; it has been a mill-stone round my neck. And yet Ellinor has never breathed a word that could wound my pride. Would her daughter be as forbearing ? Much as I love Fanny, I doubt if she has the great heart of her mother. You look incredulous ;—naturally. Oh, you think I shall sacrifice my child's happiness to a politician's ambition. Folly of youth ! Fanny would be wretched with you. She might not think so now ; she would five years hence ! Fanny will make an admirable duchess, countess, great lady ; but wife to a man who owes all to her !—no, no, don't dream it ! I shall not sacrifice her happiness, depend on it. I speak plainly, as man to man—man of the world to a man just entering it—but still man to man ! What say you ?"

"I will think over all you tell me. I know that you are speaking to me most generously—as a father would. Now let me go, and may God keep you and yours !"

"Go—I return your blessing—go ! I don't insult you now with offers of service; but, remember, you have a right to command them—in all ways, in all times. Stop !—take this comfort away with you—a sorry comfort now, a great one hereafter. In a position that might have moved anger, scorn, pity, you have made a barren-hearted man honour and admire you. You, a boy, have made me, with my grey hairs, think better of the whole world; tell your father that."

I closed the door, and stole out softly—softly. But when I got into the hall, Fanny suddenly opened the door of the breakfast parlour, and seemed, by her look, her gesture, to invite me in. Her face was very pale, and there were traces of tears on the heavy lids.

I stood still a moment, and my heart beat violently. I then muttered something inarticulately, and, bowing low, hastened to the door.

I thought, but my ears might deceive me, that I heard my name pronounced; but fortunately the tall porter started from his newspaper and his leathern chair, and the entrance stood open. I joined my father.

"It is all over," said I, with a resolute smile. "And now, my dear father, I feel how grateful I should be for all that your lessons—your life—have taught me; for, believe me, I am not unhappy."

CHAPTER IV

WE came back to my father's house, and on the stairs we met my mother, whom Roland's grave looks, and her Austin's strange absence, had alarmed. My father quietly led the way to a little room, which my mother had appropriated to Blanche and herself: and then, placing my hand in that which had helped his own steps from the stony path down the quiet vales of life, he said to me,—"Nature gives you here the soother;" and so saying, he left the room.

And it was true, O my mother! that in thy simple loving breast nature did place the deep wells of comfort! We come to men for philosophy—to women for consolation. And the thousand weaknesses and regrets—the sharp sands of the minutiæ that make up *sorrow*—all these, which I could have betrayed to no *man*—not even to him, the dearest and tenderest of all men—I showed without shame to thee! And thy tears, that fell on my cheek, had the balm of Araby; and my heart, at length, lay lulled and soothed under thy moist gentle eyes.

I made an effort, and joined the little circle at dinner; and I

o

felt grateful that no violent attempt was made to raise my spirits
—nothing but affection, more subdued, and soft, and tranquil.
Even little Blanche, as if by the intuition of sympathy, ceased
her babble, and seemed to hush her footstep as she crept to my
side. But after dinner, when we had reassembled in the drawing-
room, and the lights shone bright, and the curtains were let
down—and only the quick roll of some passing wheels reminded
us that there was a world without—my father began to talk.
He had laid aside all his work ; the younger but less perishable
child was forgotten,—and my father began to talk.

"It is," said he musingly, "a well-known thing, that particular drugs or herbs suit the body according to its particular
diseases. When we are ill, we don't open our medicine-chest
at random, and take out any powder or phial that comes to
hand. The skilful doctor is he who adjusts the dose to the
malady."

"Of that there can be no doubt," quoth Captain Roland.
"I remember a notable instance of the justice of what you say.
When I was in Spain, both my horse and I fell ill at the same
time ; a dose was sent for each ; and, by some infernal mistake,
I swallowed the horse's physic, and the horse, poor thing,
swallowed mine."

"And what was the result ?" asked my father.

"The horse died !" answered Roland mournfully—"a valuable
beast—bright bay, with a star !"

"And you ?"

"Why, the doctor said it ought to have killed me ; but it
took a great deal more than a paltry bottle of physic to kill a
man in my regiment."

"Nevertheless, we arrive at the same conclusion," pursued
my father,—"I with my theory, you with your experience,—
that the physic we take must not be chosen haphazard ; and
that a mistake in the bottle may kill a horse. But when we
come to the medicine for the mind, how little do we think of
the golden rule which common sense applies to the body !"

"Anan," said the Captain, "what medicine is there for the
mind ? Shakspeare has said something on that subject, which,
if I recollect right, implies that there is no ministering to a
mind diseased."

"I think not, brother ; he only said physic (meaning boluses
and black draughts) would not do it. And Shakspeare was the
last man to find fault with his own art ; for, verily, he has been
a great physician to the mind."

" Ah ! I take you now, brother,—books again ! So you think that, when a man breaks his heart, or loses his fortune, or his daughter—(Blanche, child, come here)—that you have only to clap a plaster of print on the sore place, and all is well. I wish you would find me such a cure."

"Will you try it ? "

" If it is not Greek," said my uncle.

CHAPTER V

MY FATHER'S CROTCHET ON THE HYGIENIC CHEMISTRY
OF BOOKS

IF," said my father—and here his hand was deep in his waist-coat—" if we accept the authority of Diodorus, as to the inscription on the great Egyptian library—and I don't see why Diodorus should not be as near the mark as any one else ? " added my father interrogatively, turning round.

My mother thought herself the person addressed, and nodded her gracious assent to the authority of Diodorus. His opinion thus fortified, my father continued,—" If, I say, we accept the authority of Diodorus, the inscription on the Egyptian library was—' The Medicine of the Mind.' Now, that phrase has become notoriously trite and hackneyed, and people repeat vaguely that books are the medicine of the mind. Yes ; but to apply the medicine is the thing ! "

"So you have told us at least twice before, brother," quoth the Captain bluffly. " And what Diodorus has to do with it, I know no more than the man of the moon."

" I shall never get on at this rate," said my father, in a tone between reproach and entreaty.

" Be good children, Roland and Blanche both," said my mother, stopping from her work, and holding up her needle threateningly—and indeed inflicting a slight puncture upon the Captain's shoulder.

" Rem *acu* tetigisti, my dear," said my father, borrowing Cicero's pun on the occasion.[1] " And now we shall go upon velvet. I say, then, that books, taken indiscriminately, are no cure to the diseases and afflictions of the mind. There is a

[1] Cicero's joke on a senator who was the son of a tailor—" Thou hast touched the thing sharply " (or with a needle—*acu*).

world of science necessary in the taking them. I have known some people in great sorrow fly to a novel, or the last light book in fashion. One might as well take a rose-draught for the plague! Light reading does not do when the heart is really heavy. I am told that Goethe, when he lost his son, took to study a science that was new to him. Ah! Goethe was a physician who knew what he was about. In a great grief like that, you cannot tickle and divert the mind; you must wrench it away, abstract, absorb—bury it in an abyss, hurry it into a labyrinth. Therefore, for the irremediable sorrows of middle life and old age, I recommend a strict chronic course of science and hard reasoning—Counter-irritation. Bring the brain to act upon the heart! If science is too much against the grain (for we have not all got mathematical heads), something in the reach of the humblest understanding, but sufficiently searching to the highest—a new language—Greek, Arabic, Scandinavian, Chinese, or Welsh! For the loss of fortune, the dose should be applied less directly to the understanding—I would administer something elegant and cordial. For as the heart is crushed and lacerated by a loss in the affections, so it is rather the head that aches and suffers by the loss of money. Here we find the higher class of poets a very valuable remedy. For observe that poets of the grander and more comprehensive kind of genius have in them two separate men, quite distinct from each other—the imaginative man, and the practical, circumstantial man; and it is the happy mixture of these that suits diseases of the mind, half imaginative and half practical. There is Homer, now lost with the gods, now at home with the homeliest, the very 'poet of circumstance,' as Gray has finely called him; and yet with imagination enough to seduce and coax the dullest into forgetting, for a while, that little spot on his desk which his banker's book can cover. There is Virgil, far below him, indeed—

> 'Virgil the wise,
> Whose verse walks highest, but not flies,'

as Cowley expresses it. But Virgil still has genius enough to be two men—to lead you into the fields, not only to listen to the pastoral reed, and to hear the bees hum, but to note how you can make the most of the glebe, and the vineyard. There is Horace, charming man of the world, who will condole with you feelingly on the loss of your fortune, and by no means undervalue the good things of this life; but who will yet show you that a man may be happy with a *vile modicum* or *parva rura*. There is Shakspeare, who, above all poets, is the mysterious dual of hard sense and empyreal fancy—and a great many more, whom I need not name; but who, if you take to them gently and quietly, will not, like your mere philosopher, your unreasonable stoic, tell you that you have lost nothing; but who will insensibly steal you out of this world, with its losses and crosses, and slip you into another world, before you know where you are!—a world where you are just as welcome, though you carry no more earth of your lost acres with you than covers the sole of your shoe. Then, for hypochondria and satiety, what is better than a brisk alterative course of travels—especially early, out-of-the-way, marvellous, legendary travels! How they freshen up the spirits! How they take you out of the humdrum yawning state you are in. See, with Herodotus, young Greece spring up into life; or note with him how already the wondrous old Orient world is crumbling into giant decay; or go with Carpini and Rubruquis to Tartary, meet 'the carts of Zagathai laden with houses, and think that a great city is travelling towards you.'[1] Gaze on that vast wild empire of the Tartar, where the descendants of Jenghis 'multiply and disperse over the immense waste desert, which is as boundless as the ocean.' Sail with the early northern discoverers, and penetrate to the heart of winter, among sea-serpents and bears, and tusked morses, with the faces of men. Then, what think you of Columbus, and the stern soul of Cortes, and the kingdom of Mexico, and the strange gold city of the Peruvians, with that audacious brute Pizarro? and the Polynesians, just for all the world like the ancient Britons? and the American Indians, and the South-sea Islanders? how petulant, and young, and adventurous, and frisky your hypochondriac must get upon a regimen like that! Then, for that vice of the mind which I call sectarianism—not in the religious sense of the word, but little, narrow prejudices, that make you hate your next-door neighbour, because he has his eggs roasted when you have yours boiled; and gossiping and prying into people's affairs, and backbiting, and thinking heaven and earth are coming together, if some broom touch a cobweb that you have let grow over the windowsill of your brains—what like a large and generous, mildly aperient (I beg your pardon, my dear) course of history! How it clears away all the fumes of the head!—better than the hellebore with which the old leeches of the middle ages purged

[1] Rubruquis, sect. xii.

the cerebellum.   There, amidst all that great whirl and *sturmbad* (storm-bath), as the Germans say, of kingdoms and empires, and races and ages, how your mind enlarges beyond that little feverish animosity to John Styles: or that unfortunate prepossession of yours, that all the world is interested in your grievances against Tom Stokes and his wife!

"I can only touch, you see, on a few ingredients in this magnificent pharmacy—its resources are boundless, but require the nicest discretion.   I remember to have cured a disconsolate widower, who obstinately refused every other medicament, by a strict course of geology.   I dipped him deep into gneiss and mica schist.   Amidst the first strata, I suffered the watery action to expend itself upon cooling crystallised masses; and, by the time I had got him into the tertiary period, amongst the transition chalks of Maestricht, and the conchiferous marls of Gosau, he was ready for a new wife.   Kitty, my dear! it is no laughing matter.   I made no less notable a cure of a young scholar at Cambridge, who was meant for the Church, when he suddenly caught a cold fit of free-thinking, with great shiverings, from wading out of his depth in Spinoza.   None of the divines, whom I first tried, did him the least good in that state; so I turned over a new leaf, and doctored him gently upon the chapters of faith in Abraham Tucker's book (you should read it, Sisty); then I threw in strong doses of Fichte; after that I put him on the Scotch metaphysicians, with plunge-baths into certain German transcendentalists; and having convinced him that faith is not an unphilosophical state of mind, and that he might believe without compromising his understanding—for he was mightily conceited on that score—I threw in my divines, which he was now fit to digest; and his theological constitution, since then, has become so robust, that he has eaten up two livings and a deanery!   In fact, I have a plan for a library that, instead of heading its compartments, 'Philology, Natural Science, Poetry,' &c., one shall head them according to the diseases for which they are severally good, bodily and mental—up from a dire calamity, or the pangs of the gout, down to a fit of the spleen or a slight catarrh; for which last your light reading comes in with a whey-posset and barley-water.   But," continued my father, more gravely, "when some one sorrow, that is yet reparable, gets hold of your mind like a monomania—. when you think, because heaven has denied you this or that, on which you had set your heart, that all your life must be a blank —oh! then diet yourself well on biography—the biography of good and great men. See how little a space one sorrow really makes in life. See scarce a page, perhaps, given to some grief similar to your own; and how triumphantly the life sails on beyond it! You thought the wing was broken!—Tut—tut—it was but a bruised feather! See what life leaves behind it when all is done!—a summary of positive facts far out of the region of sorrow and suffering, linking themselves with the being of the world. Yes, biography is the medicine here! Roland, you said you would try my prescription—here it is,"—and my father took up a book, and reached it to the Captain.

My uncle looked over it—"Life of the Reverend Robert Hall." "Brother, he was a Dissenter, and, thank Heaven! I am a Church and State man, to the backbone!"

"Robert Hall was a brave man, and a true soldier under the Great Commander," said my father artfully.

The Captain mechanically carried his forefinger to his forehead in military fashion, and saluted the book respectfully.

"I have another copy for you, Pisistratus—that is mine which I have lent Roland. This, which I bought for you to-day, you will keep."

"Thank you, sir," said I listlessly, not seeing what great good the "Life of Robert Hall" could do me, or why the same medicine should suit the old weather-beaten uncle, and the nephew yet in his teens.

"I have said nothing," resumed my father, slightly bowing his broad temples, "of the Book of Books, for that is the *lignum vitæ*, the cardinal medicine for all. These are but the subsidiaries: for, as you may remember, my dear Kitty, that I have said before —we can never keep the system quite right unless we place just in the centre of the great ganglionic system, whence the nerves carry its influence gently and smoothly through the whole frame—THE SAFFRON BAG!"

CHAPTER VI

AFTER breakfast the next morning, I took my hat to go out, when my father, looking at me, and seeing by my countenance that I had not slept, said gently—

"My dear Pisistratus, you have not tried my medicine yet."

"What medicine, sir?"

"Robert Hall."

"No, indeed, not yet," said I, smiling.

"Do so, my son, before you go out; depend on it you will enjoy your walk more."

I confess that it was with some reluctance I obeyed. I went back to my own room, and sate resolutely down to my task. Are there any of you, my readers, who have not read the "Life of Robert Hall"? If so, in the words of the great Captain Cuttle, "When found, make a note of it." Never mind what your theological opinion is—Episcopalian, Presbyterian, Baptist, Pædobaptist, Independent, Quaker, Unitarian, Philosopher, Free-thinker,—send for Robert Hall! Yea, if there exist yet on earth descendants of the arch-heresies, which made such a noise in their day—men who believe with Saturninus that the world was made by seven angels; or with Basilides, that there are as many heavens as there are days in the year; or with the Nicolaitanes, that men ought to have their wives in common (plenty of that sect still, especially in the Red Republic); or with their successors, the Gnostics, who believed in Jaldaboath; or with the Carpacratians, that the world was made by the devil; or with the Cerinthians, and Ebionites, and Nazarites (which last discovered that the name of Noah's wife was Ouria, and that she set the ark on fire); or with the Valentinians, who taught that there were thirty Æones, ages, or worlds, born out of Profundity (Bathos), male, and Silence, female; or with the Marcites, Colarbasii, and Heracleonites (who still kept up that bother about Æones, Mr. Profundity and Mrs. Silence); or with the Ophites, who are said to have worshipped the serpent; or the Cainites, who ingeniously found out a reason for honouring Judas, because he foresaw what good would come to men by betraying our Saviour; or with the Sethites, who made Seth a part of the divine substance; or with the Archonticks, Ascothyptæ, Cerdonians, Marcionites, the disciples of Apelles, and Severus (the last was a teetotaller, and said wine was begot by Satan!), or of Tatian, who thought all the descendants of Adam were irretrievably damned except themselves (some of those Tatiani are certainly extant!), or the Cataphrygians, who were also called Tascodragitæ, because they thrust their fore-fingers up their nostrils to show their devotion; or the Pepuzians, Quintilians, and Artotyrites; or—but no matter. If I go through all the follies of men in search of the truth, I shall never get to the end of my chapter, or back to Robert Hall: whatever, then, thou art, orthodox or heterodox, send for the "Life of Robert Hall." It is the life of a man that does good to manhood itself to contemplate.

I had finished the biography, which is not long, and was musing over it, when I heard the Captain's cork-leg upon the stairs. I opened the door for him, and he entered, book in hand, as I also, book in hand, stood ready to receive him.

"Well, sir," said Roland, seating himself, "has the prescription done you any good?"

"Yes, uncle—great."

"And me, too. By Jupiter, Sisty, that same Hall was a fine fellow! I wonder if the medicine has gone through the same channels in both? Tell me, first, how it has affected you."

"*Imprimis*, then, my dear uncle, I fancy that a book like this must do good to all who live in the world in the ordinary manner, by admitting us into a circle of life of which I suspect we think but little. Here is a man connecting himself directly with a heavenly purpose, and cultivating considerable faculties to that one end; seeking to accomplish his soul as far as he can, that he may do most good on earth, and take a higher existence up to heaven: a man intent upon a sublime and spiritual duty; in short, living as it were in it, and so filled with the consciousness of immortality, and so strong in the link between God and man, that, without any affected stoicism, without being insensible to pain—rather, perhaps, from a nervous temperament, acutely feeling it—he yet has a happiness wholly independent of it. It is impossible not to be thrilled with an admiration that elevates while it awes you, in reading that solemn 'Dedication of himself to God.' This offering of 'soul and body, time, health, reputation, talents,' to the divine and invisible Principle of Good, calls us suddenly to contemplate the selfishness of our own view and hopes, and awakens us from the egotism that exacts all and resigns nothing.

"But this book has mostly struck upon the chord in my own heart, in that characteristic which my father indicated as belonging to all biography. Here is a life of remarkable *fulness*, great study, great thought, and great action; and yet," said I, colouring, "how small a place those feelings, which have tyrannised over me, and made all else seem blank and void, hold in that life. It is not as if the man were a cold and hard ascetic; it is easy to see in him not only remarkable tenderness and warm affections, but strong self-will, and the passion of all vigorous natures. Yes; I understand better now what existence in a true man should be."

"All that is very well said," quoth the Captain, "but it did not strike me. What I have seen in this book is courage.

Here is a poor creature rolling on the carpet with agony; from childhood to death tortured by a mysterious incurable malady—a malady that is described as 'an internal apparatus of torture;' and who does by his heroism, more than *bear* it—he puts it out of power to affect him; and though (here is the passage) 'his appointment by day and by night was incessant pain, yet high enjoyment was, notwithstanding, the law of his existence.' Robert Hall reads me a lesson—me, an old soldier, who thought myself above taking lessons—in courage, at least. And, as I came to that passage when, in the sharp paroxysms before death, he says, 'I have not complained, have I, sir?—and I won't complain!'—when I came to that passage I started up, and cried, 'Roland de Caxton, thou hast been a coward! and, an thou hadst had thy deserts, thou hadst been cashiered, broken, and drummed out of the regiment long ago!'"

"After all, then, my father was not wrong—he placed his guns right, and fired a good shot."

"He must have been from 6° to 9° above the crest of the parapet," said my uncle thoughtfully—"which, I take it, is the best elevation, both for shot and shells, in enfilading a work."

"What say you, then, Captain?—up with our knapsacks, and on with the march!"

"Right about—face!" cried my uncle, as erect as a column.

"No looking back, if we can help it."

"Full in the front of the enemy. 'Up, guards, and at 'em!'"

"'England expects every man to do his duty!'"

"Cypress or laurel!" cried my uncle, waving the book over his head.

CHAPTER VII

I WENT out—and to see Francis Vivian; for, on leaving Mr. Trevanion, I was not without anxiety for my new friend's future provision. But Vivian was from home, and I strolled from his lodgings into the suburbs on the other side of the river, and began to meditate seriously on the best course now to pursue. In quitting my present occupations, I resigned prospects far more brilliant, and fortunes far more rapid, than I could ever hope to realise in any other entrance into life. But I felt the necessity, if I desired to keep steadfast to that more healthful frame of mind I had obtained, of some manly and continuous labour—some earnest employment. My thoughts flew back to the university; and the quiet of its cloisters—which, until I had been blinded by the glare of the London world, and grief had somewhat dulled the edge of my quick desires and hopes, had seemed to me cheerless and unaltering—took an inviting aspect. It presented what I needed most—a new scene, a new arena, a partial return into boyhood; repose for passions prematurely raised; activity for the reasoning powers in fresh directions. I had not lost my time in London: I had kept up, if not studies purely classical, at least the habits of application; I had sharpened my general comprehension, and augumented my resources. Accordingly, when I returned home, I resolved to speak to my father. But I found he had fore-stalled me; and, on entering, my mother drew me upstairs into her room, with a smile kindled by my smile, and told me that she and her Austin had been thinking that it was best that I should leave London as soon as possible; that my father found he could now dispense with the library of the Museum for some months; that the time for which they had taken their lodgings would be up in a few days; that the summer was far advanced, town odious, the country beautiful—in a word, we were to go home. There I could prepare myself for Cambridge, till the long vacation was over; and, my mother added hesitatingly, and with a prefatory caution to spare my health, that my father, whose income could ill afford the requisite allowance to me, counted on my soon lightening his burden, by getting a scholar-ship. I felt how much provident kindness there was in all this —even in that hint of a scholarship, which was meant to rouse my faculties, and spur me, by affectionate incentives, to a new ambition. I was not less delighted than grateful.

"But poor Roland," said I, "and little Blanche—will they come with us?"

"I fear not," said my mother, "for Roland is anxious to get back to his tower; and in a day or two, he will be well enough to move."

"Do you not think, my dear mother, that, somehow or other, this lost son of his had something to do with Roland's illness—that the illness was as much mental as physical?"

"I have no doubt of it, Sisty. What a sad, bad heart that young man must have!"

"My uncle seems to have abandoned all hope of finding him in London; otherwise, ill as he has been, I am sure we could not have kept him at home. So he goes back to the old tower. Poor man, he must be dull enough there! We must contrive to pay him a visit. Does Blanche ever speak of her brother?"

"No; for it seems they were not brought up much together —at all events, she does not remember him. How lovely she is! Her mother must surely have been very handsome."

"She is a pretty child, certainly, though in a strange style of beauty—such immense eyes!—and affectionate, and loves Roland as she ought."

And here the conversation dropped.

Our plans being thus decided, it was necessary that I should lose no time in seeing Vivian, and making some arrangement for the future. His manner had lost so much of its abruptness, that I thought I could venture to recommend him personally to Trevanion; and I knew, after what had passed, that Trevanion would make a point to oblige me. I resolved to consult my father about it. As yet, I had either never found, or never made the opportunity to talk to my father on the subject, he had been so occupied; and, if he had proposed to see my new friend, what answer could I have made, in the teeth of Vivian's cynic objections? However, as we were now going away, that last consideration ceased to be of importance; and, for the first, the student had not yet entirely settled back to his books. I therefore watched the time when my father walked down to the Museum, and, slipping my arm in his, I told him, briefly and rapidly, as we went along, how I had formed this strange acquaintance, and how I was now situated. The story did not interest my father quite so much as I expected, and he did not understand all the complexities of Vivian's character—how could he?—for he answered briefly, "I should think that, for a young man, apparently without a sixpence, and whose education seems so imperfect, any resource in Trevanion must be most temporary and uncertain. Speak to your Uncle Jack—he can find him some place, I have no doubt—perhaps a readership in a printer's office, or a reporter's place on some journal, if he is fit for it. But if you want to steady him, let it be something regular."

Therewith my father dismissed the matter, and vanished through the gates of the Museum. Readership to a printer— reportership on a journal—for a young gentleman with the high notions and arrogant vanity of Francis Vivian—his ambition already soaring far beyond kid gloves and a cabriolet! The idea was hopeless; and, perplexed and doubtful, I took my way to Vivian's lodgings. I found him at home, and unemployed, standing by his window, with folded arms, and in a state of such reverie that he was not aware of my entrance till I had touched him on the shoulder.

"Ha!" said he then, with one of his short, quick, impatient sighs, "I thought you had given me up, and forgotten me—but you look pale and harassed. I could almost think you had grown thinner within the last few days."

"Oh! never mind me, Vivian: I have come to speak of yourself. I have left Trevanion; it is settled that I should go to the university—and we all quit town in a few days."

"In a few days!—all!—who are all?"

"My family—father, mother, uncle, cousin, and myself. But, my dear fellow, now let us think seriously what is best to be done for you. I can present you to Trevanion."

"Ha!"

"But Trevanion is a hard, though an excellent man, and, moreover, as he is always changing the subjects that engross him, in a month or so he may have nothing to give you. You said you would work—will you consent not to complain if the work cannot be done in kid gloves? Young men who have risen high in the world have begun, it is well known, as reporters to the press. It is a situation of respectability, and in request, and not easy to obtain, I fancy; but still——"

Vivian interrupted me hastily—

"Thank you a thousand times! but what you say confirms a resolution I had taken before you came. I shall make it up with my family, and return home."

"Oh! I am so really glad. How wise in you!"

Vivian turned away his head abruptly—

"Your pictures of family life and domestic peace, you see," he said, "seduced me more than you thought. When do you leave town?"

"Why, I believe, early next week."

"So soon," said Vivian thoughtfully. "Well, perhaps I may ask you yet to introduce me to Mr. Trevanion; for—who knows?—my family and I may fall out again. But I will consider. I think I have heard you say that this Trevanion is a very old friend of your father's or uncle's?"

"He, or rather Lady Ellinor, is an old friend of both."

"And therefore would listen to your recommendations of me. But perhaps I may not need them. So you have left—left of your own accord—a situation that seemed more enjoyable, I should think, than rooms in a college;—left—why did you leave?"

And Vivian fixed his bright eyes full and piercingly on mine.

"It was only for a time, for a trial, that I was there," said I evasively; "out at nurse, as it were, till the Alma Mater opened her arms—*alma* indeed she ought to be to my father's son."

Vivian looked unsatisfied with my explanation, but did not question me farther. He himself was the first to turn the conversation, and he did this with more affectionate cordiality than was common to him. He inquired into our general plans, into the probabilities of our return to town, and drew from me a description of our rural Tusculum. He was quiet and subdued; and once or twice I thought there was a moisture in those luminous eyes. We parted with more of the unreserve and fondness of youthful friendship—at least on my part, and seemingly on his—than had yet endeared our singular intimacy; for the cement of cordial attachment had been wanting to an intercourse in which one party refused all confidence, and the other mingled distrust and fear with keen interest and compassionate admiration.

That evening, before lights were brought in, my father, turning to me, abruptly asked if I had seen my friend, and what he was about to do.

"He thinks of returning to his family," said I.

Roland, who had seemed dozing, winced uneasily.

"Who returns to his family?" asked the Captain.

"Why, you must know," said my father, "that Sisty has fished up a friend of whom he can give no account that would satisfy a policeman, and whose fortunes he thinks himself under the necessity of protecting. You are very lucky that he has not picked your pockets, Sisty; but I daresay he has! What's his name?"

"Vivian," said I—"Francis Vivian."

"A good name, and a Cornish," said my father. "Some derive it from the Romans—Vivianus; others from a Celtic word, which means——"

"Vivian!" interrupted Roland—"Vivian!—I wonder if it be the son of Colonel Vivian?"

"He is certainly a gentleman's son," said I; "but he never told me what his family and connections were."

"Vivian," repeated my uncle—"poor Colonel Vivian! So the young man is going to his father. I have no doubt it is the same. Ah!——"

"What do you know of Colonel Vivian, or his son?" said I. "Pray tell me; I am so interested in this young man."

" I know nothing of either, except by gossip," said my uncle moodily. " I did hear that Colonel Vivian, an excellent officer and honourable man, had been in—in—(Roland's voice faltered) —in great grief about his son, whom, a mere boy, he had prevented from some improper marriage, and who had run away and left him—it was supposed for America. The story affected me at the time," added my uncle, trying to speak calmly.

We were all silent, for we felt why Roland was so disturbed, and why Colonel Vivian's grief should have touched him home. Similarity in affliction makes us brothers even to the unknown.

" You say he is going home to his family—I am heartily glad of it ! " said the envying old soldier gallantly.

The lights came in then, and two minutes after, Uncle Roland and I were nestled close to each other, side by side ; and I was reading over his shoulder, and his finger was silently resting on that passage that had so struck him—" I have not complained—have I, sir ?—and I won't complain ! "

PART X

CHAPTER I

MY uncle's conjecture as to the parentage of Francis Vivian seemed to me a positive discovery. Nothing more likely than that this wilful boy had formed some headstrong attachment which no father would sanction, and so, thwarted and irritated, thrown himself on the world. Such an explanation was the more agreeable to me, as it cleared up much that had appeared discreditable in the mystery that surrounded Vivian. I could never bear to think that he had done anything mean and criminal, however I might believe he had been rash and faulty. It was natural that the unfriended wanderer should have been thrown into a society, the equivocal character of which had failed to revolt the audacity of an inquisitive mind and adventurous temper; but it was natural, also, that the habits of gentle birth, and that silent education which English gentlemen commonly receive from their very cradle, should have preserved his honour, at least, intact through all. Certainly the pride, the notions, the very faults of the well-born had remained in full force—why not the better qualities, however smothered for the time? I felt thankful for the thought that Vivian was returning to an element in which he might repurify his mind,—refit himself for that sphere to which he belonged ;—thankful that we might yet meet, and our present half-intimacy mature, perhaps, into healthful friendship.

It was with such thoughts that I took up my hat the next morning to seek Vivian, and judge if we had gained the right clue, when we were startled by what was a rare sound at our door—the postman's knock. My father was at the Museum; my mother in high conference, or close preparation for our approaching departure, with Mrs. Primmins ; Roland, I, and Blanche had the room to ourselves.

"The letter is not for me," said Pisistratus.

"Nor for me, I am sure," said the Captain, when the servant

entered and confuted him—for the letter was for him. He took
it up wonderingly and suspiciously, as Glumdalclitch took up
Gulliver, or as (if naturalists) we take up an unknown creature,
that we are not quite sure will not bite and sting us. Ah! it
has stung or bit you, Captain Roland! for you start and change
colour—you suppress a cry as you break the seal—you breathe
hard as you read—and the letter seems short—but it takes time
in the reading, for you go over it again and again. Then you
fold it up—crumple it—thrust it into your breast pocket—and
look round like a man waking from a dream. Is it a dream of
pain or of pleasure? Verily, I cannot guess, for nothing is on
that eagle face either of pain or pleasure, but rather of fear,
agitation, bewilderment. Yet the eyes are bright, too, and there
is a smile on that iron lip.

My uncle looked round, I say, and called hastily for his cane
and his hat, and then began buttoning his coat across his broad
breast, though the day was hot enough to have unbuttoned
every breast in the metropolis.

"You are not going out, uncle?"

"Yes, yes."

"But are you strong enough yet? Let me go with you."

"No, sir; no. Blanche, come here." He took the child in
his arms, surveyed her wistfully, and kissed her. "You have
never given me pain, Blanche; say, 'God bless and prosper you,
father!'"

"God bless and prosper my dear, dear papa!" said Blanche,
putting her little hands together as if in prayer.

"There—that should bring me luck, Blanche," said the
Captain gaily, and setting her down. Then seizing his cane
from the servant, and putting on his hat with a determined air,
he walked stoutly forth; and I saw him, from the window,
march along the streets as cheerfully as if he had been besieging
Badajoz.

"God prosper thee, too!" said I involuntarily.

And Blanche took hold of my hand, and said in her prettiest
way (and her pretty ways were many), "I wish you would come
with us, cousin Sisty, and help me to love papa. Poor papa!
he wants us both—he wants all the love we can give him."

"That he does, my dear Blanche; and I think it a great
mistake that we don't all live together. Your papa ought not
to go to that tower of his at the world's end, but come to our
snug, pretty house, with a garden full of flowers, for you to be
Queen of the May—from May to November; to say nothing of

P

a duck that is more sagacious than any creature in the Fables I gave you the other day."

Blanche laughed and clapped her hands—"Oh, that would be so nice! But"—and she stopped gravely, and added, "but then, you see, there would not be the tower to love papa; and I am sure that the tower must love him very much, for he loves it dearly."

It was my turn to laugh now. "I see how it is, you little witch!" said I; "you would coax us to come and live with you and the owls! With all my heart, so far as I am concerned."

"Sisty," said Blanche, with an appalling solemnity on her face, "do you know what I have been thinking?"

"Not I, miss—what?—something very deep, I can see—very horrible, indeed, I fear—you look so serious."

"Why, I've been thinking," continued Blanche, not relaxing a muscle, and without the least bit of a blush—"I've been thinking that I'll be your little wife; and then, of course, we shall all live together."

Blanche did not blush, but I did. "Ask me that ten years hence, if you dare, you impudent little thing; and now, run away to Mrs. Primmins, and tell her to keep you out of mischief, for I must say 'good morning.'"

But Blanche did not run away, and her dignity seemed exceedingly hurt at my mode of taking her alarming proposition, for she retired into a corner pouting, and sat down with great majesty. So there I left her, and went my way to Vivian. He was out; but, seeing books on his table, and having nothing to do, I resolved to wait for his return. I had enough of my father in me to turn at once to the books for company; and, by the side of some graver works which I had recommended, I found certain novels in French, that Vivian had got from a circulating library. I had a curiosity to read these—for, except the old classic novels of France, this mighty branch of its popular literature was new to me. I soon got interested, but what an interest!—the interest that a nightmare might excite, if one caught it out of one's sleep, and set to work to examine it. By the side of what dazzling shrewdness, what deep knowledge of those holes and corners in the human system, of which Goethe must have spoken when he said somewhere—(if I recollect right, and don't misquote him, which I'll not answer for)—"There is something in every man's heart which, if we could know, would make us hate him,"—by the side of all this, and of much more that showed prodigious boldness and energy

"She retired into a corner pouting
and sat down with great
majesty"

of intellect, what strange exaggeration—what mock nobility of sentiment—what inconceivable perversion of reasoning—what damnable demoralisation! The true artist, whether in Romance or the Drama, will often necessarily interest us in a vicious or criminal character—but he does not the less leave clear to our reprobation the vice or the crime. But here I found myself called upon not only to feel interest in the villain (which would be perfectly allowable,—I am very much interested in Macbeth and Lovelace),—but to admire and sympathise with the villainy itself. Nor was it the confusion of all wrong and right in individual character that shocked me the most—but rather the view of society altogether, painted in colours so hideous that, if true, instead of a revolution, it would draw down a deluge;—it was the hatred, carefully instilled, of the poor against the rich— it was the war breathed between class and class—it was that envy of all superiorities, which loves to show itself by allowing virtue only to a blouse, and asserting that a man must be a rogue if he belong to that rank of society in which, from the very gifts of education, from the necessary associations of cir- cumstance, roguery is the last thing probable or natural. It was all this, and things a thousand times worse, that set my head in a whirl, as hour after hour slipped on, and I still gazed, spellbound, on these Chimeras and Typhons—these symbols of the Destroying Principle. "Poor Vivian!" said I, as I rose at last, "if thou readest these books with pleasure, or from habit, no wonder that thou seemest to me so obtuse about right and wrong, and to have a great cavity where thy brain should have the bump of 'conscientiousness' in full salience!"

Nevertheless, to do those demoniacs justice, I had got through time imperceptibly by their pestilent help; and I was startled to see, by my watch, how late it was. I had just resolved to leave a line fixing an appointment for the morrow, and so depart, when I heard Vivian's knock—a knock that had great character in it—haughty, impatient, irregular; not a neat symmetrical, harmonious, unpretending knock, but a knock that seemed to set the whole house and street at defiance: it was a knock bullying—a knock ostentatious—a knock irritating and offensive —"impiger," and "iracundus."

But the step that came up the stairs did not suit the knock! it was a step light, yet firm—slow, yet elastic.

The maid-servant who had opened the door had, no doubt, informed Vivian of my visit, for he did not seem surprised to see me; but he cast that hurried suspicious look round the room which a man is apt to cast when he has left his papers about, and finds some idler, on whose trustworthiness he by no means depends, seated in the midst of the unguarded secrets. The look was not flattering; but my conscience was so unreproachful that I laid all the blame upon the general suspiciousness of Vivian's character.

"Three hours, at least, have I been here!" said I maliciously.

"Three hours!"—again the look.

"And this is the worst secret I have discovered,"—and I pointed to those literary Manicheans.

"Oh!" said he carelessly, "French novels!—I don't wonder you stayed so long. I can't read your English novels—flat and insipid: there are truth and life here."

"Truth and life!" cried I, every hair on my head erect with astonishment—"then hurrah for falsehood and death!"

"They don't please you; no accounting for tastes."

"I beg your pardon—I account for yours, if you really take for truth and life monsters so nefast and flagitious. For heaven's sake, my dear fellow, don't suppose that any man could get on in England—get anywhere but to the Old Bailey or Norfolk Island, if he squared his conduct to such topsy-turvy notions of the world as I find here."

"How many years are you my senior," asked Vivian sneeringly, "that you should play the mentor, and correct my ignorance of the world?"

"Vivian, it is not age and experience that speak here, it is something far wiser than they—the instinct of a man's heart, and a gentleman's honour."

"Well, well," said Vivian, rather discomposed, "let the poor books alone: you know my creed—that books influence us little one way or the other."

"By the great Egyptian library, and the soul of Diodorus! I wish you could hear my father upon that point. Come," added I, with sublime compassion—"come, it is not too late—do let me introduce you to my father. I will consent to read French novels all my life, if a single chat with Austin Caxton does not send you home with a happier face and a lighter heart. Come, let me take you back to dine with us to-day."

"I cannot," said Vivian, with some confusion—"I cannot, for this day I leave London. Some other time perhaps—for," he added, but not heartily, "we may meet again."

"I hope so," said I, wringing his hands, "and that is likely,

—since, in spite of yourself, I have guessed your secret—your birth and parentage."

"How!" cried Vivian, turning pale and gnawing his lip—"what do you mean?—speak."

"Well then, are you not the lost, runaway son of Colonel Vivian? Come, say the truth; let us be confidants."

Vivian threw off a succession of his abrupt sighs; and then, seating himself, leant his face on the table, confused, no doubt, to find himself discovered.

"You are near the mark," said he, at last, "but do not ask me farther yet. Some day," he cried impetuously, and springing suddenly to his feet—"some day you shall know all: yes; some day, if I live, when that name shall be high in the world: yes, when the world is at my feet!" He stretched his right hand as if to grasp the space, and his whole face was lighted with a fierce enthusiasm. The glow died away, and with a slight return of his scornful smile, he said—"Dreams yet; dreams! And now, look at this paper." And he drew out a memoranda, scrawled over with figures.

"This, I think, is my pecuniary debt to you; in a few days I shall discharge it. Give me your address."

"Oh!" said I, pained, "can you speak to me of money, Vivian?"

"It is one of those instincts of honour you cite so often," answered he, colouring. "Pardon me."

"That is my address," said I, stooping to write, in order to conceal my wounded feelings. "You will avail yourself of it, I hope, often, and tell me that you are well and happy."

"When I am happy you shall know."

"You do not require any introduction to Trevanion?"

Vivian hesitated. "No, I think not. If ever I do, I will write for it."

I took up my hat, and was about to go—for I was still chilled and mortified—when, as if by an irresistible impulse, Vivian came to me hastily, flung his arms round my neck, and kissed me as a boy kisses his brother.

"Bear with me!" he cried in a faltering voice; "I did not think to love any one as you have made me love you, though sadly against the grain. If you are not my good angel, it is that nature and habit are too strong for you. Certainly, some day we shall meet again. I shall have time, in the meanwhile, to see if the world can be indeed 'mine oyster, which I with sword can open.' I would be *aut Cæsar aut nullus!* Very little other Latin know I to quote from! If Cæsar, men will forgive me all the means to the end; if *nullus*, London has a river, and in every street one may buy a cord!"

"Vivian! Vivian!"

"Now go, my dear friend, while my heart is softened—go before I shock you with some return of the native Adam. Go—go!"

And taking me gently by the arm, Francis Vivian drew me from the room and re-entering, locked his door.

Ah! if I could have left him Robert Hall, instead of those execrable Typhons! But would that medicine have suited his case, or must grim Experience write sterner prescriptions with iron hand?

CHAPTER II

WHEN I got back, just in time for dinner, Roland had not returned, nor did he return till late in the evening. All our eyes were directed towards him, as we rose with one accord to give him welcome; but his face was like a mask—it was locked, and rigid, and unreadable.

Shutting the door carefully after him, he came to the hearth, stood on it, upright and calm, for a few moments, and then asked—

"Has Blanche gone to bed?"

"Yes," said my mother, "but not to sleep, I am sure; she made me promise to tell her when you came back."

Roland's brow relaxed.

"To-morrow sister," said he slowly, "will you see that she has the proper mourning made for her? My son is dead."

"Dead!" we cried with one voice, and surrounding him with one impulse.

"Dead! impossible—you could not say it so calmly. Dead—how do you know? You may be deceived. Who told you?—why do you think so?"

"I have seen his remains," said my uncle, with the same gloomy calm. "We will all mourn for him. Pisistratus, you are heir to my name now, as to your father's. Good night; excuse me, all—all you dear and kind ones; I am worn out."

Roland lighted his candle and went away, leaving us thunder-struck; but he came back again—looked round—took up his book, open in the favourite passage—nodded again, and again vanished. We looked at each other as if we had seen a ghost. Then my father rose and went out of the room, and remained in Roland's till the night was well nigh gone! We sat up—my mother and I—till he returned. His benign face looked profoundly sad.

"How is it, sir? Can you tell us more?"

My father shook his head.

"Roland prays that you may preserve the same forbearance you have shown hitherto, and never mention his son's name to him. Peace be to the living, as to the dead. Kitty, this changes our plans; we must all go to Cumberland—we cannot leave Roland thus!"

"Poor, poor Roland!" said my mother, through her tears. "And to think that father and son were not reconciled. But Roland forgives him now—oh yes; *now!*"

"It is not Roland we can censure," said my father, almost fiercely; "it is——but enough. We must hurry out of town as soon as we can: Roland will recover in the native air of his old ruins."

We went up to bed mournfully. "And so," thought I, "ends one grand object of my life!—I had hoped to have brought those two together. But, alas! what peacemaker like the grave!"

CHAPTER III

MY uncle did not leave his room for three days, but he was much closeted with a lawyer; and my father dropped some words which seemed to imply that the deceased had incurred debts, and that the poor Captain was making some charge on his small property. As Roland had said that he had seen the remains of his son, I took it, at first, for granted that we should attend a funeral, but no word of this was said. On the fourth day, Roland in deep mourning entered a hackney coach with the lawyer, and was absent about two hours. I did not doubt that he had thus quietly fulfilled the last mournful offices. On his return, he shut himself up again for the rest of the day, and would not see even my father. But the next morning he made his appearance as usual, and I even thought that he seemed more cheerful than I had yet known him—whether he played a part, or whether the worst was now over, and the grave was less cruel than uncertainty. On the following day we all set out for Cumberland.

In the interval, Uncle Jack had been almost constantly at the house, and, to do him justice, he had seemed unaffectedly shocked at the calamity that had befallen Roland. There was, indeed, no want of heart in Uncle Jack, whenever you went straight at it; but it was hard to find if you took a circuitous route towards it through the pockets. The worthy speculator had indeed much business to transact with my father before he left town. The *Anti-Publisher Society* had been set up, and it was through the obstetric aid of that fraternity that the Great Book was to be ushered into the world. The new journal, the *Literary Times*, was also far advanced—not yet out, but my father was fairly in for it. There were preparations for its *début* on a vast scale, and two or three gentlemen in black—one of whom looked like a lawyer, and another like a printer, and a third uncommonly like a Jew—called twice, with papers of a very formidable aspect. All these preliminaries settled, the last thing I heard Uncle Jack say, with a slap on my father's back, was, "Fame and fortune both made now!—you may go to sleep in safety, for you leave me wide awake. Jack Tibbets never sleeps!"

I had thought it strange that, since my abrupt exodus from Trevanion's house, no notice had been taken of any of us by himself or Lady Ellinor. But on the very eve of our departure, came a kind note from Trevanion to me, dated from his favourite country-seat (accompanied by a present of some rare books to my father), in which he said briefly that there had been illness in his family, which had obliged him to leave town for a change of air, but that Lady Ellinor expected to call on my mother the next week. He had found amongst his books some curious works of the Middle Ages, amongst others a complete set of Cardan, which he knew my father would like to have, and so sent them. There was no allusion to what had passed between us.

In reply to this note, after due thanks on my father's part, who seized upon the Cardan (Lyons edition, 1663, ten volumes folio) as a silk-worm does upon a mulberry-leaf, I expressed our joint regrets that there was no hope of our seeing Lady Ellinor, as we were just leaving town. I should have added something on the loss my uncle had sustained, but my father thought that, since Roland shrank from any mention of his son, even by his nearest kindred, it would be his obvious wish not to parade his affliction beyond that circle.

And there had beèn illness in Trevanion's family! On whom had it fallen? I could not rest satisfied with that general expression, and I took my answer myself to Trevanion's house, instead of sending it by the post. In reply to my inquiries, the porter said that all the family were expected at the end of the week; that he had heard both Lady Ellinor and Miss Trevanion had been rather poorly, but that they were now better. I left my note with orders to forward it; and my wounds bled afresh as I came away.

We had the whole coach to ourselves in our journey, and a silent journey it was, till we arrived at a little town about eight miles from my uncle's residence, to which we could only get through a cross-road. My uncle insisted on preceding us that night, and, though he had written, before we started, to announce our coming, he was fidgety lest the poor tower should not make the best figure it could; so he went alone, and we took our ease at our inn.

Betimes the next day we hired a fly-coach—for a chaise could never have held us and my father's books—and fogged through a labyrinth of villainous lanes, which no Marshal Wade had ever reformed from their primal chaos. But poor Mrs. Primmins and the canary-bird alone seemed sensible of the jolts; the former, who sat opposite to us wedged amidst a medley of packages, all marked "Care, to be kept top uppermost" (why I know not, for they were but books, and whether they lay top or bottom it could not materially affect their value),—the former, I say, contrived to extend her arms over those *disjecta membra*, and, griping a window-sill with the right hand, and a window-sill with the left, kept her seat rampant, like the split eagle of the Austrian Empire—in fact, it would be well nowadays, if the split eagle were as firm as Mrs. Primmins! As for the canary, it never failed to respond, by an astonished chirp, to every "Gracious me!" and "Lord save us!" which the delve into a rut, or the bump out of it, sent forth from Mrs. Primmins's lips, with all the emphatic dolor of the "Aῖ, aῖ!" in a Greek chorus.

But my father, with his broad hat over his brows, was in deep thought. The scenes of his youth were rising before him, and his memory went, smooth as a spirit's wing, over delve and bump. And my mother, who sat next him, had her arm on his shoulder, and was watching his face jealously. Did she think that, in that thoughtful face, there was regret for the old love? Blanche, who had been very sad, and had wept much and quietly since they put on her the mourning, and told her that she had no brother (though she had no remembrance of the lost), began now to evince infantine curiosity and eagerness to catch the first peep of her father's beloved tower.   And Blanche sat on my knee, and I shared her impatience.   At last there came in view a church spire—a church—a plain square building near it, the parsonage (my father's old home), a long straggling street of cottages and rude shops, with a better kind of house here and there—and in the hinder ground, a grey deformed mass of wall and ruin, placed on one of those eminences on which the Danes loved to pitch camp or build fort, with one high, rude, Anglo-Norman tower rising from the midst.   Few trees were round it, and those either poplars or firs, save, as we approached, one mighty oak—integral and unscathed.   The road now wound behind the parsonage, and up a steep ascent. Such a road! the whole parish ought to have been flogged for it!   If I had sent up a road like that, even on a map, to Dr. Herman, I should not have sat down in comfort for a week to come!

The fly-coach came to a full stop.

" Let us get out," cried I, opening the door, and springing to the ground to set the example.

Blanche followed, and my respected parents came next.   But when Mrs. Primmins was about to heave herself into movement—

" *Papæ !* " said my father.   " I think, Mrs. Primmins, you must remain in, to keep the books steady."

" Lord love you! " cried Mrs. Primmins, aghast.

" The subtraction of such a mass, or *moles*—supple and elastic as all flesh is, and fitting into the hard corners of the inert matter—such a subtraction, Mrs. Primmins, would leave a vacuum which no natural system, certainly no artificial organisation, could sustain.   There would be a regular dance of atoms, Mrs. Primmins; my books would fly here, there, on the floor, out of the window !

" ' Corporis officium est quoniam omnia deorsum.'

The business of a body like yours, Mrs. Primmins, is to press all things down—to keep them tight, as you will know one of these days—that is, if you will do me the favour to read Lucretius, and master that material philosophy, of which I may say, without flattery, my dear Mrs. Primmins, that you are a living illustration."

These, the first words my father had spoken since we set out from the inn, seemed to assure my mother that she need have

no apprehension as to the character of his thoughts, for her brow
cleared, and she said, laughing—

"Only look at poor Primmins, and then at that hill!"

"You may subtract Primmins, if you will be answerable for
the remnant, Kitty.   Only I warn you, that it is against all the
laws of physics."

So saying, he sprang lightly forward, and, taking hold of my
arm, paused and looked round, and drew the loud free breath
with which we draw native air.

"And yet," said my father, after that grateful and affectionate inspiration—"and yet, it must be owned, that a more
ugly country one cannot see out of Cambridgeshire."[1]

"Nay," said I, "it is bold and large, it has a beauty of its
own.   Those immense, undulating, uncultivated, treeless tracts
have surely their charm of wildness and solitude!   And how
they suit the character of the ruin!   All is feudal there!   I
understand Roland better now."

"I hope to heaven Cardan will come to no harm!" cried my
father; "he is very handsomely bound; and he fitted beautifully just into the fleshiest part of that fidgety Primmins."

Blanche, meanwhile, had run far before us, and I followed
first.   There were still the remains of that deep trench (surrounding the ruins on three sides, leaving a ragged hill-top at
the fourth) which made the favourite fortification of all the
Teutonic tribes.   A causeway, raised on brick arches, now, however, supplied the place of the drawbridge, and the outer gate
was but a mass of picturesque ruin.   Entering into the courtyard or bailey, the old castle mound, from which justice had
been dispensed, was in full view, rising higher than the broken
walls around it, and partially overgrown with brambles.   And
there stood, comparatively whole, the Tower or Keep, and from
its portals emerged the veteran owner.

His ancestors might have received us in more state, but
certainly they could not have given us a warmer greeting.   In
fact, in his own domain Roland appeared another man.   His
stiffness, which was a little repulsive to those who did not understand it, was all gone.   He seemed less proud, precisely because
he and his pride, on that ground, were on good terms with each
other.   How gallantly he extended—not his arm, in our modern

---

[1] This certainly cannot be said of Cumberland generally, one of the most
beautiful counties in Great Britain.   But the immediate district to which
Mr. Caxton's exclamation refers, if not ugly, is at least savage, bare,
and rude.

Jack-and-Jill sort of fashion—but his right hand to my mother; how carefully he led her over "brake, bush, and scaur," through the low vaulted door, where a tall servant, who, it was easy to see, had been a soldier—in the precise livery, no doubt, warranted by the heraldic colours (his stockings were red!)—stood upright as a sentry. And, coming into the hall, it looked absolutely cheerful—it took us by surprise. There was a great fireplace, and, though it was still summer, a great fire! It did not seem a bit too much, for the walls were stone, the lofty roof open to the rafters, while the windows were small and narrow, and so high and so deep sunk that one seemed in a vault. Nevertheless, I say the room looked sociable and cheerful— thanks principally to the fire, and partly to a very ingenious medley of old tapestry at one end, and matting at the other, fastened to the lower part of the walls, seconded by an arrangement of furniture which did credit to my uncle's taste for the picturesque. After we had looked about and admired to our hearts' content, Roland took us—not up one of those noble staircases you see in the later manorial residences—but a little winding stone stair, into the rooms he had appropriated to his guests. There was first a small chamber, which he called my father's study—in truth, it would have done for any philosopher or saint who wished to shut out the world—and might have passed for the interior of such a column as the Stylites inhabited; for you must have climbed a ladder to have looked out of the window, and then the vision of no short-sighted man could have got over the interval in the wall made by the narrow casement, which, after all, gave no other prospect than a Cumberland sky, with an occasional rook in it. But my father, I think I have said before, did not much care for scenery, and he looked round with great satisfaction upon the retreat assigned him.

"We can knock up shelves for your books in no time," said my uncle, rubbing his hands.

"It would be a charity," quoth my father, "for they have been very long in a recumbent position, and would like to stretch themselves, poor things. My dear Roland, this room is made for books—so round and so deep. I shall sit here like Truth in a well."

"And there is a room for you, sister, just out of it," said my uncle, opening a little, low, prison-like door into a charming room, for its window was low, and it had an iron balcony; "and out of that is the bedroom. For you, Pisistratus, my boy, I am afraid that it is soldiers' quarters, indeed, with which you will have to put up. But never mind; in a day or two we shall make all worthy a general of your illustrious name—for he was a great general, Pisistratus the First—was he not, brother?"

"All tyrants are," said my father; "the knack of soldiering is indispensable to them."

"Oh, you may say what you please here," said Roland, in high good-humour, as he drew me downstairs, still apologising for my quarters, and so earnestly, that I made up my mind that I was to be put into an *oubliette*. Nor were my suspicions much dispelled on seeing that we had to leave the keep, and pick our way into what seemed to me a mere heap of rubbish, on the dexter side of the court. But I was agreeably surprised to find, amidst these wrecks, a room with a noble casement, commanding the whole country, and placed immediately over a plot of ground cultivated as a garden. The furniture was ample, though homely; the floors and walls well matted; and, altogether, despite the inconvenience of having to cross the courtyard to get to the rest of the house, and being wholly without the modern luxury of a bell, I thought that I could not be better lodged.

"But this is a perfect bower, my dear uncle! Depend on it, it was the bower-chamber of the Dames de Caxton—Heaven rest them!"

"No," said my uncle gravely; "I suspect it must have been the chaplain's room, for the chapel was to the right of you. An earlier chapel, indeed, formerly existed in the keep tower—for, indeed, it is scarcely a true keep without chapel, well, and hall. I can show you part of the roof of the first, and the two last are entire; the well is very curious, formed in the substance of the wall at one angle of the wall. In Charles the First's time, our ancestor lowered his only son down in a bucket and kept him there six hours, while a malignant mob was storming the tower. I need not say that our ancestor himself scorned to hide from such a rabble, for *he* was a grown man. The boy lived to be a sad spendthrift, and used the well for cooling his wine. He drank up a great many good acres."

"I should scratch him out of the pedigree, if I were you. But pray, have you not discovered the proper chamber of that great Sir William, about whom my father is so shamefully sceptical?"

"To tell you a secret," answered the Captain, giving me a sly poke in the ribs, "I have put your father into it! There are the initial letters W. C. let into the cusp of the York rose, and the date three years before the battle of Bosworth, over the chimney-piece."

I could not help joining my uncle's grim, low laugh at this characteristic pleasantry; and after I had complimented him on so judicious a mode of proving his point, I asked him how he could possibly have contrived to fit up the ruin so well, especially as he had scarcely visited it since his purchase.

"Why," said he, "some years ago, that poor fellow you now see as my servant, and who is gardener, bailiff, seneschal, butler, and anything else you can put him to, was sent out of the army on the invalid list. So I placed him here; and as he is a capital carpenter, and has had a very fair education, I told him what I wanted, and put by a small sum every year for repairs and furnishing. It is astonishing how little it cost me; for Bolt, poor fellow (that is his name), caught the right spirit of the thing, and most of the furniture (which you see is ancient and suitable) he picked up at different cottages and farm-houses in the neighbourhood. As it is, however, we have plenty more rooms here and there—only, of late," continued my uncle, slightly changing colour, "I had no money to spare. But come," he resumed, with an evident effort—"come and see my barrack: it is on the other side of the hall, and made out of what no doubt were the butteries."

We reached the yard and found the fly-coach had just crawled to the door. My father's head was buried deep in the vehicle, —he was gathering up his packages, and sending out, oracle-like, various muttered objurgations and anathemas upon Mrs. Primmins, and her vacuum; which Mrs. Primmins, standing by and making a lap with her apron to receive the packages and anathemas simultaneously, bore with the mildness of an angel, lifting up her eyes to heaven and murmuring something about "poor old bones." Though, as for Mrs. Primmins's bones, they had been myths these twenty years, and you might as soon have found a Plesiosaurus in the fat lands of Romney Marsh as a bone amidst those layers of flesh in which my poor father thought he had so carefully cottoned up his Cardan.

Leaving these parties to adjust matters between them, we stepped under the low doorway, and entered Roland's room. Oh, certainly Bolt *had* caught the spirit of the thing!—certainly he had penetrated down to the pathos that lay within the deeps of Roland's character. Buffon says "the style is the man";

there, the room was the man. That nameless, inexpressible, soldier-like, methodical neatness which belonged to Roland— that was the first thing that struck one—that was the general character of the whole. Then, in details, there, on stout oak shelves, were the books on which my father loved to jest his more imaginative brother,—there they were, Froissart, Barante, Joinville, the "Mort d'Arthur," "Amadis of Gaul," Spenser's "Fairy Queen," a noble copy of Strutt's "Horda," Mallet's "Northern Antiquities," Percy's "Reliques," Pope's "Homer," books on gunnery, archery, hawking, fortification—old chivalry and modern war together cheek by jowl.

Old chivalry and modern war!—look to that tilting helmet with the tall Caxton crest, and look to that trophy near it, a French cuirass—and that old banner (a knight's pennon) sur-mounting those crossed bayonets. And over the chimney-piece there—bright, clean, and, I warrant you, dusted daily—are Roland's own sword, his holsters and pistols, yea the saddle, pierced and lacerated, from which he had reeled when that leg—I gasped—I felt it all at a glance, and I stole softly to the spot, and, had Roland not been there, I could have kissed that sword as reverently as if it had been a Bayard's or a Sydney's.

My uncle was too modest to guess my emotion; he rather thought I had turned my face to conceal a smile at his vanity, and said, in a deprecating tone of apology,—"It was all Bolt's doing, foolish fellow."

CHAPTER IV

OUR host regaled us with a hospitality that notably contrasted his economical thrifty habits in London. To be sure, Bolt had caught the great pike which headed the feast; and Bolt, no doubt, had helped to rear those fine chickens *ab ovo ;* Bolt, I have no doubt, made that excellent Spanish omelette; and, for the rest, the products of the sheep-walk and the garden came in as volunteer auxiliaries—very different from the mer-cenary recruits by which those metropolitan *condottieri,* the butcher and greengrocer, hasten the ruin of that melancholy commonwealth, called "genteel poverty."

Our evening passed cheerfully ; and Roland, contrary to his custom was talker in chief. It was eleven o'clock before Bolt appeared with a lantern to conduct me through the courtyard to my dormitory among the ruins—a ceremony which, every night, shine or dark, he insisted upon punctiliously performing.

It was long before I could sleep—before I could believe that but so few days had elapsed since Roland heard of his son's death—that son whose fate had so long tortured him; and yet, never had Roland appeared so free from sorrow! Was it natural — was it effort? Several days passed before I could answer that question, and then not wholly to my satisfaction. Effort there was, or rather resolute, systematic determination. At moments Roland's head drooped, his brows met, and the whole man seemed to sink. Yet these were only moments; he would rouse himself up, like a dozing charger at the sound of a trumpet, and shake off the creeping weight. But whether from the vigour of his determination, or from some aid, in other trains of reflection, I could not but perceive that Roland's sadness really was less grave and bitter than it had been, or than it was natural to suppose. He seemed to transfer, daily, more and more, his affections from the dead to those around him, especially to Blanche and myself. He let it be seen that he looked on me now as his lawful successor—as the future supporter of his name; he was fond of confiding to me all his little plans, and consulting me on them. He would walk with me around his domains (of which I shall say more hereafter), —point out, from every eminence we climbed, where the broad lands which his forefathers had owned stretched away to the horizon: unfold with tender hand the mouldering pedigree, and rest lingeringly on those of his ancestors who had held martial post, or had died on the field. There was a crusader who had followed Richard to Ascalon; there was a knight who had fought at Agincourt; there was a cavalier (whose picture was still extant), with fair love-locks, who had fallen at Worcester—no doubt the same who had cooled his son in that well which the son devoted to more agreeable associations. But of all these worthies there was none whom my uncle, perhaps from the spirit of contradiction, valued like that apocryphal Sir William; and why? because, when the apostate Stanley turned the fortunes of the field at Bosworth, and when that cry of despair,—"Treason! treason!" burst from the lips of the last Plantagenet, "amongst the faithless," this true soldier, "faithful found!" had fallen in that lion rush which Richard made at his foe. "Your father tells me that Richard was a murderer and usurper," quoth my uncle. "Sir, that might be true or not; but it was not on the field of battle that his followers were to reason on the character of the master who trusted them, especially when a legion of foreign hirelings stood opposed to them. I would not have descended from that turncoat Stanley to be lord of all the lands the earls of Derby can boast of. Sir, in loyalty, men fight and die for a grand principle and a lofty passion ; and this brave Sir William was paying back to the last Plantagenet the benefits he had received from the first ! "

" And yet it may be doubted," said I maliciously, " whether William Caxton the printer did not——"

" Plague, pestilence, and fire seize William Caxton the printer, and his invention too ! " cried my uncle barbarously. " When there were only a few books, at least they were good ones ; and now they are so plentiful, all they do is to confound the judgment, unsettle the reason, drive the good books out of cultivation, and draw a ploughshare of innovation over every ancient landmark ; seduce the women, womanise the men, upset states, thrones, and churches ; rear a race of chattering, conceited coxcombs, who can always find books in plenty to excuse them from doing their duty ; make the poor discontented, the rich crotchety and whimsical, refine away the stout old virtues into quibbles and sentiments ! All imagination formerly was expended in noble action, adventure, enterprise, high deeds, and aspirations ; now a man can but be imaginative by feeding on the false excitement of passions he never felt, dangers he never shared ; and he fritters away all there is of life to spare in him upon the fictitious love-sorrows of Bond Street and St. James's. Sir, chivalry ceased when the press rose ! and to fasten upon me, as a forefather, out of all men who ever lived and sinned, the very man who has most destroyed what I most valued—who, by the Lord ! with his cursed invention has well-nigh got rid of respect for forefathers, altogether—is a cruelty of which my brother had never been capable, if that printer's devil had not got hold of him ! "

That a man in this blessed nineteenth century should be such a Vandal ! and that my uncle Roland should talk in a strain that Totila would have been ashamed of, within so short a time after my father's scientific and erudite oration on the Hygeiana of Books, was enough to make one despair of the progress of intellect and the perfectibility of our species. And I have no manner of doubt that, all the while, my uncle had a brace of books in his pockets, Robert Hall one of them ! In truth, he had talked himself into a passion, and did not know what

nonsense he was saying. But this explosion of Captain Roland's
has shattered the thread of my matter. Pouff! I must take
breath and begin again!

Yes, in spite of my sauciness, the old soldier evidently took
to me more and more. And, besides our critical examination
of the property and the pedigree, he carried me with him on
long excursions to distant villages, where some memorial of a
defunct Caxton, a coat-of-arms, or an epitaph on a tombstone,
might be still seen. And he made me pore over topographical
works and county histories (forgetful, Goth that he was, that
for those very authorities he was indebted to the repudiated
printer!) to find some anecdote of his beloved dead! In truth,
the county for miles round bore the *vestigia* of those old Caxtons;
their handwriting was on many a broken wall. And, obscure as
they all were, compared to that great operative of the Sanctuary
at Westminster, whom my father clung to—still, that the yester-
days that had lighted them the way to dusty death had cast no
glare on dishonoured 'scutcheons seemed clear, from the popular
respect and traditional affection in which I found that the name
was still held in hamlet and homestead. It was pleasant to see
the veneration with which this small hidalgo of some three
hundred a year was held, and the patriarchal affection with
which he returned it. Roland was a man who would walk into
a cottage, rest his cork leg on the hearth, and talk for the hour
together upon all that lay nearest to the hearts of the owners.
There is a peculiar spirit of aristocracy amongst agricultural
peasants; they like old names and families; they identify themselves with the honours of a house, as if of its clan. They do
not care so much for wealth as townsfolk and the middle class
do; they have a pity, but a respectful one, for well-born poverty.
And then this Roland, too—who would go and dine in a cook-
shop, and receive change for a shilling, and shun the ruinous
luxury of a hack cabriolet—could be positively extravagant in
his liberalities to those around him. He was altogether another
being in his paternal acres. The shabby-genteel, half-pay
captain, lost in the whirl of London, here luxuriated into a
dignified ease of manner that Chesterfield might have admired.
And, if to please is the true sign of politeness, I wish you could
have seen the faces that smiled upon Captain Roland as he
walked down the village, nodding from side to side.

One day a frank, hearty old woman, who had known Roland
as a boy, seeing him lean on my arm, stopped us, as she said
bluffly, to take a " geud luik " at me.

Fortunately I was stalwart enough to pass muster, even in the eyes of a Cumberland matron; and after a compliment at which Roland seemed much pleased, she said to me, but pointing to the Captain—

"Hegh, sir, now you ha the bra time before you; you maun een try and be as geud as *he*. And if life last, ye wull too—for there never waur a bad ane of that stock. Wi' heads kindly stup'd to the least, and lifted manfu' oop to the heighest—that ye all war' sin ye came from the Ark. Blessins on the ould name—though little pelf goes with it—it sounds on the peur man's ear like a bit of gould!"

"Do you not see now," said Roland, as we turned away, "what we owe to a name, and what to our forefathers?—do you not see why the remotest ancestor has a right to our respect and consideration—for he was a parent? 'Honour your parents' —the law does not say, 'Honour your children!' If a child disgrace us, and the dead, and the sanctity of this great heritage of their virtues—*the name;*—if he does——" Roland stopped short, and added fervently, "But you are my heir now—I have no fear. What matter one foolish old man's sorrows?—the name, that property of generations, is saved, thank Heaven—the name!"

Now the riddle was solved, and I understood why, amidst all his natural grief for a son's loss, that proud father was consoled. For he was less himself a father than a son—son to the long dead. From every grave where a progenitor slept, he had heard a parent's voice. He could bear to be bereaved, if the fore-fathers were not dishonoured. Roland was more than half a Roman—the son might still cling to his household affections, but the *lares* were a part of his religion.

CHAPTER V

BUT I ought to be hard at work, preparing myself for Cambridge. The deuce!—how can I? The point in academical education on which I require most preparation is Greek composition. I come to my father, who, one might think, was at home enough in this. But rare indeed is it to find a great scholar who is a good teacher.

My dear father! if one is content to take you in your own way, there never was a more admirable instructor for the heart, the head, the principles, or the taste—when you have discovered that there is some one sore to be healed—one defect to be repaired : and you have rubbed your spectacles, and got your hand fairly into that recess between your frill and your waist-coat. But to go to you, cut and dry, monotonously, regularly—book and exercise in hand—to see the mournful patience with which you tear yourself from that great volume of Cardan in the very honeymoon of possession—and then to note those mild eyebrows gradually distend themselves into perplexed diagonals, over some false quantity or some barbarous collocation — till there steal forth that horrible "Papæ!" which means more on your lips than I am sure it ever did when Latin was a live language, and "Papæ!" a natural and unpedantic ejaculation! no, I would sooner blunder through the dark by myself a thousand times, than light my rushlight at the lamp of that Phlegethonian "Papæ!"

And then my father would wisely and kindly, but wondrous slowly, erase three-fourths of one's pet verses, and intercalate others that one saw were exquisite, but could not exactly see why. And then one asked why ; and my father shook his head in despair, and said—"But you ought to *feel* why!"

In short, scholarship to him was like poetry : he could no more teach it you than Pindar could have taught you how to make an ode. You breathed the aroma, but you could no more seize and analyse it, than, with the opening of your naked hand, you could carry off the scent of a rose. I soon left my father in peace to Cardan, and to the Great Book, which last, by the way, advanced but slowly. For Uncle Jack had now insisted on its being published in quarto, with illustrative plates ; and those plates took an immense time, and were to cost an immense sum—but that cost was the affair of the Anti-Publisher Society. But how can I settle to work by myself? No sooner have I got into my room—*penitus ab orbe divisus*, as I rashly think—than there is a tap at the door. Now it is my mother, who is benevolently engaged upon making curtains to all the windows (a trifling superfluity that Bolt had forgotten or disdained), and who wants to know how the draperies are fashioned at Mr. Trevanion's : a pretence to have me near her, and see with her own eyes that I am not fretting ; the moment she hears I have shut myself up in my room, she is sure that it is for sorrow. Now it is Bolt, who is making book-shelves for my father, and desires to consult me at every turn, especially as I have given him a Gothic design, which pleases him hugely. Now it is Blanche, whom, in an evil hour, I undertook to teach to draw, and who comes in on tiptoe, vowing she'll not disturb me, and sits so quiet that she fidgets me out of all patience. Now, and much more often, it is the Captain, who wants me to walk, to ride, to fish. And, by St. Hubert! (saint of the chase) bright August comes—and there is moor-game on those barren wolds —and my uncle has given me the gun he shot with at my age —single-barrelled, flint lock—but you would not have laughed at it if you had seen the strange feats it did in Roland's hands— while in mine, I could always lay the blame on the flint lock! Time, in short, passed rapidly; and if Roland and I had our dark hours, we chased them away before they could settle—shot them on the wing as they got up.

Then, too, though the immediate scenery around my uncle's was so bleak and desolate, the country within a few miles was so full of objects of interest—of landscapes so poetically grand or lovely; and occasionally we coaxed my father from the Cardan, and spent whole days by the margin of some glorious lake.

Amongst these excursions, I made one by myself to that house in which my father had known the bliss and the pangs of that stern first-love which still left its scars fresh on my own memory. The house, large and imposing, was shut up—the Trevanions had not been there for years—the pleasure-grounds had been contracted into the smallest possible space. There was no positive decay or ruin—that Trevanion would never have allowed; but there was the dreary look of absenteeship everywhere. I penetrated into the house with the help of my card and half-a-crown. I saw that memorable boudoir—I could fancy the very spot in which my father had heard the sentence that had changed the current of his life. And when I returned home, I looked with new tenderness on my father's placid brow—and blessed anew that tender helpmate who, in her patient love, had chased from it every shadow.

I had received one letter from Vivian a few days after our arrival. It had been re-directed from my father's house, at which I had given him my address. It was short, but seemed cheerful. He said, that he believed he had at last hit on the right way, and should keep to it—that he and the world were better friends than they had been—that the only way to keep friends with the world was to treat it as a tamed tiger, and have one hand on a crowbar while one fondled the beast with the other. He enclosed me a bank-note, which somewhat more than covered his debt to me, and bade me pay him the surplus when he should claim it as a millionaire. He gave me no

address in his letter, but it bore the post-mark of Godalming.
I had the impertinent curiosity to look into an old topographical
work upon Surrey, and in a supplemental itinerary I found
this passage, "To the left of the beech-wood, three miles from
Godalming, you catch a glimpse of the elegant seat of Francis
Vivian, Esq." To judge by the date of the work, the said
Francis Vivian might be the grandfather of my friend, his namesake. There could no longer be any doubt as to the parentage
of this prodigal son.

The long vacation was now nearly over, and all his guests
were to leave the poor Captain. In fact, we had made a considerable trespass on his hospitality. It was settled that I was
to accompany my father and mother to their long-neglected
penates, and start thence for Cambridge.

Our parting was sorrowful—even Mrs. Primmins wept as she
shook hands with Bolt. But Bolt, an old soldier, was of course
a lady's man. The brothers did not shake hands only—they
fondly embraced, as brothers of that time of life rarely do now-
a-days, except on the stage. And Blanche, with one arm
round my mother's neck and one round mine, sobbed in my
ear—"But I will be your little wife, I will." Finally, the fly-
coach once more received us all—all but poor Blanche, and we
looked round and missed her.

CHAPTER VI

ALMA MATER! Alma Mater! New-fashioned folks, with
their large theories of education, may find fault with thee.
But a true Spartan mother thou art—hard and stern as the old
matron who bricked up her son Pausanias, bringing the first stone
to immure him; hard and stern, I say, to the worthless, but
full of majestic tenderness to the worthy.

For a young man to go up to Cambridge (I say nothing of
Oxford, knowing nothing thereof) merely as routine work, to
lounge through three years to a degree among the οἱ πολλοι—
for such an one, Oxford Street herself, whom the immortal
Opium-Eater hath so direly apostrophised, is not a more careless and stony-hearted mother. But for him who will read,
who will work, who will seize the rare advantages proffered,
who will select his friends judiciously—yea, out of that vast
ferment of young idea in its lusty vigour, choose the good and

reject the bad—there is plenty to make those three years rich
with fruit imperishable—three years nobly spent, even though
one must pass over the Ass's Bridge to get into the Temple
of Honour.

Important changes in the Academical system have been
recently announced, and honours are henceforth to be accorded
to the successful disciples in moral and natural sciences. By
the side of the old throne of Mathesis, they have placed two
very useful *fauteuils à la Voltaire*. I have no objection; but,
in those three years of life, it is not so much the thing learned,
as the steady perseverance in learning something that is
excellent.

It was fortunate, in one respect, for me that I had seen a
little of the real world—the metropolitan, before I came to that
mimic one—the cloistral. For what were called pleasures in
the last, and which might have allured me, had I come fresh
from school, had no charm for me now. Hard drinking and
high play, a certain mixture of coarseness and extravagance,
made the fashion among the idle when I was at the University,
consule Planco—when Wordsworth was master of Trinity: it
may be altered now.

But I had already outlived such temptations, and so, naturally,
I was thrown out of the society of the idle, and somewhat into
that of the laborious.

Still, to speak frankly, I had no longer the old pleasure in
books. If my acquaintance with the great world had destroyed
the temptation to puerile excesses, it had also increased my
constitutional tendency to practical action. And alas! in spite
of all the benefit I had derived from Robert Hall, there were
times when memory was so poignant that I had no choice but
to rush from the lonely room haunted by tempting phantoms
too dangerously fair, and sober down the fever of the heart by
some violent bodily fatigue. The ardour which belongs to
early youth, and which it best dedicates to knowledge, had been
charmed prematurely to shrines less severely sacred. Therefore,
though I laboured, it was with that full *sense of labour* which
(as I found at a much later period of life) the truly triumphant
student never knows. Learning—that marble image—warms
into life, not at the toil of the chisel, but the worship of the
sculptor. The mechanical workman finds but the voiceless
stone.

At my uncle's, such a thing as a newspaper rarely made its
appearance. At Cambridge, even among reading men, the news-

papers had their due importance. Politics ran high; and I had not been three days at Cambridge before I heard Trevanion's name. Newspapers, therefore, had their charms for me. Trevanion's prophecy about himself seemed about to be fulfilled. There were rumours of changes in the Cabinet. Trevanion's name was bandied to and fro, struck from praise to blame, high and low, as a shuttlecock. Still the changes were not made, and the Cabinet held firm. Not a word in the *Morning Post,* under the head of *fashionable intelligence,* as to rumours that would have agitated me more than the rise and fall of governments—no hint of "the speedy nuptials of the daughter and sole heiress of a distinguished and wealthy·commoner;" only now and then, in enumerating the circle of brilliant guests at the house of some party chief, I gulped back the heart that rushed to my lips, when I saw the names of Lady Ellinor and Miss Trevanion.

But amongst all that prolific progeny of the periodical press—remote offspring of my great namesake and ancestor (for I hold the faith of my father)—where was the *Literary Times?*—what had so long retarded its promised blossoms? Not a leaf in the shape of advertisements had yet emerged from its mother earth. I hoped from my heart that the whole thing was abandoned, and would not mention it in my letters home, lest I should revive the mere idea of it. But, in default of the *Literary Times,* there did appear a new journal, a daily journal, too, a tall, slender, and meagre stripling, with a vast head, by way of prospectus, which protruded itself for three weeks successively at the top of the leading article;—with a fine and subtle body of paragraphs;—and the smallest legs, in the way of advertisements, that any poor newspaper ever stood upon! And yet this attenuated journal had a plump and plethoric title, a title that smacked of turtle and venison; an aldermanic, portly, grandiose, Falstaffian title—it was called THE CAPITALIST. And all those fine, subtle paragraphs were larded out with recipes how to make money. There was an El Dorado in every sentence. To believe that paper, you would think no man had ever yet found a proper return for his pounds, shillings, and pence. You would turn up your nose at twenty per cent. There was a great deal about Ireland—not her wrongs, thank Heaven! but her fisheries: a long inquiry what had become of the pearls for which Britain was once so famous: a learned disquisition upon certain lost gold mines now happily re-discovered; a very ingenious proposition to turn London smoke into manure, by a new chemical process : recommendations to the poor to hatch chickens in ovens like the ancient Egyptians ; agricultural schemes for sowing the waste lands in England with onions, upon the system adopted near Bedford—net produce one hundred pounds an acre. In short, according to that paper, every rood of ground might well maintain its man, and every shilling be like Hobson's money-bag, "the fruitful parent of a hundred more."   For three days, at the newspaper room of the Union Club, men talked of this journal ; some pished, some sneered, some wondered ; till an ill-natured mathematician, who had just taken his degree, and had spare time on his hands, sent a long letter to the *Morning Chronicle* showing up more blunders, in some article to which the editor of *The Capitalist* had specially invited attention, than would have paved the whole island of Laputa.   After that time, not a soul read *The Capitalist.*   How long it dragged on its existence I know not ; but it certainly did not die of a *maladie de langueur.*

Little thought I, when I joined in the laugh against *The Capitalist,* that I ought rather to have followed it to its grave, in black crape and weepers,—unfeeling wretch that I was ! But, like a poet, O *Capitalist !* thou wert not discovered, and appreciated, and prized, and mourned, till thou wert dead and buried, and the bill came in for thy monument !

The first term of my college life was just expiring, when I received a letter from my mother, so agitated, so alarming— at first reading so unintelligible—that I could only see that some great misfortune had befallen us ; and I stopped short and dropped on my knees to pray for the life and health of those whom that misfortune more specially seemed to menace ; and then—and then, towards the end of the last blurred sentence, read twice, thrice, over—I could cry, "Thank Heaven, thank Heaven ! it is only, then, money after all !"

PART XI

CHAPTER I

THE next day, on the outside of the Cambridge Telegraph, there was one passenger who ought to have impressed his fellow-travellers with a very respectful idea of his lore in the dead languages; for not a single syllable, in a live one, did he vouchsafe to utter from the moment he ascended that "bad eminence," to the moment in which he regained his mother earth. "Sleep," says honest Sancho, "covers a man better than a cloak." I am ashamed of thee, honest Sancho! thou art a sad plagiarist: for Tibullus said pretty nearly the same thing before thee,—

"Te somnus fusco velavit amictu."

But is not silence as good a cloak as sleep?—does it not wrap a man round with as offusc and impervious a fold? Silence—what a world it covers! — what busy schemes — what bright hopes, and dark fears—what ambition, or what despair! Do you ever see a man in any society sitting mute for hours, and not feel an uneasy curiosity to penetrate the wall he thus builds up between others and himself? Does he not interest you far more than the brilliant talker at your left—the airy wit at your right, whose shafts fall in vain on the sullen barrier of the silent man! Silence, dark sister of Nox and Erebus, how, layer upon layer, shadow upon shadow, blackness upon blackness, thou stretchest thyself from hell to heaven, over thy two chosen haunts—man's heart and the grave!

So, then, wrapped in my greatcoat and my silence, I performed my journey; and on the evening of the second day I reached the old-fashioned brick house. How shrill on my ears sounded the bell! How strange and ominous to my impatience seemed the light gleaming across the windows of

[1] Tibullus, iii. 4, 55.

the hall! How my heart beat as I watched the face of the servant who opened the gate to my summons!

"All well?" cried I.

"All well, sir," answered the servant cheerfully. "Mr. Squills, indeed, is with master, but I don't think there is anything the matter."

But now my mother appeared at the threshold, and I was in her arms.

"Sisty, Sisty!—my dear, dear son!—beggared, perhaps—and my fault—mine."

"Yours!—come into this room—out of hearing—your fault?"

"Yes—yes!—for if I had had no brother, or if I had not been led away,—if I had, as I ought, entreated poor Austin not to——"

"My dear, dearest mother, *you* accuse yourself for what, it seems, was my uncle's misfortune—I am sure not even his fault! (I made a gulp *there*.) No, lay the fault on the right shoulders —the defunct shoulders of that horrible progenitor, William Caxton the printer, for, though I don't yet know the particulars of what has happened, I will lay a wager it is connected with that fatal invention of printing. Come, come—my father is well, is he not?"

"Yes, thank Heaven."

"And I, too, and Roland, and little Blanche! Why, then you are right to thank Heaven, for your true treasures are untouched. But sit down and explain, pray."

"I cannot explain. I do not understand anything more than that he, my brother,—mine!—has involved Austin in—in——" (A fresh burst of tears.)

I comforted, scolded, laughed, preached, and adjured in a breath; and then, drawing my mother gently on, entered my father's study.

At the table was seated Mr. Squills, pen in hand, and a glass of his favourite punch by his side. My father was standing on the hearth, a shade more pale, but with a resolute expression on his countenance, which was new to its indolent thoughtful mildness. He lifted his eyes as the door opened, and then, putting his finger to his lips, as he glanced towards my mother, he said gaily, "No great harm done. Don't believe her! Women always exaggerate, and make realities of their own bugbears: it is the voice of their lively imaginations, as Wierus has clearly shown in accounting for the marks, moles, and hare lips which they inflict upon their innocent infants before they

are even born.⁴ My dear boy," added my father, as I here kissed
him and smiled in his face, " I thank you for that smile ! God
bless you ! " He wrung my hand, and turned a little aside.

" It is a great comfort," renewed my father, after a short pause,
" to know, when a misfortune happens, that it could not be
helped. Squills has just discovered that I have no bump of
cautiousness; so that, craniologically speaking, if I had escaped
one imprudence, I should certainly have run my head against
another."

"A man with your development is made to be taken in,"
said Mr. Squills consolingly.

" Do you hear that, my own Kitty ? and have you the heart
to blame Jack any longer—a poor creature cursed with a bump
that would take in the Stock Exchange ? And can any one
resist his bump, Squills ? "

"Impossible ! " said the surgeon authoritatively.

"Sooner or later it must involve him in its airy meshes—eh,
Squills ? entrap him into its fatal cerebral cell. There his fate
waits him, like the ant-lion in its pit."

"Too true," quoth Squills. " What a phrenological lecturer
you would have made ! "

" Go, then, my love," said my father, "and lay no blame but
on this melancholy cavity of mine, where cautiousness—is not !
Go, and let Sisty have some supper; for Squills says that he
has a fine development of the mathematical organs, and we
want his help. We are hard at work on figures, Pisistratus."

My mother looked broken-hearted, and, obeying submissively,
stole to the door without a word. But as she reached the
threshold she turned round, and beckoned to me to follow her.

I whispered my father and went out. My mother was
standing in the hall, and I saw by the lamp that she had dried
her tears, and that her face, though very sad, was more composed.

" Sisty," she said, in a low voice which struggled to be firm,
" promise me that you will tell me all—the worst, Sisty. They
keep it from me, and that is my hardest punishment ; for when
I don't know all that he—that Austin suffers, it seems to me
as if I had lost his heart. Oh, Sisty ! my child, my child, don't
fear me ! I shall be happy whatever befalls us, if I once get
back my privilege—my privilege, Sisty, to comfort, to share !—
do you understand me ? "

" Yes, indeed, my mother ! And with your good sense, and
clear woman's wit, if you will but feel how much we want them,

you will be the best counsellor we could have. So never fear ; you and I will have no secrets."

My mother kissed me, and went away with a less heavy step.

As I re-entered, my father came across the room and em braced me.

"My son," he said in a faltering voice, "if your modest prospects in life are ruined——"

"Father, father, can you think of me at such a moment ! Me ! —Is it possible to ruin the young, and strong, and healthy ! Ruin me, with these thews and sinews ! ruin me, with the education you have given me—thews and sinews of the mind ! Oh no ! there, Fortune is harmless ! And you forget, sir,—the saffron bag !"

Squills leapt up, and, wiping his eyes with one hand, gave me a sounding slap on the shoulder with the other.

"I am proud of the care I took of your infancy, Master Caxton. That comes of strengthening the digestive organs in early child-hood. Such sentiments are a proof of magnificent ganglions in a perfect state of order. When a man's tongue is as smooth as I am sure yours is, he slips through misfortune like an eel."

I laughed outright, my father smiled faintly ; and, seating my-self, I drew towards me a paper filled with Squills's memoranda, and said, "Now to find the unknown quantity. What on earth is this ? 'Supposed value of books, £750.' Oh, father ! this is impossible. I was prepared for anything but that. Your books —they are your life ?"

"Nay," said my father ; "after all, they are the offending party in this case, and so ought to be the principal victims. Besides, I believe I know most of them by heart. But, in truth, we are only entering all our effects, to be sure (added my father proudly) that, come what may, we are not dishonoured."

"Humour him," whispered Squills ; "we will save the books." Then he added aloud, as he laid finger and thumb on my pulse, "One, two, three, about seventy—capital pulse—soft and full— he can bear the whole : let us administer it."

My father nodded—"Certainly. But, Pisistratus, we must manage your dear mother. Why she should think of blaming herself, because poor Jack took wrong ways to enrich us, I cannot understand. But, as I have had occasion before to re-mark, Sphinx is a noun feminine."

My poor father ! that was a vain struggle for thy wonted innocent humour. The lips quivered.

Then the story came out. It seems that, when it was resolved to undertake the publication of the *Literary Times*, a certain

number of shareholders had been got together by the indefatigable energies of Uncle Jack; and in the deed of association and
partnership, my father's name figured conspicuously as the
holder of a fourth of this joint-property. If in this my father
had committed some imprudence, he had at least done nothing
that, according to the ordinary calculations of a secluded student,
could become ruinous.   But, just at the time when we were in
the hurry of leaving town, Jack had represented to my father
that it might be necessary to alter a little the plan of the
paper; and, in order to allure a larger circle of readers, touch
somewhat on the more vulgar news and interests of the day.
A change of plan might involve a change of title; and he
suggested to my father the expediency of leaving the smooth
hands of Mr. Tibbets altogether unfettered, as to the technical
name and precise form of the publication.   To this my father
had unwittingly assented, on hearing that the other shareholders
would do the same.   Mr. Peck, a printer of considerable opulence, and highly respectable name, had been found to advance
the sum necessary for the publication of the earlier numbers,
upon the guarantee of the said act of partnership and the
additional security of my father's signature to a document,
authorising Mr. Tibbets to make any change in the form or title
of the periodical that might be judged advisable, concurrent
with the consent of the other shareholders.

Now, it seems that Mr. Peck had, in his previous conferences
with Mr. Tibbets, thrown much cold water on the idea of the
Literary Times, and had suggested something that should " catch
the monied public,"—the fact being, as was afterwards discovered, that the printer, whose spirit of enterprise was congenial to Uncle Jack's, had shares in three or four speculations,
to which he was naturally glad of an opportunity to invite the
attention of the public.   In a word, no sooner was my poor
father's back turned, than the *Literary Times* was dropped incontinently, and Mr. Peck and Mr. Tibbets began to concentrate
their luminous notions into that brilliant and comet-like apparition which ultimately blazed forth under the title of *The
Capitalist.*

From this change of enterprise the more prudent and re-
sponsible of the original shareholders had altogether withdrawn.   A majority, indeed, were left; but the greater part of
those were shareholders of that kind most amenable to the
influences of Uncle Jack, and willing to be shareholders in
anything, since as yet they were possessors of nothing.

Assured of my father's responsibility, the adventurous Peck put plenty of spirit into the first launch of *The Capitalist*. All the walls were placarded with its announcements ; circular advertisements ran from one end of the kingdom to the other. Agents were engaged, correspondents levied *en masse*. The invasion of Xerxes on the Greeks was not more munificently provided for than that of *The Capitalist* upon the credulity and avarice of mankind.

But as Providence bestows upon fishes the instrument of fins, whereby they balance and direct their movements, however rapid and erratic, through the pathless deeps ; so to the cold-blooded creatures of our own species—that may be classed under the genus MONEY-MAKERS—the same protective power accords the fin-like properties of prudence and caution, where-with your true money-getter buoys and guides himself majestic-ally through the great seas of speculation. In short, the fishes the net was cast for were all scared from the surface at the first splash. They came round and smelt at the mesh with their sharp bottle-noses, and then, plying those invaluable fins, made off as fast as they could—plunging into the mud—hiding them-selves under rocks and coral banks. Metaphor apart, the capitalists buttoned up their pockets, and would have nothing to say to their namesake.

Not a word of this change, so abhorrent to all the notions of poor Augustine Caxton, had been breathed to him by Peck or Tibbets. He ate, and slept, and worked at the Great Book, occasionally wondering why he had not heard of the advent of the *Literary Times*, unconscious of all the awful responsibilities which *The Capitalist* was entailing on him, knowing no more of *The Capitalist* than he did of the last loan of the Rothschilds.

Difficult was it for all other human nature, save my father's, not to breathe an indignant anathema on the scheming head of the brother-in-law who had thus violated the most sacred obliga-tions of trust and kindred, and so entangled an unsuspecting recluse. But, to give even Jack Tibbets his due, he had firmly convinced himself that *The Capitalist* would make my father's fortune ; and if he did not announce to him the strange and anomalous development into which the original sleeping chrysalis of the *Literary Times* had taken portentous wing, it was purely and wholly in the knowledge that my father's " prejudices," as he termed them, would stand in the way of his becoming a Crœsus. And, in fact, Uncle Jack had believed so heartily in his own project, that he had put himself thoroughly into Mr. Peck's power, signed bills, in his own name, to some fabulous amount, and was actually now in the Fleet, whence his penitential and despairing confession was dated, arriving simultaneously with a short letter from Mr. Peck, wherein that respectable printer apprised my father that he had continued, at his own risk, the publication of *The Capitalist*, as far as a prudent care for his family would permit; that he need not say that a new daily journal was a very vast experiment; that the expense of such a paper as *The Capitalist* was immeasurably greater than that of a mere literary periodical, as originally suggested; and that now, being constrained to come upon the shareholders for the sums he had advanced, amounting to several thousands, he requested my father to settle with him immediately—delicately implying that Mr. Caxton himself might settle as he could with the other shareholders, most of whom, he grieved to add, he had been misled by Mr. Tibbets into believing to be men of substance, when in reality they were men of straw!

Nor was this all the evil. The "Great Anti-Bookseller Publishing Society,"—which had maintained a struggling existence—evinced by advertisements of sundry forthcoming works of solid interest and enduring nature, wherein, out of a long list, amidst a pompous array of "Poems;" "Dramas not intended for the Stage;" "Essays by Phileutheros, Philanthropos, Philopolis, Philodemus, and Philalethes," stood prominently forth, "The History of Human Error, Vols. I. and II., quarto, with illustrations,"—the "Anti-Bookseller Society," I say, that had hitherto evinced nascent and budding life by these exfoliations from its slender stem, died of a sudden blight, the moment its sun, in the shape of Uncle Jack, set in the Cimmerian regions of the Fleet; and a polite letter from another printer (O William Caxton, William Caxton!—fatal progenitor!)—informing my father of this event, stated complimentarily that it was to him "as the most respectable member of the Association," that the said printer would be compelled to look for expenses incurred, not only in the very costly edition of the "History of Human Error," but for those incurred in the print and paper devoted to "Poems," "Dramas not intended for the Stage," "Essays by Phileutheros, Philanthropos, Philopolis, Philodemus, and Philalethes," with sundry other works, no doubt of a very valuable nature, but in which a considerable loss, in a pecuniary point of view, must be necessarily expected.

I own that, as soon as I had mastered the above agreeable facts, and ascertained from Mr. Squills that my father really did seem to have rendered himself legally liable to these demands, I leant back in my chair, stunned and bewildered.

"So you see," said my father, "that as yet we are contending with monsters in the dark—in the dark all monsters look larger and uglier. Even Augustus Cæsar, though certainly he had never scrupled to make as many ghosts as suited his convenience, did not like the chance of a visit from them, and never sat alone *in tenebris*. What the amount of the sums claimed from me may be, we know not; what may be gained from the other shareholders is equally obscure and undefined. But the first thing to do is to get poor Jack out of prison."

"Uncle Jack out of prison!" exclaimed I; "surely, sir, that is carrying forgiveness too far."

"Why, he would not have been in prison if I had not been so blindly forgetful of his weakness, poor man! I ought to have known better. But my vanity misled me; I must needs publish a great book, as if (said Mr. Caxton, looking round the shelves) there were not great books enough in the world! I must needs, too, think of advancing and circulating knowledge in the form of a journal—I, who had not knowledge enough of the character of my own brother-in-law to keep myself from ruin! Come what will, I should think myself the meanest of men to let that poor creature, whom I ought to have considered as a monomaniac, rot in prison, because I, Austin Caxton, wanted common sense. And (concluded my father, resolutely) he is your mother's brother, Pisistratus. I should have gone to town at once; but, hearing that my wife had written to you, I waited till I could leave her to the companionship of hope and comfort —two blessings that smile upon every mother in the face of a son like you. To-morrow I go."

"Not a bit of it," said Mr. Squills firmly; "as your medical adviser, I forbid you to leave the house for the next six days."

CHAPTER II

SIR," continued Mr. Squills, biting off the end of a cigar which he pulled from his pocket, "you concede to me that it is a very important business on which you propose to go to London."

"Of that there is no doubt," replied my father.

"And the doing of business well or ill entirely depends upon

R

the habit of body!" cried Mr. Squills triumphantly. "Do you know, Mr. Caxton, that while you are looking so calm, and talking so quietly—just on purpose to sustain your son and delude your wife—do you know that your pulse, which is naturally little more than sixty, is nearly a hundred? Do you know, sir, that your mucous membranes are in a state of high irritation, apparent by the *papillæ* at the tip of your tongue? And if, with a pulse like this, and a tongue like that, you think of settling money matters with a set of sharp-witted tradesmen, all I can say is, that you are a ruined man."

"But—" began my father.

"Did not Squire Rollick," pursued Mr. Squills — "Squire Rollick, the hardest head at a bargain I know of—did not Squire Rollick sell that pretty little farm of his, Scranny Holt, for thirty per cent. below its value? And what was the cause, sir?—the whole country was in amaze!—what was the cause, but an incipient simmering attack of the yellow jaundice, which made him take a gloomy view of human life, and the agricultural interest? On the other hand, did not Lawyer Cool, the most prudent man in the three kingdoms—Lawyer Cool, who was so methodical, that all the clocks in the county were set by his watch — plunge one morning head over heels into a frantic speculation for cultivating the bogs in Ireland? (His watch did not go right for the next three months, which made our whole shire an hour in advance of the rest of England!) And what was the cause of that nobody knew, till I was called in, and found the cerebral membrane in a state of acute irritation, probably just in the region of his acquisitiveness and ideality. No, Mr. Caxton, you will stay at home, and take a soothing preparation I shall send you, of lettuce leaves and marsh-mallows. But I," continued Squills, lighting his cigar, and taking two determined whiffs—"but *I* will go up to town and settle the business for you, and take with me this young gentleman, whose digestive functions are just in a state to deal safely with those horrible elements of dyspepsia—the L. S. D."

As he spoke, Mr. Squills set his foot significantly upon mine.

"But," resumed my father mildly, "though I thank you very much, Squills, for your kind offer, I do not recognise the necessity of accepting it. I am not so bad a philosopher as you seem to imagine; and the blow I have received has not so deranged my physical organisation as to render me unfit to transact my affairs."

"Hum!" grunted Squills, starting up and seizing my father's

pulse; "ninety-six—ninety-six if a beat! And the tongue, sir!"

"Pshaw!" quoth my father, "you have not even seen my tongue!"

"No need of that, I know what it is by the state of the eyelids—tip scarlet, sides rough as a nutmeg-grater!"

"Pshaw!" again said my father, this time impatiently.

"Well," said Squills solemnly, "it is my duty to say (here my mother entered, to tell me that supper was ready), and I say it to you, Mrs. Caxton, and to you, Mr. Pisistratus Caxton, as the parties most nearly interested, that if you, sir, go to London upon this matter, I'll not answer for the consequences."

"Oh! Austin, Austin," cried my mother, running up and throwing her arms round my father's neck; while I, little less alarmed by Squills's serious tone and aspect, represented strongly the inutility of Mr. Caxton's personal interference at the present moment. All he could do on arriving in town would be to put the matter into the hands of a good lawyer, and that we could do for him; it would be time enough to send for him when the extent of the mischief done was more clearly ascertained. Meanwhile Squills griped my father's pulse, and my mother hung on his neck.

"Ninety-six—ninety-seven!" groaned Squills in a hollow voice.

"I don't believe it!" cried my father, almost in a passion— "never better nor cooler in my life."

"And the tongue—look at his tongue, Mrs. Caxton—a tongue, ma'am, so bright that you could see to read by it!"

"Oh! Austin, Austin!"

"My dear, it is not my tongue that is in fault, I assure you," said my father, speaking through his teeth; "and the man knows no more of my tongue than he does of the Mysteries of Eleusis."

"Put it out then," exclaimed Squills, "and if he be not as I say, you have my leave to go to London, and throw your whole fortune into the two great pits you have dug for it. Put it out!"

"Mr. Squills!" said my father, colouring—"Mr. Squills, for shame!"

"Dear, dear Austin! your hand is so hot—you are feverish, I am sure."

"Not a bit of it."

"But, sir, only just gratify Mr. Squills," said I coaxingly.

"There, there!" said my father, fairly baited into submission, and shyly exhibiting for a moment the extremest end of the vanquished organ of eloquence.

Squills darted forward his lynx-like eyes. "Red as a lobster, and rough as a gooseberry-bush!" cried Squills, in a tone of savage joy.

CHAPTER III

HOW was it possible for one poor tongue, so reviled and persecuted, so humbled, insulted, and triumphed over—to resist three tongues in league against it?

Finally, my father yielded, and Squills, in high spirits, declared, that he would go to supper with me, to see that I ate nothing that could tend to discredit his reliance on my system. Leaving my mother still with her Austin, the good surgeon then took my arm, and, as soon as we were in the next room, shut the door carefully, wiped his forehead, and said—"I think we have saved him!"

"Would it really, then, have injured my father so much?"

"So much!—why, you foolish young man, don't you see that, with his ignorance of business, where he himself is concerned— though for any other one's business, neither Rollick nor Cool has a better judgment—and with his d—d Quixotic spirit of honour worked up into a state of excitement, he would have rushed to Mr. Tibbets and exclaimed, 'How much do you owe? there it is!' settled in the same way with these printers, and come back without a sixpence; whereas you and I can look coolly about us, and reduce the inflammation to the minimum!"

"I see, and thank you heartily, Squills."

"Besides," said the surgeon, with more feeling, "your father has really been making a noble effort over himself. He suffers more than you would think—not for himself (for I do believe that, if he were alone in the world, he would be quite contented if he could save fifty pounds a year and his books), but for your mother and yourself; and a fresh access of emotional excitement, all the nervous anxiety of a journey to London on such a business, might have ended in a paralytic or epileptic affection. Now we have him here snug; and the worst news we can give him will be better than what he will make up his mind for. But you don't eat."

"Eat! How can I? My poor father!"

"The effect of grief upon the gastric juices, through the nervous system, is very remarkable," said Mr. Squills philosophically, and helping himself to a broiled bone; "it increases the thirst, while it takes away hunger. No—don't touch port!— heating! Sherry and water."

CHAPTER IV

THE house-door had closed upon Mr. Squills—that gentleman having promised to breakfast with me the next morning, so that we might take the coach from our gate—and I remained alone, seated by the supper-table, and revolving all I had heard, when my father walked in.

"Pisistratus," said he gravely, and looking round him, "your mother!—suppose the worst—your first care, then, must be to try and secure something for her. You and I are men—we can never want, while we have health of mind and body; but a woman—and if anything happens to me——"

My father's lip writhed as it uttered these brief sentences.

"My dear, dear father!" said I, suppressing my tears with difficulty, "all evils, as you yourself said, look worse by anticipation. It is impossible that your whole fortune can be involved. The newspaper did not run many weeks; and only the first volume of your work is printed. Besides, there must be other shareholders who will pay their quota. Believe me, I feel sanguine as to the result of my embassy. As for my poor mother, it is not the loss of fortune that will wound her— depend on it, she thinks very little of that; it is the loss of your confidence."

"My confidence!"

"Ah yes! tell her all your fears, as your hopes. Do not let your affectionate pity exclude her from one corner of your heart."

"It is that—it is *that*, Austin,—my husband—my joy—my pride—my soul—my all!" cried a soft broken voice.

My mother had crept in, unobserved by us.

My father looked at us both, and the tears which had before stood in his eyes forced their way. Then opening his arms, into which his Kitty threw herself joyfully—he lifted those moist eyes upward, and, by the movement of his lips, I saw that he thanked God.

I stole out of the room.   I felt that those two hearts should be left to beat and to blend alone.   And from that hour, I am convinced that Augustine Caxton acquired a stouter philosophy than that of the stoics.   The fortitude that concealed pain was no longer needed, for the pain was no longer felt.

CHAPTER V

MR. SQUILLS and I performed our journey without adventure, and, as we were not alone on the coach, with little conversation.   We put up at a small inn in the City, and the next morning I sallied forth to see Trevanion—for we agreed that he would be the best person to advise us.   But, on arriving at St. James's Square, I had the disappointment of hearing that the whole family had gone to Paris three days before, and were not expected to return till the meeting of Parliament.

This was a sad discouragement, for I had counted much on Trevanion's clear head, and that extraordinary range of accomplishment in all matters of business—all that related to practical life—which my old patron pre-eminently possessed.   The next thing would be to find Trevanion's lawyer (for Trevanion was one of those men whose solicitors are sure to be able and active). But the fact was, that he left so little to lawyers, that he had never had occasion to communicate with one since I had known him; and I was therefore in ignorance of the very name of his solicitor; nor could the porter, who was left in charge of the house, enlighten me.   Luckily, I bethought myself of Sir Sedley Beaudesert, who could scarcely fail to give me the information required, and who, at all events, might recommend to me some other lawyer.   So to him I went.

I found Sir Sedley at breakfast with a young gentleman who seemed about twenty.   The good baronet was delighted to see me; but I thought it was with a little confusion, rare to his cordial ease, that he presented me to his cousin, Lord Castleton. It was a name familiar to me, though I had never before met its patrician owner.

The Marquis of Castleton was indeed a subject of envy to young idlers, and afforded a theme of interest to grey-beard politicians.   Often had I heard of " that lucky fellow Castleton," who, when of age, would step into one of those colossal fortunes which would realise the dreams of Aladdin—a fortune that had been out to nurse since his minority. Often had I heard graver gossips wonder whether Castleton would take any active part in public life—whether he would keep up the family influence. His mother (still alive) was a superior woman, and had devoted herself, from his childhood, to supply a father's loss, and fit him for his great position. It was said that he was clever—had been educated by a tutor of great academic distinction, and was reading for a double first class at Oxford. This young marquis was indeed the head of one of those few houses still left in England that retain feudal importance. He was important, not only from his rank and his vast fortune, but from an immense circle of powerful connections; from the ability of his two predecessors, who had been keen politicians and cabinet-ministers; from the *prestige* they had bequeathed to his name; from the peculiar nature of his property, which gave him the returning interest in no less than six parliamentary seats in Great Britain and Ireland—besides the indirect ascendency which the head of the Castletons had always exercised over many powerful and noble allies of that princely house. I was not aware that he was related to Sir Sedley, whose world of action was so remote from politics; and it was with some surprise that I now heard that announcement, and certainly with some interest that I, perhaps from the verge of poverty, gazed on this young heir of fabulous El Dorados.

It was easy to see that Lord Castleton had been brought up with a careful knowledge of his future greatness, and its serious responsibilities. He stood immeasurably aloof from all the affectations common to the youth of minor patricians. He had not been taught to value himself on the cut of a coat, or the shape of a hat. His world was far above St. James's Street and the clubs. He was dressed plainly, though in a style peculiar to himself—a white neck-cloth (which was not at that day quite so uncommon for morning use as it is now), trousers without straps, thin shoes and gaiters. In his manner there was nothing of the supercilious apathy which characterises the dandy introduced to some one whom he doubts if he can nod to from the bow-window at White's—none of such vulgar coxcombries had Lord Castleton; and yet a young gentleman more emphatically coxcomb it was impossible to see. He had been told, no doubt, that, as the head of a house which was almost in itself a party in the state, he should be bland and civil to all men; and this duty being grafted upon a nature singularly cold and unsocial, gave to his politeness something so stiff, yet so con-

descending, that it brought the blood to one's cheek—though
the momentary anger was counterbalanced by a sense of the
almost ludicrous contrast between this gracious majesty of de-
portment, and the insignificant figure, with the boyish beardless
face, by which it was assumed.   Lord Castleton did not content
himself with a mere bow at our introduction.   Much to my
wonder how he came by the information he displayed, he made
me a little speech after the manner of Louis XIV. to a provincial
noble—studiously modelled upon that royal maxim of urbane
policy which instructs a king that he should know something of
the birth, parentage, and family of his meanest gentleman.   It
was a little speech, in which my father's learning, and my uncle's
services, and the amiable qualities of your humble servant, were
neatly interwoven—delivered in a falsetto tone, as if learned by
heart, though it must have been necessarily impromptu ; and
then, reseating himself, he made a gracious motion of the head
and hand, as if to authorise me to do the same.

Conversation succeeded, by galvanic jerks and spasmodic
starts—a conversation that Lord Castleton contrived to tug so
completely out of poor Sir Sedley's ordinary course of small and
polished small-talk, that that charming personage, accustomed,
as he well deserved, to be Coryphæus at his own table, was completely silenced.   With his light reading, his rich stores of
anecdote, his good-humoured knowledge of the drawing-room
world, he had scarce a word that would fit into the great,
rough, serious matters which Lord Castleton threw upon the
table, as he nibbled his toast.   Nothing but the most grave and
practical subjects of human interest seemed to attract this future
leader of mankind.   The fact is that Lord Castleton had been
taught everything that relates to *property*—(a knowledge which
embraces a very wide circumference).   It had been said to him,
" You will be an immense proprietor—knowledge is essential to
your self-preservation.   You will be puzzled, bubbled, ridiculed,
duped every day of your life, if you do not make yourself acquainted with all by which property is assailed or defended,
impoverished or increased.   You have a vast stake in the
country—you must learn all the interests of Europe—nay, of
the civilised world—for those interests react on the country, and
the interests of the country are of the greatest possible consequence to the interests of the Marquis of Castleton.   Thus the
state of the Continent—the policy of Metternich—the condition
of the Papacy—the growth of Dissent—the proper mode of
dealing with the general spirit of Democracy, which was the

"Took refuge in his easychair and the
contemplation of his snuff-box"

epidemic of European monarchies—the relative proportions of the agricultural and manufacturing population—corn-laws, currency, and the laws that regulate wages—a criticism on the leading speakers of the House of Commons, with some discursive observations on the importance of fattening cattle—the introduction of flax into Ireland—emigration—the condition of the poor—the doctrines of Mr. Owen—the pathology of potatoes; the connection between potatoes, pauperism, and patriotism; these, and such-like stupendous subjects for reflection—all branching more or less intricately from the single idea of the Castleton property—the young lord discussed and disposed of in half-a-dozen prim, poised sentences—evincing, I must say in justice, no inconsiderable information, and a mighty solemn turn of mind. The oddity was, that the subjects so selected and treated should not come rather from some young barrister, or mature political economist, than from so gorgeous a lily of the field. Of a man less elevated in rank one would certainly have said—" Cleverish, but a prig;" but there really was something so respectable in a personage born to such fortunes, and having nothing to do but to bask in the sunshine, voluntarily taking such pains with himself, and condescending to identify his own interests—the interests of the Castleton property—with the concerns of his lesser fellow-mortals, that one felt the young marquis had in him the stuff to become a very considerable man.

Poor Sir Sedley, to whom all these matters were as unfamiliar as the theology of the Talmud, after some vain efforts to slide the conversation into easier grooves, fairly gave in, and, with a compassionate smile on his handsome countenance, took refuge in his easy-chair and the contemplation of his snuff-box.

At last, to our great relief, the servant announced Lord Castleton's carriage: and, with another speech of overpowering affability to me, and a cold shake of the hand to Sir Sedley, Lord Castleton went his way.

The breakfast parlour looked on the street, and I turned mechanically to the window as Sir Sedley followed his guest out of the room. A travelling carriage with four post-horses was at the door; and a servant, who looked like a foreigner, was in waiting with his master's cloak. As I saw Lord Castleton step into the street, and wrap himself in his costly mantle lined with sables, I observed, more than I had while he was in the room, the enervate slightness of his frail form, and the more than paleness of his thin joyless face; and then, instead of envy,

I felt compassion for the owner of all this pomp and grandeur—
felt that I would not have exchanged my hardy health, and easy
humour, and vivid capacities of enjoyment in things the slightest
and most within the reach of all men, for the wealth and greatness which that poor youth perhaps deserved the more for
putting them so little to the service of pleasure.

"Well," said Sir Sedley, "and what do you think of him?"

"He is just the sort of man Trevanion would like," said I
evasively.

"That is true," answered Sir Sedley, in a serious tone of
voice, and looking at me somewhat earnestly. "Have you
heard?—but no, you cannot have heard yet."

"Heard what?"

"My dear young friend," said the kindest and most delicate
of all fine gentlemen, sauntering away that he might not observe
the emotion he caused, "Lord Castleton is going to Paris to join
the Trevanions. The object Lady Ellinor has had at heart
for many a long year is won, and our pretty Fanny will be
Marchioness of Castleton when her betrothed is of age—that
is, in six months. The two mothers have settled it all between
them!"

I made no answer, but continued to look out of the window.

"This alliance," resumed Sir Sedley, "was all that was wanting to assure Trevanion's position. When Parliament meets,
he will have some great office. Poor man! how I shall pity
him! It is extraordinary to me," continued Sir Sedley, benevolently going on, that I might have full time to recover myself,
"how contagious that disease called 'business' is in our foggy
England! Not only Trevanion, you see, has the complaint in
its very worst and most complicated form, but that poor dear
cousin of mine, who is so young (here Sir Sedley sighed), and
might enjoy himself so much, is worse than you were when
Trevanion was fagging you to death. But, to be sure, a great
name and position, like Castleton's, must be a very heavy affliction to a conscientious mind. You see how the sense of its
responsibilities has *aged* him already—positively, two great
wrinkles under his eyes. Well, after all, I admire him, and
respect his tutor; a soil naturally very thin, I suspect, has been
most carefully cultivated; and Castleton, with Trevanion's help,
will be the first man in the peerage—prime minister some day,
I dare say. And when I think of it, how grateful I ought to
feel to his father and mother, who produced him quite in their
old age; for, if he had not been born, I should have been the

most miserable of men—yes, positively, that horrible marquisate would have come to me! I never think over Horace Walpole's regrets, when he got the earldom of Orford, without the deepest sympathy, and without a shudder at the thought of what my dear Lady Castleton was kind enough to save me from—all owing to the Ems waters, after twenty years' marriage! Well, my young friend, and how are all at home?"

As when, some notable performer not having yet arrived behind the scenes, or having to change his dress, or not having yet quite recovered an unlucky extra tumbler of exciting fluids —and the green curtain has therefore unduly delayed its ascent —you perceive that the thorough-bass in the orchestra charitably devotes himself to a prelude of astonishing prolixity, calling in "Lodoiska" or "Der Freischutz" to beguile the time, and allow the procrastinating histrio leisure sufficient to draw on his flesh-coloured pantaloons, and give himself the proper complexion for a Coriolanus or Macbeth—even so had Sir Sedley made that long speech, requiring no rejoinder, till he saw the time had arrived when he could artfully close with the flourish of a final interrogative, in order to give poor Pisistratus Caxton all pre-paration to compose himself and step forward. There is certainly something of exquisite kindness, and thoughtful bene-volence, in that rarest of gifts,—*fine breeding ;* and when now, remanned and resolute, I turned round and saw Sir Sedley's soft blue eye shyly, but benignantly, turned to me—while, with a grace no other snuff-taker ever had since the days of Pope, he gently proceeded to refresh himself by a pinch of the cele-brated Beaudesert mixture—I felt my heart as gratefully moved towards him as if he had conferred on me some colossal obliga-tion. And this crowning question—"And how are all at home?" restored me entirely to my self-possession, and for the moment distracted the bitter current of my thoughts.

I replied by a brief statement of my father's involvement, dis-guising our apprehensions as to its extent, speaking of it rather as an annoyance than a possible cause of ruin, and ended by asking Sir Sedley to give me the address of Trevanion's lawyer.

The good baronet listened with great attention ; and that quick penetration which belongs to a man of the world enabled him to detect that I had smoothed over matters more than became a faithful narrator.

He shook his head, and, seating himself on the sofa, motioned me to come to his side ; then, leaning his arm over my shoulder, he said, in his seductive, winning way—

"We two young fellows should understand each other when we talk of money matters. I can say to you what I could not say to my respectable senior—by three years; your excellent father. Frankly, then, I suspect this is a bad business. I know little about newspapers, except that I have to subscribe to one in my county, which costs me a small income ; but I know that a London daily paper might ruin a man in a few weeks. And as for shareholders, my dear Caxton, I was once teased into being a shareholder in a canal that ran through my property, and ultimately ran off with £30,000 of it! The other share-holders were all drowned in the canal, like Pharaoh and his host in the Red Sea. But your father is a great scholar, and must not be plagued with such matters. I owe him a great deal. He was very kind to me at Cambridge, and gave me the taste for reading, to which I owe the pleasantest hours of my life. So, when you and the lawyers have found out what the extent of the mischief is, you and I must see how we can best settle it. What the deuce! my young friend—I have no 'encumbrances,' as the servants, with great want of politeness, call wives and children. And I am not a miserable great landed millionaire, like that poor dear Castleton, who owes so many duties to society that he can't spend a shilling, except in a grand way, and purely to benefit the public. So go, my boy, to Trevanion's lawyer: he is mine, too. Clever fellow—sharp as a needle, Mr. Pike, in Great Ormond Street—name on a brass plate ; and when he has settled the amount, we young scape-graces will help each other, without a word to the old folks."

What good it does to a man, throughout life, to meet kindness and generosity like this in his youth !

I need not say that I was too faithful a representative of my father's scholarly pride, and susceptible independence of spirit, to accept this proposal; and probably Sir Sedley, rich and liberal as he was, did not dream of the extent to which his pro-posal might involve him. But I expressed my gratitude, so as to please and move this last relic of the De Coverleys, and went from his house straight to Mr. Pike's office, with a little note of introduction from Sir Sedley. I found Mr. Pike exactly the man I had anticipated from Trevanion's character—short, quick, intelligent, in question and answer; imposing and some-what domineering in manner—not overcrowded with business, but with enough for experience and respectability ; neither young nor old ; neither a pedantic machine of parchment, nor a jaunty offhand coxcomb of West End manners.

"It is an ugly affair," said he, "but one that requires management. Leave it all in my hands for three days. Don't go near Mr. Tibbets, nor Mr. Peck; and on Saturday next, at two o'clock, if you will call here, you shall know my opinion of the whole matter." With that, Mr. Pike glanced at the clock, and I took up my hat, and went.

There is no place more delightful than a great capital, if you are comfortably settled in it—have arranged the methodical disposal of your time, and know how to take business and pleasure in due proportions. But a flying visit to a great capital, in an unsettled, unsatisfactory way—at an inn—an inn in the City, too—with a great worrying load of business on your mind, of which you are to hear no more of for three days; and an aching, jealous, miserable sorrow at the heart, such as I had— leaving you no labour to pursue, and no pleasure that you have the heart to share in—oh, a great capital then is indeed forlorn, wearisome, and oppressive! It is the Castle of Indolence, not as Thomson built it, but as Beckford drew in his Hall of Eblis —a wandering up and down, to and fro—a great awful space, with your hand pressed to your heart; and—oh for a rush on some half-tame horse, through the measureless green wastes of Australia! That is the place for a man who has no home in the Babel, and whose hand is ever pressing to his heart, with its dull, burning pain.

Mr. Squills decoyed me the second evening into one of the small theatres; and very heartily did Mr. Squills enjoy all he saw and all he heard. And while, with a convulsive effort of the jaws, I was trying to laugh too, suddenly in one of the actors, who was performing the worshipful part of a parish beadle, I recognised a face that I had seen before. Five minutes afterwards I had disappeared from the side of Squills, and was amidst that strange world—BEHIND THE SCENES.

My beadle was much too busy and important to allow me a good opportunity to accost him, till the piece was over. I then seized hold of him, as he was amicably sharing a pot of porter with a gentleman in black shorts and a laced waistcoat, who was to play the part of a broken-hearted father in the Domestic Drama in Three Acts, that would conclude the amusements of the evening.

"Excuse me," said I apologetically; "but as the Swan pertinently observes,—'Should auld acquaintance be forgot?'"

"The Swan, sir!" cried the beadle aghast—"the Swan never demeaned himself by such d——d broad Scotch as that!"

"The Tweed has its swans as well as the Avon, Mr. Peacock."

"St—st—hush—hush—h—u—sh!" whispered the beadle in great alarm, and eyeing me, with savage observation, under his corked eyebrows. Then, taking me by the arm, he jerked me away. When he had got as far as the narrow limits of that little stage would allow, Mr. Peacock said—

"Sir, you have the advantage of me; I don't remember you. Ah! you need not look!—by gad, sir, I am not to be bullied,—it was all fair play. If you will play with gentlemen, sir, you must run the consequences."

I hastened to appease the worthy man.

"Indeed, Mr. Peacock, if you remember, I refused to play with you; and, so far from wishing to offend you, I now come on purpose to compliment you on your excellent acting, and to inquire if you have heard anything lately of your young friend Mr. Vivian."

"Vivian?—never heard the name, sir. Vivian! Pooh, you are trying to hoax me; very good!"

"I assure you, Mr. Peac——"

"St—st—How the deuce did you know that I was once called Peac—, that is, people called me Peac—. A friendly nickname, no more—drop it, sir, or you 'touch me with noble anger!'"

"Well, well; 'the rose by any name will smell as sweet,' as the Swan, this time at least judiciously, observes. But Mr. Vivian, too, seems to have other names at his disposal. I mean a young, dark, handsome man—or rather boy—with whom I met you in company by the roadside, one morning."

"O—h," said Mr. Peacock, looking much relieved, "I know whom you mean, though I don't remember to have had the pleasure of seeing you before. No; I have not heard anything of the young man lately. I wish I did know something of him. He was 'a gentleman in my own way.' Sweet Will has hit him off to a hair!—

'The courtier's, soldier's, scholar's eye, tongue, sword.'

Such a hand with a cue!—you should have seen him seek the 'bubble reputation at the *cannon's* mouth.' I may say," continued Mr. Peacock emphatically, "that he was a regular trump —trump!" he reiterated with a start, as if the word had stung him—"trump! he was a BRICK!"

Then fixing his eyes on me, dropping his arms, interlacing his fingers in the manner recorded of Talma in the celebrated

"Qu'en distu!" he resumed in a hollow voice, slow and distinct—

"When—saw—you—him,—young m—m—a—n—nnn?"

Finding the tables thus turned on myself, and not willing to give Mr. Peac— any clue to poor Vivian (who thus appeared, to my great satisfaction, to have finally dropped an acquaintance more versatile than reputable), I contrived, by a few evasive sentences, to keep Mr. Peac—'s curiosity at a distance, till he was summoned in haste to change his attire for the domestic drama. And so we parted.

CHAPTER VI

I HATE law details as cordially as my readers can, and therefore I shall content myself with stating that Mr. Pike's management, at the end, not of three days, but of two weeks, was so admirable, that Uncle Jack was drawn out of prison, and my father extracted from all his liabilities, by a sum two-thirds less than was first startlingly submitted to our indignant horror—and that, too, in a manner that would have satisfied the conscience of the most punctilious formalist whose contribution to the national fund, for an omitted payment to the Income Tax, the Chancellor of the Exchequer ever had the honour to acknowledge. Still, the sum was very large in proportion to my poor father's income: and what with Jack's debts, the claims of the Anti-Publisher Society's printer—including the very expensive plates that had been so lavishly bespoken, and in great part completed, for the "History of Human Error"—and, above all, the liabilities incurred on *The Capitalist*—what with the *plant*, as Mr. Peck technically phrased a great upas-tree of a total, branching out into types, cases, printing-presses, engines, &c., all now to be resold at a third of their value; what with advertisements and bills, that had covered all the dead-walls by which rubbish might be shot, throughout the three kingdoms; what with the dues of reporters, and salaries of writers, who had been engaged for a year at least to *The Capitalist*, and whose claims survived the wretch they had killed and buried: what, in short, with all that the combined ingenuity of Uncle Jack and Printer Peck could supply for the utter ruin of the Caxton family—even after all deductions, curtailments, and after all that one could extract in the way of just contribution from the least unsubstantial of those shadows called the shareholders—my father's fortune was reduced to a sum of between seven and eight thousand pounds, which, being placed at mortgage at four per cent., yielded just £372, 10s. a year—enough for my father to live upon, but not enough to afford also his son Pisistratus the advantages of education at Trinity College, Cambridge.   The blow fell rather upon me than my father, and my young shoulders bore it without much wincing.

This settled to our universal satisfaction, I went to pay my farewell visit to Sir Sedley Beaudesert.   He had made much of me during my stay in London.   I had breakfasted and dined with him pretty often; I had presented Squills to him, who no sooner set eyes upon that splendid conformation, than he described his character with the nicest accuracy, as the necessary consequence of such a development for the rosy pleasures of life.   We had never once retouched on the subject of Fanny's marriage, and both of us tacitly avoided even mentioning the Trevanions.   But in this last visit, though he maintained the same reserve as to Fanny, he referred without scruple to her father.

"Well, my young Athenian," said he, after congratulating me on the result of the negotiations, and endeavouring again in vain to bear at least some share in my father's losses—"well, I see I cannot press this farther; but at least I *can* press on you any little interest I may have, in obtaining some appointment for yourself in one of the public offices.   Trevanion could of course be more useful, but I can understand that he is not the kind of man you would like to apply to."

"Shall I own to you, my dear Sir Sedley, that I have no taste for official employment?   I am too fond of my liberty.   Since I have been at my uncle's old Tower, I account for half my character by the Borderer's blood that is in me.   I doubt if I am meant for the life of cities; and I have old floating notions in my head, that will serve to amuse me when I get home, and may settle into schemes.   And now to change the subject, may I ask what kind of person has succeeded me as Mr. Trevanion's secretary?"

"Why, he has got a broad-shouldered, stooping fellow, in spectacles and cotton stockings, who has written upon 'Rent,' I believe—an imaginative treatise in his case, I fear, for rent is a thing he could never have received, and not often been trusted to pay.   However, he is one of your political economists, and wants Trevanion to sell his pictures, as 'unproductive capital.'

Less mild than Pope's Narcissa, 'to make a wash,' he would certainly 'stew a child.' Besides this official secretary, Trevanion trusts, however, a good deal to a clever, good-looking young gentleman, who is a great favourite with him."

"What is his name?"

"His name?—oh, Gower; a natural son, I believe, of one of the Gower family."

Here two of Sir Sedley's fellow fine gentlemen lounged in, and my visit ended.

CHAPTER VII

I SWEAR," cried my uncle, "that it *shall* be so." And with a big frown, and a truculent air, he seized the fatal instrument.

"Indeed, brother, it must not," said my father, laying one pale, scholar-like hand mildly on Captain Roland's brown, bellicose, and bony fist; and with the other, outstretched, protecting the menaced, palpitating victim.

Not a word had my uncle heard of our losses, until they had been adjusted, and the sum paid; for we all knew that the old Tower would have been gone—sold to some neighbouring squire or jobbing attorney—at the first impetuous impulse of Uncle Roland's affectionate generosity. Austin endangered! Austin ruined!—he would never have rested till he came, cash in hand, to his deliverance. Therefore, I say, not till all was settled did I write to the Captain, and tell him gaily what had chanced. And, however light I made of our misfortunes, the letter brought the Captain to the red brick house the same evening on which I myself reached it, and about an hour later. My uncle had not sold the Tower, but he came prepared to carry us off to it *vi et armis*. We must live with him, and on him—let or sell the brick house, and put out the remnant of my father's income to nurse and accumulate. And it was on finding my father's resistance stubborn, and that hitherto he had made no way, that my uncle, stepping back into the hall, in which he had left his carpet-bag, &c., returned with an old oak case, and, touching a spring roller, out flew the Caxton pedigree.

Out it flew—covering all the table, and undulating, Nile-like, till it had spread over books, papers, my mother's workbox, and the tea-service (for the table was large and compendious, em-

8

blematic of its owner's mind)—and then, flowing on the carpet, dragged its slow length along, till it was stopped by the fender.

"Now," said my uncle solemnly, "there never have been but two causes of difference between you and me, Austin.   One is over; why should the other last?   Aha! I know why you hang back; you think that we may quarrel about it!"

"About what, Roland?"

"About it, I say—and I'll be d—d if we do!" cried my uncle, reddening.   "And I have been thinking a great deal upon the matter, and I have no doubt you are right.   So I brought the old parchment with me, and you shall see me fill up the blank, just as you would have it.   Now, then, you will come and live with me, and we can never quarrel any more."

Thus saying, Uncle Roland looked round for pen and ink; and, having found them—not without difficulty, for they had been submerged under the overflow of the pedigree—he was about to fill up the *lacuna,* or *hiatus,* which had given rise to such memorable controversy, with the name of "William Caxton, printer in the Sanctuary," when my father, slowly recovering his breath, and aware of his brother's purpose, intervened.   It would have done your heart good to hear them—so completely, in the inconsistency of human nature, had they changed sides upon the question—my father now all for Sir William de Caxton, the hero of Bosworth; my uncle all for the immortal printer. And in this discussion they grew animated; their eyes sparkled, their voices rose—Roland's voice deep and thunderous, Austin's sharp and piercing.   Mr. Squills stopped his ears.   Thus it arrived at that point, when my uncle doggedly came to the end of all argumentation—"I swear that it shall be so;" and my father, trying the last resource of pathos, looked pleadingly into Roland's eyes, and said, with a tone soft as mercy, "Indeed, brother, it must not."   Meanwhile the dry parchment crisped, creaked, and trembled in every pore of its yellow skin.

"But," said I, coming in opportunely, like the Horatian deity, "I don't see that either of you gentlemen has a right so to dispose of my ancestry.   It is quite clear that a man has no possession in posterity.   Posterity may possess him; but deuce a bit will he ever be the better for his great-great-grandchildren!'

SQUILLS.—" Hear, hear !"

PISISTRATUS (warming).—" But a man's ancestry is a positive

property to him. How much, not only of acres, but of his constitution, his temper, his conduct, character, and nature, he may inherit from some progenitor ten times removed! Nay, without that progenitor would he ever have been born—would a Squills ever have introduced him into the world, or a nurse ever have carried him *upo kolpo?*"

SQUILLS.—"Hear, hear!"

PISISTRATUS (with dignified emotion).—"No man, therefore, has a right to rob another of a forefather, with a stroke of his pen, from any motives, howsoever amiable. In the present instance, you will say, perhaps, that the ancestor in question is apocryphal — it may be the printer, it may be the knight. Granted; but here, where history is in fault, shall a mére sentiment decide? While both are doubtful, my imagination appropriates both. At one time I can reverence industry and learning in the printer; at another, valour and devotion in the knight. This kindly doubt gives me two great forefathers; and, through them, two trains of idea that influence my conduct under different circumstances. I will not permit you, Captain Roland, to rob me of either forefather—either train of idea. Leave, then, this sacred void unfilled, unprofaned: and accept this compromise of chivalrous courtesy—while my father lives with the Captain, we will believe in the printer; when away from the Captain, we will stand firm to the knight."

"Good!" cried Uncle Roland, as I paused, a little out of breath.

"And," said my mother softly, "I do think, Austin, there is a way of settling the matter which will please all parties. It is quite sad to think that poor Roland, and dear little Blanche, should be all alone in the Tower; and I am sure that we should be much happier all together."

"There," cried Roland triumphantly. "If you are not the most obstinate, hard-hearted, unfeeling brute in the world—which I don't take you to be—brother Austin, after that really beautiful speech of your wife's, there is not a word to be said further."

"But we have not yet heard Kitty to the end, Roland."

"I beg your pardon a thousand times, ma'am—sister," said the Captain, bowing.

"Well, I was going to add," said my mother, "that we will go and live with you, Roland, and club our little fortunes together. Blanche and I will take care of the house, and we shall be just twice as rich together as we are separately."

"Pretty sort of hospitality that!" grunted the Captain. "I did not expect you to throw me over in that way. No, no; you must lay by for the boy there—what's to become of him?"

"But we shall *all* lay by for him," said my mother simply; "you as well as Austin. We shall have more to save, if we have more to spend."

"Ah, save!—that is easily said: there would be a pleasure in saving, then," said the Captain mournfully.

"And what's to become of me?" cried Squills, very petulantly. "Am I to be left here in my old age—not a rational soul to speak to, and no other place in the village where there's a drop of decent punch to be had! 'A plague on both your houses!' as the chap said at the theatre the other night."

"There's room for a doctor in our neighbourhood, Mr. Squills," said the Captain. "The gentleman in your profession who *does for us*, wants, I know, to sell the business."

"Humph," said Squills—"a horribly healthy neighbourhood, I suspect!"

"Why, it has that misfortune, Mr. Squills; but with your help," said my uncle slyly, "a great alteration for the better may be effected in that respect."

Mr. Squills was about to reply, when ring—a-ting—ring—ting! there came such a brisk, impatient, make-one's-self-at-home kind of tintinnabular alarum at the great gate, that we all started up and looked at each other in surprise. Who could it possibly be? We were not kept long in suspense; for in another moment, Uncle Jack's voice, which was always very clear and distinct, pealed through the hall; and we were still staring at each other when Mr. Tibbets, with a bran-new muffler round his neck, and a peculiarly comfortable great-coat—best double Saxony, equally new—dashed into the room, bringing with him a very considerable quantity of cold air, which he hastened to thaw, first in my father's arms, next in my mother's. He then made a rush at the Captain, who ensconced himself behind the dumb waiter with a "Hem! Mr.—sir—Jack—sir—hem, hem!" Failing there, Mr. Tibbets rubbed off the remaining frost upon his double Saxony against your humble servant; patted Squills affectionately on the back, and then proceeded to occupy his favourite position before the fire.

"Took you by surprise, eh?" said Uncle Jack, unpeeling himself by the hearthrug. "But no — not by surprise; you must have known Jack's heart: you at least, Austin Caxton, who know everything—you must have seen that it overflowed with the tenderest and most brotherly emotions; that once delivered from that cursed Fleet (you have no idea what a place it is, sir), I could not rest, night or day, till I had flown here—here, to the dear family nest—poor wounded dove that I am!" added Uncle Jack pathetically, and taking out his pocket-handkerchief from the double Saxony, which he had now flung over my father's arm-chair.

Not a word replied to this eloquent address, with its touching peroration. My mother hung down her pretty head, and looked ashamed. My uncle retreated quite into the corner, and drew the dumb waiter after him, so as to establish a complete fortification. Mr. Squills seized the pen that Roland had thrown down, and began mending it furiously—that is, cutting it into slivers—thereby denoting, symbolically, how he would like to do with Uncle Jack, could he once get him safe and snug under his manipular operations. I bent over the pedigree, and my father rubbed his spectacles.

The silence would have been appalling to another man: nothing appalled Uncle Jack.

Uncle Jack turned to the fire, and warmed first one foot, then the other. This comfortable ceremony performed, he again faced the company—and resumed musingly, and as if answering some imaginary observations—

"Yes, yes—you are right there—and a deuced unlucky speculation it proved too. But I was overruled by that fellow Peck. Says I to him—says I—'*Capitalist!* pshaw—no popular interest there—it don't address the great public! Very confined class the capitalists; better throw ourselves boldly on the people. Yes,' said I, 'call it the *Anti*-Capitalist.' By Jove! sir, we should have carried all before us! but I was overruled. The *Anti-Capitalist!*—what an idea! Address the whole reading world there, sir: everybody hates the capitalist—everybody would have his neighbour's money. The *Anti-Capitalist!*—sir, we should have gone off, in the manufacturing towns, like wildfire. But what could I do?——"

"John Tibbets," said my father solemnly, "Capitalist or Anti-Capitalist, thou hadst a right to follow thine own bent in either —but always provided it had been with thine own money. Thou seest not the thing, John Tibbets, in the right point of view; and a little repentance in the face of those thou hast wronged, would not have misbecome thy father's son, and thy sister's brother!"

Never had so severe a rebuke issued from the mild lips of

Austin Caxton; and I raised my eyes with a compassionate thrill, expecting to see John Tibbets gradually sink and disappear through the carpet.

"Repentance!" cried Uncle Jack, bounding up, as if he had been shot. "And do you think I have a heart of stone, of pummy-stone!—do you think I don't repent? I have done nothing but repent—I shall repent to my dying day."

"Then there is no more to be said, Jack," cried my father, softening, and holding out his hand.

"Yes!" cried Mr. Tibbets, seizing the hand, and pressing it to the heart he had thus defended from the suspicion of being pummy—"yes,—that I should have trusted that dunder-headed, rascally curmudgeon Peck: that I should have let him call it *The Capitalist*, despite all my convictions, when the *Anti*——"

"Pshaw!" interrupted my father, drawing away his hand.

"John," said my mother gravely, and with tears in her voice, "you forget who delivered you from prison,—you forget whom you have nearly consigned to prison yourself—you forg——"

"Hush, hush!" said my father, "this will never do; and it is you who forget, my dear, the obligations I owe to Jack. He has reduced my fortune one-half, it is true; but I verily think he has made the three hearts, in which lie my real treasures, twice as large as they were before. Pisistratus, my boy, ring the bell."

"My dear Kitty," cried Jack, whimpering, and stealing up to my mother, "don't be so hard on me; I thought to make all your fortunes—I did indeed."

Here the servant entered.

"See that Mr. Tibbets's things are taken up to his room, and that there is a good fire," said my father.

"And," continued Jack loftily, "I *will* make all your fortunes yet. I have it *here!*" and he struck his head.

"Stay a moment," said my father to the servant, who had got back to the door. "Stay a moment," said my father, looking extremely frightened: "perhaps Mr. Tibbets may prefer the inn!"

"Austin," said Uncle Jack, with emotion, "if I were a dog, with no home but a dog-kennel, and you came to me for shelter, I would turn out—to give you the best of the straw!"

My father was thoroughly melted this time.

"Primmins will be sure to see everything is made comfortable for Mr. Tibbets," said he, waving his hand to the servant.

"Something nice for supper, Kitty, my dear—and the largest punch-bowl. You like punch, Jack?"

" Punch, Austin!" said Uncle Jack, putting his handkerchief to his eyes.

The Captain pushed aside the dumb waiter, strode across the room, and shook hands with Uncle Jack; my mother buried her face in her apron, and fairly ran off; and Squills said in my ear, " It all comes of the biliary secretions. Nobody could account for this, who did not know the peculiarly fine organisation of your father's—liver!"

PART XII

CHAPTER I

THE Hegira is completed—we have all taken roost in the old
Tower. My father's books have arrived by the waggon, and
have settled themselves quietly in their new abode—filling up
the apartment dedicated to their owner, including the bed-
chamber and two lobbies. The duck also has arrived, under
wing of Mrs. Primmins, and has reconciled herself to the old
stewpond, by the side of which my father has found a walk that
compensates for the peach-wall—especially as he has made
acquaintance with sundry respectable carps, who permit him to
feed them after he has fed the duck—a privilege of which
(since, if any one else approaches, the carps are off in an instant)
my father is naturally vain. All privileges are valuable in proportion to the exclusiveness of their enjoyment.

Now, from the moment the first carp had eaten the bread my
father threw to it, Mr. Caxton had mentally resolved that a race
so confiding should never be sacrificed to Ceres and Primmins.
But all the fishes on my uncle's property were under the special
care of that Proteus Bolt—and Bolt was not a man likely to
suffer the carps to earn their bread without contributing their
full share to the wants of the community. But, like master,
like man! Bolt was an aristocrat fit to be hung *à la lanterne*.
He out-Rolanded Roland in the respect he entertained for
sounding names and old families; and by that bait my father
caught him with such skill, that you might see that, if Austin
Caxton had been an angler of fishes, he could have filled his
basket full any day, shine or rain.

"You observe, Bolt," said my father, beginning artfully,
"that those fishes, dull as you may think them, are creatures capable of a syllogism; and if they saw that, in proportion to their civility to me, they were depopulated by
you, they would put two and two together, and renounce my
acquaintance."

"Is that what you call being silly Jems, sir?" said Bolt; "faith, there is many a good Christian not half so wise!"

"Man," answered my father thoughtfully, "is an animal less syllogistical, or more silly-Jemical, than many creatures popularly esteemed his inferiors. Yes, let but one of those Cyprinidæ, with his fine sense of logic, see that, if his fellow-fishes eat bread, they are suddenly jerked out of their element, and vanish for ever; and though you broke a quartern loaf into crumbs, he would snap his tail at you with enlightened contempt. If," said my father, soliloquising, "I had been as syllogistic as those scaly logicians, I should never have swallowed that hook, which—hum! there—least said soonest mended. But, Mr. Bolt, to return to the Cyprinidæ."

"What's the hard name you call them 'ere carp, your honour?" asked Bolt.

"Cyprinidæ, a family of the section Malacoptergii Abdominales," replied Mr. Caxton; "their teeth are generally confined to the Pharyngeans, and their branchiostegous rays are but few —marks of distinction from fishes vulgar and voracious."

"Sir," said Bolt, glancing to the stewpond, "if I had known they had been a family of such importance, I am sure I should have treated them with more respect."

"They are a very old family, Bolt, and have been settled in England since the fourteenth century. A younger branch of the family has established itself in a pond in the garden of Peterhoff (the celebrated palace of Peter the Great, Bolt,—an emperor highly respected by my brother, for he killed a great many people very gloriously in battle, besides those whom he sabred for his own private amusement). And there is an officer or servant of the Imperial household, whose task it is to summon those Russian Cyprinidæ to dinner, by ringing a bell, shortly after which, you may see the emperor and empress, with all their waiting ladies and gentlemen, coming down in their carriages to see the Cyprinidæ eat in state. So you perceive, Bolt, that it would be a republican, Jacobinical proceeding to stew members of a family so intimately associated with royalty."

"Dear me, sir," said Bolt, "I am very glad you told me. I ought to have known they were genteel fish, they are so mighty shy—as all your real quality are."

My father smiled, and rubbed his hands gently; he had carried his point, and henceforth the Cyprinidæ of the section Malacoptergii Abdominales were as sacred in Bolt's eyes as cats and ichneumons were in those of a priest in Thebes.

My poor father! with what true and unostentatious philosophy thou didst accommodate thyself to the greatest change thy quiet, harmless life had known, since it had passed out of the brief burning cycle of the passions. Lost was the home endeared to thee by so many noiseless victories of the mind—so many mute histories of the heart—for only the scholar knoweth how deep a charm lies in monotony, in the old associations, the old ways, and habitual clockwork of peaceful time. Yet, the home may be replaced—thy heart built its home round itself everywhere— and the old Tower might supply the loss of the brick house, and the walk by the stewpond become as dear as the haunts by the sunny peach-wall. But what shall replace to thee the bright dream of thine innocent ambition,—that angel-wing which had glittered across thy manhood, in the hour between its noon and its setting? What replace to thee the Magnum Opus—the Great Book!—fair and broad-spreading tree—lone amidst the sameness of the landscape—now plucked up by the roots! The oxygen was subtracted from the air of thy life. For be it known to you, oh my compassionate readers, that with the death of the Anti-Publisher Society the blood streams of the Great Book stood still—its pulse was arrested—its full heart beat no more. Three thousand copies of the first seven sheets in quarto, with sundry unfinished plates, anatomical, architectural, and graphic, depicting various developments of the human skull (that temple of Human Error), from the Hottentot to the Greek; sketches of ancient buildings, Cyclopean and Pelasgic; Pyramids, and Pur-tors, all signs of races whose handwriting was on their walls; landscapes to display the influence of Nature upon the customs, creeds, and philosophy of men—here showing how the broad Chaldean wastes led to the contemplation of the stars; and illustrations of the Zodiac, in elucidation of the mysteries of symbol-worship; fantastic vagaries of earth fresh from the Deluge, tending to impress on early superstition the awful sense of the rude powers of Nature; views of the rocky defiles of Laconia; Sparta, neighboured by the "silent Amyclæ," explaining, as it were, geographically, the iron customs of the warrior colony (arch Tories, amidst the shift and roar of Hellenic democracies), contrasted by the seas, and coasts, and creeks of Athens and Ionia, tempting to adventure, commerce, and change. Yea, my father, in his suggestions to the artist of those few imperfect plates, had thrown as much light on the infancy of earth and its tribes as by the "shining words" that flowed from his calm, starry knowledge. Plates and copies, all rested now in peace and dust—"housed with darkness and with death," on the sepulchral shelves of the lobby to which they were consigned—rays intercepted—worlds incompleted. The Prometheus was bound, and the fire he had stolen from heaven lay imbedded in the flints of his rock. For so costly was the mould in which Uncle Jack and the Anti-Publisher Society had contrived to cast this Exposition of Human Error, that every bookseller shyed at its very sight, as an owl blinks at daylight, or human error at truth. In vain Squills and I, before we left London, had carried a gigantic specimen of the Magnum Opus into the back-parlours of firms the most opulent and adventurous. Publisher after publisher started, as if we had held a blunderbuss to his ear. All Paternoster Row uttered a "Lord deliver us!" Human Error found no man so egregiously its victim as to complete those two quartos, with the prospect of two others, at his own expense. Now I had earnestly hoped that my father, for the sake of mankind, would be persuaded to risk some portion —and that, I own, not a small one—of his remaining capital on the conclusion of an undertaking so elaborately begun. But there my father was obdurate. No big words about mankind, and the advantage to unborn generations, could stir him an inch. "Stuff!" said Mr. Caxton peevishly. "A man's duties to mankind and posterity begin with his own son; and having wasted half your patrimony, I will not take another huge slice out of the poor remainder to gratify my vanity, for that is the plain truth of it. Man must atone for sin by expiation. By the book I have sinned, and the book must expiate it. Pile the sheets up in the lobby, so that at least one man may be wiser and humbler by the sight of human error, every time he walks by so stupendous a monument of it."

Verily, I know not how my father could bear to look at those dumb fragments of himself—strata of the Caxtonian conformation lying layer upon layer, as if packed up and disposed for the inquisitive genius of some moral Murchison or Mantell. But for my part, I never glanced at their repose in the dark lobby, without thinking, "Courage, Pisistratus! courage! there's something worth living for; work hard, grow rich, and the Great Book shall come out at last."

Meanwhile, I wandered over the country, and made acquaintance with the farmers, and with Trevanion's steward—an able man, and a great agriculturist—and I learned from them a better notion of the nature of my uncle's domains. Those domains covered an immense acreage, which, save a small farm,

was of no value at present.   But land of the same sort had been
lately redeemed by a simple kind of draining, now well known
in Cumberland; and, with capital, Roland's barren moors might
become a noble property.   But capital, where was that to come
from?   Nature gives us all except the means to turn her into
marketable account.   As old Plautus saith so wittily, "Day,
night, water, sun, and moon, are to be had gratis; for everything else—down with your dust!"

CHAPTER II

NOTHING has been heard of Uncle Jack.   Before we left
the brick house, the Captain gave him an invitation to the
Tower—more, I suspect, out of compliment to my mother than
from the unbidden impulse of his own inclinations.   But Mr.
Tibbets politely declined it.   During his stay at the brick
house, he had received and written a vast number of letters—
some of those he received, indeed, were left at the village post-
office, under the alphabetical addresses of A B or X Y; for no
misfortune ever paralysed the energies of Uncle Jack.   In the
winter of adversity he vanished, it is true; but even in vanishing, he vegetated still.   He resembled those *algæ*, termed the
Prolococcus nivales, which give a rose-colour to the Polar snows
that conceal them, and flourish unsuspected amidst the general
dissolution of Nature.   Uncle Jack, then, was as lively and
sanguine as ever—though he began to let fall vague hints of
intentions to abandon the general cause of his fellow-creatures,
and to set up business henceforth purely on his own account;
wherewith my father—to the great shock of my belief in his
philanthropy—expressed himself much pleased.   And I strongly
suspect that, when Uncle Jack wrapped himself up in his new
double Saxony, and went off at last, he carried with him something more than my father's good wishes in aid of his conversion
to egotistical philosophy.

   "That man will do yet," said my father, as the last glimpse
was caught of Uncle Jack standing up on the stage-coach box,
beside the driver, partly to wave his hand to us as we stood at
the gate, and partly to array himself more commodiously in a
box-coat with six capes, which the coachman had lent him.

   "Do you think so, sir?" said I doubtfully.   "May I ask
why?"

Mr. Caxton.—"On the cat principle—that he tumbles so lightly. You may throw him down from St. Paul's, and the next time you see him he will be scrambling a-top of the Monument."

Pisistratus.—"But a cat the most viparious is limited to nine lives; and Uncle Jack must be now far gone in his eighth."

Mr. Caxton (not heeding that answer, for he has got his hand in his waistcoat).—"The earth, according to Apuleius, in his 'Treatise on the Philosophy of Plato,' was produced from right-angled triangles; but fire and air from the scalene triangle —the angles of which, I need not say, are very different from those of a right-angled triangle. Now I think there are people in the world of whom one can only judge rightly according to those mathematical principles applied to their original construction: for, if air or fire predominates in our natures, we are scalene triangles;—if earth, right-angled. Now, as air is so notably manifested in Jack's conformation, he is, *nolens volens,* produced in conformity with his preponderating element. He is a scalene triangle, and must be judged, accordingly, upon irregular, lop-sided principles; whereas you and I, commonplace mortals, are produced, like the earth, which is our preponderating element, with our triangles all right-angled, comfortable and complete; for which blessing let us thank Providence, and be charitable to those who are necessarily windy and gaseous, from that unlucky scalene triangle upon which they have had the misfortune to be constructed, and which, you perceive, is quite at variance with the mathematical constitution of the earth!"

Pisistratus.—"Sir, I am very happy to hear so simple, easy, and intelligible an explanation of Uncle Jack's peculiarities; and I only hope that, for the future, the sides of his scalene triangle may never be produced to our rectangular conformations."

Mr. Caxton (descending from his stilts, with an air as mildly reproachful as if I had been cavilling at the virtues of Socrates). —"You don't do your uncle justice, Pisistratus; he is a very clever man; and I am sure that, in spite of his scalene misfortune, he would be an honest one—that is (added Mr. Caxton, correcting himself), not romantically or heroically honest—but honest as men go—if he could but keep his head long enough above water; but, you see, when the best man in the world is engaged in the process of sinking, he catches hold of whatever comes in his way, and drowns the very friend who is swimming to save him."

Pisistratus.—"Perfectly true, sir; but Uncle Jack makes it his business to be *always* sinking!"

Mr. Caxton (with *naïveté*).—"And how could it be otherwise, when he has been carrying all his fellow-creatures in his breeches' pockets! Now he has got rid of that dead weight, I should not be surprised if he swam like a cork."

Pisistratus (who, since the *Capitalist*, has become a strong Anti-Jackian).—"But if, sir, you really think Uncle Jack's love for his fellow-creatures is genuine, that is surely not the worst part of him."

Mr. Caxton.—"O literal ratiocinator, and dull to the true logic of Attic irony! can't you comprehend that an affection may be genuine as felt by the man, yet its nature be spurious in relation to others? A man may genuinely believe he loves his fellow-creatures, when he roasts them like Torquemada, or guillotines them like St. Just! Happily Jack's scalene triangle, being more produced from air than from fire, does not give to his philanthropy the inflammatory character which distinguishes the benevolence of inquisitors and revolutionists. The philanthropy, therefore, takes a more flatulent and innocent form, and expends its strength in mounting paper balloons, out of which Jack pitches himself, with all the fellow-creatures he can coax into sailing with him. No doubt Uncle Jack's philanthropy is sincere, when he cuts the string and soars up out of sight; but the sincerity will not much mend their bruises when himself and fellow-creatures come tumbling down neck and heels. It must be a very wide heart that can take in all mankind—and of a very strong fibre to bear so much stretching. Such hearts there are, Heaven be thanked!—and all praise to them! Jack's is not of that quality. He is a scalene triangle. He is not a circle! And yet, if he would but let it rest, it is a good heart—a very good heart (continued my father, warming into a tenderness quite infantine, all things considered). Poor Jack! that was prettily said of him—'That if he were a dog, and he had no home but a dog-kennel, he would turn out to give me the best of the straw!' Poor brother Jack!"

So the discussion was dropped; and, in the meanwhile, Uncle Jack, like the short-faced gentleman in the *Spectator*, "distinguished himself by a profound silence."

CHAPTER III

BLANCHE has contrived to associate herself, if not with my more active diversions—in running over the country, and making friends with the farmers—still in all my more leisurely and domestic pursuits. There is about her a silent charm that it is very hard to define, but it seems to arise from a kind of innate sympathy with the moods and humours of those she loves. If one is gay, there is a cheerful ring in her silver laugh that seems gladness itself; if one is sad, and creeps away into a corner to bury one's head in one's hand, and muse—by-and-by, and just at the right moment, when one has mused one's fill, and the heart wants something to refresh and restore it, one feels two innocent arms round one's neck,—looks up—and lo! Blanche's soft eyes, full of wistful compassionate kindness; though she has the tact not to question—it is enough for her to sorrow with your sorrow—she cares not to know more. A strange child!—fearless, and yet seemingly fond of things that inspire children with fear; fond of tales of fay, sprite, and ghost, which Mrs. Primmins draws fresh and new from her memory, as a conjurer draws pancakes hot and hot from a hat. And yet so sure is Blanche of her own innocence, that they never trouble her dreams in her lone little room, full of caliginous corners and nooks, with the winds moaning round the desolate ruins, and the casements rattling hoarse in the dungeon-like wall. She would have no dread to walk through the ghostly keep in the dark, or cross the churchyard, what time,

"By the moon's doubtful and malignant light,"

the grave-stones look so spectral, and the shade from the yew trees lies so still on the sward. When the brows of Roland are gloomiest, and the compression of his lips makes sorrow look sternest, be sure that Blanche is couched at his feet, waiting the moment when, with some heavy sigh, the muscles relax, and she is sure of the smile if she climbs to his knee. It is pretty to chance on her gliding up broken turret-stairs, or standing hushed in the recess of shattered casements, and you wonder what thoughts of vague awe and solemn pleasure can be at work under that still little brow.

She has a quick comprehension of all that is taught to her; she already tasks to the full my mother's educational arts. My father has had to rummage his library for books, to feed (or extinguish) her desire for "farther information"; and has promised lessons in French and Italian—at some golden time in the shadowy "by-and-by"—which are received so gratefully that one might think Blanche mistook *Télémaque* and *Novelle Morali* for baby-houses and dolls. Heaven send her through French and Italian with better success than attended Mr. Caxton's lessons in Greek to Pisistratus! She has an ear for music, which my mother, who is no bad judge, declares to be exquisite. Luckily there is an old Italian settled in a town ten miles off, who is said to be an excellent music-master, and who comes the round of the neighbouring squirearchy twice a week. I have taught her to draw—an accomplishment in which I am not without skill—and she has already taken a sketch from nature, which, barring the perspective, is not so amiss; indeed, she has caught the notion of "idealising" (which promises future originality) from her own natural instincts, and given to the old witch-elm, that hangs over the stream, just the bow that it wanted to dip into the water, and soften off the hard lines. My only fear is, that Blanche should become too dreamy and thoughtful. Poor child, she has no one to play with! So I look out, and get her a dog—frisky and young, who abhors sedentary occupations—a spaniel, small and coal-black, with ears sweeping the ground. I baptize him "Juba," in honour of Addison's Cato, and in consideration of his sable curls and Mauritanian complexion. Blanche does not seem so eerie and elf-like while gliding through the ruins, when Juba barks by her side, and scares the birds from the ivy.

One day I had been pacing to and fro the hall, which was deserted; and the sight of the armour and portraits—dumb evidences of the active and adventurous lives of the old inhabitants, which seemed to reprove my own inactive obscurity—had set me off on one of those Pegaséan hobbies on which youth mounts to the skies—delivering maidens on rocks, and killing Gorgons and monsters—when Juba bounded in, and Blanche came after him, her straw hat in her hand.

BLANCHE.—"I thought you were here, Sisty: may I stay?"

PISISTRATUS.—"Why, my dear child, the day is so fine, that instead of losing it indoors, you ought to be running in the fields with Juba."

JUBA.—"Bow-wow."

BLANCHE.—"Will you come too? If Sisty stays in, Blanche does not care for the butterflies!"

Pisistratus, seeing that the thread of his day-dreams is broken, consents with an air of resignation. Just as they gain the door, Blanche pauses, and looks as if there were something on her mind.

Pisistratus.—"What now, Blanche? Why are you making knots in that ribbon, and writing invisible characters on the floor with the point of that busy little foot?"

Blanche (mysteriously).—"I have found a new room, Sisty. Do you think we may look into it?"

Pisistratus.—"Certainly; unless any Bluebeard of your acquaintance told you not. Where is it?"

Blanche.—"Upstairs—to the left."

Pisistratus.—"That little old door, going down two stone steps, which is always kept locked?"

Blanche.—"Yes! it is not locked to-day. The door was ajar, and I peeped in; but I would not do more till I came and asked you if you thought it would not be wrong."

Pisistratus.—"Very good in you, my discreet little cousin. I have no doubt it is a ghost-trap; however, with Juba's protection, I think we might venture together."

Pisistratus, Blanche, and Juba ascend the stairs, and turn off down a dark passage to the left, away from the rooms in use. We reach the arch-pointed door of oak planks nailed roughly together—we push it open, and perceive that a small stair winds down from the room: it is just over Roland's chamber.

The room has a damp smell, and has probably been left open to be aired, for the wind comes through the unbarred casement, and a billet burns on the hearth. The place has that attractive, fascinating air which belongs to a lumber-room, than which I know nothing that so captivates the interest and fancy of young people. What treasures, to them, often lie hid in those quaint odds and ends which the elder generations have discarded as rubbish! All children are by nature antiquarians and relic-hunters. Still there is an order and precision with which the articles in that room are stowed away that belies the true notion of lumber—none of the mildew and dust which give such mournful interest to things abandoned to decay.

In one corner are piled up cases, and military-looking trunks of outlandish aspect, with R. D. C. in brass nails on their sides. From these we turn with involuntary respect, and call off Juba, who has wedged himself behind in pursuit of some imaginary mouse. But in the other corner is what seems to me a child's cradle—not an English one evidently: it is of wood, seemingly

T

Spanish rosewood, with a railwork at the back, of twisted columns ; and I should scarcely have known it to be a cradle but for the fairy-like quilt and the tiny pillows, which proclaimed its uses.

On the wall above the cradle were arranged sundry little articles, that had, perhaps, once made the joy of a child's heart —broken toys with the paint rubbed off, a tin sword and trumpet, and a few tattered books, mostly in Spanish—by their shape and look, doubtless children's books. Near these stood, on the floor, a picture with its face to the wall. Juba had chased the mouse that his fancy still insisted on creating, behind this picture, and as he abruptly drew back, the picture fell into the hands I stretched forth to receive it. I turned the face to the light, and was surprised to see merely an old family portrait ; it was that of a gentleman in the flowered vest and stiff ruff which referred the date of his existence to the reign of Elizabeth —a man with a bold and noble countenance. On the corner was placed a faded coat of arms, beneath which was inscribed, " HERBERT DE CAXTON, EQ: AUR: ÆTAT: 35."

On the back of the canvas I observed, as I now replaced the picture against the wall, a label in Roland's handwriting, though in a younger and more running hand than he now wrote. The words were these :—" The best and bravest of our line. He charged by Sydney's side on the field of Zutphen ; he fought in Drake's ship against the armament of Spain. If ever I have a——" The rest of the label seemed to have been torn off.

I turned away, and felt a remorseful shame that I had so far gratified my curiosity,—if by so harsh a name the powerful interest that had absorbed me must be called. I looked round for Blanche ; she had retreated from my side to the door, and, with her hands before her eyes, was weeping. As I stole towards her, my glance fell on a book that lay on a chair near the casement, and beside those relics of an infancy once pure and serene. By the old-fashioned silver clasps, I recognised Roland's Bible. I felt as if I had been almost guilty of profanation in my thoughtless intrusion. I drew away Blanche, and we descended the stairs noiselessly ; and not till we were on our favourite spot, amidst a heap of ruins on the feudal justice-hill, did I seek to kiss away her tears and ask the cause.

" My poor brother !" sobbed Blanche, " they must have been his—and we shall never, never see him again !—and poor papa's Bible, which he reads when he is very, very sad ! I did not weep enough when my brother died. I know better what death is now! Poor papa! poor papa! Don't die, too, Sisty!"

There was no running after butterflies that morning; and it was long before I could soothe Blanche. Indeed, she bore the traces of dejection in her soft looks for many, many days; and she often asked me, sighingly, "Don't you think it was very wrong in me to take you there?" Poor little Blanche, true daughter of Eve, she would not let me bear my due share of the blame; she would have it all in Adam's primitive way of justice —"The woman tempted me, and I did eat." And since then Blanche has seemed more fond than ever of Roland, and comparatively deserts me to nestle close to him, and closer, till he looks up and says, "My child, you are pale; go and run after the butterflies;" and she says now to him, not to me, "Come too!" drawing him out into the sunshine with a hand that will not loose its hold.

Of all Roland's line, this Herbert de Caxton was "the best and bravest!" yet he had never named that ancestor to me— never put any forefather in comparison with the dubious and mythical Sir William. I now remembered once, that, in going over the pedigree, I had been struck by the name of Herbert— the only Herbert in the scroll—and had asked, "What of him, uncle?" and Roland had muttered something inaudible, and turned away. And I remembered, also, that in Roland's room there was the mark in the wall where a picture of that size had once hung. The picture had been removed thence before we first came, but must have hung there for years to have left that mark on the wall—perhaps suspended by Bolt, during Roland's long Continental absence. "If ever I have a——" What were the missing words? Alas! did they not relate to the son— missed for ever, evidently not forgotten still?

CHAPTER IV

MY uncle sat on one side the fire-place, my mother on the other; and I, at a small table between them, prepared to note down the results of their conference; for they had met in high council, to assess their joint fortunes—determine what should be brought into the common stock, and set apart for the Civil List, and what should be laid aside as a Sinking Fund. Now my mother, true woman as she was, had a womanly love of show in her own quiet way—of making "a genteel figure" in the eyes of the neighbourhood—of seeing that sixpence not only went as far as sixpence ought to go, but that, in the going, it should emit a mild but imposing splendour,—not, indeed, a gaudy flash—a startling Borealian coruscation, which is scarcely within the modest and placid idiosyncrasies of sixpence—but a gleam of gentle and benign light, just to show where a sixpence had been, and allow you time to say " Behold!" before

" The jaws of darkness did devour it up."

Thus, as I once before took occasion to apprise the reader, we had always held a very respectable position in the neighbourhood round our square brick house; been as sociable as my father's habits would permit; given our little tea-parties, and our occasional dinners, and, without attempting to vie with our richer associates, there had always been so exquisite a neatness, so notable a housekeeping, so thoughtful a disposition, in short, of all the properties indigenous to a well-spent sixpence, in my mother's management, that there was not an old maid within seven miles of us who did not pronounce our tea-parties to be perfect; and the great Mrs. Rollick, who gave forty guineas a year to a professed cook and housekeeper, used regularly, whenever we dined at Rollick Hall, to call across the table to my mother (who therewith blushed up to her ears), to apologise for the strawberry jelly. It is true, that when, on returning home, my mother adverted to that flattering and delicate compliment, in a tone that revealed the self-conceit of the human heart, my father—whether to sober his Kitty's vanity into a proper and Christian mortification of spirit, or from that strange shrewdness which belonged to him—would remark that Mrs. Rollick was of a querulous nature; that the compliment was meant not to please my mother, but to spite the professed cook and housekeeper, to whom the butler would be sure to repeat the invidious apology.

In settling at the Tower, and assuming the head of its establishment, my mother was naturally anxious that, poor battered invalid though the Tower was, it should still put its best leg foremost. Sundry cards, despite the thinness of the neighbourhood, had been left at the door; various invitations, which my uncle had hitherto declined, had greeted his occupation of the ancestral ruin, and had become more numerous since the news of our arrival had gone abroad; so that my mother saw before her a very suitable field for her hospitable accomplishments—a reasonable ground for her ambition that the Tower should hold up its head, as became a Tower that held the head of the family.

But not to wrong thee, O dear mother! as thou sittest there, opposite the grim Captain, so fair and so neat,—with thine apron as white, and thy hair as trim and as sheen, and thy morning cap, with its ribbons of blue, as coquettishly arranged as if thou hadst a fear that the least negligence on thy part might lose thee the heart of thine Austin—not to wrong thee by setting down to frivolous motives alone thy feminine visions of the social amenities of life, I know that thine heart, in its provident tenderness, was quite as much interested as ever thy vanities could be, in the hospitable thoughts on which thou wert intent. For, first and foremost, it was the wish of thy soul that thine Austin might, as little as possible, be reminded of the change in his fortunes,—might miss as little as possible those interruptions to his abstracted scholarly moods, at which, it is true, he used to fret and to pshaw and to cry Papæ! but which nevertheless always did him good, and freshened up the stream of his thoughts. And, next, it was the conviction of thine understanding that a little society, and boon companionship, and the proud pleasure of showing his ruins, and presiding at the hall of his forefathers, would take Roland out of those gloomy reveries into which he still fell at times. And, thirdly, for us young people ought not Blanche to find companions in children of her own sex and age? Already in those large black eyes there was something melancholy and brooding, as there is in the eyes of all children who live only with their elders; and for Pisistratus, with his altered prospects, and the one great gnawing memory at his heart—which he tried to conceal from himself, but which a mother (and a mother who had loved) saw at a glance—what could be better than such union and interchange with the world around us, small though that world might be, as woman, sweet binder and blender of all social links, might artfully effect?—So that thou didst not go, like the awful Florentine,

> " Sopra lor vanità che par persona,"

"over thin shadows that mocked the substance of real forms," but rather it was the real forms that appeared as shadows or *vanità*.

What a digression!—can I never tell my story in a plain straightforward way? Certainly I was born under Cancer, and all my movements are circumlocutory, sideways, and crab-like.

CHAPTER V

I THINK, Roland," said my mother, "that the establishment is settled. Bolt, who is equal to three men at least; Primmins, cook and housekeeper; Molly, a good stirring girl—and willing (though I've had some difficulty in persuading her to submit not to be called Anna Maria). Their wages are but a small item, my dear Roland."

"Hem!" said Roland, "since we can't do with fewer servants at less wages, I suppose we must call it small."

"It is so," said my mother, with mild positiveness. "And, indeed, what with the game and fish, and the garden and poultry-yard, and your own mutton, our housekeeping will be next to nothing."

"Hem!" again said the thrifty Roland, with a slight inflection of the beetle brows. "It may be next to nothing, ma'am—sister—just as a butcher's shop may be next to Northumberland House; but there is a vast deal between nothing and that next neighbour you have given it."

This speech was so like one of my father's, so *naïve* an imitation of that subtle reasoner's use of the rhetorical figure called ANTANACLASIS (or repetition of the same words in a different sense), that I laughed and my mother smiled. But she smiled reverently, not thinking of the ANTANACLASIS, as, laying her hand on Roland's arm, she replied in the yet more formidable figure of speech called EPIPHONEMA (or exclamation), "Yet, with all your economy, you would have had us——"

"Tut!" cried my uncle, parrying the EPIPHONEMA with a masterly APOSIOPESIS (or breaking off); "tut! if you had done what I wished, I should have had more pleasure for my money!"

My poor mother's rhetorical armoury supplied no weapon to meet that artful APOSIOPESIS; so she dropped the rhetoric altogether, and went on with that "unadorned eloquence" natural to her, as to other great financial reformers:—"Well, Roland, but I am a good housewife, I assure you, and—don't scold; but that you never do,—I mean, don't look as if you would like to scold; the fact is, that, even after setting aside £100 a year for our little parties——"

"Little parties!—a hundred a year!" cried the Captain aghast.

My mother pursued her way remorselessly,—"Which we can well afford; and without counting your half-pay, which you must keep for pocket-money and your wardrobe and Blanche's, I calculate that we can allow Pisistratus £150 a year, which, with the scholarship he is to get, will keep him at Cambridge" (at that, seeing the scholarship was as yet amidst the Pleasures of Hope, I shook my head doubtfully), "and," continued my mother, not heeding that sign of dissent, "we shall still have something to lay by."

The Captain's face assumed a ludicrous expression of compassion and horror; he evidently thought my mother's misfortunes had turned her head.

His tormentor continued.

"For," said my mother, with a pretty calculating shake of her head, and a movement of the right forefinger towards the five fingers of the left hand, "£370—the interest of Austin's fortune—and £50 that we may reckon for the rent of our house, make £420 a year. Add your £330 a year from the farm, sheep-walk, and cottages that you let, and the total is £750. Now, with all we get for nothing for our housekeeping, as I said before, we can do very well with £500 a year, and indeed make a handsome figure. So, after allowing Sisty £150, we still have £100 to lay by for Blanche."

"Stop, stop, stop!" cried the Captain in great agitation; "who told you that I had £330 a year?"

"Why, Bolt,—don't be angry with him."

"Bolt is a blockhead. From £330 a year take £200, and the remainder is all my income, besides my half-pay."

My mother opened her eyes, and so did I.

"To that £130 add, if you please, £130 of your own. All that you have over, my dear sister, is yours or Austin's, or your boy's; but not a shilling can go to give luxuries to a miserly, battered old soldier. Do you understand me?"

"No, Roland," said my mother, "I don't understand you at all. Does not your property bring in £330 a year?"

"Yes, but it has a debt of £200 a year on it," said the Captain, gloomily and reluctantly.

"O Roland!" cried my mother, tenderly, and approaching so near that, had my father been in the room, I am sure she would have been bold enough to kiss the stern Captain, though I never saw him look sterner, and less kissable. "O Roland!" cried my mother, concluding that famous EPIPHONEMA which my uncle's APOSIOPESIS had before nipped in the bud, "and yet you would have made us, who are twice as rich, rob you of this little all!"

"Ah!" said Roland, trying to smile, "but I should have had my own way then, and starved you shockingly. No talk then of 'little parties,' and such-like. But you must not now turn the tables against me, nor bring your £420 a year as a set-off to my £130."

"Why," said my mother generously, "you forget the money's worth that you contribute—all that your grounds supply, and all that we save by it. I am sure that that's worth a yearly £300 at the least."

"Madam—sister," said the Captain, "I'm sure you don't want to hurt my feelings. All I have to say is, that, if you add to what I bring an equal sum—to keep up the poor old ruin—it is the utmost that I can allow, and the rest is not more than Pisistratus can spend."

So saying, the Captain rose, bowed, and, before either of us could stop him, hobbled out of the room.

"Dear me, Sisty!" said my mother, wringing her hands; "I have certainly displeased him. How could I guess he had so large a debt on the property?"

"Did not he pay his son's debts? Is not that the reason that——"

"Ah!" interrupted my mother, almost crying, "and it was that which ruffled him; and I not to guess it? What shall I do?"

"Set to work at a new calculation, dear mother, and let him have his own way."

"But then," said my mother, "your uncle will mope himself to death, and your father will have no relaxation, while you see that he has lost his former object in his books. And Blanche —and you too. If we were only to contribute what dear Roland does, I do not see how, with £260 a year, we could ever bring our neighbours round us! I wonder what Austin would say! I have half a mind—no, I'll go and look over the week-books with Primmins."

My mother went her way sorrowfully, and I was left alone.

Then I looked on the stately old hall, grand in its forlorn decay. And the dreams I had begun to cherish at my heart swept over me, and hurried me along, far, far away into the golden land, whither Hope beckons youth. To restore my father's fortunes—re-weave the links of that broken ambition which had knit his genius with the world—rebuild those fallen walls—cultivate those barren moors—revive the ancient name—

Chris Hammond
Nov.' 97

'And look over the week-books
with Primmins'

glad the old soldier's age—and be to *both* the brothers what
Roland had lost—a son! These were my dreams: and when I
woke from them, lo! they had left behind an intense purpose,
a resolute object. Dream, O youth!—dream manfully and
nobly, and thy dreams shall be prophets!

CHAPTER VI

LETTER FROM PISISTRATUS CAXTON TO
ALBERT TREVANION, ESQ., M.P.

(The confession of a youth who in the Old World finds himself one too many.)

MY DEAR MR. TREVANION,—I thank you cordially, and so we
do all, for your reply to my letter, informing you of the
villainous traps through which we have passed—not indeed with
whole skins, but still whole in life and limb—which, considering
that the traps were three, and the teeth sharp, was more than
we could reasonably expect. We have taken to the wastes, like
wise foxes as we are, and I do not think a bait can be found
that will again snare the fox paternal. As for the fox filial, it
is different, and I am about to prove to you that he is burning
to redeem the family disgrace. Ah! my dear Mr. Trevanion, if
you are busy with 'blue-books' when this letter reaches you,
stop here, and put it aside for some rare moment of leisure. I
am about to open my heart to you, and ask you, who know the
world so well, to aid me in an escape from those *flammantia
mœnia*, wherewith I find that world begirt and enclosed. For
look you, sir, you and my father were right when you both
agreed that the mere book-life was not meant for me. And yet
what is not book-life, to a young man who would make his way
through the ordinary and conventional paths to fortune? All
the professions are so book-lined, book-hemmed, book-choked,
that wherever these strong hands of mine stretch towards action,
they find themselves met by octavo ramparts, flanked with quarto
crenellations. For first, this college life, opening to scholarships,
and ending, perchance, as you political economists would desire,
in Malthusian fellowships—premiums for celibacy—consider what
manner of thing it is!

"Three years, book upon book,—a great Dead Sea before
one, three years long, and all the apples that grow on the shore

full of the ashes of pica and primer! Those three years ended, the fellowship, it may be, won,—still books—books—if the whole world does not close at the college gates. Do I, from scholar, effloresce into literary man, author by profession?— books—books! Do I go into the law?—books—books. *Ars longa, vita brevis*, which, paraphrased, means that it is slow work before one fags one's way to a brief! Do I turn doctor? Why, what but books can kill time, until, at the age of forty, a lucky chance may permit me to kill something else? The Church (for which, indeed, I don't profess to be good enough),—that is book-life *par excellence*, whether inglorious and poor, I wander through long lines of divines and fathers; or, ambitious of bishoprics, I amend the corruptions, not of the human heart, but of a Greek text, and through defiles of scholiasts and commentators win my way to the See. In short, barring the noble profession of arms—which you know, after all, is not precisely the road to fortune—can you tell me any means by which one may escape these eternal books, this mental clockwork, and corporeal lethargy? Where can this passion for life that runs riot through my veins find its vent? Where can these stalwart limbs and this broad chest grow of value and worth, in this hot-bed of cerebral inflammation and dyspeptic intellect? I know what is in me; I know I have the qualities that should go with stalwart limbs and broad chest. I have some plain common sense, some promptitude and keenness, some pleasure in hardy danger, some fortitude in bearing pain—qualities for which I bless Heaven, for they are qualities good and useful in private life. But in the forum of men, in the market of fortune, are they not *flocci, nauci, nihili*?

"In a word, dear sir and friend, in this crowded Old World, there is not the same room that our bold forefathers found for men to walk about and jostle their neighbours. No; they must sit down like boys at their form, and work out their tasks, with rounded shoulders and aching fingers. There has been a pastoral age, and a hunting age, and a fighting age. Now we have arrived at the age sedentary. Men who sit longest carry all before them: puny, delicate fellows, with hands just strong enough to wield a pen, eyes so bleared by the midnight lamp that they see no joy in that buxom sun (which draws me forth into the fields, as life draws the living), and digestive organs worn and macerated by the relentless flagellation of the brain. Certainly, if this is to be the Reign of Mind, it is idle to repine, and kick against the pricks; but is it true that all these qualities of action that are within me are to go for nothing? If I were rich and happy in mind and circumstance, well and good; I should shoot, hunt, farm, travel, enjoy life, and snap my fingers at ambition. If I were so poor and so humbly bred that I could turn gamekeeper or whipper-in, as pauper gentlemen virtually did of old, well and good too; I should exhaust this trouble-some vitality of mine, by nightly battles with poachers, and leaps over double dykes and stone walls. If I were so depressed of spirit that I could live without remorse on my father's small means, and exclaim with Claudian, 'The earth gives me feasts that cost nothing,' well and good too; it were a life to suit a vegetable, or a very minor poet. But as it is!—here I open another leaf of my heart to you! To say that, being poor, I want to make a fortune, is to say that I am an Englishman. To attach ourselves to a thing positive, belongs to our practical race. Even in our dreams, if we build castles in the air, they are not *Castles of Indolence*,—indeed they have very little of the castle about them, and look much more like Hoare's Bank on the east side of Temple Bar! I desire, then, to make a fortune. But I differ from my countrymen, first, by desiring only what you rich men would call but a *small* fortune; secondly, in wishing that I may not spend my whole life in that fortune-making. Just see, now, how I am placed.

"Under ordinary circumstances, I must begin by taking from my father a large slice of an income that will ill spare paring. According to my calculation, my parents and my uncle want all they have got—and the subtraction of the yearly sum on which Pisistratus is to live, till he can live by his own labours, would be so much taken from the decent comforts of his kindred. If I return to Cambridge, with all economy, I must thus narrow still more the *res angusta domi*—and when Cambridge is over, and I am turned loose upon the world—failing, as is likely enough, of the support of a fellowship—how many years must I work, or rather, alas! not work, at the bar (which, after all, seems my best calling), before I can in my turn provide for those who, till then, rob themselves for me?—till I have arrived at middle life, and they are old and worn-out—till the chink of the golden bowl sounds but hollow at the ebbing well! I would wish that, if I can make money, those I love best may enjoy it while enjoyment is yet left to them; that my father shall see 'The History of Human Error' complete, bound in russia on his shelves; that my mother shall have the innocent pleasures that content her, before age steals the light from her happy

smile; that before Roland's hair is snow-white (alas! the snows
there thicken fast), he shall lean on my arm, while we settle
together where the ruin shall be repaired or where left to the
owls; and where the dreary bleak waste around shall laugh
with the gleam of corn:—for you know the nature of this
Cumberland soil—you, who possess much of it, and have won
so many fair acres from the wild:—you know that my uncle's
land, now (save a single farm) scarce worth a shilling an acre,
needs but capital to become an estate more lucrative than ever
his ancestors owned.   You know that, for you have applied your
capital to the same kind of land, and, in doing so, what blessings
—which you scarcely think of in your London library—you
have effected!—what mouths you feed, what hands you employ!
I have calculated that my uncle's moors, which now scarce maintain two or three shepherds, could, manured by money, maintain two hundred families by their labour.   All this is worth
trying for! therefore Pisistratus wants to make money.   Not
so much! he does not require millions—a few spare thousand
pounds would go a long way; and with a modest capital to
begin with, Roland should become a true squire, a real land-
owner, not the mere lord of a desert.   Now then, dear sir,
advise me how I may, with such qualities as I possess, arrive
at that capital—ay, and before it is too late—so that money-
making may not last till my grave.

"Turning in despair from this civilised world of ours, I have
cast my eyes to a world far older,—and yet more to a world in
its giant childhood.   India here,—Australia there!—what say
you, sir—you who will see dispassionately those things that
float before my eyes through a golden haze, looming large in the
distance?   Such is my confidence in your judgment, that you
have but to say, 'Fool, give up thine El Dorados and stay at
home—stick to the books and the desk—annihilate that re-
dundance of animal life that is in thee—grow a mental machine—
thy physical gifts are of no avail to thee—take thy place among
the slaves of the Lamp'—and I will obey without a murmur.
But if I am right—if I have in me attributes that here find no
market; if my repinings are but the instincts of nature, that,
out of this decrepit civilisation, desire vent for growth in the
young stir of some more rude and vigorous social system—then
give me, I pray, that advice which may clothe my idea in
some practical and tangible embodiments.   Have I made
myself understood?

"We take no newspaper here, but occasionally one finds its

way from the parsonage; and I have lately rejoiced at a paragraph that spoke of 'your speedy entrance into the administration as a thing certain. I write to you before you are a minister; and you see what I seek is not in the way of official patronage: A niche in an office!—oh, to me that were worse than all. Yet I did labour hard with you, but—*that* was different: I write to you thus frankly, knowing your warm, noble heart—and as if you were my father. Allow me to add my humble but earnest congratulations on Miss Trevanion's approaching marriage with one worthy, if not of her, at least of her station. I do so as becomes one whom you have allowed to retain the right to pray for the happiness of you and yours.

"My dear Mr. Trevanion, this is a long letter, and I dare not even read it over, lest, if I do, I should not send it. Take it with all its faults, and judge of it with that kindness with which you have judged ever your grateful and devoted servant,   PISISTRATUS CAXTON."

LETTER FROM ALBERT TREVANION, ESQ., M.P.,

TO PISISTRATUS CAXTON.

"LIBRARY OF THE HOUSE OF COMMONS, *Tuesday night.*

"MY DEAR PISISTRATUS,—***** is up! we are in for it for two mortal hours. I take flight to the library, and devote those hours to you. Don't be conceited, but that picture of yourself which you have placed before me has struck me with all the force of an original. The state of mind which you describe so vividly must be a very common one, in our era of civilisation, yet I have never before seen it made so prominent and life-like. You have been in my thoughts all day. Yes, how many young men must there be like you, in this Old World, able, intelligent, active, and persevering enough, yet not adapted for success in any of our conventional professions—'mute, inglorious Raleighs.' Your letter, young artist, is an illustration of the philosophy of colonising. I comprehend better, after reading it, the old Greek colonisation,—the sending out not only the paupers, the refuse of an over-populated state, but a large proportion of a better class—fellows full of pith and sap, and exuberant vitality, like yourself, blending, in those wise *cleruchiæ*, a certain portion of the aristocratic with the more democratic element; not turning a rabble loose upon a new soil, but planting in the foreign allotments all the rudiments of a harmonious state, analogous to that in the mother country —not only getting rid of hungry craving mouths, but furnishing vent for a waste surplus of intelligence and courage, which at home is really not needed, and more often comes to ill than to good ;—here only menaces our artificial embankments, but there, carried off in an aqueduct, might give life to a desert.

"For my part, in my ideal of colonisation, I should like that each exportation of human beings had, as of old, its leaders and chiefs—not so appointed from the mere quality of rank, often, indeed, taken from the humbler classes—but still men to whom a certain degree of education should give promptitude, quickness, *adaptability*—men in whom their followers can confide. The Greeks understood that. Nay, as the colony makes progress—as its principal town rises into the dignity of a Capital— a *polis* that needs a polity—I sometimes think it might be wise to go still farther, and not only transplant to it a high standard of civilisation, but draw it more closely into connection with the parent state, and render the passage of spare intellect, education, and *civility*, to and fro, more facile, by drafting off thither the spare scions of royalty itself. I know that many of my more 'liberal' friends would pooh-pooh this notion; but I am sure that the colony altogether, when arrived to a state that would bear the importation, would thrive all the better for it. And when the day shall come (as to all healthful colonies it must come sooner of later), in which the settlement has grown an independent state, we may thereby have laid the seeds of a constitution and a civilisation similar to our own—with self-developed forms of monarchy and aristocracy, though of a simpler growth than old societies accept, and not left a strange motley chaos of struggling democracy—an uncouth livid giant, at which the Frankenstein may well tremble—not because it is a giant, but because it is a giant half completed.[1] Depend on it, the New World will be friendly or hostile to the Old, *not in proportion to the kinship of race, but in proportion to the similarity of manners and institutions*—a mighty truth to which we colonisers have been blind.

[1] These pages were sent to press before the author had seen Mr. Wakefield's recent work on Colonisation, wherein the views here expressed are enforced with great earnestness and conspicuous sagacity. The author is not the less pleased at this coincidence of opinion, because he has the misfortune to dissent from certain other parts of Mr. Wakefield's elaborate theory.

" Passing from these more distant speculations to this positive present before us, you see already, from what I have said, that I sympathise with your aspirations—that I construe them as you would have me ;—looking to your nature and to your objects, I give you my advice in a word—EMIGRATE !

" My advice is, however, founded on one hypothesis—viz., that you are perfectly sincere—you will be contented with a rough life, and with a moderate fortune at the end of your probation. Don't dream of emigrating if you want to make a million, or the tenth part of a million. Don't dream of emigrating, unless you can *enjoy* its hardships,—to *bear* them is not enough !

" Australia is the land for you, as you seem to surmise. Australia is the land for two classes of emigrants : 1st, The man who has nothing but his wits, and plenty of them ; 2ndly, The man who has a small capital, and who is contented to spend ten years in trebling it. I assume that you belong to the latter class.—Take out £3000, and before you are thirty years old, you may return with £10,000 or £12,000. If that satisfies you, think seriously of Australia. By coach, to-morrow, I will send you down all the best books and reports on the subject ; and I will get you what detailed information I can from the Colonial Office. Having read these, and thought over them dispassionately, spend some months yet among the sheep-walks of Cumberland ; learn all you can, from all the shepherds you can find—from Thyrsis to Menalcas. Do more; fit yourself in every way for a life in the Bush ; where the philosophy of the division of labour is not yet arrived at. Learn to turn your hand to everything. Be something of a smith, something of a carpenter—do the best you can with the fewest tools : make yourself an excellent shot ; break in all the wild horses and ponies you can borrow and beg. Even if you want to do none of these things when in your settlement, the having learned to do them will fit you for many other things not now foreseen. *De-fine-gentlemanise* yourself from the crown of your head to the sole of your foot, and become the greater aristocrat for so doing ; for he is more than an aristocrat, he is a king, who suffices in all things for himself—who is his own master, because he wants no *valetaille*. I think Seneca has expressed that thought before me; and I would quote the passage, but the book, I fear, is not in the library of the House of Commons. But now (cheers, by Jove! I suppose ***** is down ! Ah ! it is so ; and C——— is up, and that cheer followed a sharp hit at me. How I wish I were your age, and going to Australia

with you!)—But now—to resume my suspended period—but now
to the important point—capital. You must take that, unless you
go as a shepherd, and then good-bye to the idea of £10,000 in
ten years. So, you see, it appears at the first blush that you
must still come to your father; but, you will say, with this difference, that you borrow the capital with every chance of repaying
it instead of frittering away the income year after year till you
are eight-and-thirty or forty at least. Still, Pisistratus, you don't,
in this, gain your object at a leap; and my dear old friend ought
not to lose his son and his money too. You say you write to me
as to your own father. You know I hate professions; and if you
did not mean what you say, you have offended me mortally. As
a father, then, I take a father's rights, and speak plainly. A
friend of mine, Mr. Bolding, a clergyman, has a son—a wild
fellow, who is likely to get into all sorts of scrapes in England,
but with plenty of good in him, notwithstanding—frank, bold
—not wanting in talent, but rather in prudence—easily tempted
and led away into extravagance. He would make a capital
colonist (no such temptations in the Bush!) if tied to a youth
like you. Now I propose, with your leave, that his father shall
advance him £1500, which shall not, however, be placed in his
hands, but in yours, as head partner in the firm. You, on your
side, shall advance the same sum of £1500, which you shall borrow
from me for three years without interest. At the end of that
time interest shall commence; and the capital, with the interest
on the said first three years, shall be repaid to me or my executors, on your return. After you have been a year or two in
the Bush, and felt your way, and learned your business, you may
then safely borrow £1500 more from your father; and, in the
meanwhile, you and your partner will have had together the full
sum of £3000 to commence with. You see in this proposal I
make you no gift, and I run no risk even by your death. If
you die insolvent, I will promise to come on your father, poor
fellow!—for small joy and small care will he have then in what
may be left of his fortune. There—I have said all; and I will
never forgive you if you reject an aid that will serve you so
much, and cost me so little.

"I accept your congratulations on Fanny's engagement with
Lord Castleton. When you return from Australia you will still
be a young man, she (though about your own years) almost a
middle-aged woman, with her head full of pomps and vanities.
All girls have a short period of girlhood in common; but when
they enter womanhood, the woman becomes the woman of her

class. As for me, and the office assigned to me by report, you know what I said when we parted, and—but here J—— comes, and tells me that ' I am expected to speak, and answer N——, who is just up, brimful of malice,'—the house crowded, and hungering for personalities. So I, the man of the Old World, gird up my loins, and leave you with a sigh, to the fresh youth of the New—

"'Ne tibi sit duros acuisse in prœlia dentes.'

"Yours affectionately,
"ALBERT TREVANION."

CHAPTER VII

SO, reader, thou art now at the secret of my heart.
Wonder not that I, a bookman's son, and, at certain periods of my life, a bookman myself, though of lowly grade in that venerable class—wonder not that I should thus, in that transition stage between youth and manhood, have turned impatiently from books.—Most students, at one time or other in their existence, have felt the imperious demand of that restless principle in man's nature, which calls upon each son of Adam to contribute his share to the vast treasury of human deeds. And though great scholars are not necessarily, nor usually, men of action,—yet the men of action whom History presents to our survey, have rarely been without a certain degree of scholarly nurture. For the ideas which books quicken, books cannot always satisfy. And though the royal pupil of Aristotle slept with Homer under his pillow, it was not that he might dream of composing epics, but of conquering new Ilions in the East. Many a man, how little soever resembling Alexander, may still have the conqueror's aim in an object that action can only achieve, and the book under his pillow may be the strongest antidote to his repose. And how the stern Destinies that shall govern the man weave their first delicate tissues amidst the earliest associations of the child !—Those idle tales with which the old credulous nurse had beguiled my infancy—tales of wonder, knight-errantry, and adventure, had left behind them seeds long latent—seeds that might never have sprung up above the soil—but that my boyhood was so early put under the burning-glass, and in the quick forcing-house, of the London

U

world. There, even amidst books and study, lively observation and petulant ambition broke forth from the lush foliage of romance—that fruitless leafiness of poetic youth! And there passion, which is a revolution in all the elements of individual man, had called a new state of being, turbulent and eager, out of the old habits and conventional forms it had buried—ashes that speak where the fire has been. Far from me, as from any mind of some manliness, be the attempt to create interest by dwelling at length on the struggles against a rash and misplaced attachment, which it was my duty to overcome; but all such love, as I have before implied, is a terrible unsettler :—

" Where once such fairies dance, no grass doth ever grow."

To re-enter boyhood, go with meek docility through its disciplined routine—how hard had I found that return, amidst the cloistered monotony of college! My love for my father, and my submission to his wish, had indeed given some animation to objects otherwise distasteful; but, now that my return to the University must be attended with positive privation to those at home, the idea became utterly hateful and repugnant. Under pretence that I found myself, on trial, not yet sufficiently prepared to do credit to my father's name, I had easily obtained leave to lose the ensuing college term, and pursue my studies at home. This gave me time to prepare my plans, and bring round—how shall I ever bring round to my adventurous views those whom I propose to desert? Hard it is to get on in the world—very hard! But the most painful step in the way is that which starts from the threshold of a beloved home.

How—ah, how, indeed! "No, Blanche, you cannot join me to-day; I am going out for many hours. So it will be late before I can be home."

Home!—the word chokes me! Juba slinks back to his young mistress, disconsolate; Blanche gazes at me ruefully from our favourite hill-top, and the flowers she has been gathering fall unheeded from her basket. I hear my mother's voice singing low, as she sits at work by her open casement. How,—ah, how indeed !

PART XIII

CHAPTER I

ST. CHRYSOSTOM, in his work on The Priesthood, defends deceit, if for a good purpose, by many scriptural examples; ends his first book by asserting that it is often necessary, and that much benefit may arise from it; and begins his second book by saying that it ought not to be called *deceit* but *good management.*" [1]

Good management, then, let me call the innocent arts by which I now sought to insinuate my project into favour and assent with my unsuspecting family. At first I began with Roland. I easily induced him to read some of the books, full of the charm of Australian life, which Trevanion had sent me; and so happily did those descriptions suit his own erratic tastes, and the free half-savage man that lay rough and large within that soldierly nature, that he himself, as it were, seemed to suggest my own ardent desire—sighed, as the careworn Trevanion had done, that "he was not my age," and blew the flame that consumed me with his own willing breath. So that when at last—wandering one day over the wild moors—I said, knowing his hatred of law and lawyers—"Alas, uncle, that nothing should be left for me but the bar!" Captain Roland struck his cane into the peat, and exclaimed, "Zounds, sir! the bar and lying, with truth and a world fresh from God before you!"

"Your hand, uncle—we understand each other. Now help me with those two quiet hearts at home!"

"Plague on my tongue! what have I done?" said the Captain, looking aghast. Then, after musing a little time, he turned his dark eye on me, and growled out, "I suspect, young sir, you have been laying a trap for me; and I have fallen into it, like an old fool as I am."

"Oh, sir, if you prefer the bar!——"

"Rogue!"

"Or, indeed, I might perhaps get a clerkship in a merchant's office?"

---

[1] Hohler's translation.

307

" If you do, I will scratch you out of the pedigree ! "

" Huzza, then, for Australasia ! "

" Well, well, well," said my uncle,

> " With a smile on his lip, and a tear in his eye ; "

" the old sea-king's blood will force its way—a soldier or a rover, there is no other choice for you. We shall mourn and miss you ; but who can chain the young eagles to the eyrie ? "

I had a harder task with my father, who at first seemed to listen to me as if I had been talking of an excursion to the moon. But I threw in a dexterous dose of the old Greek *Cleruchiæ*—cited by Trevanion—which set him off full trot on his hobby, till after a short excursion to Eubœa and the Chersonese, he was fairly lost amidst the Ionian colonies of Asia Minor. I then gradually and artfully decoyed him into his favourite science of Ethnology ; and, while he was speculating on the origin of the American savages, and considering the rival claims of Cimmerians, Israelites, and Scandinavians, I said quietly,—" And you, sir, who think that all human improvement depends on the mixture of races—you, whose whole theory is an absolute sermon upon emigration, and the transplanting and interpolity of our species—you, sir, should be the last man to chain your son, your elder son, to the soil, while your younger is the very missionary of rovers."

" Pisistratus," said my father, " you reason by *synecdoche*—ornamental but illogical : " and therewith resolved to hear no more, my father rose and retreated into his study.

But his observation, now quickened, began from that day to follow my moods and humours—then he himself grew silent and thoughtful, and finally he took to long conferences with Roland. The result was that, one evening in spring, as I lay listless amidst the weeds and fern that sprang up through the melancholy ruins, I felt a hand on my shoulder ; and my father, seating himself beside me on a fragment of stone, said earnestly —" Pisistratus, let us talk—I had hoped better things from your study of Robert Hall."

" Nay, dear father, the medicine did me great good : I have not repined since, and I look steadfastly and cheerfully on life. But Robert Hall fulfilled his mission, and I would fulfil mine."

" Is there no mission in thy native land, O planeticose and exallotriote spirit ? " [1] asked my father, with compassionate rebuke.

---

[1] Words coined by Mr. Caxton from πλανητικός, disposed to roaming, and ἐξαλλοτριόω, to export, to alienate.

"Alas, yes! But what the impulse of genius is to the great, the instinct of vocation is to the mediocre. In every man there is a magnet! in that thing which the man can do best there is a loadstone."

"Papæ!" said my father, opening his eyes; "and are no loadstones to be found for you nearer than the Great Australasian Bight?"

"Ah, sir, if you resort to irony I can say no more!" My father looked down on me tenderly, as I hung my head, moody and abashed.

"Son," said he, "do you think that there is any real jest at my heart, when the matter discussed is whether you are to put wide seas and long years between us?" I pressed nearer to his side, and made no answer.

"But I have noted you of late," continued my father, "and I have observed that your old studies are grown distasteful to you; and I have talked with Roland, and I see that your desire is deeper than a boy's mere whim. And then I have asked myself what prospect I can hold out at home to induce you to be contented here, and I see none; and therefore I should say to you, 'Go thy ways, and God shield thee'—but, Pisistratus, *your mother!*"

"Ah, sir, that is indeed the question! and there indeed I shrink. But, after all, whatever I were—whether toiling at the bar, or in some public office—I should be still so much from home and her. And then you, sir, she loves *you* so entirely, that——"

"No," interrupted my father; "you can advance no arguments like these to touch a mother's heart. There is but one argument that comes home there—is it for your good to leave her? If so, there will be no need of further words. But let us not decide that question hastily; let you and I be together the next two months. Bring your books and sit with me; when you want to go out, tap me on the shoulder, and say, 'Come.' At the end of those two months I will say to you 'Go,' or 'Stay.' And you will trust me; and if I say the last, you will submit?"

"Oh yes, sir—yes!"

CHAPTER II

THIS compact made, my father roused himself from all his studies—devoted his whole thoughts to me—sought with all his gentle wisdom to wean me imperceptibly from my one fixed tyrannical idea,—ranged through his wide pharmacy of books for such medicaments as might alter the system of my thoughts. And little thought he that his very tenderness and wisdom worked against him, for at each new instance of either my heart called aloud, "Is it not that thy tenderness may be repaid, and thy wisdom be known abroad, that I go from thee into the strange land, O my father!"

And the two months expired, and my father saw that the magnet had turned unalterably to the loadstone in the great Australasian Bight; and he said to me, "Go, and comfort your mother. I have told her your wish, and authorised it by my consent, for I believe now that it *is* for your good."

I found my mother in the little room she had appropriated to herself next my father's study. And in that room there was a pathos which I have no words to express; for my mother's meek, gentle, womanly soul spoke there, so that it was the Home of Home. The care with which she had transplanted from the brick house, and lovingly arranged, all the humble memorials of old times, dear to her affections—the black silhouette of my father's profile cut in paper, in the full pomp of academics, cap and gown (how had he ever consented to sit for it!) framed and glazed in the place of honour over the little hearth, and boyish sketches of mine at the Hellenic Institute, first essays in sepia and Indian ink, to animate the walls, and bring her back, when she sat there in the twilight, musing alone, to sunny hours, when Sisty and the young mother threw daisies at each other; —and covered with a great glass shade, and dusted each day with her own hand, the flower-pot Sisty had bought with the proceeds of the domino-box, on that memorable occasion on which he had learned "how bad deeds are repaired with good." There, in one corner, stood the little cottage piano, which I remembered all my life—old-fashioned, and with the jingling voice of approaching decrepitude, but still associated with such melodies as, after childhood, we hear never more! And in the modest hanging shelves, which looked so gay with ribbons, and tassels, and silken cords—my mother's own library, saying more to the heart than all the cold wise poets whose souls my father invoked in his grand Heraclea. The Bible over which, with eyes yet untaught to read, I had hung in vague awe and love, as it lay open on my mother's lap, while her sweet voice, then only serious, was made the oracle of its truths. And my first lesson-books were there, all hoarded. And bound in blue and gold, but elaborately papered up, "Cowper's Poems"—a gift from my father in the days of courtship—sacred treasure, which not

Chris Hammond
Oct /97

No—no! it is for your good—

even I had the privilege to touch; and which my mother took out only in the great crosses and trials of conjugal life, whenever some words less kind than usual had dropped unawares from her scholar's absent lips. Ah! all these poor household gods, all seemed to look on me with mild anger; and from all came a voice to my soul, "Cruel, dost thou forsake us!" And amongst them sat my mother, desolate as Rachel, and weeping silently.

"Mother! mother!" I cried, falling on her neck, "forgive me —it is past—I cannot leave you!"

CHAPTER III

NO—no! it is for your good—Austin says so. Go—it is but the first shock."

Then to my mother I opened the sluices of that deep I had concealed from scholar and soldier. To her I poured all the wild, restless thoughts which wandered through the ruins of love destroyed—to her I confessed what to myself I had scarcely before avowed. And when the picture of that, the darker, side of my mind was shown, it was with a prouder face, and less broken voice, that I spoke of the manlier hopes and nobler aims that gleamed across the wrecks and the desert, and showed me my escape.

"Did you not once say, mother, that you had felt it like a remorse, that my father's genius passed so noiselessly away,— half accusing the happiness you gave him for the death of his ambition in the content of his mind? Did you not feel a new object in life when the ambition revived at last, and you thought you heard the applause of the world murmuring round your scholar's cell? Did you not share in the day-dreams your brother conjured up, and exclaim, 'If *my* brother could be the means of raising *him* in the world!' and when you had thought we had found the way to fame and fortune, did you not sob out from your full heart, 'And it is *my* brother who will pay back to *his* son—all—all he gave up for me'?"

"I cannot bear this, Sisty!—cease, cease!"

"No; for do you not yet understand me? Will it not be better still, if *your* son—yours—restore to your Austin all that he lost, no matter how? If through your son, mother, you do indeed make the world hear of your husband's genius—restore the spring to his mind, the glory to his pursuits—if you rebuild

even that vaunted ancestral name, which is glory to our poor
sonless Roland—if your son can restore the decay of generations,
and reconstruct from the dust the whole house into which you
have entered, its meek presiding angel?—ah, mother! if this
can be done, it will be your work; for unless you can share my
ambition—unless you can dry those eyes, and smile in my face,
and bid me go, with a cheerful voice—all my courage melts from
my heart, and again I say, I cannot leave you!"

Then my mother folded her arms round me, and we both wept,
and could not speak—but we were both happy.

CHAPTER IV

NOW the worst was over, and my mother was the most heroic
of us all. So I began to prepare myself in good earnest,
and I followed Trevanion's instructions with a perseverance
which I could never, at that young day, have thrown into the
dead life of books. I was in a good school, amongst our Cumberland sheep-walks, to learn those simple elements of rural art
which belong to the ·pastoral state. Mr. Sidney, in his admirable " Australian Hand-Book," recommends young gentlemen
who think of becoming settlers in the Bush to bivouac for three
months on Salisbury Plain. That book was not then written,
or I might have taken the advice; meanwhile I think, with
due respect to such authority, that I went through a preparatory training quite as useful in seasoning the future emigrant.
I associated readily with the kindly peasants and craftsmen,
who became my teachers. With what pride I presented my
father with a desk, and my mother with a workbox, fashioned
by my own hands! I made Bolt a lock for his plate-chest,
and (that last was *my* magnum opus, my great masterpiece) I
repaired and absolutely set going an old turret-clock in the
tower, that had stood at 2 P.M. since the memory of man. I
loved to think, each time the hour sounded, that those who
heard its deep chime would remember me. But the flocks
were my main care: the sheep that I tended and helped to
shear, and the lamb that I hooked out of the great marsh, and
the three venerable ewes that I nursed through a mysterious
sort of murrain, which puzzled all the neighbourhood—are they
not written in thy loving chronicles, O House of Caxton!

And now, since much of the success of my experiment must

depend on the friendly terms I could establish with my intended partner, I wrote to Trevanion, begging him to get the young gentleman who was to join me, and whose capital I was to administer, to come and visit us. Trevanion complied, and there arrived a tall fellow, somewhat more than six feet high, answering to the name of Guy Bolding, in a cut-away sporting coat, with a dog-whistle tied to the button-hole: drab shorts and gaiters, and a waistcoat with all manner of strange furtive pockets. Guy Bolding had lived a year and a half at Oxford as a "fast man"; so "fast" had he lived that there was scarcely a tradesman at Oxford into whose books he had not contrived to run.

His father was compelled to withdraw him from the university, at which he had already had the honour of being plucked for "the little go"; and the young gentleman, on being asked for what profession he was fit, had replied with conscious pride, "That he could tool a coach!" In despair, the sire, who owed his living to Trevanion, had asked the statesman's advice, and the advice had fixed me with a partner in expatriation.

My first feeling in greeting the "fast" man was certainly that of deep disappointment and strong repugnance. But I was determined not to be too fastidious; and, having a lucky knack of suiting myself pretty well to all tempers (without which a man had better not think of loadstones in the great Australasian Bight), I contrived before the first week was out to establish so many points of connection between us, that we became the best friends in the world. Indeed, it would have been my fault if we had not, for Guy Bolding, with all his faults, was one of those excellent creatures who are nobody's enemies but their own. His good-humour was inexhaustible. Not a hardship or privation came amiss to him. He had a phrase, "Such fun!" that always rushed laughingly to his lips when another man would have cursed and groaned. If we lost our way in the great trackless moors, missed our dinner, and were half-famished, Guy rubbed hands that would have felled an ox, and chuckled out, "Such fun!" If we stuck in a bog, if we were caught in a thunderstorm, if we were pitched head-over-heels by the wild colts we undertook to break in, Guy Bolding's sole elegy was "Such fun." That grand shibboleth of philosophy only forsook him at the sight of an open book. I don't think that, at that time, he could have found "fun" even in Don Quixote. This hilarious temperament had no insensibility; a kinder heart never beat,—but, to be sure, it beat to a strange, restless, tarantula sort of measure, which kept it in a perpetual dance. It made him one of those officiously good fellows, who are never quiet themselves, and never let any one else be quiet if they can help it. But Guy's great fault, in this prudent world, was his absolute incontinence of money. If you had turned a Euphrates of gold into his pockets at morning, it would have been as dry as the great Sahara by twelve at noon. What he did with the money was a mystery as much to himself as to every one else. His father said in a letter to me, that "he had seen him shying at sparrows with half-crowns!" That such a young man could come to no good in England, seemed perfectly clear. Still, it is recorded of many great men, who did not end their days in a workhouse, that they were equally non-retentive of money. Schiller when he had nothing else to give away, gave the clothes from his back, and Goldsmith the blankets from his bed. Tender hands found it necessary to pick Beethoven's pockets at home before he walked out. Great heroes, who have made no scruple of robbing the whole world, have been just as lavish as poor poets and musicians. Alexander, in parcelling out his spoils, left himself "hope!" And as for Julius Cæsar, he was two millions in debt when he shied his last half-crown at the sparrows in Gaul. Encouraged by these illustrious examples, I had hopes of Guy Bolding; and the more as he was so aware of his own infirmity that he was perfectly contented with the arrangement which made me treasurer of his capital, and even besought me, on no account, let him beg ever so hard, to permit his own money to come in his own way. In fact, I contrived to gain a great ascendency over his simple, generous, thoughtless nature : and by artful appeals to his affections—to all he owed to his father for many bootless sacrifices, and to the duty of providing a little dower for his infant sister, whose meditated portion had half gone to pay his college debts—I at last succeeded in fixing into his mind an object to save for.

Three other companions did I select for our *Cleruchia*. The first was the son of our old shepherd, who had lately married, but was not yet encumbered with children,—a good shepherd, and an intelligent, steady fellow. The second was a very different character; he had been the dread of the whole squirearchy. A more bold and dexterous poacher did not exist. Now my acquaintance with this latter person, named Will Peterson, and more popularly "Will o' the Wisp," had commenced thus :— Bolt had managed to rear in a small copse about a mile from the house—and which was the only bit of ground in my uncle's domains that might by courtesy be called "a wood"—a young colony of pheasants, that he dignified by the title of a "preserve." This colony was audaciously despoiled and grievously depopulated, in spite of two watchers, who, with Bolt, guarded for seven nights successively the slumbers of the infant settlement. So insolent was the assault, that bang, bang, went the felonious gun—behind, before—within but a few yards of the sentinels—and the gunner was off, and the prey seized, before they could rush to the spot. The boldness and skill of the enemy soon proclaimed him, to the experienced watchers, to be Will o' the Wisp: and so great was their dread of this fellow's strength and courage, and so complete their despair of being a match for his swiftness and cunning, that after the seventh night the watchers refused to go out any longer; and poor Bolt himself was confined to his bed by an attack of what a doctor would have called rheumatism, and a moralist, rage. My indignation and sympathy were greatly excited by this mortifying failure, and my interest romantically aroused by the anecdotes I had heard of Will o' the Wisp; accordingly, armed with a thick bludgeon, I stole out at night, and took my way to the copse. The leaves were not off the trees, and how the poacher contrived to see his victims I know not; but five shots did he fire, and not in vain, without allowing me to catch a glimpse of him. I then retreated to the outskirt of the copse, and waited patiently by an angle, which commanded two sides of the wood. Just as the dawn began to peep, I saw my man emerge within twenty yards of me. I held my breath, suffered him to get a few steps from the wood, crept on so as to intercept his retreat, and then pounce—such a bound! My hand was on his shoulder—prr, prr,—no eel was ever more lubricate. He slid from me like a thing immaterial, and was off over the moors with a swiftness which might well have baffled any clodhopper —a race whose calves are generally absorbed in the soles of their hobnail shoes. But the Hellenic Institute, with its classical gymnasia, had trained its pupils in all bodily exercises; and though the Will o' the Wisp was swift for a clodhopper, he was no match at running with any youth who had spent his boyhood in the discipline of cricket, prisoner's bar, and hunt-the-hare. I reached him at length, and brought him to bay.

"Stand back!" said he, panting, and taking aim with his gun; "it is loaded."

"Yes," said I; "but though you're a brave poacher, you

dare not fire at your fellow-man. Give up the gun this instant."

My address took him by surprise; he did not fire. I struck up the barrel, and closed on him. We grappled pretty tightly, and in the wrestle the gun went off. The man loosened his hold. "Lord ha' mercy! I have not hurt you?" he said falteringly.

"My good fellow—no," said I; "and now let us throw aside gun and bludgeon, and fight it out like Englishmen, or else let us sit down and talk over it like friends."

The Will o' the Wisp scratched its head and laughed.

"Well, you're a queer one!" quoth it. And the poacher dropped the gun and sat down.

We did talk it over, and I obtained Peterson's promise to respect the preserve henceforth; and we thereon grew so cordial that he walked home with me, and even presented me, shyly and apologetically, with the five pheasants he had shot. From that time I sought him out. He was a young fellow not four-and-twenty, who had taken to poaching from the wild sport of the thing, and from some confused notions that he had a licence from Nature to poach. I soon found out that he was meant for better things than to spend six months of the twelve in prison, and finish his life on the gallows after killing a game-keeper. That seemed to me his most probable destiny in the Old World, so I talked him into a burning desire for the New One; and a most valuable aid in the Bush he proved too.

My third selection was in a personage who could bring little physical strength to help us, but who had more mind (though with a wrong twist in it) than both the others put together.

A worthy couple in the village had a son, who being slight and puny, compared to the Cumberland breed, was shouldered out of the market of agricultural labour, and went off, yet a boy, to a manufacturing town. Now about the age of thirty, this mechanic, disabled for his work by a long illness, came home to recover; and in a short time we heard of nothing but the pestilential doctrines with which he was either shocking or infecting our primitive villagers. According to report, Corcyra itself never engendered a democrat more awful. The poor man was really very ill, and his parents very poor; but his unfortu-nate doctrines dried up all the streams of charity that usually flowed through our kindly hamlet. The clergyman (an excellent man, but of the old school) walked by the house as if it were tabooed. The apothecary said, "Miles Square ought to have wine;" but he did not send him any. The farmers

held his name in execration, for he had incited all their
labourers to strike for another shilling a week. And but for
the old Tower, Miles Square would soon have found his way to
the only republic in which he could obtain that democratic
fraternisation for which he sighed—the grave being, I suspect,
the sole commonwealth which attains that dead flat of social
equality that life in its every principle so heartily abhors.

My uncle went to see Miles Square, and came back the
colour of purple. Miles Square had preached him a long
sermon on the unholiness of war. "Even in defence of your
king and country!" had roared the Captain; and Miles Square
had replied with a remark upon kings in general, that the
Captain could not have repeated without expecting to see the
old Tower fall about his ears; and with an observation about
the country in particular, to the effect that "the country would
be much better off if it *were* conquered!" On hearing the
report of these loyal and patriotic replies, my father said
"Papæ!" and, roused out of his usual philosophical indifference, went himself to visit Miles Square. My father returned
as pale as my uncle had been purple. "And to think," said
he mournfully, "that in the town whence this man comes, there
are, he tells me, ten thousand other of God's creatures who
speed the work of civilisation while execrating its laws!"

But neither father nor uncle made any opposition when,
with a basket laden with wine and arrowroot, and a neat
little Bible, bound in brown, my mother took her way to the
excommunicated cottage. Her visit was as signal a failure
as those that preceded it. Miles Square refused the basket;
"he was not going to accept alms, and eat the bread of
charity;" and on my mother meekly suggesting that, "if
Mr. Miles Square would condescend to look into the Bible, he
would see that even charity was no sin in giver or recipient,"
Mr. Miles Square had undertaken to prove that, according to
the Bible, he had as much a right to my mother's property as
she had—that all things should be in common—and, when all
things were in common, what became of charity? No; he
could not eat my uncle's arrowroot, and drink his wine, while
my uncle was improperly withholding from him and his fellow-
creatures so many unprofitable acres: the land belonged to
the people. It was now the turn of Pisistratus to go. He
went once, and he went often. Miles Square and Pisistratus
wrangled and argued—argued and wrangled—and ended by
taking a fancy to each other; for this poor Miles Square was

not half so bad as his doctrines.   His errors arose from intense sympathy with the sufferings he had witnessed, amidst the misery which accompanies the reign of *millocratism,* and from the vague aspirations of a half-taught, impassioned, earnest nature.   By degrees, I persuaded him to drink the wine and eat the arrowroot, *en attendant* that millennium which was to restore the land to the people.   And then my mother came again and softened his heart, and, for the first time in his life, let into its cold crotchets the warm light of human gratitude. I lent him some books, amongst others a few volumes on Australia.   A passage in one of the latter in which it was said "that an intelligent mechanic usually made his way in the colony, even as a shepherd, better than a dull agricultural labourer," caught hold of his fancy, and seduced his aspirations into a healthful direction.   Finally, as he recovered, he entreated me to let him accompany me.   And as I may not have to return to Miles Square, I think it right here to state, that he did go with me to Australia, and did succeed, first as a shepherd, next as a superintendent, and finally, on saving money, as a land-owner ; and that, in spite of his opinions of the unholiness of war, he was no sooner in possession of a comfortable log home-stead, than he defended it with uncommon gallantry against an attack of the aborigines, whose right to the soil was, to say the least of it, as good as his claim to my uncle's acres ; that he commemorated his subsequent acquisition of a fresh allotment, with the stock on it, by a little pamphlet, published at Sydney, on the " Sanctity of the Rights of Property ; " and that, when I left the colony, having been much pestered by two refractory " helps " that he had added to his establishment, he had just distinguished himself by a very anti-levelling lecture upon the duties of servants to their employers.   What would the Old World have done for this man ?

CHAPTER V

I HAD not been in haste to conclude my arrangements, for, independently of my wish to render myself acquainted with the small useful crafts that might be necessary to me in a life that makes the individual man a state in himself, I naturally desired to habituate my kindred to the idea of our separation, and to plan and provide for them all such substitutes or distractions, in compensation for my loss, as my fertile imagination could suggest. At first, for the sake of Blanche, Roland, and my mother, I talked the Captain into reluctant sanction of his sister-in-law's proposal, to unite their incomes and share alike, without considering which party brought the larger proportion into the firm. I represented to him that, unless he made that sacrifice of his pride, my mother would be wholly without those little notable uses and objects, those small household pleasures, so dear to woman; that all society in the neighbourhood would be impossible, and that my mother's time would hang so heavily on her hands, that her only resource would be to muse on the absent one, and fret. Nay, if he persisted in so false a pride, I told him, fairly, that I should urge my father to leave the Tower. These representations succeeded, and hospitality had commenced in the old hall, and a knot of gossips had centred round my mother—groups of laughing children had relaxed the still brow of Blanche—and the Captain himself was a more cheerful and social man. My next point was to engage my father in the completion of the Great Book. " Ah, sir," said I, " give me an inducement to toil, a reward for my industry. Let me think, in each tempting pleasure, each costly vice—No, no; I will save for the Great Book! and the memory of the father shall still keep the son from error. Ah, look you, sir! Mr. Trevanion offered me the loan of £1500 necessary to commence with; but you generously and at once said—' No; you must not begin life under the load of debt.' And I knew you were right and yielded—yielded the more gratefully that I could not but forfeit something of the just pride of manhood in incurring such an obligation to the father of—Miss Trevanion. Therefore I have taken that sum from you—a sum that would almost have sufficed to establish your younger and worthier child in the world for ever. To that child let me repay it, otherwise I will not take it. Let me hold it as a trust for the Great Book; and promise me that the Great Book shall be ready when your wanderer returns, and accounts for the missing talent."

And my father pished a little, and rubbed off the dew that had gathered on his spectacles. But I would not leave him in peace till he had given me his word that the Great Book should go on *à pas du géant*—nay, till I had seen him sit down to it with good heart, and the wheel went round again in the quiet mechanism of that gentle life.

Finally, and as the culminating acme of my diplomacy, I effected the purchase of the neighbouring apothecary's practice and goodwill for Squills, upon terms which he willingly subscribed to; for the poor man had pined at the loss of his favourite patients, though, Heaven knows, they did not add much to his income. And as for my father, there was no man who diverted him more than Squills, though he accused him of being a materialist, and set his whole spiritual pack of sages to worry and bark at him, from Plato and Zeno to Reid and Abraham Tucker.

Thus, although I have very loosely intimated the flight of time, more than a whole year elapsed from the date of our settlement at the Tower and that fixed for my departure.

In the meanwhile, despite the rarity amongst us of that phenomenon, a newspaper, we were not so utterly cut off from the sounds of the far-booming world beyond, but what the intelligence of a change in the administration and the appointment of Mr. Trevanion to one of the great offices of state reached our ears. I had kept up no correspondence with Trevanion subsequent to the letter that occasioned Guy Bolding's visit; I wrote now to congratulate him: his reply was short and hurried.

An intelligence that startled me more, and more deeply moved my heart, was conveyed to me, some three months or so before my departure, by Trevanion's steward. The ill-health of Lord Castleton had deferred his marriage, intended originally to be celebrated as soon as he arrived of age. He left the university with the honours of "a double first class"; and his constitution appeared to rally from the effects of studies more severe to him than they might have been to a man of quicker and more brilliant capacities—when a feverish cold, caught at a county meeting, in which his first public appearance was so creditable as fully to justify the warmest hopes of his party, produced inflammation of the lungs, and ended fatally. The startling contrast forced on my mind—here, sudden death and cold clay—there, youth in its first flower, princely rank, boundless wealth, the sanguine expectation of an illustrious career, and the prospect of that happiness which smiled from the eyes of Fanny—that contrast impressed me with a strange awe: death seems so near to us when it strikes those whom life most flatters and caresses. Whence is that curious sympathy that we all have with the possessors of worldly greatness, when the hour-glass is shaken and the scythe descends? If the famous meeting between Diogenes and Alexander had taken place not before, but after the achievements which gave to Alexander the name of Great, the cynic would not, perhaps, have envied the hero his pleasures nor his splendours—neither the charms of Statira nor the tiara of the Mede; but if, the day after, a cry had gone forth, "Alexander the Great is dead!" verily I believe that Diogenes would have coiled himself up in his tub, and felt that with the shadow of the stately hero, something of glory and of warmth had gone from that sun, which it should darken never more. In the nature of man, the humblest or the hardest, there is a something that lives in all of the Beautiful or the Fortunate, which hope and desire have appropriated, even in the vanities of a childish dream.

CHAPTER VI

WHY are you here all alone, cousin? How cold and still it is amongst the graves!"

"Sit down beside me, Blanche; it is not colder in the church-yard than on the village green."

And Blanche sat down beside me, nestled close to me, and leant her head upon my shoulder. We were both long silent. It was an evening in the early spring, clear and serene— the roseate streaks were fading gradually from the dark grey of long, narrow, fantastic clouds. Tall, leafless poplars, that stood in orderly level line, on the lowland between the church-yard and the hill, with its crown of ruins, left their sharp summits distinct against the sky. But the shadows coiled dull and heavy round the evergreens that skirted the churchyard, so that their outline was vague and confused; and there was a depth in that lonely stillness, broken only when the thrush flew out from the lower bushes, and the thick laurel leaves stirred reluctantly, and again were rigid in repose. There is a certain melancholy in the evenings of early spring, which is among those influences of Nature the most universally recognised, the most difficult to explain. The silent stir of reviving life, which does not yet betray signs in the bud and blossom—only in a softer clearness in the air, a more lingering pause in the slowly lengthening day; a more delicate freshness and balm in the twilight atmosphere; a more lively, yet still unquiet note from the birds, settling down into their coverts;—the vague sense under all that hush, which still outwardly wears the black sterility of winter—of the busy change, hourly, momently, at work—renewing the youth of the world, reclothing with vigorous bloom the skeletons of things—all these messages from the heart of Nature to the heart of Man may well affect and move us. But why with melancholy? No thought on our part connects and construes the low, gentle voices. It is not *thought* that replies and reasons: it is *feeling* that hears and dreams. Examine not, O child of man!—examine not that mysterious melancholy with the hard eyes of thy reason; thou canst not impale it on the spikes of thy thorny logic, nor describe its enchanted circle by problems conned from thy schools. Borderer thyself of two worlds—the Dead and the Living—give thine ear to the tones, bow thy soul to the shadows, that steal, in the Season of Change, from the dim Border Land.

BLANCHE (in a whisper).—"What are you thinking of?—speak, pray!"

PISISTRATUS.—"I was not thinking, Blanche; or, if I were, the thought is gone at the mere effort to seize or detain it."

BLANCHE (after a pause).—"I know what you mean. It is the same with me often—so often, when I am sitting by myself, quite still. It is just like the story Primmins was telling us the other evening, 'how there was a woman in her village who saw things and people in a piece of crystal, not bigger than my hand:[1] they passed along as large as life, but they were only pictures in the crystal.' Since I heard the story, when aunt asks me what I am thinking of, I long to say, 'I'm not thinking! I am seeing pictures in the crystal!'"

PISISTRATUS.—"Tell my father *that*; it will please him. There is more philosophy in it than you are aware of, Blanche. There are wise men who have thought the whole world, its 'pride, pomp, and circumstance,' only a phantom image—a picture in the crystal."

BLANCHE.—"And I shall see you—see us both, as we are sitting here—and that star which has just risen yonder—see it

[1] In primitive villages in the west of England, the belief that the absent may be seen in a piece of crystal is, or was not many years ago, by no means an uncommon superstition. I have seen more than one of these magic mirrors, which Spenser, by the way, has beautifully described. They are about the size and shape of a Swan's egg. It is not every one, however, who can be a crystal-seer; like second-sight, it is a special gift. *N. B.*—Since the above note (appended to the first edition of this work) was written, crystals and crystal-seers have become very familiar to those who interest themselves in speculations upon the disputed phenomena ascribed to Mesmerical *Clairvoyance.*

all in my crystal—when you are gone!—gone, cousin!" (And Blanche's head drooped.)

There was something so quiet and deep in the tenderness of this poor motherless child, that it did not affect one superficially, like a child's loud momentary affection, in which we know that the first toy will replace us. I kissed my little cousin's pale face, and said, "And I too, Blanche, have my crystal; and when I consult it, I shall be very angry if I see you sad and fretting, or seated alone. For you must know, Blanche, that that is all selfishness. God made us, not to indulge only in crystal pictures, weave idle fancies, pine alone, and mourn over what we cannot help—but to be alert and active—givers of happiness. Now, Blanche, see what a trust I am going to bequeath you. You are to supply my place to all whom I leave. You are to bring sunshine wherever you glide with that shy, soft step—whether to your father, when you see his brows knit and his arms crossed (that, indeed, you always do), or to mine, when the volume drops from his hand—when he walks to and fro the room, restless, and murmuring to himself—then you are to steal up to him, put your hand in his, lead him back to his books, and whisper, 'What will Sisty say if his younger brother, the Great Book, is not grown up when he comes back?'—And my poor mother, Blanche!—ah, how can I counsel you there—how tell you where to find comfort for her? Only, Blanche, steal into her heart and be her daughter. And, to fulfil this threefold trust, you must not content yourself with seeing pictures in the crystal—do you understand me?"

"Oh yes," said Blanche, raising her eyes, while the tears rolled from them, and folding her arms resolutely on her breast.

"And so," said I, "as we two, sitting in this quiet burial-ground, take new heart for the duties and cares of life, so see, Blanche, how the stars come out, one by one, to smile upon us; for they, too, glorious orbs as they are, perform their appointed tasks. Things seem to approximate to God in proportion to their vitality and movement. Of all things, least inert and sullen should be the soul of man. How the grass grows up over the very graves—quickly it grows and greenly—but neither so quick nor so green, my Blanche, as hope and comfort from human sorrows."

PART XIV

CHAPTER I

THERE is a beautiful and singular passage in Dante (which has not perhaps attracted the attention it deserves), wherein the stern Florentine defends Fortune from the popular accusations against her. According to him, she is an angelic power appointed by the Supreme Being to direct and order the course of human splendours: she obeys the will of God; she is blessed, and, hearing not those who blaspheme her, calm and aloft amongst the other angelic powers, revolves her spheral course, and rejoices in her beatitude.[1]

This is a conception very different from the popular notion which Aristophanes, in his true instinct of things popular, expresses by the sullen lips of his Plutus. That deity accounts for his blindness by saying, that "when a boy, he had indiscreetly promised to visit only the good," and Jupiter was so envious of the good that he blinded the poor money-god. Whereon Chremylus asks him, whether, "if he recovered his sight, he would frequent the company of the good?" "Certainly," quoth Plutus, "for I have not seen them ever so long." "Nor I either," rejoins Chremylus pithily, "for all I can see out of both eyes."

But that misanthropical answer of Chremylus is neither here nor there, and only diverts us from the real question, and that is, "Whether Fortune be a heavenly, Christian angel, or a blind, blundering, old heathen deity?" For my part, I hold with Dante—for which, if I were so pleased, or if, at this period of my memoirs, I had half-a-dozen pages to spare, I could give many good reasons. One thing, however, is quite clear—that, whether Fortune be more like Plutus or an angel,

[1] Dante here evidently associates Fortune with the planetary influences of judicial astrology. It is doubtful whether Schiller ever read Dante; but in one of his most thoughtful poems he undertakes the same defence of Fortune, making the Fortunate a part of the beautiful.

it is no use abusing her—one may as well throw stones at a star. And I think, if one looked narrowly at her operations, one might perceive that she gives every man a chance, at least once in his life; if he take and make the best of it, she will renew her visits; if not, *itur ad astra!* And therewith I am reminded of an incident quaintly narrated by Mariana in his "History of Spain," how the army of the Spanish kings got out of a sad hobble among the mountains at the Pass of Losa, by the help of a shepherd, who showed them the way. "But," saith Mariana parenthetically, "some do say the shepherd was an angel; for, after he had shown the way, he was never seen more." That is, the angelic nature of the guide was proved by being only once seen, and, after having got the army out of the hobble, leaving it to fight or run away, as it had most mind to. Now, I look upon that shepherd, or angel, as a very good type of my fortune at least. The apparition showed me my way in the rocks to the great "Battle of Life": after that,—hold fast and strike hard!

Behold me in London with Uncle Roland. My poor parents naturally wished to accompany me, and take the last glimpse of the adventurer on board ship; but I, knowing that the parting would seem less dreadful to them by the hearthstone, and while they could say, "He is with Roland—he is not yet gone from the land"—insisted on their staying behind; and thus the farewell was spoken. But Roland, the old soldier, had so many practical instructions to give—could so help me in the choice of the outfit and the preparations for the voyage, that I could not refuse his companionship to the last. Guy Bolding, who had gone to take leave of his father, was to join me in town, as well as my humbler Cumberland colleagues.

As my uncle and I were both of one mind upon the question of economy, we took up our quarters at a lodging-house in the City; and there it was that I first made acquaintance with a part of London, of which few of my politer readers even pretend to be cognisant. I do not mean any sneer at the City itself, my dear alderman; that jest is worn out. I am not alluding to streets, courts, and lanes; what I mean may be seen at the West-end—not so well as at the East, but still seen very fairly! I mean—THE HOUSE-TOPS!

CHAPTER II

BEING A CHAPTER ON HOUSE-TOPS

THE HOUSE-TOPS! what a soberising effect that prospect produces on the mind.   But a great many requisites go towards
the selection of the right point of survey.   It is not enough
to secure a lodging in the attic; you must not be fobbed off
with a front attic that faces the street.   First, your attic must
be unequivocally a back attic; secondly, the house in which
it is located must be slightly elevated above its neighbours;
thirdly, the window must not lie slant on the roof, as is
common with attics—in which case you only catch a peep of
that leaden canopy which infatuated Londoners call the sky
—but must be a window perpendicular, and not half blocked
up by the parapets of that fosse called the gutter; and, lastly,
the sight must be so humoured that you cannot catch a glimpse
of the pavements : if you once see the world beneath, the whole
charm of that world above is destroyed.   Taking it for granted
that you have secured these requisites, open your window, lean
your chin on both hands, the elbows propped commodiously
on the sill, and contemplate the extraordinary scene which
spreads before you.   You find it difficult to believe life can be
so tranquil on high, while it is so noisy and turbulent below.
What astonishing stillness!   Eliot Warburton (seductive en-
chanter!) recommends you to sail down the Nile if you want
to lull the vexed spirit.   It is easier and cheaper to hire an
attic in Holborn!   You don't have the crocodiles, but you
have animals no less hallowed in Egypt—the cats!   And how
harmoniously the tranquil creatures blend with the prospect
—how noiselessly they glide along at the distance, pause, peer
about, and disappear.   It is only from the attic that you can
appreciate the picturesque which belongs to our domesticated
tigerkin!   The goat should be seen on the Alps, and the cat
on the house-top.

By degrees the curious eye takes the scenery in detail : and
first, what fantastic variety in the heights and shapes of the
chimney-pots!   Some all level in a row, uniform and respectable, but quite uninteresting; others, again, rising out of all
proportion, and imperatively tasking the reason to conjecture
why they are so aspiring.   Reason answers that it is but a

homely expedient to give freer vent to the smoke; wherewith
Imagination steps in, and represents to you all the fretting, and
fuming, and worry, and care, which the owners of that chimney,
now the tallest of all, endured, before, by building it higher,
they got rid of the vapours. You see the distress of the cook,
when the sooty invader rushed down, "like a wolf on the fold,"
full spring on the Sunday joint. You hear the exclamations
of the mistress (perhaps a bride—house newly furnished) when,
with white apron and cap, she ventured into the drawing-room,
and was straightway saluted by a joyous dance of those monads,
called vulgarly *smuts*. You feel manly indignation at the brute
of a bridegroom, who rushes out from the door, with the smuts
dancing after him, and swears, "Smoked out again! By the
Arch-smoker himself! I'll go and dine at the club." All
this might well have been, till the chimney-pot was raised a
few feet nearer heaven; and now perhaps that long-suffering
family owns the happiest home in the Row. Such contrivances
to get rid of the smoke! It is not every one who merely
heightens his chimney; others clap on the hollow tormentor
all sorts of odd head-gear and cowls. Here, patent contrivances act the purpose of weathercocks, swaying to and fro
with the wind; there, others stand as fixed, as if, by a "*sic
jubeo*," they had settled the business. But of all those houses
that, in the street, one passes by, unsuspicious of what's the
matter within, there is not one in a hundred but what there
has been the devil to do, to cure the chimneys of smoking!
At that reflection, Philosophy dismisses the subject; and de-
cides that, whether one lives in a hut or a palace, the first
thing to do is to look to the hearth—and get rid of the
vapours.

New beauties demand us. What endless undulations in the
various declivities and ascents; here a slant, there a zig-zag!
With what majestic disdain yon roof rises up to the left!
Doubtless a palace of Genii or Gin (which last is the proper
Arabic word for those builders of halls out of nothing, employed
by Aladdin). Seeing only the roof of that palace boldly breaking the sky-line—how serene your contemplations! Perhaps a
star twinkles over it, and you muse on soft eyes far away; while
below at the threshold—No, phantoms! we see you not from
our attic. Note, yonder, that precipitous fall—how ragged and
jagged the roof-scene descends in a gorge. He who would
travel on foot through the pass of that defile, of which we see
but the picturesque summits, stops his nose, averts his eyes,

guards his pockets, and hurries along through the squalor of the
grim London lazzaroni.   But, seen *above,* what a noble break in
the sky-line !   It would be sacrilege to exchange that fine gorge
for the dead flat of dull roof-tops.   Look here—how delightful !
—that desolate house with no roof at all—gutted and skinned
by the last London fire !   You can see the poor green-and-white
paper still clinging to the walls, and the chasm that once was a
cupboard, and the shadows gathering black on the aperture that
once was a hearth !   Seen below, how quickly you would cross
over the way !   That great crack forebodes an avalanche ; you
hold your breath, not to bring it down on your head.   But seen
above, what a compassionate, inquisitive charm in the skeleton
ruin !   How your fancy runs riot—repeopling the chambers,
hearing the last cheerful good night of that destined Pompeii—
creeping on tiptoe with the mother, when she gives her farewell
look to the baby.   Now all is midnight and silence ; then the
red, crawling serpent comes out.   Lo ! his breath ; hark ! his
hiss.   Now, spire after spire he winds and he coils ; now he
soars up erect—crest superb, and forked tongue—the beautiful
horror !   Then the start from the sleep, and the doubtful
awaking, and the run here and there, and the mother's rush to
the cradle ; the cry from the window, and the knock at the
door, and the spring of those on high towards the stair that
leads to safety below, and the smoke rushing up like the surge
of a hell !   And they run back stifled and blinded, and the floor
heaves beneath them like a bark on the sea.   Hark ! the grating
wheels thundering low ; near and nearer comes the engine.   Fix
the ladders !—there ! there ! at the window, where the mother
stands with the babe !   Splash and hiss comes the water ; pales,
then flares out, the fire ; foe defies foe ; element, element.
How sublime is the war !   But the ladder, the ladder !—there,
at the window !   All else are saved : the clerk and his books !
the lawyer with that tin box of title-deeds ; the landlord, with
his policy of insurance ; the miser, with his bank-notes and gold :
all are saved—all, but the babe and the mother.   What a crowd
in the streets ! how the light crimsons over the gazers, hundreds
on hundreds !   All those faces seem as one face, with fear.   Not
a man mounts the ladder.   Yes, there—gallant fellow !   God
inspires—God shall speed thee !   How plainly I see him ! his
eyes are closed, his teeth set.   The serpent leaps up, the forked
tongue darts upon him, and the reek of the breath wraps him
round.   The crowd has ebbed back like a sea, and the smoke
rushes over them all.   Ha ! what dim forms are those on the

ladder? Near and nearer—crash come the roof-tiles. Alas,
and alas!—no! a cry of joy—a "Thank Heaven!" and the
women force their way through the men to come round the
child and the mother. All is gone save that skeleton ruin.
But the ruin is seen from *above*. O Art! study life from the
roof-tops!

CHAPTER III

I WAS again foiled in seeing Trevanion. It was the Easter
recess, and he was at the house of one of his brother
ministers, somewhere in the north of England. But Lady
Ellinor was in London, and I was ushered into her presence.
Nothing could be more cordial than her manner, though she
was evidently much depressed in spirits, and looked wan and
careworn.

After the kindest inquiries relative to my parents and the
Captain, she entered with much sympathy into my schemes
and plans, which she said Trevanion had confided to her. The
sterling kindness that belonged to my old patron (despite his
affected anger at my not accepting his proffered loan), had not
only saved me and my fellow-adventurer all trouble as to allotment orders, but procured advice as to choice of site and soil,
from the best practical experience, which we found afterwards
exceedingly useful. And as Lady Ellinor gave me the little
packet of papers, with Trevanion's shrewd notes on the margin,
she said with a half sigh, "Albert bids me say that he wishes
he were as sanguine of his success in the Cabinet as of yours
in the Bush." She then turned to her husband's rise and
prospects, and her face began to change. Her eyes sparkled,
the colour came to her cheeks—"But you are one of the few
who know him," she said, interrupting herself suddenly; "you
know how he sacrifices all things—joy, leisure, health—to his
country. There is not one selfish thought in his nature. And
yet such envy—such obstacles still! and" (her eyes dropped on
her dress, and I perceived that she was in mourning, though
the mourning was not deep), "and," she added, "it has pleased
Heaven to withdraw from his side one who would have been
worthy his alliance."

I felt for the proud woman, though her emotion seemed
more that of pride than sorrow. And perhaps Lord Castleton's

highest merit in her eyes had been that of ministering to her husband's power and her own ambition. I bowed my head in silence, and thought of Fanny. Did she, too, pine for the lost rank, or rather mourn the lost lover?

After a time, I said hesitatingly, "I scarcely presume to condole with you, Lady Ellinor! yet believe me, few things ever shocked me like the death you allude to. I trust Miss Trevanion's health has not much suffered. Shall I not see her before I leave England?"

Lady Ellinor fixed her keen bright eyes searchingly on my countenance, and perhaps the gaze satisfied her, for she held out her hand to me with a frankness almost tender, and said— "Had I had a son, the dearest wish of my heart had been to see you wedded to my daughter."

I started up—the blood rushed to my cheeks, and then left me pale as death. I looked reproachfully at Lady Ellinor, and the word "cruel!" faltered on my lips.

"Yes," continued Lady Ellinor mournfully, "that was my real thought, my impulse of regret, when I first saw you. But, as it is, do not think me too hard and worldly, if I quote the lofty old French proverb, *Noblesse oblige*. Listen to me, my young friend—we may never meet again, and I would not have your father's son think unkindly of me, with all my faults. From my first childhood I was ambitious—not as women usually are, of mere wealth and rank—but ambitious as noble men are, of power and fame. A woman can only indulge such ambition by investing it in another. It was not wealth, it was not rank, that attracted me to Albert Trevanion: it was the nature that dispenses with the wealth, and commands the rank. Nay," continued Lady Ellinor, in a voice that slightly trembled, "I may have seen in my youth, before I knew Trevanion, one (she paused a moment, and went on hurriedly)—one who wanted but ambition to have realised my ideal. Perhaps, even when I married—and it was said for love—I loved less with my whole heart than with my whole mind. I may say this now, for *now* every beat of this pulse is wholly and only true to him with whom I have schemed, and toiled, and aspired; with whom I have grown as one; with whom I have shared the struggle, and now partake the triumph, realising the visions of my youth."

Again the light broke from the dark eyes of this grand daughter of the world, who was so superb a type of that moral contradiction—*an ambitious woman*.

"I cannot tell you," resumed Lady Ellinor, softening, "how

pleased I was when you came to live with us. Your father has perhaps spoken to you of me, and of our first acquaintance ! "

Lady Ellinor paused abruptly, and surveyed me as she paused. I was silent.

" Perhaps, too, he has blamed me ? " she resumed, with a heightened colour.

" He never blamed you, Lady Ellinor ! "

" He had a right to do so—though I doubt if he would have blamed me on the true ground. Yet no ; he never could have done me the wrong that your uncle did, when, long years ago, Mr. De Caxton in a letter—the very bitterness of which disarmed all anger—accused me of having trifled with Austin— nay, with himself ! And *he*, at least, had *no* right to approach me," continued Lady Ellinor warmly, and with a curve of her haughty lip; " for if I felt interest in his wild thirst for some romantic glory, it was but in the hope that, what made the one brother so restless might at least wake the other to the ambition that would have become his intellect, and aroused his energies. But these are old tales of follies and delusions now no more : only this will I say, that I have ever felt, in thinking of your father, and even of your sterner uncle, as if my conscience reminded me of a debt which I longed to discharge—if not to them, to their children. So, when we knew you, believe me, that your interests, your career, instantly became to me an object. But mistaking you—when I saw your ardent industry bent on serious objects, and accompanied by a mind so fresh and buoyant; and, absorbed as I was in schemes or projects far beyond a woman's ordinary province of hearth and home— I never dreamed, while you were our guest—never dreamed of danger to you or Fanny. I wound you—pardon me ; but I must vindicate myself. I repeat that, if we had a son to inherit our name, to bear the burden which the world lays upon those who are born to influence the world's destinies, there is no one to whom Trevanion and myself would sooner have entrusted the happiness of a daughter. But my daughter is the sole representative of the mother's line, of the father's name : it is not her happiness alone that I have to consult, it is her duty— duty to her birthright, to the career of the noblest of England's patriots—duty, I may say, without exaggeration, to the country for the sake of which that career is run ! "

" Say no more, Lady Ellinor ; say no more. I understand you. I have no hope—I never had hope—it was a madness—it is over. It is but as a friend that I ask again, if I may see

Miss Trevanion in your presence, before—before I go alone into this long exile, to leave, perhaps, my dust in a stranger's soil! Ay, look in my face—you cannot fear my resolution, my honour, my truth. But once, Lady Ellinor—but once more. Do I ask in vain?"

Lady Ellinor was evidently much moved. I bent down almost in the attitude of kneeling; and, brushing away her tears with one hand, she laid the other on my head tenderly, and said in a very low voice—

"I entreat you not to ask me; I entreat you not to see my daughter. You have shown that you are not selfish—conquer yourself still. What if such an interview, however guarded you might be, were but to agitate, unnerve my child, unsettle her peace, prey upon——"

"Oh, do not speak thus—she did not share my feelings!"

"Could her mother own it if she did! Come, come, remember how young you both are. When you return, all these dreams will be forgotten; then we can meet as before—then I will be your second mother, and again your career shall be my care; for do not think that we shall leave you so long in this exile as you seem to forebode. No, no; it is but an absence—an excursion—not a search after fortune. Your fortune—leave that to us when you return!"

"And I am ,to see her no more!" I murmured, as I rose and went silently towards the window to conceal my face. The great struggles in life are limited moments. In the drooping of the head upon the bosom—in the pressure of the hand upon the brow—we may scarcely consume a second in our threescore years and ten; but what revolutions of our whole being may pass within us, while that single sand drops noiseless down to the bottom of the hour-glass.

I came back with firm step to Lady Ellinor, and said calmly, "My reason tells me that you are right, and I submit. Forgive me! and do not think me ungrateful and over-proud, if I add, that you must leave me still the object in life that consoles and encourages me through all."

"What object is that?" asked Lady Ellinor hesitatingly.

"Independence for myself, and ease to those for whom life is still sweet. This is my twofold object; and the means to effect it must be my own heart and my own hands. And now, convey all my thanks to your noble husband, and accept my warm prayers for yourself and *her*—whom I will not name. Farewell, Lady Ellinor."

"I rose and went silently towards
the window to conceal my face"

Chris Hammond
nov. 97

"No, do not leave me so hastily; I have many things to discuss with you—at least to ask of you. Tell me how your father bears his reverse?—tell me, at least, if there be·aught he will suffer us to do for him? There are many appointments in Trevanion's range of influence that would suit even the wilful indolence of a man of letters. Come, be frank with me!"

I could not resist so much kindness; so I sat down, and, as collectedly as I could, replied to Lady Ellinor's questions, and sought to convince her that my father only felt his losses so far as they affected me, and that nothing in Trevanion's power was likely to tempt him from his retreat, or calculated to compensate for a change in his habits. Turning at last from my parents, Lady Ellinor inquired for Roland, and, on learning that he was with me in town, expressed a strong desire to see him. I told her I would communicate her wish, and she then said thoughtfully—

"He has a son, I think, and I have heard that there is some unhappy dissension between them."

"Who could have told you that?" I asked in surprise, knowing how closely Roland had kept the secret of his family afflictions.

"Oh, I heard so from some one who knew Captain Roland— I forget when and where I heard it—but is it not the fact?"

"My uncle Roland has no son."

"How!"

"His son is dead."

"How such a loss must grieve him."

I did not speak.

"But is he sure that his son is dead? What joy if he were mistaken—if the son yet lived!"

"Nay, my uncle has a brave heart, and he is resigned;—but, pardon me, have you heard anything of that son?"

"I!—what should I hear? I would fain learn, however, from your uncle himself, what he might like to tell me of his sorrows —or if, indeed, there be any chance that——"

"That—what?"

"That—that his son still survives."

"I think not," said I; "and I doubt whether you will learn much from my uncle. Still there is something in your words that belies their apparent meaning, and makes me suspect that you know more than you will say."

"Diplomatist!" said Lady Ellinor, half smiling; but then, her face settling into a seriousness almost severe, she added— "It is terrible to think that a father should hate his son!"

"Hate!—Roland *hate* his son! What calumny is this?"

"He does not do so, then! Assure me of that; I shall be so glad to know that I have been misinformed."

"I can tell you this, and no more—for no more do I know—that if ever the soul of a father were wrapt up in a son—fear, hope, gladness, sorrow, all reflected back on a father's heart from the shadows on a son's life—Roland was that father while the son lived still."

"I cannot disbelieve you!" exclaimed Lady Ellinor, though in a tone of surprise. "Well, do let me see your uncle."

"I will do my best to induce him to visit you, and learn all that you evidently conceal from me."

Lady Ellinor evasively replied to this insinuation, and shortly afterwards I left that house in which I had known the happiness that brings the folly, and the grief that bequeaths the wisdom.

CHAPTER IV

I HAD always felt a warm and almost filial affection for Lady Ellinor, independently of her relationship to Fanny, and of the gratitude with which her kindness inspired me; for there is an affection very peculiar in its nature, and very high in its degree, which results from the blending of two sentiments not often allied,—viz., pity and admiration. It was impossible not to admire the rare gifts and great qualities of Lady Ellinor, and not to feel pity for the cares, anxieties, and sorrows which tormented one who, with all the sensitiveness of woman, went forth into the rough world of man.

My father's confession had somewhat impaired my esteem for Lady Ellinor, and had left on my mind the uneasy impression that she *had* trifled with his deep and Roland's impetuous heart. The conversation that had just passed allowed me to judge her with more justice—allowed me to see that she had really shared the affection she had inspired in the student, but that ambition had been stronger than love—an ambition, it might be, irregular, and not strictly feminine, but still of no vulgar nor sordid kind. I gathered, too, from her hints and allusions, her true excuse for Roland's misconception of her apparent interest in himself: she had but seen, in the wild energies of the elder brother, some agency by which to arouse the serener faculties of the younger. She had but sought, in the strange comet that flashed

before her, to fix a lever that might move the star.   Nor could
I withhold my reverence from the woman who, not being married
precisely from love, had no sooner linked her nature to one
worthy of it, than her whole life became as fondly devoted to
her husband's as if he had been the object of her first romance
and her earliest affections.   If even her child was so secondary
to her husband—if the fate of that child was but regarded by
her as one to be rendered subservient to the grand destinies of
Trevanion—still it was impossible to recognise the error of that
conjugal devotion without admiring the wife, though one might
condemn the mother.   Turning from these meditations, I felt
a lover's thrill of selfish joy, amidst all the mournful sorrow
comprised in the thought that I should see Fanny no more.
Was it true, as Lady Ellinor implied, though delicately, that
Fanny still cherished a remembrance of me—which a brief
interview, a last farewell, might reawaken too dangerously for
her peace ?   Well, that was a thought that it became me not
to indulge.

What could Lady Ellinor have heard of Roland and his son ?
Was it possible that the lost lived still ?   Asking myself these
questions, I arrived at our lodgings, and saw the Captain himself
before me, busied with the inspection of sundry specimens of
the rude necessaries an Australian adventurer requires.   There
stood the old soldier, by the window, examining narrowly into
the temper of hand-saw and tenon-saw, broad-axe and drawing-
knife ; and as I came up to him, he looked at me from under
his black brows, with gruff compassion, and said peevishly—

" Fine weapons these for the son of a gentleman !—one bit of
steel in the shape of a sword were worth them all."

" Any weapon that conquers fate is noble in the hands of a
brave man, uncle."

" The boy has an answer for everything," quoth the Captain,
smiling, as he took out his purse and paid the shopman.

When we were alone, I said to him—" Uncle, you must go
and see Lady Ellinor ; she desires me to tell you so."

" Pshaw ! "

" You will not ? "

" No ! "

" Uncle, I think that she has something to say to you with
regard to—to—pardon me !—to my cousin."

" To Blanche ? "

" No, no—the cousin I never saw."   Roland turned pale, and
sinking down on a chair, faltered out—" To him—to my son ? "

"Yes; but I do not think it is news that will afflict you. Uncle, are you sure that my cousin is dead?"

"What!—how dare you!—who doubts it? Dead—dead to me for ever! Boy, would you have him to live to dishonour these grey hairs?"

"Sir, sir, forgive me—uncle, forgive me: but, pray, go to see Lady Ellinor; for whatever she has to say, I repeat that I am sure it will be nothing to wound you."

"Nothing to wound me—yet relate to *him!*"

It is impossible to convey to the reader the despair that was in those words.

"Perhaps," said I, after a long pause, and in a low voice—for I was awe-stricken—"perhaps—if he be dead—he may have repented of all offence to you before he died."

"Repented—ha, ha!"

"Or, if he be not dead——"

"Hush, boy—hush!"

"While there is life, there is hope of repentance."

"Look you, nephew," said the Captain, rising and folding his arms resolutely on his breast—"look you, I desired that that name might never be breathed. I have not cursed my son yet; could he come to life—the curse might fall! You do not know what torture your words have given me, just when I had opened my heart to another son, and found that son in you. With respect to the lost, I have now but one prayer, and you know it—the heart-broken prayer—that his name never more may come to my ears!"

As he closed these words, to which I ventured no reply, the Captain took long, disordered strides across the room: and suddenly, as if the space imprisoned, or the air stifled him, he seized his hat, and hastened into the streets. Recovering my surprise and dismay, I ran after him; but he commanded me to leave him to his own thoughts, in a voice so stern, yet so sad, that I had no choice but to obey. I knew, by my own experience, how necessary is solitude in the moments when grief is strongest and thought most troubled.

CHAPTER V

HOURS elapsed, and the Captain had not returned home. I began to feel uneasy, and went forth in search of him, though I knew not whither to direct my steps. I thought it, however, at least probable that he had not been able to resist

visiting Lady Ellinor, so I went first to St. James's Square. My
suspicions were correct; the Captain had been there two hours
before.   Lady Ellinor herself had gone out shortly after the
Captain left.   While the porter was giving me this information,
a carriage stopped at the door, and a footman, stepping up,
gave the porter a note and a small parcel, seemingly of books,
saying simply, "From the Marquis of Castleton."   At the
sound of that name I turned hastily, and recognised Sir Sedley
Beaudesert seated in the carriage, and looking out of the
window with a dejected, moody expression of countenance,
very different from his ordinary aspect, except when the rare
sight of a grey hair or a twinge of the toothache reminded
him that he was no longer twenty-five.   Indeed, the change
was so great that I exclaimed dubiously—" Is that Sir Sedley
Beaudesert ? "   The footman looked at me, and touching his
hat said, with a condescending smile,—" Yes, sir—now the
Marquis of Castleton."

Then, for the first time since the young lord's death, I remembered Sir Sedley's expressions of gratitude to Lady Castleton, and the waters of Ems, for having saved him from " that
horrible marquisate."   Meanwhile, my old friend had perceived
me, exclaiming—

"What! Mr. Caxton! I am delighted to see you.   Open the
door, Thomas.   Pray come in, come in."

I obeyed; and the new Lord Castleton made room for me by
his side.

"Are you in a hurry?" said he; "if so, shall I take you anywhere?—if not, give me half-an-hour of your time, while I
drive to the City."

As I knew not now in what direction, more than another, to
prosecute my search for the Captain, and as I thought I might
as well call at our lodgings to inquire if he had not returned,
I answered that I should be very happy to accompany his
lordship; "though the City," said I, smiling, "sounds to me
strange upon the lips of Sir Sedley—I beg pardon, I should
say of Lord——"

"Don't say any such thing; let me once more hear the
grateful sound of Sedley Beaudesert.   Shut the door, Thomas;
to Gracechurch Street—Messrs. Fudge & Fidget."

The carriage drove on.

"A sad affliction has befallen me," said the marquis, "and
none sympathise with me!"

"Yet all, even unacquainted with the late lord, must have

felt shocked at the death of one so young, and so full of promise."

"So fitted in every way to bear the burthen of the great Castleton name and property—and yet you see it killed him!— Ah! if he had been but a simple gentleman, or if he had had a less conscientious desire to do his duties, he would have lived to a good old age. I know what it is already. Oh, if you saw the piles of letters on my table! I positively dread the post. Such colossal improvement on the property which the poor boy had begun, for me to finish. What do you think takes me to Fudge & Fidget's? Sir, they are the agents for an infernal coal-mine which my cousin had re-opened in Durham, to plague my life out with another thirty thousand pounds a year! How am I to spend the money?—how am I to spend it? There's a cold-blooded head steward, who says that charity is the greatest crime a man in high station can commit; it demoralises the poor. Then, because some half-a-dozen farmers sent me a round-robin, to the effect that their rents were too high, and I wrote them word that the rents should be lowered, there was such a hullabaloo—you would have thought heaven and earth were coming together. 'If a man in the position of the Marquis of Castleton set the example of letting land below its value, how could the poorer squires in the country exist?—or if they did exist, what injustice to expose them to the charge that they were grasping landlords, vampires, and bloodsuckers! Clearly if Lord Castleton lowered his rents (they were too low already), he struck a mortal blow at the property of his neighbours, if they followed his example: or at their characters if they did not.' No man can tell how hard it is to do good, unless fortune gives him a hundred thousand pounds a year, and says—'Now, do good with it!' Sedley Beaudesert might follow his whims, and all that would be said against him was, 'good-natured, simple fellow!' But if Lord Castleton follow his whims, you would think he was a second Catiline—unsettling the peace, and undermining the prosperity, of the entire nation!" Here the wretched man paused, and sighed heavily; then, as his thoughts wandered into a new channel of woe, he resumed,— "Ah! if you could but see the forlorn great house I am expected to inhabit, cooped up between dead walls, instead of my pretty rooms, with the windows full on the park; and the balls I am expected to give, and the parliamentary interest I am to keep up: and the villainous proposal made to me to become a lord-steward or lord-chamberlain, because it suits

my rank to be a sort of a servant. O Pisistratus! you lucky
dog—not twenty-one, and with, I dare say, not two hundred
pounds a year in the world!"

Thus bemoaning and bewailing his sad fortunes, the poor
marquis ran on, till at last he exclaimed, in a tone of yet deeper
despair—

"And everybody says I must marry, too!—that the Castleton
line must not be extinct! The Beaudeserts are a good old
family eno'—as old, for what I know, as the Castletons; but
the British empire would suffer no loss if they sunk into the
tomb of the Capulets. But that the Castleton peerage should
expire, is a thought of crime and woe, at which all the mothers
of England rise in a phalanx! And so, instead of visiting the
sins of the fathers on the sons, it is the father that is to be
sacrificed for the benefit of the third and fourth generation!"

Despite my causes for seriousness, I could not help laughing;
my companion turned on me a look of reproach.

"At least," said I, composing my countenance, "Lord Castleton has one comfort in his afflictions—if he must marry, he may
choose as he pleases."

"That is precisely what Sedley Beaudesert could, and Lord
Castleton cannot do," said the marquis gravely. "The rank of
Sir Sedley Beaudesert was a quiet and comfortable rank—he
might marry a curate's daughter, or a duke's—and please his
eye or grieve his heart as the caprice took him. But Lord
Castleton must marry, not for a wife, but for a marchioness,—
marry some one who will *wear his rank* for him,—take the
trouble of splendour off his hands, and allow him to retire into
a corner, and dream that he is Sedley Beaudesert once more!
Yes, it must be so—the crowning sacrifice must be completed
at the altar. But a truce to my complaints. Trevanion informs
me you are going to Australia,—can that be true?"

"Perfectly true."

"They say there is a sad want of ladies there."

"So much the better,—I shall be all the more steady."

"Well, there's something in that. Have you seen Lady
Ellinor?"

"Yes—this morning."

"Poor woman!—a great blow to her—we have tried to console
each other. Fanny, you know, is staying at Oxton, in Surrey,
with Lady Castleton—the poor lady is so fond of her—and no
one has comforted her like Fanny."

"I was not aware that Miss Trevanion was out of town."

"Only for a few days, and then she and Lady Ellinor join Trevanion in the north—you know he is with Lord N——, settling measures on which—but alas! they consult me now on those matters — force their secrets on me. I have, Heaven knows how many votes! Poor me! Upon my word, if Lady Ellinor was a widow, I should certainly make up to her; very clever woman, nothing bores her." (The marquis yawned— Sir Sedley Beaudesert never yawned.) "Trevanion has provided for his Scotch secretary, and is about to get a place in the Foreign Office for that young fellow Gower, whom, between you and me, I don't like. But he has bewitched Trevanion!"

"What sort of a person is this Mr. Gower?—I remember you said that he was clever, and good-looking."

"He is both, but it is not the cleverness of youth; he is as hard and sarcastic as if he had been cheated fifty times, and jilted a hundred! Neither are his good looks that letter of recommendation which a handsome face is said to be. He has an expression of countenance very much like that of Lord Hertford's pet bloodhound, when a stranger comes into the room. Very sleek, handsome dog, the bloodhound is certainly—well-mannered, and I dare say exceedingly tame; but still you have but to look at the corner of the eye, to know that it is only the habit of the drawing-room that suppresses the creature's constitutional tendency to seize you by the throat, instead of giving you a paw. Still this Mr. Gower has a very striking head—something about it Moorish or Spanish, like a picture by Murillo: I half suspect that he is less a Gower than a gipsy!"

"What!"—I cried, as I listened with rapt and breathless attention to this description. "He is then very dark, with high narrow forehead, features slightly aquiline, but very delicate, and teeth so dazzling that the whole face seems to sparkle when he smiles—though it is only the lip that smiles, not the eye."

"Exactly as you say; you have seen him, then?"

"Why, I am not sure, since you say his name is Gower."

"He says his name is Gower," returned Lord Castleton dryly, as he inhaled the Beaudesert mixture.

"And where is he now?—with Mr. Trevanion?"

"Yes, I believe so. Ah! here we are—Fudge & Fidget! But, perhaps," added Lord Castleton, with a gleam of hope in his blue eye—"perhaps they are not at home!"

Alas! that was an illusive "imagining," as the poets of the nineteenth century unaffectedly express themselves. Messrs. Fudge & Fidget were never out to such clients as the Marquis of Castleton: with a deep sigh, and an altered expression of face, the Victim of Fortune slowly descended the steps of the carriage.

"I can't ask you to wait for me," said he: "Heaven only knows how long I shall be kept! Take the carriage where you will, and send it back to me."

"A thousand thanks, my dear lord, I would rather walk—but you will let me call on you before I leave town."

"Let you!—I insist on it. I am still at the old quarters—under pretence," said the marquis, with a sly twinkle of the eyelid, "that Castleton House wants painting!"

"At twelve to-morrow, then?"

"Twelve to-morrow. Alas! that's just the hour at which Mr. Screw, the agent for the London property (two squares, seven streets, and a lane!) is to call."

"Perhaps two o'clock will suit you better!"

"Two! just the hour at which Mr. Plausible, one of the Castleton members, insists upon telling me why his conscience will not let him vote with Trevanion!"

"Three o'clock?"

"Three!—just the hour at which I am to see the Secretary of the Treasury, who has promised to relieve Mr. Plausible's conscience! But come and dine with me—you will meet the executors to the will!"

"Nay, Sir Sedley—that is, my dear lord—I will take my chance, and look in after dinner."

"Do so; my guests are not lively! What a firm step the rogue has! Only twenty, I think—twenty! and not an acre of property to plague him!" So saying, the marquis dolorously shook his head, and vanished through the noiseless mahogany doors, behind which Messrs. Fudge & Fidget awaited the unhappy man,—with the accounts of the Great Castleton coal-mine.

CHAPTER VI

ON my way towards our lodgings, I resolved to look in at a humble tavern, in the coffee-room of which the Captain and myself habitually dined. It was now about the usual hour in which we took that meal, and he might be there waiting for me. I had just gained the steps of this tavern, when a stage-coach came rattling along the pavement, and drew up at an

inn of more pretensions than that which we favoured, situated
within a few doors of the latter.   As the coach stopped, my eye
was caught by the Trevanion livery, which was very peculiar.
Thinking I must be deceived, I drew near to the wearer of the
livery, who had just descended from the roof, and while he paid
the coachman, gave his orders to a waiter who emerged from
the inn—" Half-and-half, cold without ! "   The tone of the
voice struck me as familiar, and the man now looking up, I
beheld the features of Mr. Peacock.   Yes, unquestionably it
was he.   The whiskers were shaved—there were traces of
powder in the hair or the wig—the livery of the Trevanions
(ay, the very livery—crest-button, and all) upon that portly
figure, which I had last seen in the more august robes of a
beadle.   But Mr. Peacock it was—Peacock travestied, but
Peacock still.   Before I had recovered my amaze, a woman got
out of a cabriolet, that seemed to have been in waiting for the
arrival of the coach, and, hurrying up to Mr. Peacock, said in
the loud impatient tone common to the fairest of the fair sex,
when in haste—" How late you are !—I was just going.   I must
get back to Oxton to-night."

Oxton—Miss Trevanion was staying at Oxton !   I was now
close behind the pair—I listened with my heart in my ear.

"So you shall, my dear—so you shall ; just come in, will
you."

" No, no ; I have only ten minutes to catch the coach.   Have
you any letter for me from Mr. Gower ?   How can I be sure, if
I don't see it under his own hand, that——"

" Hush ! " said Peacock, sinking his voice so low that I could
only catch the words, " no names—letter, pooh, I'll tell you."
He then drew her apart, and whispered to her for some
moments.   I watched the woman's face, which was bent towards
her companion's, and it seemed to show quick intelligence.   She
nodded her head more than once, as if in impatient assent to
what was said ; and, after a shaking of hands, hurried off to
the cab ; then, as if a thought struck her, she ran back, and
said—

" But in case my lady should not go—if there's any change of
plan."

" There'll be no change, you may be sure—positively to-
morrow—not too early ; you understand ? "

"Yes, yes ; good-bye"—and the woman, who was dressed with
a quiet neatness, that seemed to stamp her profession as that
of an abigail (black cloak with long cape—of that peculiar silk

which seems spun on purpose for ladies'-maids—bonnet to match, with red and black ribbons), hastened once more away, and in another moment the cab drove off furiously.

What could all this mean? By this time the waiter brought Mr. Peacock the half-and-half. He despatched it hastily, and then strode on towards a neighbouring stand of cabriolets. I followed him; and just as, after beckoning one of the vehicles from the stand, he had ensconed himself therein, I sprang up the steps and placed myself by his side. "Now, Mr. Peacock," said I, "you will tell me at once how you come to wear that livery, or I shall order the cabman to drive to Lady Ellinor Trevanion's, and ask her that question myself."

"And who the devil!—Ah, you're the young gentleman that came to me behind the scenes—I remember."

"Where to, sir?" asked the cabman.

"To—to London Bridge," said Mr. Peacock.

The man mounted the box, and drove on.

"Well, Mr. Peacock, I wait your answer. I guess by your face that you are about to tell me a lie; I advise you to speak the truth."

"I don't know what business you have to question me," said Mr. Peacock sullenly; and raising his glance from his own clenched fists, he suffered it to wander over my form with so vindictive a significance, that I interrupted the survey by saying, "'Will you encounter the house?' as the Swan interrogatively puts it—shall I order the cabman to drive to St. James's Square?"

"Oh, you know my weak point, sir? any man who can quote Will—sweet Will—has me on the hip," rejoined Mr. Peacock, smoothing his countenance, and spreading his palms on his knees. But if a man does fall in the world, and, after keeping servants of his own, is obliged to be himself a servant,

> —— 'I will not shame
> To tell you what I am.'"

"The Swan says, 'To tell you what I *was*,' Mr. Peacock. But enough of this trifling; who placed you with Mr. Trevanion?"

Mr. Peacock looked down for a moment, and then fixing his eyes on me, said—"Well, I'll tell you: you asked me, when we met last, about a young gentleman—Mr.—Mr. Vivian."

Pisistratus.—"Proceed."

Peacock.—"I know you don't want to harm him. Besides,

'He hath a prosperous art,' and one day or other,—mark my words, or rather my friend Will's—

> 'He will bestride this narrow world
> Like a Colossus.'

Upon my life he will—like a Colossus,

> 'And we petty men——'"

PISISTRATUS (savagely).—"Go on with your story."

PEACOCK (snappishly).—"I am going on with it! You put me out; where was I—oh—ah—yes. I had just been sold up —not a penny in my pocket; and if you could have seen my coat—yet that was better than the small-clothes! Well, it was in Oxford Street—no, it was in the Strand, near the Lowther—

> 'The sun was in the heavens and the proud day
> Attended with the pleasures of the world.'"

PISISTRATUS (lowering the glass).—"To St. James's Square?"
PEACOCK.—"No, no; to London Bridge.

> 'How use doth breed a habit in a man!'

I will go on—honour bright. So I met Mr. Vivian, and as he had known me in better days, and has a good heart of his own, he says—

> 'Horatio,—or I do forget myself.'"

Pisistratus puts his hand on the check-string.

PEACOCK (correcting himself).—"I mean—'Why, Johnson, my good fellow.'"

PISISTRATUS.—"Johnson!—oh, that's your name—not Peacock."

PEACOCK. — "Johnson and Peacock both (with dignity). When you know the world as I do, sir, you will find that it is ill travelling this 'naughty world' without a change of names in your portmanteau.

"'Johnson,' says he, 'my good fellow,' and he pulled out his purse. 'Sir,' said I, 'if, "exempt from public haunt," I could get something to do when this dross is gone. In London there are sermons in stones, certainly, but not "good in everything," an observation I should take the liberty of making to the Swan, if he were not now, alas! "the baseless fabric of a vision."'"

PISISTRATUS.—"Take care!"

PEACOCK (hurriedly).—"Then says Mr. Vivian, 'If you don't mind wearing a livery, till I can provide for you more suitably, my old friend, there's a vacancy in the establishment of Mr. Trevanion.' Sir, I accepted the proposal, and that's why I wear this livery."

PISISTRATUS.—"And pray, what business had you with that young woman, whom I take to be Miss Trevanion's maid ? and why should she come from Oxton to see you ? "

I had expected that these questions would confound Mr. Peacock ! but if there really were anything in them to cause embarrassment, the *ci-devant* actor was too practised in his profession to exhibit it.   He merely smiled, and smoothing jauntily a very tumbled shirt front, he said, " Oh, sir, fie !

> ' Of this matter
> Is little Cupid's crafty arrow made.'

If you must know my love affairs, that young woman is, as the vulgar say, my sweetheart."

" Your sweetheart ! " I exclaimed, greatly relieved, and acknowledging at once the probability of the statement.   " Yet," I added suspiciously—" yet, if so, why should she expect Mr. Gower to write to her ? "

" You're quick of hearing, sir ; but though

> ——' All adoration, duty, and observance :
> All humbleness, and patience, and impatience,'

the young woman won't marry a livery servant—proud creature ! —very proud ! and Mr. Gower, you see, knowing how it was, felt for me, and told her, if I may take such liberty with the Swan, that she should

> ——' Never lie by Johnson's side
> With an unquiet soul,'

for that he would get me a place in the Stamps ! The silly girl said she would have it in black and white—as if Mr. Gower would write to her !

" And now, sir," continued Mr. Peacock, with a simpler gravity, " you are at liberty, of course, to say what you please to my lady, but I hope you'll not try to take the bread out of my mouth because I wear a livery, and am fool enough to be in love with a waiting-woman—I, sir, who could have married ladies who have played the first parts in life—on the metropolitan stage."

I had nothing to say to these representations—they seemed plausible ; and though at first I had suspected that the man had only resorted to the buffoonery of his quotations in order to gain

time for invention, or to divert my notice from any flaw in his
narrative, yet at the close, as the narrative seemed probable, so
I was willing to believe the buffoonery was merely characteristic.
I contented myself, therefore, with asking—

"Where do you come from now?"

"From Mr. Trevanion, in the country, with letters to Lady
Ellinor."

"Oh! and so the young woman knew you were coming to
town?"

"Yes, sir; Mr. Trevanion told me, some days ago, the day I
should have to start."

"And what do you and the young woman propose doing
to-morrow, if there is no change of plan?"

Here I certainly thought there was a slight, scarce perceptible, alteration in Mr. Peacock's countenance, but he answered
readily, "To-morrow, a little assignation, if we can both get
out—

> 'Woo me, now I am in a holiday humour,
> And like enough to consent.'

Swan again, sir."

"Humph!—so then Mr. Gower and Mr. Vivian are the same
person?"

Peacock hesitated. "That's not *my* secret, sir; 'I am combined by a sacred vow.' You are too much the gentleman
to peep through the blanket of the dark, and to ask me, who
wear the whips and stripes—I mean the plush small-clothes
and shoulder-knots—the secrets of another gent, to whom 'my
services are bound.'"

How a man past thirty foils a man scarcely twenty!—what
superiority the mere fact of living-on gives to the dullest dog!
I bit my lip and was silent.

"And," pursued Mr. Peacock, "if you knew how the Mr.
Vivian you inquired after loves you! When I told him incidentally, how a young gentleman had come behind the scenes
to inquire after him, he made me describe you, and then said,
quite mournfully, 'If ever I am what I hope to become, how
happy I shall be to shake that kind hand once more,'—very
words, sir!—honour bright!

> 'I think there's ne'er a man in Christendom
> Can lesser hide his hate or love than he.'

And if Mr. Vivian has some reason to keep himself concealed
still—if his fortune or ruin depend on your not divulging his

secret for a while—I can't think you are the man he need fear.
'Pon my life—

> 'I wish I was as sure of a good dinner,'

as the Swan touchingly exclaims. I dare swear that was a
wish often on the Swan's lips in the privacy of his domestic
life !"

My heart was softened, not by the pathos of the much pro-
faned and desecrated Swan, but by Mr. Peacock's unadorned
repetition of Vivian's words; I turned my face from the sharp
eyes of my companion—the cab now stopped at the foot of
London Bridge.

I had no more to ask, yet still there was some uneasy
curiosity in my mind, which I could hardly define to myself,
—was it not jealousy? Vivian so handsome and so daring—
he at least might see the great heiress; Lady Ellinor perhaps
thought of no danger there. But—I—I was a lover still, and
—nay, such thoughts were folly indeed !

"My man," said I to the ex-comedian, "I neither wish to
harm Mr. Vivian (if I am so to call him), nor you who imitate
him in the variety of your names. But I tell you fairly, that
I do not like your being in Mr. Trevanion's employment, and
I advise you to get out of it as soon as possible. I say nothing
more as yet, for I shall take time to consider well what you
have told me."

With that I hastened away, and Mr. Peacock continued his
solitary journey over London Bridge.

CHAPTER VII

AMIDST all that lacerated my heart, or tormented my thoughts,
that eventful day, I felt at least one joyous emotion, when,
on entering our little drawing-room, I found my uncle seated
there.

The Captain had placed before him on the table a large
Bible, borrowed from the landlady. He never travelled, to
be sure, without his own Bible, but the print of that was
small, and the Captain's eyes began to fail him at night. So
this was a Bible with large type ; and a candle was placed
on either side of it ; and the Captain leant his elbows on the
table, and both his hands were tightly clasped upon his fore-

head—tightly, as if to shut out the tempter, and *force* his whole soul upon the page.

He sat the image of iron courage ; in every line of that rigid form there was resolution. " I will *not* listen to my heart ; I *will* read the Book, and learn to suffer as becomes a Christian man."

There was such a pathos in the stern sufferer's attitude, that it spoke those words as plainly as if his lips had said them.

Old soldier ! thou hast done a soldier's part in many a bloody field ; but if I could make visible to the world thy brave soldier's soul, I would paint thee as I saw thee then !—Out on this tyro's hand !

At the movement I made, the Captain looked up, and the strife he had gone through was written upon his face.

" It has done me good," said he simply, and he closed the book.

I drew my chair near to him, and hung my arm over his shoulder.

" No cheering news, then ? " asked I in a whisper.

Roland shook his head, and gently laid his finger on his lips.

CHAPTER VIII

IT was impossible for me to intrude upon Roland's thoughts, whatever their nature, with a detail of those circumstances which had aroused in me a keen and anxious interest in things apart from his sorrow.

Yet as "restless I roll'd around my weary bed," and re-volved the renewal of Vivian's connection with a man of character so equivocal as Peacock, the establishment of an able and unscrupulous tool of his own in the service of Tre-vanion, the care with which he had concealed from me his change of name, and his intimacy at the very house to which I had frankly offered to present him ; the familiarity which his creature had contrived to effect with Miss Trevanion's maid, the words that had passed between them—plausibly accounted for, it is true, yet still suspicious—and, above all, my painful recollections of Vivian's reckless ambition and unprincipled sentiments—nay, the effect that a few random words upon Fanny's fortune, and the luck of winning an heiress, had sufficed to produce upon his heated fancy and audacious temper ;

when all these thoughts came upon me, strong and vivid, in the darkness of night, I longed for some confidant, more experienced in the world than myself, to advise me as to the course I ought to pursue. Should I warn Lady Ellinor ? But of what ?—the character of a servant, or the designs of the fictitious Gower ? Against the first I could say, if nothing very positive, still enough to make it prudent to dismiss him. But of Gower or Vivian, what could I say without—not indeed betraying his confidence, for that he had never given me—but without belying the professions of friendship that I myself had lavishly made to him ? Perhaps, after all, he might have disclosed whatever were his real secrets to Trevanion ; and, if not, I might indeed ruin his prospects by revealing the aliases he assumed. But wherefore reveal, and wherefore warn ? Because of suspicions that I could not myself analyse—suspicions founded on circumstances most of which had already been seemingly explained away. Still, when morning came, I was irresolute what to do ; and after watching Roland's countenance, and seeing on his brow so great a weight of care, that I had no option but to postpone the confidence I pined to place in his strong understanding and unerring sense of honour, I wandered out, hoping that in the fresh air I might recollect my thoughts, and solve the problem that perplexed me. I had enough to do in sundry small orders for my voyage, and commissions for Bolding, to occupy me some hours. And, this business done, I found myself moving westward : mechanically, as it were, I had come to a kind of half-and-half resolution to call upon Lady Ellinor, and question her, carelessly and incidentally, both about Gower and the new servant admitted to the household.

Thus I found myself in Regent Street, when a carriage, borne by post-horses, whirled rapidly over the pavement—scattering to the right and left all humbler equipages—and hurried, as if on an errand of life and death, up the broad thoroughfare leading into Portland Place. But, rapidly as the wheels dashed by, I had seen distinctly the face of Fanny Trevanion in the carriage, and that face wore a strange expression, which seemed to me to speak of anxiety and grief ; and by her side—was not that the woman I had seen with Peacock ? I did not see the face of the woman, but I thought I recognised the cloak, the bonnet, and peculiar turn of the head. If I could be mistaken there, I was not mistaken at least as to the servant on the seat behind. Looking back at a butcher's boy, who had just escaped being run over, and was revenging himself by all the imprecations the Diræ of London slang could suggest, the face of Mr. Peacock was exposed in full to my gaze.

My first impulse, on recovering my surprise, was to spring after the carriage ; in the haste of that impulse, I cried " Stop ! " But the carriage was out of sight in a moment, and my word was lost in air.   Full of presentiments of some evil—I knew not what—I then altered my course, and stopped not, till I found myself panting and out of breath, in St. James's Square—at the door of Trevanion's house—in the hall.   The porter had a newspaper in his hand as he admitted me.

" Where is Lady Ellinor ?—I must see her instantly."

" No worse news of master, I hope, sir ? "

" Worse news of what ?—of whom ?—of Mr. Trevanion ? "

" Did you not know he was suddenly taken ill, sir ; that a servant came express to say so last night ?   Lady Ellinor went off at ten o'clock to join him."

" At ten o'clock last night ? "

" Yes, sir ; the servant's account alarmed her ladyship so much."

" The new servant, who had been recommended by Mr. Gower ? "

" Yes, sir— Henry," answered the porter, staring at me. " Please, sir, here is an account of master's attack in the paper. I suppose Henry took it to the office before he came here, which was very wrong in him ; but I am afraid he's a very foolish fellow."

" Never mind that.   Miss Trevanion—I saw her just now— *she* did not go with her mother ; where was she going, then ? "

" Why, sir—but pray step into the parlour."

" No, no—speak ! "

" Why, sir, before Lady Ellinor set out, she was afraid that there *might* be something in the papers to alarm Miss Fanny, and so she sent Henry down to Lady Castleton's, to beg her ladyship to make as light of it as she could ; but it seems that Henry blabbed the worst to Mrs. Mole."

" Who is Mrs. Mole ? "

" Miss Trevanion's maid, sir—a new maid ; and Mrs. Mole blabbed to my young lady, and so she took fright, and insisted on coming to town.   And Lady Castleton, who is ill herself in bed, could not keep her, I suppose,—especially as Henry said, though he ought to have known better, ' that she would be in time to arrive before my lady set off.'   Poor Miss Trevanion was so disappointed when she found her mamma gone. And then she would order fresh horses, and would go on, though Mrs. Bates (the housekeeper, you know, sir) was very angry with Mrs. Mole, who encouraged Miss; and——"

"Good heavens! Why did not Mrs. Bates go with her?"

"Why, sir, you know how old Mrs. Bates is, and my young lady is always so kind that she would not hear of it, as she is going to travel night and day; and Mrs. Mole said she had gone all over the world with her last lady, and that——"

"I see it all. Where is Mr. Gower?"

"Mr. Gower, sir!"

"Yes! Can't you answer?"

"Why, with Mr. Trevanion, I believe, sir."

"In the north—what is the address?"

"Lord N——, C—— Hall, near W——."

I heard no more.

The conviction of some villainous snare struck me as with the swiftness and force of lightning. Why, if Trevanion were really ill, had the false servant concealed it from me? Why suffered me to waste his time, instead of hastening to Lady Ellinor? How, if Mr. Trevanion's *sudden* illness had brought the man to London—how had he known so long beforehand (as he himself told me, and his appointment with the waiting-woman proved) the day he should arrive? Why now, if there were no design of which Miss Trevanion was the object—why so frustrate the provident foresight of her mother, and take advantage of the natural yearning of affection, the quick impulse of youth, to hurry off a girl whose very station forbade her to take such a journey without suitable protection—against what must be the wish, and what clearly were the instructions, of Lady Ellinor? Alone, worse than alone! Fanny Trevanion was then in the hands of two servants, who were the instruments and confidants of an adventurer like Vivian; and that conference between those servants—those broken references to the morrow, coupled with the name Vivian had assumed: needed the unerring instincts of love more cause for terror?—terror the darker, because the exact shape it should assume was obscure and indistinct.

I sprang from the house.

I hastened into the Haymarket, summoned a cabriolet, drove home as fast as I could (for I had no money about me for the journey I meditated); sent the servant of the lodging to engage a chaise-and-four, rushed into the room, where Roland fortunately still was, and exclaimed—" Uncle, come with me !--take money, plenty of money !—some villainy I know, though I can't explain it, has been practised on the Trevanions. We may defeat it yet. I will tell you all by the way—come, come ! "

" Certainly.   But villainy !—and to people of such a station—pooh !—collect yourself.   Who is the villain ? "

" Oh, the man I had loved as a friend—the man whom I myself helped to make known to Trevanion—Vivian—Vivian ! "

" Vivian !—ah, the youth I have heard you speak of. But how ?—villainy to whom—to Trevanion ? "

" You torture me with your questions.   Listen—this Vivian (I know him)—he has introduced into the house, as a servant, an agent capable of any trick and fraud ; that servant has aided him to win over her maid—Fanny's—Miss Trevanion's. Miss Trevanion is an heiress, Vivian an adventurer. My head swims round, I cannot explain now.   Ha !   I will write a line to Lord Castleton—tell him my fears and suspicions—he will follow us, I know, or do what is best."

I drew ink and paper towards me, and wrote hastily.   My uncle came round and looked over my shoulder.

Suddenly he exclaimed, seizing my arm, " Gower, Gower ! What name is this ?   You said Vivian."

" Vivian or Gower—the same person."

My uncle hurried out of the room.   It was natural that he should leave me to make our joint and brief preparations for departure.

I finished my letter, sealed it, and when, five minutes after-wards, the chaise came to the door, I gave it to the ostler who accompanied the horses, with injunctions to deliver it forthwith to Lord Castleton himself.

My uncle now descended, and stepped from the threshold with a firm stride.   " Comfort yourself," he said, as he entered the chaise, into which I had already thrown myself.   " We may be mistaken yet."

" Mistaken !   You do not know this young man.   He has every quality that could entangle a girl like Fanny, and not, I fear, one sentiment of honour, that would stand in the way of his ambition.   I judge him now as by a revelation—too late —oh heavens, if it be too late."

A groan broke from Roland's lips.   I heard in it a proof of his sympathy with my emotion, and grasped his hand ; it was as cold as the hand of the dead.

PART XV

CHAPTER I

THERE would have been nothing in what had chanced to justify the suspicions that tortured me, but for my impressions as to the character of Vivian.

Reader, hast thou not, in the easy, careless sociability of youth, formed acquaintance with some one, in whose more engaging or brilliant qualities thou hast—not lost that dislike to defects or vices which is natural to an age when, even while we err, we adore what is good, and glow with enthusiasm for the ennobling sentiment and the virtuous deed—no, happily, not lost dislike to what is bad, nor thy quick sense of it—but conceived a keen interest in the struggle between the bad that revolted, and the good that attracted thee, in thy companion? Then, perhaps, thou hast lost sight of him for a time—suddenly thou hearest that he has done something out of the way of ordinary good or commonplace evil! and, in either—the good or the evil—thy mind runs rapidly back over its old reminiscences, and of either thou sayest, " How natural!—only So-and-so could have done this thing!"

Thus I felt respecting Vivian. The most remarkable qualities in his character were his keen power of calculation, and his unhesitating audacity—qualities that lead to fame or to infamy, according to the cultivation of the moral sense and the direction of the passions. Had I recognised those qualities in some agency apparently of good—and it seemed yet doubtful if Vivian were the agent—I should have cried, " It is he! and the better angel has triumphed!" With the same (alas! with a yet more impulsive) quickness, when the agency was of evil, and the agent equally dubious, I felt that the qualities revealed the man, and that the demon had prevailed.

Mile after mile, stage after stage, were passed, on the dreary, interminable, high north road. I narrated to my companion, more intelligibly than I had yet done, my causes for apprehen-

sion.   The Captain at first listened eagerly, then checked me on
the sudden.   " There may be nothing in all this," he cried.
" Sir, we must be men here—have our heads cool, our reason
clear; stop ! "   And, leaning back in the chaise, Roland refused
farther conversation, and, as the night advanced, seemed to
sleep.   I took pity on his fatigue, and devoured my heart in
silence.   At each stage we heard of the party of which we were
in pursuit.   At the first stage or two we were less than an hour
behind ; gradually, as we advanced, we lost ground, despite the
most lavish liberality to the post-boys.   I supposed, at length,
that the mere circumstance of changing, at each relay, the
chaise as well as the horses, was the cause of our comparative
slowness ; and on saying this to Roland, as we were changing
horses, somewhere about midnight, he at once called up the
master of the inn, and gave him his own price for permission
to retain the chaise till the journey's end.   This was so
unlike Roland's ordinary thrift, whether dealing with my money
or his own—so unjustified by the fortune of either, that I
could not help muttering something in apology.

" Can you guess why I was a miser ? " said Roland calmly.

" A miser !—anything but that !   Only prudent—military men
often are so."

" I was a miser," repeated the Captain, with emphasis.   " I
began the habit first when my son was but a child.   I thought
him high-spirited, and with a taste for extravagance.   ' Well,'
said I to myself, ' I will save for him ; boys will be boys.'   Then,
afterwards, when he was no more a child (at least he began to
have the vices of a man), I said to myself, ' Patience, he may
reform still ! if not, I will save money, that I may have power
over his self-interest, since I have none over his heart.   I will
bribe him into honour ! '   And then—and then—God saw that
I was very proud, and I was punished.   Tell them to drive
faster—faster—why, this is a snail's pace ! ' "

All that night, all the next day, till towards the evening, we
pursued our journey, without pause, or other food than a crust
of bread and a glass of wine.   But we now picked up the ground
we had lost, and gained upon the carriage.   The night had
closed in when we arrived at the stage at which the route to
Lord N——'s branched from the direct north road.   And here,
making our usual inquiry, my worst suspicions were confirmed.
The carriage we pursued had changed horses an hour before,
but had not taken the way to Lord N——'s ;—continuing the
direct road into Scotland.   The people of the inn had not seen

the lady in the carriage, for it was already dark, but the man-servant (whose livery they described) had ordered the horses.

The last hope that, in spite of appearances, no treachery had been designed here vanished. The Captain, at first, seemed more dismayed than myself, but he recovered more quickly. "We will continue the journey on horseback," he said; and hurried to the stables. All objections vanished at the sight of his gold. In five minutes we were in the saddle, with a postillion also mounted, to accompany us. We did the next stage in little more than two-thirds of the time which we should have occupied in our former mode of travel—indeed, I found it hard to keep pace with Roland. We remounted; we were only twenty-five minutes behind the carriage. We felt confident that we should overtake it before it could reach the next town—the moon was up—we could see far before us.—We rode at full speed. Milestone after milestone glided by; the carriage was not visible. We arrived at the post-town, or rather village; it contained but one posting-house. We were long in knocking up the ostlers—no carriage had arrived just before us; no carriage had passed the place since noon.

What mystery was this?

"Back, back, boy!" said Roland, with a soldier's quick wit, and spurring his jaded horse from the yard. "They will have taken a cross-road or by-lane. We shall track them by the hoofs of the horses or the print of the wheels."

Our postillion grumbled, and pointed to the panting sides of our horses. For answer, Roland opened his hand—full of gold. Away we went back through the dull sleeping village, back into the broad moonlit thoroughfare. We came to a cross-road to the right, but the track we pursued still led us straight on. We had measured back nearly half the way to the post-town at which we had last changed, when lo! there emerged from a by-lane two postillions and their horses!

At that sight our companion, shouting loud, pushed on before us and hailed his fellows. A very few words gave us the information we sought. A wheel had come off the carriage just by the turn of the road, and the young lady and her servants had taken refuge in a small inn not many yards down the lane. The man-servant had dismissed the post-boys after they had baited their horses, saying they were to come again in the morning, and bring a blacksmith to repair the wheel.

"How came the wheel off?" asked Roland sternly.

"Why, sir, the linch-pin was all rotted away, I suppose, and came out."

"Did the servant get off the dickey after you set out, and before the accident happened?"

"Why, yes. He said the wheels were catching fire, that they had not the patent axles, and he had forgot to have them oiled."

"And he looked at the wheels, and shortly afterwards the linch-pin came out? Eh?"

"Anan, sir!" said the post-boy, staring; "why, and indeed so it was!"

"Come on, Pisistratus, we are in time; but pray God—pray God—that"—the Captain dashed his spurs into the horse's sides, and the rest of his words were lost to me.

A few yards back from the causeway, a broad patch of green before it, stood the inn—a sullen, old-fashioned building of cold grey stone, looking livid in the moonlight, with black firs at one side, throwing over half of it a dismal shadow. So solitary! not a house, not a hut near it. If they who kept the inn were such that villainy might reckon on their connivance, and innocence despair of their aid—there was no neighbourhood to alarm—no refuge at hand. The spot was well chosen.

The doors of the inn were closed; there was a light in the room below; but the outside shutters were drawn over the windows on the first floor. My uncle paused a moment, and said to the postillion—

"Do you know the back way to the premises?"

"No, sir: I doesn't often come by this way, and they be new folks that have taken the house—and I hear it don't prosper over much."

"Knock at the door; we will stand a little aside while you do so. If any one ask what you want—merely say you would speak to the servant—that you have found a purse;—here, hold up mine."

Roland and I had dismounted, and my uncle drew me close to the wall by the door. Observing that my impatience ill submitted to what seemed to me idle preliminaries—

"Hist!" whispered he; "if there be anything to conceal within, they will not answer the door till some one has reconnoitred; were they to see us, they would refuse to open. But seeing only the post-boy, whom they will suppose at first to be one of those who brought the carriage, they will have no suspicion. Be ready to rush in the moment the door is unbarred."

My uncle's veteran experience did not deceive him.—There was a long silence before any reply was made to the post-boy's summons; the light passed to and fro rapidly across the window, as if persons were moving within. Roland made sign to the post-boy to knock again; he did so twice—thrice—and at last, from an attic window in the roof, a head obtruded, and a voice cried, "Who are you?—what do you want?"

"I'm the post-boy at the Red Lion; I want to see the servant with the brown carriage: I have found this purse!"

"Oh, that's all—wait a bit."

The head disappeared; we crept along under the projecting eaves of the house; we heard the bar lifted from the door; the door itself cautiously opened; one spring and I stood within, and set my back to the door to admit Roland.

"Ho, help!—thieves!—help!" cried a loud voice, and I felt a hand gripe at my throat. I struck at random in the dark, and with effect, for my blow was followed by a groan and a curse.

Roland, meanwhile, had detected a ray through the chinks of a door in the hall, and, guided by it, found his way into the room at the window of which we had seen the light pass and go, while without. As he threw the door open, I bounded after him, and saw, in a kind of parlour, two females—the one a stranger, no doubt the hostess, the other the treacherous abigail. Their faces evinced their terror.

"Woman," I said, seizing the last, "where is Miss Trevanion?" Instead of replying, the woman set up a loud shriek. Another light now gleamed from the staircase which immediately faced the door; and I heard a voice, that I recognised as Peacock's, cry out, "Who's there?—What's the matter?"

I made a rush at the stairs. A burly form (that of the landlord, who had recovered from my blow) obstructed my way for a moment, to measure its length on the floor at the next. I was at the top of the stairs; Peacock recognised me, recoiled, and extinguished the light. Oaths, cries, and shrieks now resounded through the dark. Amidst them all, I suddenly heard a voice exclaim, "Here, here!—help!" It was the voice of Fanny. I made my way to the right, whence the voice came, and received a violent blow. Fortunately, it fell on the arm which I extended, as men do who feel their way through the dark. It was not the right arm, and I seized and closed on my assailant. Roland now came up, a candle in his hand, and at that sight my antagonist, who was no other than

Peacock, slipped from me, and made a rush at the stairs.   But
the Captain caught him with his grasp of iron.   Fearing nothing
for Roland in a contest with any single foe, and all my thoughts
bent on the rescue of her whose voice again broke on my ear,
I had already (before the light of the candle which Roland held
went out in the struggle between himself and Peacock) caught
sight of a door at the end of the passage, and thrown myself
against it : it was locked, but it shook and groaned to my
pressure.

"Hold back, whoever you are !" cried a voice from the room
within, far different from that wail of distress which had guided
my steps.   "Hold back, at the peril of your life !"

The voice, the threat, redoubled my strength ; the door flew
from its fastenings.   I stood in the room.   I saw Fanny at my
feet, clasping my hands ; then raising herself, she hung on my
shoulder and murmured "Saved !"   Opposite to me, his face
deformed by passion, his eyes literally blazing with savage fire,
his nostrils distended, his lips apart, stood the man I have
called Francis Vivian.

"Fanny—Miss Trevanion—what outrage—what villainy is
this ?   You have not met this man at your free choice,—oh
speak !"   Vivian sprang forward.

"Question no one but me.   Unhand that lady,—she is my
betrothed—shall be my wife."

"No, no, no,—don't believe him," cried Fanny ; "I have
been betrayed by my own servants—brought here, I know not
how !   I heard my father was ill ; I was on my way to him :
that man met me here, and dared to——"

"Miss Trevanion—yes, I dared to say I loved you."

"Protect me from him !—you will protect me from him !"

"No, madam !" said a voice behind me, in a deep tone, "it
is I who claim the right to protect you from that man ; it is I
who now draw around you the arm of one sacred, even to him ;
it is I who, from this spot, launch upon his head—a father's
curse.   Violator of the hearth !   Baffled ravisher !—go thy way
to the doom which thou hast chosen for thyself.   God will be
merciful to me yet, and give me a grave before thy course find
its close in the hulks—or at the gallows !"

A sickness came over me—a terror froze my veins—I reeled
back, and leant for support against the wall.   Roland had passed
his arm round Fanny, and she, frail and trembling, clung to his
broad breast, looking fearfully up to his face.   And never in
that face, ploughed by deep emotions, and dark with unutterable

Chris Hammond
Oct '97

"She hung on my shoulder and
murmured "Saved"

sorrows, had I seen an expression so grand in its wrath, so sublime in its despair. Following the direction of his eye, stern, and fixed as the look of one who prophesies a destiny and denounces a doom, I shivered as I gazed upon the son. His whole frame seemed collapsed and shrinking, as if already withered by the curse; a ghastly whiteness overspread the cheek, usually glowing with the dark bloom of oriental youth; the knees knocked together; and, at last, with a faint exclamation of pain, like the cry of one who receives a death-blow, he bowed his face over his clasped hands, and so remained—still, but cowering.

Instinctively I advanced, and placed myself between the father and the son, murmuring, "Spare him; see, his own heart crushes him down." Then stealing towards the son, I whispered, "Go, go; the crime was not committed, the curse can be recalled." But my words touched a wrong chord in that dark and rebellious nature. The young man withdrew his hands hastily from his face and reared his front in passionate defiance.

Waving me aside, he cried, "Away! I acknowledge no authority over my actions and my fate; I allow no mediator between this lady and myself. Sir," he continued, gazing gloomily on his father—"sir, you forget our compact. Our ties were severed, your power over me annulled; I resigned the name you bear: to you I was, and am still, as the dead. I deny your right to step between me and the object dearer to me than life."

"Oh!" (and here he stretched forth his hands towards Fanny)—"Oh, Miss Trevanion, do not refuse me one prayer, however you condemn me. Let me see you alone but for one moment; let me but prove to you that, guilty as I may have been, it was not from the base motives you will hear imputed to me—that it was not the heiress I sought to decoy, it was the woman I sought to win; oh, hear me——"

"No, no," murmured Fanny, clinging closer to Roland; "do not leave me. If, as it seems, he is your son, I forgive him: but let him go—I shudder at his very voice!"

"Would you have me, indeed, annihilate the memory of the bond between us?" said Roland, in a hollow voice; "would you have me see in you only the vile thief, the lawless felon,—deliver you up to justice, or strike you to my feet? Let the memory still save you, and begone!"

Again I caught hold of the guilty son, and again he broke from my grasp.

"It is," he said, folding his arms deliberately on his breast—
"it is for me to command in this house; all who are within it
must submit to my orders.   You, sir, who hold reputation, name,
and honour at so high a price, how can you fail to see that you
would rob them from the lady whom you would protect from
the insult of my affection?   How would the world receive the
tale of your rescue of Miss Trevanion? how believe that—oh,
pardon me, madam—Miss Trevanion—Fanny—pardon me—I
am mad; only hear me—alone—alone—and then if you, too,
say 'Begone,' I submit without a murmur; I allow no arbiter
but you."

But Fanny still clung closer, and closer still, to Roland.   At
that moment I heard voices and the trampling of feet below,
and supposing that the accomplices in this villainy were muster-
ing courage, perhaps, to mount to the assistance of their em-
ployer, I lost all the compassion that had hitherto softened my
horror of the young man's crime, and all the awe with which
that confession had been attended.   I therefore, this time,
seized the false Vivian with a gripe that he could no longer
shake off, and said sternly—

"Beware how you aggravate your offence.   If strife ensues,
it will not be between father and son, and——"

Fanny sprang forward.   "Do not provoke this bad dangerous
man.   I fear him not.   Sir, I *will* hear you, and alone."

"Never!" cried I and Roland simultaneously.

Vivian turned his look fiercely to me, and with a sullen
bitterness to his father, and then, as if resigning his former
prayer, he said—"Well, then, be it so; even in the presence
of those who judge me so severely, I will speak, at least."   He
paused, and throwing into his voice a passion that, had the
repugnance at his guilt been less, would not have been without
pathos, he continued to address Fanny: "I own that, when I
first saw you, I might have thought of love, as the poor and
ambitious think of the way to wealth and power.   Those
thoughts vanished, and nothing remained in my heart but love
and madness.   I was as a man in a delirium when I planned
this snare.   I knew but one object—saw but one heavenly
vision.   Oh! mine—mine at least in that vision—are you
indeed lost to me for ever!"

There was that in this man's tone and manner which, whether
arising from accomplished hypocrisy, or actual, if perverted,
feeling, would, I thought, find its way at once to the heart of
a woman who, however wronged, had once loved him; and,

with a cold misgiving, I fixed my eyes on Miss Trevanion. Her look, as she turned with a visible tremor, suddenly met mine, and I believe that she discerned my doubt, for, after suffering her eyes to rest on my own, with something of mournful reproach, her lips curved as with the pride of her mother, and for the first time in my life I saw anger on her brow.

"It is well, sir, that you have thus spoken to me in the presence of others, for in their presence I call upon you to say, by that honour which the son of this gentleman may for a while forget, but cannot wholly forfeit,—I call upon you to say, whether by deed, word, or sign, I, Frances Trevanion, ever gave you cause to believe that I returned the feeling you say you entertained for me, or encouraged you to dare this attempt to place me in your power."

"No!" cried Vivian readily, but with a writhing lip—"no; but where I loved so deeply, perilled all my fortune for one fair and free occasion to tell you so alone, I would not think that such love could meet only loathing and disdain. What!—has Nature shaped me so unkindly, that where I love no love can reply? What!—has the accident of birth shut me out from the right to woo and mate with the high-born? For the last, at least that gentleman in justice should tell you, since it has been his care to instil the haughty lesson into me, that my lineage is one that befits lofty hopes, and warrants fearless ambition. My hopes, my ambition—they were you! Oh, Miss Trevanion, it is true that to win you I would have braved the world's laws, defied every foe, save him who now rises before me. Yet, believe me, believe me, had I won what I dared to aspire to, you would not have been disgraced by your choice; and the name, for which I thank not my father, should not have been despised by the woman who pardoned my presumption, nor by the man who now tramples on my anguish and curses me in my desolation."

Not by a word had Roland sought to interrupt his son—nay, by a feverish excitement, which my heart understood in its secret sympathy, he had seemed eagerly to court every syllable that could extenuate the darkness of the offence, or even imply some less sordid motive for the baseness of the means. But as the son now closed with the words of unjust reproach, and the accents of fierce despair—closed a defence that showed, in its false pride and its perverted eloquence, so utter a blindness to every principle of that Honour which had been the father's idol, Roland placed his hand before the eyes that he had previously,

as if spellbound, fixed on the hardened offender, and once more
drawing Fanny towards him, said—

"His breath pollutes the air that innocence and honesty
should breathe. He says, 'All in this house are at his command,'—why do we stay?—let us go." He turned towards the
door, and Fanny with him.

Meanwhile the louder sounds below had been silenced for
some moments, but I heard a step in the hall. Vivian started,
and placed himself before us.

"No, no, you cannot leave me thus, Miss Trevanion. I resign
you—be it so; I do not even ask for pardon. But to leave
this house thus, without carriage, without attendants, without
explanation!—the blame falls on me—it shall do so. But at
least vouchsafe me the right to repair what I yet can repair of
the wrong, to protect all that is left to me—your name."

As he spoke, he did not perceive (for he was facing us, and
with his back to the door) that a new actor had noiselessly
entered on the scene, and, pausing by the threshold, heard his
last words.

"The name of Miss Trevanion, sir—and from what?" asked
the newcomer, as he advanced and surveyed Vivian with a look
that, but for its quiet, would have seemed disdain.

"Lord Castleton!" exclaimed Fanny, lifting up the face she
had buried in her hands.

Vivian recoiled in dismay, and gnashed his teeth.

"Sir," said the marquis, "I await your reply; for not even
you, in my presence, shall imply that one reproach can be
attached to the name of that lady."

"Oh, moderate your tone to me, my Lord Castleton!" cried
Vivian; "in you, at least, there is one man I am not forbidden
to brave and defy. It was to save that lady from the cold
ambition of her parents—it was to prevent the sacrifice of her
youth and beauty, to one whose sole merits are his wealth and
his titles—it was this that impelled me to the crime I have
committed, this that hurried me on to risk all for one hour,
when youth at least could plead its cause to youth; and this
gives me now the power to say that it does rest with me to
protect the name of the lady, whom your very servility to that
world which you have made your idol forbids you to claim from
the heartless ambition that would sacrifice the daughter to the
vanity of the parents. Ha! the future Marchioness of Castleton
on her way to Scotland with a penniless adventurer! Ha! if
my lips are sealed, who but I can seal the lips of those below

in my secret? The secret shall be kept, but on this condition
—you shall not triumph where I have failed; I may lose what
I adored, but I do not resign it to another. Ha; have I foiled
you, my Lord Castleton?—ha, ha!"

"No, sir; and I almost forgive you the villainy you have *not*
effected, for informing me, for the first time, that had I presumed to address Miss Trevanion, her parents at least would
have pardoned the presumption. Trouble not yourself as to
what your accomplices may say. They have already confessed
their infamy and your own. Out of my path, sir!"

Then, with the benign look of a father, and the lofty grace of
a prince, Lord Castleton advanced to Fanny. Looking round
with a shudder, she hastily placed her hand in his, and, by so
doing, perhaps prevented some violence on the part of Vivian,
whose heaving breast, and eye bloodshot, and still unquailing,
showed how little even shame had subdued his fiercer passions.
But he made no offer to detain them, and his tongue seemed to
cleave to his lips. Now, as Fanny moved to the door, she passed
Roland, who stood motionless and with vacant looks, like an
image of stone; and with a beautiful tenderness, for which (even
at this distant date recalling it), I say, "God requite thee,
Fanny," she laid her other hand on Roland's arm, and said,
"Come, too; *your* arm still."

But Roland's limbs trembled and refused to stir; his head, relaxing, drooped on his breast, his eyes closed. Even Lord Castleton was so struck (though unable to guess the true and terrible
cause of his dejection) that he forgot his desire to hasten from
the spot, and cried with all his kindliness of heart, "You are ill
—you faint; give him your arm, Pisistratus."

"It is nothing," said Roland feebly, as he leant heavily on
my arm, while I turned back my head with all the bitterness of
that reproach which filled my heart, speaking in the eyes that
sought *him*, whose place should have been where mine now was.
And, oh!—thank Heaven, thank Heaven!—the look was not
in vain. In the same moment the son was at the father's
knees.

"Oh, pardon—pardon! Wretch, lost wretch though I be, I
bow my head to the curse. Let it fall—but on me, and on me
only—not on your own heart too."

Fanny burst into tears, sobbing out, "Forgive him, as I do."
Roland did not heed her.

"He thinks that the heart was not shattered before the curse
could come," he said, in a voice so weak as to be scarcely audible.

Then, raising his eyes to heaven, his lips moved as if he prayed inly. Pausing, he stretched his hands over his son's head, and averting his face, said, " I revoke the curse. Pray to thy God for pardon."

Perhaps not daring to trust himself further, he then made a violent effort, and hurried from the room.

We followed silently. When we gained the end of the passage, the door of the room we had left closed with a sullen jar.

As the sound smote on my ear, with it came so terrible a sense of the solitude upon which that door had closed—so keen and quick an apprehension of some fearful impulse, suggested by passions so fierce, to a condition so forlorn—that instinctively I stopped, and then hurried back to the chamber. The lock of the door having been previously forced, there was no barrier to oppose my entrance. I advanced, and beheld a spectacle of such agony, as can only be conceived by those who have looked on the grief which takes no fortitude from reason, no consolation from conscience—the grief which tells us what would be the earth were man abandoned to his passions, and the CHANCE of the atheist reigned alone in the merciless heavens. Pride humbled to the dust; ambition shivered into fragments; love (or the passion mistaken for it) blasted into ashes; life, at the first onset, bereaved of its holiest ties, forsaken by its truest guide; shame that writhed for revenge, and remorse that knew not prayer—all, all blended, yet distinct, were in that awful spectacle of the guilty son.

And I had told but twenty years, and my heart had been mellowed in the tender sunshine of a happy home, and I had loved this boy as a stranger, and, lo!—he was Roland's son! I forgot all else, looking upon that anguish; and I threw myself on the ground by the form that writhed there, and folding my arms round the breast which in vain repelled me, I whispered, " Comfort—comfort—life is long. You shall redeem the past, you shall efface the stain, and your father shall bless you yet! "

CHAPTER II

I COULD not stay long with my unhappy cousin, but still I stayed long enough to make me think it probable that Lord Castleton's carriage would have left the inn: and when, as I passed the hall, I saw it standing before the open door, I was seized with fear for Roland; his emotions might have ended in some physical attack. Nor were those fears without foundation. I found Fanny kneeling beside the old soldier in the parlour where we had seen the two women, and bathing his temples, while Lord Castleton was binding his arm; and the marquis's favourite valet, who, amongst his other gifts, was something of a surgeon, was wiping the blade of the penknife that had served instead of a lancet. Lord Castleton nodded to me, "Don't be uneasy— a little fainting fit—we have bled him. He is safe now—see, he is recovering."

Roland's eyes, as they opened, turned to me with an anxious, inquiring look. I smiled upon him as I kissed his forehead, and could, with a safe conscience, whisper words which neither father nor Christian could refuse to receive as a comfort.

In a few minutes more we had left the house. As Lord Castleton's carriage only held two, the marquis, having assisted Miss Trevanion and Roland to enter, quietly mounted the seat behind, and made a sign to me to come by his side, for there was room for both. (His servant had taken one of the horses that had brought thither Roland and myself, and already gone on before.) No conversation took place between us then. Lord Castleton seemed profoundly affected, and I had no words at my command.

When we had reached the inn at which Lord Castleton had changed horses, about six miles distant, the marquis insisted on Fanny's taking some rest for a few hours, for indeed she was thoroughly worn out.

I attended my uncle to his room, but he only answered my assurances of his son's repentance with a pressure of the hand, and then, gliding from me, went into the farthest recess of the room, and there knelt down. When he rose, he was passive and tractable as a child. He suffered me to assist him to undress; and when he had lain down on the bed, he turned his face quietly from the light, and, after a few heavy sighs, sleep seemed mercifully to steal upon him. I listened to his breathing till it grew low and regular, and then descended to the sitting-room in which I had left Lord Castleton, for he had asked me in a whisper to seek him there.

I found the marquis seated by the fire, in a thoughtful and dejected attitude.

"I am glad you are come," said he, making room for me on the hearth, "for I assure you I have not felt so mournful for many years; we have much to explain to each other. Will you begin? they say the sound of the bell dissipates the thunder-cloud. And there is nothing like the voice of a frank, honest nature to dispel all the clouds that come upon us when we think of our own faults and the villainy of others. But I beg you a thousand pardons—that young man, your relation!—your brave uncle's son! Is it possible?"

My explanations to Lord Castleton were necessarily brief and imperfect. The separation between Roland and his son, my ignorance of its cause, my belief in the death of the latter, my chance acquaintance with the supposed Vivian; the interest I took in him; the relief it was to the fears for his fate with which he inspired me, to think he had returned to the home I ascribed to him: and the circumstances which had induced my suspicions, justified by the result—all this was soon hurried over.

"But, I beg your pardon," said the marquis, interrupting me, "did you, in your friendship for one so unlike you, even by your own partial account, never suspect that you had stumbled upon your lost cousin?"

"Such an idea never could have crossed me."

And here I must observe, that though the reader, at the first introduction of Vivian, would divine the secret,—the penetration of a reader is wholly different from that of the actor in events. That I had chanced on one of those curious coincidences in the romance of real life, which a reader looks out for and expects in following the course of narrative, was a supposition forbidden to me by a variety of causes. There was not the least family resemblance between Vivian and any of his relations; and, some-how or other, in Roland's son I had pictured to myself a form and a character wholly different from Vivian's. To me it would have seemed impossible that my cousin could have been so little curious to hear any of our joint family affairs; been so un-heedful, or even weary, if I spoke of Roland—never, by a word or tone, have betrayed a sympathy with his kindred. And my other conjecture was so probable!—son of the Colonel Vivian whose name he bore. And that letter, with the post-mark of "Godalming!" and my belief, too, in my cousin's death; even now I am not surprised that the idea never occurred to me.

I paused from enumerating these excuses for my dulness, angry with myself, for I noticed that Lord Castleton's fair brow darkened;—and he exclaimed, "What deceit he must have gone through before he could become such a master in the art!"

"That is true, and I cannot deny it," said I. "But his

punishment now is awful: let us hope that repentance may follow the chastisement. And, though certainly it must have been his own fault that drove him from his father's home and guidance, yet, so driven, let us make some allowance for the influence of evil companionship on one so young—for the suspicions that the knowledge of evil produces, and turns into a kind of false knowledge of the world. And in this last and worst of all his actions——"

"Ah, how justify that?"

"Justify it!—good heavens! justify it!—no. I only say this, strange as it may seem, that I believe his affection for Miss Trevanion was for herself: so he says, from the depth of an anguish in which the most insincere of men would cease to feign. But no more of this,—she is saved, thank Heaven!"

"And you believe," said Lord Castleton musingly, "that he spoke the truth when he thought that I——" The marquis stopped, coloured slightly, and then went on. "But no; Lady Ellinor and Trevanion, whatever might have been in their thoughts, would never have so forgot their dignity as to take him, a youth—almost a stranger—nay, take any one into their confidence on such a subject."

"It was but by broken gasps, incoherent, disconnected words, that Vivian,—I mean my cousin,—gave me any explanation of this. But Lady N——, at whose house he was staying, appears to have entertained such a notion, or at least led my cousin to think so."

"Ah! that is possible," said Lord Castleton, with a look of relief. "Lady N—— and I were boy and girl together; we correspond; she has written to me suggesting that——Ah! I see,—an indiscreet woman. Hum! this comes of lady correspondents!"

Lord Castleton had recourse to the Beaudesert mixture; and then, as if eager to change the subject, began his own explanation. On receiving my letter, he saw even more cause to suspect a snare than I had done, for he had that morning received a letter from Trevanion, not mentioning a word about his illness; and on turning to the newspaper, and seeing a paragraph headed, "Sudden and alarming illness of Mr. Trevanion," the marquis had suspected some party manœuvre or unfeeling hoax, since the mail that had brought the letter must have travelled as quickly as any messenger who had given the information to the newspaper. He had, however, immediately sent down to the office of the journal to inquire on what authority the paragraph had been inserted, while he despatched another messenger to St. James's Square. The reply from the office was, that the message had been brought by a servant in Mr. Trevanion's livery, but was not admitted as news until it had been ascertained by inquiries at the minister's house that Lady Ellinor had received the same intelligence and actually left town in consequence.

" I was extremely sorry for poor Lady Ellinor's uneasiness," said Lord Castleton, " and extremely puzzled, but I still thought there could be no real ground for alarm until your letter reached me. And when you there stated your conviction that Mr. Gower was mixed up in this fable, and that it concealed some snare upon Fanny, I saw the thing at a glance. The road to Lord N——'s, till within the last stage or two, would be the road to Scotland. And a hardy and unscrupulous adventurer, with the assistance of Miss Trevanion's servants, might thus entrap her to Scotland itself, and there work on her fears ; or, if he had hope in her affections, entrap her into consent to a Scotch marriage. You may be sure, therefore, that I was on the road as soon as possible. But as your messenger came all the way from the City, and not so quickly perhaps as he might have come ; and then, as there was the carriage to see to, and the horses to send for, I found myself more than an hour and a half behind you. Fortunately, however, I made good ground, and should probably have overtaken you half-way, but that, on passing between a ditch and waggon, the carriage was upset, and that somewhat delayed me. On arriving at the town where the road branched off to Lord N——'s, I was rejoiced to learn you had taken what I was sure would prove the right direction, and finally I gained the clue to that villainous inn, by the report of the post-boys who had taken Miss Trevanion's carriage there, and met you on the road. On reaching the inn, I found two fellows conferring outside the door. They sprang in as we drove up, but not before my servant Summers—a quick fellow, you know, who has travelled with me from Norway to Nubia—had quitted his seat, and got into the house, into which I followed him with a step, you dog, as active as your own ! Egad ! I was twenty-one then ! Two fellows had already knocked down poor Summers and showed plenty of fight. Do you know," said the marquis, interrupting himself with an air of serio-comic humiliation—" do you know that I actually—no, you never will believe it—mind 'tis a secret—actually broke my cane over one fellow's shoulders ?—look ! " (and the marquis held up the fragment of the lamented weapon). " And I half suspect, but I can't say positively, that I had even the necessity to demean myself by a blow with the naked hand—clenched too!—quite Eton again—upon my honour it was. Ha, ha !"

And the marquis—whose magnificent proportions, in the full vigour of man's strongest, if not his most combative, age, would have made him a formidable antagonist, even to a couple of prize-fighters, supposing he had retained a little of Eton skill in such encounters—laughed with the glee of a schoolboy, whether at the thought of his prowess, or his sense of the contrast between so rude a recourse to primitive warfare, and his own indolent habits, and almost feminine good temper. Composing himself, however, with the quick recollection how little I could share his hilarity, he resumed gravely, " It took us some time —I don't say to defeat our foes; but to bind them, which I thought a necessary precaution;—one fellow, Trevanion's servant, all the while stunning me with quotations from Shakspeare. I then gently laid hold of a gown, the bearer of which had been long trying to scratch me ; but, being luckily a small woman, had not succeeded in reaching to my eyes. But the gown escaped, and fluttered off to the kitchen. I followed, and there I found Miss Trevanion's Jezebel of a maid. She was terribly frightened, and affected to be extremely penitent. I own to you that I don't care what a man says in the way of slander, but a woman's tongue against another woman—especially if that tongue be in the mouth of a lady's lady—I think it always worth silencing : I therefore consented to pardon this woman on condition she would find her way here before morning. No scandal shall come from her. Thus you see some minutes elapsed before I joined you ; but I minded that the less, as I heard you and the Captain were already in the room with Miss Trevanion ; and not, alas ! dreaming of your connection with the culprit, I was wondering what could have delayed you so long,—afraid, I own it, to find that Miss Trevanion's heart might have been seduced by that — hem — hem !—handsome — young — hem — hem !— There's no fear of that?" added Lord Castleton anxiously, as he bent his bright eyes upon mine.

I felt myself colour as I answered firmly, " It is just to Miss Trevanion to add, that the unhappy man owned, in her presence and in mine, that he had never had the slightest encouragement for his attempt—never one cause to believe that she approved the affection which, I try to think, blinded and maddened himself,"

2 A

"I believe you; for I think"—Lord Castleton paused uneasily, again looked at me, rose, and walked about the room with evident agitation; then, as if he had come to some resolution, he returned to the hearth and stood facing me.

"My dear young friend," said he, with his irresistible kindly frankness, "this is an occasion that excuses all things between us, even my impertinence. Your conduct from first to last has been such, that I wish, from the bottom of my heart, that I had a daughter to offer you, and that you felt for her as I believe you feel for Miss Trevanion. These are not mere words; do not look down as if ashamed. All the marquisates in the world would never give me the pride I should feel, if I could see in my life one steady self-sacrifice to duty and honour, equal to that which I have witnessed in you."

"Oh, my lord! my lord!"

"Hear me out. That you love Fanny Trevanion I know; that she may have innocently, timidly, half-unconsciously returned that affection, I think probable. But——"

"I know what you would say; spare me—I know it all."

"No! it is a thing impossible; and, if Lady Ellinor could consent, there would be such a life-long regret on her part, such a weight of obligation on yours, that—no, I repeat, it is impossible! But let us both think of this poor girl. I know her better than you can—have known her from a child; know all her virtues—they are charming; all her faults—they expose her to danger. These parents of hers—with their genius and ambition—may do very well to rule England, and influence the world; but to guide the fate of that child—no!" Lord Castleton stopped, for he was affected. I felt my old jealousy return, but it was no longer bitter.

"I say nothing," continued the marquis, "of this position, in which, without fault of hers, Miss Trevanion is placed: Lady Ellinor's knowledge of the world, and woman's wit, will see how all that can be best put right. Still it is awkward, and demands much consideration. But, putting this aside altogether, if you do firmly believe that Miss Trevanion is lost to you, can you bear to think that she is to be flung as a mere cipher into the account of the worldly greatness of an aspiring politician—married to some minister, too busy to watch over her; or some duke, who looks to pay off his mortgages with her fortune—minister or duke only regarded as a prop to Trevanion's power against a counter cabal, or as giving his section a preponderance in the cabinet? Be assured such is her most likely destiny, or rather the beginning of a destiny yet more mournful.   Now, I tell you this, that he who marries Fanny Trevanion should have little other object, for the first few years of marriage, than to correct her failings and develop her virtues.   Believe one who, alas! has too dearly bought his knowledge of woman—hers is a character to be formed.   Well, then, if this prize be lost to you, would it be an irreparable grief to your generous affection to think that it has fallen to the lot of one who at least knows his responsibilities, and who will redeem his own life, hitherto wasted, by the steadfast endeavour to fulfil them? Can you take this hand still, and press it, even though it be a rival's?"

"My lord!   This from you to me, is an honour that——"

"You will not take my hand?   Then, believe me, it is not I that will give that grief to your heart."

Touched, penetrated, melted, by this generosity in a man of such lofty claims, to one of my age and fortunes, I pressed that noble hand, half raising it to my lips—an action of respect that would have misbecome neither; but he gently withdrew the hand, in the instinct of his natural modesty.   I had then no heart to speak further on such a subject, but faltering out that I would go and see my uncle, I took up the light, and ascended the stairs.   I crept noiselessly into Roland's room, and shading the light, saw that, though he slept, his face was very troubled.   And then I thought, "What are my young griefs to his?" and sitting beside the bed, communed with my own heart and was still !

CHAPTER III

AT sunrise I went down into the sitting-room, having resolved to write to my father to join us; for I felt how much Roland needed his comfort and his counsel, and it was no great distance from the old Tower.   I was surprised to find Lord Castleton still seated by the fire; he had evidently not gone to bed.

"That's right," said he; "we must encourage each other to recruit nature," and he pointed to the breakfast things on the table.

I had scarcely tasted food for many hours, but I was only aware of my own hunger by a sensation of faintness.   I ate unconsciously, and was almost ashamed to feel how much the food restored me.

"I suppose," said I, "that you will soon set off to Lord N.'s?"

"Nay, did I not tell you that I have sent Summers express, with a note to Lady Ellinor, begging her to come here? I did not see, on reflection, how I could decorously accompany Miss Trevanion alone, without even a female servant, to a house full of gossiping guests. And even had your uncle been well enough to go with us, his presence would but have created an additional cause for wonder; so, as soon as we arrived, and while you went up with the Captain, I wrote my letter and despatched my man. I expect Lady Ellinor will be here before nine o'clock. Meanwhile, I have already seen that infamous waiting-woman, and taken care to prevent any danger from her garrulity. And you will be pleased to hear that I have hit upon a mode of satisfying the curiosity of our friend Mrs. Grundy—that is, 'the World'—without injury to any one. We must suppose that that footman of Trevanion's was out of his mind—it is but a charitable, and your good father would say, a philosophical supposition. All great knavery is madness! The world could not get on if truth and goodness were not the natural tendencies of sane minds. Do you understand?"

"Not quite."

"Why, the footman, being out of his mind, invented this mad story of Trevanion's illness, frightened Lady Ellinor and Miss Trevanion out of their wits with his own chimera, and hurried them both off, one after the other. I having heard from Trevanion, and knowing he could not have been ill when the servant left him, set off, as was natural in so old a friend of the family, saved her from the freaks of a maniac, who, getting more and more flighty, was beginning to play the Jack o' Lantern, and leading her, Heaven knows where, over the country:—and then wrote to Lady Ellinor to come to her. It is but a hearty laugh at our expense, and Mrs. Grundy is content. If you don't want her to pity, or backbite, let her laugh. She is a she Cerberus—she wants to eat you; well— stop her mouth with a cake.

"Yes," continued this better sort of Aristippus, so wise under all his seeming levities; "the cue thus given, everything favours it. If that rogue of a lackey quoted Shakspeare as much in the servants' hall as he did while I was binding him neck and heels in the kitchen, that's enough for all the household to declare he was moon-stricken; and if we find it necessary to do anything more, why, we must induce him to go into Bedlam for a month or two. The disappearance of the waiting-woman is natural; either I or Lady Ellinor send her about her business for her folly in being so gulled by the lunatic. If that's unjust, why, injustice to servants is common enough—public and private. Neither minister nor lackey can be forgiven, if he help us into a scrape. One must vent one's passion on something. Witness my poor cane: though, indeed, a better illustration would be the cane that Louis XIV. broke on a footman, because his Majesty was out of humour with the prince, whose shoulders were too sacred for royal indignation.

"So you see," concluded Lord Castleton, lowering his voice, "that your uncle, amongst all his other causes of sorrow, may think at least that his name is spared in his son's. And the young man himself may find reform easier, when freed from that despair of the possibility of redemption, which Mrs. Grundy inflicts upon those who—Courage, then; life is long!"

"My very words!" I cried; "and so repeated by you, Lord Castleton, they seem prophetic."

"Take my advice, and don't lose sight of your cousin while his pride is yet humbled, and his heart perhaps softened. I don't say this only for his sake. No, it is your poor uncle I think of: noble old fellow! And now, I think it right to pay Lady Ellinor the respect of repairing, as well as I can, the havoc three sleepless nights have made on the exterior of a gentleman who is on the shady side of remorseless forty."

Lord Castleton here left me, and I wrote to my father, begging him to meet us at the next stage (which was the nearest point from the high road to the Tower), and I sent off the letter by a messenger on horseback. That task done, I leant my head upon my hand, and a profound sadness settled upon me, despite all my efforts to face the future, and think only of the duties of life—not its sorrows.

CHAPTER IV

BEFORE nine o'clock, Lady Ellinor arrived, and went straight into Miss Trevanion's room. I took refuge in my uncle's, Roland was awake and calm, but so feeble that he made no effort to rise; and it was his calm, indeed, that alarmed me the most—it was like the calm of nature thoroughly

exhausted. He obeyed me mechanically, as a patient takes
from your hand the draught, of which he is almost unconscious,
when I pressed him to take food. He smiled on me faintly,
when I spoke to him ; but made me a sign that seemed to implore
silence. Then he turned his face from me, and buried it in the
pillow ; and I thought that he slept again, when, raising himself
a little, and feeling for my hand, he said, in a scarcely audible
voice—

"Where is he ?"

"Would you see him, sir ?'

"No, no ; that would kill me—and then—what would become
of him ?"

"He has promised me an interview, and in that interview I
feel assured he will obey your wishes, whatever they are."

Roland made no answer.

"Lord Castleton has arranged all, so that his name and madness (thus let us call it) will never be known."

"Pride, pride ! pride still !"—murmured the old soldier.
"The name, the name—well, that is much; but the living
soul !—I wish Austin were here."

"I have sent for him, sir."

Roland pressed my hand, and was again silent. Then he
began to mutter, as I thought, incoherently, about the Peninsula
and obeying orders ; and how some officer woke Lord Wellington at night, and said that something or other (I could not
catch what—the phrase was technical and military) was impossible ; and how Lord Wellington asked " Where's the order-
book ?" and looking into the order-book, said, " Not at all
impossible, for it is in the order-book ;" and so Lord Wellington
turned round and went to sleep again. Then suddenly Roland
half rose, and said, in a voice clear and firm, " But Lord Wellington, though a great captain, was a fallible man, sir, and the
order-book was his own mortal handiwork.—Get me the Bible!"

O Roland, Roland ! and I had feared that thy mind was
wandering !

So I went down and borrowed a Bible, in large characters,
and placed it on the bed before him, opening the shutters, and
letting in God's day upon God's Word.

I had just done this, when there was a slight knock at the
door. I opened it, and Lord Castleton stood without. He
asked me, in a whisper, if he might see my uncle. I drew him
in gently, and pointed to the soldier of life, "learning what was
not impossible " from the unerring Order-Book.

Lord Castleton gazed with a changing countenance, and, without disturbing my uncle, stole back. I followed him, and gently closed the door.

"You must save his son," he said, in a faltering voice—"you must; and tell me how to help you. That sight!—no sermon ever touched me more. Now come down, and receive Lady Ellinor's thanks. We are going. She wants me to tell my own tale to my old friend, Mrs. Grundy; so I go with them. Come!"

On entering the sitting-room, Lady Ellinor came up and fairly embraced me. I need not repeat her thanks, still less the praises, which fell cold and hollow on my ear. My gaze rested on Fanny where she stood apart—her eyes, heavy with fresh tears, bent on the ground. And the sense of all her charms—the memory of the tender, exquisite kindness she had shown to the stricken father! the generous pardon she had extended to the criminal son; the looks she had bent upon me on that memorable night—looks that had spoken such trust in my presence—the moment in which she had clung to me for protection, and her breath been warm upon my cheek—all these rushed over me; and I felt that the struggle of months was undone—that I had never loved her as I loved her then—when I saw her but to lose her evermore! And then there came for the first, and, I now rejoice to think, for the only time, a bitter, ungrateful accusation against the cruelty of fortune and the disparities of life. What was it that set our two hearts eternally apart, and made hope impossible? Not nature, but the fortune that gives a second nature to the world. Ah, could I then think that it is in that second nature that the soul is ordained to seek its trials, and that the elements of human virtue find their harmonious place! What I answered I know not. Neither know I how long I stood there listening to sounds which seemed to have no meaning, till there came other sounds which indeed woke my sense, and made my blood run cold to hear,—the tramp of the horses, the grating of the wheels, the voice at the door that said, "All was ready."

Then Fanny lifted her eyes, and they met mine; and then involuntarily and hastily she moved a few steps towards me, and I clasped my right hand to my heart, as if to still its beating, and remained still. Lord Castleton had watched us both. I felt that watch was upon us, though I had till then shunned his looks: now, as I turned my eyes from Fanny's, that look came full upon me—soft, compassionate, benignant. Suddenly, and with an unutterable expression of nobleness, the marquis

turned to Lady Ellinor, and said—" Pardon me for telling you
an old story. A friend of mine—a man of my own years—had
the temerity to hope that he might one day or other win the
affections of a lady young enough to be his daughter, and whom
circumstances and his own heart led him to prefer from all her
sex. My friend had many rivals; and you will not wonder—for
you have seen the lady. Among them was a young gentleman,
who for months had been an inmate of the same house—(Hush,
Lady Ellinor! you will hear me out; the interest of my story is
to come)—who respected the sanctity of the house he had
entered, and had left it when he felt he loved, for he was poor
and the lady rich. Some time after, this gentleman saved the
lady from a great danger, and was then on the eve of leaving
England—(Hush! again—hush!) My friend was present when
these two young persons met, before the probable absence of
many years, and so was the mother of the lady to whose hand
he still hoped one day to aspire. He saw that his young rival
wished to say ' Farewell!' and without a witness; that farewell
was all that his honour and his reason could suffer him to say.
My friend saw that the lady felt the natural gratitude for a
great service, and the natural pity for a generous and unfortunate
affection ; for so, Lady Ellinor, he only interpreted the sob that
reached his ear! What think you my friend did? Your high
mind at once conjectures. He said to himself—' If I am ever to
be blest with the heart which, in spite of disparity of years, I
yet hope to win, let me show how entire is the trust that I
place in its integrity and innocence: let the romance of first
youth be closed—the farewell of pure hearts be spoken—un-
embittered by the idle jealousies of one mean suspicion.' With
that thought, which *you*, Lady Ellinor, will never stoop to blame,
he placed his hand on that of the noble mother, drew her gently
towards the door, and calmly confident of the result, left these
two young natures to the unwitnessed impulse of maiden honour
and manly duty."

All this was said and done with a grace and earnestness that
thrilled the listeners: word and action suited to each with so
inimitable a harmony, that the spell was not broken till the
voice ceased and the door closed.

That mournful bliss for which I had so pined was vouchsafed:
I was alone with her to whom, indeed, honour and reason forbade me to say more than the last farewell.

It was some time before we recovered—before we *felt* that
we were alone.

It was some time before we recovered — before we felt that we were alone

Oh, ye moments, that I can now recall with so little sadness in the mellow and sweet remembrance, rest ever holy and undisclosed in the solemn recesses of the heart. Yes!—whatever confession of weakness was interchanged, we were not unworthy of the trust that permitted the mournful consolation of the parting. No trite love-tale—with vows not to be fulfilled, and hopes that the future must belie—mocked the realities of the life that lay before us. Yet on the confines of the dream we saw the day rising cold upon the world: and if—children as we well-nigh were—we shrunk somewhat from the light, we did not blaspheme the sun, and cry "There is darkness in the dawn!"

All that we attempted was to comfort and strengthen each other for that which must be: not seeking to conceal the grief we felt, but promising, with simple faith, to struggle against the grief. If vow were pledged between us—*that* was the vow— each for the other's sake would strive to enjoy the blessings Heaven left us still. Well may I say that we were children! I know not, in the broken words that passed between us, in the sorrowful hearts which those words revealed—I know not if there were that which they who own, in human passion, but the storm and the whirlwind, would call the love of maturer years—the love that gives fire to the song, and tragedy to the stage; but I know that there was neither a word nor a thought which made the sorrow of the children a rebellion to the heavenly Father.

And again the door unclosed, and Fanny walked with a firm step to her mother's side, and, pausing there, extended her hand to me, and said, as I bent over it, "Heaven WILL be with you!"

A word from Lady Ellinor; a frank smile from him—the rival; one last, last glance from the soft eyes of Fanny, and then Solitude rushed upon me—rushed, as something visible, palpable, overpowering. I felt it in the glare of the sunbeam—I heard it in the breath of the air! like a ghost it rose there—where *she* had filled the space with her presence but a moment before. A something seemed gone from the universe for ever; a change like that of death passed through my being; and when I woke to feel that my being lived again, I knew that it was my youth and its poet-land that were no more, and that I had passed, with an unconscious step, which never could retrace its way, into the hard world of laborious man!

PART XVI

CHAPTER I

"PLEASE, sir, be this note for you?" asked the waiter.
"For me—yes; it is my name."

I did not recognise the handwriting, and yet the note was from one whose writing I had often seen. But formerly the writing was cramped, stiff, perpendicular (a feigned hand, though I guessed not it was feigned); now it was hasty, irregular, impatient—scarce a letter formed, scarce a word that seemed finished—and yet strangely legible withal, as the handwriting of a bold man almost always is. I opened the note listlessly, and read—

"I have watched for you all the morning. I saw her go. Well! —I did not throw myself under the hoofs of the horses. I write this in a public-house, not far. Will you follow the bearer, and see once again the outcast whom all the rest of the world will shun?"

Though I did not recognise the hand, there could be no doubt who was the writer.

"The boy wants to know if there's an answer," said the waiter.

I nodded, took up my hat, and left the room. A ragged boy was standing in the yard, and scarcely six words passed between us, before I was following him through a narrow lane that faced the inn, and terminated in a turnstile. Here the boy paused, and making me a sign to go on, went back his way whistling. I passed the turnstile, and found myself in a green field, with a row of stunted willows hanging over a narrow rill. I looked round, and saw Vivian (as I intend still to call him) half kneeling, and seemingly intent upon some object in the grass.

My eye followed his mechanically. A young unfledged bird that had left the nest too soon, stood, all still and alone, on the bare short sward—its beak open as for food, its gaze fixed on us with a wistful stare. Methought there was something in the forlorn bird that softened me more to the forlorner youth, of whom it seemed a type.

"Now," said Vivian, speaking half to himself, half to me, "did the bird fall from the nest, or leave the nest at its own wild whim? The parent does not protect it. Mind, I say not it is the parent's fault—perhaps the fault is all with the wanderer. But, look you, though the parent is not here, the foe is!—yonder, see!"

And the young man pointed to a large brindled cat, that, kept back from its prey by our unwelcome neighbourhood, still remained watchful, a few paces off, stirring its tail gently backwards and forwards, and with that stealthy look in its round eyes—dulled by the sun—half fierce, half frightened—which belongs to its tribe, when man comes between the devourer and the victim.

"I do see," said I; "but a passing footstep has saved the bird!"

"Stop!" said Vivian, laying my hand on his own—and with his old bitter smile on his lip—"stop! do you think it mercy to save the bird? What from and what for? From a natural enemy—from a short pang and a quick death? Fie!—is not that better than slow starvation? or, if you take more heed of it, than the prison-bars of a cage? You cannot restore the nest, you cannot recall the parent! Be wiser in your mercy: leave the bird to its gentlest fate!"

I looked hard on Vivian: the lip had lost the bitter smile. He rose and turned away. I sought to take up the poor bird, but it did not know its friends, and ran from me, chirping piteously—ran towards the very jaws of the grim enemy. I was only just in time to scare away the beast, which sprang up a tree, and glared down through the hanging boughs. Then I followed the bird, and, as I followed, I heard, not knowing at first whence the sound came, a short, quick, tremulous note. Was it near? was it far?—from the earth? in the sky?—Poor parent bird like parent-love, it seemed now far and now near; now on earth, now in sky!

And at last, quick and sudden, as if born of the space, lo! the little wings hovered over me!

The young bird halted, and I also.

"Come," said I, "ye have found each other at last; settle it between you!"

I went back to the outcast.

CHAPTER II

PISISTRATUS.—" How came you to know we had stayed in
the town ?"

VIVIAN.—" Do you think I could remain where you left me ?
I wandered out—wandered hither. Passing at dawn through
yon streets, I saw the ostlers loitering by the gates of the yard,
overheard them talk, and so knew you were all at the inn—
all ! " [He sighed heavily.]

PISISTRATUS.—" Your poor father is very ill ! O cousin, how
could you fling from you so much love ! "

VIVIAN.—" Love !—his !—my father's ! "

PISISTRATUS.—" Do you really not believe, then, that your
father loved you ? "

VIVIAN.—" If I had believed it, I had never left him. All the
gold of the Indies had never bribed me to leave my mother ! "

PISISTRATUS.—" This is indeed a strange misconception of
yours. If we can remove it, all may be well yet. Need there
now be any secrets between us ? [Persuasively].—Sit down, and
tell me all, cousin."

After some hesitation, Vivian complied; and by the clearing of
his brow, and the very tone of his voice, I felt sure that he was no
longer seeking to disguise the truth. But, as I afterwards learned
the father's tale as well as now the son's, so, instead of repeating
Vivian's words, which—not by design, but by the twist of a mind
habitually wrong—distorted the facts, I will state what appears
to me the real case, as between the parties so unhappily opposed. Reader, pardon me if the recital be tedious. And if
thou thinkest that I bear not hard enough on the erring hero of
the story, remember, that he who recites judges as Austin's son
must judge of Roland's.

CHAPTER III

VIVIAN

AT THE ENTRANCE OF LIFE SITS—THE MOTHER

IT was during the war in Spain that a severe wound, and
the fever which ensued, detained Roland at the house of a
Spanish widow. His hostess had once been rich; but her

fortune had been ruined in the general calamities of the country. She had an only daughter, who assisted to nurse and tend the wounded Englishman; and when the time approached for Roland's departure, the frank grief of the young Ramouna betrayed the impression that the guest had made upon her affections. Much of gratitude, and something, it might be, of an exquisite sense of honour, aided, in Roland's breast, the charm naturally produced by the beauty of his young nurse, and the knightly compassion he felt for her ruined fortunes and desolate condition.

In one of those hasty impulses common to a generous nature —and which too often fatally vindicate the rank of Prudence amidst the tutelary Powers of Life—Roland committed the error of marriage with a girl of whose connections he knew nothing, and of whose nature little more than its warm spontaneous susceptibility. In a few days subsequent to these rash nuptials, Roland rejoined the march of the army; nor was he able to return to Spain till after the crowning victory of Waterloo.

Maimed by the loss of a limb, and with the scars of many a noble wound still fresh, Roland then hastened to a home, the dreams of which had soothed the bed of pain, and now replaced the earlier visions of renown. During his absence a son had been born to him—a son whom he might rear to take the place he had left in his country's service; to renew, in some future fields, a career that had failed the romance of his own antique and chivalrous ambition. As soon as that news had reached him, his care had been to provide an English nurse for the infant—so that, with the first sounds of the mother's endearments, the child might yet hear a voice from the father's land. A female relation of Bolt's had settled in Spain, and was induced to undertake this duty. - Natural as this appointment was to a man so devotedly English, it displeased his wild and passionate Ramouna. She had that mother's jealousy, strongest in minds uneducated: she had also that peculiar pride which belongs to her country-people, of every rank and condition; the jealousy and the pride were both wounded by the sight of the English nurse at the child's cradle.

That Roland, on regaining his Spanish hearth, should be disappointed in his expectations of the happiness awaiting him there, was the inevitable condition of such a marriage; since, not the less for his military bluntness, Roland had that refinement of feeling, perhaps over-fastidious, which belongs to all natures essentially poetic : and as the first illusions of love died away, there could have been little indeed congenial to his stately temper in one divided from him by an utter absence of education, and by the strong, but nameless, distinctions of national views and manners.   The disappointment, probably, however, went deeper than that which usually attends an ill-assorted union ; for, instead of bringing his wife to his old Tower (an expatriation which she would doubtless have resisted to the utmost), he accepted, maimed as he was, not very long after his return to Spain, the offer of a military post under Ferdinand.   The Cavalier doctrines and intense loyalty of Roland attached him, without reflection, to the service of a throne which the English arms had contributed to establish ; while the extreme unpopularity of the Constitutional Party in Spain, and the stigma of irreligion fixed to it by the priests, aided to foster Roland's belief that he was supporting a beloved king against the professors of those revolutionary and Jaco-binical doctrines, which to him were the very atheism of politics. The experience of a few years in the service of a bigot so con-temptible as Ferdinand, whose highest object of patriotism was the restoration of the Inquisition, added another disappointment to those which had already embittered the life of a man who had seen in the grand hero of Cervantes no follies to satirise, but high virtues to imitate.   Poor Quixote himself—he came mournfully back to his La Mancha, with no other reward for his knight-errantry than a decoration which he disdained to place beside his simple Waterloo medal, and a grade for which he would have blushed to resign his more modest, but more honourable English dignity.

But, still weaving hopes, the sanguine man returned to his Penates.   His child now had grown from infancy into boyhood —the child would pass naturally into his care.   Delightful occupation !—At the thought, home smiled again.

Now behold the most pernicious circumstance in this ill-omened connection.

The father of Ramouna had been one of that strange and mysterious race which presents in Spain so many features dis-tinct from the characteristics of its kindred tribes in more civilised lands.   The Gitano, or gipsy of Spain, is not the mere vagrant we see on our commons and roadsides.   Retaining, indeed, much of his lawless principles and predatory inclina-tions, he lives often in towns, exercises various callings, and not unfrequently becomes rich.   A wealthy Gitano had married a Spanish woman:[1] Roland's wife had been the offspring of this marriage. The Gitano had died while Ramouna was yet extremely young, and her childhood had been free from the influences of her paternal kindred. But, though her mother, retaining her own religion, had brought up Ramouna in the same faith, pure from the godless creed of the Gitano—and, at her husband's death, had separated herself wholly from his tribe—still she had lost caste with her own kin and people. And while struggling to regain it, the fortune, which made her sole chance of success in that attempt, was swept away, so that she had remained apart and solitary, and could bring no friends to cheer the solitude of Ramouna during Roland's absence. But, while my uncle was still in the service of Ferdinand, the widow died; and then the only relatives who came round Ramouna were her father's kindred. They had not ventured to claim affinity while her mother lived; and they did so now by attentions and caresses to her son. This opened to them at once Ramouna's heart and doors. Meanwhile the English nurse—who, in spite of all that could render her abode odious to her, had, from strong love to her charge, stoutly maintained her post—died, a few weeks after Ramouna's mother, and no healthful influence remained to counteract those baneful ones to which the heir of the honest old Caxtons was subject. But Roland returned home in a humour to be pleased with all things. Joyously he clasped his wife to his breast, and thought, with self-reproach, that he had forborne too little, and exacted too much—he would be wiser now. Delightedly he acknowledged the beauty, the intelligence, and manly bearing of the boy, who played with his sword-knot, and ran off with his pistols as a prize.

The news of the Englishman's arrival at first kept the lawless kinsfolk from the house: but they were fond of the boy, and the boy of them, and interviews between him and his wild comrades, if stolen, were not less frequent. Gradually Roland's eyes became opened. As, in habitual intercourse, the boy abandoned the reserve which awe and cunning at first imposed, Roland was inexpressibly shocked at the bold principles his son affected, and at his utter incapacity even to comprehend that plain honesty and that frank honour which, to the English soldier, seemed ideas innate and heaven-planted. Soon after-

[1] A Spaniard very rarely indeed marries a Gitano, or female gipsy. But occasionally (observes Mr. Borrow) a wealthy Gitano marries a Spanish female.

wards, Roland found that a system of plunder was carried on in his household, and tracked it to the connivance of the wife and the agency of his son, for the benefit of lazy bravos and dissolute vagrants. A more patient man than Roland might well have been exasperated—a more wary man confounded by this discovery. He took the natural step—perhaps insisting on it too summarily—perhaps not allowing enough for the un-cultured mind and lively passions of his wife—he ordered her instantly to prepare to accompany him from the place, and to abandon all communication with her kindred.

A vehement refusal ensued; but Roland was not a man to give up such a point, and at length a false submission, and a feigned repentance, soothed his resentment and obtained his pardon. They moved several miles from the place; but where they moved, there, some at least, and those the worst, of the baleful brood, stealthily followed. Whatever Ramouna's earlier love for Roland had been, it had evidently long ceased, in the thorough want of sympathy between them, and in that absence which, if it renews a strong affection, destroys an affection already weakened. But the mother and son adored each other with all the strength of their strong, wild natures. Even under ordinary circumstances the father's influence over a boy yet in childhood is exerted in vain, if the mother lend herself to baffle it. And in this miserable position, what chance had the blunt, stern, honest Roland (separated from his son during the most ductile years of infancy) against the ascendency of a mother who humoured all the faults, and gratified all the wishes, of her darling?

In his despair, Roland let fall the threat that, if thus thwarted, it would become his duty to withdraw his son from the mother. This threat instantly hardened both hearts against him. The wife represented Roland to the boy as a tyrant, as an enemy—as one who had destroyed all the happiness they had before enjoyed in each other—as one whose severity showed that he hated his own child; and the boy believed her. In his own house a firm union was formed against Roland, and protected by the cunning which is the force of the weak against the strong.

In spite of all, Roland could never forget the tenderness with which the young nurse had watched over the wounded man, nor the love—genuine for the hour, though not drawn from the feelings which withstand the wear and tear of life—that lips so beautiful had pledged him in the bygone days. These thoughts must have come perpetually between his feelings and his judgment, to embitter still more his position—to harass still more his heart. And if, by the strength of that sense of duty which made the force of his character, he could have strung himself to the fulfilment of the threat, humanity, at all events, compelled him to delay it—his wife promised to be again a mother. Blanche was born. How could he take the infant from the mother's breast, or abandon the daughter to the fatal influences from which only, by so violent an effort, he could free the son?

No wonder, poor Roland, that those deep furrows contracted thy bold front, and thy hair grew grey before its time.

Fortunately, perhaps, for all parties, Roland's wife died while Blanche was still an infant. She was taken ill of a fever—she died delirious, clasping her boy to her breast, and praying the saints to protect him from his cruel father. How often that deathbed haunted the son, and justified his belief that there was no parent's love in the heart which was now his sole shelter from the world, and the " pelting of its pitiless rain." Again I say, poor Roland! for I know that, in that harsh, unloving disrupture of such solemn ties, thy large, generous heart forgot its wrongs, again didst thou see tender eyes bending over the wounded stranger—again hear low murmurs breathe the warm weakness which the women of the south deem it no shame to own. And now did it all end in those ravings of hate, and in that glazing gaze of terror!

CHAPTER IV

THE PRECEPTOR

ROLAND removed to France, and fixed his abode in the environs of Paris. He placed Blanche at a convent in the immediate neighbourhood, going to see her daily, and gave himself up to the education of his son. The boy was apt to learn, but to unlearn was here the arduous task—and for that task it would have needed either the passionless experience, the exquisite forbearance of a practised teacher, or the love and confidence, and yielding heart of a believing pupil. Roland felt that he was not the man to be the teacher, and that his son's heart remained obstinately closed to him. He looked round,

2 B

and found at the other side of Paris what seemed a suitable
preceptor—a young Frenchman of some distinction in letters,
more especially in science, with all a Frenchman's eloquence of
talk, full of high-sounding sentiments that pleased the romantic
enthusiasm of the Captain; so Roland, with sanguine hopes,
confided his son to this man's care. The boy's natural quickness
mastered readily all that pleased his taste; he learned to speak
and write French with rare felicity and precision. His tenacious
memory, and those flexile organs in which the talent for
languages is placed, served, with the help of an English master,
to revive his earlier knowledge of his father's tongue, and to
enable him to speak it with fluent correctness—though there
was always in his accent something which had struck me as
strange; but not suspecting it to be foreign, I had thought it
a theatrical affectation. He did not go far into science—little
farther, perhaps, than a smattering of French mathematics; but
he acquired a remarkable facility and promptitude in calculation.
He devoured eagerly the light reading thrown in his way, and
picked up thence that kind of knowledge which novels and
plays afford, for good or evil, according as the novel or the play
elevates the understanding and ennobles the passions, or merely
corrupts the fancy, and lowers the standard of human nature.
But of all that Roland desired him to be taught, the son remained as ignorant as before. Among the other misfortunes
of this ominous marriage, Roland's wife had possessed all the
superstitions of a Roman Catholic Spaniard, and with these the
boy had unconsciously intermingled doctrines far more dreary,
imbibed from the dark paganism of the Gitanos.

Roland had sought a Protestant for his son's tutor. The preceptor was nominally a Protestant—a biting derider of all superstitions, indeed! He was such a Protestant as some defender
of Voltaire's religion says the Great Wit would have been had
he lived in a Protestant country. The Frenchman laughed the
boy out of his superstitions, to leave behind them the sneering
scepticism of the *Encyclopédie,* without those redeeming ethics
on which all sects of philosophy are agreed, but which, unhappily, it requires a philosopher to comprehend.

This preceptor was, doubtless, not aware of the mischief he
was doing; and for the rest, he taught his pupil after his own
system—a mild and plausible one, very much like the system
we at home are recommended to adopt—"Teach the understanding,—all else will follow;" "Learn to read *something,* and
it will all come right;" "Follow the bias of the pupil's mind;

thus you develop genius, not thwart it." Mind, understanding, genius—fine things! But, to educate the whole man, you must educate something more than these. Not for want of mind, understanding, genius, have Borgias and Neros left their names as monuments of horror to mankind. Where, in all this teaching, was one lesson to warm the heart, and guide the soul?

"Oh, mother mine! that the boy had stood by thy knee, and heard from thy lips why life was given us, in what life shall end, and how heaven stands open to us night and day! Oh, father mine; that thou hadst been his preceptor, not in book-learning, but the heart's simple wisdom! Oh that he had learned from thee, in parables closed with practice, the happiness of self-sacrifice, and how "good deeds should repair the bad!"

It was the misfortune of this boy, with his daring and his beauty, that there was in his exterior and his manner that which attracted indulgent interest, and a sort of compassionate admiration. The Frenchman liked him—believed his story—thought him ill-treated by that hard-visaged English soldier. All English people were so disagreeable, particularly English soldiers; and the Captain once mortally offended the Frenchman by calling Vilainton *un grand homme,* and denying, with brutal indignation, that the English had poisoned Napoleon! So, instead of teaching the son to love and revere his father, the Frenchman shrugged his shoulders when the boy broke into some unfilial complaint, and at most said, *" Mais, cher enfant, ton père est Anglais,—c'est tout dire."* Meanwhile, as the child sprang rapidly into precocious youth, he was permitted a liberty in his hours of leisure of which he availed himself with all the zest of his earlier habits and adventurous temper. He formed acquaintances among the loose young haunters of *cafés* and spendthrifts of that capital—the wits! He became an excellent swordsman and pistol-shot—adroit in all games in which skill helps fortune. He learned betimes to furnish himself with money, by the cards and the billiard-balls.

But, delighted with the easy home he had obtained, he took care to school his features and smooth his manner in his father's visits—to make the most of what he had learned of less ignoble knowledge, and, with his characteristic imitativeness, to cite the finest sentiments he had found in his plays and novels. What father is not credulous? Roland believed, and wept tears of joy. And now he thought the time was come to take back the boy—to return with a worthy heir to the old Tower. He thanked and blessed the tutor—he took the son. But under pretence that he had yet some things to master, whether in book knowledge or manly accomplishments, the youth begged his father, at all events, not yet to return to England—to let him attend his tutor daily for some months. Roland consented, moved from his old quarters, and took a lodging for both in the same suburb as that in which the teacher resided. But soon, when they were under one roof, the boy's habitual tastes, and his repugnance to all paternal authority, were betrayed. To do my unhappy cousin justice (such as that justice is), though he had the cunning for a short disguise, he had not the hypocrisy to maintain systematic deceit. He could play a part for a while, from an exulting joy in his own address; but he could not wear a mask with the patience of cold-blooded dissimulation. Why enter into painful details, so easily divined by the intelligent reader? The faults of the son were precisely those to which Roland would be least indulgent. To the ordinary scrapes of high-spirited boyhood, no father, I am sure, would have been more lenient; but to anything that seemed low, petty—that grated on him as a gentleman and soldier—there, not for worlds would I have braved the darkness of his frown, and the woe that spoke like scorn in his voice. And when, after all warning and prohibition were in vain, Roland found his son in the middle of the night, in a resort of gamblers and sharpers, carrying all before him with his cue, in the full flush of triumph, and a great heap of five-franc pieces before him, you may conceive with what wrath the proud, hasty, passionate man drove out, cane in hand, the obscene associates, flinging after them the son's ill-gotten gains; and with what resentful humiliation the son was compelled to follow the father home. Then Roland took the boy to England, but not to the old Tower; that hearth of his ancestors was still too sacred for the footsteps of the vagrant heir!

CHAPTER V

THE HEARTH WITHOUT TRUST, AND THE WORLD WITHOUT A GUIDE

AND then, vainly grasping at every argument his blunt sense could suggest—then talked Roland much and grandly of the duties men owed—even if they threw off all love to their father—still to their father's name; and then his pride, always so lively, grew irritable and harsh, and seemed, no doubt, to the perverted ears of the son, unlovely and unloving. And that pride, without serving one purpose of good, did yet more mischief: for the youth caught the disease, but in a wrong way. And he said to himself—

"Ho, then, my father is a great man, with all these ancestors and big words! And he has lands and a castle—and yet how miserably we live, and how he stints me! But, if he has cause for pride in all these dead men, why, so have I. And are these lodgings, these appurtenances, fit for the 'gentleman' he says I am?"

Even in England, the gipsy blood broke out as before, and the youth found vagrant associates, Heaven knows how or where; and strange-looking forms, gaudily shabby and disreputably smart, were seen lurking in the corner of the street, or peering in at the window, slinking off if they saw Roland—and Roland could not stoop to be a spy. And the son's heart grew harder and harder against his father, and his father's face now never smiled on him. Then bills came in, and duns knocked at the door. Bills and duns to a man who shrunk from the thought of a debt as an ermine from a spot on its fur! And the son's short answer to remonstrance was,—"Am I not a gentleman?—these are the things gentlemen require." Then perhaps Roland remembered the experiment of his French friend, and left his bureau unlocked, and said, "Ruin me if you will, but no debts. There is money in those drawers—they are unlocked." That trust would for ever have cured of extravagance a youth with a high and delicate sense of honour: the pupil of the Gitanos did not understand the trust; he thought it conveyed a natural, though ungracious permission to take out what he wanted—and he took! To Roland this seemed a theft, and a theft of the coarsest kind; but when he so said, the son started indignant, and saw in that which had been so touching an appeal to his honour, but a trap to decoy him into disgrace. In short, neither could understand the other. Roland forbade his son to stir from the house; and the young man the same night let himself out, and stole forth into the wide world, to enjoy or defy it in his own wild way.

It would be tedious to follow him through his various adventures and experiments on fortune (even if I knew them all, which I do not). And now putting altogether aside his right name, which he had voluntarily abandoned, and not embarrassing the reader with the earlier aliases assumed, I shall give to my unfortunate kinsman the name by which I first knew him,

and continue to do so until—Heaven grant the time may come !
—having first redeemed, he may reclaim, his own.   It was in
joining a set of strolling players that Vivian became acquainted
with Peacock ; and that worthy, who had many strings to his
bow, soon grew aware of Vivian's extraordinary skill with the
cue, and saw therein a better mode of making their joint
fortunes than the boards of an itinerant Thespis furnished to
either.   Vivian listened to him, and it was while their intimacy
was most fresh that I met them on the high-road.   That chance
meeting produced (if I may be allowed to believe his assurance)
a strong, and, for the moment, a salutary effect upon Vivian.
The comparative innocence and freshness of a boy's mind were
new to him ; the elastic healthful spirits with which those gifts
were accompanied startled him, by the contrast to his own
forced gaiety and secret gloom.   And this boy was his own
cousin !

Coming afterwards to London, he adventured inquiry at the
hotel in the Strand at which I had given my address ; learned
where we were ; and passing one night into the street, saw
my uncle at the window—to recognise and to fly from him.
Having then some money at his disposal, he broke off abruptly
from the set in which he had been thrown.   He had resolved
to return to France—he would try for a more respectable mode
of existence.   He had not found happiness in that liberty he
had won, nor room for the ambition that began to gnaw him, in
those pursuits from which his father had vainly warned him.
His most reputable friend was his old tutor ; he would go to
him.   He went ; but the tutor was now married, and was himself a father, and that made a wonderful alteration in his
practical ethics.   It was no longer moral to aid the son in
rebellion to his father.   Vivian evinced his usual sarcastic
haughtiness at the reception he met, and was requested civilly
to leave the house.   Then again he flung himself on his wits at
Paris.   But there were plenty of wits there sharper than his
own.   He got into some quarrel with the police—not, indeed,
for any dishonest practices of his own, but from an unwary
acquaintance with others less scrupulous, and deemed it prudent
to quit France.   Thus had I met him again, forlorn and ragged,
in the streets of London.

Meanwhile Roland, after the first vain search, had yielded to
the indignation and disgust that had long rankled within him.
His son had thrown off his authority, because it preserved him
from dishonour.   His ideas of discipline were stern, and patience

had been well-nigh crushed out of his heart. He thought he could bear to resign his son to his fate—to disown him, and to say, "I have no more a son." It was in this mood that he had first visited our house. But when, on that memorable night in which he had narrated to his thrilling listeners the dark tale of a fellow-sufferer's woe and crime—betraying in the tale, to my father's quick sympathy, his own sorrow and passion—it did not need much of his gentler brother's subtle art to learn or guess the whole, nor much of Austin's mild persuasion to convince Roland that he had not yet exhausted all efforts to track the wanderer and reclaim the erring child. Then he had gone to London—then he had sought every spot which the outcast would probably haunt—then had he saved and pinched from his own necessities to have wherewithal to enter theatres and gaming-houses, and fee the agencies of police; then had he seen the form for which he had watched and pined, in the street below his window, and cried, in a joyous delusion, " He repents!" One day a letter reached my uncle, through his banker's, from the French tutor (who knew of no other means of tracing Roland but through the house by which his salary had been paid), informing him of his son's visit. Roland started instantly for Paris. Arriving there, he could only learn of his son through the police, and from them only learn that he had been seen in the company of accomplished swindlers, who were already in the hands of justice; but that the youth himself, whom there was nothing to criminate, had been suffered to quit Paris, and had taken, it was supposed, the road to England. Then, at last, the poor Captain's stout heart gave way. His son the companion of swindlers!—could he be sure that he was not their accomplice? If not yet, how small the step between companionship and participation! He took the child left him still from the convent, returned to England, and arrived there to be seized with fever and delirium—apparently on the same day (or a day before that on which) the son had dropped, shelterless and penniless, on the stones of London.

CHAPTER VI

THE ATTEMPT TO BUILD A TEMPLE TO FORTUNE OUT OF
THE RUINS OF HOME

BUT," said Vivian, pursuing his tale, "but when you came to
my aid, not knowing me—when you relieved me—when
from your own lips, for the first time, I heard words that praised
me, and for qualities that implied I might yet be ' worth much '
—Ah ! (he added mournfully) I remember the very words—a
new light broke upon me—struggling and dim, but light still.
The ambition with which I had sought the truckling Frenchman
revived, and took worthier and more definite form.   I would lift
myself above the mire, make a name, rise in life ! "
    Vivian's head drooped, but he raised it quickly, and laughed
his low, mocking laugh.   What follows of this tale may be told
succinctly.   Retaining his bitter feelings towards his father, he
resolved to continue his incognito—he gave himself a name
likely to mislead conjecture, if I conversed him to my family,
since he knew that Roland was aware that a Colonel Vivian had
been afflicted by a runaway son—and, indeed, the talk upon
that subject had first put the notion of flight into his own head.
He caught at the idea of becoming known to Trevanion ; but
he saw reasons to forbid his being indebted to me for the introduction—to forbid my knowing where he was : sooner or later
that knowledge could scarcely fail to end in the discovery of his
real name.   Fortunately, as he deemed, for the plans he began
to meditate, we were all leaving London—he should have the
stage to himself.   And then boldly he resolved upon what he
regarded as the master-scheme of life—viz., to obtain a small
pecuniary independence, and to emancipate himself formally
and entirely from his father's control.   Aware of poor Roland's
chivalrous reverence for his name, firmly persuaded that Roland
had no love for the son, but only the dread that the son might
disgrace him, he determined to avail himself of his father's
prejudices in order to effect his purpose.
    He wrote a short letter to Roland (that letter which had
given the poor man so sanguine a joy—that letter after reading
which he had said to Blanche, " pray for me "), stating simply
that he wished to see his father ; and naming a tavern in the
City for the meeting.

The interview took place. And when Roland, love and forgiveness in his heart,—but (who shall blame him?) dignity on his brow and rebuke in his eye—approached, ready at a word to fling himself on the boy's breast, Vivian, seeing only the outer signs, and interpreting them by his own sentiments—recoiled, folded his arms on his bosom, and said coldly, "Spare me reproach, sir—it is unavailing. I seek you only to propose that you shall save your name and resign your son."

Then, intent perhaps but to gain his object, the unhappy youth declared his fixed determination never to live with his father, never to acquiesce in his authority, resolutely to pursue his own career, whatever that career might be, explaining none of the circumstances that appeared most in his disfavour—rather, perhaps, thinking that, the worse his father judged of him, the more chance he had to achieve his purpose. "All I ask of you," he said, "is this: Give me the least you can afford to preserve me from the temptation to rob, or the necessity to starve; and I, in my turn, promise never to molest you in life—never to degrade you in my death; whatever my misdeeds, they will never reflect on yourself, for you shall never recognise the misdoer! The name you prize so highly shall be spared." Sickened and revolted, Roland attempted no argument—there was that in the son's cold manner which shut out hope, and against which his pride rose indignant. A meeker man might have remonstrated, implored, and wept—that was not in Roland's nature. He had but the choice of three evils, to say to his son: "Fool, I command thee to follow me!" or say, "Wretch, since thou wouldst cast me off as a stranger, as a stranger I say to thee—Go, starve or rob as thou wilt!" or lastly, to bow his proud head, stunned by the blow, and say, "Thou refusest me the obedience of the son, thou demandest to be as the dead to me. I can control thee not from vice, I can guide thee not to virtue. Thou wouldst sell me the name I have inherited stainless, and have as stainless borne. Be it so!—Name thy price!"

And something like this last was the father's choice.

He listened and was long silent; and then he said slowly, "Pause before you decide."

"I have paused long—my decision is made! this is the last time we meet. I see before me now the way to fortune, fairly, honourably; you can aid me in it only in the way I have said. Reject me now, and the option may never come again to either!"

And then Roland said to himself, "I have spared and saved

for this son; what care I for aught else than enough to live without debt, creep into a corner, and await the grave! And the more I can give, why, the better chance that he will abjure the vile associate and the desperate course." And so, out of his small income, Roland surrendered to the rebel child more than the half.

Vivian was not aware of his father's fortune—he did not suppose the sum of two hundred pounds a year was an allowance so disproportioned to Roland's means—yet when it was named, even he was struck by the generosity of one to whom he himself had given the right to say, "I take thee at thy word; 'just enough not to starve!'"

But then that hateful cynicism which, caught from bad men and evil books, he called "knowledge of the world," made him think "it is not for me, it is only for his name;" and he said aloud, "I accept these terms, sir; here is the address of a solicitor with whom yours can settle them. Farewell for ever."

At those last words Roland started, and stretched out his arms vaguely like a blind man. But Vivian had already thrown open the window (the room was on the ground floor) and sprang upon the sill. "Farewell," he repeated; "tell the world I am dead."

He leapt into the street, and the father drew in the outstretched arms, smote his heart, and said—"Well, then, my task in the world of man is over! I will back to the old ruin—the wreck to the wrecks—and the sight of tombs I have at least rescued from dishonour shall comfort me for all!"

CHAPTER VII

THE RESULTS—PERVERTED AMBITION—SELFISH PASSION—THE
INTELLECT DISTORTED BY THE CROOKEDNESS OF THE HEART

VIVIAN'S schemes thus prospered. He had an income that permitted him the outward appearances of a gentleman—an independence, modest indeed, but independence still. We were all gone from London. One letter to me with the postmark of the town near which Colonel Vivian lived, sufficed to confirm my belief in his parentage, and in his return to his friends. He then presented himself to Trevanion as the young man whose pen I had employed in the member's service; and

Chris
Hammond
'97

"*Roland started, and stretched out his arms vaguely like a blind man*"

knowing that I had never mentioned his name to Trevanion—
for, without Vivian's permission, I should not, considering his
apparent trust in me, have deemed myself authorised to do so
—he took that of Gower, which he selected, haphazard, from
an old Court Guide, as having the advantage—in common with
most names borne by the higher nobility of England—of not
being confined, as the ancient names of untitled gentlemen
usually are, to the members of a single family. And when, with
his wonted adaptability and suppleness, he had contrived to lay
aside, or smooth over, whatever in his manners would be calculated to displease Trevanion, and had succeeded in exciting the
interest which that generous statesman always conceived for
ability, he owned, candidly, one day, in the presence of Lady
Ellinor—for his experience had taught him the comparative
ease with which the sympathy of woman is enlisted in anything
that appeals to the imagination, or seems out of the ordinary
beat of life—that he had reasons for concealing his connections
for the present—that he had cause to believe I suspected what
they were, and from mistaken regard for his welfare, might
acquaint his relations with his whereabout. He therefore
begged Trevanion, if the latter had occasion to write to me, not
to mention him. This promise Trevanion gave, though reluctantly; for the confidence volunteered to him seemed to
exact the promise; but as he detested mystery of all kinds, the
avowal might have been fatal to any farther acquaintance; and
under auspices so doubtful, there would have been no chance
of his obtaining that intimacy in Trevanion's house which he
desired to establish, but for an accident which at once opened
that house to him almost as a home.

Vivian had always treasured a lock of his mother's hair, cut
off on her deathbed; and when he was at his French tutor's,
his first pocket-money had been devoted to the purchase of a
locket, on which he had caused to be inscribed his own name
and his mother's. Through all his wanderings he had worn
this relic : and in the direst pangs of want, no hunger had been
keen enough to induce him to part with it. Now, one morning
the ribbon that suspended the locket gave way, and his eye
resting on the names inscribed on the gold, he thought, in his
own vague sense of right, imperfect as it was, that his compact
with his father obliged him to have the names erased. He took
it to a jeweller in Piccadilly for that purpose, and gave the
requisite order, not taking notice of a lady in the further part of
the shop. The locket was still on the counter after Vivian had

left, when the lady coming forward observed it, and saw the
names on the surface. She had been struck by the peculiar
tone of the voice, which she had heard before ; and that very
day Mr. Gower received a note from Lady Ellinor Trevanion,
requesting to see him. Much wondering, he went. Presenting
him with the locket, she said, smiling, "There is only one
gentleman in the world who calls himself *De* Caxton, unless it
be his son. Ah ! I see now why you wished to conceal yourself
from my friend Pisistratus. But how is this ? can you have any
difference with your father ? Confide in me, or it is my duty to
write to him."

Even Vivian's powers of dissimulation abandoned him, thus
taken by surprise. He saw no alternative but to trust Lady
Ellinor with his secret, and implore her to respect it. And
then he spoke bitterly of his father's dislike to him, and his own
resolution to prove the injustice of that dislike by the position
he would himself establish in the world. At present his father
believed him dead, and perhaps was not ill-pleased to think so.
He would not dispel that belief, till he could redeem any boyish
errors, and force his family to be proud to acknowledge him.

Though Lady Ellinor was slow to believe that Roland could
dislike his son, she could yet readily believe that he was harsh
and choleric, with a soldier's high notions of discipline : the
young man's story moved her, his determination pleased her
own high spirit ;—always with a touch of romance in her, and
always sympathising with each desire of ambition, she entered
into Vivian's aspirations with an alacrity that surprised himself.
She was charmed with the idea of ministering to the son's
fortunes, and ultimately reconciling him to the father,—through
her own agency ;—it would atone for any fault of which Roland
could accuse herself in the old time.

She undertook to impart the secret to Trevanion, for she
would have no secrets from him, and to secure his acquiescence
in its concealment from all others.

And here I must a little digress from the chronological course
of my explanatory narrative, to inform the reader that, when
Lady Ellinor had her interview with Roland, she had been
repelled by the sternness of his manner from divulging Vivian's
secret. But on her first attempt to sound or conciliate him,
she had begun with some eulogies on Trevanion's new friend
and assistant, Mr. Gower, and had awakened Roland's suspicions
of that person's identity with his son—suspicions which had
given him a terrible interest in our joint deliverance of Miss

Trevanion. But so heroically had the poor soldier sought to resist his own fears, that on the way he shrank to put to me the questions that might paralyse the energies which, whatever the answer, were then so much needed. "For," said he to my father, "I felt the blood surging to my temples; and if I had said to Pisistratus, 'Describe this man,' and by his description I had recognised my son, and dreaded lest I might be too late to arrest him from so treacherous a crime, my brain would have given way;—and so I did not care!"

I return to the thread of my story. From the time that Vivian confided in Lady Ellinor, the way was cleared to his most ambitious hopes; and though his acquisitions were not sufficiently scholastic and various to permit Trevanion to select him as a secretary, yet, short of sleeping at the house, he was little less intimate there than I had been.

Among Vivian's schemes of advancement, that of winning the hand and heart of the great heiress had not been one of the least sanguine. This hope was annulled when, not long after his intimacy at her father's house, she became engaged to young Lord Castleton. But he could not see Miss Trevanion with impunity (alas! who, with a heart yet free, could be insensible to attractions so winning?) He permitted the love—such love as his wild, half-educated, half-savage nature acknowledged—to creep into his soul—to master it; but he felt no hope, cherished no scheme while the young lord lived. With the death of her betrothed, Fanny was free; then he began to hope—not yet to scheme. Accidently he encountered Peacock—partly from the levity that accompanied a false good-nature that was constitutional with him, partly from a vague idea that the man might be useful, Vivian established his quondam associate in the service of Trevanion. Peacock soon gained the secret of Vivian's love for Fanny, and, dazzled by the advantages that a marriage with Miss Trevanion would confer on his patron, and might reflect on himself, and delighted at an occasion to exercise his dramatic accomplishments on the stage of real life, he soon practised the lesson that the theatres had taught him—viz., to make a sub-intrigue between maid and valet serve the schemes and ensure the success of the lover. If Vivian had some opportunities to imply his admiration, Miss Trevanion gave him none to plead his cause. But the softness of her nature, and that graceful kindness which surrounded her like an atmosphere, emanating unconsciously from a girl's harmless desire to please, tended to deceive him. His own personal gifts were so rare, and, in his wandering life, the effect they had produced had so increased his reliance on them, that he thought he wanted but the fair opportunity to woo in order to win. In this state of mental intoxication, Trevanion having provided for his Scotch secretary, took him to Lord N——'s. His hostess was one of those middle-aged ladies of fashion, who like to patronise and bring forward young men, accepting gratitude for condescension, as a homage to beauty. She was struck by Vivian's exterior, and that "picturesque" in look and in manner which belonged to him. Naturally garrulous and indiscreet, she was unreserved to a pupil whom she conceived the whim to make "*au fait* to society." Thus she talked to him among other topics in fashion, of Miss Trevanion, and expressed her belief that the present Lord Castleton had always admired her; but it was only on his accession to the marquisate that he had made up his mind to marry, or, from his knowledge of Lady Ellinor's ambition, thought that the Marquis of Castleton might achieve the prize which would have been refused to Sir Sedley Beaudesert. Then, to corroborate the predictions she hazarded, she repeated, perhaps with exaggeration, some passages from Lord Castleton's replies to her own suggestions on the subject. Vivian's alarm became fatally excited; unregulated passions easily obscured a reason so long perverted, and a conscience so habitually dulled. There is an instinct in all intense affection (whether it be corrupt or pure) that usually makes its jealousy prophetic. Thus, from the first, out of all the brilliant idlers round Fanny Trevanion, my jealousy had pre-eminently fastened on Sir Sedley Beaudesert, though, to all seeming, without a cause. From the same instinct, Vivian had conceived the same vague jealousy—a jealousy, in his instance, coupled with a deep dislike to his supposed rival, who had wounded his self-love. For the marquis, though to be haughty or ill-bred was impossible to the blandness of his nature, had never shown to Vivian the genial courtesies he had lavished upon me, and kept politely aloof from his acquaintance—while Vivian's personal vanity had been wounded by that drawing-room effect which the proverbial winner of all hearts produced without an effort—an effect that threw into the shade the youth and the beauty (more striking but infinitely less prepossessing) of the adventurous rival. Thus animosity to Lord Castleton conspired with Vivian's passion for Fanny to rouse all that was worst by nature and by rearing in this audacious and turbulent spirit.

His confidant Peacock suggested, from his stage experience, the outlines of a plot, to which Vivian's astuter intellect instantly gave tangibility and colouring. Peacock had already found Miss Trevanion's waiting-woman ripe for any measure that might secure himself as her husband, and a provision for life as a reward. Two or three letters between them settled the preliminary engagements. A friend of the ex-comedian's had lately taken an inn on the north road, and might be relied upon. At that inn it was settled that Vivian should meet Miss Trevanion, whom Peacock, by the aid of the abigail, engaged to lure there. The sole difficulty that then remained would, to most men, have seemed the greatest—viz., the consent of Miss Trevanion to a Scotch marriage. But Vivian hoped all things from his own eloquence, art, and passion; and by an inconsistency, however strange, still not unnatural in the twists of so crooked an intellect, he thought that, by insisting on the intention of her parents to sacrifice her youth to the very man of whose attractions he was most jealous—by the picture of disparity of years, by the caricature of his rival's foibles and frivolities, by the commonplaces of "beauty bartered for ambition," &c., he might enlist her fears of the alternative on the side of the choice urged upon her. The plan proceeded, the time came: Peacock pretended the excuse of a sick relation to leave Trevanion; and Vivian a day before, on pretence of visiting the picturesque scenes in the neighbourhood, obtained leave of absence. Thus the plot went on to its catastrophe.

"And I need not ask," said I, trying in vain to conceal my indignation, "how Miss Trevanion received your monstrous proposition!"

Vivian's pale cheek grew paler, but he made no reply.

"And if we had not arrived, what would you have done? Oh, dare you look into the gulf of infamy you have escaped!"

"I cannot, and I will not bear this!" exclaimed Vivian, starting up. "I have laid my heart bare before you, and it is ungenerous and unmanly thus to press upon its wounds. You can moralise, you can speak coldly—but—I—I loved!"

"And do you think," I burst forth,—"do you think that I did not love too!—love longer than you have done; better than you have done; gone through sharper struggles, darker days, more sleepless nights than you,—and yet——"

Vivian caught hold of me.

"Hush!" he cried; "is this indeed true! I thought you might have had some faint and fleeting fancy for Miss Trevanion,

but that you curbed and conquered it at once.   Oh no! it was
impossible to have loved really, and to have surrendered all
chance as you did!—have left the house, have fled from her
presence!   No—no! that was not love!"

"It *was* love! and I pray Heaven to grant that, one day, you
may know how little your affection sprang from those feelings
which make true love sublime as honour, and meek as is religion!
Oh! cousin, cousin—with these rare gifts, what you might have
been! what, if you will pass through repentance, and cling to
atonement—what, I dare hope, you may yet be.   Talk not now
of your love; I talk not of mine!   Love is a thing gone from the
lives of both.   Go back to earlier thoughts, to heavier wrongs!
—your father!—that noble heart which you have so wantonly
lacerated, which you have so little comprehended!"

Then with all the warmth of emotion I hurried on—showed
him the true nature of honour and of Roland (for the names
were one!)—showed him the watch, the hope, the manly
anguish I had witnessed, and wept—I, not his son—to see;
showed him the poverty and privation to which the father, even
at the last, had condemned himself, so that the son might have
no excuse for the sins that Want whispers to the weak.   This,
and much more, and I suppose with the pathos that belongs to
all earnestness, I enforced, sentence after sentence—yielding to
no interruption, over-mastering all dissent! driving in the truth,
nail after nail, as it were, into the obdurate heart, that I constrained and grappled to.   And at last, the dark, bitter, cynical
nature gave way, and the young man fell sobbing at my feet, and
cried aloud, "Spare me, spare me!   I see it all now!   Wretch
that I have been!"

CHAPTER VIII

ON leaving Vivian I did not presume to promise him Roland's
immediate pardon.   I did not urge him to attempt to see
his father.   I felt the time was not come for either pardon
or interview.   I contented myself with the victory I had
already gained.   I judged it right that thought, solitude, and
suffering should imprint more deeply the lesson, and prepare
the way to the steadfast resolution of reform.   I left him seated
by the stream, and with the promise to inform him at the small
hostelry, where he took up his lodging, how Roland struggled
through his illness.

On returning to the inn, I was uneasy to see how long a time had elapsed since I had left my uncle. But on coming into his room, to my surprise and relief, I found him up and dressed, and with a serene, though fatigued, expression of countenance. He asked me no questions where I had been—perhaps from sympathy with my feelings in parting with Miss Trevanion—perhaps from conjecture that the indulgence of those feelings had not wholly engrossed my time.

But he said simply, " I think I understood from you that you had sent for Austin—is it so ? "

" Yes, sir ; but I named ——, as the nearest point to the Tower, for the place of meeting."

" Then let us go hence forthwith—nay, I shall be better for the change. And here, there must be curiosity, conjecture—torture ! "—said he, locking his hands tightly together : " order the horses at once ! "

I left the room accordingly ; and while they were getting ready the horses, I ran to the place where I had left Vivian. He was still there, in the same attitude, covering his face with his hands, as if to shut out the sun. I told him hastily of Roland's improvement, of our approaching departure, and asked him an address in London at which I could find him. He gave me as his direction the same lodging at which I had so often visited him. " If there be no vacancy there for me," said he, " I shall leave word where I am to be found. But I would gladly be where I was before—" He did not finish the sentence. I pressed his hand, and left him.

CHAPTER IX

SOME days have elapsed : we are in London, my father with us ; and Roland has permitted Austin to tell me his tale, and received through Austin all that Vivian's narrative to me suggested, whether in extenuation of the past, or in hope of redemption in the future. And Austin has inex pressibly soothed his brother. And Roland's ordinary roughness has gone, and his looks are meek, and his voice low. But he talks little, and smiles never. He asks me no questions ; does not to *me* name his son, nor recur to the voyage to Australia, nor ask " why it is put off ; " nor interest himself as before in preparations for it—he has no heart for anything.

2 c

The voyage *is* put off till the next vessel sails, and I have seen Vivian twice or thrice, and the result of the interviews has disappointed and depressed me. It seems to me that much of the previous effect I had produced is already obliterated. At the very sight of the great Babel—the evidence of the ease, the luxury, the wealth, the pomp;—the strife, the penury, the famine, and the rags, which the focus of civilisation, in the disparities of old societies, inevitably gathers together—the fierce combative disposition seemed to awaken again; the perverted ambition, the hostility to the world; the wrath, the scorn; the war with man, and the rebellious murmur against Heaven. There was still the one redeeming point of repentance for his wrongs to his father—his heart was still softened there; and, attendant on that softness, I hailed a principle more like that of honour than I had yet recognised in Vivian. He cancelled the agreement which had assured him of a provision at the cost of his father's comforts. "At least, there," he said, "I will injure him no more!"

But while, on this point, repentance seemed genuine, it was not so with regard to his conduct towards Miss Trevanion. His gipsy nurture, his loose associates, his extravagant French romances, his theatrical mode of looking upon love intrigues and stage plots, seemed all to rise between his intelligence and the due sense of the fraud and treachery he had practised. He seemed to feel more shame at the exposure than at the guilt; more despair at the failure of success than gratitude at escape from crime. In a word, the nature of a whole life was not to be remodelled at once—at least by an artificer so unskilled as I.

After one of these interviews, I stole into the room where Austin sat with Roland, and, watching a seasonable moment when Roland, shaking off a reverie, opened his Bible, and sat down to it, with each muscle in his face set, as I had seen it before, into iron resolution, I beckoned my father from the room.

PISISTRATUS.—"I have again seen my cousin. I cannot make the way I wished. My dear father, *you* must see him."

MR. CAXTON.—"I?—yes, assuredly, if I can be of any service. But will he listen to me?"

PISISTRATUS.—"I think so. A young man will often respect in his elder what he will resent as a presumption in his contemporary."

MR. CAXTON.—"It may be so: (then more thoughtfully), but you describe this strange boy's mind as a wreck!—in what part of the mouldering timbers can I fix the grappling-hook? Here, it seems that most of the supports on which we can best rely, when we would save another, fail us. Religion, honour, the associations of childhood, the bonds of home, filial obedience— even the intelligence of self-interest, in the philosophical sense of the word. And I, too!—a mere bookman! My dear son!— I despair!"

PISISTRATUS.—"No, you do not despair—no, you must succeed; for, if you do not, what is to become of Uncle Roland? Do you not see his heart is fast breaking?"

MR. CAXTON.—"Get me my hat; I will go. I will save this Ishmael—I will not leave him till he is saved!"

PISISTRATUS (some minutes after, as they are walking towards Vivian's lodging).—"You ask me what support you are to cling to. A strong and a good one, sir."

MR. CAXTON.—"Ah! what is that?"

PISISTRATUS.—"Affection! there is a nature capable of strong affection at the core of this wild heart! He could love his mother; tears gush to his eyes at her name—he would have starved rather than part with the memorial of that love. It was his belief in his father's indifference, or dislike, that hardened and embruted him—it is only when he hears how that father loved him, that I now melt his pride and curb his passions. You have affection to deal with!—do you despair now?"

My father turned on me those eyes so inexpressibly benign and mild, and replied softly, "No!"

We reached the house; and my father said, as we knocked at the door, "If he is at home, leave me. This is a hard study to which you have set me; I must work at it alone."

Vivian was at home, and the door closed on his visitor. My father stayed some hours.

On returning home, to my great surprise I found Trevanion with my uncle. He had found us out—no easy matter, I should think. But a good impulse in Trevanion was not of that feeble kind which turns home at the sight of a difficulty. He had come to London on purpose to see and to thank us.

I did not think there had been so much of delicacy—of what I may call the "beauty of kindness"—in a man whom incessant business had rendered ordinarily blunt and abrupt. I hardly recognised the impatient Trevanion in the soothing, tender, subtle respect that rather implied than spoke gratitude, and sought to insinuate what he owed to the unhappy father, without touching on his wrongs from the son. But of this kindness

—which showed how Trevanion's high nature of gentleman raised him aloof from that coarseness of thought which those absorbed wholly in practical affairs often contract—of this kindness, so noble and so touching, Roland seemed scarcely aware. He sat by the embers of the neglected fire, his hands grasping the arms of his elbow-chair, his head drooping on his bosom ; and only by a deep hectic flush on his dark cheek could you have seen that he distinguished between an ordinary visitor and the man whose child he had helped to save.   This minister of state—this high member of the elect, at whose gift are places, peerages, gold sticks, and ribbons—has nothing at his command for the bruised spirit of the half-pay soldier.   Before that poverty, that grief, and that pride, the King's Counsellor was powerless.   Only when Trevanion rose to depart, something like a sense of the soothing intention which the visit implied seemed to rouse the repose of the old man, and to break the ice at its surface ; for he followed Trevanion to the door, took both his hands, pressed them, then turned away, and resumed his seat.   Trevanion beckoned to me, and I followed him downstairs, and into a little parlour which was unoccupied.

After some remarks upon Roland, full of deep and considerate feeling, and one quick, hurried reference to the son—to the effect that his guilty attempt would never be known by the world—Trevanion then addressed himself to me with a warmth and urgency that took me by surprise.   " After what has passed," he exclaimed, " I cannot suffer you to leave England thus.   Let me not feel with you, as with your uncle, that there is nothing by which I can repay—no, I will not so put it—stay and serve your country at home : it is my prayer—it is Ellinor's.   Out of all at my disposal, it will go hard but what I shall find something to suit you."   And then, hurrying on, Trevanion spoke flatteringly of my pretensions, in right of birth and capabilities, to honourable employment, and placed before me a picture of public life—its prizes and distinctions—which, for the moment at least, made my heart beat loud and my breath come quick. But still, even then, I felt (was it an unreasonable pride ?) that there was something that jarred, something that humbled, in the thought of holding all my fortunes as a dependency on the father of the woman I loved, but might not aspire to ;—something even of personal degradation in the mere feeling that I was thus to be repaid for a service, and recompensed for a loss. But these were not reasons I could advance ; and, indeed, so for the time did Trevanion's generosity and eloquence overpower me, that I could only falter out my thanks, and my promise that I would consider and let him know.

With that promise he was forced to content himself; he told me to direct to him at his favourite country seat, whither he was going that day, and so left me. I looked round the humble parlour of the mean lodging-house, and Trevanion's words came again before me like a flash of golden light. I stole into the open air, and wandered through the crowded streets, agitated and disturbed.

CHAPTER X

SEVERAL days elapsed—and of each day my father spent a considerable part at Vivian's lodgings. But he maintained a reserve as to his success, begged me not to question him, and to refrain also for the present from visiting my cousin. My uncle guessed or knew his brother's mission; for I observed that, whenever Austin went noiseless away, his eye brightened, and the colour rose in a hectic flush to his cheek. At last my father came to me one morning, his carpet-bag in his hand, and said, "I am going away for a week or two. Keep Roland company till I return."

"Going with *him* ?"

"With him."

"That is a good sign."

"I hope so: that is all I can say now."

The week had not quite passed when I received from my father the letter I am about to place before the reader, and you may judge how earnestly his soul must have been in the task it had volunteered, if you observe how little, comparatively speaking, the letter contains of the subtleties and pedantries (may the last word be pardoned, for it is scarcely a just one) which ordinarily left my father, a scholar even in the midst of his emotions. He seemed here to have abandoned his books, to have put the human heart before the eyes of his pupil, and said, "Read and *un*-learn!"

To Pisistratus Caxton.

"MY DEAR SON,—It were needless to tell you all the earlier difficulties I have had to encounter with my charge, nor to repeat all the means which, acting on your suggestion (a correct

one), I have employed to arouse feelings long ,dormant and
confused, and allay others, long prematurely active and terribly
distinct.   The evil was simply this: here was the intelligence
of a man in all that is evil—and the ignorance of an infant in all
that is good. In matters merely worldly, what wonderful acumen!
in the plain principles of right and wrong, what gross and stolid
obtuseness!   At one time, I am straining all my poor wit to
grapple in an encounter on the knottiest mysteries of social life;
at another, I am guiding reluctant fingers over the horn-book of
the most obvious morals.   Here hieroglyphics, and there pot-
hooks!   But as long as there is affection in a man, why, there is
Nature to begin with!   To get rid of all the rubbish laid upon
her, clear back the way to that Nature, and start afresh—that is
one's only chance.

"Well, by degrees I won my way, waiting patiently till the
bosom, pleased with the relief, disgorged itself of all ' its perilous
stuff,'—not chiding—not even remonstrating, seeming almost
to sympathise, till I got him, Socratically, to disprove himself.
When I saw that he no longer feared me—that my company
had become a relief to him—I proposed an excursion, and did
not tell him whither.

"Avoiding as much as possible the main north road (for I did
not wish, as you may suppose, to set fire to a train of associations
that might blow us up to the dog-star), and, where that avoid-
ance was not possible, travelling by night, I got him into the
neighbourhood of the old Tower.   I would not admit him under
its roof.   But you know the little inn, three miles off, near the
trout stream ?—we made our abode there.

"Well, I have taken him into the village, preserving his incognito.   I have entered with him into cottages, and turned the
talk upon Roland.   You know how your uncle is adored ; you
know what anecdotes of his bold, warm-hearted youth once,
and now of his kind and charitable age, would spring up from
the garrulous lips of gratitude!   I made him see with his own
eyes, hear with his own ears, how all who knew Roland loved
and honoured him—except his son.   Then I took him round the
ruins—(still not suffering him to enter the house), for those
ruins are the key to Roland's character—seeing them, one sees
the pathos in his poor foible of family pride.   There, you dis-
tinguish it from the insolent boasts of the prosperous, and feel
that it is little more than the pious reverence to the dead—
'the tender culture of the tomb.'   We sat down on heaps of
mouldering stone, and it was there that I explained to him

what Roland was in youth, and what he had dreamed that a son would be to him. I showed him the graves of his ancestors, and explained to him why they were sacred in Roland's eyes! I had gained a great way, when he longed to enter the home that should have been his; and I could make him pause of his own accord, and say, ' No, I must first be worthy of it.' Then you would have smiled—sly satirist that you are—to have heard me impressing upon this acute, sharp-witted youth, all that we plain folk understand by the name of HOME—its perfect trust and truth, its simple holiness, its exquisite happiness—being to the world what conscience is to the human mind. And after that, I brought in his sister, whom till then he had scarcely named—for whom he scarcely seemed to care—brought her in to aid the father, and endear the home. ' And you know,' said I, 'that if Roland were to die, it would be a brother's duty to supply his place; to shield her innocence—to protect her name! A good name is something, then. Your father was not so wrong to prize it. You would like yours to be that which your sister would be proud to own!'

" While we were talking, Blanche suddenly came to the spot, and rushed to my arms. She looked on him as a stranger; but I saw his knees tremble. And then she was about to put her hand in his—but I drew her back. Was I cruel? He thought so. But when I dismissed her, I replied to his reproach, ' Your sister is a part of Home. If you think yourself worthy of either, go and claim both; I will not object.'—' She has my mother's eyes,' said he, and walked away. I left him to muse amidst the ruins, while I went in to see your poor mother, and relieve her fears about Roland, and make her understand why I could not yet return *home*.

" This brief sight of his sister has sunk deep into him. But I now approach what seems to me the great difficulty of the whole. He is fully anxious to redeem his name—to regain his home. So far so well. But he cannot yet see ambition, except with hard, worldly eyes. He still fancies that all he has to do is to get money and power, and some of those empty prizes in the Great Lottery which we often win more easily by our sins than our virtues. (Here follows a long passage from Seneca, omitted as superfluous.) He does not yet even understand me—or, if he does, he fancies me a mere bookworm indeed, when I imply that he might be poor, and obscure, at the bottom of fortune's wheel, and yet be one we should be proud of! He supposes that, to redeem his name, he has only got to lacker it. Don't think me merely the fond father, when I add my hope that I shall use you to advantage here. I mean to talk to him to-morrow, as we return to London, of you, and of your ambition : you shall hear the result.

" At this moment (it is past midnight), I hear his step in the room above me. The window-sash aloft opens—for the third time : would to Heaven he could read the true astrology of the stars ! There they are—bright, luminous, benignant. And I seeking to chain this wandering comet into the harmonies of heaven ! Better task than that of astrologers, and astronomers to boot ! Who among them can ' loosen the band of Orion ' ?— but who amongst us may not be permitted by God to have sway over the action and orbit of the human soul ?—Your ever affectionate father,   A. C."

Two days after the receipt of this letter, came the following ; and though I would fain suppress those references to myself which must be ascribed to a father's partiality, yet it is so needful to retain them in connection with Vivian, that I have no choice but to leave the tender flatteries to the indulgence of the kind.

" MY DEAR SON,—I was not too sanguine as to the effect that your simple story would produce upon your cousin. Without implying any contrast to his own conduct, I described that scene in which you threw yourself upon our sympathy, in the struggle between love and duty, and asked for our counsel and support; when Roland gave you his blunt advice to tell all to Trevanion ; and when, amidst such sorrow as the heart in youth seems scarcely large enough to hold, you caught at truth impulsively, and the truth bore you safe from the shipwreck. I recounted your silent and manly struggles—your resolution not to suffer the egotism of passion to unfit you for the aims and ends of that spiritual probation which we call LIFE. I showed you as you were, still thoughtful for us, interested in our interests— smiling on us, that we might not guess that you wept in secret ! Oh, my son—my son ! do not think that, in those times, I did not feel and pray for you ! And while he was melted by my own emotion, I turned from your love to your ambition. I made him see that you, too, had known the restlessness which belongs to young ardent natures ; that you, too, had your dreams of fortune, and aspirations for success. But I painted that ambition in its true colours : it was not the desire of a selfish intellect, to be in yourself a somebody—a something—raised a step or two in the social ladder, for the pleasure of looking down on those at the foot, but the warmer yearning of a generous heart: your ambition was to repair your father's losses—minister to your father's very foible, in *his* idle desire of fame—supply to your uncle what he had lost in his natural heir —link your success to useful objects, your interests to those of your kind, your reward to the proud and grateful smiles of those you loved. That was thine ambition O my tender Anachronism! And when, as I closed the sketch, I said, 'Pardon me: you know not what delight a father feels when, while sending a son away from him into the world, he can speak and think thus of him! But this, you see, is not your kind of ambition. Let us talk of making money, and driving a coach-and-four through this villainous world,'—your cousin sank into a profound reverie; and when he woke from it, it was like the waking of the earth after a night in spring—the bare trees had put forth buds!

"And, some time after, he startled me by a prayer that I would permit him, with his father's consent, to accompany you to Australia. The only answer I have given him as yet, has been in the form of a question: 'Ask yourself if I ought? I cannot wish Pisistratus to be other than he is, and unless you agree with him in all his principles and objects, ought I to incur the risk that you should give him your knowledge of the world, and inoculate him with your ambition?' He was struck, and had the candour to attempt no reply.

"Now, Pisistratus, the doubt I expressed to him is the doubt I feel. For, indeed, it is only by home-truths, not refining arguments, that I can deal with this unscholastic Scythian, who, fresh from the Steppes, comes to puzzle me in the Portico.

"On the one hand, what is to become of him in the Old World? At his age, and with his energies, it would be impossible to cage him with us in the Cumberland ruins; weariness and discontent would undo all we could do. He has no resource in books—and, I fear, never will have! But to send him forth into one of the overcrowded professions;—to place him amidst all those 'disparities of social life,' on the rough stones of which he is perpetually grinding his heart; turn him adrift amongst all the temptations to which he is most prone—this is a trial which, I fear, will be too sharp for a conversion so incomplete. In the New World, no doubt, his energies would find a safer field; and even the adventurous and desultory habits of his childhood might there be put to

healthful account.   Those complaints of the disparities of the
civilised world find, I suspect, an easier, if a bluffer, reply from
the political economist than the Stoic philosopher.   'You don't
like them, you find it hard to submit to them,' says the political
economist ; 'but they are the laws of a civilised state, and you
can't alter them.   Wiser men than you have tried to alter
them, and never succeeded, though they turned the earth
topsy-turvy !   Very well ; but the world is wide—go into a
state that is not so civilised.   The disparities of the Old World
vanish amidst the New !   Emigration is the reply of Nature
to the rebellious cry against Art.'   Thus would say the political
economist ; and, alas, even in your case, my son, I found no
reply to the reasonings !   I acknowledge, then, that Australia
might open the best safety-valve to your cousin's discontent
and desires; but I acknowledge also a counter-truth, which is
this—' It is not permitted to an honest man to corrupt himself
for the sake of others.'   That is almost the only maxim of
Jean Jacques to which I can cheerfully subscribe !   Do you
feel quite strong enough to resist all the influences which a
companionship of this kind may subject you to—strong enough
to bear his burden as well as your own—strong enough, also—
ay, and alert and vigilant enough—to prevent those influences
harming the others, whom you have undertaken to guide, and
whose lots are confided to you ?   Pause well, and consider
maturely, for this must not depend upon a generous impulse.
I think that your cousin would now pass under your charge
with a sincere desire for reform ; but between sincere desire
and steadfast performance there is a long and dreary interval—
even to the best of us.   Were it not for Roland, and had I one
grain less confidence in you, I could not entertain the thought
of laying on your young shoulders so great a responsibility.
But every new responsibility to an earnest nature is a new
prop to virtue ;—and all I now ask of you is—to remember
that it *is* a solemn and serious charge, not to be undertaken
without the most deliberate gauge and measure of the strength
with which it is to be borne.

  "In two days we shall be in London.—Yours, my Anachronism, anxiously and fondly,   A. C."

  I was in my own room while I read this letter, and I had
just finished it when, as I looked up, I saw Roland standing
opposite to me.   "It is from Austin," said he ; then he paused
a moment, and added, in a tone that seemed quite humble,

"May I see it?—and dare I?" I placed the letter in his hands, and retired a few paces, that he might not think I watched his countenance while he read it. And I was only aware that he had come to the end by a heavy, anxious, but not disappointed sigh. Then I turned, and our eyes met, and there was something in Roland's look, inquiring—and, as it were, imploring. I interpreted it at once.

"Oh yes, uncle," I said, smiling; "I have reflected, and I have no fear of the result. Before my father wrote, what he now suggests had become my secret wish. As for our other companions, their simple natures would defy all such sophistries as—but he is already half-cured of those. Let him come with me, and when he returns he shall be worthy of a place in your heart, beside his sister Blanche. I feel, I promise it—do not fear for me! Such a change will be a talisman to myself. I will shun every error that I might otherwise commit, so that he may have no example to entice him to err."

I know that in youth, and the superstition of first love, we are credulously inclined to believe that love, and the possession of the beloved, are the only happiness. But when my uncle folded me in his arms, and called me the hope of his age, and stay of his house—the music of my father's praise still ringing on my heart—I do affirm that I knew a prouder bliss than if Trevanion had placed Fanny's hand in mine, and said, "She is yours."

And now the die was cast—the decision made. It was with no regret that I wrote to Trevanion to decline his offers. Nor was the sacrifice so great—even putting aside the natural pride which had before inclined to it—as it may seem to some; for, restless though I was, I had laboured to constrain myself to other views of life than those which close the vistas of ambition with images of the terrestrial deities—Power and Rank. Had I not been behind the scenes, noted all of joy and of peace that the pursuit of power had cost Trevanion, and seen how little of happiness rank gave even to one of the polished habits and graceful attributes of Lord Castleton? Yet each nature seemed fitted so well—the first for power, the last for rank! It is marvellous with what liberality Providence atones for the partial dispensations of Fortune. Independence, or the vigorous pursuit of it; affection, with its hopes and its rewards; a life only rendered by Art more susceptible to Nature—in which the physical enjoyments are pure and healthful—in which the moral faculties expand harmoniously with the intellectual—and

the heart is at peace with the mind; is this a mean lot for
ambition to desire—and is it so far out of human reach?
"Know thyself," said the old philosophy. "Improve thyself,"
saith the new. The great object of the Sojourner in Time is
not to waste all his passions and gifts on the things external,
that he must leave behind—that which he cultivates within is
all that he can carry into the Eternal Progress. We are here
but as schoolboys, whose life begins where school ends; and the
battles we fought with our rivals, and the toys that we shared
with our playmates, and the names that we carved, high or low,
on the wall, above our desks—will they so much bestead us
hereafter! As new fates crowd upon us, can they more than
pass through the memory with a smile or a sigh? Look back
to thy schooldays, and answer.

CHAPTER XI

TWO weeks since the date of the preceding chapter have
passed; we have slept our last, for long years to come, on
the English soil. It is night—and Vivian has been admitted
to an interview with his father. They have been together
alone an hour and more, and I and my father will not disturb
them. But the clock strikes—the hour is late—the ship sails
to-night—we should be on board. And as we two stand below,
the door opens in the room above, and a heavy step descends
the stairs; the father is leaning on the son's arm. You should
see how timidly the son guides the halting step. And now as
the light gleams on their faces, there are tears on Vivian's
cheek; but the face of Roland seems calm and happy. Happy!
when about to be separated, perhaps for ever, from his son?
Yes, happy, because he has found a son for the first time; and
is not thinking of years and absence, and the chance of death
—but thankful for the Divine Mercy, and cherishing celestial
hope. If ye wonder why Roland is happy in such an hour, how
vainly have I sought to make him breathe, and live, and move
before you!

　　.　　　.　　　.　　　.　　　.　　　.　　　.　　　.

We are on board; our luggage all went first. I had had time,
with the help of a carpenter, to knock up cabins for Vivian,
Guy Bolding, and myself, in the hold. For, thinking we could
not too soon lay aside the pretensions of Europe—"*de*-fine-

gentlemanise" ourselves, as Trevanion recommended—we had engaged steerage passage, to the great humouring of our finances. We had, too, the luxury to be by ourselves, and our own Cumberland folks were round us, as our friends and servants both.

We are on board, and have looked our last on those we are to leave, and we stand on deck leaning on each other. We are on board, and the lights, near and far, shine from the vast City; and the stars are on high, bright and clear, as for the first mariners of old. Strange noises, rough voices, and crackling cords, and here and there the sobs of women mingling with the oaths of men. Now the swing and heave of the vessel— the dreary sense of exile that comes when the ship fairly moves over the waters. And still we stood, and looked, and listened; silent, and leaning on each other.

Night deepened, the City vanished—not a gleam from its myriad lights! The river widened and widened. How cold comes the wind!—is that a gale from the sea? The stars grow faint—the moon has sunk. And now, how desolate seem the waters in the comfortless grey of dawn! Then we shivered and looked at each other, and muttered something that was not the thought deepest at our hearts, and crept into our berths—feeling sure it was not for sleep. And sleep came on us, soft and kind. The ocean lulled the exiles as on a mother's breast.

PART XVII

CHAPTER I

THE stage-scene has dropped. Settle yourselves, my good audience; chat each with his neighbour. Dear madam, in the boxes, take up your opera-glass and look about you. Treat Tom and pretty Sal to some of those fine oranges, O thou happy-looking mother in the two-shilling gallery! Yes, brave 'prentice boys, in the tier above, the cat-call by all means! And you, "most potent, grave, and reverend seigneurs," in the front row of the pit — practised critics and steady old playgoers — who shake your heads at new actors and playwrights, and, true to the creed of your youth (for the which all honour to you!) firmly believe that we are shorter by the head than those giants our grandfathers—laugh or scold as you will, while the drop-scene still shuts out the stage. It is just that you should all amuse yourselves in your own way, O spectators! for the interval is long. All the actors have to change their dresses; all the scene-shifters are at work, sliding the "sides" of a new world into their grooves; and in high disdain of all unity of time, as of place, you will see in the play-bills that there is a great demand on your belief. You are called upon to suppose that we are older by five years than when you last saw us "fret our hour upon the stage." Five years! the author tells us especially to humour the belief by letting the drop-scene linger longer than usual between the lamps and the stage.

Play up! O ye fiddles and kettledrums! the time is elapsed. Stop that cat-call, young gentleman!—heads down in the pit there! Now the flourish is over—the scene draws up: look before.

A bright, clear, transparent atmosphere—bright as that of the East, but vigorous and bracing as the air of the North; a broad and fair river, rolling through wide grassy plains; yonder, far in the distance, stretch away vast forests of evergreen, and gentle slopes break the line of the cloudless horizon; see the

pastures, Arcadian with sheep in hundreds and thousands—
Thyrsis and Menalcas would have had hard labour to count
them, and small time, I fear, for singing songs about Daphne.
But, alas! Daphnes are rare: no nymphs with garlands and
crooks trip over those pastures.

Turn your eyes to the right, nearer the river; just parted by
a low fence from the thirty acres or so that are farmed for
amusement or convenience, not for profit—*that* comes from the
sheep—you catch a glimpse of a garden. Look not so scornfully at the primitive horticulture—such gardens are rare in the
Bush. I doubt if the stately King of the Peak ever more
rejoiced in the famous conservatory, through which you may
drive in your carriage, than do the sons of the Bush in the
herbs and blossoms which taste and breathe of the old father-
land. Go on, and behold the palace of the patriarchs—it is of
wood, I grant you, but the house we build with our own hands
is always a palace. Did you ever build one when you were a
boy? And the lords of that palace are lords of the land,
almost as far as you can see, and of those numberless flocks;
and better still, of a health which an antediluvian might have
envied, and of nerves so seasoned with horse-breaking, cattle-
driving, fighting with wild blacks—chases from them and after
them, for life and for death—that if any passion vex the breast
of those kings of the Bushland, fear at least is erased from
the list.

See here and there through the landscape, rude huts like the
masters'—wild spirits and fierce dwell within. But they are
tamed into order by plenty and hope; by the hand open but
firm, by the eye keen but just.

Now, out from those woods, over those green rolling plains,
harum-scarum, helter-skelter, long hair flying wild, and all
bearded, as a Turk or a pard, comes a rider you recognise.
The rider dismounts, and another old acquaintance turns from
a shepherd, with whom he has been conversing on matters that
never plagued Thyrsis and Menalcas, whose sheep seem to have
been innocent of foot-rot and scab—and accosts the horseman.

PISISTRATUS.—"My dear Guy, where on earth have you been?"

GUY (producing a book from his pocket, with great triumph).
—"There! Dr. Johnson's 'Lives of the Poets.' I could not
get the squatter to let me have 'Kenilworth,' though I offered
him three sheep for it. Dull old fellow, that Dr. Johnson, I
suspect; so much the better, the book will last all the longer.
And here's a Sydney paper, too, only two months old!" (Guy

takes a short pipe, or *dodeen*, from his hat, in the band of which it had been stuck, fills and lights it.)

PISISTRATUS.—"You must have ridden thirty miles at the least. To think of *your* turning book-hunter, Guy!"

GUY BOLDING (philosophically).—"Ay, one don't know the worth of a thing till one has lost it. No sneers at me, old fellow; you, too, declared that you were bothered out of your life by those books, till you found how long the evenings were without them. Then, the first new book we got—an old volume of the *Spectator!*—such fun!"

PISISTRATUS.—"Very true. The brown cow has calved in your absence. Do you know, Guy, I think we shall have no scab in the fold this year. If so, there will be a rare sum to lay by! Things look up with us now, Guy."

GUY BOLDING.—"Yes! Very different from the first two years. You drew a long face then. How wise you were, to insist on our learning experience at another man's station before we hazarded our own capital! But, by Jove! those sheep, at first, were enough to plague a man out of his wits. What with the wild dogs, just as the sheep had been washed and ready to shear; then that cursed scabby sheep of Joe Timmes's, that we caught rubbing his sides so complacently against our unsuspecting poor ewes. I wonder we did not run away. But '*Patientia fit*'—what is that line in Horace? Never mind now. 'It is a long lane that has no turning' does just as well as anything in Horace, and Virgil to boot. I say, has not Vivian been here?"

PISISTRATUS.—"No; but he will be sure to come to-day."

GUY BOLDING.—"He has much the best berth of it. Horse-breeding and cattle-feeding; galloping after those wild devils; lost in a forest of horns; beasts lowing, scampering, goring, tearing off like mad buffaloes; horses galloping up hill, down hill, over rocks, stones, and timber; whips cracking, men shouting—your neck all but broken; a great bull making at you full rush. Such fun! Sheep are dull things to look at after a bull-hunt and a cattle-feast."

PISISTRATUS.—"Every man to his taste in the Bush. One may make one's money more easily and safely, with more adventure and sport, in the bucolic department. But one makes larger profit and quicker fortune, with good luck and good care, in the pastoral—and our object, I take it, is to get back to England as soon as we can."

GUY BOLDING.—"Humph! I should be content to live and die in the Bush—nothing like it, if women were not so scarce.

To think of the redundant spinster population at home, and not a spinster here to be seen within thirty miles, save Bet Goggins, indeed—and she has only one eye! But to return to Vivian—why should it be our object, more than his, to get back to England as soon as we can?"

PISISTRATUS.—"Not more, certainly. But you saw that an excitement more stirring than that we find in the sheep had become necessary to him. You know he was growing dull and dejected; the cattle station was to be sold a bargain. And then the Durham bulls, and the Yorkshire horses, which Mr. Trevanion sent you and me out as presents, were so tempting, I thought we might fairly add one speculation to another; and since one of us must superintend the bucolics, and two of us were required for the pastorals, I think Vivian was the best of us three to entrust with the first; and, certainly, it has succeeded as yet."

GUY.—"Why, yes, Vivian is quite in his element—always in action, and always in command. Let him be first in everything, and there is not a finer fellow, nor a better tempered—present company excepted. Hark! the dogs, the crack of the whip; there he is. And now, I suppose, we may go to dinner."

Enter VIVIAN.

His frame has grown more athletic; his eye, more steadfast and less restless, looks you full in the face. His smile is more open; but there is a melancholy in his expression, almost approaching to gloom. His dress is the same as that of Pisistratus and Guy—white vest and trousers; loose neckcloth, rather gay in colour; broad cabbage-leaf hat; his moustache and beard are trimmed with more care than ours. He has a large whip in his hand, and a gun slung across his shoulders. Greetings are exchanged; mutual inquiries as to cattle and sheep, and the last horses despatched to the Indian market. Guy shows the "Lives of the Poets;" Vivian asks if it is possible to get the "Life of Clive," or "Napoleon," or a copy of "Plutarch." Guy shakes his head—says, if a "Robinson Crusoe" will do as well, he has seen one in a very tattered state, but in too great request to be had a bargain.

The party turn into the hut. Miserable animals are bachelors in all countries; but most miserable in Bushland. A man does not know what a helpmate of the soft sex is in the Old World, where women seem a matter of course. But in the Bush, a

2 D

wife is literally bone of your bone, flesh of your flesh—your
better half, your ministering angel, your Eve of the Eden—in
short, all that poets have sung, or young orators say at public
dinners, when called upon to give the toast of "The Ladies."
Alas! we are three bachelors, but we are better off than
bachelors often are in the Bush.   For the wife of the shepherd
I took from Cumberland does me and Bolding the honour to
live in our hut, and make things tidy and comfortable.   She has
had a couple of children since we have been in the Bush; a
wing has been added to the hut for that increase of family.
The children, I dare say, one might have thought a sad nuisance
in England; but I declare that, surrounded as one is by great
bearded men, from sunrise to sunset, there is something humanis-
ing, musical, and Christian-like in the very squall of the baby.
There it goes—bless it!   As for my other companions from
Cumberland, Miles Square, the most aspiring of all, has long
left me, and is superintendent to a great sheep-owner some two
hundred miles off.   The Will-o'-the-Wisp is consigned to the
cattle station, where he is Vivian's head man, finding time now
and then to indulge his old poaching propensities at the expense of parrots, black cockatoos, pigeons, and kangaroos.   The
shepherd remains with us, and does not seem, honest fellow, to
care to better himself; he has a feeling of clanship, which keeps
down the ambition common in Australia.   And his wife—such
a treasure!   I assure you, the sight of her smooth, smiling
woman's face, when we return home at nightfall, and the very
flow of her gown, as she turns the "dampers" [1] in the ashes,
and fills the tea-pot, have in them something holy and angelical.
How lucky our Cumberland swain is not jealous!   Not that
there is any cause, enviable dog though he be; but where
Desdemonas are so scarce, if you could but guess how green-
eyed their Othellos generally are!   Excellent husbands, it is
true—none better; but you had better think twice before you
attempt to play the Cassio in Bushland!   There, however, she
is, dear creature!—rattling among knives and forks, smoothing
the tablecloth, setting on the salt beef, and that rare luxury of
pickles (the last pot in our store), and the produce of our garden
and poultry-yard, which few Bushmen can boast of—and the
dampers, and a pot of tea to each banqueter; no wine, beer,
nor spirits—those are only for shearing-time.   We have just
said grace (a fashion retained from the holy mother-country),

---

[1] A damper is a cake of flour baked without yeast, in the ashes.

when, bless my soul! what a clatter without, what a tramping of feet, what a barking of dogs! Some guests have arrived. They are always welcome in Bushland! Perhaps a cattle-buyer in search of Vivian; perhaps that cursed squatter, whose sheep are always migrating to ours. Never mind, a hearty welcome to all—friend or foe. The door opens; one, two, three strangers. More plates and knives; draw your stools: just in time. First eat, then—what news?

Just as the strangers sit down, a voice is heard at the door—

" You will take particular care of this horse, young man: walk him about a little; wash his back with salt and water. Just unbuckle the saddle-bags; give them to me. Oh! safe enough, I dare say—but papers of consequence. The prosperity of the colony depends on these papers. What would become of you all if any accident happened to them, I shudder to think."

And here, attired in a twill shooting-jacket, budding with gilt buttons, impressed with a well-remembered device; a cabbage-leaf hat shading a face rarely seen in the Bush—a face smooth as razor could make it: neat, trim, respectable-looking as ever—his arm full of saddle-bags, and his nostrils gently distended, inhaling the steam of the banquet, walks in— Uncle Jack.

PISISTRATUS (leaping up).—" Is it possible? *You* in Australia! —you in the Bush!"

Uncle Jack, not recognising Pisistratus in the tall-bearded man who is making a plunge at him, recedes in alarm, exclaiming—" Who are you?—never saw you before, sir! I suppose you'll say next that *I owe you something!*"

PISISTRATUS.—" Uncle Jack!"

UNCLE JACK (dropping his saddle-bags).—"Nephew!—Heaven be praised! Come to my arms!"

They embrace; mutual introductions to the company—Mr. Vivian, Mr. Bolding, on the one side—Major MacBlarney, Mr. Bullion, Mr. Emanuel Speck, on the other. Major MacBlarney is a fine portly man, with a slight Dublin brogue, who squeezes your hand as he would a sponge. Mr. Bullion—reserved and haughty—wears green spectacles, and gives you a forefinger. Mr. Emanuel Speck—unusually smart for the Bush, with a blue satin stock, and one of those blouses common in Germany, with elaborate hems, and pockets enough for Briareus to have put all his hands into at once—is thin, civil, and stoops—bows, smiles, and sits down to dinner again, with the air of a man accustomed to attend to the main chance.

UNCLE JACK (his mouth full of beef).—" Famous beef!—breed it yourself, eh? Slow work that cattle-feeding!—" (Empties the rest of the pickle-jar into his plate.) " Must learn to go ahead in the New World—railway times these! We can put him up to a thing or two—eh, Bullion?" (Whispering me)—" Great capitalist, that Bullion! LOOK AT HIM!"

MR. BULLION (gravely).—" A thing or two! If he has capital —you have said it, Mr. Tibbets." (Looks round for the pickles—the green spectacles remain fixed upon Uncle Jack's plate.)

UNCLE JACK.—" All that this colony wants is a few men like us, with capital and spirit. Instead of paying paupers to emigrate, they should pay rich men to come—eh, Speck?"

While Uncle Jack turns to Mr. Speck, Mr. Bullion fixes his fork in a pickled onion in Jack's plate, and transfers it to his own—observing—not as incidentally to the onion but to truth in general—" A man, gentlemen, in this country, has only to keep his eyes on the look-out, and seize on the first advantage!— resources are incalculable!"

Uncle Jack, returning to the plate and missing the onion, forestalls Mr. Speck in seizing the last potato—observing also, and in the same philosophical and generalising spirit as Mr. Bullion—" The great thing in this country is to be always beforehand: discovery and invention, promptitude and decision! —that's your go. 'Pon my life, one picks up sad vulgar sayings among the natives here!—' that's your go!' shocking! What would your poor father say? How is he—good Austin? Well?—that's right: and my dear sister? Ah, that damnable Peck!—still harping on the *Anti-Capitalist*, eh? But I'll make it up to you all now. Gentlemen, charge your glasses—a bumper-toast."

MR. SPECK (in an affected tone).—" I respond to the sentiment in a flowing cup. Glasses are not forthcoming."

UNCLE JACK.—" A bumper-toast to the health of the future millionaire, whom I present to you in my nephew and sole heir —Pisistratus Caxton, Esq. Yes, gentlemen, I here publicly announce to you that this gentleman will be the inheritor of all my wealth—freehold, leasehold, agricultural, and mineral; and when I am in the cold grave "—(takes out his pocket-hand-kerchief)—" and nothing remains of poor John Tibbets, look upon that gentleman, and say, ' John Tibbets lives again!' "

MR. SPECK (chauntingly)—

" Let the bumper toast go round."

GUY BOLDING.—"Hip, hip, hurrah!—three times three! What fun!"

Order is restored; dinner-things are cleared; each gentleman lights his pipe.

VIVIAN.—"What news from England?"

MR. BULLION.—"As to the funds, sir?"

MR. SPECK.—"I suppose you mean, rather, as to the railways: great fortunes will be made there, sir; but still I think that our speculations here will——"

VIVIAN.—"I beg pardon for interrupting you, sir; but I thought, in the last papers, that there seemed something hostile in the temper of the French. No chance of a war?"

MAJOR MACBLARNEY.—"Is it the wars you'd be after, young gintleman? If me interest at the Horse Guards can avail you, bedad! you'd make a proud man of Major MacBlarney."

MR. BULLION (authoritatively).—"No, sir, we won't have a war: the capitalists of Europe and Australia won't have it. The Rothschilds, and a few others that shall be nameless, have only got to do *this*, sir"—(Mr. Bullion buttons up his pockets)—"and we'll do it, too; and then what becomes of your war, sir?" (Mr. Bullion snaps his pipe in the vehemence with which he brings his hand on the table, turns round the green spectacles, and takes up Mr. Speck's pipe, which that gentleman had laid aside in an unguarded moment.)

VIVIAN.—"But the campaign in India?"

MAJOR MACBLARNEY. — "Oh! — and if it's the Ingees you'd——"

MR. BULLION (refilling Speck's pipe from Guy Bolding's exclusive tobacco-pouch, and interrupting the Major).—"India—that's another matter: I don't object to that! War there—rather good for the money market than otherwise."

VIVIAN.—"What news there, then?"

MR. BULLION.—"Don't know—haven't got India stock."

MR. SPECK.—"Nor I either. The day for India is over: this is our India now." (Misses his tobacco-pipe; sees it in Bullion's mouth, and stares aghast!—*N.B.*—The pipe is not a clay *dodeen*, but a small meerschaum—irreplaceable in Bushland.)

PISISTRATUS.—"Well, uncle, but I am at a loss to understand what new scheme you have in hand. Something benevolent, I am sure—something for your fellow-creatures—for philanthropy and mankind?"

MR. BULLION (starting).—"Why, young man, are you as green as all that?"

PISISTRATUS.—" I, sir—no—Heaven forbid ! But my——"
(Uncle Jack holds up his forefinger imploringly, and spills his
tea over the pantaloons of his nephew !)

Pisistratus, wroth at the effect of the tea, and therefore
obdurate to the sign of the forefinger, continues rapidly, " But
my uncle *is !*—some Grand National-Imperial-Colonial-Anti-
Monopoly——"

UNCLE JACK.—" Pooh ! pooh ! What a droll boy it is ! "

MR. BULLION (solemnly).—" With these notions, which not
even in jest should be fathered on my respectable and intelligent friend here "—(Uncle Jack bows)—" I am afraid you will
never get on in the world, Mr. Caxton. I don't think our
speculations will suit *you !* It is growing late, gentlemen : we
must push on."

UNCLE JACK (jumping up).—" And I have so much to say to
the dear boy. Excuse us : you know the feelings of an uncle ! "
(Takes my arm, and leads me out of the hut.)

UNCLE JACK (as soon as we are in the air).—" You'll ruin us—
you, me, and your father and mother. Yes ! What do you
think I work and slave myself for but for you and yours ? Ruin
us all, I say, if you talk in that way before Bullion ! His heart
is as hard as the Bank of England's—and quite right he is, too.
Fellow-creatures !—stuff ! I have renounced that delusion—
the generous follies of my youth ! I begin at last to live for myself—that is, for self and relatives ! I shall succeed this time,
you'll see ! "

PISISTRATUS.—" Indeed, uncle, I hope so sincerely ; and, to do
you justice, there is always something very clever in your ideas
—only they don't——"

UNCLE JACK (interrupting me with a groan).—" The fortunes
that other men have gained by my ideas !—shocking to think of
—What !—and shall I be reproached if I live no longer for
such a set of thieving, greedy, ungrateful knaves ? No, no !
Number One shall be my maxim ; and I'll make you a Crœsus,
my boy—I will."

Pisistratus, after grateful acknowledgments for all prospective
benefits, inquires how long Jack has been in Australia ; what
brought him into the colony ; and what are his present views.
Learns, to his astonishment, that Uncle Jack has been four years
in the colony ; that he sailed the year after Pisistratus—induced,
he says, by that illustrious example, and by some mysterious
agency or commission, which he will not explain, emanating
either from the Colonial Office or an Emigration Company.

Uncle Jack has been thriving wonderfully since he abandoned his fellow-creatures. His first speculation, on arriving at the colony, was in buying some houses in Sydney, which (by those fluctuations in prices common to the extremes of the colonial mind—which is one while skipping up the rainbow with Hope, and at another plunging into Acherontian abysses with Despair) he bought excessively cheap, and sold excessively dear. But his grand experiment has been in connection with the infant settlement of Adelaide, of which he considers himself one of the first founders; and as, in the rush of emigration which poured to that favoured establishment in the earlier years of its existence,—rolling on its tide all manner of credulous and inexperienced adventurers,—vast sums were lost, so, of those sums, certain fragments and pickings were easily gripped and gathered up by a man of Uncle Jack's readiness and dexterity. Uncle Jack had contrived to procure excellent letters of introduction to the colonial grandees: he got into close connection with some of the principal parties seeking to establish a monopoly of land (which has since been in great measure effected, by raising the price, and excluding the small fry of petty capitalists); and effectually imposed on them, as a man with a vast knowledge of public business—in the confidence of great men at home—considerable influence with the English press, &c. &c. And no discredit to their discernment; for Jack, when he pleased, had a way with him that was almost irresistible. In this manner he contrived to associate himself and his earnings with men really of large capital, and long practical experience in the best mode by which that capital might be employed. He was thus admitted into partnership (so far as his means went) with Mr. Bullion, who was one of the largest sheep-owners and landholders in the colony; though, having many other nests to feather, that gentleman resided in state at Sydney, and left his runs and stations to the care of overseers and superintendents. But land-jobbing was Jack's special delight; and an ingenious German having lately declared that the neighbourhood of Adelaide betrayed the existence of those mineral treasures which have since been brought to day, Mr. Tibbets had persuaded Bullion and the other gentleman now accompanying him, to undertake the land journey from Sydney to Adelaide, privily and quietly, to ascertain the truth of the German's report, which was at present very little believed. If the ground failed of mines, Uncle Jack's account convinced his associates that mines quite as profitable might be found in the pockets of the raw adventurers, who were ready to buy one year at the dearest market, and driven to sell the next at the cheapest.

"But," concluded Uncle Jack, with a sly look, and giving me a poke in the ribs, "I've had to do with mines before now, and know what they are. I'll let nobody but you into my pet scheme; you shall go shares if you like. The scheme is as plain as a problem in Euclid,—if the German is right, and there are mines, why, the mines will be worked. Then miners must be employed; but miners must eat, drink, and spend their money. The thing is to get *that* money. Do you take?"

PISISTRATUS.—"Not at all!"

UNCLE JACK (majestically).—"A Great Grog and Store Depôt! The miners want grog and stores, come to your depôt; you take their money; Q.E.D.! Shares—eh, you dog? Cribs, as we said at school. Put in a paltry thousand or two, and you shall go halves."

PISISTRATUS (vehemently).—"Not for all the mines of Potosi."

UNCLE JACK (good-humouredly).—"Well, it shan't be the worse for you. I shan't alter my will, in spite of your want of confidence. Your young friend,—that Mr. Vivian, I think you call him—intelligent-looking fellow, sharper than the other, I guess,—would *he* like a share?"

PISISTRATUS.—"In the grog depôt? You had better ask him!"

UNCLE JACK.—"What! you pretend to be aristocratic in the Bush! Too good. Ha, ha—they're calling to me—we must be off."

PISISTRATUS.—"I will ride with you a few miles. What say you, Vivian? and you, Guy?——"

The whole party now joined us.

Guy prefers basking in the sun, and reading the "Lives of the Poets." Vivian assents; we accompany the party till sunset. Major MacBlarney prodigalises his offers of service in every conceivable department of life, and winds up with an assurance that, if we want anything in those departments connected with engineering—such as mining, mapping, surveying, &c.,—he will serve us, bedad, for nothing, or next to it. We suspect Major MacBlarney to be a civil engineer, suffering under the innocent hallucination that he has been in the army.

Mr. Speck lets out to me, in a confidential whisper, that Mr. Bullion is monstrous rich, and has made his fortune from small beginnings, by never letting a good thing go. I think of Uncle Jack's pickled onion, and Mr. Speck's meerschaum, and perceive, with respectful admiration, that Mr. Bullion acts uniformly on one grand system. Ten minutes afterwards, Mr. Bullion observes, in a tone equally confidential, that Mr. Speck, though so smiling and civil, is as sharp as a needle; and that if I want any shares in the new speculation, or indeed in any other, I had better come at once to Bullion, who would not deceive me for my weight in gold. "Not," added Bullion, "that I have anything to say against Speck. He is well enough to do in the world—a warm man, sir; and when a man is really warm, I am the last person to think of his little faults, and turn on him the cold shoulder."

"Adieu," said Uncle Jack, pulling out once more his pocket-handkerchief; "my love to all at home." And sinking his voice into a whisper, "If ever you think better of the grog and store depôt, nephew, you'll find an uncle's heart in this bosom!"

CHAPTER II

IT was night as Vivian and myself rode slowly home. Night in Australia! How impossible to describe its beauty! Heaven seems, in that new world, so much nearer to earth! Every star stands out so bright and particular, as if fresh from the time when the Maker willed it. And the moon like a large silvery sun;—the least object on which it shines so distinct and so still.[1] Now and then a sound breaks the silence, but a sound so much in harmony with the solitude that it only deepens its charms. Hark! the low cry of a night-bird, from yonder glen amidst the small grey gleaming rocks. Hark! as night deepens, the bark of the distant watch-dog, or the low strange howl of his more savage species, from which he defends the fold. Hark! the echo catches the sound, and flings it sportively from hill to hill —farther, and farther, and farther down, till all again is hushed, and the flowers hang noiseless over your head, as you ride through a grove of the giant gum-trees. Now the air is literally charged with the odours, and the sense of fragrance grows almost painful in its pleasure. You quicken your pace, and escape again

---

[1] "I have frequently," says Mr. Wilkinson, in his invaluable work upon South Australia, at once so graphic and so practical, "been out in a journey in such a night, and whilst allowing the horse his own time to walk along the road, have solaced myself by reading in the still moonlight."

into the open plains and the full moonlight, and through the slender tea-trees catch the gleam of the river, and in the exquisite fineness of the atmosphere hear the soothing sound of its murmur.

PISISTRATUS.—" And this land has become the heritage of our people ! Methinks I see, as I gaze around, the scheme of the All-beneficent Father disentangling itself clear through the troubled history of mankind. How mysteriously, while Europe rears its populations, and fulfils its civilising mission, these realms have been concealed from its eyes—divulged to us just as civilisation needs the solution to its problems ; a vent for feverish energies, baffled in the crowd ; offering bread to the famished, hope to the desperate ; in very truth enabling the ' New World to redress the balance of the Old.' Here, what a Latium for the wandering spirits—

' On various seas by various tempests toss'd.'

Here, the actual Æneid passes before our eyes. From the huts of the exiles scattered over this hardier Italy, who cannot see in the future—

' A race from whence new Alban sires shall come,
And the long glories of a future Rome ? ' "

VIVIAN (mournfully).—" Is it from the outcasts of the workhouse, the prison, and the transport-ship, that a second Rome is to arise ? "

PISISTRATUS.—" There is something in this new soil—in the labour it calls forth, in the hope it inspires, in the sense of property, which I take to be the core of social morals—that expedites the work of redemption with marvellous rapidity. Take them altogether, whatever their origin, or whatever brought them hither, they are a fine, manly, frank-hearted race, these colonists now !—rude, not mean, especially in the Bush, and, I suspect, will ultimately become as gallant and honest a population as that now springing up in South Australia, from which convicts are excluded—and happily excluded—for the distinction will sharpen emulation. As to the rest, and in direct answer to your question, I fancy even the emancipist part of our population every whit as respectable as the mongrel robbers under Romulus."

VIVIAN.—" But were *they* not soldiers ? —I mean the first Romans ? "

PISISTRATUS.—" My dear cousin, we are in advance of those

grim outcasts, if we can get lands, houses, and wives (though the last is difficult, and it is well that we have no white Sabines in the neighbourhood), without that same soldiering which was the necessity of their existence."

VIVIAN (after a pause).—" I have written to my father, and to yours more fully—stating in the one letter my wish, in the other trying to explain the feelings from which it springs."

PISISTRATUS.—" Are the letters gone ? "

VIVIAN.—" Yes."

PISISTRATUS.—" And you would not show them to me ! "

VIVIAN.—" Do not speak so reproachfully. I promised your father to pour out my whole heart to him, whenever it was troubled and at strife. I promise you now that I will go by his advice."

PISISTRATUS (disconsolately).—" What is there in this military life for which you yearn that can yield you more food for healthful excitement and stirring adventure than your present pursuits afford ? "

VIVIAN.—" Distinction ! You do not see the difference between us. You have but a fortune to make, I have a name to redeem ; you look calmly on to the future ; I have a dark blot to erase from the past."

PISISTRATUS (soothingly).—" It is erased. Five years of no weak bewailings, but of manly reform, steadfast industry, conduct so blameless that even Guy (whom I look upon as the incarnation of blunt English honesty) half doubts whether you are *'cute* enough for ' a station '—a character already so high that I long for the hour when you will again take your father's spotless name, and give me the pride to own our kinship to the world, —all this surely redeems the errors arising from an uneducated childhood and a wandering youth."

VIVIAN (leaning over his horse, and putting his hand on my shoulder).—" My dear friend, what do I owe you ! " Then recovering his emotion, and pushing on at a quicker pace, while he continues to speak, " But can you see that, just in proportion as my comprehension of right would become clear and strong, so my conscience would become also more sensitive and reproachful ; and the better I understand my gallant father, the more I must desire to be as he would have had his son. Do you think it would content him, could he see me branding cattle, and bargaining with bullock-drivers ?—Was it not the strongest wish of his heart that I should adopt his own career ? Have I not heard you say that he would have had you too a soldier, but for your mother? I have no mother! If I made thousands, and tens of thousands, by this ignoble calling, would they give my father half the pleasure that he would feel at seeing my name honourably mentioned in a despatch? No, no! You have banished the gipsy blood, and now the soldier's breaks out! Oh for one glorious day in which I may clear my way into fair repute, as our fathers before us!—when tears of proud joy may flow from those eyes that have wept such hot drops at my shame. When *she*, too, in her high station beside that sleek lord, may say, 'His heart was not so vile, after all!' Don't argue with me—it is in vain! Pray, rather, that I may have leave to work out my own way; for I tell you that, if condemned to stay here, I may not murmur aloud—I may go through this round of low duties as the brute turns the wheel of a mill! but my heart will prey on itself, and you shall soon write on my gravestone the epitaph of the poor poet you told us of, whose true disease was the thirst of glory—'Here lies one whose name was written in water.'"

I had no answer: that contagious ambition made my own veins run more warmly, and my own heart beat with a louder tumult. Amidst the pastoral scenes, and under the tranquil moonlight of the New, the Old World, even in me, rude Bushman, claimed for awhile its son. But as we rode on, the air, so inexpressibly buoyant, yet soothing as an anodyne, restored me to peaceful Nature. Now the flocks, in their snowy clusters, were seen sleeping under the stars; hark! the welcome of the watch-dogs; see the light gleaming far from the chink of the door! And, pausing, I said aloud, "No, there is more glory in laying these rough foundations of a mighty state, though no trumpets resound with your victory—though no laurels shall shadow your tomb—than in forcing the onward progress of your race over burning cities and hecatombs of men!" I looked round for Vivian's answer; but, ere I spoke, he had spurred from my side, and I saw the wild dogs slinking back from the hoofs of his horse, as he rode at speed, on the sward, through the moonlight.

CHAPTER III

THE weeks and the months rolled on, and the replies to Vivian's letters came at last; I foreboded too well their purport. I knew that my father could not set himself in opposition to the deliberate and cherished desire of a man who had now arrived at the full strength of his understanding, and must be left at liberty to make his own election of the paths of life. Long after that date, I saw Vivian's letter to my father; and even his conversation had scarcely prepared me for the pathos of that confession of a mind remarkable alike for its strength and its weakness. If born in the age, or submitted to the influences, of religious enthusiasm, here was a nature that, awaking from sin, could not have been contented with the sober duties of mediocre goodness—that would have plunged into the fiery depths of monkish fanaticism—wrestled with the fiend in the hermitage, or marched barefoot on the infidel with a sackcloth for armour—the cross for a sword. Now, the impatient desire for redemption took a more mundane direction, but with something that seemed almost spiritual in its fervour. And this enthusiasm flowed through strata of such profound melancholy! Deny it a vent, and it might sicken into lethargy, or fret itself into madness—give it the vent, and it might vivify and fertilise as it swept along.

My father's reply to this letter was what might be expected. It gently reinforced the old lessons in the distinctions between aspirations towards the perfecting ourselves—aspirations that are never in vain—and the morbid passion for applause from others, which shifts conscience from our own bosoms to the confused Babel of the crowd, and calls it "fame." But my father, in his counsels, did not seek to oppose a mind so obstinately bent upon a single course—he sought rather to guide and strengthen it in the way it should go. The seas of human life are wide. Wisdom may suggest the voyage, but it must first look to the condition of the ship, and the nature of the merchandise to exchange. Not every vessel that sails from Tarshish can bring back the gold of Ophir; but shall it therefore rot in the harbour? No; give its sails to the wind!

But I had expected that Roland's letter to his son would have been full of joy and exultation—joy there was none in it, yet exultation there might be, though serious, grave, and

subdued.   In the proud assent that the old soldier gave to his
son's wish, in his entire comprehension of motives so akin to
his own nature, there was yet a visible sorrow; it seemed
even as if he constrained himself to the assent he gave.   Not
till I had read it again and again could I divine Roland's feelings
while he wrote.   At this distance of time, I comprehend them
well.   Had he sent from his side, into noble warfare, some boy
fresh to life, new to sin, with an enthusiasm pure and single-
hearted as his own young chivalrous ardour, then, with all a
soldier's joy, he had yielded a cheerful tribute to the hosts of
England; but here he recognised, though perhaps dimly, not
the frank military fervour, but the stern desire of expiation,
and in that thought he admitted forebodings that would have
been otherwise rejected, so that, at the close of the letter, it
seemed not the fiery war-seasoned Roland that wrote, but rather
some timid, anxious mother.   Warnings and entreaties and
cautions not to be rash, and assurances that the best soldiers
were ever the most prudent : were these the counsels of the
fierce veteran, who, at the head of the forlorn hope, had
mounted the wall at ——, his sword between his teeth !

But, whatever his presentiments, Roland had yielded at once
to his son's prayer—hastened to London at the receipt of his
letter—obtained a commission in a regiment now in active
service in India ; and that commission was made out in his son's
name.   The commission, with an order to join the regiment as
soon as possible, accompanied the letter.

And Vivian, pointing to the name addressed to him, said,
"Now, indeed, I may resume this name, and, next to Heaven,
will I hold it sacred !   It shall guide me to glory in life, or my
father shall read it, without shame, on my tomb !"   I see him
before me, as he stood then—his form erect, his dark eyes
solemn in their light, a serenity in his smile, a grandeur on his
brow, that I had never marked till then !   Was that the same
man I had recoiled from as the sneering cynic, shuddered at as
the audacious traitor, or wept over as the cowering outcast ?
How little the nobleness of aspect depends on symmetry of
feature, or the mere proportions of form !   What dignity robes
the man who is filled with a lofty thought !

CHAPTER IV

HE is gone! he has left a void in my existence. I had grown to love him so well; I had been so proud when men praised him. My love was a sort of self-love—I had looked upon him in part as the work of my own hands. I am a long time ere I can settle back, with good heart, to my pastoral life. Before my cousin went, we cast up our gains, and settled our shares. When he resigned the allowance which Roland had made him, his father secretly gave to me, for his use, a sum equal to that which I and Guy Bolding brought into the common stock. Roland had raised the sum upon mortgage ; and, while the interest was a trivial deduction from his income, compared to the former allowance, the capital was much more useful to his son than a mere yearly payment could have been. Thus, between us, we had a considerable sum for Australian settlers— £4500. For the first two years we made nothing ; indeed, great part of the first year was spent in learning our art, at the station of an old settler. But, at the end of the third year, our flocks having then become very considerable, we cleared a return beyond my most sanguine expectations. And when my cousin left, just in the sixth year of exile, our shares amounted to £4000 each, exclusive of the value of the two stations. My cousin had, at first, wished that I should forward his share to his father, but he soon saw that Roland would never take it ; and it was finally agreed that it should rest in my hands, for me to manage for him, send him out an interest at five per cent., and devote the surplus profits to the increase of his capital. I had now, therefore, the control of £12,000, and we might consider ourselves very respectable capitalists. I kept on the cattle station, by the aid of the Will-o'-the-Wisp, for about two years after Vivian's departure (we had then had it altogether for five). At the end of that time, I sold it and the stock to great advantage. And the sheep—for the " brand " of which I had a high reputation—having wonderfully prospered in the meanwhile, I thought we might safely extend our speculations into new ventures. Glad, too, of a change of scene, I left Bolding in charge of the flocks, and bent my course to Adelaide, for the fame of that new settlement had already disturbed the peace of the Bush. I found Uncle Jack residing near Adelaide, in a very handsome villa, with all the signs and appurtenances of colonial opulence ; and report, perhaps, did not exaggerate the gains he had made :—so many strings to his bow—and each arrow, this time, seemed to have gone straight to the white of the butts. I now thought I had acquired knowledge and caution sufficient to avail myself of Uncle Jack's ideas, without ruining myself by following them out in his company ; and I saw a kind of retributive justice in making his brain minister to the fortunes which his ideality and constructiveness, according to Squills, had served so notably to impoverish. I must here gratefully acknowledge, that I owed much to this irregular genius. The investigation of the supposed mines had proved unsatisfactory to Mr. Bullion ; and they were not fairly discovered till a few years after. But Jack had convinced himself of their existence, and purchased, on his own account, " for an old song," some barren land, which he was persuaded would prove to him a Golconda, one day or other, under the euphonious title (which, indeed, it ultimately established) of the " Tibbets' Wheal." The suspension of the mines, however, fortunately suspended the existence of the Grog and Store Depôt, and Uncle Jack was now assisting in the foundation of Port Philip. Profiting by his advice, I adventured in that new settlement some timid and wary purchases, which I resold to considerable advantage. Meanwhile, I must not omit to state briefly what, since my departure from England, had been the ministerial career of Trevanion.

That refining fastidiousness,—that scrupulosity of political conscience, which had characterised him as an independent member, and often served, in the opinion both of friend and of foe, to give the attribute of *general* impracticability to a mind that, in all *details*, was so essentially and laboriously practical—might perhaps have founded Trevanion's reputation as a minister, if he could have been a minister without colleagues—if, standing alone, and from the necessary height, he could have placed, clear and single, before the world, his exquisite honesty of purpose, and the width of a statesmanship marvellously accomplished and comprehensive. But Trevanion could not amalgamate with others, nor subscribe to the discipline of a cabinet in which he was not the chief, especially in a policy which must have been thoroughly abhorrent to such a nature—a policy that, of late years, has distinguished not one faction alone, but has seemed so forced upon the more eminent political leaders, on either side, that they who take the more charitable view of things may, perhaps, hold it to arise from the necessity of the age, fostered by the temper of the public—I mean the policy of *Expediency*. Certainly not in this book will I introduce the angry elements of party politics; and how should I know much about them? All that I have to say is, that, right or wrong, such a policy must have been at war, every moment, with each principle of Trevanion's statesmanship, and fretted each fibre of his moral constitution. The aristocratic combinations which his alliance with the Castleton interest had brought to his aid served perhaps to fortify his position in the cabinet; yet aristocratic combinations were of small avail against what seemed the atmospherical epidemic of the age. I could see how his situation had preyed on his mind, when I read a paragraph in the newspapers, "that it was reported, on good authority, that Mr. Trevanion had tendered his resignation, but had been prevailed upon to withdraw it, as his retirement at that moment would break up the government." Some months afterwards came another paragraph, to the effect, "that Mr. Trevanion was taken suddenly ill, and that it was feared his illness was of a nature to preclude his resuming his official labours." Then parliament broke up. Before it met again, Mr. Trevanion was gazetted as Earl of Ulverstone—a title that had been once in his family—and had left the administration, unable to encounter the fatigues of office. To an ordinary man, the elevation to an earldom, passing over the lesser honours in the peerage, would have seemed no mean close to a political career; but I felt what profound despair of striving against circumstance for utility—what entanglements with his colleagues, whom he could neither conscientiously support, nor, according to his high old-fashioned notions of party honour and etiquette, energetically oppose—had driven him to abandon that stormy scene in which his existence had been passed. The House of Lords, to that active intellect, was as the retirement of some warrior of old into the cloisters of a convent. The Gazette that chronicled the earldom of Ulverstone was the proclamation that Albert Trevanion lived no more for the world of public men. And, indeed, from that date his career vanished out of sight. Trevanion died—the Earl of Ulverstone made no sign.

I had hitherto written but twice to Lady Ellinor during my exile—once upon the marriage of Fanny with Lord Castleton, which took place about six months after I sailed from England, and again, when thanking her husband for some rare animals, equine, pastoral, and bovine, which he had sent as presents to Bolding and myself. I wrote again after Trevanion's elevation

to the peerage, and received, in due time, a reply, confirming
all my impressions—for it was full of bitterness and gall, accusations of the world, fears for the country : Richelieu himself
could not have taken a gloomier view of things, when his levees
were deserted, and his power seemed annihilated before the
"Day of Dupes." Only one gleam of comfort appeared to
visit Lady Ulverstone's breast, and thence to settle prospectively
over the future of the world—a second son had been born to
Lord Castleton ; to that son would descend the estates of
Ulverstone, and the representation of that line distinguished
by Trevanion, and enriched by Trevanion's wife. Never was
there a child of such promise ! Not Virgil himself, when he
called on the Sicilian Muses to celebrate the advent of a son
to Pollio, ever sounded a loftier strain. Here was one, now,
perchance, engaged on words of two syllables, called—

> " By labouring nature to sustain
> The nodding frame of heaven, and earth, and main,
> See to their base restored, earth, sea, and air,
> And joyful ages from behind in crowding ranks appear ! "

Happy dream which Heaven sends to grand-parents ! rebaptism of Hope in the font whose drops sprinkle the grand-
child !

Time flies on ; affairs continue to prosper. I am just leaving
the bank at Adelaide with a satisfied air, when I am stopped in
the street by bowing acquaintances, who never shook me by
the hand before. They shake me by the hand now, and cry—
"I wish you joy, sir. That brave fellow, your namesake, is of
course your near relation."

"What do you mean ? "

"Have not you seen the papers ? Here they are."

"Gallant conduct of Ensign de Caxton—promoted to a lieu-
tenancy on the field."—I wipe my eyes, and cry—"Thank
Heaven—it is my cousin ! " Then new hand-shakings, new
groups gather round. I feel taller by the head than I was
before ! We, grumbling English, always quarrelling with each
other—the world not wide enough to hold us ; and yet, when
in the far land some bold deed is done by a countryman, how
we feel that we are brothers ! how our hearts warm to each other !
What a letter I wrote home ! and how joyously I went back to the
Bush ! The Will-o'-the-Wisp has attained to a cattle-station of
his own. I go fifty miles out of my way to tell him the news and
give him the newspaper ; for he knows now that his old master,

Vivian, is a Cumberland man—a Caxton. Poor Will-o'-the-Wisp! The tea that night tasted uncommonly like whisky-punch! Father Mathew, forgive us—but if you had been a Cumberland man, and heard the Will-o'-the-Wisp roaring out, "Blue Bonnets over the Borders," I think your tea, too, would not have come out of the—caddy!

CHAPTER V

A GREAT change has occurred in our household. Guy's father is dead—his latter years cheered by the accounts of his son's steadiness and prosperity, and by the touching proofs thereof which Guy has exhibited. For he insisted on repaying to his father the old college debts, and the advance of the £1500, begging that the money might go towards his sister's portion. Now, after the old gentleman's death, the sister resolved to come out and live with her dear brother Guy. Another wing is built to the hut. Ambitious plans for a new stone house, to be commenced the following year, are entertained; and Guy has brought back from Adelaide not only a sister, but, to my utter astonishment, a wife, in the shape of a fair friend by whom the sister is accompanied.

The young lady did quite right to come to Australia if she wanted to be married. She was very pretty, and all the beaux in Adelaide were round her in a moment. Guy was in love the first day—in a rage with thirty rivals the next—in despair the third—put the question the fourth—and before the fifteenth was a married man, hastening back with a treasure, of which he fancied all the world was conspiring to rob him. His sister was quite as pretty as her friend, and she, too, had offers enough the moment she landed—only she was romantic and fastidious, and I fancy Guy told her that "I was just made for her."

However, charming though she be—with pretty blue eyes and her brother's frank smile—I am not enchanted. I fancy she lost all chance of my heart by stepping across the yard in a pair of silk shoes. If I were to live in the Bush, give me a wife as a companion who can ride well, leap over a ditch, walk beside me when I go forth, gun in hand, for a shot at the kangaroos. But I dare not go on with the list of a Bush husband's requisites. This change, however, serves, for various reasons, to quicken my desire of return. Ten years have now elapsed, and I have already obtained a much larger fortune than I had calculated

to make.   Sorely to Guy's honest grief, I therefore wound up
our affairs, and dissolved partnership : for he had decided to
pass his life in the colony—and with his pretty wife, who has
grown very fond of him, I don't wonder at it.   Guy takes my
share of the station and stock off my hands ; and, all accounts
squared between us, I bid farewell to the Bush.   Despite all
the motives that drew my heart homeward, it was not without
participation in the sorrow of my old companions, that I took
leave of those I might never see again on this side the grave.
The meanest man in my employ had grown a friend ; and when
those hard hands grasped mine, and from many a breast that
once had waged fierce war with the world came the soft blessing
to the Homeward-bound—with a tender thought for the Old
England, that had been but a harsh stepmother to them—I
felt a choking sensation, which I suspect is little known to the
friendships of Mayfair and St. James's.   I was forced to get off
with a few broken words, when I had meant to part with a long
speech : perhaps the broken words pleased the audience better.
Spurring away, I gained a little eminence and looked back.
There were the poor faithful fellows gathered in a ring, watching
me—their hats off—their hands shading their eyes from the sun.
And Guy had thrown himself on the ground, and I heard his
loud sobs distinctly.   His wife was leaning over his shoulder,
trying to soothe.   Forgive him, fair helpmate, you will be all in
the world to him—to-morrow !   And the blue-eyed sister, where
was she ?   Had she no tears for the rough friend who laughed
at the silk shoes, and taught her how to hold the reins, and
never fear that the old pony would run away with her ?   What
matter ?—if the tears were shed, they were hidden tears.   No
shame in them, fair Ellen ?—since then, thou hast wept happy
tears over thy first-born—those tears have long ago washed away
all bitterness in the innocent memories of a girl's first fancy.

CHAPTER VI

DATED FROM ADELAIDE

IMAGINE my wonder— Uncle Jack has just been with me, and
—but hear the dialogue—

UNCLE JACK.—" So you are positively going back to that
smoky, fusty, Old England, just when you are on your high
road to a plumb.   A plumb, sir, at least !   They all say there is

not a more rising young man in the colony. I think Bullion
would take you into partnership. What are you in such a
hurry for?"

PISISTRATUS.—"To see my father and mother and uncle
Roland, and——" (was about to name some one else, but stops).
"You see, my dear uncle, I came out solely with the idea of
repairing my father's losses in that unfortunate speculation of
The Capitalist."

UNCLE JACK (coughs and ejaculates).—"That villain Peck!"

PISISTRATUS.—"And to have a few thousands to invest in poor
Roland's acres. The object is achieved: why should I stay?"

UNCLE JACK.—"A few paltry thousands, when in twenty years
more, at the farthest, you would wallow in gold!"

PISISTRATUS.—"A man learns in the Bush how happy life can
be with plenty of employment and very little money. I shall
practise that lesson in England."

UNCLE JACK.—"Your mind's made up?"

PISISTRATUS.—"And my place in the ship taken."

UNCLE JACK.—"Then there's no more to be said." (Hums,
haws, and examines his nails—filbert nails, not a speck on them.
Then suddenly, and jerking up his head)—"That *Capitalist!*
it has been on my conscience, nephew, ever since; and, somehow or other, since I have abandoned the cause of my fellow-
creatures, I think I have cared more for my relations."

PISISTRATUS (smiling as he remembers his father's shrewd predictions thereon).—"Naturally, my dear uncle: any child who
has thrown a stone into a pond knows that a circle disappears as
it widens."

UNCLE JACK.—"Very true—I shall make a note of that, appli-
cable to my next speech, in defence of what they call the
'land monopoly.' Thank you—stone—circle!" (Jots down notes
in his pocket-book.) "But, to return to the point: I am well
off now—I have neither wife nor child; and I feel that I ought
to bear my share in your father's loss: it was our joint speculation. And your father, good, dear Austin! paid my debts into
the bargain. And how cheering the punch was that night, when
your mother wanted to scold poor Jack! And the £300 Austin
lent me when I left him: nephew, that was the remaking of
me—the acorn of the oak I have planted. So here they are"
(added Uncle Jack, with a heroical effort—and he extracted from
the pocket-book bills for a sum between three and four thousand pounds). "There, it is done; and I shall sleep better for
it!" (With that Uncle Jack got up, and bolted out of the room.)

" Ought I to take the money ?   Why, I think yes !—it is but
fair.   Jack must be really rich, and can well spare the money ;
besides, if he wants it again, I know my father will let him have
it.   And, indeed, Jack caused the loss of the whole sum lost on
The Capitalist, &c. : and this is not quite the half of what my
father paid away.   But is it not fine in Uncle Jack !   Well, my
father was quite right in his milder estimate of Jack's scalene
conformation, and it is hard to judge of a man when he is needy
and down in the world.   When one grafts one's ideas on one's
neighbour's money, they are certainly not so grand as when
they spring from one's own."

UNCLE JACK (popping his head into the room).—" And, you see,
you can double that money if you will just leave it in my hands
for a couple of years—you have no notion what I shall make of
the Tibbets' Wheal !   Did I tell you—the German was quite
right—I have been offered already seven times the sum which I
gave for the land.   But I am now looking out for a company : let
me put you down for shares to the amount at least of those
trumpery bills.   Cent. per cent.—I guarantee cent. per cent. ! "
(And Uncle Jack stretches out those famous smooth hands of
his, with a tremulous motion of the ten eloquent fingers.)

PISISTRATUS.—" Ah ! my dear uncle, if you repent——"

UNCLE JACK.—" Repent ! when I offer you cent. per cent., on
my personal guarantee ! "

PISISTRATUS (carefully putting the bills into his breast coat
pocket).—" Then, if you don't repent, my dear uncle allow me
to shake you by the hand, and say that I will not consent to
lessen my esteem and admiration for the high principle which
prompts this restitution, by confounding it with trading associations of loans, interests, and copper mines.   And, you see, since
this sum is paid to my father, I have no right to invest it
without his permission."

UNCLE JACK (with emotion).—" ' Esteem, admiration, high
principle ! '—these are pleasant words from you, nephew."
(Then, shaking his head, and smiling).—" You sly dog ! you are
quite right : get the bills cashed at once.   And hark ye, sir,
just keep out of my way, will you ? and don't let me coax from
you a farthing."   (Uncle Jack slams the door and rushes out.
Pisistratus draws the bills warily from his pocket, half-suspecting
they must already have turned into withered leaves, like fairy
money; slowly convinces himself that the bills are good bills ;
and, by lively gestures, testifies his delight and astonishment.)
Scene changes.

PART XVIII

CHAPTER I

ADIEU, thou beautiful land! Canaan of the exiles, and Ararat to many a shattered Ark! Fair cradle of a race for whom the unbounded heritage of a future, that no sage can conjecture, no prophet divine, lies afar in the golden promise-light of Time!—destined, perchance, from the sins and sorrows of a civilisation struggling with its own elements of decay, to renew the youth of the world, and transmit the great soul of England through the cycles of Infinite Change. All climates that can best ripen the products of earth, or form into various character and temper the different families of man, "rain influences" from the heaven, that smiles so benignly on those who had once shrunk, ragged, from the wind, or scowled on the thankless sun. Here, the hardy air of the chill Mother Isle, there the mild warmth of Italian autumns, or the breathless glow of the tropics. And with the beams of every climate, glides subtle HOPE. Of her there, it may be said, as of Light itself, in those exquisite lines of a neglected poet—

> " Through the soft ways of heaven, and air, and sea,
>   Which open all their pores to thee;
>   Like a clear river thou dost glide—
> .   .   .   .
>   All the world's bravery that delights our eyes,
>   Is but thy several liveries;
>   Thou the rich dye on them bestowest;
>   Thy nimble pencil paints the landscape as thou goest." [1]

Adieu, my kind nurse and sweet foster-mother!—a long and a last adieu! Never had I left thee but for that louder voice of Nature which calls the child to the parent, and woos us from the labours we love the best by the chime in the Sabbath-bells of Home.

[1] Cowley's "Ode to Light."

No one can tell how dear the memory of that wild Bush life becomes to him who has tried it with a *fitting spirit* How often it haunts him in the commonplace of more civilised scenes! Its dangers, its risks, its sense of animal health, its bursts of adventure, its intervals of careless repose: the fierce gallop through a very sea of wide rolling plains—the still saunter, at night, through woods, never changing their leaves; with the moon, clear as sunshine, stealing slant through their clusters of flowers. With what an effort we reconcile ourselves to the trite cares and vexed pleasures, "the quotidian ague of frigid impertinences," to which we return! How strong and black stands my pencil-mark in this passage of the poet from whom I have just quoted before!—

"We are here among the vast and noble scenes of Nature—we are there among the pitiful shifts of policy; we walk here, in the light and open ways of the Divine Bounty—we grope there, in the dark and confused labyrinth of human malice." [1]

But I weary you, reader. The New World vanishes—now a line—now a speck; let us turn away, with the face to the Old.

Amongst my fellow-passengers, how many there are returning home disgusted, disappointed, impoverished, ruined, throwing themselves again on those unsuspecting poor friends, who thought they had done with the luckless good-for-naughts for ever. For, don't let me deceive thee, reader, into supposing that every adventurer to Australia has the luck of Pisistratus. Indeed, though the poor labourer, and especially the poor operative from London and the great trading towns (who has generally more of the quick knack of learning—the *adaptable faculty*—required in a new colony, than the simple agricultural labourer), are pretty sure to succeed, the class to which I belong is one in which failures are numerous and success the exception —I mean young men with scholastic education and the habits of gentlemen—with small capital and sanguine hopes. But this, in ninety-nine times out of a hundred, is not the fault of the colony, but of the emigrants. It requires, not so much intellect as a peculiar turn of intellect, and a fortunate combination of physical qualities, easy temper, and quick mother-wit, to make a small capitalist a prosperous Bushman.[2] And if you

---

[1] Cowley on *Town and Country*. (Discourse on Agriculture.)

[2] How true are the following remarks :—

"Action is the first great requisite of a colonist (that is, a pastoral or agricultural settler). With a young man, the tone of his mind is more important than his previous pursuits. I have known men of an active,

could see the sharks that swim round a man just dropped at Adelaide or Sydney, with one or two thousand pounds in his pocket! Hurry out of the towns as fast as you can, my young emigrant; turn a deaf ear, for the present at least, to all jobbers and speculators; make friends with some practised old Bushman; spend several months at his station before you hazard your capital; take with you a temper to bear everything and sigh for nothing; put your whole heart in what you are about; never call upon Hercules when your cart sticks in the rut, and, whether you feed sheep or breed cattle, your success is but a question of time.

But, whatever I owed to nature, I owed also something to fortune. I bought my sheep at little more than 7s. each. When I left, none were worth less than 15s., and the fat sheep were worth £1.[1] I had an excellent shepherd, and my whole care, night and day, was the improvement of the flock. I was fortunate, too, in entering Australia before the system miscalled

energetic, contented disposition, with a good flow of animal spirits, who had been bred in luxury and refinement, succeed better than men bred as farmers, who were always hankering after bread and beer, and market ordinaries of Old England. . . . To be dreaming when you should be looking after your cattle is a terrible drawback. . . . There are certain persons who, too lazy and too extravagant to succeed in Europe, sail for Australia under the idea that fortunes are to be made there by a sort of legerdemain, spend or lose their capital in a very short space of time, and return to England to abuse the place, the people, and everything connected with colonisation." — *Sidney's Australian Handbook* — admirable for its wisdom and compactness.

[1] Lest this seem an exaggeration, I venture to annex an extract from a MS. letter to the author from Mr. George Blakeston Wilkinson, author of "South Australia":—

"I will instance the case of one person, who had been a farmer in England, and emigrated with about £2000 about seven years since. On his arrival he found that the prices of sheep had fallen from about 30s. to 5s. or 6s. per head, and he bought some well-bred flocks at these prices. He was fortunate in obtaining a good and extensive *run*, and he devoted the whole of his time to improving his flocks, and encouraged his shepherds by rewards; so that, in about four years, his original number of sheep had increased from 2500 (which cost him £700) to 7000; and the breed and wool were also so much improved, that he could obtain £1 per head for 2000 fat sheep, and 15s. per head for the other 5000, and this at a time when the general price of sheep was from 10s. to 16s. This alone increased his original capital, invested in sheep, from £700 to £5700. The profits from the wool paid the whole of his expenses and wages for his men."

"The Wakefield"[1] had diminished the supply of labour, and raised the price of land. When the change came (like most of those with large allotments and surplus capital), it greatly increased the value of my own property, though at the cost of a terrible blow on the general interests of the colony. I was lucky, too, in the additional venture of a cattle-station, and in the breed of horses and herds, which, in the five years devoted to that branch establishment, trebled the sum invested therein, exclusive of the advantageous sale of the station.[2] I was lucky, also, as I have stated, in the purchase and resale of lands, at Uncle Jack's recommendation. And, lastly, I left in time, and escaped a very disastrous crisis in colonial affairs, which I take the liberty of attributing entirely to the mischievous crotchets of theorists at home, who want to set all clocks by Greenwich time, forgetting that it is morning in one part of the world at the time they are tolling the curfew in the other.

CHAPTER II

LONDON once more! How strange, lone, and savage I feel in the streets! I am ashamed to have so much health and strength, when I look at these slim forms, stooping backs, and pale faces. I pick my way through the crowd with the merciful timidity of a good-natured giant. I am afraid of jostling against

---

[1] I felt sure from the first, that the system called "The Wakefield" could never fairly represent the ideas of Mr. Wakefield himself, whose singular breadth of understanding, and various knowledge of mankind, belied the notion that fathered on him the clumsy execution of a theory wholly inapplicable to a social state like Australia. I am glad to see that he has vindicated himself from the discreditable paternity. But I grieve to find that he still clings to one cardinal error of the system, in the discouragement of small holdings, and that he evades, more ingeniously than ingenuously, the important question—"What should be the minimum price of land?"

[2] "The profits of cattle-farming are smaller than those of the sheepowner (if the latter have good luck, for much depends upon that), but cattle-farming is much more safe as a speculation, and less care, knowledge, and management are required. £2000, laid out on 700 head of cattle, if good runs be procured, might increase the capital in five years from £2000 to £6000, besides enabling the owner to maintain himself, pay wages, &c."—*MS. letter from G. B. Wilkinson.*

a man, for fear the collision should kill him. I get out of the way of a thread-paper clerk, and 'tis a wonder I am not run over by the omnibuses;—I feel as if I could run over them! I perceive too, that there is something outlandish, peregrinate, and lawless about me. Beau Brummell would certainly have denied me all pretension to the simple air of a gentleman, for every third passenger turns back to look at me. I retreat to my hotel—send for bootmaker, hatter, tailor, and haircutter. I humanise myself from head to foot. Even Ulysses is obliged to have recourse to the arts of Minerva, and, to speak unmetaphorically, "smarten himself up," before the faithful Penelope condescends to acknowledge him.

The artificers promise all despatch. Meanwhile, I hasten to remake acquaintance with my mother country over files of the *Times, Post, Chronicle,* and *Herald.* Nothing comes amiss to me, but articles on Australia; from those I turn aside with the true pshaw-supercilious of your practical man.

No more are leaders filled with praise and blame of Trevanion. "Percy's spur is cold." Lord Ulverstone figures only in the *Court Circular,* or *"Fashionable Movements."* Lord Ulverstone entertains a royal duke at dinner, or dines in turn with a royal duke, or has come to town, or gone out of it. At most (faint Platonic reminiscence of the former life), Lord Ulverstone says in the House of Lords a few words on some question, not a party one; and on which (though affecting perhaps the interests of some few thousands, or millions, as the case may be) men speak without "hears," and are inaudible in the gallery: or Lord Ulverstone takes the chair at an agricultural meeting, or returns thanks when his health is drunk at a dinner at Guildhall. But the daughter rises as the father sets, though over a very different kind of world.

"First ball of the season at Castleton House!" Long description of the rooms and the company; above all, of the hostess. Lines on the Marchioness of Castleton's picture in the "Book of Beauty," by the Hon. Fitzroy Fiddledum, beginning with "Art thou an angel from," &c.—a paragraph that pleased me more, on "Lady Castleton's Infant School at Raby Park;" then again—"Lady Castleton, the new patroness at Almack's;" a criticism more rapturous than ever gladdened living poet, on Lady Castleton's superb diamond stomacher, just reset by Storr and Mortimer; Westmacott's bust of Lady Castleton; Landseer's picture of Lady Castleton and her children, in the costume of the olden time. Not a month in that long file of the *Morning Post* but what Lady Castleton shone forth from the rest of womankind—

"——Velut inter ignes
Luna minores."

The blood mounted to my cheek. Was it to this splendid constellation in the patrician heaven that my obscure, portionless youth had dared to lift its presumptuous eyes? But what is this? "Indian Intelligence—Skilful retreat of the Sepoys under Captain de Caxton!" A captain already—what is the date of the newspaper?—three months ago. The leading article quotes the name with high praise. Is there no leaven of envy amidst the joy at my heart? How obscure has been my career —how laurelless my poor battle with adverse fortune! Fie, Pisistratus! I am ashamed of thee. Has this accursed Old World, with its feverish rivalries, diseased thee already? Get thee home, quick, to the arms of thy mother, the embrace of thy father—hear Roland's low blessing, that thou hast helped to minister to the very fame of that son. If thou wilt have ambition, take it, not soiled and foul with the mire of London. Let it spring fresh and hardy in the calm air of wisdom; and fed, as with dews, by the loving charities of Home.

CHAPTER III

IT was at sunset that I stole through the ruined courtyard, having left my chaise at the foot of the hill below. Though they whom I came to seek knew that I had arrived in England, they did not, from my letter, expect me till the next day. I had stolen a march upon them; and now, in spite of all the impatience which had urged me thither, I was afraid to enter— afraid to see the change more than ten years had made in those forms, for which, in my memory, Time had stood still. And Roland had, even when we parted, grown old before his time. Then my father was in the meridian of life, now he had approached to the decline. And my mother, whom I remembered so fair, as if the freshness of her own heart had preserved the soft bloom to the cheek—I could not bear to think that she was no longer young. Blanche, too, whom I had left a child— Blanche, my constant correspondent during those long years of exile, in letters crossed and recrossed, with all the small details

that make the eloquence of letter-writing, so that in those
epistles I had seen her mind gradually grow up in harmony
with the very characters; at first vague and infantine—then
somewhat stiff with the first graces of running hand, then dash-
ing off, free and facile; and, for the last year before I left, so
formed, yet so airy—so regular, yet so unconscious of effort—
though, in truth, as the caligraphy had become thus matured, I
had been half vexed and half pleased to perceive a certain
reserve creeping over the style—wishes for my return less expressed from herself than as messages from others; words of
the old childlike familiarity repressed; and "Dearest Sisty"
abandoned for the cold form of "Dear Cousin." Those letters,
coming to me in a spot where maiden and love had been as
myths of the by-gone, phantasms and *eidola*, only vouchsafed
to the visions of fancy, had, by little and little, crept into secret
corners of my heart; and out of the wrecks of a former
romance, solitude and reverie had gone far to build up the
fairy domes of a romance yet to come. My mother's letters
had never omitted to make mention of Blanche—of her forethought and tender activity, of her warm heart and sweet
temper—and, in many a little home picture, presented her
image where I would fain have placed it, not "crystal seeing,"
but joining my mother in charitable visits to the village, instructing the young, and tending on the old, or teaching herself to illuminate, from an old missal in my father's collection,
that she might surprise my uncle with a new genealogical table,
with all shields and quarterings, blazoned *or sable*, and *argent;*
or flitting round my father where he sat, and watching when
he looked round for some book he was too lazy to rise for.
Blanche had made a new catalogue, and got it by heart, and
knew at once from what corner of the Heraclea to summon the
ghost. On all these little traits had my mother been eulogisti-
cally minute; but somehow or other she had never said, at
least for the last two years, whether Blanche was pretty or
plain. That was a sad omission. I had longed just to ask
that simple question, or to imply it delicately and diplomati-
cally; but I know not why, I never dared—for Blanche would
have been sure to have read the letter, and what business was
it of mine? And if she *was* ugly, what question more awkward
both to put and to answer? Now, in childhood, Blanche had
just one of those faces that might become very lovely in youth,
and would yet quite justify the suspicion that it might become
gryphonesque, witch-like, and grim. Yes, Blanche, it is per-

fectly true! If those large, serious black eyes took a fierce light, instead of a tender—if that nose, which seemed then undecided whether to be straight or to be aquiline, arched off in the latter direction, and assumed the martial, Roman and imperative character of Roland's manly proboscis—if that face, in childhood too thin, left the blushes of youth to take refuge on two salient peaks by the temples (Cumberland air, too, is famous for the growth of the cheekbone!)—if all that should happen, and it very well might, then, O Blanche, I wish thou hadst never written me those letters; and I might have done wiser things than steel my heart so obdurately to pretty Ellen Bolding's blue eyes and silk shoes. Now, combining together all these doubts and apprehensions, wonder not, O reader, why I stole so stealthily through the ruined courtyard, crept round to the other side of the tower, gazed wistfully on the sun setting slant, on the high casements of the hall (too high, alas! to look within) and shrunk yet to enter;—doing battle, as it were, with my heart.

Steps!—one's sense of hearing grows so quick in the Bushland!—steps, though as light as ever brushed the dew from the harebell! I crept under the shadow of the huge buttress mantled with ivy. A form comes from the little door at an angle in the ruins—a woman's form. Is it my mother's? It is too tall, and the step is more bounding. It winds round the building, it turns to look back, and a sweet voice—a voice strange, yet familiar, calls, tender but chiding, to a truant that lags behind. Poor Juba! he is trailing his long ears on the ground; he is evidently much disturbed in his mind; now he stands still, his nose in the air. Poor Juba! I left thee so slim and so nimble—

> "Thy form that was fashioned as light as a fay's,
> Has assumed a proportion more round;"

years have sobered thee strangely, and made thee obese and Primmins-like.—They have taken too good care of thy creature comforts, O sensual Mauritanian! still, in that mystic intelligence we call instinct, thou art chasing something that years have not swept from thy memory. Thou art deaf to thy lady's voice, however tender and chiding. That's right, come near—nearer—my cousin Blanche; let me have a fair look at thee. Plague take the dog! he flies off from her: he has found the scent, he is making up to the buttress! Now—pounce—he is caught!—whining ungallant discontent. Shall I not yet see

the face ! it is buried in Juba's black curls.   Kisses too !   Wicked
Blanche ! to waste on a dumb animal what, I heartily hope,
many a good Christian would be exceedingly glad of !   Juba
struggles in vain, and is borne off !   I don't think that those
eyes can have taken the fierce turn, and Roland's eagle nose
can never go with that voice, which has the coo of the dove.

I leave my hiding-place, and steal after the Voice, and its
owner.   Where can she be going ?   Not far.   She springs up
the hill whereon the lords of the castle once administered
justice—that hill which commands the land far and wide, and
from which can be last caught the glimpse of the westering
sun.   How gracefully still is that attitude of wistful repose !
Into what delicate curves do form and drapery harmoniously
flow !   How softly distinct stands the lithe image against the
purple hues of the sky !   Then again comes the sweet voice,
gay and carolling as a bird's—now in snatches of song, now in
playful appeals to that dull, four-footed friend.   She is telling
him something that must make the black ears stand on end, for
I just catch the words, " He is coming," and " home."

I cannot see the sun set where I lurk in my ambush, amidst
the brake and the ruins ; but I *feel* that the orb has passed
from the landscape, in the fresher air of the twilight, in the
deeper silence of eve.   Lo !   Hesper comes forth ; at his signal,
star after star, come the hosts—

> " Ch'eran con lui, quando l'amor divino,
>   Mosse da primà quelle cose belle ! "

And the sweet voice is hushed.

Then slowly the watcher descends the hill on the opposite
side—the form escapes from my view.   What charm has gone
from the twilight ?   See, again, where the step steals through
the ruins and along the desolate court.   Ah ! deep and true
heart, do I divine the remembrance that leads thee ?   I pass
through the wicket, down the dell, skirt the laurels, and behold
the face, looking up to the stars—the face which had nestled to
my breast in the sorrow of parting years, long years ago : on the
grave where we had sat, I the boy, thou the infant—there, O
Blanche ! is thy fair face—(fairer than the fondest dream that
had gladdened my exile)—vouchsafed to my gaze !

" Blanche, my cousin !—again, again—soul with soul, amidst
the dead !   Look up, Blanche ; it is I."

CHAPTER IV

G̲O in first and prepare them, dear Blanche; I will wait by
the door.   Leave it ajar, that I may see them."

Roland is leaning against the wall—old armour suspended
over the grey head of the soldier.   It is but a glance that I
give to the dark cheek and high brow; no change there for the
worse—no new sign of decay.   Rather, if anything, Roland
seems younger than when I left.   Calm is the brow—no shame
on it now, Roland; and the lips, once so compressed, smile
with ease—no struggle now, Roland, "not to complain."   A
glance shows me all this.

"Papæ!" says my father, and I hear the fall of a book, "I
can't read a line.   He is coming to-morrow!—to-morrow!   If
we lived to the age of Methuselah, Kitty, we could never
reconcile philosophy and man; that is, if the poor man's to be
plagued with a good, affectionate son!"

And my father gets up and walks to and fro.   One minute
more, father—one minute more—and I am on thy breast!
Time, too, has dealt gently with thee, as he doth with those
for whom the wild passions and keen cares of the world never
sharpen his scythe.   The broad front looks more broad, for the
locks are more scanty and thin; but still not a furrow.

Whence comes that short sigh!

"What is really the time, Blanche?   Did you look at the
turret clock?   Well, just go and look again."

"Kitty," quoth my father, "you have not only asked what
time it is thrice within the last ten minutes, but you have got
my watch, and Roland's great chronometer, and the Dutch
clock out of the kitchen, all before you, and they all concur in
the same tale—to-day is not to-morrow."

"They are all wrong, I know," said my mother, with mild
firmness; "and they've never gone right since he left."

Now out comes a letter—for I hear the rustle—and then a
step glides towards the lamp; and the dear, gentle, womanly
face—fair still, fair ever for me, fair as when it bent over my
pillow, in childhood's first sickness, or when we threw flowers
at each other on the lawn, at sunny noon!   And now Blanche
is whispering; and now the flutter, the start, the cry—"It is
true! it is true!   Your arms, mother.   Close, close round my
neck, as in the old time.   Father!   Roland, too!   Oh, joy! joy!
joy! home again—home till death!"

CHAPTER V

FROM a dream of the Bushland, howling dingoes,[1] and the war-whoop of the wild men, I wake and see the sun shining in through the jasmine that Blanche herself has had trained round the window—old school-books, neatly ranged round the wall—fishing-rods, cricket-bats, foils, and the old-fashioned gun—and my mother seated by the bedside—and Juba whining and scratching to get up. Had I taken thy murmured blessing, my mother, for the whoop of the blacks, and Juba's low whine for the howl of the dingoes?

Then what days of calm exquisite delight!—the interchange of heart with heart: what walks with Roland, and tales of him once our shame, now our pride; and the art with which the old man would lead those walks round by the village, that some favourite gossips might stop and ask, "What news of his brave young honour?"

I strive to engage my uncle in my projects for the repair of the ruins—for the culture of those wide bogs and moorlands: why is it that he turns away and looks down embarrassed? Ah, I guess! his true heir now is restored to him. He cannot consent that I should invest this dross, for which (the Great Book once published) I have no other use, in the house and the lands that will pass to his son. Neither would he suffer me so to invest even his son's fortune, the bulk of which I still hold in trust for that son. True, in his career, my cousin may require to have his money always forthcoming. But *I*, who have no career,—pooh! these scruples will rob me of half the pleasure my years of toil were to purchase. I must contrive it somehow or other; what if he would let me house and moorland on a long improving lease? Then, for the rest, there is a pretty little property to be sold close by, on which I can retire, when my cousin, as heir of the family, comes, perhaps with a wife, to reside at the Tower. I must consider of all this, and talk it over with Bolt, when my mind is at leisure from happiness to turn to such matters; meanwhile I fall back on my favourite proverb,—" *Where there's a will there's a way.*"

What smiles and tears, and laughter and careless prattle with my mother, and roundabout questions from her, to know if I had never lost my heart in the Bush? and evasive answers from

---

[1] *Dingoes*—the name given by Australian natives to the wild dogs.

me, to punish her for not letting out that Blanche was so charming. "I fancied Blanche had grown the image of her father, who has a fine martial head certainly, but not seen to advantage in petticoats! How could you be so silent with a theme so attractive?"

"Blanche made me promise."

Why? I wonder. Therewith I fell musing.

What quiet delicious hours are spent with my father in his study, or by the pond, where he still feeds the carps, that have grown into Cyprinidian leviathans. The duck, alas! has departed this life—the only victim that the Grim King has carried off; so I mourn, but am resigned to that lenient composition of the great tribute to Nature. I am sorry to say the Great Book has advanced but slowly—by no means yet fit for publication, for it is resolved that it shall not come out as first proposed, a part at a time, but *totus, teres, atque rotundus*. The matter has spread beyond its original compass; no less than five volumes—and those of the amplest—will contain the History of Human Error. However, we are far in the fourth, and one must not hurry Minerva.

My father is enchanted with Uncle Jack's "noble conduct," as he calls it; but he scolds me for taking the money, and doubts as to the propriety of returning it. In these matters my father is quite as Quixotical as Roland. I am forced to call in my mother as umpire between us, and she settles the matter at once by an appeal to feeling. "Ah, Austin! do you not humble me, if you are too proud to accept what is due to you from my brother?"

"*Velit, nolit, quod amica*," answered my father, taking off and rubbing his spectacles—"which means, Kitty, that when a man's married he has no will of his own. To think," added Mr. Caxton, musingly, "that in this world one cannot be sure of the simplest mathematical definition! You see, Pisistratus, that the angles of a triangle so decidedly scalene as your Uncle Jack's, may be equal to the angles of a right-angled triangle after all!"[1]

The long privation of books has quite restored all my appetite

---

[1] Not having again to advert to Uncle Jack, I may be pardoned for informing the reader, by way of annotation, that he continues to prosper surprisingly in Australia, though the Tibbets' Wheal stands still for want of workmen. Despite of a few ups and downs, I have had no fear of his success until this year (1849), when I tremble to think what effect the discovery of the gold mines in California may have on his lively imagination. If thou escapest that snare, Uncle Jack, *res age tutus eris,*—thou art safe for life.

for them. How much I have to pick up!—what a compendious scheme of reading I and my father chalk out! I see enough to fill up all the leisure of life. But, somehow or other, Greek and Latin stand still: nothing charms me like Italian. Blanche and I are reading Metastasio, to the great indignation of my father, who calls it "rubbish," and wants to substitute Dante. I have no associations at present with the souls

" Che son contenti
Nel fuoco ; "

I am already one of the "*beate gente.*" Yet, in spite of Metastasio, Blanche and I are not so intimate as cousins ought to be. If we are by accident alone, I become as silent as a Turk,—as formal as Sir Charles Grandison. I caught myself calling her *Miss* Blanche the other day.

I must not forget thee, honest Squills!—nor thy delight at my health and success; nor thy exclamation of pride (one hand on my pulse and the other griping hard the "ball" of my arm). " It all comes of my citrate of iron ; nothing like it for children; it has an effect on the cerebral developments of hope and combativeness." Nor can I wholly omit mention of poor Mrs. Primmins, who still calls me "Master Sisty," and is breaking her heart that I will not wear the new flannel waistcoats she had such pleasure in making—"Young gentlemen just growing up are so apt to go off in a galloping 'sumption!'" "She knew just such another as Master Sisty, when she lived at Torquay, who wasted away, and went out like a *snuff,* all because he would not wear flannel waistcoats." Therewith my mother looks grave, and says, "One can't take too much precaution."

Suddenly the whole neighbourhood is thrown into commotion. Trevanion—I beg his pardon, Lord Ulverstone—is coming to settle for good at Compton. Fifty hands are employed daily in putting the ground into hasty order. Fourgons, and waggons, and vans have disgorged all the necessaries a great man requires, where he means to eat, drink, and sleep; books, wines, pictures, furniture. I recognise my old patron still. He is in earnest, whatever he does. I meet my friend, his steward, who tells me that Lord Ulverstone finds his favourite seat, near London, too exposed to interruption; and moreover that, as he has there completed all improvements that wealth and energy can effect, he has less occupation for agricultural pursuits, to which he has grown more and more partial, than on the wide and princely domain which has hitherto wanted the master's eye. "He is a bra' farmer, I know," quoth the steward, "so far as the theory goes; but I don't think we in the north want great lords to teach us how to follow the pleugh." The steward's sense of dignity is hurt; but he is an honest fellow, and really glad to see the family come to settle in the old place.

They have arrived, and with them the Castletons, and a whole *posse comitatus* of guests. The county paper is full of fine names.

"What on earth did Lord Ulverstone mean by pretending to get out of the way of troublesome visitors?"

"My dear Pisistratus," answered my father to that exclamation, "it is not the visitors who come, but the visitors who stay away, that most trouble the repose of a retired minister. In all the procession, he sees but the images of Brutus and Cassius— that are *not* there! And depend on it also, a retirement so near London did not make noise enough. You see, a retiring statesman is like that fine carp—the farther he leaps from the water, the greater splash he makes in falling into the weeds! But," added Mr. Caxton, in a repentant tone, "this jesting does not become us; and, if I indulged it, it is only because I am heartily glad that Trevanion is likely now to find out his true vocation. And as soon as the fine people he brings with him have left him alone in his library, I trust he will settle to that vocation, and be happier than he has been yet."

"And that vocation, sir, is——"

"Metaphysics!" said my father. "He will be quite at home in puzzling over Berkeley, and considering whether the Speaker's chair, and the official red boxes, were really things whose ideas of figure, extension, and hardness were all in the mind. It will be a great consolation to him to agree with Berkeley, and to find that he has only been baffled by immaterial phantasma!"

My father was quite right. The repining, subtle, truth-weighing Trevanion, plagued by his conscience into seeing all sides of a question (for the least question has more than two sides, and is hexagonal at least), was much more fitted to discover the origin of ideas than to convince Cabinets and Nations that two and two make four—a proposition on which he himself would have agreed with Abraham Tucker, where that most ingenious and suggestive of all English metaphysicians observes, "Well, persuaded as I am that two and two make four, if I were to meet with a person of credit, candour, and understanding, who should sincerely call it in question, I would give him a hearing; for I am not more certain of that than of the whole being greater than a part. And yet I could myself suggest

some considerations that might seem to controvert this point."[1] I can
so well imagine Trevanion listening to "some person of credit,
candour, and understanding," in disproof of that vulgar proposition that twice two make four! But the news of this arrival,
including that of Lady Castleton, disturbed me greatly, and I
took to long wanderings alone. In one of these rambles, they
all called at the Tower—Lord and Lady Ulverstone, the Castletons, and their children. I escaped the visit ; and on my return
home, there was a certain delicacy respecting old associations
that restrained much talk, before me, on so momentous an event.
Roland, like me, had kept out of the way. Blanche, poor child,
ignorant of the antecedents, was the most communicative. And
the especial theme she selected—was the grace and beauty of
Lady Castleton!

A pressing invitation to spend some days at the castle had
been cordially given to all. It was accepted only by myself: I
wrote word that I would come.

Yes: I longed to prove the strength of my own self-conquest,
and accurately test the nature of the feelings that had disturbed
me. That any sentiment which could be called love remained
for Lady Castleton, the wife of another, and that other a man
with so many claims on my affection as her lord, I held as a
moral impossibility. But, with all those lively impressions of
early youth still engraved on my heart—impressions of the
image of Fanny Trevanion as the fairest and brightest of human
beings—could I feel free to love again ? Could I seek to woo,
and rivet to myself for ever, the entire and virgin affections of
another, while there was a possibility that I might compare and
regret ? No; either I must feel that, if Fanny were again
single—could be mine without obstacle, human or divine—she
had ceased to be the one I would single out of the world ; or,
though regarding love as the dead, I would be faithful to its
memory and its ashes. My mother sighed, and looked fluttered
and uneasy all the morning of the day on which I was to repair
to Compton. She even seemed cross, for about the third time
in her life, and paid no compliment to Mr. Stultz, when my
shooting-jacket was exchanged for a black frock, which that
artist had pronounced to be "splendid" ; neither did she honour
me with any of those little attentions to the contents of my
portmanteau, and the perfect "getting up" of my white waist-

---

[1] *Light of Nature—chapter on Judgment.*—See the very ingenious illustration of doubt, "whether the part is always greater than the whole "—
taken from time, or rather eternity.

coats and cravats, which made her natural instincts on such memorable occasions. There was also a sort of querulous, pity- ing tenderness in her tone, when she spoke to Blanche, which was quite pathetic; though, fortunately, its cause remained dark and impenetrable to the innocent comprehension of one who could not see where the past filled the urns of the future at the fountain of life. My father understood me better, shook me by the hand as I got into the chaise, and muttered, out of Seneca—

"Non tanquam transfuga, sed tanquam explorator."
"Not to desert, but examine."

Quite right.

CHAPTER VI

AGREEABLY to the usual custom in great houses, as soon as I arrived at Compton, I was conducted to my room, to adjust my toilet, or compose my spirits by solitude :—it wanted an hour to dinner. I had not, however, been thus left ten minutes, before the door opened, and Trevanion himself (as I would fain still call him) stood before me. Most cordial were his greeting and welcome; and, seating himself by my side, he continued to converse in his peculiar way—bluntly eloquent, and carelessly learned—till the half-hour bell rang. He talked on Australia, the Wakefield system—cattle—books, his trouble in arranging his library—his schemes for improving his property, and embellishing his grounds—his delight to find my father look so well—his determination to see a great deal of him, whether his old college friend would or not. He talked, in short, of everything except politics, and his own past career— showing only his soreness in that silence. But (independently of the mere work of time) he looked yet more worn and jaded in his leisure than he had done in the full tide of business; and his former abrupt quickness of manner now seemed to partake of feverish excitement. I hoped that my father *would* see much of him, for I felt that the weary mind wanted soothing.

Just as the second bell rang, I entered the drawing-room. There were at least twenty guests present—each guest, no doubt, some planet of fashion or fame, with satellites of its own. But I saw only two forms distinctly; first, Lord Castleton, conspicuous with star and garter—somewhat ampler and portlier in proportions, and with a frank dash of grey in the silky waves of his hair; but still as pre-eminent as ever for that beauty—

the charm of which depends less than any other upon youth—arising, as it does, from a felicitous combination of bearing and manner, and that exquisite suavity of expression which steals into the heart, and pleases so much that it becomes a satisfaction to admire! Of Lord Castleton, indeed, it might be said, as of Alcibiades, "that he was beautiful at every age." I felt my breath come thick, and a mist passed before my eyes, as Lord Castleton led me through the crowd, and the radiant vision of Fanny Trevanion, how altered—and how dazzling!—burst upon me.

I felt the light touch of that hand of snow; but no guilty thrill shot through my veins. I heard the voice, musical as ever —lower than it was once, and more subdued in its key, but steadfast and untremulous—it was no longer the voice that made "my soul plant itself in the ears." [1] The event was over, and I knew that the dream had fled from the waking world for ever.

"Another old friend!" as Lady Ulverstone came forth from a little group of children, leading one fine boy of nine years old, while one, two or three years younger, clung to her gown. "Another old friend!—and," added Lady Ulverstone, after the first kind greetings, "two new ones when the old are gone." The slight melancholy left the voice, as after presenting to me the little viscount, she drew forward the more bashful Lord Albert, who indeed had something of his grandsire's and namesake's look of refined intelligence in his brow and eyes.

The watchful tact of Lord Castleton was quick in terminating whatever embarrassment might belong to these introductions, as, leaning lightly on my arm, he drew me forward, and presented me to the guests more immediately in our neighbourhood, who seemed by their earnest cordiality to have been already prepared for the introduction.

Dinner was now announced, and I welcomed that sense of relief and segregation with which one settles into one's own "particular" chair at your large miscellaneous entertainment.

I stayed three days at that house. How truly had Trevanion said that Fanny would make "an excellent great lady." What perfect harmony between her manners and her position; just retaining enough of the girl's seductive gaiety and bewitching desire to please, to soften the new dignity of bearing she had unconsciously assumed—less, after all, as great lady, than as wife and mother: with a fine breeding, perhaps a little languid and artificial, as compared with her lord's—which sprang, fresh

[1] Sir Philip Sidney.

and healthful, wholly from nature—but still so void of all the
chill of condescension, or the subtle impertinence that belongs
to that order of the inferior *noblesse*, which boasts the name of
" exclusives "; with what grace, void of prudery, she took the
adulation of the flatterers, turning from them to her children,
or escaping lightly to Lord Castleton, with an ease that drew
round her at once the protection of hearth and home.

And certainly Lady Castleton was more incontestably beautiful than Fanny Trevanion had been.

All this I acknowledged, not with a sigh and a pang, but
with a pure feeling of pride and delight. I might have loved
madly and presumptuously, as boys will do; but I had loved
worthily—the love left no blush on my manhood; and Fanny's
very happiness was my perfect and total cure of every wound
in my heart, not quite scarred over before. Had she been
discontented, sorrowful, without joy in the ties she had formed,
there might have been more danger that I should brood over
the past, and regret the loss of its idol. Here there was none.
And the very improvement in her beauty had so altered its
character—*so* altered—that Fanny Trevanion and Lady Castleton seemed two persons. And, thus observing and listening
to her, I could now dispassionately perceive such differences in
our nature as seemed to justify Trevanion's assertion, which
once struck me as so monstrous, "that we should not have
been happy had fate permitted our union." Pure-hearted and
simple though she remained in the artificial world, still that
world was her element; its interests occupied her; its talk,
though just chastened from scandal, flowed from her lips. To
borrow the words of a man who was himself a courtier, and one
so distinguished that he could afford to sneer at Chesterfield,[1]
"*She* had the routine of that style of conversation which is a
sort of gold leaf, that is a great embellishment where it is
joined to anything else." I will not add, " but makes a very
poor figure by itself "—for *that* Lady Castleton's conversation
certainly did not do—perhaps, indeed, because it was not " by
itself "—and the gold leaf was all the better for being thin,
since it could not cover even the surface of the sweet and
amiable nature over which it was spread. Still this was not
the mind in which now, in maturer experience, I would seek
to find sympathy with manly action, or companionship in the
charms of intellectual leisure.

There was about this same beautiful favourite of nature

[1] Lord Hervey's " Memoirs of George II."

and fortune a certain helplessness, which had even its grace in that high station, and which, perhaps, tended to ensure her domestic peace, for it served to attach her to those who had won influence over her, and was happily accompanied by a most affectionate disposition. But still, if less favoured by circumstances, less sheltered from every wind that could visit her too roughly—if, as the wife of a man of inferior rank, she had failed of that high seat and silken canopy reserved for the spoiled darlings of fortune—that helplessness might have become querulous. I thought of poor Ellen Bolding and her silken shoes. Fanny Trevanion seemed to have come into the world with silk shoes—not to walk where there was a stone or a brier! I heard something, in the gossip of those around, that confirmed this view of Lady Castleton's character, while it deepened my admiration of her lord, and showed me how wise had been her choice, and how resolutely he had prepared himself to vindicate his own. One evening, as I was sitting, a little apart from the rest, with two men of the London world, to whose talk—for it ran upon the *on-dits* and anecdotes of a region long strange to me—I was a silent but amused listener; one of the two said—"Well, I don't know anywhere a more excellent creature than Lady Castleton; so fond of her children —and her tone to Castleton so exactly what it ought to be—so affectionate, and yet, as it were, respectful. And the more credit to her, if, as they say, she was not in love with him when she married (to be sure, handsome as he is, he is twice her age)! And no woman could have been more flattered and courted by Lotharios and lady-killers than Lady Castleton has been. I confess, to my shame, that Castleton's luck puzzles me, for it is rather an exception to my general experience."

"My dear ——," said the other, who was one of those wise men of pleasure, who occasionally startle us into wondering how they come to be so clever, and yet rest contented with mere drawing-room celebrity—men who seem always idle, yet appear to have read everything; always indifferent to what passes before them, yet who know the character and divine the secrets of everybody—"my dear ——," said the gentleman, "you would not be puzzled if you had studied Lord Castleton, instead of her ladyship. Of all the conquests ever made by Sedley Beaudesert —when the two fairest dames of the Faubourg are said to have fought for his smiles, in the Bois de Boulogne—no conquest ever cost him such pains, or so tasked his knowledge of women, as that of his wife after marriage! He was not satisfied with her hand, he was resolved to have her whole heart, 'one entire and perfect chrysolite,' and he has succeeded! Never was husband so watchful and so little jealous—never one who confided so generously in all that was best in his wife, yet was so alert in protecting and guarding her, wherever she was weakest! When in the second year of marriage, that dangerous German Prince Von Leibenfels attached himself so preseveringly to Lady Castleton, and the scandle-mongers pricked up their ears, in hopes of a victim, I watched Castleton with as much interest as if I had been looking over Deschapelles playing at chess. You never saw anything so masterly; he pitted himself against his highness with the cool confidence, not of a blind spouse, but a fortunate rival. He surpassed him in the delicacy of his attentions, he outshone him by his careless magnificence. Leibenfels had the impertinence to send Lady Castleton a bouquet of some rare flowers just in fashion. Castleton, an hour before, had filled her whole balcony with the same costly exotics, as if they were too common for nosegays, and only just worthy to bloom for her a day. Young and really accomplished as Leibenfels is, Castleton eclipsed him by his grace, and fooled him with his wit; he laid little plots to turn his moustache and guitar into ridicule; he seduced him into a hunt with the buckhounds (though Castleton himself had not hunted before, since he was thirty), and drew him, spluttering German oaths, out of the slough of a ditch; he made him the laughter of the clubs: he put him fairly out of fashion—and all with such suavity and politeness, and bland sense of superiority, that it was the finest piece of high comedy you ever beheld. The poor prince, who had been coxcomb enough to lay a bet with a Frenchman as to his success with the English in general, and Lady Castleton in particular, went away with a face as long as Don Quixote's. If you had but seen him at S—— House, the night before he took leave of the island, and his comical grimace when Castleton offered him a pinch of the Beaudesert mixture! No! the fact is, that Castleton made it the object of his existence, the masterpiece of his art, to secure to himself a happy home, and the entire possession of his wife's heart. The first two or three years, I fear, cost him more trouble than any other man ever took, with his own wife, at least; but he may now rest in peace—Lady Castleton is won, and for ever."

As my gentleman ceased, Lord Castleton's noble head rose above the group standing round him; and I saw Lady Castleton turn with a look of well-bred fatigue from a handsome young fop, who had affected to lower his voice while he spoke to her, and, encountering the eyes of her husband, the look changed at once into one of such sweet smiling affection, such frank, unmistakable wife-like pride, that it seemed a response to the assertion—"Lady Castleton is won, and for ever."

Yes, that story increased my admiration for Lord Castleton: it showed me with what forethought and earnest sense of responsibility he had undertaken the charge of a life, the guidance of a character yet undeveloped: it lastingly acquitted him of the levity that had been attributed to Sedley Beaudesert. But I felt more than ever contented that the task had devolved on one whose temper and experience had so fitted him to discharge it. That German prince made me tremble from sympathy with the husband, and in a sort of relative shudder for myself! Had that episode happened to me, I could never have drawn "high comedy" from it!—I could never have so happily closed the fifth act with a pinch of the Beaudesert mixture! No, no; to my homely sense of man's life and employment, there was nothing alluring in the prospect of watching over the golden tree in the garden, with a "woe to the Argus, if Mercury once lull him to sleep!" Wife of mine shall need no watching, save in sickness and sorrow! Thank Heaven that my way of life does not lead through the roseate thoroughfares, beset with German princes laying bets for my perdition, and fine gentlemen admiring the skill with which I play at chess for so terrible a stake! To each rank and each temper, its own laws. I acknowledge that Fanny is an excellent marchioness, and Lord Castleton an incomparable marquis. But, Blanche! if I can win thy true, simple heart, I trust I shall begin at the fifth act of high comedy, and say at the altar—

"Once won, won for ever."

CHAPTER VII

I RODE home on a horse my host lent me; and Lord Castleton rode part of the way with me, accompanied by his two boys, who bestrode manfully their Shetland ponies, and cantered on before us. I paid some compliment to the spirit and intelligence of these children—a compliment they well deserved.

"Why, yes," said the marquis, with a father's becoming pride,

"I hope neither of them will shame his grandsire, Trevanion. Albert (though not quite the wonder poor Lady Ulverstone declares him to be) is rather too precocious; and it is all I can do to prevent his being spoilt by flattery to his cleverness, which, I think, is much worse than even flattery to rank—a danger to which, despite Albert's destined inheritance, the elder brother is more exposed. Eton soon takes out the conceit of the latter and more vulgar kind. I remember Lord —— (you know what an unpretending, good-natured fellow he is now) strutting into the playground, a raw boy, with his chin up in the air, and burly Dick Johnson (rather a tuft-hunter now, I'm afraid) coming up, and saying, 'Well, sir, and who the deuce are you?' 'Lord ——,' says the poor devil unconsciously, 'eldest son of the Marquis of ——.' 'Oh, indeed!' cries Johnson; 'then, there's one kick for my lord, and two for the marquis!' I am not fond of kicking, but I doubt if anything ever did —— more good than those three kicks! But," continued Lord Castleton, "when one flatters a boy for his cleverness, even Eton itself cannot kick the conceit out of him. Let him be last in the form, and the greatest dunce ever flogged, there are always people to say that your public schools don't do for your great geniuses. And it is ten to one but what the father is plagued into taking the boy home, and giving him a private tutor, who fixes him into a prig for ever. A coxcomb in dress," said the marquis smiling, "is a trifler it would ill become me to condemn, and I own that I would rather see a youth a fop than a sloven; but a coxcomb in ideas—why, the younger he is, the more unnatural and disagreeable. Now, Albert, over that hedge, sir."

"That hedge, papa? The pony will never do it."

"Then," said Lord Castleton, taking off his hat with politeness, "I fear you will deprive us of the pleasure of your company."

The boy laughed, and made gallantly for the hedge, though I saw by his change of colour that it a little alarmed him. The pony could not clear the hedge; but it was a pony of tact and resources, and it scrambled through like a cat, inflicting sundry rents and tears on a jacket of Raphael blue.

Lord Castleton said, smiling, "You see, I teach them to get through a difficulty one way or the other. Between you and me," he added seriously, "I perceive a very different world rising round the next generation from that in which I first went forth and took my pleasure. I shall rear my boys accordingly.

Rich noblemen must nowadays be useful men; and if they can't leap over briers, they must scramble through them. Don't you agree with me?"

"Yes, heartily."

"Marriage makes a man much wiser," said the marquis, after a pause. "I smile now, to think how often I sighed at the thought of growing old. Now I reconcile myself to the grey hairs without dreams of a wig, and enjoy youth still—for," pointing to his sons, "it is *there!*"

"He has very nearly found out the secret of the saffron bag now," said my father, pleased and rubbing his hands, when I repeated this talk with Lord Castleton. "But I fear poor Trevanion," he added, with a compassionate change of countenance, "is still far away from the sense of Lord Bacon's receipt. And his wife, you say, out of very love for him, keeps always drawing discord from the one jarring wire."

"You must talk to her, sir."

"I will," said my father angrily; "and scold her too—foolish woman! I shall tell her Luther's advice to the Prince of Anhalt."

"What was that, sir?"

"Only to throw a baby into the river Maldon, because it had sucked dry five wet-nurses besides the mother, and must therefore be a changeling. Why, that ambition of hers would suck dry all the mother's milk in the genus mammalian. And such a withered, rickety, malign little changeling too! She shall fling it into the river, by all that is holy!" cried my father; and, suiting the action to the word, away into the pond went the spectacles he had been rubbing indignantly for the last three minutes. "Papæ!" faltered my father, aghast, while the Ceprinidæ, mistaking the dip of the spectacles for an invitation to dinner, came scudding up to the bank. "It is all your fault," said Mr. Caxton, recovering himself. "Get me the new tortoise-shell spectacles and a large slice of bread. You see that when fish are reduced to a pond they recognise a benefactor, which they never do when rising at flies, or groping for worms, in the waste world of a river. Hem!—a hint for the Ulverstones. Besides the bread and the spectacles, just look out and bring me the old black-letter copy of St. Anthony's 'Sermon to Fishes.'"

CHAPTER VIII

SOME weeks now have passed since my return to the Tower:
the Castletons are gone, and all Trevanion's gay guests.
And since these departures, visits between the two houses have
been interchanged often, and the bonds of intimacy are growing
close. Twice has my father held long conversations apart with
Lady Ulverstone (my mother is not foolish enough to feel a
pang now at such confidences), and the result has become
apparent. Lady Ulverstone has ceased all talk against the
world and the public—ceased to fret the galled pride of her
husband with irritating sympathy. She has made herself the
true partner of his present occupations, as she was of those in
the past ; she takes interest in farming, and gardens, and flowers,
and those philosophical peaches which come from trees academical that Sir William Temple reared in his graceful retirement.
She does more—she sits by her husband's side in the library,
reads the books he reads, or, if in Latin, coaxes him into construing them. Insensibly she leads him into studies farther
and farther remote from Blue Books and Hansard ; and, taking
my father's hint,

> " Allures to brighter worlds, and leads the way."

They are inseparable. Darby-and-Joan-like, you see them
together in the library, the garden, or the homely little pony-
phaeton, for which Lord Ulverstone has resigned the fast-trotting
cob, once identified with the eager looks of the busy Trevanion.
It is most touching, most beautiful! And to think what a
victory over herself the proud woman must have obtained !—
never a thought that seems to murmur, never a word to recall
the ambitious man back from the philosophy into which his
active mind flies for refuge. And with the effort, her brow has
become so serene ! That careworn expression, which her fine
features once wore, is fast vanishing. And what affects me
most, is to think that this change (which is already settling into
happiness) has been wrought by Austin's counsels and appeals
to her sense and affection. "It is to you," he said, "that
Trevanion must look for more than comfort—for cheerfulness
and satisfaction. Your child is gone from you—the world ebbs
away—you two should be all in all to each other. Be so."
Thus, after paths so devious, meet those who had parted in
youth, now on the verge of age. There, in the same scenes
where Austin and Ellinor had first formed acquaintance, he,

aiding her to soothe the wounds inflicted by the ambition that had separated their lots, and both taking counsel to ensure the happiness of the rival she had preferred.

After all this vexed public life of toil, and care, and ambition—to see Trevanion and Ellinor, drawing closer and closer to each other, knowing private life and its charms for the first time—verily, it would have been a theme for an elegiast like Tibullus.

But all this while a younger love, with no blurred leaves to erase from the chronicle, has been keeping sweet account of the summer time. "Very near are two hearts that have no guile between them," saith a proverb, traced back to Confucius. "Oh ye days of still sunshine, reflected back from ourselves—Oh ye haunts, endeared evermore by a look, tone, or smile, or rapt silence ; when more and more with each hour unfolded before me, that nature, so tenderly coy, so cheerful though serious, so attuned by simple cares to affection, yet so filled, from soft musings and solitude, with a poetry that gave grace to duties the homeliest—setting life's trite things to music ! Here nature and fortune concurred alike ; equal in birth and pretensions—similar in tastes and in objects—loving the healthful activity of purpose, but content to find it around us—neither envying the wealthy nor vying with the great; each framed by temper to look on the bright side of life, and find founts of delight, and green spots fresh with verdure, where eyes but accustomed to cities could see but the sands and the mirage : while afar (as man's duty) I had gone through the travail that, in wrestling with fortune, gives pause to the heart to recover its losses, and know the value of love, in its graver sense of life's earnest realities ; Heaven had reared, at the thresholds of home, the young tree that should cover the roof with its blossoms, and embalm with its fragrance the daily air of my being.

It had been the joint prayer of those kind ones I left, that such might be my reward ; and each had contributed, in his or her several way, to fit that fair life for the ornament and joy of the one that now asked to guard and to cherish it. From Roland came that deep, earnest honour—a man's in its strength, and a woman's in its delicate sense of refinement. From Roland, that quick taste for all things noble in poetry, and lovely in nature—the eye that sparkled to read how Bayard stood alone at the bridge, and saved an army—or wept over the page that told how the dying Sydney put the bowl from his burning lips. Is that too masculine a spirit for some ? Let each please himself. Give me the woman who can echo all

thoughts that are noblest in men! And that eye, too—like
Roland's—could pause to note each finer mesh in the wonderful
web-work of beauty. No landscape to her was the same
yesterday and to-day—a deeper shade from the skies could
change the face of the moors—the springing up of fresh wild
flowers, the very song of some bird unheard before, lent variety
to the broad rugged heath. Is that too simple a source of
pleasure for some to prize? Be it so to those who need the
keen stimulants that cities afford. But, if we were to pass all
our hours in those scenes, it was something to have the tastes
which own no monotony in Nature.

All this came from Roland; and to this, with thoughtful
wisdom, my father had added enough knowledge from books to
make those tastes more attractive, and to lend to impulsive
perception of beauty and goodness the culture that draws finer
essence from beauty, and expands the Good into the Better by
heightening the sight of the survey; hers, knowledge enough to
sympathise with intellectual pursuits, not enough to dispute on
man's province—Opinion. Still, whether in nature or in lore, still

> " The fairest garden in her looks,
> And in her mind the choicest books ! "

And yet, thou wise Austin—and thou, Roland, poet that never
wrote a verse—yet your work had been incomplete, but then
Woman stepped in, and the mother gave to her she designed
for a daughter the last finish of meek everyday charities—the
mild household virtues—" the soft word that turneth away
wrath "—the angelic pity for man's rougher faults—the patience
that bideth its time—and, exacting no " rights of woman,"
subjugates us, delighted, to the invisible thrall.

Dost thou remember, my Blanche, that soft summer evening
when the vows our eyes had long interchanged stole at last
from the lip? Wife mine! come to my side—look over me
while I write: there, thy tears (happy tears are they not,
Blanche?) have blotted the page! Shall we tell the world
more? Right, my Blanche; no words should profane the place
where those tears have fallen　　.　　　　.　　　.　　　.　　　.

And here I would fain conclude; but alas, and alas! that I
cannot associate with our hopes, on this side the grave, him who,
we fondly hoped (even on the bridal-day, that gave his sister to
my arms), would come to the hearth where his place now stood
vacant, contented with glory, and fitted at last for the tranquil
happiness which long years of repentance and trial had deserved.

HERBERT DE CAXTON
AS FELL ON THE FIELD
HIS
COUNTRY REQUIRING IT
AND
HIS FATHER IS RESIGNED

"And his father is resigned"

Clara Hammond
oct 19 ⁄

Within the first year of my marriage, and shortly after a gallant share in a desperate action, which had covered his name with new honours, just when we were most elated, in the blinded vanity of human pride, came the fatal news! The brief career was run. He died, as I knew he would have prayed to die, at the close of a day ever memorable in the annals of that marvellous empire, which valour without parallel has annexed to the Throne of the Isles. He died in the arms of Victory, and his last smile met the eyes of the noble chief, who, even in that hour, could pause from the tide of triumph by the victim it had cast on its bloody shore. "One favour," faltered the dying man; "I have a father at home—he, too, is a soldier. In my tent is my will: it gives all I have to him—he can take it without shame. That is not enough! Write to him—you— with your own hand, and tell him how his son fell!" And the hero fulfilled the prayer, and that letter is dearer to Roland than all the long roll of the ancestral dead! Nature has reclaimed her rights, and the forefathers recede before the son.

In a side chapel of the old Gothic church, amidst the mouldering tombs of those who fought at Acre and Agincourt, a fresh tablet records the death of HERBERT DE CAXTON, with the simple inscription—

> HE FELL ON THE FIELD:
> HIS COUNTRY MOURNED HIM,
> AND HIS FATHER IS RESIGNED.

Years have rolled away since that tablet was placed there, and changes have passed on that nook of earth which bounds our little world: fair chambers have sprung up amidst the desolate ruins; far and near, smiling corn-fields replace the bleak dreary moors. The land supports more retainers than ever thronged to the pennon of its barons of old; and Roland can look from his Tower over domains that are reclaimed, year by year, from the waste, till the ploughshare shall win a lordship more opulent than those feudal chiefs ever held by the tenure of the sword. And the hospitable mirth that had fled from the ruin has been renewed in the hall; and rich and poor, great and lowly, have welcomed the rise of an ancient house from the dust of decay. All those dreams of Roland's youth are fulfilled; but they do not gladden his heart like the thought that his son, at the last, was worthy of his line, and the hope that no gulf shall yawn between the two when the Grand Circle is rounded, and man's past and man's future meet where Time disappears. Never was that lost one forgotten!—never was his name breathed but tears rushed to the eyes; and each morning the peasant going to his labour might see Roland steal down the dell to the deep-set door of the chapel. None presume there to follow his steps, or intrude on his solemn thoughts; for there, in sight of that tablet, are his orisons made, and the remembrance of the dead forms a part of the commune with Heaven. But the old man's step is still firm, and his brow still erect; and you may see in his face that it was no hollow boast which proclaimed that the "father was resigned": and ye who doubt if too Roman a hardness might not be found in that Christian resignation, think what it is to have feared for a son the life of shame, and ask them if the sharpest grief to a father is in a son's death of honour!

Years have passed, and two fair daughters play at the knees of Blanche, or creep round the footstool of Austin, waiting patiently for the expected kiss when he looks up from the Great Book, now drawing fast to its close; or, if Roland enter the room, forget all their sober demureness, and, unawed by the terrible "Papæ!" run clamorous for the promised swing in the orchard, or the fiftieth recital of "Chevy Chase."

For my part, I take the goods the gods provide me, and am contented with girls that have the eyes of their mother; but Roland, ungrateful man, begins to grumble that we are so neglectful of the rights of heirs-male. He is in doubt whether to lay the fault on Mr. Squills or on us: I am not sure that he does not think it a conspiracy of all three to settle the representation of the martial De Caxtons on the "spindle side." Whosoever be the right person to blame, an omission so fatal to the straight line in the pedigree is rectified at last, and Mrs. Primmins again rushes, or rather rolls—in the movement natural to forms globular and spheral—into my father's room, with—

"Sir, sir—it is a boy!"

Whether my father asked also this time that question so puzzling to metaphysical inquirers, "What is a boy?" I know not: I rather suspect he had not leisure for so abstract a question: for the whole household burst on him, and my mother, in that storm peculiar to the elements of the Mind Feminine—a sort of sunshiny storm between laughter and crying—whirled him off to behold the *Neogilos.*

Now, some months after that date, on a winter's evening, we were all assembled in the hall, which was still our usual apartment, since its size permitted to each his own segregated and peculiar employment. A large screen fenced off from interruption my father's erudite settlement; and quite out of sight, behind that impermeable barrier, he was now calmly winding up that eloquent peroration which will astonish the world, whenever, by Heaven's special mercy, the printer's devils have done with "The History of Human Error." In another nook my uncle had ensconced himself—stirring his coffee (in the cup my mother had presented to him so many years ago, and which had miraculously escaped all the ills the race of crockery is heir to), a volume of "Ivanhoe" in the other hand, and, despite the charm of the Northern Wizard, his eye *not* on the page. On the wall, behind him, hangs the picture of Sir Herbert de Caxton, the soldier-comrade of Sidney and Drake; and, at the foot of the picture, Roland has slung his son's sword beside the letter that spoke of his death, which is framed and glazed: sword and letter had become as the last, nor least honoured, Penates of the hall:—the son was grown an ancestor.

Not far from my uncle sat Mr. Squills, employed in mapping out phrenological divisions on a cast he had made from the skull of one of the Australian aborigines—a ghastly present which (in compliance with a yearly letter to that effect) I had brought him over, together with a stuffed "wombat" and a large bundle of sarsaparilla. (For the satisfaction of his patients, I may observe, parenthetically, that the skull and the wombat"—that last is a creature between a miniature pig and a very small badger—were not precisely packed up with the sarsaparilla!) Farther on stood open, but idle, the new pianoforte, at which, before my father had given his preparatory hem, and sat down to the Great Book, Blanche and my mother had been trying hard to teach me to bear the third in the glee of "The Chough and Crow to roost have gone,"—vain task, in spite of all flattering assurances that I have a very fine "bass," if I could but manage to humour it. Fortunately for the ears of the audience, that attempt is now abandoned. My mother is hard at work on her tapestry—the last pattern in fashion—to wit, a rosy-cheeked young troubadour playing the lute under a salmon-coloured balcony; the two little girls look gravely on, prematurely in love, I suspect, with the troubadour; and Blanche and I have stolen away into a corner, which, by some strange delusion, we consider out of sight, and in that corner is the cradle of the *Neogilos*. Indeed, it is not our fault that it is there—Roland would have it so; and the baby is so good, too, he never cries—at least so say Blanche and my mother: at all events, he does not cry to-night. And, indeed, that child is a wonder! He seems to know and respond to what was uppermost at our hearts when he was born; and yet more, when Roland (contrary, I dare say, to all custom) permitted neither mother, nor nurse, nor creature of womankind, to hold him at the baptismal font, but bent over the new Christian his own dark high-featured face, reminding one of the eagle that hid the infant in its nest, and watched over it with wings that had battled with the storm: and from that moment the child, who took the name of HERBERT, seemed to recognise Roland better than his nurse, or even mother— seemed to know that, in giving him that name, we sought to give Roland his son once more! Never did the old man come near the infant but it smiled, and crowed, and stretched out its little arms; and then the mother and I would press each other's hand secretly, and were not jealous. Well, then, Blanche and Pisistratus were seated near the cradle, and talking in low whispers, when my father pushed aside the screen, and said—

"There—the work is done!—and now it may go to press as soon as you will."

Congratulations poured in. My father bore them with his usual equanimity; and standing on the hearth, his hand in his waistcoat, he said musingly, "Among the last delusions of Human Error, I have had to notice Rousseau's phantasy of Perpetual Peace, and all the like pastoral dreams, which preceded the bloodiest wars that have convulsed the earth for more than a thousand years!"

"And to judge by the newspapers," said I, "the same delusions are renewed again. Benevolent theorists go about prophesying peace as a positive certainty, deduced from that sibyl-book the ledger; and we are never again to buy cannons, provided only we can exchange cotton for corn."

MR. SQUILLS (who, having almost wholly retired from general business, has, from want of something better to do, attended sundry "Demonstrations in the North," since which he has talked much about the march of improvement, the spirit of the age, and "us of the nineteenth century").—"I heartily hope that those benevolent theorists *are* true prophets. I have found, in the course of my professional practice, that men go out of the world quite fast enough, without hacking them into pieces or blowing them up into the air. War is a great evil."

BLANCHE (passing by Squills, and glancing towards Roland).— "Hush!"

Roland remains silent.

MR. CAXTON.—"War is a great evil; but evil is admitted by

Providence into the agency of creation, physical and moral. The existence of evil has puzzled wiser heads than ours, Squills. But, no doubt, there is One above who has His reasons for it. The combative bump seems as common to the human skull as the philoprogenitive,—if it is in our organisation, be sure it is not there without cause. Neither is it just to man, nor wisely submissive to the Disposer of all events, to suppose that war is wholly and wantonly produced by human crimes and follies— that it conduces *only* to ill, and does not as often arise from the necessities interwoven in the framework of society, and speed the great ends of the human race, conformably with the designs of the Omniscient. Not one great war has ever desolated the earth, but has left behind it seeds that have ripened into blessings incalculable!"

MR. SQUILLS (with the groan of a dissentient at a "Demonstration").—"*Oh! oh!* OH!"

Luckless Squills! Little could he have foreseen the showerbath, or rather *douche*, of erudition that fell splash on his head, as he pulled the string with that impertinent *Oh! oh!* Down first came the Persian War, with Median myriads disgorging all the rivers they had drunk up in their march through the East—all the arts, all the letters, all the sciences, all the notions of liberty that we inherit from Greece—my father rushed on with them all, sousing Squills with his proofs that, without the Persian War, Greece would never have risen to be the teacher of the world. Before the gasping victim could take breath, down came Hun, Goth, and Vandal, on Italy and Squills.

"What, sir!" cried my father, "don't you see that from those eruptions on demoralised Rome came the regeneration of manhood; the rebaptism of earth from the last soils of paganism; and the remote origin of whatever of Christianity yet exists, free from the idolatries with which Rome contaminated the faith?"

Squills held up his hands and made a splutter. Down came Charlemagne—paladins and all! There my father was grand! What a picture he made of the broken, jarring, savage elements of barbaric society. And the iron hand of the great Frank— settling the nations and founding existent Europe. Squills was now fast sinking into coma, or stupefaction; but, catching at a straw, as he heard the word "Crusades," he stuttered forth, "Ah! *there* I defy you."

"Defy me there!" cries my father; and one would think the ocean was in the shower-bath, it came down in such a rattle. My father scarcely touched on the smaller points in excuse for the Crusades, though he recited very volubly all the humaner arts introduced into Europe by that invasion of the East; and showed how it had served civilisation, by the vent it afforded for the rude energies of chivalry—by the element of destruction to feudal tyranny that it introduced—by its use in the emancipation of burghs, and the disrupture of serfdom. But he painted, in colours vivid, as if caught from the skies of the East, the great spread of Mahometanism, and the danger it menaced to Christian Europe—and drew up the Godfreys, and Tancreds, and Richards, as a league of the Age and Necessity, against the terrible progress of the sword and the Koran. "You call them madmen," cried my father, "but the frenzy of nations is the statesmanship of fate! How know you that—but for the terror inspired by the hosts who marched to Jerusalem—how know you that the Crescent had not waved over other realms than those which Roderic lost to the Moor? If Christianity had been less a passion, and the passion had less stirred up all Europe—how know you that the creed of the Arab (which was then, too, a passion) might not have planted its mosques in the forum of Rome, and on the site of Notre Dame? For in the war between creeds—when the creeds are embraced by vast races—think you that the reason of sages can cope with the passion of millions? Enthusiasm must oppose enthusiasm. The crusader fought for the tomb of Christ, but he saved the life of Christendom."

My father paused. Squills was quite passive; he struggled no more—he was drowned.

"So," resumed Mr. Caxton, more quietly—"so, if later wars yet perplex us as to the good that the All-wise One draws from their evils, our posterity may read their uses as clearly as we now read the finger of Providence resting on the barrows of Marathon, or guiding Peter the Hermit to the battle-fields of Palestine. Nor, while we admit the evil to the passing generation, can we deny that many of the virtues that make the ornament and vitality of peace sprung up first in the convulsion of war!" Here Squills began to evince faint signs of resuscitation, when my father let fly at him one of those numberless waterworks which his prodigious memory kept in constant supply. "Hence," said he, "hence, not unjustly, has it been remarked by a philosopher, shrewd at least in worldly experience"—(Squills again closed his eyes, and became exanimate)—"'It is strange to imagine that war, which of all things appears the most savage, should be the passion of the most heroic spirits.

But 'tis in war that the knot of fellowship is closest drawn; 'tis in war that mutual succour is most given—mutual danger run, and common affection most exerted and employed; for heroism and philanthropy are almost one and the same!' " [1]

My father ceased, and mused a little. Squills, if still living, thought it prudent to feign continued extinction.

"Not," said Mr. Caxton, resuming—"not but what I hold it our duty never to foster into a passion what we must rather submit to as an awful necessity. You say truly, Mr. Squills—war is an evil; and woe to those who, on slight pretences, open the gates of Janus—

> ——'The dire abode,
> And the fierce issues of the furious god.' "

Mr. Squills, after a long pause—employed in some of the more handy means for the reanimation of submerged bodies, supporting himself close to the fire in a semi-erect posture, with gentle friction, self-applied, to each several limb, and copious recourse to certain steaming stimulants which my compassionate hands prepared for him—stretches himself, and says feebly, " In short, then, not to provoke farther discussion, you would go to war in defence of your country. Stop, sir—stop, for Heaven's sake! I agree with you—I agree with you! But, fortunately, there is little chance now that any new Boney will build boats at Boulogne to invade us."

MR. CAXTON.—"I am not so sure of that, Mr. Squills." (Squills falls back with a glassy stare of deprecating horror.) " I don't read the newspapers very often, but the past helps me to judge of the present."

Therewith my father earnestly recommended to Mr. Squills the careful perusal of certain passages in Thucydides, just previous to the outbreak of the Peloponnesian war (Squills hastily nodded the most servile acquiescence), and drew an ingenious parallel between the signs and symptoms foreboding that outbreak, and the very apprehension of coming war which was evinced by the recent *Io pæans* to peace.[2] And, after sundry notable and shrewd remarks, tending to show where elements for war were already ripening, amidst clashing opinions and

---

[1] Shaftesbury.

[2] When this work was first published, Mr. Caxton was generally deemed a very false prophet in these anticipations, and sundry critics were pleased to consider his apology for war neither seasonable nor philosophical. That Mr. Caxton was right, and the politicians opposed to him have been somewhat ludicrously wrong, may be briefly accounted for—Mr. Caxton had read history.

disorganised states, he wound up with saying—"So that, all
things considered, I think we had better just keep up enough
of the bellicose spirit, not to think it a sin if we are called upon
to fight for our pestles and mortars, our three-per-cents, goods,
chattels, and liberties. Such a time must come, sooner or
later, even though the whole world were spinning cotton and
printing sprigged calicoes. *We* may not see it, Squills, but
that young gentleman in the cradle, whom you have lately
brought into light, may."

"And if so," said my uncle abruptly, speaking for the first
time—"if indeed it be for altar and hearth!" My father suddenly drew in and pished a little, for he saw that he was caught
in the web of his own eloquence.

Then Roland took down from the wall his son's sword. Stealing to the cradle, he laid it in its sheath by the infant's side, and
glanced from my father to us with a beseeching eye. Instinctively Blanche bent over the cradle, as if to protect the *Neogilos*,
but the child, waking, turned from her, and attracted by the
glitter of the hilt, laid one hand lustily thereon, and pointed with
the other, laughingly, to Roland.

"Only on my father's proviso," said I hesitatingly. "For
hearth and altar—nothing less!"

"And even in that case," said my father, "add the shield to the
sword!" and on the other side of the infant he placed Roland's
well-worn Bible, blistered in many a page with secret tears.

There we all stood, grouping round the young centre of so
many hopes and fears—in peace or in war, born alike for the
Battle of Life. And he, unconscious of all that made our lips
silent, and our eyes dim, had already left that bright bauble of
the sword, and thrown both arms round Roland's bended neck.

"*Herbert!*" murmured Roland; and Blanche gently drew
away the sword—and left the Bible.